PATTERN RECOGNITION TECHNIQUES

PATTERN RECOGNITION TECHNIQUES

J. R. ULLMANN, M.A., Ph.D.
Division of Computer Science,
National Physical Laboratory

LONDON BUTTERWORTHS

THE BUTTERWORTH GROUP

ENGLAND
Butterworth & Co (Publishers) Ltd
London: 88 Kingsway, WC2B 6AB

AUSTRALIA
Butterworths Pty Ltd
Sydney: 586 Pacific Highway NSW 2067
Melbourne: 343 Little Collins Street, 3000
Brisbane: 240 Queen Street, 4000

CANADA
Butterworth & Co (Canada) Ltd
Toronto: 14 Curity Avenue, 374

NEW ZEALAND
Butterworths of New Zealand Ltd
Wellington: 26–28 Waring Taylor Street, 1
Auckland: 35 High Street, 1

SOUTH AFRICA
Butterworth & Co (South Africa) (Pty) Ltd
Durban: 152–154 Gale Street

First published in 1973

ISBN 0 408 70441 1

Set in 10pt IBM Press Roman,
printed by photolithography,
and bound in Great Britain at
The Pitman Press, Bath

PREFACE

This book is a fairly broad informal introduction to techniques of automatic pattern recognition. It is written for engineers, computer scientists, and biologists who have no specialist knowledge of the subject. Incursions into fields such as statistics, switching theory, Fourier theory, graph theory, linguistics, and optics are at an elementary level and are introduced from first principles, so that this book is practically self-contained.

Automation of pattern recognition may be useful in practical situations where the number of patterns to be recognised, or the required speed of recognition, is too great for available human effort. Such situations arise in the recognition of chromosomes, blood cells, finger-prints, faces, speech, electrocardiograms, electro-encephalograms, seismic signals, bubble or spark chamber events, vehicles, defects in printed circuits or in glass items, targets in aerial photographs, etc. Of all the possible applications of automatic pattern recognition, character recognition is the best known and most clearly established.

There is a section on speech recognition, but, for the sake of unity and clarity, most of the basic techniques introduced in this book are illustrated in terms of character recognition, even though many of them are more widely applicable. This book is an introductory sketch, not an exhaustive treatise, and there is no attempt to trace the historical origins of ideas. The references listed at the end constitute only a small sample from the massive and diffuse literature on automatic pattern recognition.

As far as possible the terminology used in this book is the same as that most widely used in the literature, even though terms such as *recognition, learning,* and *training set* may be philosophically objectionable, and terms such as *peephole mask* may be quaint and ingenuous.

The performance of a recognition system depends on the variability and diversity of the patterns to be recognised. A quantitative assessment of performance should therefore include measurements of the variability and diversity of the data, and of error rates of the system. Except in restricted circumstances, no scientifically reproducible measure of variability or diversity is available, and therefore the recognition performance of different systems on different data cannot be compared accurately. The error rates of a recognition system depend not only on the data and the principles of operation of the system, but also on the skill and diligence with which these principles are implemented. This means that, if two recognition machines which work on different principles are tested on the same data, a comparison of the error rates is not necessarily a true comparison of the merits of the principles. Because of these difficulties, this book says little about the actual quantitative performance of recognition systems.

Nevertheless, there is a certain amount of agreement as to what can and what cannot be done, at acceptable cost, at the present state of the art, particularly in character recognition[29]. Roughly speaking, satisfactory techniques are available for recognising printed characters in known fonts and controlled print quality. When print quality and font are entirely uncontrolled, as on a random collection of typed or printed envelopes in the mail, error rates of contemporary machines tend to be high (e.g. greater than 1% per character); but, even when error rates are comparatively high, automatic recognition may still be commercially worthwhile. There are machines in quite widespread commercial use which recognise hand-printed characters written in accordance with rules of constraint. Automatic recognition, at viable cost and error rate, of the complete set 0, . . ., 9, A, . . ., Z of unconstrained hand-printed characters, as on envelopes in the mail, does not appear to have been achieved. Recognition of cursive script (not in real time) is more clearly beyond the state of the art in 1972.

A general impression is that character recognition is not just one problem so much as a progression of increasingly difficult problems. At the least difficult end of this progression, characters are constrained or controlled, and recognition of such characters is the basis of a firmly established multimillion pound industry[17, 67, 361]. At the most difficult end of this progression, there is very little constraint on characters, and much research remains to be done on recognition[222].

I am very grateful to Dr C. N. Liu and Dr G. L. Shelton for providing Figure 1.1, to Dr J. D. Armitage and Professor A. W. Lohman for providing Figure 9.8, and to Mr S. R. Hyde for providing Figures 9.12, 9.13, and 9.14. This book has been written during evenings and weekends, not as part of my official work at the National Physical Laboratory, and I am very grateful to my wife for her forbearance.

CONTENTS

Chapter One

MASK MATCHING

1.1 OPTICAL MASK MATCHING

In 1929 Tauschek[430] described a machine which recognised numerals printed in a single font. Tauschek's machine employed 10 masks, one for each of the 10 numerals. A mask was like a stencil or a photographic negative transparency. For instance, the mask for '2' was such that a positive image of a '2' could be projected onto this mask so that black parts of the projected '2' covered all transparent parts of the mask and very little light passed through the mask. The black parts of a projected '2' would not cover all transparent parts of any other mask. To recognise a numeral on a document, Tauschek's machine projected an image of this numeral onto each of the 10 masks in turn. The total light transmitted through each mask was measured by a photocell, and the numeral was recognised as the numeral whose mask transmitted less than a prescribed minimum amount of light. In other words, a numeral was recognised as the numeral whose mask it *matched.*

Handel[198] described a further machine of this type, in which there was one output channel per numeral. For instance, if a numeral on the document matched the '2' mask, one voltage was applied to the '2' output channel, and a different voltage was applied to all other output channels. If a numeral matched the '3' mask, one voltage was applied to the '3' output channel, and a different voltage was applied to all other output channels, and so on. The machine *recognised* a character correctly if it produced output voltages which were appropriate to that character. The machine *misrecognised* a '2' if it produced output voltages appropriate to '3', for instance.

In a machine such as Tauschek's or Handel's the positive image of a character must be accurately positioned on each of the masks. To achieve this positioning, Tauschek and Handel required characters to be printed in prescribed positions on the document. In practice, characters printed by a typewriter or a high-speed printer are seldom positioned with sufficient accuracy. To allow tolerance for horizontal misalignment, a mask matching machine described by Bryce[66] employed (e.g.) five masks for each character. The five masks for '2' were mutually identical except that they were located in slightly different horizontal positions with respect to the image of a character to be recognised, and the same was true for the five masks for each of the other numerals. To allow tolerance for vertical misalignment, Bryce's machine moved all the masks in a vertical direction with respect to the image of a numeral. If any one of the '2' masks matched a numeral in any vertical position, that numeral was recognised as '2'. If any one of the '3' masks matched a numeral in any vertical position, that numeral was recognised as '3', and so on.

In imperfect printing, some of the regions of a character which should ideally be black may in fact be more like white, as for example in Figure 1.1. Furthermore, even if a character is accurately aligned

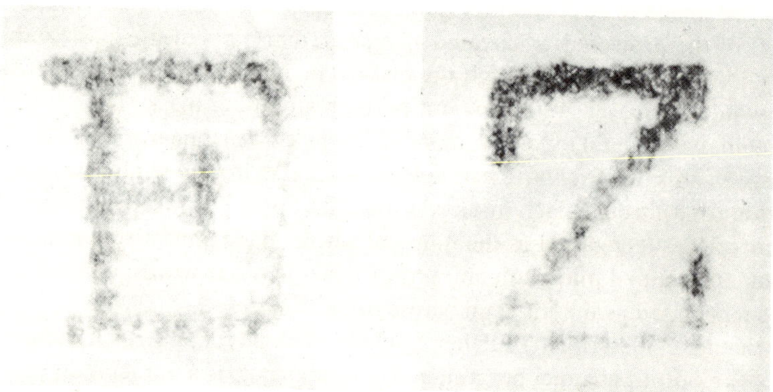

Figure 1.1. *Photographs of poorly printed characters. From Reference 283, with permission*

horizontally and vertically with a mask, it may be slightly rotated with respect to the mask, perhaps because of imperfect adjustment of the printing mechanism. To allow for such imperfections, a character was deemed to match a mask if the amount of light reaching the appropriate photocell did not exceed a prescribed threshold. This threshold was (ideally) made low enough to prevent misrecognition, yet high enough to allow tolerance for imperfect printing. If, for instance, a '2' was poorly printed, the total amount of light passing through the '2' mask in Tauschek's machine might exceed the prescribed threshold, yet be less than that passing through any other mask. This '2' would not be recognised by Tauschek's machine, but might be recognised by a machine using a *best match* condition for recognition. In such a machine, a character would be recognised as a '2' if it matched the '2' mask better than any other mask; a character would be recognised as a '3' if it matched the '3' mask better than any other mask; and so on. One such machine was described by Howard[227], and we shall introduce this in a little detail, because Howard's alignment technique is of interest.

Howard's machine[227] employed one mask per character, and all the masks were placed in the same plane. The document to be read was flooded with light. Light reflected from the document passed through a rectangular aperture somewhat larger than any character to be recognised, and was reflected by a rotating mirror onto an array of lenses arranged so that one image of a character was focused onto each of the masks. The total light passing through each mask was measured by a separate photocell. The document moved from right to left in a direction parallel to the row of characters to be recognised. The axis of rotation of the mirror was also parallel to this row, and images of a character were repeatedly swept vertically across the masks by the mirror via the lenses. The speed of this vertical sweep was much greater than the horizontal speed of the document, and successive vertical sweeps were associated with only a small horizontal movement of the document. During the course of vertical and horizontal motion, the images of a character came into and out of alignment with the masks. At the instant of alignment a character was recognised as the character whose mask it matched best.

For use in determining *when* character images were aligned with the masks, the plane containing the character masks also contained two rectangular transparent apertures, each of these being approximately 25% wider and taller than any of the characters to be recognised. The array of lenses included two lenses which focused images of a character onto these apertures. Light reached these lenses via the rotating mirror, so that images of a character were swept vertically across the apertures. One of the apertures was positioned so that a character image would lie entirely within this aperture shortly before the character images were aligned vertically with the character masks. The second aperture was positioned so that a character image would lie entirely within this aperture shortly after the character images were aligned vertically with the character masks. The total light passing through each aperture was measured by a separate photocell. The outputs of these two photocells, and also of each of the photocells associated with the character masks, were amplified by separate amplifiers, and each amplifier was adjusted so that, if the document was blank and bore no black marks or characters, the output was zero. The output of an amplifier was a measure of the amount of black in the image falling on the transparent area of the corresponding mask or aperture.

The two rectangular apertures were positioned so that, *only* when a character image was in accurate alignment with the correct character mask, would the output of the amplifier associated with this mask exceed the outputs of all other amplifiers, including those associated with the two rectangular apertures. When an amplifier associated with a rectangular aperture gave the largest output, the character images were not aligned with the character masks, and the machine continued the vertical sweep and horizontal document movement until one of the amplifiers associated with a character mask gave the largest output. The character on the document was then recognised as the character whose amplifier gave the largest output.

In Tauschek's, Handel's, Bryce's, and Howard's machines, and in many others[424], positive character images were matched with (photographically) negative masks. For reading microfilm, for instance, it may be more convenient to use negative character images and positive masks[364], and to find the mask which transmits a minimum, or less than a threshold amount, of light when properly aligned. Whether the masks are held stationary and character images are moved, as for example in Howard's machine, or whether character images are held stationary and the masks are moved, as for example in Bryce's machine, can also be resolved in accordance with practical expediency.

A positive 'E' properly aligned with a negative 'F' would transmit no light, and a simple mask matching machine might thus confuse 'E' and 'F'. One way of avoiding such confusions is to restrict the repertoire and the shapes of the characters so that no character is wholly, or almost wholly, included in any other. Another method[364, 424] exploits the fact that, if a positive character matches the negative 'C', 'O', and 'Q' masks, then it is a 'Q'. If a positive character only matches the negative 'C' and 'O' masks, then it is an 'O'. A positive character which matches the negative 'F', 'E' and 'L' masks is an 'E'; a positive character which matches the negative 'P' and 'B' masks is a 'B', and so on. In this method, characters either do or do not match masks, and the principle of best match, as in Howard's machine[227], is not used. One method of avoiding confusion between 'E' and 'F', between 'P' and 'B', etc., while retaining the principle of best match, is to normalise as will be explained in Section 3.5. A further method is used in all the systems which are introduced in the remainder of this chapter.

Hannan[200] (cf. Scarrott[392]) described a machine which employed one positive and one negative mask for each character to be recognised. Positive images of a character were projected onto all negative masks simultaneously, and at the same time negative images were projected onto all the positive masks. A negative image of a character on a document was obtained electronically, and simultaneous projection of positive and negative images onto the array of masks was accomplished by means of an optic tunnel, which produced multiple images by multiple reflection in parallel plane mirrors. For each character, the two masks, one positive and one negative, were placed side by side, and the total light passing through both masks were measured by a single photomultiplier. A character on a document, after alignment of its images with the masks, was recognised as the character whose photomultiplier gave the least output.

Figure 1.2 indicates how Hannan's machine avoided confusions such as that between 'E' and 'F'. In Figure 1.2(a) the positive 'F' mask transmits the bottom horizontal bar of a negative 'E', and in Figure 1.2(b) the negative 'E' mask transmits some of the light from a positive 'F'. If positive–negative pairs of E's were projected onto negative–positive pairs of 'E' masks, then (ideally) no light would reach the 'E' photomultiplier; and if positive–negative pairs of F's were projected onto negative–positive pairs of 'F' masks, then (ideally) no light would reach the 'F' photomultiplier.

The chance of misrecognition, that is, the chance of signalling that one character was present when in fact a different character was present, was reduced by the following elaboration of the recognition rule in Hannan's machine. A character was recognised as the character whose photomultiplier output was lower than every other photomultiplier output by at least a threshold amount, ρ. If there was no such photomultiplier, the machine gave a special output signal to indicate that the character on the document was *rejected.* A character was rejected if the machine could not recognise it with sufficient confidence.

Misrecognition of a '3' as a '5', for example, is called a *substitution error* or simply an *error.* The *substitution error rate* is the percentage of input characters for which a machine makes substitution errors. The

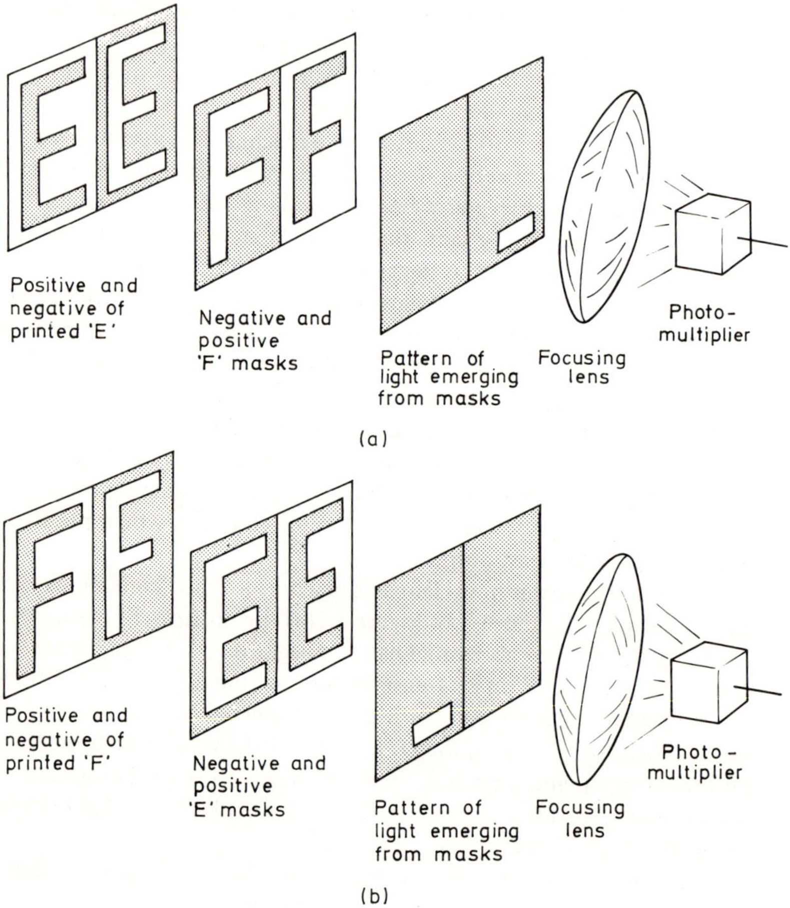

Figure 1.2. (*a*) *Input* E's *aligned with* 'F' *masks;* (*b*) *Input* F's *aligned with* 'E' *masks*

reject rate is the percentage of input characters which a machine rejects, and

$$\text{success rate} = 100 - \text{substitution error rate} - \text{reject rate}$$

By raising the *reject threshold*, ρ, the substitution error rate of Hannan's machine could be reduced at the cost of increasing the reject rate.

Reject thresholds are used in many recognition systems, and a fairly typical trade-off between reject and substitution error rates is shown in Figure 3.2.

1.2 ELECTRONIC MASK MATCHING USING ANALOGUE GREY SCALE

The machine described by Hannan[200] recognised 500 characters per second, whereas electronic mask matching machines (e.g. Ref. 366) have recognised more than 2000 characters per second. Alignment between characters and masks can be accomplished more rapidly by electronic than by optical–mechanical means. Furthermore, unequal *weighting* of masks, as will be explained later, is easier in electronic than in optical implementation, because it is difficult to control accurately the grey scale in a photographic transparency.

To introduce what is roughly an electronic counterpart of Hannan's optical mask matching system, let us consider by way of example a system in which an image of a character is projected onto an array of 35 photocells, arranged in seven rows and five columns. In this system, the output voltage of a photocell is a measure of the total light reflected from a small area of the document. In other words, a photocell produces a voltage which is a measure of the average grey scale value of a small area of the document. An array of photocells is not the only means of transducing a visual pattern into an array of voltages, and other techniques will be outlined in Section 2.1. Methods of alignment will be discussed in Section 2.3, and we shall assume in the remainder of the present chapter that characters have already been aligned. Specifically, we shall assume that the size and position of a character image are such that the lowermost and rightmost black parts of the image are aligned with the lowermost row and rightmost column of our 7 x 5 array of photocells, and that no black part of the image protrudes outside the array.

Hannan's optical system worked with positive and negative images of a character to be recognised. In our electronic counterpart of Hannan's system, the output of each photocell is fed to a separate amplifier which has two output channels, called the *black* and *white* output channels, as indicated in Figure 1.3. Each amplifier is adjusted so that, when the corresponding photocell is aligned with the whitest area on the document, the *white* output channel is at, for example,

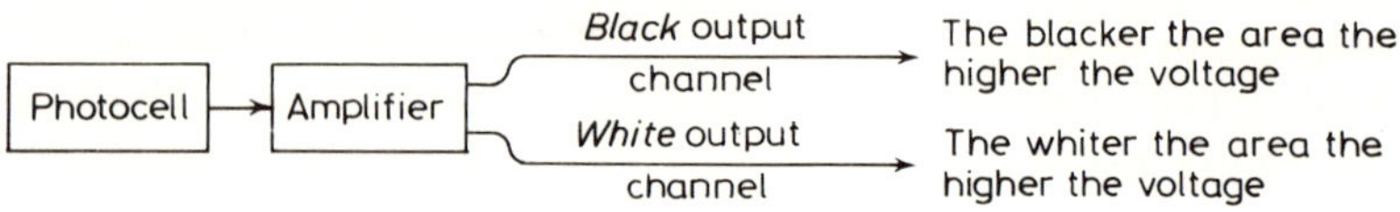

Figure 1.3.

10 V, and the *black* output channel is at 0 V. When the corresponding photocell is aligned with the blackest area on the document, the *white* output channel is at 0 V and the *black* output channel is at 10 V. For intermediate shades of grey the *black* and *white* output voltages are in the range 0–10 V.

In Figure 1.4 each of the 35 small squares corresponds to one of the 35 photocells. By way of example let us say that each square marked 'b' in Figure 1.4 is one for which the corresponding photocell would detect mainly white in a perfectly printed and aligned '2'. Each square marked 'w' in Figure 1.4 is one for which the corresponding photocell would detect mainly black in a perfectly aligned and printed '2'. For every square marked 'w', the *white* output of the corresponding amplifier is connected via a separate resistor to a common current-measuring device. For every square marked 'b' the *black* output channel of the corresponding amplifier is connected via a separate resistor to the same current-measuring device. Although for simplicity only 11 of the 35 resistors are shown in Figure 1.4, all of the 35 resistors are in fact connected to the same current-measuring device, which measures the total current in all of the 35 resistors. The set of 35 resistors is called a *resistor mask.*

The system employs a separate resistor mask for each character to be recognised, each mask having its own current-measuring device. In the resistor mask for any character other than '2', the pattern of

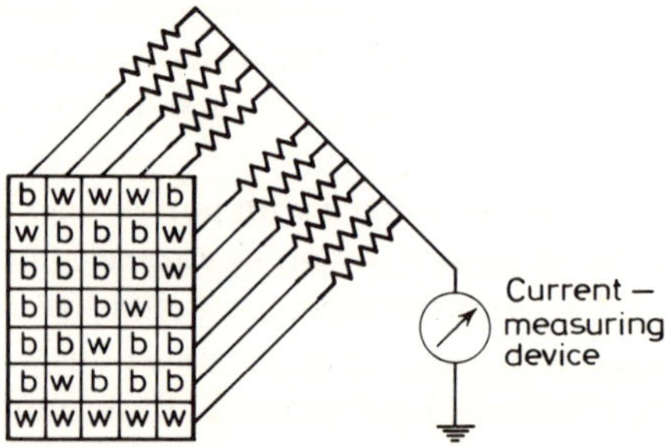

Figure 1.4. *Resistor mask connections*

connections of resistors to *black* and *white* output channels is not as indicated by b's and w's in Figure 1.4, but instead is in accordance with the distribution of white and black in a perfectly printed and aligned specimen of that character. For each photocell which ideally detects mainly white, the *black* output of the corresponding amplifier is connected to the resistor mask; and for each photocell which ideally detects mainly black, the *white* output of the corresponding amplifier is connected to the resistor mask. A character on a document is recognised as the character whose current-measuring device measures a current smaller than that for any other character by at least a threshold amount.

If all resistors in all masks have the same resistance value, a current-measuring device in the present system is roughly the counterpart of a photocell in Hannan's system. The present system differs from Hannan's in that it employs *spatial sampling*, that is, it only 'looks at' a set of small areas of a character. If these areas are each quite large compared with the size of a character, information as to the exact shape of a character may be lost.

In the present system, an amplifier output provides an *analogue* representation of grey scale value, since it varies *continuously* with variations in grey scale value.

1.3 DIGITAL GREY SCALE

Instead of using an analogue grey scale, it is often more convenient to restrict the grey scale values to two discrete values, usually known as *black* and *white*. The analogue output of a photocell can be classified as *white* or *black* according as it does or does not exceed a threshold which is known as a *binarising threshold*. The use of a fixed binarising threshold is not generally satisfactory and methods of determining variable thresholds will be introduced in Section 2.2. A circuit which classifies a photocell output as *black* or *white* is known as a *binarising circuit*.

Let us modify the Section 1.2 recognition system by replacing every Figure 1.3 amplifier by a Figure 1.5 binarising circuit. In the resulting system, there is one binarising circuit per photocell. If a photocell output exceeds the binarising threshold, the *black* output channel of the corresponding binarising circuit is at 0 V, and the *white* output channel is at 10 V. If a photocell output does not exceed the binarising

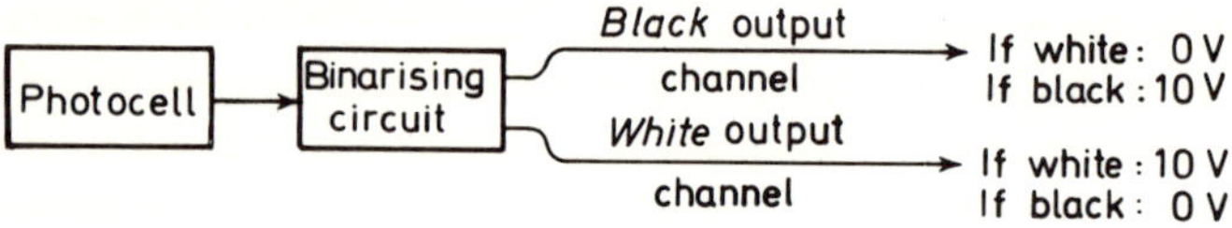

Figure 1.5.

threshold, the *black* output channel of the corresponding binarising circuit is at 10 V, and the *white* output channel is at 0 V. The *black* and *white* output channels are connected to one resistor mask per character, precisely as in Section 1.2, and a character is recognised as the character whose current-measuring device measures a current smaller than that for any other character by at least a threshold amount[362].

To formulate this mathematically, let us index the 35 binarising circuits as indicated in Figure 1.6 and, for $j = 1, 2, \ldots, 35$, let x_j be a variable whose value is 1 or 0 according as the *black* output channel of the jth binarising circuit is at 10 V or 0 V. The array $\boldsymbol{X} = \{x_1, x_2, \ldots, x_{35}\}$ is called a binary *pattern*, and $x_1, \ldots, x_{35}$ are the *elements* of the binary pattern $\boldsymbol{X}$. Before $\boldsymbol{X}$ has been recognised, $\boldsymbol{X}$ is said to be an *unknown* pattern.

1	2	3	4	5
6	7	8	9	10
11	12	13	14	15
16	17	18	19	20
21	22	23	24	25
26	27	28	29	30
31	32	33	34	35

Figure 1.6. *Horizontal raster sequence*

For $j = 1, \ldots, 35$, let q_{rj} be a variable whose value is 1 or 0 according as the *white* or *black* output of the jth binarising circuit is connected to the resistor mask for the rth character. The array $Q_r = \{q_{r1}, q_{r2}, \ldots, q_{rN}\}$ is called the rth *reference pattern.* Different values of r correspond to different characters: let us say, for instance, that Q_1 is the reference pattern for the character '1', Q_2 is the reference pattern for the character '2', and so on. If the resistor mask for '2' is as indicated in Figure 1.4, then Q_2 is as indicated in Figure 1.7, which is simply a binary version of (what we assume here to be) a perfectly printed and aligned specimen '2'.

0	1	1	1	0
1	0	0	0	1
0	0	0	0	1
0	0	0	1	0
0	0	1	0	0
0	1	0	0	0
1	1	1	1	1

Figure 1.7. *A Binarised '2'*

Only one of the output channels of the jth binarising circuit is connected to a resistor in the resistor mask for the rth character. This channel is at 10 V if and only if

$$q_{rj} = 1 \text{ and } x_j = 0, \text{ or } q_{rj} = 0 \text{ and } x_j = 1$$

Now $|q_{rj} - x_j| = 1$ if and only if

$$q_{rj} = 1 \text{ and } x_j = 0, \text{ or } q_{rj} = 0 \text{ and } x_j = 1$$

and therefore the total current in the resistor mask for the rth character is proportional to the *Hamming distance*, h_r, between X and Q_r, which is defined by

$$h_r = \sum_{j=1}^{35} |q_{rj} - x_j|$$

The constants of proportionality are the same for all masks, and can therefore be ignored for purposes of finding the *best* match between X

and a mask. Thus the following is an abstract statement of the recognition rule which, in effect, is used in our resistor mask system:

$$\text{recognise } \boldsymbol{X} \text{ as the } s\text{th character if } h_s < h_r - \rho, \text{ for all } r \text{ except } r = s, \quad (1.1)$$

where ρ is a reject threshold. If the condition is not satisfied for any s, $\boldsymbol{X}$ is rejected. 'Recognise $\boldsymbol{X}$ as the sth character' of course does *not* mean 'recognise $\boldsymbol{X}$ as the actual character 's' '. Here 's' is used as an algebraic unknown, standing, in this particular context, for the index number of the reference pattern which has the smallest Hamming distance to $\boldsymbol{X}$. If, instead of having 35 elements, $\boldsymbol{X}$ and $\boldsymbol{Q}_r$ have N elements, the Hamming distance, h_r, between $\boldsymbol{X}$ and $\boldsymbol{Q}_r$ is defined by

$$h_r = \sum_{j=1}^{N} | q_{rj} - x_j |$$

A weakness of the Hamming distance rule (1.1) is illustrated in Figure 1.8, where pattern elements are presented by black and white squares rather than 1's and 0's. The pattern in Figure 1.8(c) has Hamming distance 32 to the pattern in Figure 1.8(a) and Hamming distance 23 to the pattern in Figure 1.8(b). The pattern in Figure 1.8(d)

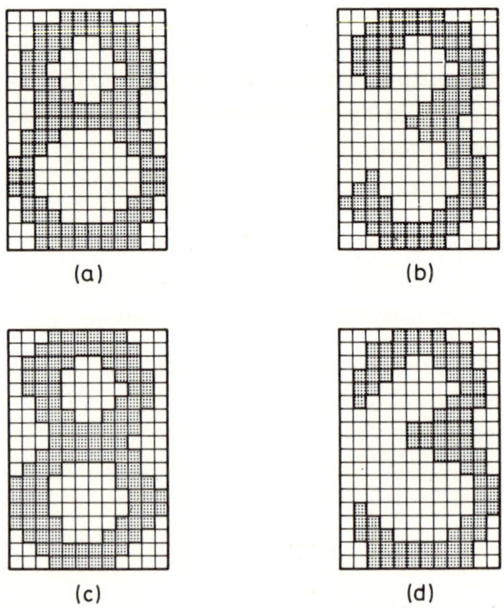

Figure 1.8.

has Hamming distance 22 to the pattern in Figure 1.8(a) and 28 to the pattern in Figure 1.8(b). If character shapes are designed so as to maximise the Hamming distance between all pairs of characters, rule (1.1) becomes more practical[436].

We have associated 10 V with $x_j = 1$ and 0 V with $x_j = 0$ only by way of example, and the actual voltages can be chosen in accordance with practical expediency, except that the voltage associated with $x_j = 1$ should be greater than that associated with $x_j = 0$. If a channel is at the voltage associated with $x_j = 1$, we say that that channel is in *state 1*, and, if a channel is at the voltage associated with $x_j = 0$, we say that that channel is in *state 0*.

For reasons arising from methods of alignment (Section 2.3) it is more usual to connect bistables, instead of binarising circuits, to resistor masks[75, 188, 362]. A *bistable*, for the purposes of this book, is a circuit which has two states, two input channels, and two output channels, as indicated in Figure 1.9. A channel is in state 1 or 0 according as it is at one or other of two arbitrary voltages, as above. If the '1' input channel changes to state 1, then the '1' output channel, if not already in state 1, adopts state 1, and the '0' output channel adopts state 0. The states of the output channels remain unchanged, whatever the subsequent state of the '1' input channel, until such time as the '0' input channel is in state 1, whereupon the '0' output channel adopts state 1 and the '1' output channel adopts state 0. The states of the output channels remain unchanged whatever the subsequent state of the '0' input channel, until such time as the '1' input channel is in state 1. The bistable itself is said to be in state 1 or state 0 according as the '1' output channel is in state 1 or state 0.

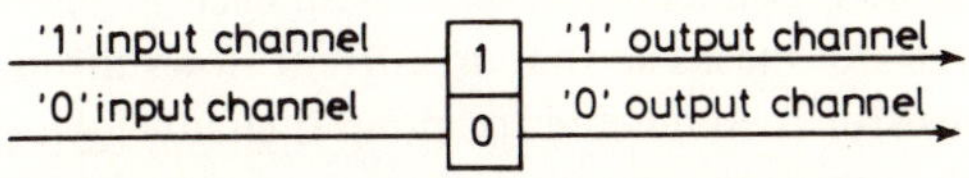

Figure 1.9.

The interposition of bistables between binarising circuits and resistor masks makes no difference to recognition: if we connect each of the Figure 1.5 binarising circuits to a separate bistable, as in Figure 1.10, and if we connect the '1' and '0' output channel of the jth bistable to a resistor in the rth mask according as $q_{rj} = 0$ or 1, then the total current in the rth mask is proportional to h_r, as above.

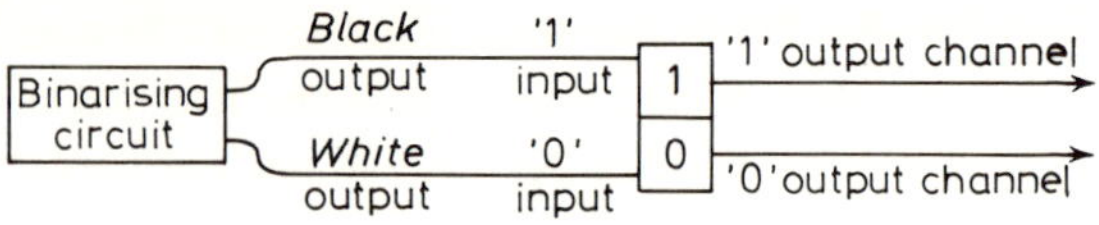

Figure 1.10.

As a compromise between, on the one hand, using a two-level grey scale, and on the other hand, using a continuum of levels in an analogue grey scale, we can use more than two discrete levels. For instance, we can use 16 discrete levels, or 32 discrete levels, or any other number of discrete levels in the grey scale, except that it is usually convenient to choose the number of levels to be a power of two. When there are only two levels, these can be represented by the two states of a bistable, as above. Four levels can be represented by the combinations 00, 01, 10, 11 of states of two bistables[359], and 2^n levels can be represented by the 2^n different combinations of states of n bistables, where n is a positive integer. This is known as *digital* representation of the grey scale.

Let us briefly return to the case where all patterns are binary, and let us again say that states 1 and 0 correspond to 10 V and 0 V respectively. If N, the number of elements per pattern, is large, then implementation of (1.1) may require that error tolerances of circuit components be very small. For instance, if $N = 100$, then when h_r increases by 1 the total current in the rth mask increases by 1% of the amount associated with $h_r = N$. If this 1% increase is to be reliably detected, then the error tolerances of circuit components (e.g. resistors) must be very much less than 1%.

The requirement for low-error circuitry can be mitigated as follows[360]. A separate diode is connected in series with each of the N resistors in each of the resistor masks so that no current flows through a resistor unless that resistor is connected to an input channel which is in state 1. Further, each current-measuring device is connected to earth via a series resistor which has (let us say for simplicity) the same resistance value as any one of the resistors in a mask. The circuit for the mask for the rth character is now as indicated in Figure 1.11 (cf. Figure 15 in Ref. 391 a); and the result of this modification is that the current measured by the current-measuring device is no longer linearly proportional to h_r. A simple application of Ohm's law shows that the current measured by the current-measuring device associated with the rth character is proportional to $h_r/(h_r + 1)$. If h_r increases from $h_r = 1$

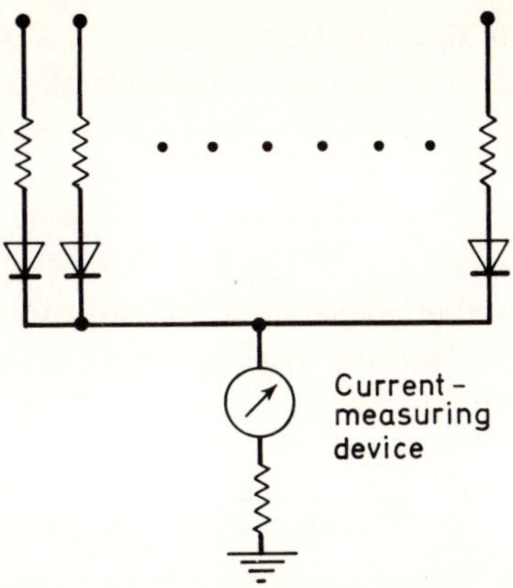

Figure 1.11. *Resistor mask with series diodes. Only three of the N diodes are shown*

to $h_r = 2$, then the total current increases by 66·6% – 50% = 16·6%; and if h_r changes from $h_r = 2$ to $h_r = 3$, then the total current increases by 75% – 66·6% = 8·3%, and so on. Such changes can be more readily detected than, for example, 1% changes.

1.4 SCORE MAXIMISATION

The sth character for which (1.1) is satisfied is also the sth character such that, for all r except $r = s$,

$$N - h_s > N - h_r + \rho \tag{1.2}$$

where N is the number of elements per pattern. Instead of recognising characters in accordance with (1.1), a machine can equivalently recognise characters in accordance with (1.2). To implement (1.2) we only need to make a slight modification to the resistor mask circuitry (without diodes) which implemented (1.1) in Section 1.3, as will now be explained.

Let z be the number of *different* characters to be recognised. For instance, if the 10 numerals 0, . . ., 9 are to be recognised, then $z = 10$, whatever the actual number of 1's, whatever the actual number of 2's, etc. In the implementation of (1.2), we require that, for all $r = 1, \ldots, z$ and for all $j = 1, \ldots, N$, the jth resistor in the mask for the rth character be connected to the '1' or '0' output of the jth bistable according as $q_{rj} = 1$ or 0, where $Q_r = \{q_{r1}, q_{r2}, \ldots, q_{rj}, \ldots, q_{rz}\}$ is as defined in Section 1.3. The jth resistor in the mask for the rth character is now connected to the voltage associated with state 1 only if $q_{rj} = x_j$; that is, if

$$1 - | q_{rj} - x_j | = 1$$

Apart from this reversal of connections, the resistor masks are the same as in Section 1.3. Thus the total current in the mask for the rth character is proportional to

$$\sum_{j=1}^{N} (1 - |q_{rj} - x_j|) = N - h_r$$

and X should be recognised as the character whose current-measuring device measures a *greater* total current than that for any other character by at least a threshold amount[75, 188, 237, 433a]. A current-maximising counterpart of the Section 1.2 analogue system can be obtained by reversal of connections between the *black* and *white* output channels of the Figure 1.3 amplifiers and the resistor masks.

Recognition Equipment Incorporated (REI) have used a current-maximising system in which both binary and analogue voltages are applied to resistor masks[366]. During the 'reading' of a document, the analogue grey scale is automatically adjusted so that the highest analogue voltage always represents the whiteness of the background on which characters are printed, even though this whiteness, when measured absolutely, may vary from document to document, or, due for example to smudging, may be different in different regions of the same document. In this REI system, each photocell is connected to a separate circuit which has two output channels which are called the *black* and *white* output channels respectively, as in Figure 1.12. If the analogue output of a photocell is greater than the average analogue

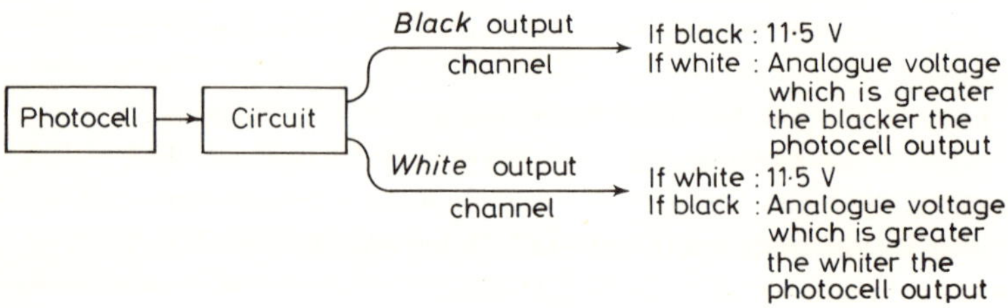

Figure 1.12.

outputs of the 20 nearest-neighbouring photocells, the corresponding Figure 1.12 circuit classifies the photocell output as *white,* and as *black* otherwise. If the photocell output is classified as *black* the Figure 1.12 circuit applies 11·5 V to the *black* output channel. If the photocell output is classified as *white,* the Figure 1.12 circuit applies to the *black* output channel an analogue voltage which is greater the blacker the photocell output, but never greater than 11·5 V. Corresponding conditions apply to the *white* output channel, as indicated in Figure 1.12. The machine uses resistor masks like those used for implementation of (1.2), except that the resistor values are not now all equal. Thus, for $r = 1, \ldots, z$ and $j = 1, \ldots, N$, the *black* or *white* output channel is connected to the jth resistor in the rth mask according as $q_{rj} = 1$ or 0. At a time when the largest total current in any resistor mask exceeds a prescribed absolute threshold, a character on a document is recognised as the character whose mask has a larger total current than any other mask by at least a threshold amount. If there is no such mask, the character is rejected.

1.5 PEEPHOLE MASKS

In Sections 1.3 and 1.4, Q_r is a simple abstract representation of the mask for the rth character. For many purposes we can disregard the distinction between Q_r and the mask for the rth character, and say loosely that Q_r *is* the mask for the rth character. We shall disregard the corresponding distinction when using the term peephole mask. A peephole mask is a subset of the elements of a mask. For example, let $C_r = \{c_{r1}, \ldots, c_{rj}, \ldots, c_{rN}\}$ be a pattern of 1's and 0's whose elements correspond 1:1 with those of Q_r. Let Q_{rc} be the array of all q_{rj}'s such that $c_{rj} = 1$. Then Q_{rc} is a peephole mask if at least one element of C_r is 0. A peephole mask is so called because it only 'looks at' some, not all, of the elements of a pattern[29, 424]. Peephole masks are used in various different ways in pattern recognition, as we shall see in later chapters. The remainder of the present section introduces, as an example, just one of the ways in which peephole masks have been used.

Along a black/white edge of a character there may not be an abrupt change from black to white, but instead there may be a region containing intermediate shades of grey. A photocell which is positioned so as to measure the average grey scale value of a small area near an edge of a limb may produce an output which is binarised as *black* for some specimens, and *white* for other specimens of the same character. This is because the average grey scale value of the small area may be close to the binarising threshold, and slight misalignment, or slight variation in the widths of character limbs, may cause the binarising threshold to be exceeded for some specimens and not for other specimens of the same character. A photocell which is positioned so as to measure the average grey scale value over a small area which is *not* near an edge of a limb can be expected to produce a more consistent output for different specimens of the same character. By taking account of this we may be able to improve the recognition performance of, for instance, the Section 1.3 recognition system, as follows.

For all $r = 1, \ldots, s, \ldots, z$ and $j = 1, \ldots, N$, let $c_{rj} = 1$ if $q_{rj} = x_j$ in all or almost all specimens of the rth character, and let $c_{rj} = 0$ otherwise[188]. Lower recognition error rates may perhaps be obtained by recognising X as the sth character such that, for all r except $r = s$,

$$\sum_{j=1}^{N} c_{sj} \,|\, x_j - q_{sj} \,|< \sum_{j=1}^{N} c_{rj} \,|\, x_j - q_{rj} \,| - \rho$$

instead of using (1.1). This peephole mask recognition rule can be implemented by a resistor mask system which differs from the Section 1.3 system only in that, for all $r = 1, \ldots, z$ and $j = 1, \ldots, N$, the jth resistor in the rth mask is absent if $c_{rj} = 0$ and present only if $c_{rj} = 1$. When some of the resistors are removed from one of the Section 1.3 resistor masks, the result is a resistor peephole mask.

If we let $c_{rj} = 1$ only if $q_{rj} = x_j$ in all or in almost all specimens of the rth character, the resistor peephole mask for the rth character may turn out to include an *unnecessarily* large number of resistors for achieving reliable recognition. It may be possible to leave out further resistors without impairing recognition performance, and with the advantage of economy[137, 452].

1.6 NEGATIVE WEIGHTS

The resistor mask implementation of (1.2) which was introduced in Section 1.4 is not the only possible implementation, and may sometimes not be the most convenient. To introduce an alternative implementation of (1.2), we note that, since the values of x_j and q_{rj} are restricted to 1 and 0,

$$x_j = x_j^2 \quad \text{and} \quad q_{rj} = q_{rj}^2$$

and

$$|x_j - q_{rj}| = |x_j - q_{rj}|^2 = x_j^2 - 2q_{rj}x_j + q_{rj}^2 = x_j(1 - 2q_{rj}) + q_{rj}$$

Therefore

$$N - h_r = N + \sum_{j=1}^{N} x_j(2q_{rj} - 1) - \sum_{j=1}^{N} q_{rj} \tag{1.3}$$

For maximisation purposes N can be omitted since it is the same for all characters, and X can be recognised as the sth character such that, for all r except $r = s$

$$\sum_{j=1}^{N} w_{sj}x_j + w_{s0} > \sum_{j=1}^{N} w_{rj}x_j + w_{r0} + \rho \tag{1.4}$$

where $w_{rj} = 2q_{rj} - 1$ and $w_{r0} = -\sum_{j=1}^{N} q_{rj}$, and ρ is as usual a reject threshold. The w_{rj}'s are called *weights*, and w_{r0} is sometimes called an *additive bias*. Note that $w_{rj} = 1$ or -1 according as $q_{rj} = 1$ or 0.

The peephole mask counterpart of (1.2) is

$$\sum_{j=1}^{N} c_{sj}(1 - |x_j - q_{sj}|) > \sum_{j=1}^{N} c_{rj}(1 - |x_j - q_{rj}|) + \rho$$

and this is the same as (1.4) if

$$w_{rj} = c_{rj}(2q_{rj} - 1) \quad \text{and} \quad w_{r0} = \sum_{j=1}^{N} c_{rj}(1 - q_{rj})$$

Note that the possible values of w_{rj} are now +1, 0, and −1.

To implement (1.4) we can use an array of N photocells and binarising circuits as in Sections 1.3, 1.4, and 1.5. Let us say that the output of each binarising circuit is now connected to a separate circuit as indicated in Figure 1.13, instead of a bistable as in Figure 1.10.

In Figure 1.13, 10 V is specified only by way of example. There is a separate resistor mask for each character. The resistor mask for the rth character has one resistor corresponding to each of $w_{r1}, \ldots, w_{rj}, \ldots, w_{rN}$, and an $(N + 1)$th resistor corresponding to w_{r0}. For

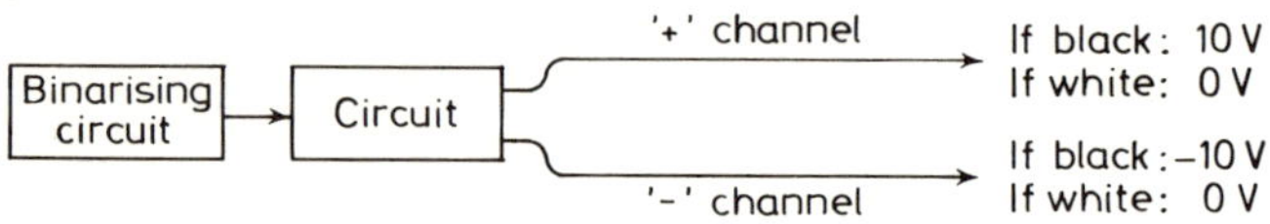

Figure 1.13.

$j = 0, 1, \ldots, N$, the resistance value of the jth resistor is $\alpha/|w_{rj}|\ \Omega$, where α is a constant, and the jth resistor is connected to the '+' or '−' output channel of the jth Figure 1.13 circuit according as w_{rj} is positive or negative[213]. The total current through all the $N + 1$ resistors is measured by a single current-measuring device. The connections of four of the resistors of the rth mask are shown in Figure 1.14, it being assumed, by way of example, that w_{r0}, w_{r1}, and w_{r3} are negative, and that w_{r2} is positive. A pattern X is recognised as the character whose current-measuring device measures a larger current than that for any other character by at least a threshold amount. This resistor mask system remains an implementation of (1.4) even when the weights are not restricted to ±1. Methods of automatic determination of weights will be introduced in Chapter 3.

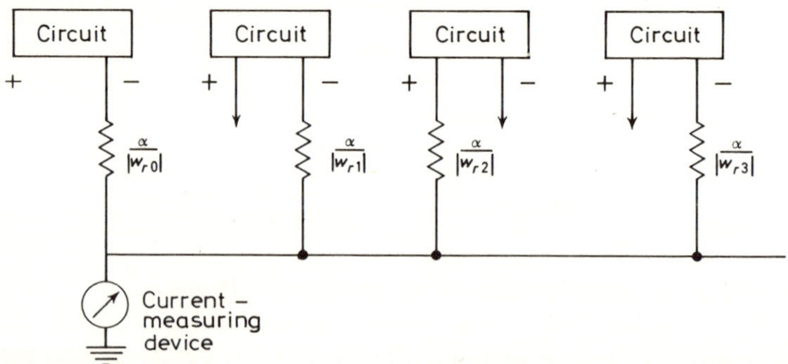

Figure 1.14. *Resistor mask implementation of positive and negative weights*

With only the following trivial modification the present system will work with an analogue grey scale. Let us extend our definition of $X = \{x_1, \ldots, x_j, \ldots, x_N\}$ so that x_j is now an analogue quantity which is a measure of the blackness of the jth photocell output. For all $r = 1, \ldots, z$ and $j = 1, \ldots, N$, the jth resistor in the rth mask is connected to a source of $+\beta x_j$ or $-\beta x_j$ V, according as w_{rj} is positive or negative, where β is a constant[413]. The w_{r0} resistor is connected to $+\beta$ or $-\beta$ V according as w_{r0} is positive or negative. The total current in the rth mask is proportional to

$$\sum_{j=0}^{N} x_j w_{rj} + w_{r0}$$

A resistor mask is not the only simple hardware for computing $\sum_{j=0}^{N} x_j w_{rj} + w_{r0}$. For instance, for application with binary patterns, Gorbatenko has described a system which uses capacitors[179].

Chapter 2

PREPROCESSING FOR CHARACTER RECOGNITION

2.1 CONVERSION FROM VISUAL TO ELECTRICAL PATTERNS

2.1.1 Nipkow disc

A Nipkow disc mechanical scanner can be used instead of an array of photocells for transducing visual into electrical patterns. Figure 2.1 is a diagram of a Nipkow disc scanner. Light reflected from the document is focused via a vertical slit aperture onto the Nipkow disc and thence into a photomultiplier via a condensing lens[181]. The Nipkow disc is opaque except for spiral[145] sets of holes, only two of the spirals being shown in

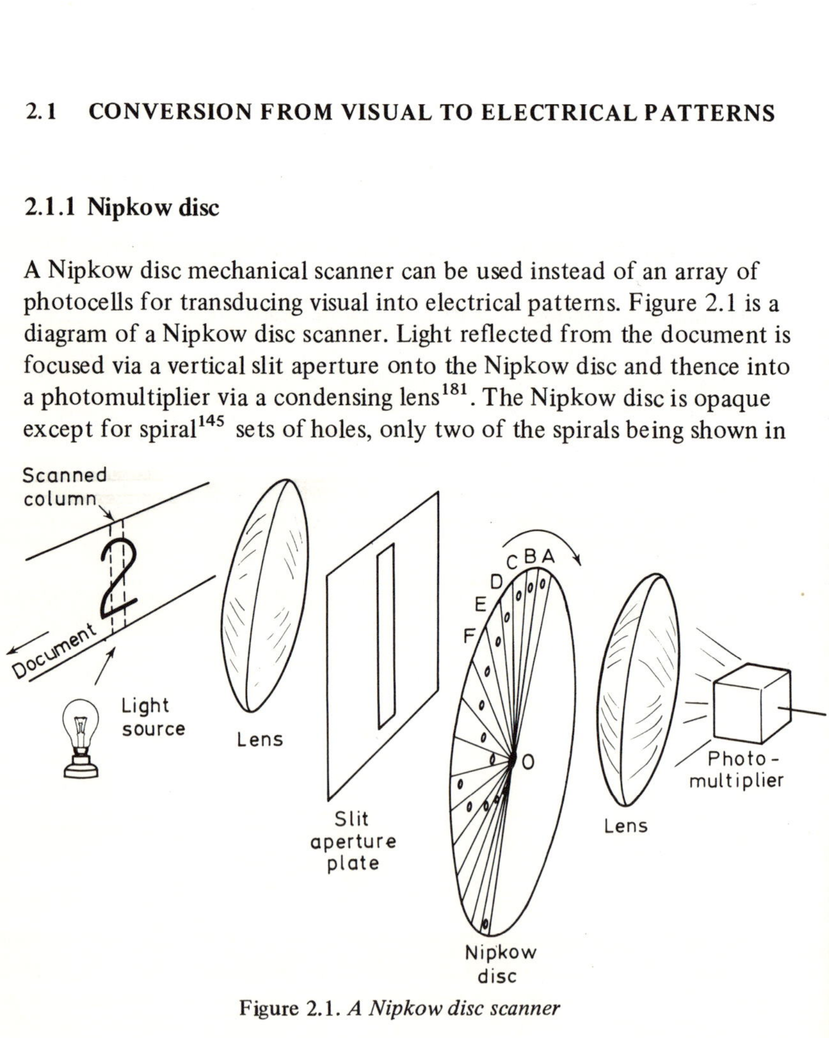

Figure 2.1. *A Nipkow disc scanner*

Figure 2.1. The disc rotates so that at successive instants radial segments AO, BO, CO, DO, etc., are parallel to the slit aperture. Each segment contains a hole, which in successive segments is nearer to the axis of the disc, and at a given instant the only light to reach the photomultiplier is that passing through the hole in the segment which is aligned with the slit aperture. At successive instants the light reaching the photomultiplier comes from successively lower small areas within the scanned column, indicated in Figure 2.1, on the input document.

After the last hole belonging to a spiral has come into alignment with the slit, the first hole of the next spiral comes into alignment, and so on. If the document were stationary this would result in the same column on the document being scanned again. But actually the document itself moves relatively slowly from right to left so that a new column is scanned by each successive spiral. Thus the sequence of output voltages from the photomuliplier refers to successive small areas whose positions are indicated by successive numbers in Figure 2.2. This sequence is known as a vertical *raster*, and the sequence shown in Figure 1.6 is an example of a horizontal raster.

1	9	17	25	33
2	10	18	26	34
3	11	19	27	35
4	12	20	28	36
5	13	21	29	37
6	14	22	30	38
7	15	23	31	39
8	16	24	32	40

Figure 2.2. *Vertical raster sequence*

Other mechanical scanning systems have been devised in which slits are aligned with a slit, rather than holes with a slit[334, 397, 403]. Mechanical scanning is comparatively cheap and robust, but slower than electronic methods. It is only suitable for recognition of characters whose positions on the document are fairly well known. Mechanical scanning has been used in several Farrington readers[17], and also in the IBM 1418 and 1428, where there are in fact 24 spirals each comprising 68 holes in the disc[145]. The maximum reading speed of the IBM 1418 is 480 characters per second[62].

2.1.2 Vidicon

Figure 2.3 is a schematic diagram of a vidicon, which is one of the most stable and durable of the devices which are used as television camera tubes[16, 39a, 188, 340a]. Magnetic-deflection coils direct a low-energy electron beam from an electron gun onto a phototarget. The phototarget includes a *signal plate* which is a transparent conductive layer on the inside of the glass onto which the visual picture is focused. The other component of the phototarget is a layer, on the signal plate, of for example sponge-textured antimony trisulphide, onto which the electron beam is pin-point focused. Antimony trisulphide is a photoconductor, that is, a substance whose electrical conductivity depends on the intensity of light incident upon it.

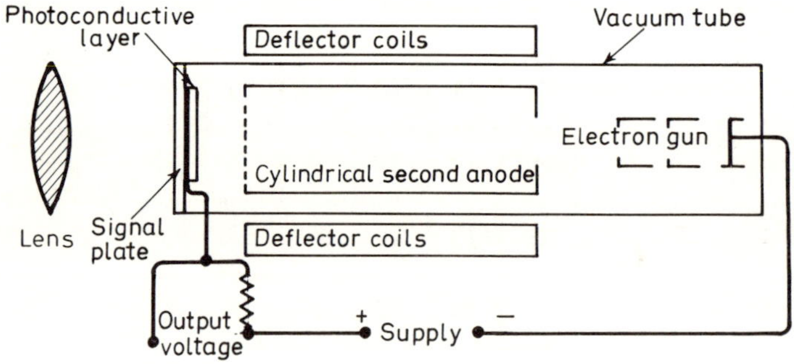

Figure 2.3. *A vidicon*

The pin-point electron beam traces out a raster over the photoconductive surface, thus providing the surface with negative charge. The signal plate is connected to a positive supply voltage which causes current to flow through the thickness of the photoconductive layer (in which the sponge texturing reduces lateral current). The current depends on the resistance of the antimony trisulphide and this varies across the picture in accordance with the variation in greyness.

Consequently the pattern of electric charge on the surface of the photoconductor facing the electron gun is an analogue version of the visual picture, and this in turn means that during the next raster scan the current in the electron beam is modulated in accordance with the visual picture. The current, or the voltage across a resistor in series with the signal plate, can be sampled at discrete time intervals and fed into recognition circuitry.

A disadvantage of the vidicon is that the charge pattern is imperfectly discharged by the electron beam and each pattern read out has a faint ghost of the previous pattern superimposed on it. Hall[195] has mentioned a system in which each pattern is stored in a delay line and an attenuated version of it is subtracted from the next pattern scanned, to balance out the ghosting effect. The resolution, that is, the limit of fineness of the grid of picture elements, which is attainable with a vidicon is somewhat less than that attainable with a flying-spot scanner, and the scanning speed is also generally somewhat less.

2.1.3 Flying-spot scanner

In the Nipkow disc and vidicon techniques the document is flooded with light, and reflected light is 'read' off, point by point. The flying-spot scanning technique is the opposite of this, in that the document is not flooded with light but instead is illuminated at any given instant only by a single sharply focused spot of light[206, 311, 357]. The bright spot originates from the screen of a cathode-ray tube, and can be deflected magnetically into successive positions which constitute a raster scan. In practice the brightness of the spot is liable to vary with its position. An important source of such variation is irregularity in the phosphor of the cathode-ray tube screen, which results in *bright-up noise.* The total light reflected from the document is measured by a photomultiplier, and the total light emanating from the cathode-ray tube screeen is measured by a second photomultiplier. To compensate for bright-up noise, the *difference* between the outputs of the two photomultipliers can be fed into recognition circuitry[374] (cf. Ref. 462).

An advantage of the flying-spot scanner is that the whole raster can be deflected electronically to any position within a 6 in by 6 in area on the document without calling for mechanical movement of the document or scanning apparatus[141]. This is important when the location of characters on the document is not known in advance, as, for example, in reading addresses on envelopes in the mail. A flying-spot scanner can readily scan in an irregular non-raster fashion which can be useful, for instance, in searching for lines of text[290]. It is possible to scan several thousand characters per second with a flying-spot scanner.

A disadvantage is that the document has to be scanned in a light-tight box, and this can be troublesome when high-speed automatic document handling is used. The scanning speed of a flying-spot scanner is limited by the time taken for a bright spot on the cathode-ray tube screen to fade away when the electron beam has moved on to another position. In the fastest tubes the spot is blue, with ultraviolet components which may cause unwelcome fluorescence of various inks and papers[62]. A further disadvantage is that the spot has to be bright, which means that the cathode-ray tube may deteriorate and have to be replaced quite often.

2.1.4 Arrays of photocells

In one method the document is flooded with light and the reflected light is focused onto a single vertical column of photocells, the column being about three times the maximum height of any character, to allow for misalignment. Photocells are commonly used in this application because they are physically more compact than photomultipliers, although they require a higher level of illumination. The document[235, 362], or an image of the document reflected by a rotating mirror[11], moves continuously in a horizontal direction, so that the vertical column of photocells is aligned with successive vertical strips of the document. The document does not have to be in a light-tight box. A photocell column is more rugged and compact than a vidicon, and does not suffer from a ghosting effect.

Retina systems employ a two-dimensional array composed of a plurality of parallel columns of photocells[366, 413]. The array is made wide enough to span the widest character to be recognised, and about three times the maximum height of any character. An advantage of a retina is that the analogue outputs of the photocells are all available at once for parallel processing. Since fast and accurate storage of analogue information is difficult, or at least expensive, to accomplish, it is usual for non-retina systems to make only limited use of analogue information.

High speeds of operation, e.g. 2400 characters per second[366], may be achieved with a single column of photocells or a full retina. However, it is desirable to know in advance the approximate location of characters on the document. Otherwise the document, or a reflected image of it, must be moved line-by-line past the photocells until the required characters are found.

2.1.5 Facsimile transmitter

In Figure 2.4 the document to be read is wrapped round a cylindrical drum, which is rotated about its axis by an electric motor. The motor is also geared to rotate a screw so that the box moves in a direction parallel to the axis of the drum by a prescribed amount, e.g. 0.005 in,

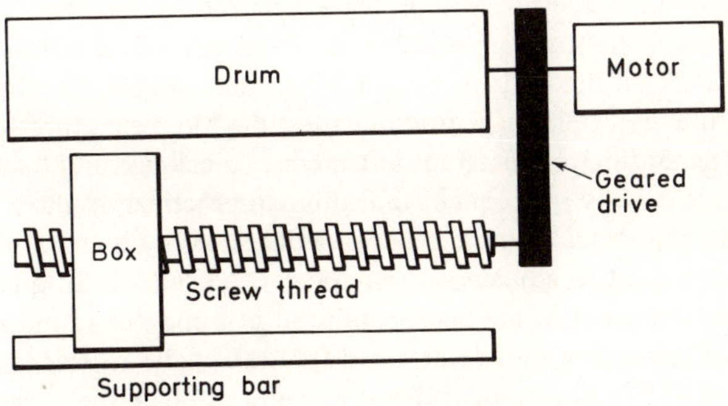

Figure 2.4. *Facsimile transmitter*

for each rotation of the drum. The supporting bar merely steadies the box. The box contains a light source which illuminates the document on the drum. Light reflected from the document is focused through a pinhole onto a photocell which is situated in the box and arranged so that light from only a small (e.g. 0·005 in diameter) area of the document is measured by the photocell[93, 255]. This method of transducing a visual pattern into an electrical pattern has been extensively used for transmitting pictures for journalistic purposes. It has the advantages of being relatively cheap and robust. For character recognition it has the disadvantages of being slow and of transducing pattern points from the document in an inconvenient order.

2.2 BINARISATION

2.2.1 Threshold determined by contrast

The blackness of typed or printed characters is liable to vary from character to character, and sometimes across a single character. Typing or printing is liable to be accompanied by spattering of ink, and new ribbons or dirty type elements may cause the centre of an 'o', for example, to be somewhat blackened. Differences in colour and gloss of different documents mean that the background on which characters are printed is at a variable level of whiteness. Documents are liable to be dirtied during the automatic document handling process, and electronic processing of transduced data contributes further noise.

Binarisation is achieved by applying a threshold to the grey scale, and a pattern element is deemed black or white according as it is more black or less black than this threshold. When the blackness of characters and the whiteness of the background varies, the binarising threshold must vary accordingly. Variations in character blackness and background whiteness are usually so frequent that it is not practical to make appropriate adjustments to the binarising threshold by hand, and instead the threshold must be adjusted automatically. A crude technique is to find the whitest point in the neighbourhood of a character, and set the binarising threshold as a predetermined fraction of the whiteness of this point. But this technique is liable to count as black the somewhat blackened centre of an 'o'; and an 'E' which gets progressively fainter (less black) from top to bottom due to misalignment of the printing mechanism is liable to be truncated.

In a binarising technique known as the *focus–defocus* technique[75], the character to be recognised is scanned by a flying spot, the diameter of the focused spot being roughly half the expected width of a character limb. The spot pauses in a (raster) series of positions across the character. In each position the spot is first focused and then defocused so that it grows to three or four times its original diameter, though the total amount of light incident on the document remains the same whether the spot is focused or defocused. At each position the small area of the character is deemed *black* only if the photomultiplier output is less for the focused spot than for the defocused one, and *white* otherwise. A practical elaboration of this is that, to count as *black*, the photomultiplier output for the focused spot must be less by some small prescribed amount than that for the defocused spot.

To relate the focus–defocus technique to a Laplacian operation, consider the spot moving from a white region into a black region, as in Figure 2.5. The difference in photomultiplier output for the focused and defocused spot varies as indicated by the dotted curve in Figure 2.5, and the crosses correspond to the five illustrated positions of the spot. If a sharply focused spot were to move vertically from white to black, the photomultiplier output, regarded as a measure of whiteness, would be as shown in Figure 2.6(a). The first and second differentials of Figure 2.6(a) with respect to vertical displacement would be as shown in Figures 2.6(b) and (c) respectively. Figure 2.6(b) is a rounded peak rather than a discontinuous delta function because the diameter of the sharply focused spot is not infinitesimal. Because Figure 2.6(c) resembles the dotted curve in Figure 2.5, and because the double differentiation is generally two dimensional, or in other words Laplacian, the focus–defocus technique roughly performs a Laplacian operation[246].

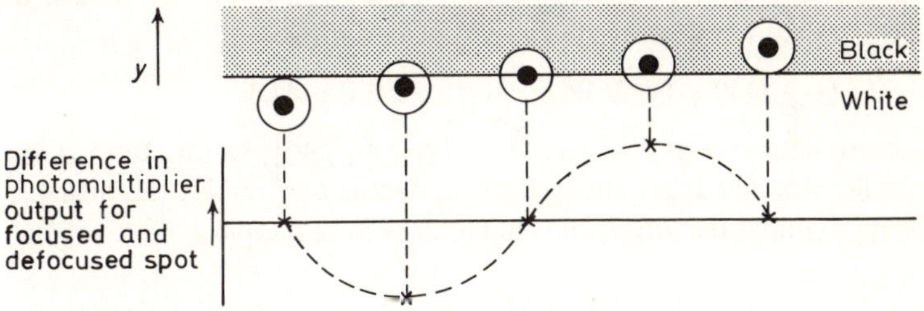

Figure 2.5. *Focus–defocused spot moving across black/white boundary*

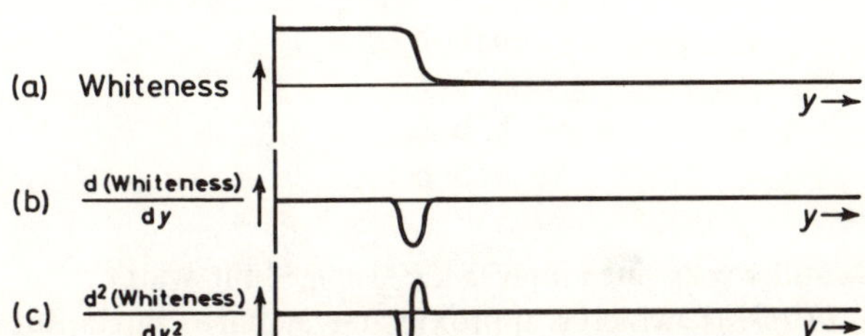

Figure 2.6. *Differentials of whiteness with respect to vertical displacement*

An analogous technique can be employed in systems using a retina: the output of a given photocell can be deemed *white* or *black* according as it does or does not exceed the average output of (e.g.) the 20 nearest-neighbouring photocells[366, 431]. This is redolent of the function of ganglion cells in the mammalian retina[61].

2.2.2 Threshold determined by measurement of limb width

It is possible to adjust the binarisation threshold so as to bring the average limb width approximately to a prescribed value. Average limb width can be estimated as follows[31, 180a, 386]. Let A be the total number of black elements in the input character, with the binarising threshold set at some arbitrary level, and let us start by considering a particular idealised character consisting of a tall narrow black rectangle of L rows and W columns of black bits. The number, Q', of positions in which the four bits

```
b b
b b
```

are all included in this character is $(L-1)(W-1)$, where 'b' stands for black. If $L >> 1$ we can write as an approximation

$$Q' = L(W-1) = LW(W-1)/W = A(W-1)/W$$

which can be rearranged to give $W = 1/[1-(Q'/A)]$, so that limb width can be determined approximately from counts of Q' and A. If, instead of being a simple rectangle, the character is for example a 'T':

```
b b b b b b b
b b b b b b b
b b b b b b b
    b b b
    b b b
    b b b
    b b b
    b b b
```

the formula still works since it gives the average limb width $W = 1/[1-(19/33)]$, which is approximately equal to three. But the formula does not work if the limb width is less than two, nor in characters containing diagonals, such as the '7':

```
b b b b b b
b b b b b b
        b b
      b b
    b b
  b b
```

To cater for diagonals the system[31] counts not merely the number of positions in which

```
b b
b b
```

is completely included in the input character, but instead the system counts the number, Q, of positions in which *at least one of*

```
b b       b b     b b
b b ,   b b   ,     b b
```

relatively positioned so that the left-hand three b's in

```
  b b          b b                       b b
b b    and       b b    are covered by   b b
```

is completely included in the character. Approximate average limb width is now given by $W = 1/[1 - (Q/A)]$. In the 'T' shown above,

```
b b
b b
```

fits in every position where

```
  b b      b b
b b    or    b b
```

fits so $Q = Q'$. But in the '7' shown above, $Q \neq Q'$, and only the formula using Q instead of Q' gives the right answer $W = 1/[1 - (9/21)]$, which is approximately equal to two.

In one recognition system[402], Q and A are determined for a given character while that character is being submitted to a recognition process. If at the end of the recognition process the character is classified as a *reject*, the binarising threshold is moved nearer to black if W exceeds a prescribed value, or moved nearer to white if W is less than this prescribed value, and a second attempt at recognition is made. An alternative way of making use of the estimate of W is to adjust the binarising threshold for the *next* character to be encountered in the text. Again the binarising threshold is adjusted so as to bring W nearer to a prescribed value. This technique, among others, is used in the highly developed binarising system of the IBM 1975 optical page reader[31].

2.3 ALIGNMENT

2.3.1 Vertical alignment by measurement

An REI machine[366] employs a retina which is 48 photocells high and 13 wide, but the input array for the resistor masks is only 16 elements high and 13 elements wide. The 16 rows which provide the input to the masks are 16 consecutive rows out of the 48 which constitute the retina, and they are selected as follows. For each of the 48 rows in the retina there is a separate circuit which has a binary output indicating whether or not there are any black elements in that row. Further circuits detect the highest row in the retina which

(1) contains at least one black element, and
(2) is such that the row immediately below it contains at least one black element, and
(3) is such that neither of the two rows immediately above it contain at least one black element.

These circuits are intended to find the top of the *top* character which is in registration with the retina. To reduce time spent searching for lines of text, the retina, together with a special line-finding extension, is made high enough to cover two lines of text at once.

Circuits are also provided for finding the bottom row of the top character, and this is taken to be the highest row which

(1) contains at least one black element, and
(2) is such that none of the three rows immediately below it contains any black elements.

Having found the position of the top and bottom rows of the top character, the system computes the midpoint between these positions, and selects 16 rows centred on this midpoint. Transistor switches connect these 16 rows to the recognition circuitry. After 5 μs, transistor switches connect a new set of 16 rows to the recognition circuitry, such that the top row of the new 16 rows is one row higher than the top row of the previous 16 rows. After a further 5 μs, transistor switches connect a further new set of 16 rows to the recognition circuitry, such that the top row of the new 16 rows is one row lower than the top row of the first set of 16 rows. In each of these three positions, the total current in each resistor mask is measured. If the total current in any mask exceeds a prescribed threshold, the total currents in all masks are compared and the input character is recognised as the character whose mask produces a total current which is larger than that from any other mask by at least a threshold amount[366]. Because of the finite resolution of the retina, and because of minute imperfections in the printing of characters, the up-and-down-one-row 5 μs *jitter* sometimes results in recognition of a character which has been missed in the central alignment position.

During reading, the text moves continuously past the reading head at 200 in/s, and the centring and up-and-down jitter cycle is repeated every 15 μs. The document does not move by more than half of the width of a photocell in 15 μs. Thus vertical alignment is achieved by centring on the midpoint between the top and bottom rows of a character and jittering; and horizontal alignment is achieved by testing, at *all* successive horizontal alignments, whether any mask matching score exceeds a prescribed limit.

We now outline two other methods of alignment, which are perhaps less sensitive to spurious marks at the top and bottom of a character. If black and white pattern elements are regarded as having unit and zero mass respectively, the centre of gravity of an unknown character can be determined, and the recognition system can be aligned on the position of the centre of gravity[212, 255]. Whether a given element is black or white has more influence on the position of the centre of gravity the further this element is from the centre of gravity. To avoid this distance weighting, the *centre of black*[362] can be used instead of the centre of gravity: an imaginary horizontal line is found such that the total number of black points above the line is equal to the total number of black points below it. The vertical position of this line is used to determine the vertical alignment of the recognition system. Note that if, due to imperfect printing, limb width is greater at the top than at the bottom of a character, both the centre of black and the centre of gravity methods may misalign the character.

2.3.2 Vertical alignment by exhaustive trial

The following important technique requires the use of a *shift register,* which is a string of bistables with its input at one end and its output at the other end. A shift register is controlled by timing pulses, and on receipt of a timing pulse each bistable adopts the state of its immediate neighbour on the side nearest the input. At the same time one bit is lost off the output end of the shift register, and one bit is fed in at the input end. The input bit determines the state of the bistable at the input end of the string.

Consider for example a shift register consisting of six bistables, with input on the left, and the states of the bistables represented by 1's and 0's. If at a given time the states of the bistables are 1,0,1,1,0,0, we say that the shift register *contains* 101100. If, when the next three timing pulses are received, the input bits are respectively 0, 1, and 1, then the shift register contains successively 010110, 101011, and 110101. This illustrates the idea of a shift register.

Suppose now that a vertical raster is used in a recognition system, and to illustrate the following idea [75, 181, 188, 235] let us suppose that each vertical scan of the raster only includes five pattern elements, and let us consider only four successive vertical scans. Binarisation of the scanner output provides successive inputs to a shift register which is composed of 20 bistables. The 20 bistables are arranged physically in a 5 x 4 array, the sequence of bistables being

20	15	10	5
19	14	9	4
18	13	8	3
17	12	7	2
16	11	6	1

In this the bottom of one column is connected to the top of the next. Representing the states of the 20 bistables by $a, b, c, \ldots, t$, we see that at successive times the bit pattern in the top left-hand 3 x 3 sub-array or *window* in Figure 2.7(a) is the one marked out in the corresponding diagram in Figure 2.7(b). In Figure 2.7(b) the original pattern remains unshifted, and the 3 x 3 window moves across it as shown, whilst in Figure 2.7(a) the original pattern is electronically shifted through the shift register and the 3 x 3 window remains fixed in position. This shows that, if we look at the shift register through a

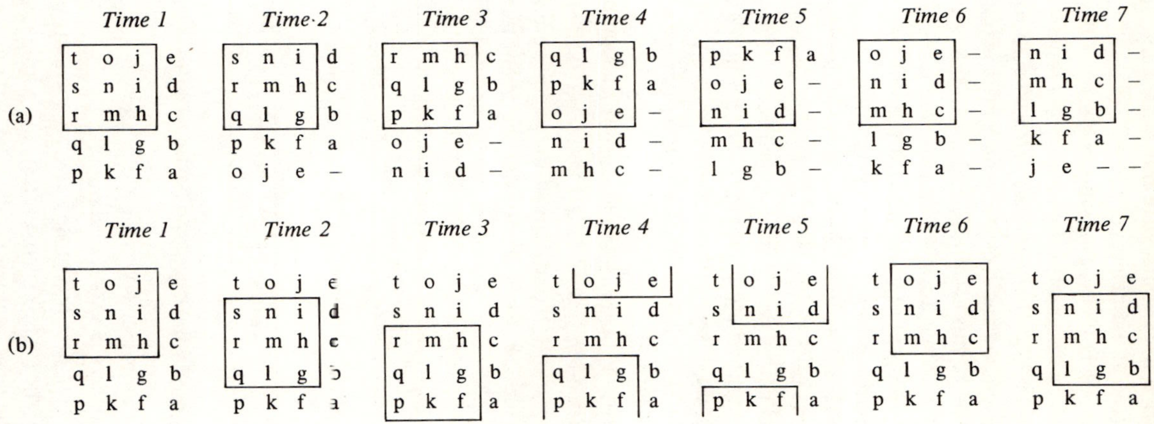

Figure 2.7. *Elements appearing in a* 3 × 3 *window in a* 4 × 5 *shift register*

fixed window while the pattern shifts through the shift register, we see what we would see if the pattern were not shifted and instead the window were shifted as indicated in Figure 2.7(b).

This small example has served merely to illustrate the technique. By way of a more realistic example let us consider a resistor mask recognition system in which binarised characters are fed into a 36 row by 20 column shift register, and the largest character fits within a 24 row by 16 column window. In this system the inputs to the resistor masks are derived from a 24 x 16 window of bistables, and recognition is attempted after each step of an input pattern through the shift register. This is equivalent to attempting to recognise the unknown pattern in each position in turn within the 36 x 20 array. It may not matter that, for instance, after some of the steps of a '2' through the shift register, the bottom horizontal bar of the '2' may appear *above* the curved top of the '2' in the 24 x 16 element window, cf. times 4 and 5 in Figure 2.7. If we wish to avoid this, we design the system so that the total number of rows in the shift register is at least twice the number of consecutive rows which contain black in any character.

If the printing or typing of characters is not carefully controlled, lines of text may be skewed or bowed as in Figure 2.8. If the loci of the uppermost and lowermost excursions of the raster were the horizontal lines drawn in Figure 2.8, the shift register alignment technique would not work, because the raster would not always completely cover the

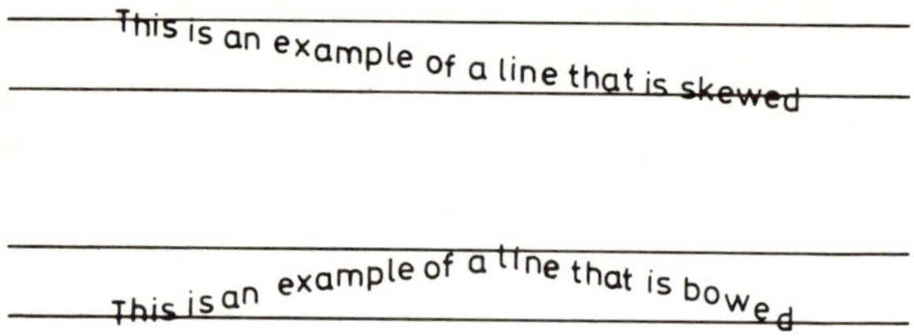

Figure 2.8. *Skewed and bowed lines of text*

characters to be recognised. To remedy this, the whole raster must be moved so that it always covers the characters. If, on its way through the shift register, a character is recognised at a time which signifies that the character is below the middle of the raster, the whole raster can be lowered so that the next character to be read will more nearly lie in the middle of the raster[353]. Similarly, if recognition occurs when the character is high in the raster, the raster can be raised.

In some recognition systems, such as the IBM 1975[210], the character in the shift register does not come into alignment at a unique time, but instead recognition is based on fulfilment, possibly at somewhat different times, of a number of separate logical conditions. In such systems the above technique for following lines cannot be used. Instead the whole raster can be vertically positioned so that, roughly speaking, above and below each successive character the numbers of rows of the raster containing no black elements are more or less equal. IBM patents[107a, 290] describe practical techniques for achieving this, and also for *finding* straight, skewed, or bowed lines of text on a document.

2.3.3 Horizontal alignment and segmentation of text

Reading machines are usually required to recognise characters belonging to words or to strings of numbers and letters. *Segmentation* is the process of dividing up a string of characters into separate characters. This is easy when between each pair of successive characters there is at least one column containing no black elements. The first such column immediately to the right of a character can be used as a vertical reference line for horizontal alignment of the recognition system with the character[34, 362]. This simple method, which is known as *right justification,* suffers more from spurious black marks to the right of a character than does the method[414] of centring on the mid-line between the first all-white column each side of the character.

Sometimes two characters almost touch, and if they are binarised there is a continuous black path from one to the other. But if they are *not* binarised we may find, looking at the total analogue black in successive columns of the raster, that this total has a minimum at the column where the characters should be segmented[180, 210]. It would be fairly safe to segment the characters at this column if its position were roughly what would be expected in the light of the known range of *pitch* and the known position of recognition of the previous character.

The *pitch* is the distance between the centre lines of successive characters. Touching characters are sometimes produced by typewriters which have constant pitch for all characters, rather than, for example, spacing 'mt' and 'it' differently. When pitch is constant it can be determined, automatically if necessary, and used to force segmentation if all else fails[35, 362].

In Figure 2.9 there is no continuous black path from the 'A' to the 'T', yet there is no purely white column between these two characters. If a pair of successive vertical columns can be found which do not contain

$$\mathrm{b\ b} \quad \text{or} \quad \begin{matrix} & \mathrm{b} \\ \mathrm{b} & \end{matrix} \quad \text{or} \quad \begin{matrix} \mathrm{b} & \\ & \mathrm{b} \end{matrix}$$

in any vertical position, it is correct to take a mid-line between these two columns as a segmentation line. This is known as *snake* segmentation[362].

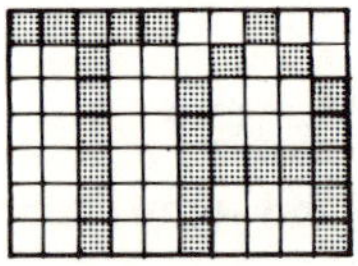

Figure 2.9. *Characters which can be segmented by snake segmentation*

Let us consider all possible adjacent pairs of bits in any given row of black and white bits. If the given row has a white bit at each end, then the total number of bw (that is, black white) pairs is necessarily equal to the total number of wb pairs. Therefore, over all the rows of a binarised character, the total number of bw pairs is equal to the total number of wb pairs. One of the segmentation techniques of Hoffman and McCullough[219a] is a development of the following idea. While a character is scanned from right to left, all bw and wb pairs are counted. When the scan nears the left-hand side of the character, the total number of wb pairs approaches the total number of bw pairs. As soon as the difference between the total numbers of bw pairs and wb pairs is less than a prescribed threshold, the system searches for a cue, such as the ending of a limb (or serif), which determines precisely the segmentation line.

In the REI system[366] discussed above, the masks are designed, so that, when a character is in perfect alignment, the mask does not protrude horizontally beyond the ideally black portion of the character. This means that it does not matter whether successive characters touch. Segmentation is based on testing at all successive horizontal alignments to find whether any resistor mask has a total current exceeding a prescribed threshold. Ideally this threshold is only exceeded when the character is in perfect horizontal alignment, and *therefore* segmented.

This idea can also be used in the Section 2.3.2 shift register method[75]. As a line of text passes through the shift register, each character passes through many vertical alignments and also through all horizontal alignments. Recognition is attempted after every step through the shift register and the masks or recognition logic circuits are of minimal width so that, when a character is perfectly aligned, the presence of touching characters will not alter the total currents in the resistor masks or upset logical recognition conditions.

Roughly speaking, this method amounts to looking at the text through a window which is the same width as a character, and recognising any adequate character appearing in the window. But it is possible to look at a touching '1' and '0' and recognise 'K', or to look at two touching 0's and recognise 'X', as in Figure 2.10. This can be remedied

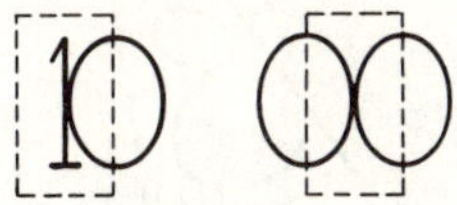

Figure 2.10. *Touching characters*

by making use of approximate knowledge of character width. After a character has been recognised, all recognition processes are inhibited until a time long enough for that character to pass almost out of the window. This technique permits recognition of a character within a range of horizontal positions which is determined by the position at which the preceding character is recognised. Holt and Hill[222a] have described a technique which uses the position of the preceding character and also uses the position of the character immediately following the character which is to be recognised.

2.3.4 Size and perspective normalisation

In the shift register technique introduced in Section 2.3.2, at the time when the bottom of a character lies in some arbitrarily prescribed row of the shift register, suitable circuitry can detect the highest row in the shift register containing at least one black element. This amounts to measuring the height of the character. If the character is bigger than required, the height of the raster and the speed of the scan are proportionately increased, and when the character is scanned a second time it has the required height in the shift register. If the character is too small the first time, the height of the raster and speed of the scan are proportionately reduced, and the character is rescanned[25, 290, 353]. Normalisation of shear[26, 71] and height-to-width ratio[210] have also been employed.

Nagy and Tuong have described a technique of normalisation by perspective transformation[329]. To introduce the idea which they have developed, let us imagine a character standing up from the paper in bas-relief. Nagy and Tuong find the four points where a string drawn tightly round the character passes through ±45° to the horizontal. In Figure 2.11(a) the string is represented by a dotted line and the ±45° points lie at the tops of the four arrows. Nagy and Tuong expand

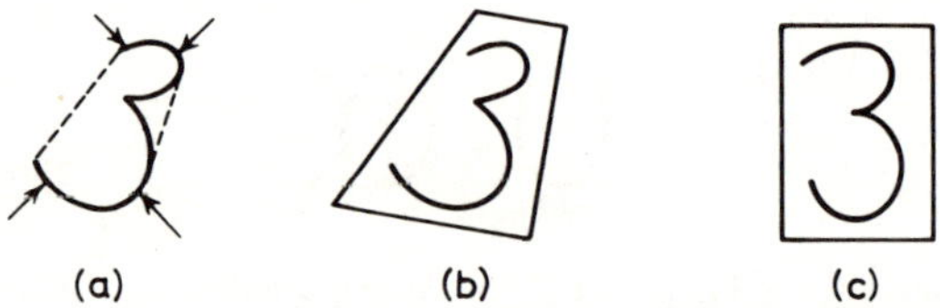

Figure 2.11. *Steps of perspective normalisation procedure*

the quadrilateral whose vertices are the ±45° points so that this quadrilateral just includes the character, as in Figure 2.11(b). They then apply a perspective transformation to the quadrilateral and the character so that the quadrilateral becomes a rectangle of standard size, as in Figure 2.11(c).

2.4 SMOOTHING, EDGE DETECTION, AND THINNING

2.4.1 Smoothing

Due to spattering of ink and imperfect printing and binarisation, a binarised character may contain isolated black elements, as in the right-hand column of Figure 2.12(a), or contain white elements (known as *voids*) which should ideally be black. For instance, one or two voids have, at one place, reduced the width of the right-hand vertical portion of the '2' in Figure 2.12(a) to a single element. *Smoothing* is a technique for reducing the numbers of voids and spurious black elements, that is, for reducing black and white *noise*.

In Dineen's smoothing technique[122] an $n \times n$ element window is moved in turn into all positions in the binary pattern. In each position the *black* elements contained within the window are counted. A new pattern is formed in which each element corresponds to one position of the window, and an element in the new pattern is made *black* only if the count obtained in the corresponding position of the window is greater than or equal to a threshold, θ. For instance, taking $n = \theta = 3$, we obtain Figure 2.12(b) from Figure 2.12(a). The count of *black* elements in a 3 x 3 window in Figure 2.12(a) determines the state of the element in Figure 2.12(b) which is at the centre of the window.

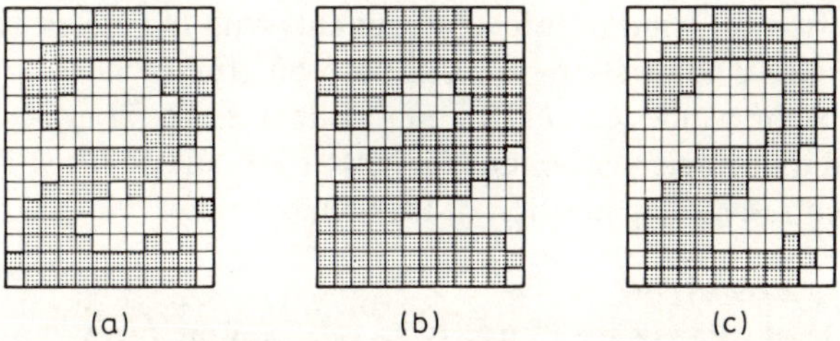

Figure 2.12. *(a) A binarised printed '2'; (b) and (c) Results of smoothing Figure 2.12(a) with thresholds* $\theta = 3$ *and 5 respectively*

For instance, the top left-hand 3 x 3 sub-array of Figure 2.12(a) contains only one *black* element, so there is a *white* element in the second row and second column of Figure 2.12(b). Shifting the window one element to the right, we now find three *black* elements within the window, so there is a *black* element in the second row and third column of Figure 2.12(b). Note that the isolated black element in the right-hand column of Figure 2.12(a) is not carried into Figure 2.12(b).

Figure 2.12(c) is obtained from Figure 2.12(a) by the same technique, but with $\theta = 5$. In general, the smaller the value of θ, the greater the resulting limb width, and, the larger the value of θ, the less the resulting limb width.

A pattern element is deemed *black* if the total whiteness over a small area of the document is less than a threshold amount. By judicious choice of this area and threshold we can achieve a certain amount of denoising, and this is more direct than Dineen's technique. If the area is made too big and the threshold is set too low, we lose resolution: for instance the white area between the horizontal limbs of 'F' may be deemed *black*. If the area is made too small we suffer unnecessarily from noise. In practice, for multifont print the optimum diameter of the spot has been found to be between 0·005 in and 0·007 in[293].

Instead of smoothing by averaging, Unger[445] applied explicit logical rules to the pattern element appearing within a 3 x 3 window. Let us index these elements as

$$\begin{matrix} x_e & x_h & x_k \\ x_f & x_i & x_l \\ x_g & x_j & x_m \end{matrix}$$

Unger shifted the window into all alignments with the unknown pattern and generated a new pattern in which each bit corresponded to one position of the window, as in Dineen's technique. To fill in voids, Unger stipulated that an element in the new pattern should be *black* if and only if in the corresponding position of the window either

(1) x_i was *black*, or
(2) at least three of the elements x_f, x_h, x_l, x_j were *black*.

This resulted in a pattern to which Unger applied the following rules for eliminating small black bumps and isolated black elements. An element in the new pattern was made *black* if and only if x_i was *black* and either

(1) at least one of x_f, x_e, x_h and at least one of x_j, x_m, x_l were *black*, or
(2) at least one of x_h, x_k, x_l and at least one of x_f, x_g, x_j were *black*.

Another method of denoising is by means of spatial frequency filtering, and to introduce this we must anticipate the subject matter of Section 9.4.1. A simple optical set-up is shown in Figure 2.13, where

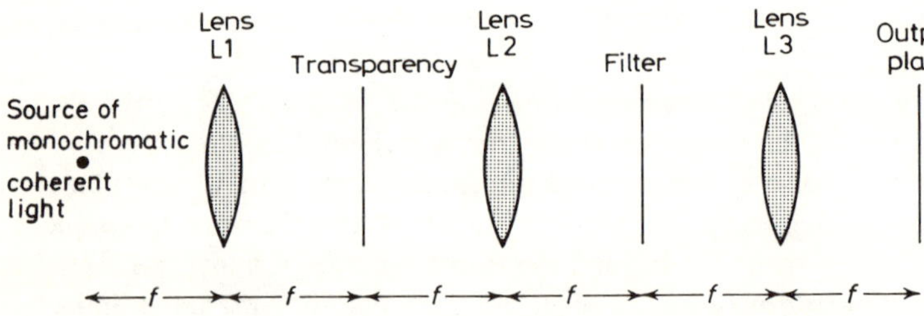

Figure 2.13. *A simple set-up for optical spatial frequency filtering*

for simplicity the three lenses all have the same focal length, *f*. The input pattern is in the form of a photographic transparency, and the Fourier transform of this transparency is in focus in the focal plane of lens L2. Noise which is associated with high spatial frequencies can be eliminated by means of a stop which is opaque except for a circular transparent area centred on the optic axis in the focal plane of L2. The Fourier transform of the pattern of light emerging from the stop is in focus in the focal plane of lens L3. Thus the focal plane of L3 contains a denoised version of the pattern in the input transparency[206]. The diameter of the transparent area of the stop determines the lowest spatial frequency eliminated by this system. Instead of using a stop which is partly opaque and partly transparent, it may be expedient to use intermediate transmission coefficients[332].

2.4.2 Edge detection

An edge detector developed at Stanford Research Institute matches peephole masks with a 24 x 24 bit binary pattern[323]. The peephole masks are variously orientated versions of the configuration shown in Figure 2.14. If the number of *black* pattern elements coincident with the +'s in any given peephole mask exceeds by at least six the number of *black* elements coincident with the −'s, the output of that mask is '1', and otherwise '0'. A peephole mask (or, more accurately, a threshold circuit to which the output of that peephole mask is fed) gives output '1' when aligned at least roughly with a black/white edge. The use of this in character recognition will be outlined in Section 7.2.

+ + + + + + + +
+ + + + + + + +
− − − − − − − −
− − − − − − − −

Figure 2.14. *An SRI edge detector*

+		−
+		−
+		−

+	+	+
−	−	−

	+	+
−		+
−	−	

−	−	
−		+
	+	+

Figure 2.15. *Nadler's edge detectors*

To detect edges, Nadler[325] used peephole masks as shown in Figure 2.15. The output of a peephole mask was the sum of the *analogue* pattern elements coincident with the +'s minus the sum of the *analogue* pattern elements coincident with the −'s. The four Figure 2.15 peephole masks were aligned so that their central elements coincided with each input pattern element in turn. For each alignment of the four peephole masks, the peephole mask with the largest absolute output, regardless of sign, was found. If the magnitude of the largest output was below a prescribed threshold, the central element was deemed *not* to lie on a black/white edge in the input pattern. Otherwise the central element was deemed to lie on an edge in the direction corresponding to the mask with largest absolute output. The sign of the largest output was used for determining whether the edge was black/white or white/black. For example, if the peephole mask producing the largest output, regardless of sign, was the left-hand peephole mask in Figure 2.15, the centre element would be counted as lying on a vertical black/white edge. If the sign of the largest output were negative, this would mean that black was on the right and white on the left (if the analogue value of a pattern element increases with blackness).

For purposes other than character recognition, more-elaborate edge detectors have been described by, for example, Herskovits and Binford[211], Hueckel[230], Kelly[252], Rosenfeld and Thurston[383], and Sakai *et al.*[388]

Contour tracing is a means of edge detection. To illustrate this, let us consider a computer programme for tracing the black/white edge of a character which has been binarised and stored in a rectangular array. The programme starts by choosing arbitrarily an element on the black/white edge of a character, such as the element labelled '1' in Figure 2.16. Starting at the element immediately above the element which is labelled '1', the programme works clockwise round the eight immediate neighbours of the element labelled '1' until two successive neighbours are found such that the first is white and the second is black. In the present example this black element is the element labelled '2' in Figure 2.16. The programme now works clockwise round the eight immediate neighbours of '2' applying the same rule, so that the programme next works round the element labelled '3', and so on[379]. The output of the programme could be a binary pattern in which the elements corresponding to the elements labelled '1', '2', '3', '4', . . . in Figure 2.16 were 1's and all other elements were 0's. More usually a contour tracing programme is written so as to give its output in the form of a one-dimensional *chain* of directions. This chain gives the direction of '2' relative to '1', of '3' relative to '2', and so on. In terms of compass directions the chain starting at '1' in Figure 2.16 is NE, E, NE, E, E, SE [151, 264, 455a]. Freeman[152] has extensively studied such chains.

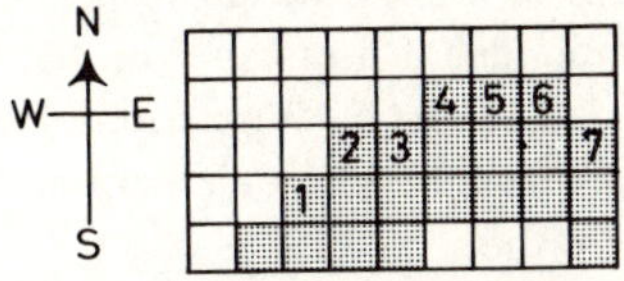

Figure 2.16. *Part of a character*

Using a non-raster flying-spot scanner, the IBM 1287 [374] traces the character contour directly on the document. The flying spot executes a circular scan such that the diameter of the circle is roughly twice as great when the spot is on white than when it is on black. Such diameter modulation automatically causes the circular scan to follow the contour[183], as in Figure 2.17. An important advantage of this

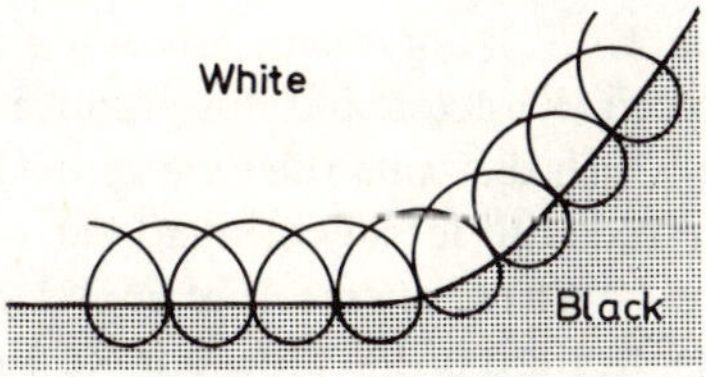

Figure 2.17. Cycloidal traversal of a black/white boundary

technique (cf. Ref. 407a) is that it avoids the coarseness of a finite grid of pattern elements, and the direction of a tangent to a character contour can be determined with greater accuracy than in a contour tracing technique which works with characters which have previously been raster scanned and stored. A further advantage is that it is possible to vary the binarising threshold while the scan works round the contour, and the IBM 1287 can cope successfully with big variations in black/white contrast across a single character.

2.4.3 Thinning

For some purposes we wish to reduce the width of the limbs of a character to one pattern element, so as to be left with a skeleton of the original character. Using the contour tracing technique which was introduced in terms of Figure 2.16, Sherman's thinning technique[404] places the centre element of a 3 x 3 window on successive black elements of a black/white edge, for instance on the elements labelled '1', '2', '3', . . . in Figure 2.16. At each position of the window, Sherman's procedure changes the black element at the centre of the window to white unless either

(1) this would remove the only black element connecting two non-adjacent black elements, as in Figure 2.18(a), or
(2) the element at the centre of the window only has one black neighbour, as in Figure 2.18(b).

Figure 2.18. *(a) Centre element which is the only element connecting two 'black' elements; (b) Centre element which has only one 'black' neighbour*

Figure 2.19(a) shows the pattern that remains after this process has been applied to Figure 2.12(a). Sherman's procedure then applies the same rules to the reduced character, and this produces a further reduced character, to which the same rules are applied again, and so on, until the contour is traced without any element being changed from black to white. Figure 2.19(b) is the result of applying the rules to Figure 2.19(a); and application of the procedure to Figure 2.19(b) results in no further changes from black to white.

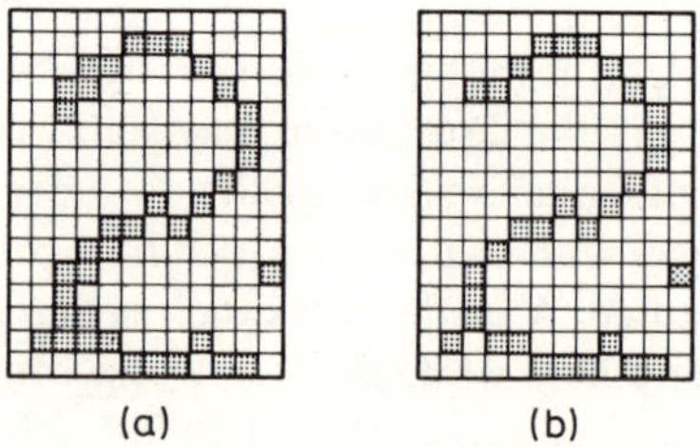

Figure 2.19. *Thinning of Figure 2.12(a)*

The '2' in Figure 2.12(a) contains no point at which more than two character limbs join, and it may be important for this to be true also of the thinned version of the character. But the black element in the third from left column and third from bottom row in Figure 2.19(b) has three black neighbours. The leftmost black element in the second from bottom row is a spurious *tail* attached to the string of elements constituting the thinned '2'. As a remedy for spurious tails, Fraser[150 a] has modified Sherman's condition (1). Specifically, a black element having only one black neighbour is changed to white unless no black element has been changed to white since the previous point (if any) on the contour where a black element had only one black neighbour.

Golay[177], Triendl[437], and Stefanelli and Rosenfeld[421 a] have devised thinning techniques which, unlike Sherman's, may simultaneously change many black elements to white. Hilditch[214] has provided a method of thinning non-binary patterns. We shall briefly return to a further thinning technique, the medial axis transformation, in Section 8.5.1.

Instead of thinning patterns which are stored versions of raster-scanned characters, it is possible to read a skeleton version of a character directly from a document by using a special flying-spot[393] or vidicon[159, 297, 396] scanner. With the exception of movements of the spot during the finding of character limbs, the spot (or electron beam) executes a circular or cycloidal motion. This motion is servocontrolled so that the centre of the circle moves along the centre of a character limb. The locus of the centre of the circle constitutes a thinned version of a character[466].

Chapter 3

LINEAR TECHNIQUES

3.1 RECOGNITION CLASS

Different specimens of, for example, the character '2', are generally somewhat different spatial distributions of black, white, and grey. We now require a clear terminology for specifying different variants of '2'. The most common terminological convention defines pattern so that each distinct variant of '2' is a different pattern. A *pattern* is defined to be an ordered array of pattern elements, and if any element of a pattern is changed we thereby obtain a different pattern. In the present chapter, a *pattern element* is a real number, and the terms *pattern* and *vector* are synonymous. A pattern element might, for example, be a measure of the average grey scale value over a small area of a document.

What we regard as a pattern for recognition purposes is generally part of a more extensive scene. For instance, a character in a line of text is part of the text. Most recognition machines effectively place a window over the text or scene. What is inside the window is taken as the pattern, and what is outside the window is at least temporarily ignored. The window bounds the pattern, and the choice of the dimensions and position of the window was the subject of Section 2.3.

The class of somewhat different patterns which are 2's is an example of a recognition class. A *recognition class* is a set of patterns for each of which a recognition machine is required to give the same output response. When we say that a pattern has been recognised as '2', we mean that the pattern has been classified as a member of the recognition class '2'. Alternatively we may say that the pattern has been *assigned* to the recognition class '2'.

3.2 MINIMUM ERROR BAYESIAN CLASSIFIER

Bayes' rule, which is of basic importance in statistical pattern recognition, can be introduced, though not proved, in terms of Figure 3.1. Figure 3.1 shows an array of points, and also shows two arbitrary overlapping regions A and B. Let $P(\mathrm{A})$ be the probability that an arbitrarily chosen point in Figure 3.1 lies in the region A, let $P(\mathrm{B})$ be the probability that an arbitrarily chosen point in Figure 3.1 lies in the region B, and let $P(\mathrm{A}\ \&\ \mathrm{B})$ be the probability that an arbitrarily chosen point in Figure 3.1 belongs to the overlap region common to A and B. Let $P(\mathrm{B}/\mathrm{A})$ be the conditional probability that, given that a point is in A, it is also in B: 'B/A' here means 'B given A'. Let $P(\mathrm{A}/\mathrm{B})$ be the conditional probability that, given that a point is in B, it is also in A.

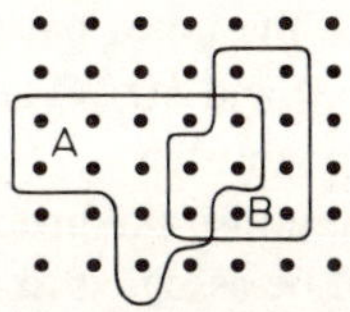

Figure 3.1. *An example to illustrate Bayes' Rule*

If we make a large number, M, of random choices of points in the array, $P(\mathrm{A}) \times M$ of these points will belong to A. Out of this set of $P(\mathrm{A}) \times M$ points, altogether $P(\mathrm{B}/\mathrm{A}) \times P(\mathrm{A}) \times M$ points will belong to the region of overlap between A and B. But the number of points belonging to the overlap region will also be given by $P(\mathrm{A}\ \&\ \mathrm{B}) \times M$.

Thus

$$P(\mathrm{B}/\mathrm{A}) \,.\, P(\mathrm{A}) = P(\mathrm{A}\ \&\ \mathrm{B})$$

and similarly

$$P(\mathrm{A}/\mathrm{B}) \,.\, P(\mathrm{B}) = P(\mathrm{A}\ \&\ \mathrm{B})$$

and therefore

$$P(\mathrm{B}/\mathrm{A}) \,.\, P(\mathrm{A}) = P(\mathrm{A}/\mathrm{B}) \,.\, P(\mathrm{B})$$

which exemplifies Bayes' rule.

Let us now consider a pattern recognition problem in which there are z recognition classes $R_1, R_2, \ldots, R_r, R_s, \ldots, R_z$. For each r from 1 to z, let

$P(r)$ be the probability of the input pattern belonging to R_r,
$P(X)$ be the probability of the input pattern being the particular pattern X,
$P(X/r)$ be the conditional probability of the input pattern being the particular pattern X, given that the input pattern belongs to R_r, and let
$P(r/X)$ be the conditional probability of the input pattern belonging to R_r, given that the input pattern is the particular pattern X.

Before an input pattern is seen by an observer or fed to a recognition machine, the probability that this pattern belongs to the rth class is $P(r)$. After the input pattern has been observed to be the particular pattern X, the probability that the input pattern belongs to the rth class is $P(r/X)$. Accordingly $P(r)$ and $P(r/X)$ are known respectively as *a priori* and *a posteriori* probabilities.

It can be shown that, to minimise the probability of misrecognition, an unknown pattern X should be assigned to the class R_s such that, for all r except $r = s$,

$$P(s/X) > P(r/X)$$

This is known as the *maximum likelihood* decision rule. If, for example, the cost of misrecognising '2' as '3' is different to the cost of misrecognising '2' as '5', then a more elaborate decision rule should be employed to minimise the total cost of misrecognition[41, 76, 81, 87, 103].

The maximum likelihood rule requires estimates of $P(r/X)$ for all r, and in principle these estimates can be obtained by a method of direct counting. For this we require many specimens of every pattern which ever occurs as an input pattern. Each specimen must in some way be labelled according to its recognition class. It may sometimes happen that two specimens of precisely the same pattern will be labelled as belonging to different recognition classes. $P(r/X)$ can be estimated by

$$P(r/X) = \frac{\text{number of occurrences of } X \text{ with the } r\text{th class label}}{\text{total number of occurrences of } X \text{ regardless of label}}$$

and of course this applies for all r and X. But this method of estimating $P(r/X)$ is hopelessly impractical because the number of input patterns which may actually occur is generally astronomical.

For example, to collect at least one specimen of each of 10^6 *different* 2's we might have to inspect 10^8 specimens of '2'; and in this case, to estimate $P(2/X)$ for the 10^6 different 2's, we would have to inspect many more than 10^8 specimens of '2'.

A more practical method of estimating $P(r/X)$ is to make assumptions concerning the statistics of the recognition classes, and examples of this method will be introduced below in Sections 3.3 and 3.4. This method leads to estimates of $P(X/r)$, and to use these we combine the maximum likelihood rule with Bayes' rule and assign X to the class R_s such that, for all r except $r = s$;

$$P(s) \,.\, P(X/s)/P(X) > P(r) \,.\, P(X/r)/P(X)$$

Since $P(X)$ is independent of recognition class, it can be omitted for maximisation purposes, and we obtain the maximum likelihood rule in the form: assign X to the sth class such that, for all r except $r = s$,

$$P(s) \,.\, P(X/s) > P(r) \,.\, P(X/r) \tag{3.1}$$

3.3 STATISTICAL INDEPENDENCE

The assumption of statistical independence of pattern elements leads to a practical method of estimating $P(X/r)$. The method requires a collection of specimen patterns from all recognition classes. Such a collection is commonly known as a *training set*, and the patterns which belong to the training set and also to the rth class are said to belong to the *rth class training set*. For $r = 1, \ldots, z$, let the number of patterns in the rth class training set be t_r.

Let indices be assigned to pattern elements as in Section 1.3, so that a pattern X is composed of elements $x_1, x_2, \ldots, x_j, \ldots, x_N$. In the present section we only consider the case where all patterns are binary, and $x_j = 1$ or 0 according as the jth element of X is *black* or *white*. Let n_{rj} be the number of patterns which

(1) belong to the rth class training set, and
(2) have the jth element black.

For all $r = 1, \ldots, z$ and $j = 1, \ldots, N$ we obtain the value of n_{rj} by counting. The quantity defined by $m_{rj} = n_{rj}/t_r$ is subsequently used as an estimate of the conditional probability that the jth element of X is black, given that X is a member of the rth class. The quantity $1 - m_{rj}$ is used as an estimate of the conditional probability that the jth element of X is white, given that X is a member of the rth class. As a very trivial example, if the rth class training set consists of the five 4-bit patterns 1010, 0011, 0111, 1100, and 0111, then $m_{r1} = 0{\cdot}4$, $m_{r2} = 0{\cdot}6$, $m_{r3} = 0{\cdot}8$, and $m_{r4} = 0{\cdot}6$.

If there is no correlation between the values of x_i and x_j in patterns belonging to the rth class, then the ith and jth pattern elements are *statistically independent.* Let us now *assume* that, for all $r = 1, \ldots, z$, the elements of rth class patterns are statistically independent. In this case $P(X/r)$ is given by the *product*

$$P(X/r) = P(x_1/r) \times P(x_2/r) \times \ldots \times P(x_j/r) \times \ldots \times P(x_N/r)$$

If $x_j = 1$, then $P(x_j/r) = m_{rj} = m_{rj}{}^{x_j}$, and if $x_j = 0$, then $P(x_j/r) = 1 - m_{rj} = (1 - m_{rj})^{(1-x_j)}$. Whether $x_j = 1$ or $x_j = 0$, it is true that $P(x_j/r) = m_{rj}{}^{x_j} . (1 - m_{rj})^{(1-x_j)}$, and hence

$$P(X/r) = \prod_{j=1}^{N} m_{rj}{}^{x_j} . (1 - m_{rj})^{(1-x_j)} \tag{3.2}$$

This expression[318] can be substituted into the maximum likelihood rule (3.1). But it is easier in practice to add than to multiply, and to convert the recognition rule into a form involving summation rather than multiplication, we take logs. The unknown pattern is assigned to the sth class such that $\log P(X/s) + \log P(s)$ is greater than for any other class; and this is equivalent to (3.1) because the logarithm of a number is a single-valued function of that number which increases as that number increases. For simplicity let us assume that $P(r)$ is the same for all r, or in other words that the *a priori* probabilities of all classes are equal. Then the term $\log P(s)$ can be omitted for maximisation purposes, and X can be assigned to the class for which $\log P(X/s)$ is greatest.

Taking logs of (3.2),

$$\begin{aligned}\log P(X/r) &= \sum_{j=1}^{N} [x_j \log m_{rj} + (1 - x_j) \log (1 - m_{rj})] \\ &= \sum_{j=1}^{N} x_j [\log m_{rj} - \log (1 - m_{rj})] + \sum_{j=1}^{N} \log (1 - m_{rj}) \\ &= \sum_{j=1}^{N} x_j \log [m_{rj}/(1 - m_{rj})] + \sum_{j=1}^{N} \log (1 - m_{rj}) \\ &= \sum_{j=1}^{N} x_j w_{rj} + w_{r0}\end{aligned}$$

where $w_{rj} = \log[m_{rj}/(1 - m_{rj})]$ and $w_{r0} = \sum_{j=1}^{N} \log(1 - m_{rj})$.

To control the trade-off between reject and substitution errors, a reject threshold ρ can be introduced, and the following recognition rule can be applied: assign X to the sth class such that, for all r except $r = s$,

$$\sum_{j=1}^{N} x_j w_{sj} + w_{s0} > \sum_{j=1}^{N} x_j w_{rj} + w_{r0} + \rho$$

This recognition rule can be implemented by a system of resistor masks, as in Section 1.6, the weights not now being restricted to ±1. Figure 3.2 shows a typical reject/substitution curve obtained by varying

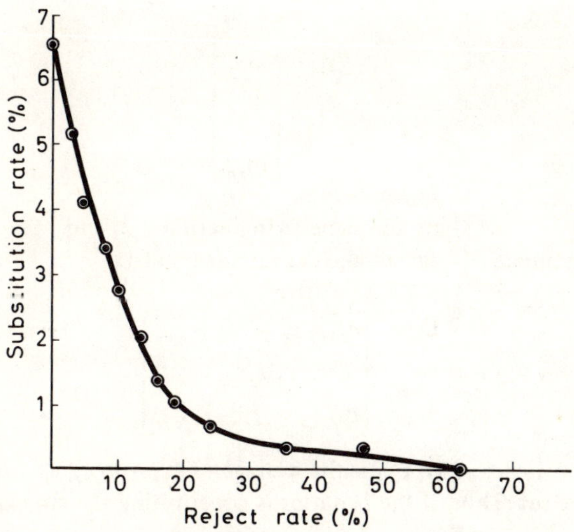

Figure 3.2. *A plot of substitution rate versus reject error rate, obtained by varying the reject threshold. From Reference* 444, *with permission*

ρ in a small-scale experiment with typewritten numerals[444]. Control of substitution error rates by varying ρ is not the statistically optimal method of control[85] but it is simple and widely used.

3.4 GAUSSIAN DISTRIBUTION

As we have seen, the assumption of statistical independence leads to a formula for computing an estimate of $P(X/r)$ from X and parameters $M_r = \{m_{r1}, m_{r2}, \ldots, m_{rN}\}$. This exemplifies the *parametric* approach to the estimation of $P(X/r)$, wherein we *assume* a specific functional relationship between $P(X/r)$, X, and various parameters whose estimated values are obtained from a training set. The assumption that patterns are normally distributed leads to a workable parametric alternative to the independence assumption, and may be valid when the independence assumption is not.

According to the assumption of normality[3, 18, 294, 336],

$$P(X/r) = \frac{\exp[-(1/2)(X-M_r)^{\mathrm{T}} C_r^{-1} (X-M_r)]}{(2\pi)^{N/2}(\det C_r)^{1/2}} \tag{3.3}$$

In this, X is not restricted to being binary, X and M_r are column vectors,

$$M_r = \begin{bmatrix} m_{r1} \\ m_{r2} \\ \vdots \\ m_{rn} \end{bmatrix}$$

where $m_{r1}, \ldots, m_{rN}$ are the same as in Section 3.3, and C_r is (an estimate of) the rth class covariance matrix

$$C_r = \begin{bmatrix} c_{r11}, c_{r12}, \ldots, c_{r1N} \\ \vdots \\ \ldots\ldots, c_{rij}, \ldots\ldots \\ \vdots \\ c_{rN1}, \ldots\ldots, c_{rNN} \end{bmatrix}$$

For all $i, j = 1, 2, \ldots, N$, c_{rij} is the average of $(x_i - m_{ri})(x_j - m_{rj})$ over the training set. Thus, if the t_r patterns constituting the rth class training set are $X_1, X_2, \ldots, X_h, \ldots, X_{t_r}$,

$$c_{rij} = (1/t_r) \sum_{h=1}^{t_r} (x_{hi} - m_{ri})(x_{hj} - m_{rj}) \tag{3.4}$$

c_{rij} is a measure of the extent of correlation between x_i and x_j in patterns belonging to the rth class. For example, if, in the rth class training set, usually $x_j = 1$ when $x_i = 1$ and usually $x_j = 0$ when $x_i = 0$, then c_{rij} turns out to be positive. If $x_j = 1$ or $x_j = 0$ are just as likely whether $x_i = 1$ or $x_i = 0$, c_{rij} turns out to be zero. $\mathbf{C}_r^{-1}$ and det $\mathbf{C}_r$ are respectively the inverse and determinant of $\mathbf{C}_r$, and superscript T denotes transposition. Formula (3.3) is only strictly valid when the normality assumption is valid and when the number of patterns in the training set tends to infinity. When the training set is small discrepancies may arise[3, 336], but for introductory purposes we shall ignore this difficulty, and anyway the normality assumption is seldom precisely valid in pattern recognition.

Let us assume that the *a priori* probabilities of all recognition classes are equal, as in Section 3.3, and let us again apply the logarithmic version of the maximum likelihood decision rule, so that X is assigned to the class for which log $P(X/r)$ is greatest. Taking logs in (3.3) and expanding

$$\log P(X/r) = \tfrac{1}{2}(-N \log 2\pi - \log \det \mathbf{C}_r - X^{\mathrm{T}}\mathbf{C}_r^{-1} X + 2X^{\mathrm{T}}\mathbf{C}_r^{-1}\mathbf{M}_r - \mathbf{M}_r^{\mathrm{T}}\mathbf{C}_r^{-1}\mathbf{M}_r) \quad (3.5)$$

Note that this expression is quadratic[102], and also that the term $-N \log 2\pi$ can be omitted for maximisation purposes, since it is constant.

In the special case where the covariance matrices for all classes are equal, the terms $-\log \det \mathbf{C}_r$ and $-X^{\mathrm{T}}\mathbf{C}_r^{-1} X$ can be omitted from (3.5) since they are independent of r, and the remaining function

$$X^{\mathrm{T}}\mathbf{C}_r^{-1}M_r - \tfrac{1}{2}M_r^{\mathrm{T}}\mathbf{C}_r^{-1}M_r \quad (3.6)$$

is linear in X. The class for which (3.6) is maximal can be determined by a system of resistor masks, as in Section 1.6, using $N + 1$ weights per class; whereas, in general, (3.5) requires $\frac{1}{2}N(N + 2) + 1$ weights per class.

A further simplification is obtained if the covariance matrices for all classes are equal and, for all $i, j = 1, \ldots, N$,

(1) $c_{rij} = 0$ unless $i = j$, and
(2) $c_{rii} = c_{rjj}$

This means that

(1) pattern elements are statistically independent, and
(2) the statistical variability of all pattern elements is equal.

In this case $\mathbf{C}_r^{-1}$ is scalar and can be omitted from (3.6) for maximisation purposes. Thus X should be assigned to the class for which

$$X^{\mathrm{T}}M_r - M_r{}^{\mathrm{T}}M_r/2 \tag{3.7}$$

is greatest. This rule is equivalent to the minimum Euclidean distance rule, as will now be demonstrated.

The components of X can be regarded as the coordinates of a point in N-dimensional Euclidean space, and this point is known as the *representative point* of X. According to the minimum Euclidean distance rule, X is assigned to the sth class such that the representative point of X is closer to the representative point whose coordinates are $m_{s1}, \ldots, m_{sN}$ than to any representative point whose coordinates are $m_{r1}, \ldots, m_{rN}$, for all r except $r = s$. By the N-dimensional extension of Pythagoras' theorem, the Euclidean distance between the representative points of X and $\mathbf{M}_r = \{m_{r1}, \ldots, m_{rN}\}$ is

$$d_r = \left[\sum_{j=1}^{N} (x_j - m_{rj})^2\right]^{1/2} \tag{3.8}$$

Now d_r^2 is a monotonic increasing function of d_r and therefore instead of minimising d_r we can equivalently assign X to the class for which

$$d_r^2 = \sum_{j=1}^{N} x_j^2 - 2\sum_{j=1}^{N} x_j m_{rj} + \sum_{j=1}^{N} m^2{}_{rj}$$

is minimal. Since $\sum_{j=1}^{N} x_j^2$ is independent of r it can be ignored for minimisation purposes, and instead of assigning X to the class for which

$$-2\sum_{j=1}^{N} x_j m_{rj} + \sum_{j=1}^{N} m_{rj}^2$$

is minimal, we can equivalently assign X to the class for which

$$\sum_{j=1}^{N} x_j m_{rj} - \tfrac{1}{2}\sum_{j=1}^{N} m_{rj}^2 \tag{3.9}$$

is maximal. This is the same as (3.7), which shows that, when covariance matrices are scalar and equal for all classes, the normality assumption leads to the minimum Euclidean distance rule[336].

In the special case where X and M_r are binary, the minimum Euclidean distance rule is equivalent to the minimum Hamming distance rule introduced in Section 1.3. Expression (1.3) in Section 1.6 can be rewritten

$$N - h_r = N - \sum_{j=1}^{N} x_j + \sum_{j=1}^{N} 2q_{rj}x_j - \sum_{j=1}^{N} q_{rj}$$

and for maximisation purposes $N - \sum_{j=1}^{N} x_j$ can be omitted since it is the same for all recognition classes. Thus, according to the Hamming distance rule, X should be assigned to the class for which

$$\sum_{j=1}^{N} q_{rj}x_j - \tfrac{1}{2} \sum_{j=1}^{N} q_{rj}$$

is maximal, and this is the same as (3.9) since in the binary case $q_{rj} = q_{rj}^2$. This also follows from the fact that the Hamming distance between X and M_r is the square of the Euclidean distance, since $h_r = \sum_{j=1}^{N} (x_j - m_{rj})^2$, so that the class for which the Hamming distance is minimal is also the class for which the Euclidean distance is minimal.

3.5 CROSS CORRELATION WITH NORMALISED AVERAGE MASKS

In character recognition a change in the overall whiteness of a pattern X_A can be represented by the multiplication of X_A by a scalar constant, k. For instance X_A might be a grey 'F' on a white background, and $X_B = kX_A$ might be a black 'F' on a grey background. The class to which the minimum Euclidean distance rule assigns an unknown pattern may sometimes be altered by multiplication of the pattern by a scalar, and in some applications this is undesirable. For example a grey 'F' on a white background might be recognised as 'F' whilst a black 'F' on a grey background might be misrecognised as 'E'.

For simplicity let us discuss this in terms of an example where $N = 2$ and $X_A = \{x_{A1}, x_{A2}\}$ and $X_B = \{kx_{A1}, kx_{A2}\}$ are as shown in

Figure 3.3. Because $X_B = kX_A$, the representative point of X_A necessarily lies on the line OX_B, where O is the origin. Since X_A is closer to M_s than to M_r, X_A is assigned by the minimum Euclidean distance rule to the sth class rather than the rth; but the reverse assignation is made for X_B since X_B is closer to M_r than to M_s. Reversal of assignation can be avoided by replacing the minimum Euclidean distance rule by the rule: assign X to the class R_s such that the cosine of the angle between OX and OM_s is greater than the cosine of the angle between OX and OM_r for all r except $r = s$. The rationale of this rule can be appreciated in terms of the Figure 3.3 example: the angle between OM_r and OX_B, where $X_B = kX_A$, is independent of k. We now have a recognition rule whose assignations are unchanged when patterns are multiplied by scalars.

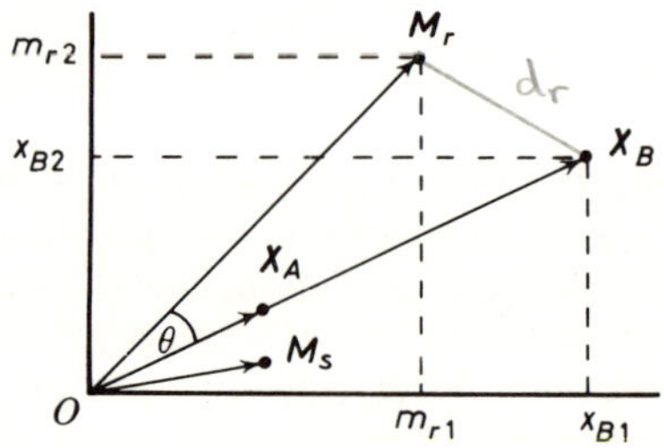

Figure 3.3.

Denoting the Euclidean distance between M_r and X_B by d_r, a well-known trigonometrical formula gives

$$d_r^2 = (OX_B)^2 + (OM_r)^2 - 2(OX_B)(OM_r)\cos\theta$$

$$= x_{B1}^2 + x_{B2}^2 + m_{r1}^2 + m_{r2}^2 -$$
$$2(x_{B1}^2 + x_{B2}^2)^{1/2}(m_{r1}^2 + m_{r2}^2)^{1/2}\cos\theta$$

Equating this with d_r^2 given by (3.8), cancelling common terms, and rearranging we obtain

$$\cos\theta = \frac{x_{B1}m_{r1} + x_{B2}m_{r2}}{(x_{B1}^2 + x_{B2}^2)^{1/2}(m_{r1}^2 + m_{r2}^2)^{1/2}}$$

When N is not restricted to $N=2$, a similar equation holds, and for any X,

$$\cos\theta = \frac{X \cdot M_r}{\left(\sum_{j=1}^{N} x_j^2\right)^{1/2} \left(\sum_{j=1}^{N} m_{rj}^2\right)^{1/2}} \tag{3.10}$$

where θ is the angle between OX and OM_r, and $X \cdot M_r = \sum_{j=1}^{N} x_j m_{rj}$ is the *dot product* of X and M_r. For maximisation purposes, division by $\left(\sum_{j=1}^{N} x_j^2\right)^{1/2}$ can be omitted, since this is independent of r, and X can be assigned to the class such that $X \cdot W_r$ is greater than for any other class[212], where W_r is the vector

$$W_r = \left\{ \frac{m_{r1}}{\left(\sum_{j=1}^{N} m_{rj}^2\right)^{1/2}}, \ldots, \frac{m_{rN}}{\left(\sum_{j=1}^{N} m_{rj}^2\right)^{1/2}} \right\}$$

$\left(\sum_{j=1}^{N} m_{rj}^2\right)^{1/2}$ is the length OM_r, and thus we see that the length of the vector W_r is one unit. Reduction of a vector M_r to a vector of unit length is an example of *normalisation*.

To control the reject/substitution trade-off we can, as before, introduce a reject threshold ρ, and assign X to the sth class such that, for all r except $r = s$,

$$X \cdot W_s > X \cdot W_r + \rho$$

If this condition is not fulfilled for any class, X is rejected. Note that this recognition rule can be applied directly to analogue patterns, whereas the Section 3.3 rule cannot.

3.6 LINEAR DISCRIMINANT FUNCTIONS

A single-valued function $g_r(X)$ of X is said to be a *discriminant function* when we employ the recognition rule: assign X to the sth class such that, for all r except $r = s$,

$$g_s(X) > g_r(X) + \rho \tag{3.11}$$

Sections 1.6, 3.3, 3.4, and 3.5 have lead to *linear* discriminant functions of the form

$$g_r(X) = w_{r0} + \boldsymbol{X} \,.\, \boldsymbol{W}_r \tag{3.12}$$

The importance of linear discriminant functions arises from the relatively low cost of their physical implementation, for instance by the Section 1.6 resistor mask method, and also from their theoretical tractability[336].

It is convenient now to redefine the weight vector $\boldsymbol{W}_r$ to be the $(N + 1)$-component vector $\{w_{r0}, w_{r1}, \ldots, w_{rj}, \ldots, w_{rN}\}$, and to define an *augmented pattern vector*

$$\boldsymbol{Y} = \{1, x_1, \ldots, x_j, \ldots, x_N\}$$

in which the first of the $N + 1$ components is always unity. Equation (3.12) can now be rewritten

$$g_r(\boldsymbol{Y}) = \boldsymbol{Y} \,.\, \boldsymbol{W}_r \tag{3.13}$$

In order to introduce a basic idea, let us consider a problem in which there are only two recognition classes, R_1 and R_2, and let the training sets for R_1 and R_2 be R_1' and R_2' respectively. To each pattern $\boldsymbol{X}$ there corresponds a unique augmented pattern $\boldsymbol{Y}$, and let

$$R_1^* = \{\boldsymbol{Y}_{11}, \boldsymbol{Y}_{12}, \ldots, \boldsymbol{Y}_{1t_1}\} \quad \text{and} \quad R_2^* = \{\boldsymbol{Y}_{21}, \boldsymbol{Y}_{22}, \ldots, \boldsymbol{Y}_{2t_2}\}$$

be the training sets of augmented patterns corresponding respectively to R_1' and R_2'. In our introductory problem, a linear discriminant function is used, and $\boldsymbol{X}$ is assigned to R_1 if $\boldsymbol{Y} . \boldsymbol{W}_1 > \boldsymbol{Y} . \boldsymbol{W}_2$, to R_2 if $\boldsymbol{Y} . \boldsymbol{W}_1 < \boldsymbol{Y} . \boldsymbol{W}_2$, and rejected if $\boldsymbol{Y} . \boldsymbol{W}_1 = \boldsymbol{Y} . \boldsymbol{W}_2$. (To simplify the discussion we omit the reject threshold ρ.) Equivalently $\boldsymbol{X}$ can be assigned to R_1 or R_2 or rejected according as $\boldsymbol{Y} . \boldsymbol{W} > 0$ or $\boldsymbol{Y} . \boldsymbol{W} < 0$ or $\boldsymbol{Y} . \boldsymbol{W} = 0$, where

$$\boldsymbol{W} = \boldsymbol{W}_1 - \boldsymbol{W}_2 = \{w_{10} - w_{20}, w_{11} - w_{21}, \ldots, w_{1N} - w_{2N}\}$$

For 100% correct recognition of the training sets, $\boldsymbol{W}$ must satisfy the $t = t_1 + t_2$ inequalities

$$\left.\begin{array}{l} \boldsymbol{W} . \boldsymbol{Y}_{11} > 0 \\ \boldsymbol{W} . \boldsymbol{Y}_{12} > 0 \\ \quad\vdots \\ \boldsymbol{W} . \boldsymbol{Y}_{1t_1} > 0 \\ \boldsymbol{W} . \boldsymbol{Y}_{21} < 0 \\ \quad\vdots \\ \boldsymbol{W} . \boldsymbol{Y}_{2t_2} < 0 \end{array}\right\} \tag{3.14}$$

The procedures introduced above for determining weights do not necessarily lead to a $\boldsymbol{W}$ which satisfies these inequalities. The basic idea which we now introduce is the idea of determining $\boldsymbol{W}$ *so as to* satisfy inequalities (3.14), if this is possible. Weight determining procedures based on this idea will be introduced in Sections 3.7 and 3.8, and they differ from procedures introduced above in that weights are not computed straightforwardly from probabilities.

The rule that $\boldsymbol{X}$ is assigned to R_1 or to R_2 or rejected according as $\boldsymbol{Y} . \boldsymbol{W} > 0$ or $\boldsymbol{Y} . \boldsymbol{W} < 0$ or $\boldsymbol{Y} . \boldsymbol{W} = 0$ has an important geometrical interpretation which will now be introduced for the case where $N = 3$. Figure 3.4 shows a point $\boldsymbol{X}$ lying on a plane, and also shows a vector

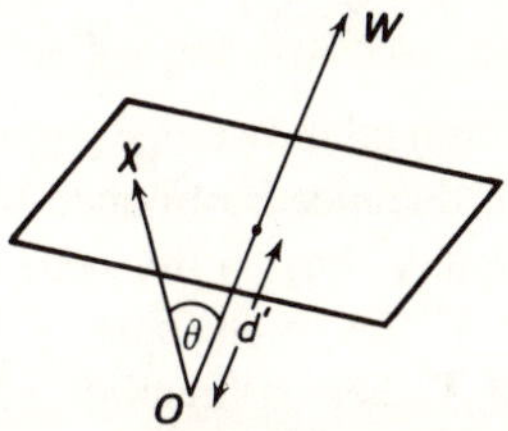

Figure 3.4.

$\boldsymbol{W}$ which is normal (i.e. perpendicular) to the plane. The origin, O, lies at a perpendicular distance d' from the plane, and θ is the angle between OX and OW. The distance or length OX is the *modulus* of vector $\boldsymbol{X}$, written $|\boldsymbol{X}|$, and similarly $|\boldsymbol{W}|$ is the length of vector $\boldsymbol{W}$. We see that $|\boldsymbol{X}| \cos\theta = d'$, and from (3.10)

$$\cos\theta = \frac{\boldsymbol{X} . \boldsymbol{W}}{|\boldsymbol{X}||\boldsymbol{W}|}$$

By combining these two equations we obtain

$$\frac{\boldsymbol{X} . \boldsymbol{W}}{|\boldsymbol{W}|} - d' = 0 \qquad (3.15)$$

Since this equation holds for all points $\boldsymbol{X}$ on the plane and no points off the plane it is an equation for the plane. In general, any equation of the form $\boldsymbol{X} . \boldsymbol{W} =$ constant is the equation of a plane, if $N = 3$. If $N > 3$, the equation $\boldsymbol{X} . \boldsymbol{W} =$ constant is the equation of a hyperplane. A *hyperplane* is a surface in hyperspace (i.e. in an N-dimensional space) which is mathematically analogous to a plane in three-dimensional space.

Let us now consider a point $\boldsymbol{X}''$ which does not lie on the plane specified by (3.15), and derive an expression for the perpendicular distance of $\boldsymbol{X}''$ from that plane. The first step is to construct a plane through $\boldsymbol{X}''$ parallel to the plane specified by (3.15), as indicated in Figure 3.5. Let the perpendicular distance of the new plane from the origin be d'', so that the equation of the new plane is

$$\frac{\boldsymbol{X}'' \cdot \boldsymbol{W}}{|\boldsymbol{W}|} - d'' = 0$$

Thus the perpendicular distance between the two planes is

$$d' - d'' = d' - \frac{\boldsymbol{X}'' \cdot \boldsymbol{W}}{|\boldsymbol{W}|} \tag{3.16}$$

and this is also the perpendicular distance from $\boldsymbol{X}''$ to the plane specified by (3.15). Note that this distance is obtained by substituting $\boldsymbol{X}''$ for $\boldsymbol{X}$ in (3.15), and is positive if $\boldsymbol{X}''$ lies on the same side of the plane (3.15) as the origin, negative if $\boldsymbol{X}''$ lies on the side of the plane (3.15) opposite to the origin, and zero if $\boldsymbol{X}''$ lies on the plane (3.15). Analogous results are true when $N > 3$.

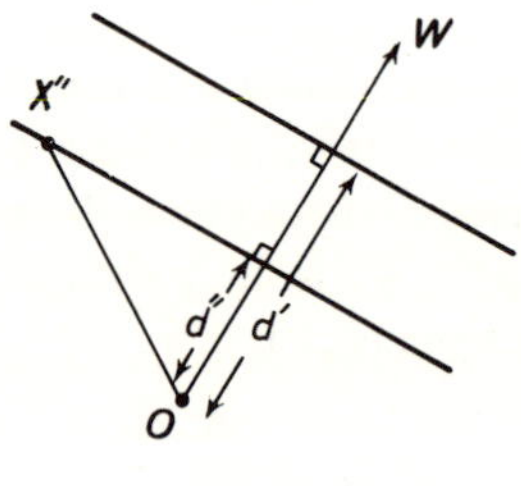

Figure 3.5.

The hyperplane $\boldsymbol{Y} \cdot \boldsymbol{W} = 0$ passes *through* the origin in $(N + 1)$-dimensional hyperspace, since the perpendicular distance of this hyperplane from the origin is zero. The rule: assign $\boldsymbol{X}$ to R_1 or R_2 according as $\boldsymbol{Y} \cdot \boldsymbol{W} > 0$ or $\boldsymbol{Y} \cdot \boldsymbol{W} < 0$ can be interpreted: assign $\boldsymbol{X}$ to R_1 or R_2 according to the side of the hyperplane $\boldsymbol{Y} \cdot \boldsymbol{W} = 0$ on which the representative point of $\boldsymbol{Y}$ lies. The hyperplane $\boldsymbol{Y} \cdot \boldsymbol{W} = 0$ separates the $(N + 1)$-dimensional hyperspace into two parts, all $\boldsymbol{Y}$'s in one part being assigned to R_1 and all $\boldsymbol{Y}$'s in the other to R_2. It is often loosely said that the hyperplane separates *patterns* rather than *representative points* of patterns or of augmented patterns.

Let us suppose that the representative points of the patterns belonging to R'_1 and R'_2 occupy respectively the regions marked '1' and '2' in Figure 3.6(a). If $\boldsymbol{W}$ is such that $\boldsymbol{Y}.\boldsymbol{W}$ is represented by the solid straight line in Figure 3.6(a), some of the R'_2 patterns will be misrecognised; that is, some of the inequalities (3.14) will not be satisfied. This situation is liable to arise when $\boldsymbol{W}$ is determined by the procedures introduced in Sections 3.3, 3.4, and 3.5. The procedures introduced in Sections 3.7 and 3.8 are guaranteed to determine $\boldsymbol{W}$ such that the regions '1' and '2' are separated by a hyperplane $\boldsymbol{Y}.\boldsymbol{W} = 0$, for example by the dotted line in Figure 3.6(a), if any separating hyperplane can be found.

Figure 3.6. *Regions which are (a) linearly separable, and (b) not linearly separable*

If the regions '1' and '2', which contain R'_1 and R'_2 respectively, are as in Figure 3.6(b), then no hyperplane can be found to separate them, and we say that R'_1 and R'_2 are not *linearly separable*. In this case no $\boldsymbol{W}$ can be found which satisfies inequalities (3.14). The simplest example where R'_1 and R'_2 are not linearly separable is where $N = 2$ and $R'_1 = \{00, 11\}$ and $R'_2 = \{01, 10\}$, as can be seen by considering a square whose corners are the points 00, 01, 11, and 10.

3.7 FIXED INCREMENT PROCEDURE

3.7.1 The two-class case

Given training sets R_1^* and R_2^* of augmented patterns, the fixed increment procedure determines a hyperplane $\boldsymbol{Y}.\boldsymbol{W} = 0$ which separates R_1^* from R_2^* if any separating hyperplane can be found. At the start of the procedure we are free to choose on which side of the hyperplane the members of R_1^* will lie, and by way of example let us choose the positive side, so that the members of R_2^* will lie on the negative side. At the start of the procedure we are also free to make an arbitrary choice of the components $w_0, w_1, \ldots, w_N$ of W: for instance the components of W may initially be chosen randomly, or chosen to be all zero's, or determined by a statistical method.

The procedure works through all the Y's in R_1^* and R_2^* as follows. The dot product of W with the first Y is computed, and W is changed according to the following rules:

If $W . Y \leqslant 0$ and Y belongs to R_1^*, then W is changed to, that is, replaced by, $W + Y$.

If $W . Y \geqslant 0$ and Y belongs to R_2^*, then W is changed to $W - Y$.

If $W . Y > 0$ and Y belongs to R_1^* or if $W . Y < 0$ and Y belongs to R_2^*, then W is unchanged.

The dot product of the resulting weight vector with the *second* Y in the training set is then computed and the same rules applied. The dot product of the resulting weight vector with the *third* Y is then computed and the same rules applied, and so on. When all the Y's belonging to R_1^* or R_2^* have been processed in this way, they are all processed in this same way over again, and so on, until there is a pass through the members of R_1^* and R_2^* in the course of which W remains unaltered. The procedure is then said to have *converged.* A pass through all the members of R_1^* and R_2^* is called an *iteration,* and when W remains unaltered during an iteration this necessarily means that, for each Y belonging to R_1^*, $Y . W > 0$, and for each Y belonging to R_2^*, $Y . W < 0$; so it would be pointless to perform further iterations after convergence. If R_1^* and R_2^* are not linearly separable, the procedure does not converge, and iterations continue indefinitely, or, in practice, until stopped after an arbitrary time limit, or when weight vectors vary in a cyclic manner characteristic of non-convergence.

A small-scale example is provided in Table 3.1, in which R_1^* and R_2^* consist of 3-bit patterns which have been augmented to 4-bit patterns by including a first bit which is always '1'. The members of R_1^* are 1101 and 1011, and of R_2^* are 1110 and 1010. The weight vector shown in any given row of Table 3.1 is the weight vector *resulting* from applying the fixed increment procedure to the Y shown in that row. Initially $W = \{0, 0, 0, 0\}$. The Table 3.1 example is only a simple

Table 3.1. SIMPLE ILLUSTRATION OF FIXED INCREMENT PROCEDURE

Y	*Desired sign of Y . W*	*Resulting weight vector*	*Iteration*
1101	+	1 1 0 1	
1011	+	1 1 0 1	1
1110	−	0 0-1 1	
1010	−	0 0-1 1	
1101	+	0 0-1 1	
1011	+	1 0 0 2	2
1110	−	0-1-1 2	
1010	−	0-1-1 2	
1101	+	0-1-1 2	
1011	+	0-1-1 2	3
1110	−	0-1-1 2	
1010	−	0-1-1 2	

one. If R_1^* and R_2^* are linearly separable, the procedure will necessarily converge even if

(1) the patterns are non-binary,
(2) the training set augmented patterns belonging to R_1^* and R_2^* are shuffled up together into any order, and the order need not be the same in different iterations,
(3) R_1^* and R_2^* contain different numbers of *Y*'s,
(4) any arbitrary initial weight vector is chosen.

3.7.2 Proof of convergence

The following paragraphs contain a proof that, if R_1^* and R_2^* are linearly separable, the fixed increment procedure will necessarily converge. A number of proofs of this are known, and the following is a version of Ridgeway's proof[336].

It is convenient to replace R_1^* and R_2^* by a single training set *R*, which consists of all the *Y*'s belonging to R_1^*, together with *negatives* of all the *Y*'s belonging to R_2^*. For example, if R_1^* and R_2^* are as in Table 3.1, the four members of *R* are 1 1 0 1, 1 0 1 1, −1−1−1 0, and −1 0 −1 0. It will be seen that the following error correction rule, when applied to *R*, is exactly equivalent to the fixed increment procedure applied to R_1^* and R_2^*. According to the new rule, $\boldsymbol{Y} . \boldsymbol{W}$ is computed for the current weight vector and each member of R in turn. If $\boldsymbol{Y} . \boldsymbol{W} \leqslant 0$, $\boldsymbol{W}$ is changed to $\boldsymbol{W} + \boldsymbol{Y}$, and if $\boldsymbol{Y} . \boldsymbol{W} > 0$, $\boldsymbol{W}$ is left unchanged. The procedure works iteratively through the training set R, until convergence. If we prove convergence of this procedure, we thereby prove convergence of the equivalent procedure which was introduced in Section 3.7.1.

To prove convergence, we assume that R_1^* and R_2^* are linearly separable, i.e. that there exists a weight vector $\boldsymbol{W}$ such that, for all $\boldsymbol{Y}$'s belonging to R, $\boldsymbol{Y} . \boldsymbol{W} > 0$. Any such $\boldsymbol{W}$ can be multiplied by a positive scalar to ensure that, for all $\boldsymbol{Y}$'s in R, $\boldsymbol{Y} . \boldsymbol{W}$ is greater than some arbitrary positive constant. Let us consider one particular solution vector $\boldsymbol{W}_s$ which obeys the arbitrary condition

$$\boldsymbol{W}_s . \boldsymbol{Y} > M, \text{ for all } \boldsymbol{Y}\text{'s belonging to } R \tag{3.17}$$

where M is the square of the modulus of the training set pattern which has the largest modulus, that is, $M = \max(|\boldsymbol{Y}|^2)$.

Regarding $\boldsymbol{W}$ as a variable and the $\boldsymbol{Y}$'s as constant vectors, we see that each $\boldsymbol{Y}$ belonging to R defines a hyperplane $\boldsymbol{W} . \boldsymbol{Y} = 0$. It follows from (3.16) and (3.17) that $\boldsymbol{W}_s$ lies at a Euclidean distance greater than $M/|\boldsymbol{Y}|$ from $\boldsymbol{W} . \boldsymbol{Y} = 0$ for each $\boldsymbol{Y}$ in R. Any weight vector whose distance from $\boldsymbol{W}_s$ is less than $M/|\boldsymbol{Y}|$ lies on the same side of $\boldsymbol{W} . \boldsymbol{Y} = 0$ as $\boldsymbol{W}_s$. This is true for all of the t hyperplanes, and therefore any weight vector whose distance from $\boldsymbol{W}_s$ is less than $M/|\boldsymbol{Y}|$ is a solution vector. Therefore, if we can prove that, during the fixed increment procedure, every change in the current weight vector $\boldsymbol{W}$ decreases its Euclidean distance, or equivalently its squared Euclidean distance, from $\boldsymbol{W}_s$, then since the number of changes of $\boldsymbol{W}$ is unlimited, we shall have proved that the procedure is bound to arrive at a solution vector.

To prove this consider the kth change in the weight vector, such that

$$\boldsymbol{W}_{k+1} = \boldsymbol{W}_k + \boldsymbol{Y} \tag{3.18}$$

The decrease, e_{k+1}, in squared Euclidean distance between $\boldsymbol{W}_k$ and $\boldsymbol{W}_s$ and $\boldsymbol{W}_{k+1}$ and $\boldsymbol{W}_s$ is given by

$$\begin{aligned} e_{k+1} &= |\boldsymbol{W}_s - \boldsymbol{W}_k|^2 - |\boldsymbol{W}_s - \boldsymbol{W}_{k+1}|^2 \\ &= -2\boldsymbol{W}_s . \boldsymbol{W}_k + \boldsymbol{W}_k . \boldsymbol{W}_k + 2\boldsymbol{W}_s . \boldsymbol{W}_{k+1} \\ &\quad - \boldsymbol{W}_{k+1} . \boldsymbol{W}_{k+1} \end{aligned}$$

Substituting (3.18) in this gives

$$e_{k+1} = -2W_k \,.\, Y + 2W_s \,.\, Y - Y \,.\, Y$$

But $\max(Y \,.\, Y) = M$, and since the weight vector is being changed, $W_k \,.\, Y \leqslant 0$, whence

$$e_{k+1} \geqslant 2W_s \,.\, Y - M$$

and from (3.17),

$$e_{k+1} \geqslant 0$$

This proves that every change of W brings W nearer to W_s by a non-infinitesimal amount greater than zero. Starting from any arbitrary W, changes of W continue to be made until convergence, and therefore the procedure necessarily converges if W_s exists, that is, if R_1^* and R_2^* are linearly separable.

Note that, if the initial W is zero, the solution weight vector determined by the fixed increment rule is a linear combination of training set patterns:

$$W_{\text{solution}} = \sum_{i=1}^{t} \alpha_i Y_i \tag{3.19}$$

where α_i is the number of times when Y_i is added to the weight vector during the procedure. If we modify the procedure so that W is changed to $W = W + \lambda Y$ if $W \,.\, Y \leqslant 0$ and left unchanged if $W \,.\, Y > 0$, where λ is a positive constant, the effect is merely to multiply the solution vector by λ, since

$$\sum_{i=0}^{t} \alpha_i \lambda Y_i = \lambda \sum_{i=1}^{t} \alpha_i Y_i$$

and this does not affect recognition performance. But if R_1^* and R_2^* are not linearly separable, recognition performance may be improved if λ is decreased gradually during successive iterations[126], and we shall briefly return to this in Section 4.7.

3.7.3 Multiclass case of the fixed increment procedure

We now extend the Section 3.7.1 version of the fixed increment procedure, in which none of the Y's are multiplied by -1. The aim of the multiclass procedure is to determine, if possible, weight vectors $W_1, \ldots, W_r, W_s, \ldots, W_z$, one per class, such that, for all r except $r = s$,

$$W_s \,.\, Y > W_r \,.\, Y \qquad (3.20)$$

for all Y's belonging to the sth class training set R_s^*; and this is to be true for all $s = 1, \ldots, z$, that is, for all classes.

Initially the weight vectors $W_1, \ldots, W_z$ are arbitrarily chosen. The error correcting procedure is, as before, iterative, and each Y is processed in turn. If Y belongs to R_s^* and $W_s \,.\, Y \leqslant W_r \,.\, Y$ for any r other than $r = s$, W_s is changed to $W_s + \lambda Y$ and W_r is changed to $W_r - \lambda Y$; and if there is more than one such r, W_r is changed to $W_r - \lambda Y$ for all such r. If Y belongs to R_s^* and $W_s \,.\, Y > W_r \,.\, Y$ for all r except $r = s$, then $W_1, \ldots, W_z$ are left unchanged. When all the members of $R_1^*, \ldots, R_z^*$ have been processed in this way, they are processed in this same way again, or, in other words, a further iteration takes place. Iterations continue until one occurs during which there is no change in any weight vector, and the procedure is then said to have converged. Nilsson[336] provides a proof that this procedure will necessarily converge in a finite number of iterations if there exist weight vectors $W_1, \ldots, W_z$ which satisfy (3.20). If no such weight vectors exist the procedure does not converge, and it should be terminated when an arbitrary time limit expires or when the weight vectors start cycling in a characteristic manner. After training, an unknown Y is assigned to the sth class such that (3.20) holds.

3.7.4 Dead zones

To introduce the idea of a *dead zone*, let us temporarily return to the Section 3.7.1 two-class problem. Consider a simple example in which the representative points of the members of R_1^* and R_2^* are indicated by circles and crosses respectively in Figure 3.7(a). In this example R_1^* and R_2^* are linearly separable. The fixed increment procedure is liable to terminate when a hyperplane has been found which *only just* separates R_1^* and R_2^*, as indicated by the solid line in Figure 3.7(a). The small square in Figure 3.7(a) is at the representative point of an augmented pattern which belongs to R_1 but not to R_1^*. This pattern will be misrecognised because it lies on the R_2^* side of the line. Such misrecognition can be rendered less likely by modifying the fixed increment procedure as follows.

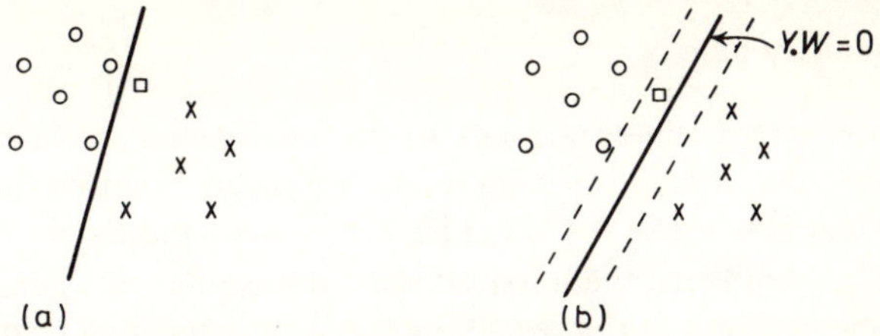

Figure 3.7.*(a) A hyperplane which only just separates two training sets; (b) Training sets separated by a dead zone*

As in Section 3.7.1, the procedure works iteratively through R_1^* and R_2^*, but the following rules are now applied:

If Y belongs to R_1^* and $Y \,.\, W > \delta$, where δ is a positive constant, W is left unchanged.

If Y belongs to R_1^* and $Y \,.\, W \leqslant \delta$, W is changed to $W + Y$.

If Y belongs to R_2^* and $Y \,.\, W \geqslant -\delta$, W is changed to $W - Y$.

If Y belongs to R_2^* and $Y \,.\, W < -\delta$, W is left unchanged.

If this procedure converges, R_1^* and R_2^* are separated by a *dead zone* which is the region between two parallel hyperplanes $Y \,.\, W = \pm\delta$. From (3.16) it follows that the perpendicular distance between these two hyperplanes is $2\delta/|W|$. In the Figure 3.7 example these hyperplanes are represented by dotted lines in Figure 3.7(b). The hyperplane $Y \,.\, W = 0$ is now at a safer distance from members of R_1^* and R_2^*, so that there is more chance of a pattern such as the one represented by a square in Figures 3.7(a) and (b) being correctly recognised. It is also very important that the dead zone leaves a margin for inaccuracy in the physical implementation of weights and thresholds[277].

In the multiclass case, Duda and Fossum[126] have used a procedure which works iteratively through the training set: if Y belongs to R_r^* and $W_r \,.\, Y > W_s \,.\, Y + \delta$ for all s except $s = r$, then $W_1, \ldots, W_z$ are left unchanged. If Y belongs to R_r^* and $W_r \,.\, Y \leqslant W_s \,.\, Y + \delta$ for any $s \neq r$, then W_r is changed to $W_r + \lambda Y$ and W_s is changed to $W_s - \lambda Y$.

If the classes are linearly separable, weight vectors with maximal dead zones can be determined by linear programming[266, 347] (cf. Refs 292 and 376). Lewis and Coates[277] provide an introduction to linear programming for weight determination, and Gass[168] provides a more general introduction to linear programming.

3.7.5 Boundary matrix

The following idea relates not only to the fixed increment rule but also to any other method of weight determination. Suppose for example that $N = 3$, $R'_1 = \{111, 110, 100, 010\}$, and $R'_2 = \{101, 011, 000, 001\}$. By plotting these patterns as corners of a cube, one can see that the problem of finding a hyperplane to separate R'_1 and R'_2, or the problem of maximising a dead zone between R'_1 and R'_2, is the same whether or not we eliminate 110 from R'_1 and 001 from R'_2. In general, if two training sets R'_1 and R'_2 are linearly separable, there exist subsets R''_1 of R'_1 and R''_2 of R'_2 such that a hyperplane which separates R''_1 and R''_2 also separates R'_1 and R'_2 [105, 301]. The use of R''_1 and R''_2 as training sets instead of R'_1 and R'_2 would reduce the amount of computation required for weight determination; but the computation required for determining R''_1 and R''_2 might be comparable with the computation required for determining a weight vector directly from R'_1 and R'_2.

3.8 PATTERN ERROR

To introduce the notion of pattern error let us consider a two-class recognition problem as in Section 3.7.2 where all $\boldsymbol{Y}$'s belonging to R_2^* are multiplied by -1. Let the total number of patterns in R_1^* and R_2^* be t, as before. We require a weight vector such that, for all $i = 1, \ldots, t$, $\boldsymbol{W} . \boldsymbol{Y}_i > 0$. When this condition is not satisfied an *error* is said to exist. Quantitatively, the *pattern error* h_i associated with the ith augmented training set pattern $\boldsymbol{Y}_i$ is defined by[411]

$$h_i = \boldsymbol{W} . \boldsymbol{Y}_i \qquad \text{if } \boldsymbol{W} . \boldsymbol{Y}_i < 0, \text{ and}$$

$$h_i = 0 \qquad \text{if } \boldsymbol{W} . \boldsymbol{Y}_i \geqslant 0$$

For a given $\boldsymbol{W}$, the total pattern error H_w associated with R_1^* and R_2^* is defined by $H_w = -\sum_{i=1}^{t} h_i$. Note that H_w is always non-negative, since h_i is necessarily negative or zero. Even when the classes are not linearly separable, it is surely reasonable to choose the weight vector *so that* the pattern error H_w associated with the chosen weight vector is minimal.

To minimise H_w we can apply the method of steepest descent, which is here intuitively introduced by means of an analogy.

Suppose that a man wishes to walk to the top of a hill, but he does not know where the top of the hill is located: he has no map and the entire hill is covered with thick fog so that the summit is invisible. He knows, however, that the hill has only one peak. If he is already on the hill but not at the top, a sensible strategy is to determine the gradient of the ground where he is standing, walk a little way up the direction of maximum slope, determine the gradient again, walk a little way up the direction of maximum slope, and so on[460]. If instead of trying to reach the top of a hill, he were trying to reach the bottom of a geographical basin, he should keep walking downwards in the direction of maximum gradient.

Pattern error is analogous to height, and $\boldsymbol{W}$ is analogous to position. Starting from arbitrary $\boldsymbol{W}$, $\boldsymbol{W}$ should be reduced by some function of the gradient vector ∇H_w at each step. In the simplest form of this procedure of steepest descent, $\boldsymbol{W}$ is changed to $\boldsymbol{W} - \nabla H_w$, ∇H_w is detemined again, $\boldsymbol{W}$ is changed again to $\boldsymbol{W} - \nabla H_w$, and so on until a minimum ($\nabla H_w = 0$) is reached[260]. Now

$$\nabla H_w = \left\{ \frac{\partial H_w}{\partial w_0}, \frac{\partial H_w}{\partial w_1}, \ldots, \frac{\partial H_w}{\partial w_j}, \ldots, \frac{\partial H_w}{\partial w_N} \right\} \tag{3.21}$$

and

$$\frac{\partial H_w}{\partial w_j} = \frac{\partial(-\sum_{\text{error}} Y_i \,.\, W)}{\partial w_j} = -\sum_{\text{error}} y_{ij}$$

where $\sum_{\text{error}}$ denotes summation over all i such that $h_i \neq 0$. Thus

$$\nabla H_w = -\sum_{\text{error}} Y_i$$

The steepest-descent procedure is therefore: choose an initial $\boldsymbol{W}$ arbitrarily and compute dot products of $\boldsymbol{W}$ with all members of R_1^* and R_2^* and *then* change $\boldsymbol{W}$ to $\boldsymbol{W} + \sum_{\text{error}} \boldsymbol{Y}_i$. Then compute dot products of the new $\boldsymbol{W}$ with all members of R_1^* and R_2^* and change $\boldsymbol{W}$ to $\boldsymbol{W} + \sum_{\text{error}} \boldsymbol{Y}_i$, and so on until convergence, if the classes are linearly separable. This procedure is known as the *many patterns* version of the fixed increment procedure, because *all* training set patterns are processed prior to any change in $\boldsymbol{W}$. The version considered in Section 3.7.2 is the *single patterns* version, so called because $\boldsymbol{W}$ may be changed immediately after $\boldsymbol{Y}_i \,.\, \boldsymbol{W}$ and immediately before $\boldsymbol{Y}_{i+1} \,.\, \boldsymbol{W}$ is computed. The single patterns version is not exactly equivalent to the many patterns version, and is only approximately a method of steepest descent[260, 411].

If R_1^* and R_2^* are not linearly separable, the fixed increment procedure does not converge, and instead the weight vector fluctuates randomly about the minimum pattern error weight vector during successive iterations. This difficulty is avoided in F. W. Smith's linear programming technique which determines the minimum pattern error weight vector even when R_1^* and R_2^* are not linearly separable[192, 410].

Instead of minimising the pattern error function H_w, it may be expedient to minimise a more elaborate pattern error function, for instance that defined by

$$E_w = \sum_{i=1}^{t} h_i^2$$

E_w is known as the *squared error.* To minimise E_w, the steepest-descent procedure starts with an arbitrary $\boldsymbol{W}$ and after each iteration $\boldsymbol{W}$ is changed to $\boldsymbol{W} - \nabla E_w$, where

$$\nabla E_w = \left\{\frac{\partial E_w}{\partial w_0}, \ldots, \frac{\partial E_w}{\partial w_j}, \ldots, \frac{\partial E_w}{\partial w_N}\right\}$$

and

$$\frac{\partial E_w}{\partial w_j} = \frac{\partial \sum_{i=1}^{t} h_i^2}{\partial w_j} = \sum_{i=1}^{t} \frac{\partial h_i^2}{\partial w_j}$$

$$= \sum_{i=1}^{t} \frac{\mathrm{d} h_i^2}{\mathrm{d} h_i} \cdot \frac{\partial h_i}{\partial w_j} = 2 \sum_{i=1}^{t} h_i \frac{\partial h_i}{\partial w_j}$$

Now

$$\frac{\partial h_i}{\partial w_j} = \frac{\partial (\boldsymbol{Y}_i \,.\, \boldsymbol{W})}{\partial w_j} = \frac{\partial}{\partial w_j}(y_{i0} \,.\, w_0 + \ldots + y_{ij} \,.\, w_j + \ldots + y_{iN} \,.\, w_N) = y_{ij}$$

Therefore

$$\frac{\partial E_w}{\partial w_j} = 2 \sum_{i=1}^{t} h_i y_{ij}$$

and

$$\nabla E_w = 2 \left\{ \sum_{i=0}^{t} h_i y_{i0}, \ldots, \sum_{i=0}^{t} h_i y_{ij}, \ldots, \sum_{i=0}^{t} h_i y_{iN} \right\} = 2 \sum_{i=1}^{t} h_i Y_i \quad (3.22)$$

Thus in the procedure for determining $\boldsymbol{W}$, after each iteration $\boldsymbol{W}$ is changed to $\boldsymbol{W} - \nabla E = \boldsymbol{W} - 2 \sum_{\text{error}} (\boldsymbol{Y}_i \,.\, \boldsymbol{W})\boldsymbol{Y}_i$. Note that $-\nabla E$ is always positive since there is no error unless $\boldsymbol{Y}_i \,.\, \boldsymbol{W} < 0$. Iterations continue until convergence, if the classes are linearly separable. The above derivation is not a proof that the procedure will necessarily converge when the classes are linearly separable, since we have not proved that the procedure $\boldsymbol{W} = \boldsymbol{W} - \nabla E$ will converge. In fact if the classes are linearly separable the procedure does not necessarily converge in a finite number of iterations, for the following reason[299]. It may happen that ∇E is very small, so that a small change is made in $\boldsymbol{W}$, resulting in a smaller ∇E, resulting in turn in a smaller change in $\boldsymbol{W}$, and so on *ad infinitum.* To avoid this, Mays has modified the procedure whilst retaining its essential characteristic that the magnitude of each change in $\boldsymbol{W}$ depends on the magnitude of the pattern error.

The single patterns version of Mays' *modified relaxation procedure* passes iteratively through the training set[300]. If $\boldsymbol{Y}_i \,.\, \boldsymbol{W} \geqslant \delta$, where δ is a constant such that $0 < \delta < 1$, $\boldsymbol{W}$ is left unchanged. If $\boldsymbol{Y}_i \,.\, \boldsymbol{W} < \delta$, $\boldsymbol{W}$ is changed to $\boldsymbol{W} + \lambda(1 - \boldsymbol{Y}_i \,.\, \boldsymbol{W})\boldsymbol{Y}_i$, where λ is a constant of proportionality such that $0 < \lambda \leqslant 2/(N+1)$. By stipulating $\delta < 1$, Mays ensures that the increment is never infinitesimal, and he has proved that convergence occurs after a *finite* number of iterations when R_1^* and R_2^* are linearly separable[299]. The modified relaxation procedure has been found to converge in fewer iterations than the fixed increment procedure[300]. A disadvantage of attempting to determine $\boldsymbol{W}$ to minimise E_w when the classes are not linearly separable is that $\boldsymbol{Y}_i$ with large h_i has a relatively big influence on the choice of $\boldsymbol{W}$; but if $\boldsymbol{Y}_i$ is going to be misrecognised anyway, it does not matter how large h_i is, and overall recognition performance may be no better if $\boldsymbol{W}$ is chosen so as to reduce this h_i somewhat. In practice we usually want to minimise the *number* of patterns misrecognised, rather than the average squared error.

Returning to the method of steepest descent, it is obvious that if R_1^* and R_2^* are linearly separable, the minimum value of E_w is zero, and a correction strategy which leads to minimum E_w will therefore lead to a separating weight vector. This idea can be developed by redefining h_i by $h_i = \boldsymbol{Y}_i \cdot \boldsymbol{W} - \delta_i$, where δ_i is a non-negative value associated with Y_i. A procedure which determines a vector $\boldsymbol{W}$ and a vector $\boldsymbol{\delta} = \{\delta_1, \ldots, \delta_i, \ldots, \delta_t\}$ such that

$$E_w = \sum_{i=1}^{t} h_i^2$$

is minimised in fact determines a separating weight vector if one exists (but this is not true if δ is rigidly fixed[459]). To pursue this development just a little further, let A be the matrix whose rows are the augmented training set patterns $\boldsymbol{Y}_1, \ldots, \boldsymbol{Y}_t$, and note that (3.22) can be rewritten

$$\nabla E_w = 2\mathbf{A}^{\mathrm{T}} \begin{bmatrix} h_1 \\ \vdots \\ h_i \\ \vdots \\ h_t \end{bmatrix} = 2\mathbf{A}^{\mathrm{T}}(\mathbf{A}\boldsymbol{W} - \delta)$$

where δ and $\boldsymbol{W}$ are column vectors and superscript T denotes transposition. For minimum $E, \nabla E_w = 0$, which implies that

$$\boldsymbol{W} = \mathbf{A}^{\#}\delta \qquad (3.23)$$

where $\mathbf{A}^{\#}$ is the generalised inverse of $\mathbf{A}$. Ho and Kashyap's procedure[218] is to determine $\boldsymbol{W}$ from (3.23), starting from arbitrary initial $\boldsymbol{\delta}$, (e.g. $\boldsymbol{\delta} = \{1, 1, 1, \ldots, 1\}$). If $\boldsymbol{W}$ is not a solution, a steepest-descent correction is applied to $\boldsymbol{\delta}$, and a new $\boldsymbol{W}$ is obtained from (3.23), and so on until convergence, if the classes are linearly separable. If the classes are linearly separable a solution is reached after very few iterations, but the computation in each iteration is more elaborate than that in, for instance, the fixed increment procedure. Wee[456] has developed a generalised inverse method for the multiclass case.

3.9 DICHOTOMISATION SCHEMES

3.9.1 One/many dichotomisation

Let us consider a recognition system employing z weight vectors in the recognition of z classes. Let the weight vectors be chosen so that, ideally, for all Y's in the rth class, $W_r \,.\, Y > \rho$, and for all patterns not belonging to the rth class $W_r \,.\, Y < \rho$, where ρ is a constant. In this system, the hyperplane $W_r \,.\, Y = \rho$ separates the representative points of all Y's belonging to the rth class from all Y's belonging to classes other than the rth. The hyperplane $W_r \,.\, Y = \rho$ can therefore be said to perform one/many dichotomisation. We find it convenient to extend this nomenclature by saying that the hyperplanes in all the many-class systems which we have considered above in previous sections perform one/many dichotomisation. In these systems, Y is assigned to the rth class if, for all s except $s = r$,

$$Y \,.\, W_r > Y \,.\, W_s \tag{3.24}$$

Here the Y's belonging to the rth class are not separated from the Y's belonging to all other classes by a single hyperplane $Y \,.\, W_r$ = constant, but one weight vector per class is employed, and this is not true in one/one and many/many dichotomisation schemes, as we shall see below.

One/many dichotomisation schemes can be subclassified into two types, according as specimen patterns from one or from more than one class are used in determining the weight vector for any given class. These two types are considered in the following two subsections.

3.9.1.1 Single-class parameter determination

One possible application for automatic pattern recognition is for identifying people by recognising their signatures or speech[153, 238a, 278, 320] The idea is to use this for ensuring, for example, that a sum of money is given to the right man rather than to an impostor. A man's signature is not always the precisely the same, and its variants constitute a recognition class; whereas the fraudulent signatures of (imperfect) impostors constitute different recognition classes. Training sets embracing all possible forgeries are not available during the design of an automatic system for distinguishing authentic signatures from forgeries. In this circumstance there is an obvious advantage in methods which *only* use specimen members of one class in the determination of a weight vector for that class[111]. For example, in the statistical independence method of Section 3.3, the weight vector $\{w_{r0}, \ldots, w_{rN}\}$ only depends on the rth class training set patterns. Training set patterns belonging to classes other than the rth need not be available during the determination of the rth class weight vector.

3.9.1.2 Many-class parameter determination

In the Section 3.7.3 multiclass version of the fixed increment procedure, for example, training set patterns belonging to *all* classes are actively used in the determination of the weight vector for each class. If the same class occurs in a number of different multiclass recognition problems, its weight vector is generally different in each problem: each weight vector is tailor-made for a given multiclass problem. For instance, if one multiclass problem is to recognise 2's, 3's, and 4's, and another multiclass problem is to recognise 2's, 5's, and 6's, the Section 3.7.3 procedure will generally yield a different weight vector for 2's in these two problems.

When training sets from all classes to be recognised are available at the time of weight determination, the advantage of using all of them in the determination of each and every weight vector is that this makes more use of the available information. Results obtained by Casey *et al.*[70] imply appreciably better performance by the Section 3.7.3 fixed increment method than by the Section 3.3 statistical independence method.

3.9.2 One/one dichotomisation

In a one/one dichotomisation scheme, one hyperplane separates R_r from R_s, for all r and s except $r = s$. This scheme of pairwise separation of classes requires altogether $z(z-1)/2$ hyperplanes, where z is, as usual, the number of classes. The hyperplane which (ideally) separates R_r from R_s can be determined, for example, by the two-class version of the fixed increment rule applied to R_r and R_s training sets. As in Section 3.7.1, we are free to choose initially whether R_r lies on the positive or negative side of the R_r/R_s hyperplane. In recognition, an unknown pattern is assigned to the rth class if its representative point lies on the rth class side of each of the $(z-1)$ hyperplanes which separate R_r from other classes[213].

The main advantage of one/one dichotomisation over one/many dichotomisation will be discussed below in Section 3.9.3. An obvious *disadvantage* is that a one/one system may require $z(z-1)/2$ hyperplanes instead of z hyperplanes, and this disadvantage may be serious if z is large.

Given a one/many system which uses recognition rule (3.24), we can always construct a one/one system having exactly the same recognition performance[213]. To see this, note that, if Y lies on the R_r side of the $(z-1)$ hyperplanes $Y.(W_r - W_1) = 0, \ldots, Y.(W_r - W_s) = 0, \ldots, Y.(W_r - W_z) = 0$, then Y satisfies condition (3.24). But this is also the condition for assignment of Y to R_r in a one/one dichotomisation scheme which separates R_r from R_s, for all r except $r = s$, by means of the hyperplane $Y.(W_r - W_s) = 0$. Therefore this one/one scheme has the same performance as the one/many scheme using (3.24).

But the converse is not true: for any given one/one system will not not necessarily an equivalent one/many system. In particular, if we determine one/one hyperplanes using the two-class fixed increment procedure of Section 3.7.1, the resulting one/one system will not generally give the same recognition performance as a one/many system using hyperplanes determined by the multiclass fixed increment procedure of Section 3.7.3.

Instead of determining one/one hyperplanes by an error correcting procedure such as the fixed increment procedure, we can use a statistical technique. In particular, if the recognition classes are normally distributed and their covariance matrices are unequal, it can be shown that is is sensible[19, 349] to employ one/one dichotomisation such that, for $r = 1, \ldots, z$, R_r and R_s are separated by the *Fisher* hyperplane $Y.W = 0$, where

$$W = (C_r + C_s)^{-1}\,(M_r - M_s)$$

in the notation of Section 3.4. This has been used experimentally by, for example, Bakis *et al.*[26], and Lambert[266].

3.9.3 The chance of linear separability

To introduce an idea, let us take *any t N*-element patterns, *arbitrarily* assign them to two classes, and determine whether these classes are linearly separable. Let us make then a different arbitrary assignment of these same t patterns to two classes, and determine whether these two classes are linearly separable. Let us repeat this for all possible assignments of the same t patterns to two arbitrary classes, and count the number of assignments for which the two classes are linearly separable. Cover[105] has shown that, if our t patters are chosen randomly, and if N is large, we shall find either that almost all or almost none of the assignments produce linearly separable classes according as $t < 2N$ or $t > 2N$. Thus, if two classes each contain more than N random patterns of N elements, they are very unlikely to be linearly separable.

In practice, recognition classes usually contain very many more than N N-element patterns. But this does not necessarily mean that recognition classes are not in practice linearly separable, because recognition classes are generally not random collections of patterns. To illustrate this it is easy to make up examples where two classes are linearly separable, but both contain many orders of magnitude more than N patterns. For instance let $N = 100$, and let us say that arbitrary recognition class R_1 consists of all binary patterns which have Hamming distance not greater than 10 from a given pattern Q_1, and arbitrary recognition class R_2 consists of all binary patterns which have Hamming distance not greater than 10 from a further given pattern Q_2, and that the Hamming distance between Q_1 and Q_2 is 22. From equation (1.3) of Section 1.6, all patterns with Hamming distance 11 from Q_1 lie on the hyperplane

$$\sum_{j=1}^{N} x_j(1 - 2q_{1j}) + \sum_{j=1}^{N} q_{1j} = 11$$

where

$$Q_1 = \{q_{11}, \ldots, q_{1j}, \ldots, q_{1N}\}$$

But the Hamming distance between Q_1 and any pattern belonging to R_2 is not less than 12, and similarly the Hamming distance between Q_2 and any pattern belonging to R_1 is not less than 12. Therefore this hyperplane separates R_1 from R_2. The number of patterns in R_1 is

$$\sum_{i=1}^{10} \frac{N(N-1)\ldots(N-i)}{1 \times 2 \times \ldots\ldots \times i}$$

which is very much greater than $2N$. Because the patterns belonging to R_1 lie close to the single pattern Q_1, they form a cluster.

Practical recognition classes cannot always be expected to form compact non-overlapping clusters, and the only way to determine whether classes are linearly separable is by experiment. However, as a rough general rule of thumb, it can be said that the more closely recognition classes resemble compact clusters, the greater the chance of linear separability. In the simplest type of one/many dichotomisation scheme, each hyperplane separates one class from many others. There is obviously a better chance that a single class will form a single compact cluster than that a collection of many classes will resemble a single compact cluster. Therefore linear separability is more likely in a one/one dichotomisation scheme, and this is the main advantage of one/one dichotomisation[233].

3.9.4 Many/many dichotomisation

In many/many dichotomisation schemes, each hyperplane is used to separate many classes from many others. To introduce this, let us consider an example where the problem is to recognise the numerals 0, . . ., 9. Let us assume that four hyperplanes can be found which separate

(1) the classes 8, 9, 0 from 1, 2, 3, 4, 5, 6, 7
(2) the classes 4, 5, 6, 7 from 1, 2, 3, 8, 9, 0
(3) the classes 2, 3, 6, 7, 0 from 1, 4, 5, 8, 9
(4) the classes 1, 3, 5, 7, 9 from 2, 4, 6, 8, 0

Corresponding to each hyperplane, let us define a variable which takes the value 1 or 0 according to the side of the hyperplane on which the representative point of an augmented input pattern, $\boldsymbol{Y}$, lies. The four variables corresponding to the four hyperplanes constitute a 4-bit pattern. In the present example we arbitrarily arrange that the left-hand bit in the 4-bit pattern corresponds to the first hyperplane, and the right-hand bit to the fourth. The 4-bit pattern corresponding to $\boldsymbol{Y}$ depends on the class to which $\boldsymbol{Y}$ belongs, according to Table 3.2.

Table 3.2. 4-BIT PATTERNS CORRESPONDING TO 10 RECOGNITION CLASSES

Class of Y	*4-bit pattern*
1	0 0 0 1
2	0 0 1 0
3	0 0 1 1
4	0 1 0 0
5	0 1 0 1
6	0 1 1 0
7	0 1 1 1
8	1 0 0 0
9	1 0 0 1
0	1 0 1 0

To recognise an unknown $\boldsymbol{Y}$, we first find the side of each of the four hyperplanes on which the representative point of $\boldsymbol{Y}$ lies, and this gives us a 4-bit pattern. We assign $\boldsymbol{Y}$ to the class to which this 4-bit pattern corresponds.

In this example, four hyperplanes are used for recognising 10 classes, instead of the 10 hyperplanes which would be required by a one/many system, or the 45 that would be required by a one/one system. More generally, assuming many/many linear separability, a many/many system using τ hyperplanes can recognise 2^τ classes, since there are 2^τ possible distinct patterns of τ bits. Conversely, a many/many system for recognising z classes will require a number of hyperplanes not less than the smallest integer greater than $\log_2 z$. For large z, $\log_2 z$ is very much smaller than z, so there would be a big economical advantage in many/many dichotomisation. If $N \gg \tau$, the cost of τ-bit masks for recognising τ-bit patterns by mask matching is only a small proportion of the total cost of the system. Unfortunately, a hyperplane for separating many classes from many others is *not* separating two compact clusters; and according to the discussion in Section 3.9.3, many/many linear separability is less likely than one/many linear separability, which in turn is less likely than one/one linear separability.

In our example we have assumed many/many linear separability. Although in practice it may be impossible to find a hyperplane which separates *all* 2's, 3's, 6's, 7's, and 0's from *all* 1's, 4's, 5's, 8's, and 9's, it may be possible to find a hyperplane which separates a *large proportion* of 2's, 3's, 6's, 7's, and 0's, from a *large proportion* of 1's, 4's, 5's, 8's, and 9's. In that this hyperplane does not perfectly separate these two sets of classes, it is *unreliable*. To achieve tolerably reliable overall recognition performance using unreliable hyperplanes we must increase the *number* of hyperplanes, or, in other words, introduce *redundancy*.

This can be illustrated by introducing a fifth hyperplane into the above example, so that the 5-bit patterns which *usually* correspond to the 10 numerals are as in Table 3.3.

Fairly reliable recognition can be achieved if

(1) any given input $\boldsymbol{Y}$ is very unlikely to lie on the wrong side of more than one hyperplane, and
(2) we use the recognition rule that the unknown pattern is assigned to the class whose 5-bit pattern is Hamming distance 0 or 1 from the 5-bit pattern derived from $\boldsymbol{Y}$. If there is no such class, $\boldsymbol{Y}$ is rejected.

If there is an appreciable chance of any given Y lying on the wrong side of more than one hyperplane, we must incorporate further hyperplanes into the system. Even so, the total number of weights may perhaps be less than in a one/many system applied to the same recognition task.

Table 3.3. 5-BIT PATTERNS CORRESPONDING TO 10 RECOGNITION CLASSES

Class of Y	*5-bit pattern*
1	1 0 0 0 1
2	1 0 0 1 0
3	0 0 0 1 1
4	1 0 1 0 0
5	0 0 1 0 1
6	0 0 1 1 0
7	1 0 1 1 1
8	1 1 0 0 0
9	0 1 0 0 1
0	0 1 0 1 0

Generally speaking, the τ hyperplanes in a many/many system are not all equally unreliable, and we need not be restricted to the Hamming distance rule mentioned above by way of example. It is only necessary that the τ-bit patterns derived from 2's, for example, should constitute a recognition class which is distinguishable from the classes of τ-bit patterns derived from other classes of input patterns. The τ hyperplanes transform the problem of recognising N-element patterns into that of recognising τ-bit patterns, and the τ hyperplanes should be such that no two N-element patterns belonging to different recognition classes are ever transformed into the same τ-bit pattern. It is economically expedient to impose the additional restriction that the z recognition classes of τ-bit patterns should be recognisable by a one/many linear system.

We then have altogether a two-layer linear system. The τ hyperplanes constituting the first layer can be implemented by resistor masks as in Section 1.6, except that a threshold circuit, instead of a current-measuring device, is now associated with each mask. A threshold circuit here produces an output voltage which is digital '1' or digital '0' according as the total current in the corresponding mask is positive or negative. A threshold circuit together with its corresponding mask constitutes a *threshold logic circuit*[336]. The outputs from the τ threshold logic circuits are the τ inputs to a resistor mask system as in Section 1.6, which now forms the second layer of the two-layer system illustrated diagrammatically in Figure 3.8. (Note that with appropriately chosen hyperplanes at the first and second levels, this becomes an implementation of a one/one dichotomisation scheme.)

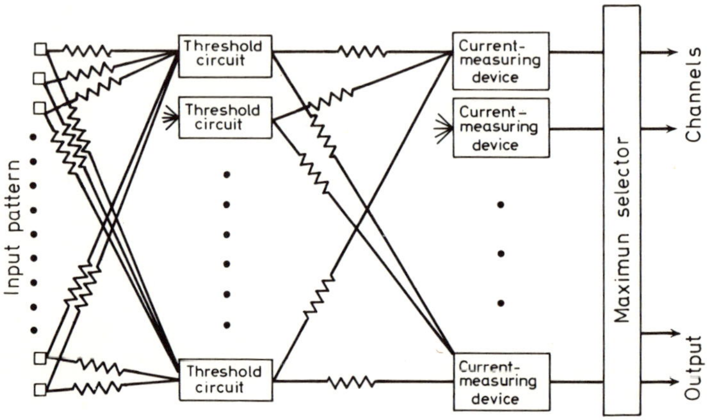

Figure 3.8. *A two-layer linear recognition system*

There are two possible advantages in many/many systems. First, the possibility of economy, as indicated at the beginning of this section. Secondly, because there is no very obvious limit to the number of many/many hyperplanes which can be used, and because none of them need be perfectly reliable, it may perhaps be possible to obtain better performance from many/many than from one/many or one/one schemes, since one/many and one/one schemes demand reliability of dichotomisation. It is not clear from the published literature whether better performance has in fact been achieved this way.

We now outline four of the methods which have been proposed for determining the first-level hyperplanes. None of these methods is entirely satisfactory, but they are all basic, and remarkably different from each other. In each of these four methods, the second layer is not restricted to being linear: the second layer can be any recognition system, and this may or may not be linear.

3.9.4.1 Construction of ideal τ-bit patterns

In this approach, we start by constructing z arbitrary τ-bit patterns, preferably such that the Hamming distance between all pairs of arbitrary τ-bit patterns is maximal. We arbitrarily associate one τ-bit pattern with each recognition class. Using, for example, the Section 3.7.1 fixed increment procedure, we attempt to find a hyperplane to separate all classes for which the first bit in the associated τ-bit pattern is '1' from all those for which the first bit is '0'. We attempt to find a second hyperplane to separate all classes for which the second of the τ bits is '1' from those for which the second bit is '0', and so on, until τ hyperplanes have been determined[97, 110, 355].

The τ hyperplanes serve to transform any input pattern into a τ-bit pattern. This transformation can be applied to training set patterns, and the resulting τ-bit patterns can be used, for instance, for determining second-level hyperplanes, by the Section 3.7.3 fixed increment procedure or any other method. The value of τ is chosen to be just large enough to ensure adequate recognition performance, if this is possible.

To recognise the 10 numerals, this approach might for example prescribe linear separation of 1, 3, 5, 6, 9 from 2, 4, 7, 8, 0. These sets of classes might not be linearly separable, and the minimum pattern error associated with this dichotomy might be high. The minimum pattern error associated with a dichotomy such as 1, 2, 4, 7, 9/3, 5, 6, 8, 0 might be lower, but the present first-level design procedure might not call for this dichotomy. A disadvantage of this approach is that it does not necessarily find or use the most reliable dichotomies.

3.9.4.2 Statistical selection

A simple but not very effective technique is to choose the first-level hyperplanes at random. It is convenient in this case to restrict the weights to −1, 0, and +1. There is no reason to believe that if this restriction were removed the *random* hyperplanes would be more useful, and this consideration justifies the restriction. The τ randomly chosen hyperplanes transform training set patterns into τ-bit patterns which can be used to determine the weights of a linear second layer. The resulting two-layer linear system is known as an α-perceptron[46, 377].

Better recognition performance can be obtained by

(1) generating the first-level hyperplanes not at random but in accordance with a rough statistical strategy,
(2) generating more hyperplanes than will finally be required, and
(3) selecting from among these hyperplanes a collection which pass a statistical test of effectiveness[427, 428].

Because some of the first-level weights are zero, this technique happens to fall within the scope of Chapter 5, and we shall defer further discussion of it until Section 5.5.

3.9.4.3 Dissecting planes algorithm

A simple version of Braverman's dissecting planes algorithm[57] works with training set patterns belonging to z recognition classes. The training set patterns are shuffled up into a random sequence, such that, given the class of a pattern in the sequence, it is impossible to predict the class of the next pattern. The patterns in this sequence are processed in turn. If the first two patterns belong to different classes, the algorithm determines the hyperplane which perpendicularly bisects the line joining the representative points of these two patterns. When each subsequent pattern is processed, perpendicularly bisecting hyperplanes are constructed between this and the representative points of all previous patterns in other classes from which this pattern is not already separated by at least one hyperplane. When the training sequence is exhausted, the set of hyperplanes which have been determined during the sequence forms the first layer of a two-layer recognition system. This technique is introduced in more general and complete form in Arkadev and Braverman's book[22]. In practice the number of first-layer hyperplanes may become very large[268].

3.9.4.4 Common subpatterns

The seven black bars in Figure 3.9(a) can be put together in 17 different ways to make up the stylised characters shown in Figure 3.9(b). Each of the Figure 3.9(a) bars could be detected by a separate peephole mask. According to this idea there is, for each Figure 3.9(a) bar, a hyperplane which separates all patterns containing that bar from all patterns not containing that bar. A pattern can be recognised as one of the Figure 3.9(b) characters according to the Figure 3.9(a) bars which it does or does not contain. Here we have a two-layer recognition system in which the first layer has one hyperplane per bar, and this may be more economical than a one/many linear system for recognising the Figure 3.9(b) characters directly, not in terms of bars.

Although stylised characters can be designed so that different characters are composed of a few common parts[208], it is less obvious

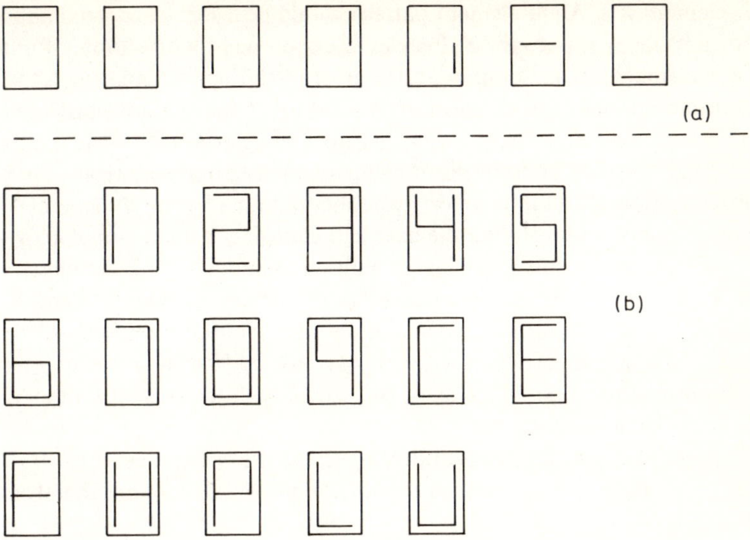

Figure 3.9. (*a*) *Bars out of which the stylised characters in Figure* 3.9(*b*) *are composed*

that ordinary non-stylised characters can usefully be regarded as made up of common parts analogous to those in the Figure 3.9 example[1,47,327]. In Chapter 7 we shall consider the idea that ordinary non-stylised characters contain *features* in a rather more general sense than in the Figure 3.9 example: the idea of the present section is rather limited in that it presumes only one sub-pattern per f-class (*see* Section 7.5).

3.10 KARHUNEN–LOÈVE EXPANSION

In the techniques which were introduced in Section 3.9.4, a pattern X was transformed into a new pattern whose jth component was 1 or 0 according as the dot product of X with the jth weight vector was positive or negative. In the present section, X is transformed into a new pattern whose jth component is simply the dot product of X with the jth weight vector.

In an N-element pattern recognition problem, it may be possible to economise by ignoring $(N-M)$ elements of each pattern X, particularly if the problem of recognising the resulting M-element patterns is not very much more difficult than the problem of recognising the original

N-element X's. An M-element pattern would be a sort of approximation to an N-element pattern, X. Instead of enquiring how to choose M out of N elements so as to minimise the error of this approximation, let us consider a more general question. A rotation of the N axes transforms a pattern $X = \{x_1, \ldots, x_j, \ldots, x_N\}$ into a new pattern $Z = \{z_1, \ldots, z_j, \ldots, z_N\}$. Instead of choosing M elements of X, a mathematical investigation shows that we can generally obtain a better M-element approximation by rotating the axes and choosing M elements of Z. By rotating the axes and applying recognition techniques to M elements of Z, we can reduce the *dimensionality* of our recognition problem from N to M without introducing more than a minimal amount of error. The questions which we must now ask are first, how to determine the optimal rotation of the axes, and secondly, how to choose the best M elements of Z.

After rotation, let the coordinate axes be the column vectors $W_1, \ldots, W_j, \ldots, W_N$. These are mutually perpendicular and, therefore for all $i, j = 1, \ldots, N$,

$$W_i^T W_j = \begin{cases} 1 \text{ if } i = j \\ 0 \text{ if } i \neq j \end{cases} \tag{3.25}$$

$W_i^T W_j$ means the same as $W_i \cdot W_j$ but it is convenient here to use matrix notation; superscript T denotes transposition. X and Z are column vectors, and

$$X = \sum_{j=1}^{N} z_j W_j \tag{3.26}$$

Applying (3.25) to this, we obtain

$$W_j^T X = W_j^T (z_1 W_1 + z_2 W_2 + \ldots + z_j W_j + \ldots + z_N W_N) = z_j \tag{3.27}$$

Equations (3.26) and (3.27) are particularly familiar in the case where $N = 2$, where rotation is through $\theta°$, and $W_1 = \begin{bmatrix} \cos\theta \\ \sin\theta \end{bmatrix}$ and $W_2 = \begin{bmatrix} -\sin\theta \\ \cos\theta \end{bmatrix}$.

If we ignore the $(M+1)$th to the Nth elements of Z, we loose the $(M+1)$th to Nth terms of (3.26), and X is approximated according to

$$X = \sum_{j=1}^{M} z_j W_j$$

(which is the K-L expansion of X)

The squared error of this approximation is

$$\epsilon_x^2 = \left(\sum_{j=M+1}^{N} z_j W_j\right)^{\mathrm{T}} \left(\sum_{j=M+1}^{N} z_j W_j\right) = \sum_{j=M+1}^{N} z_j^2 \quad \text{using 3.25}$$

and from (3.25) and (3.27)

$$\epsilon_x^2 = \sum_{j=M+1}^{N} z_j^2 = \sum_{j=M+1}^{N} (W_j{}^{\mathrm{T}} X)(W_j{}^{\mathrm{T}} X) = \sum_{j=M+1}^{N} W_j^{\mathrm{T}} X X^{\mathrm{T}} W_j$$

If we make this approximation not just for one pattern X but for t patterns, $X_1, \ldots, X_t$, the mean squared error is the mean of ϵ_x^2 for all the X's, that is

$$\overline{\epsilon^2} = \sum_{j=M+1}^{N} W_j^{\mathrm{T}} \mathbf{S} W_j \tag{3.28}$$

where $\mathbf{S}$ is the matrix which is the average of $X_1 X_1^{\mathrm{T}}, X_2 X_2^{\mathrm{T}}, \ldots, X_t X_t^{\mathrm{T}}$. The Karhunen–Loève expansion is such that the vectors $W_1, \ldots, W_N$ are eigenvectors of $\mathbf{S}$, so that for $j = 1, \ldots, N$, $\lambda_j W_j = \mathbf{S} W_j$, where $\lambda_1, \lambda_2, \ldots, \lambda_N$ are the eigenvalues of $\mathbf{S}$. In this case (3.28) becomes

$$\overline{\epsilon^2} = \sum_{j=M+1}^{N} \lambda_j$$

Let $W_1, \ldots, W_N$ be indexed so that $\lambda_1 \geqslant \lambda_2 \geqslant \ldots \geqslant \lambda_N$. It can be proved[450, 454] that $\overline{\epsilon^2}$ is not greater when $W_1, \ldots, W_N$ are eigenvectors of $\mathbf{S}$ than when $W_1, \ldots, W_N$ are arbitrary vectors conforming to (3.25) which are not eigenvectors of $\mathbf{S}$. In other words, we minimise the mean squared error of the approximation by using the Karhunen–Loève expansion.

This technique, which is essentially the same as *factor analysis* or *discriminant analysis*, has been used in various ways in pattern recognition, *see* for example Refs 60, 256, 320, 455. One way is to obtain

$$\mathbf{S}_r = \frac{1}{t_r} \sum_{i=1}^{t_r} X_{ri} X_{ri}{}^{\mathrm{T}}$$

from the rth class training set $\{X_{r1}, \ldots, X_{ri}, \ldots, X_{rt}\}$, and select the set of, say, M_r eigenvectors of $\mathbf{S}_r$ corresponding to the M_r largest eigenvalues. This is repeated for all $r = 1, \ldots, z$, and the $\tau = M_1 + M_2 + \ldots$

$+M_r + \ldots + M_z$ selected eigenvectors transform a pattern X into a τ-component pattern whose components are $X^T W_{11}, X^T W_{12}, \ldots, X^T W_{rj}, \ldots, X^T W_{rM_r}$, where W_{rj} is the jth eigenvector of $\mathbf{S}_r$. Recognition techniques are applied to this τ-component pattern.

Alternatively[455], we can obtain the average, A, of all training set X's, regardless of class,

$$A = \frac{1}{\sum_{r=1}^{z} t_r} \sum_{r=1}^{z} \sum_{i=1}^{t_r} X_{ri}$$

and choose $W_1, \ldots, W_M$ to be the eigenvectors of

$$\mathbf{S} = \frac{1}{\sum_{r=1}^{z} t_r} \sum_{r=1}^{z} \sum_{i=1}^{t_r} (X_{ri} - A)(X_{ri} - A)^T$$

corresponding to the M largest eigenvalues of $\mathbf{S}$. Recognition techniques are applied to the vector whose M components are $W_1^T X, \ldots, W_M^T X$. The idea here is that the retained variables are those with the greatest statistical variability over all classes. Unfortunately this does not distinguish variability *between* classes from variability *within* classes.

A general disadvantage of the Karhunen–Loève approach to pattern recognition is that patterns belonging to different recognition classes may be transformed into the same or similar patterns[161, 326]. The transformation does not necessarily enhance differences between members of different recognition classes.

Chapter 4

PIECEWISE LINEAR TECHNIQUES, THE METHOD OF POTENTIALS, AND STOCHASTIC APPROXIMATION

4.1 PIECEWISE LINEAR DISCRIMINANT FUNCTIONS

In Sections 3.3, 3.5, and 3.7, a pattern X was assigned to the sth class if $W_s . Y > W_r . Y$ for all r except $r = s$, where W_r is the rth class weight vector. In piecewise linear systems, we employ more than one weight vector per class. Let $W_{r1}, \ldots, W_{ri}, W_{rj}, \ldots, W_{r\gamma_r}$ be the weight vectors for the rth class, for $r = 1, \ldots, z$. A piecewise linear recognition rule is[336]: assign X to the sth class such that there exists i in the range $1, \ldots, \gamma_s$ such that

$$W_{si} . Y > W_{rj} . Y \tag{4.1}$$

for all $j = 1, \ldots, \gamma_r$ and for all $r = 1, \ldots, z$ except $r = s$.

To introduce a geometrical interpretation of piecewise linear discrimination, let us consider a very simple example in which $N = 2$ and there are only two recognition classes, R_1 and R_2. In this introductory example there are two weight vectors, W_{11} and W_{12}, corresponding to R_1, and only one weight vector, W_2, corresponding to R_2. Let $W' = W_{11} - W_2$ and $W'' = W_{12} - W_2$. Recognition rule (4.1) becomes here: assign X to R_1 if $Y . W' > 0$ *or* $Y . W'' > 0$. Thus X is assigned to R_1 if the representative point of Y lies on the positive side of either $Y . W' = 0$ or $Y . W'' = 0$ and X is assigned to R_2 if the representative point of Y lies on the negative side of $Y . W' = 0$ and $Y . W'' = 0$. In Figure 4.1, regions '1' and '2' contain all members of R_1 and R_2 respectively, and the two hyperplanes $Y . W' = 0$ and $Y . W'' = 0$ are represented by straight lines with their positive and negative sides labelled '+' and '–' respectively. In this example, R_1 and R_2 are not linearly separable, but perfect recognition is achieved by using two hyperplanes instead of one, which illustrates the general advantage of piecewise linear discrimination.

When two regions are not linearly separable, we can separate them by means of a curved surface or by means of a piecewise system of hyperplanes which *approximate* a curved surface.

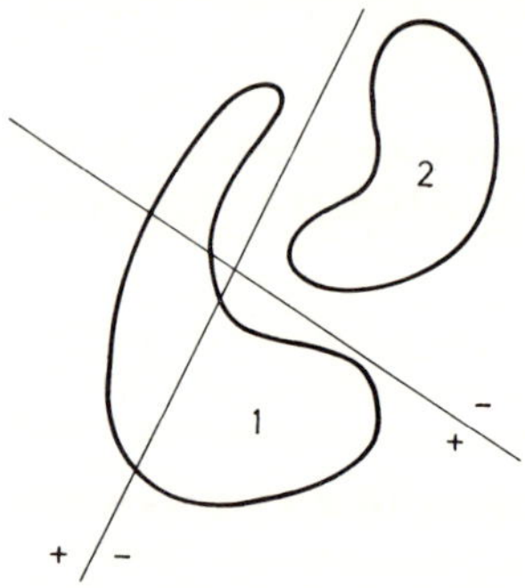

Figure 4.1. *Piecewise linear separation of two regions*

For any given s, i the set of patterns which satisfy (4.1) is the ith *subclass* of the sth class. Thus there is one subclass per weight vector, and one weight vector per subclass. Ideally the union of the γ_s subclasses corresponding to $W_{s1}, \ldots, W_{s\gamma_s}$ should include all patterns belonging to the sth class and no patterns belonging to any class other than the sth. In this case, if we establish that X belongs to any subclass of the sth class, we thereby establish that X belongs to the sth class.

4.2 INTUITIVELY DETERMINED SUBCLASSES

When a machine is to recognise, for example, print from different known fonts, the most obvious way of splitting up classes into subclasses may prove to be the most useful. For instance, all 2's in one font might constitute one subclass of '2', all 2's in another font might constitute another subclass of '2', and so on[283]. To obtain one weight vector per subclass by straightforward application of the methods of Chapter 3, we would require a separate training set for each subclass. For instance, a training set of 2's in a given font could be used in the determination of a weight vector by the Section 3.3 method. A training set of 2's in a different font could be used in the determination of a further weight vector by the Section 3.3 method, and so on. An unknown pattern could be recognised in accordance with (4.1).

4.3 NEAREST-NEIGHBOUR METHOD

The nearest-neighbour method is one of the most rudimentary techniques of pattern recognition, and in its simplest implementation it is piecewise linear. Training set patterns belonging to all recognition classes are simply stored in the recognition machine. The machine determines the distance of an unknown pattern X from every pattern in the training set, and finds the training set pattern which is nearest to X. Then X is assigned to the class to which the nearest training set pattern belongs[107]. Distance, for this purpose, need not be Euclidean distance, and other metrics may be used.

The error rate of the nearest-neighbour method in the case where the number of patterns in the training set tends to infinity has been the subject of virtuoso statistical investigations[106, 107, 348]. It is perhaps sufficient for present purposes to note that in the case where

(1) the number of patterns in the training set tends to infinity, and
(2) each pattern, X, has non-zero class membership probability, $P(r/X)$, for not more than one class,

the nearest-neighbour method would give 100% correct recognition. This follows because an unknown pattern would lie at zero distance from a stored pattern.

When Euclidean distance is used in the nearest-neighbour method, it follows from our discussion of minimum Euclidean distance in Section 3.4 that the nearest-neighbour recognition rule is equivalent to: assign X to the sth class such that there exists i in the range $1, \ldots, t_s$ such that

$$X \,.\, X_{si} - \frac{X_{si} \,.\, X_{si}}{2} > X \,.\, X_{rj} - \frac{X_{rj} \,.\, X_{rj}}{2} \qquad (4.2)$$

for all $j = 1, \ldots, t_r$ and all $r = 1, \ldots, z$ except $r = s$, where $\{x_{r1}, \ldots, X_{rj}, \ldots, X_{rt_r}\}$ is the rth class training set. This shows that when Euclidean distance is used, the nearest-neighbour method is piecewise linear. We can write (4.2) in the form $Y \,.\, W_{si} > Y \,.\, W_{rj}$, where for all r, j the first component of W_{rj} is $(-X_{rj} \,.\, X_{rj})/2$, and the remaining N components of W_{rj} are the N components of X_{rj}. Instead of storing all training set patterns, it is more efficient to store all W_{rj}'s and compute $Y \,.\, W_{rj}$ instead of Euclidean distance.

If the number of stored training set patterns or W_{rj}'s is large, recognition by the nearest-neighbour method involves much computation. Hart[203] has devised a method of reducing the amount of stored data, and experiments with the nearest neighbour method have been reported by, for instance, Hart[203] and Munson, *et al.*[324]

Whereas the normality assumption method of Section 3.4 was a clear example of a parametric statistical recognition technique, the nearest-neighbour method is a clear example of a non-parametric technique.

4.4 FIRSCHEIN AND FISCHLER'S METHOD

When the rth class is normally distributed, its contours of equal probability in hyperspace are hyperellipsoidal. We see this by setting the exponent in equation (3.3) equal to a constant, since only the exponent depends upon X. When $\mathbf{C}_r$ is scalar the contours of equal probability for the rth class are hyperspherical, in accordance with $(X-M_r)^{\mathrm{T}}(X-M_r)$ = constant, and thus the rth class forms a hyperspherical cluster. We have seen in Section 3.4 that when the covariance matrices of all classes are scalar and equal, it is appropriate to assign X to the sth class if X is nearer to M_s than to M_r for all $r \neq s$. This minimum distance rule is appropriate only when recognition classes form hyperspherical, or at least approximately hyperspherical, clusters, The nearest-neighbour method, on the other hand, merely presupposes that closely neighbouring points in hyperspace belong to the same recognition class: the representative points of a class need not form a single cluster, and there is scarcely any restriction on the shapes of clusters. For direct application to hand-printed characters, for example, this is more realistic than the demand for roughly hyperspherical clusters. But the nearest-neighbour method in practice makes far greater demands on storage and computation than does the simple minimum Euclidean distance rule of Section 3.4.

Firschein and Fischler's method[142] can be regarded as a compromise which avoids the restrictiveness of the minimum Euclidean distance rule and the extravagance of the nearest-neighbour method. Firschein and Fischler's method *automatically* splits up each class into a set of subclasses, and for each subclass a mean vector is obtained by the method used for whole classes in Section 3.3. The subclasses are such that each training set pattern is nearer to the mean vector of its own subclass than to the mean vector of any other subclass. Firschein and Fischler's method was originally formulated[142] in terms of a somewhat questionable[444] discriminant which can easily be shown equivalent to $X . M_r - \frac{1}{2} \sum_{j=1}^{N} m_{rj}$. Rosen and Hall[375] replaced this with Euclidean distance. The method is introduced here in terms of Euclidean distance, rather than the more practical and equivalent discriminant $X . M_r - \frac{1}{2} M_r . M_r$, because distance is intuitively more meaningful. To simplify the wording of the following paragraphs, we shall leave out the words *training set*, and it is to be understood that *rth class* in fact means *rth class training set*.

Initially a mean vector, M_r, is obtained for each class as in Sections 3.3 and 3.4, and Firschein and Fischler's procedure then works through each class in turn, as follows. The Euclidean distances between the means of all classes and all patterns in the first class are computed. The pattern, if any, is found which

(1) lies closer to any mean vector other than that of the first class, and
(2) lies further from the mean vector of the first class than does any other pattern which obeys condition (1).

If there is no such pattern, the procedure simply passes on to the second class. If, however, there is such a pattern, it is regarded as the mean of a new subclass, and this pattern is excluded when the remaining patterns in the first class are averaged to yield a new mean vector, which itself can be regarded as a subclass mean. So the first class has been resolved into two subclasses, and this illustrates the method of generating new subclasses. Condition (2) limits the rate of birth of new subclasses.

At an intermediate stage in the procedure, each class generally comprises a number of subclasses, and each subclass is a collection of training set patterns. As well as a mechanism for generating subclasses, the procedure includes an important mechanism for transferring patterns between subclasses belonging to the same class, and this allows growth in the membership of new subclasses, as we shall now see.

The procedure works through each subclass determining the Euclidean distance between each pattern in this subclass and the mean of *every* other subclass, regardless of class, in order to find the nearest mean to each pattern. If, while any given subclass is being worked through, a pattern in this subclass is found which is nearest to the mean of some other class in the same class, that pattern is transferred to this other subclass, and the means of both subclasses are recomputed. The procedure then starts again at the beginning of the subclass through which it was working, and applies these same rules. When the procedure eventually reaches the end of a subclass, the pattern, if any, is selected which

(1) lies closer to the mean of a subclass belonging to a different class than to the mean of its own subclass, and
(2) lies further from the mean of its own subclass than does any other pattern which satisfies condition (1).

If there is no such pattern the procedure passes on and processes the next subclass according to these rules. But if there is such a pattern it is removed from the subclass to which it belonged and taken as the mean of a new subclass, and the mean of the subclass to which it belonged is recomputed.

When all the subclasses in a given class have been processed in this way, they are all processed in this way again, and so on, until there is no change in the membership of any subclass during a pass through the subclasses. The next class is then processed in this way, and so on. When the last class has been processed, the procedure starts again with with the first subclass in the first class, and so on. The procedure terminates when there has been a complete iteration through all classes with no change in the membership of any class, or when an arbitrary time limit expires. Convergence of the procedure implies 100% correct recognition of the training set, but it has not been proved that the procedure will necessarily converge. In recognition, an unknown pattern is assigned to the class of the nearest subclass mean.

A training set may perhaps include a few patterns which are not representative of their classes, possibly because of accidental mutilation. A disadvantage of Firschein and Fischler's procedure is that it is liable to count such patterns as subclass means; and these non-representative means have the same significance, in recognition, as means of large subclasses. This trouble can be mitigated by eliminating all subclasses with less than a certain number of members[375].

4.5 A PIECEWISE LINEAR FIXED INCREMENT PROCEDURE

Automatic subclass determination is required only when the splitting up of classes into subclasses is not obvious as it was in Section 4.2.

Firschein and Fischler's method is not the only known method of automatically determining a plurality of weight vectors per class, and we now introduce a further method which is a simple generalisation of the fixed increment procedure of Section 3.7.3.

We decide in advance the number of weight vectors per class, and initially the components of all weight vectors have arbitrary values. During successive iterations through the training sets of all classes, weights are adjusted according to the rules:

If X belongs to the sth class and the largest dot product of Y with any sth class weight vector is $Y \,.\, W_{si}$, and for any r, j, $Y.\ W_{si} \leqslant Y \,.\, W_{rj}$, then W_{si} is changed to $W_{si} + \lambda Y$, and W_{rj} is changed to $W_{rj} - \lambda Y$, and all other weight vectors are left unchanged.

If X belongs to the sth class and the largest dot product of Y with any sth class weight vector is $Y \,.\, W_{si}$, and if $Y \,.\, W_{si} > Y \,.\, W_{rj}$ for all r, j, no weight vectors are changed.

Iterations continue until convergence, or until an arbitrary time limit has expired. In Duda and Fossum's experiments[126] the coefficient λ was gradually decreased over successive iterations. Unknown patterns were recognised according to (4.1).

Since the number of weight vectors per class has to be chosen in advance, too few may be used for some classes, and unnecessarily many for others. Firschein and Fischler's procedure does not suffer from this disadvantage, but it is possible that, if the fixed increment procedure converges with, say, γ weight vectors per class, then on the same data Firschein and Fischler's procedure will converge with an average of more than γ weight vectors per class.

4.6 THE METHOD OF POTENTIALS

4.6.1 Approximation of unknown probability distributions

The method of potentials is a basic method of pattern recognition which is best introduced in the trivial case where $N = 1$ and a pattern X consists of a single element x. Suppose, for example, that the distributions of $P(x/r)$ and $P(x/s)$ are as in Figure 4.2. We do not assume that these distributions are defined by equations known in advance, nor indeed that they can ever be accurately defined by reasonably simple formulae. Instead we attempt to approximate unknown distributions by the following method[32, 344].

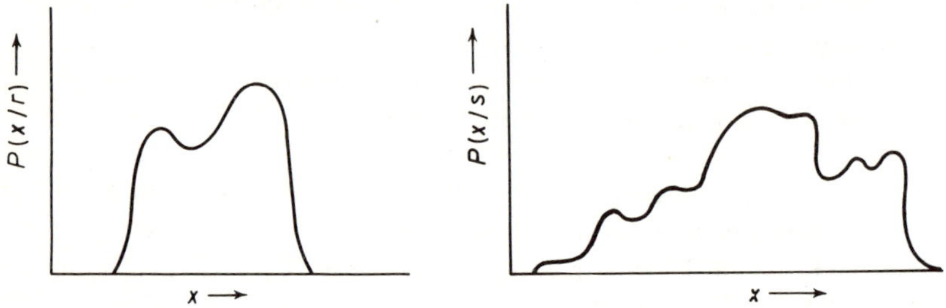

Figure 4.2. *Arbitrary conditional probability distributions*

A training set is required for each recognition class. A training set, in the one-dimensional case, is of course simply a set of values of x, and let x_{rj} be the jth member of the rth class training set. We arbitrarily define a function $f(d(x, x_{rj}))$, such as the one shown in Figure 4.3,

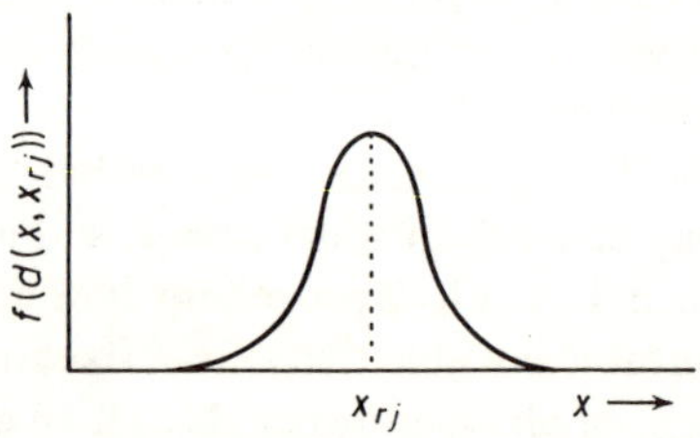

Figure 4.3. *Example of an interpolating function*

which is smooth and continuous, expressible by a simple formula, and falls to zero at infinite distance from x_{rj}. The function $d(x,x_{rj})$ is a measure of distance between x and x_{rj}: usually $d(x,x_{rj})$ is the Euclidean distance between x and x_{rj}. The arbitrary function $f(d(x,x_{rj}))$, which is known as an *interpolating function*, has been defined for example as[32]

$$f(d(x,x_{rj})) = 1/[1 + b(d(x,x_{rj}))^2] \tag{4.3}$$

where b is a constant, or as[4, 309, 415]

$$f(d(x,x_{rj})) = a \exp(-c(d(x,x_{rj}))^2) \tag{4.4}$$

where a and c are constants.

The idea is that if we simply add up $f(d(x,x_{rj}))$ for all j, that is, for all members of the rth class, the resulting sum will be roughly proportional to $P(x/r)$. Suppose, for example, that the members of the rth class training set are the values of x represented by dots on the x axis in Figure 4.4. For each dot there is an interpolating function $f(d(x,x_{rj}))$, as indicated by solid curves in Figure 4.4. The dotted curve in Figure 4.4 is the sum of the solid curves, and is roughly the same shape as $P(x/r)$ in Figure 4.2. The success of this approximation depends on the width of the peak of the interpolating function, which in turn depends, for instance, on the constant b or c. The optimal width depends on the number of patterns in the training set, and should be determined experimentally[4, 416].

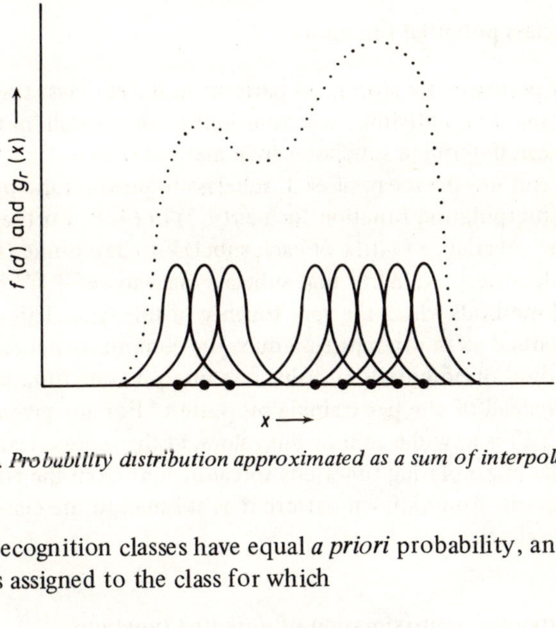

Figure 4.4. *Probability distribution approximated as a sum of interpolating functions*

If all recognition classes have equal *a priori* probability, an unknown pattern is assigned to the class for which

$$g_r(x) = (1/t_r) \sum_{j=1}^{t_r} f(d(x,x_{rj}))$$

is maximal, where t_r is the number of patterns in the rth class training set. Division by t_r is intended[32] to take care of the case where the training sets for different classes have different numbers of members.

The N-dimensional generalisation of $g_r(x)$ is straightforward:

$$g_r(X) = (1/t_r) \sum_{j=1}^{t_r} f(d(X,X_{rj})) \qquad (4.5)$$

A disadvantage of the method of potentials is that it requires the explicit storage of all members of all training sets. This is also true of the nearest-neighbour method, where recognition is based on finding the minimum $d(X,X_{rj})$. For a given training set size, minimising $d(X,X_{rj})$ requires less computation than does maximising $g_r(X)$. An experimental comparison of the nearest-neighbour method and method of potentials on the same data, using the same training sets, does not appear to have been published.

4.6.2 Subclass potential functions

Instead of permanently storing all patterns in the rth class training set and summing their individual contributions to the overall 'potential', $g_r(X)$, we can determine subclasses by a method such as Firschein and Fischler's and use the mean of each subclass to position the peak of a decaying interpolation function such as (4.3) or (4.4). Further, we can use the covariance matrix of each subclass to determine the width of the peak corresponding to that subclass. Sebestyen[394, 395] has developed methods which are very roughly of this type. This approach can be regarded as an attempt to reduce the computational extravagance of the method of potentials by using one interpolating function per subclass, instead of one per training set pattern. For any given X, the value of $g_r(X)$ is now the sum of the values, at the representative point of X, of the interpolating functions spreading out from the rth class subclass means. An unknown pattern X is assigned to the class for which $g_r(X)$ is maximal.

4.6.3 Polynomial approximation of potential functions

Specht[416] has employed the interpolating function

$$f(d(x,x_{rj})) = a \,.\, \exp(-(X - X_{rj})^2/2\sigma^2) \qquad (4.6)$$

where a and σ are constants, [cf. (4.4) and (3.3)]. (4.6) can be rewritten

$$f(d(x,x_{rj})) = a \,.\, \exp(-X^2/2\sigma^2) \,.\, \exp(-X_{rj}^2/2\sigma^2) \,.\, \exp(X \,.\, X_{rj}/\sigma^2) \qquad (4.7)$$

and the last term of this can be expanded in the Taylor series:

$$\exp\left(\frac{X \,.\, X_{rj}}{\sigma^2}\right) = 1 + \frac{X \,.\, X_{rj}}{\sigma^2} + \frac{1}{2!}\left(\frac{X \,.\, X_{rj}}{\sigma^2}\right)^2 + \frac{1}{3!}\left(\frac{X \,.\, X_{rj}}{\sigma^2}\right)^3 + \ldots$$

$$= \sum_{h=0}^{\infty} \frac{1}{h!\sigma^{2h}} (X \,.\, X_{rj})^h \qquad (4.8)$$

Now $(X \,.\, X_{rj})^h = (x_1 x_{rj1} + x_2 x_{rj2} + \ldots + x_N x_{rjN})^h$, and this can be expanded according to the multinomial theorem:

$$(X \,.\, X_{rj})^h = \sum_{\text{all } k} \frac{h!}{z_{k1}! z_{k2}! \ldots ! z_{kN}!} (x_1 x_{rj1})^{z_{k1}} (x_2 x_{rj2})^{z_{k2}} \ldots (x_N x_{rjN})^{z_{kN}} \qquad (4.9)$$

where each value of the index k corresponds to a different combination of values of non-negative integers $z_{k1}, z_{k2}, \ldots, z_{kN}$ such that $z_{k1} + z_{k2} + \ldots + z_{kN} = h$. From (4.5) and (4.7),

$$g_r(X) = (a/t_r) \exp(-X^2/2\sigma^2) \sum_{j=1}^{t_r} \exp(-X_{rj}^2/2\sigma^2) \,.\, \exp(X \,.\, X_{rj}/\sigma^2)$$

For maximisation purposes the term in X^2 can be omitted since it is independent of r, and an unknown pattern X can be assigned to the rth class such that

$$g_r(X) = \frac{1}{t_r} \sum_{j=1}^{t_r} \beta_{rj} \,.\, \exp(X \,.\, X_{rj}/\sigma^2) \qquad (4.10)$$

is maximal, where

$$\beta_{rj} = \exp(-X_{rj}^2/2\sigma^2)$$

Using (4.8), (4.9), and (4.10) we obtain

$$g_r(X) = \sum_{h=0}^{\infty} \sum_{\text{all } k} w_{rjk} (x_1^{z_{k1}} \,.\, x_2^{z_{k2}} \,\ldots\ldots\, x_N^{z_{kN}}) \qquad (4.11)$$

where

$$w_{rjk} = \frac{1}{t_r \,.\, z_{k1}! z_{k2}! \ldots ! z_{kN}! \sigma^{2h}} \sum_{j=1}^{t_r} \beta_{rj} (x_{rj1}^{z_{k1}} \,.\, x_{rj2}^{z_{k2}} \,\ldots\ldots\, x_{rjN}^{z_{kN}})$$

The discriminant function (4.11) can be *approximated* by truncating the infinite series after a reasonable number of terms. In experiments with recognition of electrocardiograms, using $N = 46$ and only 30 coefficients w_{rjk} in (4.11), Specht[415] obtained performance on test data which was as good as when (4.10) was used as the discriminant.

The advantage of this approximation is that after training, only a limited number of coefficients w_{rjk} need be stored in the machine, and the training set patterns need *not* be stored. Recognition involves evaluating the selected products, each of which has the form $x_1^{z_{k1}} . x_2^{z_{k2}} \ldots\ldots x_N^{z_{kN}}$, multiplying each product by the corresponding coefficient w_{rjk}, summing the products for each class, and selecting the maximum sum. This is simpler than the computation required in the Section 4.6.1 method of potentials. Because (4.11) is polynomial, the technique[416] which has been introduced in the present section is of theoretical interest as a link between the method of potentials and the n-tuple methods of Chapter 5.

4.6.4 Error correction in the method of potentials

In Sections 4.6.2 and 4.6.3 we have considered ways of mitigating the computational requirements of the Section 4.6.1 method. In the present section we modify the basic idea of the Section 4.6.1 method of potentials. We no longer attempt to approximate probability distributions, and instead attempt to determine discriminant functions which achieve error-free recognition of the training sets.

Let us consider an example where the training set members of two classes R_1 and R_2 are represented by dots in regions '1' and '2' respectively in Figure 4.5. In the simple method of potentials of Section 4.6.1, patterns lying in the vicinity 'a' in region '1' in Figure 4.5 may be mistakenly assigned to R_2 because of their proximity to a

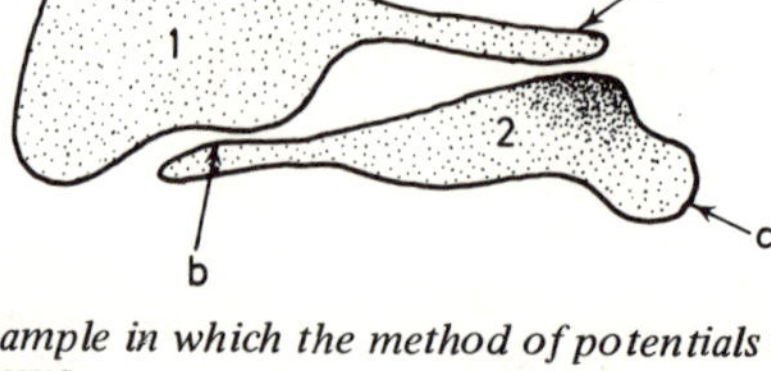

Figure 4.5. *An example in which the method of potentials of Section 4.6.1 may misrecognise patterns*

densely populated part of region '2'. Patterns lying in the vicinity 'b' may be misrecognised because of their proximity to a large chunk of region '1'.

To deal with this difficulty, Bashkirov *et al.*[32] have used the following procedure. Initially discriminants $g_1(X), \ldots, g_z(X)$ as given by (4.5) for $r = 1, \ldots, z$ are used. The procedure works iteratively through the training sets, applying the following rules for all s, i.

If, for X_{si}, which is the ith training set pattern in the sth class, $g_s(X_{si}) > g_r(X_{si})$ for all r except $r = s$, then $g_s(X)$ is left unchanged, and the procedure passes on to the next training set pattern.

If, for any r, $g_s(X_{si}) \leqslant g_r(X_{si})$, then $g_s(X)$ is changed to $g_s(X) + \lambda f(d(X, X_{si}))$, where λ is a constant of proportionality, and the procedure then passes on to the next training set pattern.

These rules are applied to all training set patterns iteratively until convergence. It is easy to see that after convergence

$$g_r(X) = \frac{1}{t_r} \sum_{j=1}^{t_r} \nu_{rj} f(d(X, X_{rj}))$$

where $\nu_{rj} = 1 + \lambda\alpha_{rj}$, and α_{rj} is the number of times that the training set pattern X_{rj} has occasioned a change in $g_r(X)$ during training. The quantity ν_{rj} is relatively large when X_{rj} lies in a vicinity such as 'a' or 'b' in Figure 4.5, and can be interpreted[32] as a weighting factor which, where necessary, counterbalances sparseness of statistical population. (For the vicinity 'c' in Figure 4.5, no counterbalancing would be necessary for avoidance of confusion with R_1.) Bashkirov *et al.*[32] did not provide a proof of convergence of their error correcting method, but they reported experimental results which were 3·3% better with their error correcting method than with the Section 4.6.1 method of potentials.

On page 834 of Ref 4, Aizerman *et al.* have formulated the two-class case of an error correcting procedure which is similar to that of Bashkirov *et al.* This procedure works through a training set of unlimited size which contains members of R_1 and R_2 in any order. At the start of training, no patterns are stored, but various patterns are stored while training progresses, as we shall see. Suppose that, at an intermediate stage of training, the training set patterns $X_1, X_2, \ldots, X_i, \ldots, X_l$ have been stored, and that it is now the turn of the training set pattern X to be processed. The value of

$$K(X) = \sum_{i=1}^{l} \gamma_i f(d(X, X_i)) \tag{4.12}$$

is computed, where $\gamma_i = +1$ or -1 according as the ith stored pattern belongs to R_1 or R_2. If X belongs to R_1 and $K(X) > 0$, or if X belongs to R_2 and $K(X) < 0$, then X is not stored, and the procedure passes on to the next training set pattern. Otherwise X is stored, and $\gamma_{l+1} = +1$ or -1 according to X belongs to R_1 or R_2. Training stops at some arbitrary time, and an unknown pattern X is assigned to R_1 or R_2 according as $K(X)$ is greater than or less than zero.

At an intermediate stage of training in the Section 3.7.1 fixed increment procedure, if all components of the initial weight vector are zero,

$$W = \sum_{i=1}^{t} \alpha_i Y_i$$

where the sign of α_i is + or − according as X_i belongs to R_1 or R_2, and the magnitude of α_i is the number of times when X_i has occasioned an error correction during training, cf. (3.19). At an intermediate stage of training, the discriminant function used in the fixed increment procedure can be written

$$(g(X))_j = (W \,.\, Y)_j = \sum_{i=1}^{t} \alpha_i Y_i \,.\, Y$$

where t is the total number of training set patterns. When the weight vector is altered during training, the discriminant function is thereby altered according to

$$(g(X))_{j+1} = (W \,.\, Y)_{j+1} = (W \,.\, Y)_j \pm (Y_j \,.\, Y)$$

where X_j is the training set pattern which occasions this change in the weight vector. The expression for $(g(X))_{j+1}$ can be written more abstractly

$$(g(X))_{j+1} = (g(X))_j \pm \text{function}\,(X_j, X) \tag{4.13}$$

In the modified method of potentials using (4.12), if X_j is stored, the discriminant function is thereby changed according to

$$(K(X))_{j+1} = \sum_{i=1}^{l} f(\mathrm{d}(X, X_i)) + f(\mathrm{d}(X, X_j))$$

and this can be written more abstractly

$$(K(X))_{j+1} = (K(X))_j \pm \text{function}\ (X, X_j)$$

which at this abstract level, is the same as (4.13). Equation (4.13) is a special case of

$$(g(X))_{j+1} = \mu_j(g(X))_j \pm \lambda_j \text{ function } (X_j, X) \quad (4.14)$$

where the coefficients λ_j, μ_j may be different for every value of j. Aizerman *et al.*[7] call all of the many procedures including various stochastic approximation procedures, which conform to (4.14), *methods of potential functions.* We shall not follow this nomenclature, but instead reserve the term *method of potentials* for methods involving decaying interpolation functions, such as (4.3) or (4.4), or approximations thereto.

Note that, whilst the fixed increment procedure and the method of potentials using (4.12) both conform to (4.13), the method of potentials demands explicit storage of patterns, and recognition involves much computation; whereas the fixed increment procedure leads to a linear discriminant system which expends less computational effort in recognition.

4.7 STOCHASTIC APPROXIMATION IN PATTERN RECOGNITION

Stochastic approximation is introduced here rather than in Chapter 3 only because of the association between stochastic approximation and the method of potentials in the Russian literature. Indeed stochastic approximation can be applied *in* the method of potentials. An elementary introduction to stochastic approximation has been provided by Wilde[460]. The following paragraphs relate only to stochastic approximation in pattern recognition.

In Section 3.8 we discussed the determination of a weight vector by a steepest-descent procedure which minimised H_w. We now consider the more general problem of determining a weight vector such that the associated pattern error H_w is minimised not just for a given R_1, R_2 training set, but for the entire classes R_1 and R_2. We tackle this problem by attempting to determine a weight vector whose *average* H_w over a large number of different R_1 and R_2 training sets is minimal.

According to stochastic approximation theory, we can determine a weight vector whose average H_w over many training sets is minimal by means of a steepest-descent procedure which uses a different R_1, R_2 training set during each successive iteration. The first training set consists of t_1 randomly chosen members of R_1 and t_2 randomly chosen members of R_2. The second training set consists of a further t_1 randomly chosen members of R_1 and a further t_2 randomly chosen members of R_2, and so on. At the end of the kth iteration W is changed according to

$$W_{k+1} = W_k - \lambda_k \nabla H_w \tag{4.15}$$

where

$$\sum_{k=1}^{\infty} \lambda_k = \infty \tag{4.16}$$

and

$$\sum_{k=1}^{\infty} \lambda_k^2 < \infty \tag{4.17}$$

For instance, $\lambda_k = 1/k$, i.e., $\lambda_1, \lambda_2, \lambda_3, \lambda_4, \ldots = 1, \frac{1}{2}, \frac{1}{3}, \frac{1}{4}, \ldots$, satisfies (4.16) and (4.17) and illustrates the important condition that, according to (4.17), λ_k must decrease as k increases. Using the reasoning of Section 3.8 we find that (4.15) leads to a procedure of which the single patterns version is: if X belongs to R_1 and $Y \cdot W > 0$, or if X belongs to R_2 and $Y \cdot W < 0$, W is not changed; otherwise W is changed to $W \pm \lambda_k Y$, where λ_k conforms to (4.16) and (4.17). This procedure can be applied *once* to a single quasi-infinite R_1, R_2 training set, rather than iteratively to a training set of limited size[6, 42, 439].

If, after the kth iteration of procedure (4.15) we did not alter W, but instead, using the same W, determined the value of ∇H_w for many different training sets, we would find that the ∇H_w's for the different training sets varied randomly about a mean value. Because of random fluctuations of this sort, if we were to apply the Section 3.8 procedure $W_{k+1} = W_k - \nabla H_w$, with a different training set for each iteration, this procedure would not converge, and instead the weight vector would fluctuate about its optimal value during an infinite number of iterations. In stochastic approximation, the decrease of successive coefficients $\lambda_1, \lambda_2, \lambda_3, \ldots$, in accordance with (4.17) prevents indefinite fluctuation about optimal W. Condition (4.16) ensures[460] that λ_k does not vanish before the procedure reaches optimal W. Procedure (4.15), which is a *Robbins–Monro* procedure, is said to be *stochastic* because it can cope with random variations in ∇H_w, whereas the Section 3.8 methods are said to be *deterministic* because they are applicable only when no randomness is present.

If the deterministic single patterns version of the fixed increment procedure is applied iteratively to a training set of limited size when the classes are not linearly separable, convergence is not reached, and instead the weight vector fluctuates randomly about the minimum error weight vector during successive iterations. To avoid this, we can use a fixed increment procedure with coefficients λ conforming to (4.16) and (4.17). This *stochastic* procedure necessarily converges to a minimum error weight vector, even when the classes are not linearly separable, although convergence may be reached only after an exceedingly large number of iterations. Duda and Fossum[126] have used coefficients λ which decrease very much less rapidly than λ's which conform to (4.17), so that the procedure does not necessarily converge to minimum error weight vectors, but serviceable weight vectors are determined without a prohibitive number of iterations.

Stochastic approximation can be applied to the error function E_w, which was defined in Section 3.8, instead of H_w. This leads to a stochastic counterpart of Mays' modified relaxation procedure[6, 465]. Indeed many possible error functions have been considered. For each choice of error function and coefficients λ_k, μ_k in (4.14) we obtain a somewhat different stochastic approximation procedure[119]. (A different genus of stochastic approximation procedures arise from implementations of the multivariate Kieffer–Wolfovitz procedure[98, 119, 439].) Generally speaking, stochastic approximation procedures suffer from the serious drawback of being exceedingly slow to converge[217]. Although various techniques have been devised for accelerating convergence[247, 284], stochastic approximation does not appear to be used in practical pattern recognition.

Chapter 5

POLYNOMIAL DISCRIMINANTS AND N-TUPLE METHODS

5.1 LEAST SQUARE APPROXIMATION

5.1.1 Orthonormal expansion

The method of potentials of Section 4.6.1 is a method of approximating unknown probability distributions. In Sections 5.1 and 5.2 we introduce two further methods of approximating unknown probability distributions. In particular, Section 5.1 is concerned with orthonormal expansion of probability functions. To introduce the idea of orthonormal expansion of a function $f(X)$ of X, we consider a trivial example in which $N = 3$, and the 2^N possible binary patterns are

$$
\begin{aligned}
X_0 &= \{0, 0, 0\} & X_4 &= \{1, 0, 0\} \\
X_1 &= \{0, 0, 1\} & X_5 &= \{1, 0, 1\} \\
X_2 &= \{0, 1, 0\} & X_6 &= \{1, 1, 0\} \\
X_3 &= \{0, 1, 1\} & X_7 &= \{1, 1, 1\}
\end{aligned}
$$

We define eight functions of X as follows:

$$
\left.
\begin{aligned}
\phi_0(X) &= (1-x_1)(1-x_2)(1-x_3) &&= 1 - x_1 - x_2 - x_3 + x_1x_2 \\
& &&\quad + x_1x_3 + x_2x_3 - x_1x_2x_3 \\
\phi_1(X) &= (1-x_1)(1-x_2)x_3 &&= x_3 - x_1x_3 - x_2x_3 + x_1x_2x_3 \\
\phi_2(X) &= (1-x_1)x_2(1-x_3) &&= x_2 - x_1x_2 - x_3x_2 + x_1x_2x_3 \\
\phi_3(X) &= (1-x_1)x_2x_3 &&= x_2x_3 - x_1x_2x_3 \\
\phi_4(X) &= x_1(1-x_2)(1-x_3) &&= x_1 - x_1x_2 - x_1x_3 + x_1x_2x_3 \\
\phi_5(X) &= x_1(1-x_2)x_3 &&= x_1x_3 - x_1x_2x_3 \\
\phi_6(X) &= x_1x_2(1-x_3) &&= x_1x_2 - x_1x_2x_3 \\
\phi_7(X) &= x_1x_2x_3 &&= x_1x_2x_3
\end{aligned}
\right\} \quad (5.1)
$$

It is easy to check that these functions are such that

$$\phi_i(X_j) = \begin{cases} 1 \text{ if } i = j \\ 0 \text{ if } i \neq j \end{cases} \tag{5.2}$$

and therefore

$$\sum_{\text{all } X} \phi_i(X)\phi_j(X) = \begin{cases} 1 \text{ if } i = j \\ 0 \text{ if } i \neq j \end{cases} \tag{5.3}$$

Because (5.2) holds, any real-valued function $g(X_i)$ can be written

$$g(X_i) = \phi_i(X_i)\, g(X_i) = \sum_{j=0}^{7} \phi_j(X_i)\, g(X_j)$$

and, since this is true for any $i = 0, 1, \ldots, 7$, we can write

$$g(X) = \sum_{j=0}^{7} \phi_j(X)\, g(X_j) \tag{5.4}$$

which has the general form

$$g(X) = \sum_{j=0}^{2^N-1} w_j \phi_j(X) \tag{5.5}$$

where the w's are scalar coefficients. This introduces and illustrates the basic fact that any real-valued function of X can be expressed as a unique linear combination of ϕ's, as in (5.5), provided that the ϕ's form a complete orthonormal set[10]. The ϕ's are *orthonormal* if they satisfy (5.3) for all i, j.

In the above example, $w_j = g(X_j)$, but this is only true for ϕ's such as those defined by (5.1). Whatever the complete orthonomal set of ϕ's, we can determine the w's by multiplying both sides of (5.5) by $\phi_i(X)$ and summing over all X to obtain

$$\sum_{\text{all } X} g(X)\phi_i(X) = \sum_{\text{all } X} \sum_{j=0}^{2^N-1} w_j \phi_j(X)\phi_i(X)$$

$$= \sum_{j=0}^{2^N-1} w_j \sum_{\text{all } X} \phi_j(X)\phi_i(X)$$

and by using (5.3),

$$w_i = \sum_{all\ X} g(X)\phi_i(X) \tag{5.6}$$

Let us now consider a further example, in which $N = 3$, but the ϕ's are not those defined in (5.1). Instead, the ϕ's are *Rademacher–Walsh* functions[84, 238] defined by

$$\left.\begin{array}{ll} \phi_0(X) = 1 & \phi_4(X) = (2x_1 - 1) \\ \phi_1(X) = (2x_3 - 1) & \phi_5(X) = (2x_1 - 1)(2x_3 - 1) \\ \phi_2(X) = (2x_2 - 1) & \phi_6(X) = (2x_1 - 1)(2x_2 - 1) \\ \phi_3(X) = (2x_2 - 1)(2x_3 - 1) & \phi_7(X) = (2x_1 - 1)(2x_2 - 1)(2x_3 - 1) \end{array}\right\} \tag{5.7}$$

It is easy to check that

$$\sum_{all\ X} \phi_i(X)\phi_j(X) = \begin{cases} 2^N = 8 & \text{if } i = j \\ 0 & \text{if } i \neq j \end{cases} \tag{5.8}$$

Multiplying both sides of (5.5) by $\phi_i(X)$, summing over all X, and using (5.8), we obtain

$$w_i = 2^{-N} \sum_{all\ X} g(X)\phi_i(X)$$

If $g(X) = P(X/r)$, we have

$$w_{ri} = 2^{-N} \sum_{all\ X} P(X/r)\phi_i(X)$$

which can reasonably be approximated by[84]

$$w_{ri} = \frac{1}{2^N t_r} \sum_{k=1}^{t_r} \phi_i(X_{rk}) \tag{5.9}$$

that is, by 2^{-N} times the average of $\phi_i(X)$ over the patterns $X_{r1}, \ldots, X_{rk}, \ldots, X_{rt_r}$ which constitute the rth class training set. According to the maximum likelihood decision rule and equation (5.5), an unkown pattern X should be assigned to the rth class such that

$$P(r)P(X/r) = P(r) \sum_{i=0}^{2^N-1} w_{ri}\phi_i(X) \tag{5.10}$$

is maximal.

Instead of confining our attention to the $N = 3$ case, let us now define Rademacher–Walsh functions for any given value of N. Corresponding to each of the 2^N binary patterns $X_1, \ldots, X_i, \ldots, X_{2N}$ we define a unique ϕ function which is a product of N terms. The product corresponding to the ith pattern $X_i = \{x_{i1}, \ldots, x_{iN}\}$ is

$$\phi_i(X) = (2x_1 - 1)^{x_{i1}} (2x_2 - 1)^{x_{i2}} \ldots (2x_N - 1)^{x_{iN}} \tag{5.11}$$

It is easy to check that (5.7) conforms to this.

For large N, for example $N > 12$, estimation of $P(X/r)$ using functions (5.11) as in (5.10) becomes economically impractical. In this case we can, as an approximation, simply omit some of the 2^N functions (5.11) and work with many fewer than 2^N of them[84]. For instance, we may choose to omit all ϕ_i's such that

$$\sum_{j=1}^{N} x_{ij}$$

exceeds a prescribed limit. By increasing this limit we can obtain a better approximation to $P(X/r)$, but at increased cost.

Let τ be the number of ϕ functions (5.11) which we retain. These retained functions have the property that

$$\sum_{\text{all } X} \phi_i(X)\phi_j(X) = \begin{cases} \tau & \text{if } i = j \\ 0 & \text{if } i \neq j \end{cases} \tag{5.12}$$

$P(X/r)$ is now approximated, according to

$$P(X/r) = \sum_{j=0}^{\tau-1} w_{rj}\phi_j(X) \tag{5.13}$$

Multiplying both sides of this by $\phi_i(X)$, summing over all X, and using (5.12), we find that

$$w_{ri} = \frac{1}{\tau} \sum_{\text{all } X} P(X/r)\phi_i(X)$$

which can be approximated according to

$$w_{ri} = \frac{1}{\tau t_r} \sum_{k=1}^{t_r} \phi_i(X_{rk}) \tag{5.14}$$

An unknown pattern X is assigned to the class for which

$$P(r) \sum_{i=0}^{\tau-1} w_{ri}\phi_i(X)$$

is maximal.

5.1.2 Least square approximation

The approximation of $P(X/r)$ according to (5.13) is in fact a least square approximation, as will now be explained. This explanation holds not only when the ϕ's in (5.13) are Rademacher–Walsh functions, but also when the ϕ's in (5.13) are *any* set of τ orthonormal functions, and this set need not be complete in the sense that the set of 2^N functions (5.11) is complete[308, 440].

If coefficients $u_{r0}, \ldots, u_{rj}, \ldots, u_{r(\tau-1)}$ are chosen so that

$$\int_{\text{all } X} \left[P(X/r) - \sum_{j=0}^{\tau-1} u_{rj}\phi_j(X) \right]^2 \mathrm{d}X \tag{5.15}$$

is minimised, $\sum_{j=0}^{\tau-1} u_{rj}\phi_j(X)$ is said to be a *least square approximation* to $P(X/r)$. Expression (5.15) is minimised when its partial derivatives with respect to $u_{r0}, \ldots, u_{ri}, \ldots, u_{r(\tau-1)}$ are zero. Setting the derivative of (5.15) with respect to u_{ri} equal to zero gives

$$\int_{\text{all } X} \phi_i(X)P(X/r)\mathrm{d}X = \int_{\text{all } X} \sum_{j=0}^{\tau-1} u_{rj}\phi_j(X)\phi_i(X)\mathrm{d}X$$

$$= \sum_{j=0}^{\tau-1} u_{rj} \int_{\text{all } X} \phi_j(X)\phi_i(X)\mathrm{d}X \tag{5.16}$$

The left-hand side of this can reasonably be approximated by the average of $\phi_i(X)$ over the rth class training set. Since the ϕ's are orthonormal,

$$\int_{\text{all } X} \phi_i(X)\phi_j(X) = \begin{cases} 1 & \text{if } i = j \\ 0 & \text{if } i \neq j \end{cases} \tag{5.17}$$

and hence the right-hand side of (5.16) reduces to u_{ri}. Thus the coefficients $u_{r0}, \ldots, u_{ri}, \ldots, u_{r(\tau-1)}$ which provide the least square approximation to $P(X/r)$ are given by

$$u_{ri} = \frac{1}{t_r} \sum_{k=1}^{t_r} \phi_i(X_{rk}) \tag{5.18}$$

for $i = 0, \ldots, \tau - 1$.

If the ϕ's are Rademacher–Walsh functions, (5.12) holds instead of (5.17), which leads to

$$u_{rj} = \frac{1}{\tau t_r} \sum_{k=1}^{t_r} \phi_j(X_{rk})$$

in place of (5.18). This agrees with (5.14), and thus we see that (5.13) is a least square approximation to $P(X/r)$.

The function (5.13) is not a probability distribution, because it can possibly assume negative values for some X [84]. However, in Sections 3.7, 3.8, and 4.6.4 we were not alarmed when a discriminant function was not proportional to an estimate of conditional probability. Note that we have seen no reason to believe that the least square approximation leads to minimal error rates in pattern recognition. Note also that neither E_w nor H_w in Section 3.8 is a measure of the percentage of patterns which are not correctly recognised by a recognition system.

5.1.3 Implementation by stochastic approximation

Let us consider the averaging of the t values $y_1, y_2, \ldots, y_i, \ldots, y_t$ of the variable y. If we are given all these values at once we can simply compute the average

$$a_t = \frac{1}{t} \sum_{i=1}^{t} y_i$$

Alternatively, if these values become available one by one, we need not store them explicitly, and instead we can use them to update a running average a_i according to

$$a_{i+1} = [1/(i+1)]\,[ia_i + y_{i+1}]$$

This can be rewritten in the form of a trivial stochastic approximation algorithm

$$a_{i+1} = a_i + [1/(i+1)]\,[y_{i+1} - a_i]$$

where the coefficients $1/(i+1)$ in fact conform to (4.16) and (4.17) in Section 4.7 [460].

A similar algorithm can be applied in the determination of the averages of $\phi_0(X), \ldots, \phi_{T-1}(X)$ to yield values of the coefficients $w_{r0}, \ldots, w_{r(T-1)}$ or $u_{r0}, \ldots, u_{r(T-1)}$ in accordance with (5.14) or (5.18)[5, 308, 440].

5.2 MAXIMUM LIKELIHOOD *n*-TUPLE METHOD

In Section 3.3 the assumption of statistical independence provided a technique for estimating $P(X/r)$. Since the independence assumption is seldom strictly justified in practice, the Section 3.3 method can usually be regarded as providing only an approximate estimate of $P(X/r)$. The purpose of the present section is to generalise the Section 3.3 method in order to obtain a better approximation to $P(X/r)$.

For present purposes, an *n-tuple* is a set of n x's and the *state* of the n-tuple is the set of values of these x's. For example the six pattern elements marked by heavy squares in Figure 5.1 constitute a 6-tuple.

Figure 5.1. *Example of an n-tuple and an n-tuple state*

Representing *black* by '1' and *white* by '0', the state of this 6-tuple is 101001, the bits being ordered arbitrarily as indicated by dotted lines in Figure 5.1. We say that the '2' in Figure 5.1 *includes* this n-tuple state.

Prior to training, a number, m, say, of n-tuples are chosen randomly or arbitrarily. An rth class training set is used in the estimation of the conditional probability of occurrence of each possible state of each of the m n-tuples, given that X belongs to the rth class. For instance let us denote a particular state of a particular n-tuple by S. Then $P(S/r)$ is estimated by the usual method of averaging:

$$P(S/r) = \left(\frac{1}{t_r}\right) \text{(number of } r\text{th class training set patterns which include } S\text{)}$$

To recognise an unknown pattern X, the maximum likelihood rule is applied and $P(r)P(X/r)$ is maximised as in Section 3.2. Here $P(X/r)$ is estimated as the product[275] of the rth class conditional probabilities of the states, included in X, of the m n-tuples[2, 44, 82]. In practice, as in Section 3.3, it is expedient to take logs and add, replacing log 0 by an arbitrary negative number. In the limiting case where $n = 1$ and $m = N$, the present system is identical to the Section 3.3 system.

To formulate the maximum likelihood n-tuple method more precisely, we employ an n-dimensional generalisation of functions (5.1). Let us consider the ith of the m n-tuples, and for notational simplicity, and without loss of generality, let us denote the elements of the ith n-tuple by $x_1, x_2, \ldots, x_n$. These elements could, for example, be the six elements in heavy squares in Figure 5.1. Corresponding to each of the 2^n possible n-element binary patterns $Z_1, \ldots, Z_j, \ldots, Z_{2^n}$ we define a unique function $\phi_{ij}(X)$ which is the product of $2n$ terms. For $j=1, \ldots, 2^n$, the function corresponding to $Z_j = \{z_{j1}, \ldots, z_{jn}\}$ is defined by

$$\phi_{ij}(X) = x_1^{z_{j1}}(1-x_1)^{(1-z_{j1})}x_2^{z_{j2}}(1-x_2)^{(1-z_{j2})} \ldots x_n^{z_{jn}}(1-x_n)^{(1-z_{jn})} \tag{5.19}$$

Functions (5.1) provide an example of this where $n = N = 3$.

The present method estimates $P(X/r)$ as the product of the n-tuple state conditional probabilities for all n-tuples. This can be written

$$P(X/r) = \prod_{i=1}^{m} \sum_{j=1}^{2^n} w_{rij}\phi_{ij}(X) \tag{5.20}$$

where

$$w_{rij} = \sum_{\text{all } X} P(X/r)\phi_{ij}(X)$$

or in practice w_{rij} is approximated according to

$$w_{rij} = \frac{1}{t_r}\sum_{k=1}^{t_r} \phi_{ij}(X_{rk}) \tag{5.21}$$

that is, the average of $\phi_{ij}(X)$ over the rth class training set. For given X,

$\phi_{ij}(X) = 1$ for one and only one value of j in the range $1, \ldots, 2^n$, and for all other values of j, $\phi_{ij}(X) = 0$. So we can write

$$\log \sum_{j=1}^{2^n} w_{rij}\phi_{ij}(X) = \sum_{j=1}^{2^n} \phi_{ij}(X) \log w_{rij}$$

and taking logs of (5.20) we obtain

$$\log P(X/r) = \sum_{i=1}^{m} \sum_{j=1}^{2^n} \phi_{ij}(X) \log w_{rij} \tag{5.22}$$

When this is used in the logarithmic version of the maximum likelihood decision rule of Section 3.2, this method of recognition is called the *maximum likelihood n-tuple method*[44].

Figure 5.2 shows the percentage correct recognition versus n when the maximum likelihood n-tuple method was applied to 10 classes of unconstrained hand-printed numerals, with training sets of 10, 20, 70, 200, and 630 per class, using 40 randomly chosen n-tuples. With training sets of 630 per class the Figure 5.2 curve is clearly peaked and the maximum lies at about $n = 10$. As n increases from 2 to 10 the maximum likelihood n-tuple method makes a better and better estimate of $\log P(X/r)$ by taking more account of the statistical dependence between pattern elements. As n increases above $n = 10$, n-tuple states have lower and lower probabilities of occurrence, and therefore these probabilities are less accurately estimated, which effects recognition performance adversely. In other words, performance deteriorates when n increases above $n = 10$ because $\frac{1}{t_r} \sum_{k=1}^{t_r} \phi_{ij}(X_{rk})$ becomes a poorer and poorer estimate of $\sum_{\text{all } X} P(X/r)\phi_{ij}(X)$. For instance, in experiments with the data used in Figure 5.2, with $n = 18$ and with training sets of 650 per class, rather more than half the occurrences of n-tuple states during training were occurrences of states which occurred only once per n-tuple per class[442]. One occurrence is obviously inadequate for the estimation of conditional probability, and this illustrates the reason for the decline

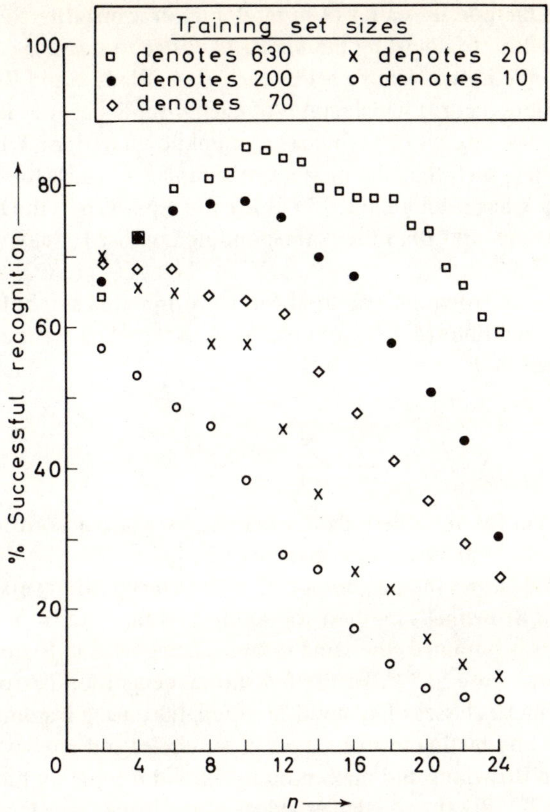

Figure 5.2. *Percentage successful recognition versus n for maximum likelihood n-tuple method. From reference* 442, *with permission*

in performance above $n = 10$. This decline can be understood more fully in the light of a statistical investigation by Hughes[231]. Kanal and Chandrasekaran[245a] have made a general study of relationships between error rates, dimensionality, training set size, and test set size.

5.3 BLEDSOE AND BROWNING'S METHOD

Bledsoe and Browning's paper[45] in 1959 introduced various weighted versions and other developments of the basic method which we now introduce. Like the maximum likelihood n-tuple method, Bledsoe and

Browning's method uses a set of m randomly or arbitrarily chosen n-tuples. Instead of counting the numbers of occurrences of each state of each n-tuple in the training set of each class, Bledsoe and Browning's method simply records which states of each n-tuple occur at least once in the training set of each class. An unknown pattern X is assigned to the rth class such that the number of n-tuples in which the state included in X has been included in at least one pattern in the rth class training set is greater than the corresponding number for any other class[43, 45, 89, 421].

Bledsoe and Browning's method can be formulated symbolically[385] in terms of functions (5.19). An unknown pattern X is assigned to the rth class such that

$$\sum_{i=1}^{m} \sum_{j=1}^{2^n} u_{rij}\phi_{ij}(X) \tag{5.23}$$

is greater than for any other class, where $u_{rij} = 1$ or 0 according as $w_{rij} > 0$ or $w_{rij} = 0$, and w_{rij} is given by (5.21).

Figure 5.3 shows the percentage of correct recognition versus n when Bledsoe and Browning's method was applied to the data from which Figure 5.2 was obtained, the same n-tuples being used in Figure 5.3 as were used in Figure 5.2[442]. Figure 5.4 shows recognition performance versus n with 10 classes of typewritten numerals, using training sets of 92 per class and testing sets of 20 per class, circles and crosses indicating Bledsoe and Browning and maximum likelihood n-tuple method results respectively[444]. Because for larger values of n a bigger training set is required for adequate estimation of n-tuple state conditional probabilities, and because Bledsoe and Browning's method does not depend on this estimation, it is not surprising that Bledsoe and Browning's method peaks in performance at higher n than the maximum likelihood n-tuple method in Figure 5.4. But it is remarkable that the actual optimal performance of Bledsoe and Browning's method is better than that of the maximum likelihood n-tuple method in Figure 5.4. The fact that the maxima in Figure 5.4 are at values of n greater than $n = 1$ indicates that, in these experiments, pattern bits were not statistically independent.

Figure 5.5 is a plot of percentage correct recognition versus number of 14-tuples when the Bledsoe and Browning method was applied to 10 classes of unconstrained hand-printed numerals, training with 600 per class and testing with 50 per class[442]. This shows that there is no advantage in using more than a limited number of n-tuples.

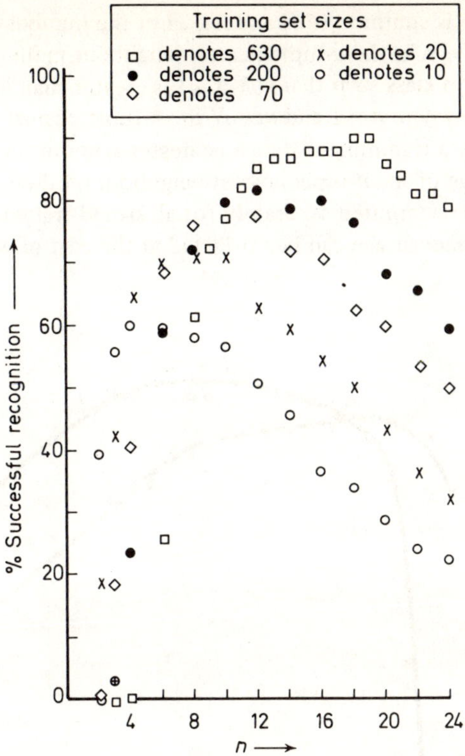

Figure 5.3. *Percentage successful recognition versus n for Bledsoe and Browning's method. From Reference* 442, *with permission*

Bledsoe and Browning's method is a degenerate form of an *n*-tuple nearest-neighbour method. An *n*-tuple nearest-neighbour method is a nearest-neighbour method which uses *n*-tuples as follows. As in Bledsoe and Browning's method, a collection of *m n*-tuples are arbitrarily chosen, and let us call this collection of *m n*-tuples *M*. As is usual in nearest-neighbour methods, training set patterns from every recognition class are simply stored in the recognition machine. Let X_{rk} be the *k*th stored training set pattern belonging to the *r*th class. Let us define a subset M_{rk} of *M* by saying that, if an *n*-tuple belonging to *M* has the same state in X_{rk} as this *n*-tuple has in an unknown pattern *X*, then this *n*-tuple belongs to M_{rk}: M_{rk} includes all such *n*-tuples and only such *n*-tuples. Thus M_{rk} is the subset of *M* such that on each *n*-tuple belonging to M_{rk}, the state is common to X and X_{rk}. Let the number of members of M_{rk} be $g(X,X_{rk})$. In the n-tuple nearest-neighbour method, X is assigned to the rth class such that $g(X,X_{rk})$ is greater than for any other class. In the case where $n = 1$ and $m = N$ the n-tuple nearest-neighbour method is simply a Hamming-distance nearest-neighbour method.

A disadvantage of the n-tuple nearest-neighbour method is that $g(X,X_{rk})$ must be computed separately for all stored training set patterns. This disadvantage can be mitigated at the cost of weakening

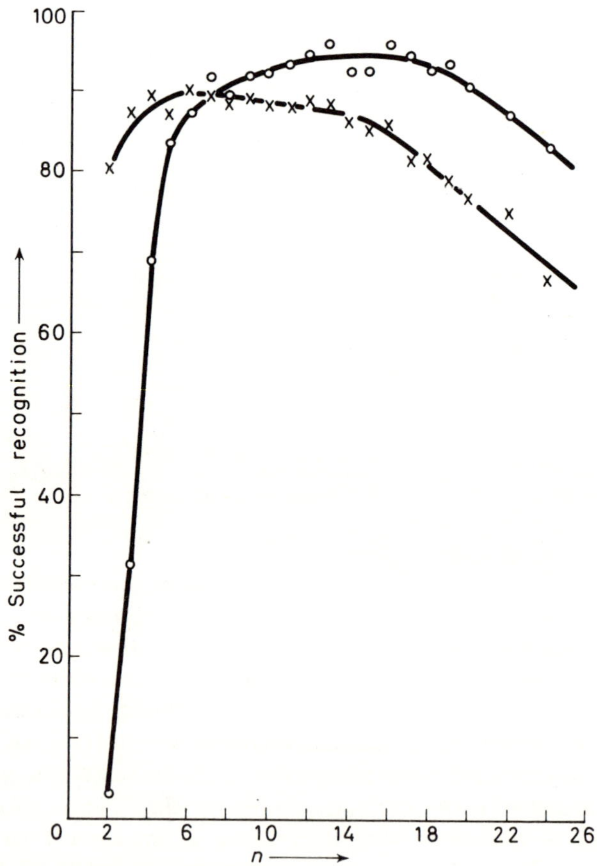

Figure 5.4. *Percentage successful recognition versus n for maximum likelihood (crosses) and Bledsoe and Browning (circles) n-tuple methods applied to multifont printed numerals. From Reference 444, with permission*

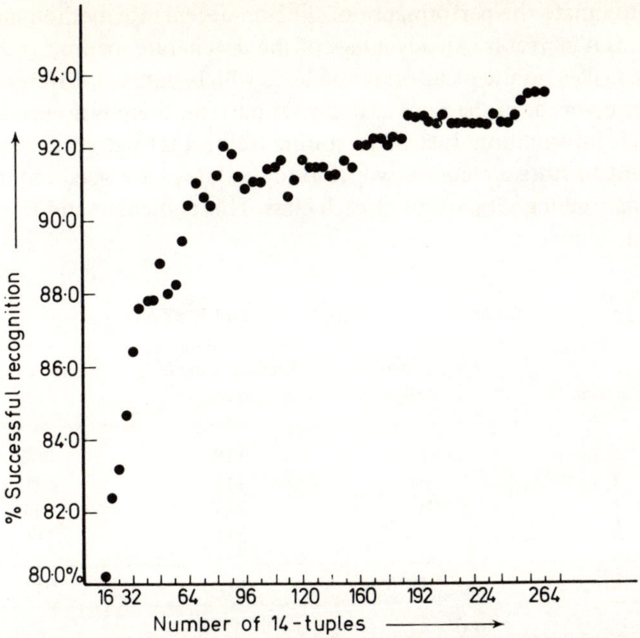

Figure 5.5. *Percentage successful recognition versus number of* 14*-tuples for Bledsoe and Browning's method applied to hand-printed numerals. From Reference* 442, *with permission*

the method as follows. Let us define M_r to be the union

$$M_r = M_{r1} \cup M_{r2} \cup \ldots \cup M_{rk} \cup \ldots \cup M_{rt_r}$$

where t_r is the number of patterns in the rth class training set. M_r is thus the subset of M such that the state in X of each n-tuple belonging to M_r occurs in at least one of the training set patterns $X_{r1}, \ldots, X_{rt_r}$. Let us assign X to the rth class such that the number of members of M_r is greater than for any other class. This is a *degenerate* nearest-neighbour method, since it takes no account of joint occurrences of n-tuple states in the same training set pattern. To illustrate this, suppose that M has three members, that $n = 3$, $t = 4$, and that the n-tuple states are as in Table 5.1.

To see the difference between the non-degenerate and degenerate n-tuple nearest-neighbour methods, note that in the Table 5.1 example $g(X,X_{rk}) = 1$, for $k = 1, 2, 3, 4$, whereas the number of members of M_r is three. The performance of the degenerate method can be expected to approximate the performance of the non-degenerate method more closely as n increases. An advantage of the degenerate method is that, since it makes no use of information as to which states of different n-tuples co-occur in the same training set pattern, there is no need to store this information. Instead of storing training set patterns, it is sufficient to store a record of which n-tuple states have occurred in at least one training set pattern of each class. This is Bledsoe and Browning's method.

Table 5.1. EXAMPLE OF n-TUPLE STATES

Pattern	*First n-tuple state*	*Second n-tuple state*	*Third n-tuple state*
X_{r1}	001	110	000
X_{r2}	010	111	010
X_{r3}	011	111	011
X_{r4}	010	011	100
X	010	110	011

In principle, Bledsoe and Browning's method, and also the maximum likelihood n-tuple method, can be applied when pattern elements are restricted to a q-level discrete grey scale. If $q \neq 2$, functions (5.19) must be appropriately generalised. There are then q^n possible states per n-tuple, which is usually too many for practical purposes. Even when $q = 2$, if n is not very small, Bledsoe and Browning's method tends to be extravagant from the point of view of storage requirements.

5.4 POLYNOMIAL DISCRIMINANT FUNCTIONS

5.4.1 Polynomial discriminant functions with statistically determined coefficients

The methods of recognition which have been introduced so far in this chapter employ polynomial discriminant functions. To show that Bledsoe and Browning's method employs polynomial discriminants, we multiply out the ϕ_{ij}'s in (5.23) as at the right-hand side of (5.1).

Expression (5.23) is then seen to be a polynomial of order of n. Similarly we can multiply out the ϕ_{ij}'s in (5.22) in order to see that the discriminant function used in the maximum likelihood n-tuple method is a polynomial of order n. Furthermore, we can see that (5.13) is polynomial by multiplying out the Rademacher–Walsh functions (5.11). It will be remembered also that Specht's technique, Section 4.6.3, leads to polynomial discriminant functions; and that the normality assumption in Section 3.4, with unequal covariance matrices, leads to quadratic discriminant functions, that is, to discriminant functions which are polynomials of order two.

5.4.2 Coefficients determined by error correcting procedures

Let $g_r(X)$ be the rth class polynomial discriminant function in any one of the methods mentioned in Section 5.4.1. This can be written as the dot product

$$g_r(X) = Z \cdot W_r$$

where W_r is the τ-component vector whose first component is the constant term in $g_r(X)$ and whose remaining components are the coefficients of the $\tau - 1$ product terms in $g_r(X)$, and Z is the τ-component pattern or vector whose first component is unity and whose remaining components are the $\tau - 1$ product terms in $g_r(X)$. We can think of a polynomial discriminant method as separating N-element patterns by means of polynomial (generally curved) surfaces in N-dimensional space. Alternatively we can think of a polynomial method as transforming an N-element pattern X into a τ-element pattern Z and recognising Z linearly.

For a given choice of product terms, none of the Section 5.4.1 methods is guaranteed to determine τ-component weight vectors $W_1, \ldots, W_r, \ldots, W_z$ which give error-free recognition of training set patterns. If the training sets of τ-element patterns are linearly separable, we can determine weight vectors which yield error-free recognition of training sets as follows. For $r = 1, \ldots, z$ and $i = 1, \ldots, t_r$, for each training set pattern X_{ri} we can compute the values of the $\tau - 1$ products and thus obtain a τ-component training set pattern Z_{ri}. Then τ-component weight vectors $W_1, \ldots, W_r, \ldots, W_z$ can be determined by applying, for example, the Section 3.7.3 fixed increment procedure to the training sets of Z_{ri}'s. In practice, instead of using $\tau - 1$ product terms which happen to be those used in one of the Section 5.4.1 methods, we may perhaps obtain equally good results with $\tau - 1$ arbitrarily or randomly chosen product terms of order n.

If τ is considerably greater than N, there is a clear theoretical advantage in applying a method such as the Section 3.7.3 method to τ-element patterns rather than directly to untransformed N-element patterns. For simplicity let us consider the case where there are only two recognition classes, R_1 and R_2, and the total number of patterns in the R_1 and R_2 training sets is t. Further, let us assume that the R_1 and R_2 training sets do not form clusters and that they can be regarded as containing randomly chosen patterns. Then according to Cover (Section 3.9.3) the R_1 and R_2 training sets are very unlikely to be linearly separable if $t > 2N$. If the training sets are transformed into training sets of τ-component patterns, the R_1 and R_2 training sets of τ-component patterns are unlikely to be linearly separable if $t > 2\tau$. Thus, if τ is greater than N, the advantage of the transformation is that it increases the maximum value of t for which linear separability can be expected. [But note that, for example, in Figure 5.2, with training sets of 70 per class, error rates on test sets (not included in training sets) became *worse* as n, and thus τ, was increased.]

Generally speaking, an advantage of transforming patterns into further patterns with higher dimensionality is that this increases the chance of linear separability of the transformed patterns. As a simple example[82], suppose that $N = 2$ and $R_1 = \{00, 11\}$ and $R_2 = \{01, 10\}$, as at the end of Section 3.6, where we remarked that R_1 and R_2 are not linearly separable. Let us now transform each two-element pattern into a three-element pattern, such that the first two elements of the transformed pattern are the same as the two elements of the original pattern, and the third element of the transformed pattern is the product of the first two elements. The transformed classes $R_1 = \{000, 111\}$ and $R_2 = \{010, 100\}$ are linearly separable, as can be seen by plotting the transformed patterns as the corners of a cube.

Instead of transforming an N-element pattern into a τ-element pattern by means of τ product terms, we can use τ hyperplanes, as in Section 3.9.4. Later chapters will introduce further examples of systems which employ τ functions $\phi_1(X), \ldots, \phi_\tau(X)$ of X such that the values of these functions constitute a τ-element pattern which is a transform of X. Any machine which uses such a transformation and which recognises transformed patterns linearly is called by Nilsson[336] a Φ-machine.

5.5 AUTOMATIC SELECTION BY MEANS OF AN INFORMATION CRITERION

In this section we consider the problem of choosing a *good* set of τ functions for transforming N-element patterns into τ-element patterns. The most direct way to find the best τ functions would be to try out all possible sets of τ functions and select the set giving the lowest error rates in recognition. This would involve a prohibitive number of trials. An alternative approach would be to restrict our attention to functions of a particular sort, e.g. linear functions, and start by making a random choice of, say, 10 functions. Then add an 11th randomly chosen function. By applying our 11 functions to training sets of N-elements patterns, we could obtain training sets of 11-element patterns. These could be used for training a system to recognise 11-element patterns, and after training we could evaluate the recognition performance of this system on test data. Then we could replace the 11th function by an alternative randomly chosen function, train the recognition system, and evaluate it on test data. We could repeat this with a total of, say, 1000 alternative randomly chosen functions, and select from these the function giving the best recognition performance. This function would be accepted as the final and permanent 11th function. We could then try out 1000 alternative 12th functions, and select the best; then 1000 13th functions and select the best, and so on, until the use of further functions no longer improved recognition performance.

The main disadvantages of this evolutionary idea are that

(1) even with only 1000 alternative functions at each step, the amount of computation required in training and testing would be great, and
(2) compared with the number of possible sets of functions, the number actually tried out would be exceedingly small, so the best functions, and sets of functions, would probably be missed.

Because of these difficulties, various methods, e.g. Refs. 26, 157, 242, 243, 262a, 276, 295, 320, 322a, and 435, have been developed for selecting functions according to criteria *other than* recognition performance. Mohn[320] has drawn a distinction between two types of selection methods:

(1) A set of τ functions are selected from a very much larger set of functions. Let the number of functions in this larger set be T. In

recognition, an input pattern is transformed into a τ-component pattern whose components are the values of the τ selected functions.

(2) Each pattern is first transformed into a T-component pattern whose components are the values of the T functions. A set of τ T-component weight vectors are determined, and a T-component pattern is transformed into a τ-component pattern whose components are the values of the dot products of the T-component pattern with the τ weight vectors. The weight vectors can be determined by the method of Section 3.10, applied to T-component instead of N-component patterns.

Type (1) is clearly a trivial case of type (2) in which each weight vector has one component which is unity and $T - 1$ components which are zero. According to Section 3.10 it is generally possible to obtain a better approximation by the type (2) method which was introduced in Section 3.10. But note that the error of this approximation is measured by $\overline{\epsilon^2}$, which is not obviously a useful function of pattern recognition error rate. Furthermore, in recognising an unknown pattern, methods of type (2) require computation of the values of all of the T functions, whereas methods of type (1) require computation of the values of only the τ selected functions. In cases where T is very large, say > 1000, methods of type (2) tend to be impractical.

For introductory purposes, we shall discuss just one method of type (1). This method of selection was originally developed for use in the Section 5.6 recognition system but the applicability of this method is not restricted to the Section 5.6 recognition system. For instance, this method can be applied in the selection of first-level hyperplanes for an α-perceptron (Section 3.9.4.2) as follows (cf. Swonger[427, 428]).

(a) If all patterns in all classes lie on the same side of a given hyperplane, and no pattern in any class lies on the other side of it, or
(b) in every class, half the patterns lie on one side of the given hyperplane, and the other half lie on the other side of it,

then this hyperplane is likely to be of no use in the first level of a many/many recognition system, and should be discarded.

If we choose hyperplanes randomly, many will not conform perfectly to (a) or (b) but will *almost* conform to (a) or (b). For instance, all members of all but one of the classes might lie on the same side of a given hyperplane, in which case this hyperplane would *almost* conform to (a). At least as a rough rule of thumb, we can say that the more closely a hyperplane conforms to (a) or (b), the less likely it is to be useful in the first level of a many/many system. To automate the application of this rule of thumb, we require for each hyperplane a statistical measure which has a lower value the more closely this hyperplane conforms to (a) or (b). A computer can evaluate this measure for a large number of candidate hyperplanes and reject those for which the value of this measure lies below a prescribed threshold level.

One such measure is[243, 244]

$$I(v_j) = \log_2 z + P(v_j = 1) \sum_{r=1}^{z} P(r/v_j = 1)\log_2 P(r/v_j = 1) +$$

$$P(v_j = 0) \sum_{r=1}^{z} P(r/v_j = 0) \log_2 P(r/v_j = 0) \qquad (5.24)$$

where z is the total number of classes to be recognised, and the training sets of all classes are assumed to contain the same number of patterns. Here v_j is a variable whose value is 1 or 0 according to the result of a binary test applied to an input pattern; or in other words, v_j is a binary function of an input pattern. In the α-perceptron example which we are discussing, $v_j = 1$ or $v_j = 0$ according to the side of the jth candidate hyperplane on which a pattern X lies. $P(r/v_j = 1)$ is the conditional probability that X belongs to the rth class given that $v_j = 1$ and $P(v_j = 1)$ is a probability which is estimated according to

$$P(v_j = 1) = \frac{\text{total number of training set patterns, regardless of class, in which } v_j = 1}{\text{total number of training set patterns for all classes}}$$

$P(r/v_j = 0)$ and $P(v_j = 0)$ are defined correspondingly.

To illustrate the conformity of (5.24) to the requirements introduced intuitively above, the four right-hand columns of Table 5.2 list values of $P((v_j = 1)/r)$ for the four j's $j = 1, 2, 3, 4$. The rows of Table 5.2 correspond to recognition classes of upper-case letters $A, \ldots, Z$ and lower-case letters $a, \ldots, z$ as indicated in the left-hand column. $P((v_j = 1)/r)$ is the conditional probability that $v_j = 1$ given that X belongs to the rth class: for instance, the figure 0·76 at the top of the $j = 1$ column in Table 5.2 means that $v_j = 1$ in 76% of members of the recognition class of upper-case A's. For $j = 1, 2, 3, 4$ the value of $I(v_j)$, as given by (5.24), is given at the foot of the corresponding column in Table 5.2.

In Table 5.2, $I(\nu_4)$ is low because condition (a) is almost perfectly fulfilled in the case of ν_4. Condition (a) is less nearly fulfilled in the case of ν_3, and $I(\nu_3)$ is higher than $I(\nu_4)$. Although condition (a) is not fulfilled for ν_2, condition (b) is fulfilled to some extent instead, and this is why $I(\nu_2)$ is not much higher than $I(\nu_3)$. Neither (a) nor (b) is fulfilled for ν_1, and $I(\nu_1)$ turns out to be roughly twice as great as $I(\nu_2)$. Formula (5.24) is such that the highest possible value of $I(\nu_j)$ is unity, and this value is attained when $P((\nu_j = 1)/r) = 1$ for half the r's and $P((\nu_j = 0)/r) = 1$ for the remaining r's. $I(\nu_j)$ can be regarded as a measure of the *information*[243] provided by ν_j.

We might generate at random a large number of hyperplanes and reject all but those with high $I(\nu_j)$. But the retained hyperplanes would *not* necessarily constitute a satisfactory set for recognition purposes.

Table 5.2. EXAMPLES OF INFORMATION MEASURE $I(\nu_j)$. THE FIGURES ARE TAKEN FROM REF. 243, WITH PERMISSION

Class	$P((\nu_1 = 1)/r)$	$P((\nu_2 = 1)/r)$	$P((\nu_3 = 1)/r)$	$P((\nu_4 = 1)/r)$
A	0·76	0	0	1·00
B	1·00	0·88	0·27	1·00
C	0·94	0·24	0	1·00
D	0·97	0·91	0·03	1·00
E	0·97	0·85	0·12	1·00
F	0·21	0·67	0·03	1·00
G	0·91	0·30	0·03	1·00
H	1·00	0·89	0·09	1·00
I	0	0·73	0·03	1·00
J	0	0·97	0·03	1·00
K	1·00	0·89	0·21	1·00
L	1·00	0·82	0	1·00
M	1·00	0·24	0·06	1·00
N	0·61	0·36	0·06	1·00
O	0·82	0·33	0	1·00
P	1·00	0·97	0·06	1·00
Q	1·00	0·24	0·03	1·00
R	1·00	0·82	0·21	1·00
S	1·00	0	0·12	1·00
T	0	0·91	0	1·00
U	1·00	1·00	0·06	1·00
V	1·00	0·45	0·09	1·00
W	1·00	0·45	0·09	1·00
X	1·00	0·89	0·45	1·00
Y	1·00	0·76	0·12	1·00
Z	0·03	0·48	0·12	1·00

Table 5.2 (*contd.*)

Class	$P((\nu_1 = 1)/r)$	$P((\nu_2 = 1)/r)$	$P((\nu_3 = 1)/r)$	$P((\nu_4 = 1)/r)$
a	0	0·27	0·33	1·00
b	0·39	0·42	0·03	1·00
c	0	0·09	0	1·00
d	0	0·06	0·03	1·00
e	0	0·55	0·24	1·00
f	0	0·36	0	1·00
g	0	0·48	0·91	1·00
h	0·12	0·36	0	1·00
i	0	0	0	1·00
j	0	0·03	0	1·00
k	0	0·67	0·03	1·00
l	0	0	0	1·00
m	1·00	1·00	0·15	1·00
n	0·52	0·70	0	1·00
o	0	0·12	0·06	1·00
p	0·45	0·94	0·03	1·00
q	0	0·15	0	1·00
r	0	0·06	0	1·00
s	0	0·18	0·97	1·00
t	0	0·70	0	0·89
u	0·06	0·06	0·68	1·00
v	0·27	0·09	0·03	1·00
w	1·00	0·24	0·21	1·00
x	0·48	0·15	0·27	1·00
y	0·33	0·06	0·58	0·97
z	0	0·33	0·33	1·00
value of $I(\nu_j)$	0·784	0·380	0·215	0·025

To illustrate this, suppose, for the sake of a simple example, that we wish to recognise the 10 numerals, and that we are lucky enough to find 20 hyperplanes for which $I(\nu_j) = 1$. It is (remotely) possible that all these hyperplanes will effect precisely the *same* dichotomy, for example 1, 2, 3, 4, 5/6, 7, 8, 9, 0. In this case there is no advantage in retaining more than one of these hyperplanes.

To avoid difficulties of this sort, Liu's programme[282] selected a set of ν's for which $I(\nu_j)$ was high. Let the number of ν's in this set be σ. For all possible pairs of recognition classes, *r*, *s*, Liu's programme computed the value of the 'distance' D_{rs} defined by

$$D_{rs} = \sum_{j=1}^{\sigma} |\log P((\nu_j = 1)/r) - \log P((\nu_j = 1)/s)|$$

(In the above simple example with 20 hyperplanes, D_{rs} would be zero for all r, s.) Liu's programme rejected any of the σ ν's which were unnecessary for ensuring that, for all r, s, D_{rs} exceeded a prescribed minimum value. New ν's were generated specifically to increase D_{rs} for any pairs of classes such that D_{rs} did not exceed the prescribed minimum value. The final set of ν's were used in recognition.

When economic limits are imposed on computer usage, a disadvantage of the present technique is that it evaluates $I(\nu_j)$ for an exceedingly small proportion of all possible ν's (e.g. hyperplanes). Therefore it is likely to miss the best ones. Another disadvantage is that this technique does not take account of statistical dependence between ν's. This technique is essentially heuristic: if it is used to select two different sets of ν's, and one set turns out to have higher average $I(\nu_j)$ than the other, the set with the higher average $I(\nu_j)$ will not necessarily yield the better recognition performance. Although this technique is not *guaranteed* to find an optimal set of ν's, it has been shown experimentally[243] to select a set of ν's yielding considerably better recognition performance than that yielded by a set of randomly chosen ν's. This is also true of the selection technique described by Bakis *et al.*[26] which does not use formula (5.24). In Section 10.3 we will reconsider the problem of selection.

5.6 SHIFTED PEEPHOLE MASK SYSTEMS

5.6.1 With binary patterns

Figure 5.6 represents a peephole mask. In the present section we say that for a binary pattern to *match* a peephole mask the elements of the pattern which are aligned with 1's in the peephole mask must all be 1's, and the elements of the pattern which are aligned with 0's in the peephole mask must all be 0's. Elements aligned with –'s can either be '0' or '1'. In the present section, *match* means *perfect match* (i.e. zero Hamming distance) between the pattern and those elements of the peephole mask which are not '–'. A character can be aligned in all positions with a peephole mask by passing the character through a shift register to which the peephole mask is connected, as in Section 2.3.2. Kamentsky and Liu[243], Liu[282], and Liu and Shelton[283] have used this technique for determining whether a peephole mask matches a given character in *any* alignment of that character and peephole mask.

For recognition of multifont print, Kamentsky and Liu[243] used peephole masks which were chosen so that, generally speaking, each

```
– – – – – – – – – –
– – – – – – – – – –
– – – – – – – – – –
– – 1 – – 0 – – – –
– – – – 1 – – – – –
– – – – – – – – – –
– 0 – – – – – – – –
– – – 0 – – – – – –
– – – – – – – – – 0
– – – – – – – – – –
```

Figure 5.6. *Example of a peephole mask*

peephole mask matched, in at least one alignment, the characters belonging to *more than one* recognition class. Let τ be the total number of different peephole masks used in the system. An unknown binary pattern $\boldsymbol{X}$ was transformed into a τ-bit binary pattern $\{\nu_1, \ldots, \nu_j, \ldots, \nu_\tau\}$ where, for all $j = 1, \ldots, \tau$, ν_j was 1 or 0 according as the jth peephole mask did or did not match $\boldsymbol{X}$ *in at least one alignment.* The τ-bit patterns were recognised by the independence assumption method of Section 3.3; or by a piecewise linear counterpart of this[283], where different subclasses corresponded to different fonts, as mentioned in Section 4.2. (Liu and Shelton[283] also experimented with a compromise between the extremes of one weight vector per class and one weight vector per font per class.)

The τ peephole masks were selected from a set of candidate peephole masks by a computer using the information measure method of Section 5.5. Instead of applying the information measure $I(\nu_j)$ to randomly generated peephole masks, Liu[282] gained efficiency by generating the candidate set of peephole masks as follows. Training set characters from all classes were roughly aligned into a standard position by means of left justification and bottom justification (Section 2.3.3). Liu's programme then computed $I(x_j)$ for all binary pattern elements, and typically 60 elements turned out to have relatively high $I(x_j)$. To generate a peephole mask, roughly seven out of these 60 points were chosen at random, a state of this 7-tuple was chosen at random, and this state was used as a peephole mask.

Liu's plot[282] of substitution error rate versus number of peephole masks was roughly the same shape as in Figure 5.5, and the improvement in performance gained by using more than 96 peephole masks would not have outweighed the cost.

For recognition of uncontrolled poor-quality multifont print, Liu's system was superseded by the IBM 1975, which will be briefly introduced in Section 6.2.3. In Section 7.5 we shall briefly discuss the logical structure of Liu's and Bledsoe and Browning's systems. The systems of Bledsoe and Browning and of Kamentsky and Liu were linked historically by the system of Uhr and Vossler[441], which determined the average positions of alignment where peephole masks matched patterns.

5.6.2 With analogue patterns

With very poor-quality printed characters it is difficult to accomplish binarisation so that the binarised characters have faithfully the same shape as the originals. A shifted peephole mask system was developed at the National Physical Laboratory for direct application to analogue patterns, in order to avoid the problem of binarisation of poor-quality print. We shall introduce one version of this system simply by noting how it differs from Liu's which was introduced in Section 5.6.1.

Liu's shift register is replaced by a delay line, which stores analogue rather than binary patterns. The counterpart of one of Liu's peephole masks is a device which computes the product of all the analogue pattern elements which are aligned with 1's in the peephole mask, and divides this product by the product of all the analogue pattern elements which are aligned with 0's in the peephole mask[342]. The outputs of this device in all possible alignments with the input pattern are summed. By the use of τ such devices, an input pattern is transformed into a τ-element analogue pattern, the τ elements being the sums obtained from the τ devices. The τ-element patterns are recognised by the cross-correlation technique of Section 3.5. In practice this system suffers from the instabilities and inaccuracies of analogue delay lines and analogue multiplication and division.

A somewhat different analogue peephole mask system has been developed by the Plessey Company[64]. In this, the counterpart of one of Liu's peephole masks is a device which determines whether the whitest analogue pattern element coincident with any '1' in the peephole masks is more than a prescribed amount blacker than the blackest element coincident with any '0' in the peephole mask. If this condition is fulfilled, the device *matches* the pattern. By using these devices the Plessey company have avoided the practical difficulties both of binarisation and of analogue multiplication.

Chapter 6

BOOLEAN AND SEQUENTIAL DECISION MAKING

6.1 BOOLEAN FUNCTIONS

Boolean functions are important in pattern recognition because of their widespread use in commercial character recognition, and because of their mathematical generality. The present section provides a very elementary and perfunctory introduction to Boolean functions[144, 303].

Boolean functions are functions of binary variables. We shall call the two possible values of a Boolean variable, x_j, *true* and *false*. *True* and *false* are *truth values*, not numerical values. For the purposes of this book it is convenient to define a Boolean *pattern*, X, to be an array $X = \{x_1, \ldots, x_j, \ldots, x_N\}$ of N Boolean variables*. We shall also use the term *pattern* to mean the ordered array of T's and F's which are the truth values of the elements $x_1, \ldots, x_N$, where T and F stand for *true* and *false* respectively. We shall denote the 2^N different Boolean patterns of N elements by $X_1, \ldots, X_i, \ldots, X_{2N}$. A Boolean *function* $f(X)$ of X is a set of 2^N pairs

$$
\begin{array}{c}
\{X_1, f(X_1)\} \\
\{X_2, f(X_2)\} \\
\vdots \\
\{X_i, f(X_i)\} \\
\vdots \\
\{X_{2N}, f(X_{2N})\}
\end{array}
$$

where, for all i from 1 to 2^N, the value of $f(X_i)$ is T or F. This set of 2^N pairs maps X onto the truth value of $f(X)$ for all X. Thus a Boolean function specifies a truth value of $f(X)$ for each X.

*The symbol X will be used for a binary pattern regarded as a Boolean pattern, and the symbol $\mathbf{X}$ will be used for a binary or for a non-binary pattern which is regarded as a vector with numerical components.

To define a particular Boolean function of N variables, we can simply list the pairs $\{X_i, f(X_i)\}$ for $i = 1, \ldots, 2^N$. It is usual to write this list in the form of a table, called a *truth table,* which has $N + 1$ columns and 2^N rows. The first N entries in the ith row constitute the pattern X_i; and the $(N + 1)$th entry, that is, the entry in the ith row and $(N + 1)$th column, is the truth value of $f(X_i)$. If two Boolean functions have the same truth table, then these two functions are identical. On the other hand, if we change any entry in the $(N + 1)$th column of a truth table, we thereby change the Boolean function which is defined by that truth table. The entries in the $(N + 1)$th column of a truth table constitute a binary pattern which has 2^N elements. 2^{2^N} such patterns are possible, and therefore there are 2^{2^N} possible different Boolean functions of N variables.

Let us now consider some simple examples. Table 6.1 is the truth table of a function, $f(X)$, which is *true* if and only if x_1 *and* x_2 are both *true.* We write $f(X) = x_1 . x_2$, where '.' means *and*: Table 6.1 specifies exactly what we mean by *and*. Table 6.2 is the truth table of the function $f(X)$

Table 6.1. *And* FUNCTION OF TWO VARIABLES

x_1	x_2	$f(X)$
F	F	F
F	T	F
T	F	F
T	T	T

which is *true* if and only if x_1 and x_2 and x_3 are all *true*, and we write $f(X) = x_1 . x_2 . x_3$. The function, $f(X)$, which is *true* if and only if $x_1, x_2, \ldots, x_N$ are all *true* is the *and* function of N variables, and we write $f(X) = x_1 . x_2 . x_3 . \ldots . x_N$.

Table 6.3 is the truth table of a function, $f(X)$, which is *true* if and only if at least one of x_1, x_2 is *true*; and we write $f(X) = x_1 \vee x_2$, where '$\vee$' means *'inclusive or'*. The function, $f(X)$, which is *true* if and only if at least one of $x_1, x_2, \ldots, x_N$ is *true,* is the inclusive *or* function of N variables; and we write $f(X) = x_1 \vee x_2 \vee x_3 \vee \ldots \vee x_N$. Many authors use the symbols 1, 0, +, instead of T, F, and $\vee$, respectively.

Table 6.4 is the truth table of a function, $f(X)$, which is *true* if X is *false* and *false* if x is *true*; and we write $f(x) = \overline{x}$, where $\overline{x}$ is the *negation* of x. It is quite usual to refer to $\overline{x}$ as *not x* or as the *complement of x*.

The negation, $\overline{f(X)}$, of a Boolean function, $f(X)$, is *true* or *false* according as $f(X)$ is *false* or *true*. For instance $\overline{x_1 . x_2}$ is *true* or *false*

Table 6.2. *And* FUNCTION OF THREE VARIABLES

x_1	x_2	x_3	$f(X)$
F	F	F	F
F	F	T	F
F	T	F	F
F	T	T	F
T	F	F	F
T	F	T	F
T	T	F	F
T	T	T	T

Table 6.3. *Or* FUNCTION OF TWO VARIABLES

x_1	x_2	$f(X)$
F	F	F
F	T	T
T	F	T
T	T	T

Table 6.4. *Negation* OF X

x	$f(X)$
F	T
T	F

according as $x_1 . x_2$ is *false* or *true*. Thus the truth table for $f(X) = \overline{x_1 . x_2}$ can be obtained by changing each F to T and each T to F in the third column of Table 6.1. The truth table for $f(X) = \overline{x_1 . x_2}$ is Table 6.5. By checking row by row it is easy to see that

Table 6.5. TRUTH TABLE FOR $f(X) = \overline{x_1 . x_2}$

x_1	x_2	$f(X)$
F	F	T
F	T	T
T	F	T
T	T	F

Table 6.5 is also the truth table for $f(X) = \bar{x}_1 \vee \bar{x}_2$. Therefore $\bar{x}_1 \vee \bar{x}_2 = \overline{x_1 . x_2}$. The following are further formulae whose validity can be checked by checking that the truth table for the left-hand side is the same as the truth table for the right-hand side of each equation.

$$x_1 . x_2 . x_3 = x_1 . (x_2 . x_3) = (x_1 . x_2) . x_3 \tag{6.1}$$
$$x_1 \vee x_2 \vee x_3 = x_1 \vee (x_2 \vee x_3) = (x_1 \vee x_2) \vee x_3 \tag{6.2}$$
$$x_1 . (x_2 \vee x_3) = x_1 . x_2 \vee x_1 . x_3 \tag{6.3}$$
$$x_1 \vee x_2 . x_3 = (x_1 \vee x_2) . (x_1 \vee x_3) \tag{6.4}$$
$$x_1 \vee x_1 . x_2 = x_1 . (x_1 \vee x_2) = x_1 \tag{6.5}$$
$$x_1 \vee \bar{x}_1 = x_1 \vee T = \overline{x_1 . F} = \bar{F} = T \tag{6.6}$$
$$x_1 . x_1 = x_1 \vee x_1 = x_1 . T = x_1 \vee F = x_1 \tag{6.7}$$
$$\bar{x}_1 . \bar{x}_2 = \overline{x_1 \vee x_2} \tag{6.8}$$
$$\bar{x}_1 \vee \bar{x}_2 = \overline{x_1 . x_2} \tag{6.9}$$

Here we are using brackets in the same way as in the ordinary algebra of numbers. Just as '$x_1 + x_2 \times x_3$', means '$x_1 + (x_2 \times x_3)$' in ordinary algebra, '$x_1 \vee x_2 . x_3$' means '$x_1 \vee (x_2 . x_3)$' in Boolean algebra. In this sense, *and* has priority over *or*, just as in ordinary algebra we use the convention that multiplication has priority over addition.

Table 6.6 is the truth table for an *arbitrary* Boolean function of three variables. From Table 6.6 we see that this function, $f(X)$, is *true* if and only if $\bar{x}_1 . x_2 . x_3$ is *true* or $x_1 . \bar{x}_2 . \bar{x}_3$ is *true* or $x_1 . \bar{x}_2 . x_3$ is *true* or $x_1 . x_2 . \bar{x}_3$ is *true*. This can be expressed symbolically

$$f(X) = \bar{x}_1 . x_2 . x_3 \vee x_1 . \bar{x}_2 . \bar{x}_3 \vee x_1 . \bar{x}_2 . x_3 \vee x_1 . x_2 . \bar{x}_3 \tag{6.10}$$

The four *and* terms of three variables in (6.10) correspond to the four rows of Table 6.6 for which $f(X) = T$. Any Boolean function, $f(X)$, of N variables can be expressed in a form in which there is one *and* term of N variables corresponding to each row of the truth table for which $f(X) = T$, and these *and* terms are *or*'ed together, as for instance in (6.10). This is called a *normal form* because any Boolean function can be expressed in this form. Specifically, this is called a *disjunctive normal form* because the *and* terms are *or*'ed together. Thus (6.10) is the disjunctive normal form of the Table 6.6 function.

Table 6.6. TRUTH TABLE FOR AN ARBITRARY BOOLEAN FUNCTION

x_1	x_2	x_3	$f(X)$
F	F	F	F
F	F	T	F
F	T	F	F
F	T	T	T
T	F	F	T
T	F	T	T
T	T	F	T
T	T	T	F

To check the validity of an equation in Boolean algebra we can check that the truth table for the left-hand side is the same as for the right-hand side. Alternatively we can make use of formulae such as (6.1), . . ., (6.9) whose validity has already been established. To illustrate this, let us manipulate (6.10) into a more economical form. Using (6.3) we can write the second and fourth terms of (6.10)

$$x_1 . \bar{x}_3 . \bar{x}_2 \vee x_1 . \bar{x}_3 . x_2 = x_1 . \bar{x}_3 . (\bar{x}_2 \vee x_2)$$
$$= x_1 . \bar{x}_3$$

from (6.6) and (6.7).

Substituting this into (6.10) and using (6.3),

$$\overline{x}_1 . x_2 . x_3 \vee x_1 . \overline{x}_2 . x_3 \vee x_1 . \overline{x}_3 = \overline{x}_1 . x_2 . x_3 \vee x_1(\overline{x}_2 . x_3 \vee \overline{x}_3) \quad (6.11)$$

From (6.4), (6.6), and (6.7)

$$\begin{aligned}\overline{x}_2 . x_3 \vee \overline{x}_3 &= (\overline{x}_3 \vee \overline{x}_2) . (\overline{x}_3 \vee x_3)\\ &= (\overline{x}_3 \vee \overline{x}_2)\end{aligned}$$

which, from (6.9),

$$= \overline{x_3 . x_2}$$

Substituting this into (6.11) we obtain

$$f(X) = \overline{x}_1 . x_2 . x_3 \vee x_1 . \overline{x_2 . x_3} \qquad (6.12)$$

which is more economical than (6.10) as an expression of the Table 6.6 function. Generally speaking, for most Boolean functions there exists a form which is, in some sense, more economical than the disjunctive normal form. Various techniques have been devised for facilitating the finding of economical forms of Boolean functions[303].

Let us now very briefly discuss hardware implementation of Boolean functions. In electronic implementation[303], the truth values *true* and *false* can be represented by different voltages: for instance by 10 V and 0 V respectively, as in Section 1.3. Figure 6.1 is a schematic representation of a circuit which implements $f(X) = x_1 . x_2$. A potential difference of 10 V between the terminals a and d represents $x_1 = \text{T}$, and a potential difference of 0 V between a and d represents $x_1 = \text{F}$. Similarly, $x_2 = \text{T}$ and $x_2 = \text{F}$ are respectively represented by 10 V and 0 V between b and d. The circuit in the box marked '&' in Figure 6.1 produces 10 V between

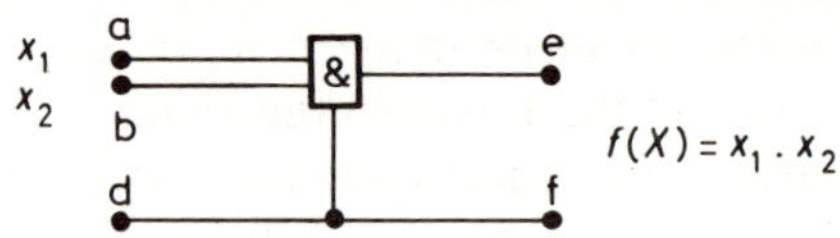

Figure 6.1. *Schematic diagram of 'and' circuit*

terminals e and f if and only if terminals a and b are both at 10 V. Thus the voltage between e and f represents $f(X) = x_1 . x_2$. In schematic representations, it is usual to leave out lines such as that joining d and f in Figure 6.1, since a reference line is *always* needed. Figure 6.2 shows the British Standard symbol which is used instead of Figure 6.1 in schematic diagrams. Figure 6.2 is the same whether $f(X) = x_1 . x_2$ is implemented by relays, valves, transistors, or an integrated circuit[458]:

Figure 6.2 merely indicates the logical job that the circuit does, without specifying the physical details of how it does it.

The actual hardware which implements $f(X) = x_1 . x_2$ is called an *and element* or *and gate.* Hardware which implements $f(X) = x_1 \vee x_2$ is called an *or element* or *or gate.* Generically, all such elements are known as *logic elements.* Figure 6.3 lists the American[15] and British[63] standard symbols for some of the common logic elements. The inputs to each symbol are on the left and are indexed $x_1, x_2, \ldots$ from top to bottom.

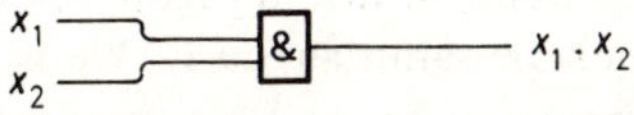

Figure 6.2. *Standard symbol for 'and' element*

Description	American Standard symbol	British Standard symbol	Function
AND element		 &	$f(X) = x_1 . x_2 . x_3$
OR element		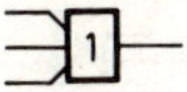 1	$f(X) = x_1 \vee x_2 \vee x_3$
THRESHOLD element		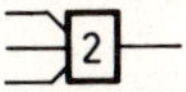 2	$f(X) = T$ if at least two of x_1, x_2, x_3 are *true*
NOR element		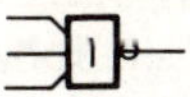 1	$f(X) = \overline{x_1 \vee x_2 \vee x_3}$
NEGATER	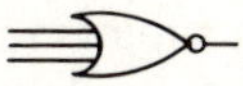	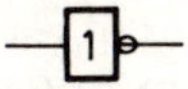 1	$f(X) = \bar{x}$
NAND element or NOT-AND element	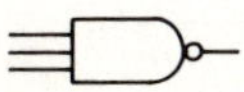	 &	$f(X) = \overline{x_1 . x_2 . x_3}$
The symbol for negated input illustrated by examples	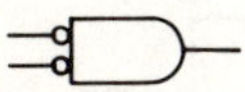	 &	$f(X) = \bar{x}_1 . \bar{x}_2$
		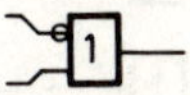 1	$f(X) = \bar{x}_1 \vee x_2$

Figure 6.3. *British and American Standard symbols for some of the more common logic elements*

The output is on the right. Although only a three-input *and* gate is shown in Figure 6.3, the same symbol, though with n inputs, would be used for an n-input *and* gate. The other symbols generalise similarly. British Standard 3939 does not speak of the *truth value* of an input or output, but instead of the *state* of an input or output line. The states which correspond to *true* and *false* are represented by the symbols '1' and '0' respectively.

To illustrate the manner in which simple logic elements can be interconnected to implement an arbitrary Boolean function, Figure 6.4 shows an implementation of (6.12). A circuit of logic elements in known as a *logic circuit*. The logic circuit shown in Figure 6.4 requires that the inputs x_1, x_2, x_3 be available simultaneously. We shall call any circuit which requires all its inputs to be available simultaneously a *parallel* circuit, in contradistinction to a *sequential* circuit, in which not all of the inputs need to be available simultaneously.

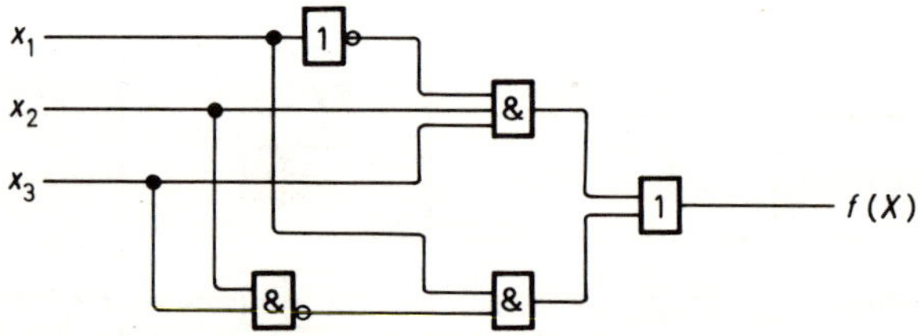

Figure 6.4. *A logic circuit which computes the Table* 6.6 *function*

There are generally many alternative parallel logic circuits for implementing any given Boolean function. One circuit may have the advantage of a minimum number of logic gates, another the advantage of a minimum number of gate inputs, yet another may have no economic advantage. Any Boolean function can be implemented by a

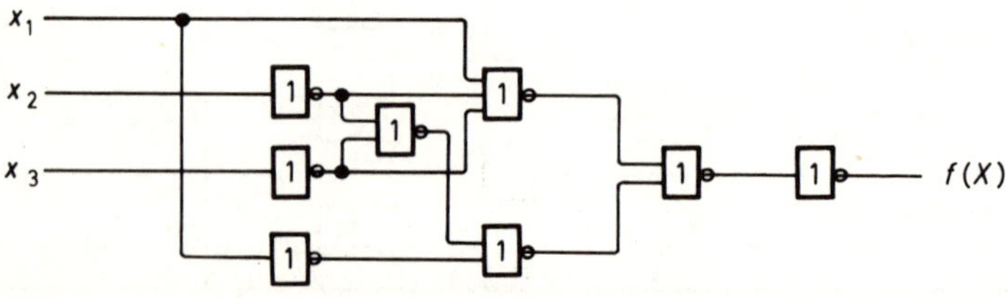

Figure 6.5. *A logic circuit which computes the Table* 6.6 *function using only* NOR *and* NEGATER *elements*

logic circuit which employs no logic elements other than NOR elements and NEGATERS. Figure 6.5 illustrates this for the Table 6.6 function. In practice it is common to work mainly with NAND and NOR elements, which can be purchased ready-made in integrated circuits[458].

6.2 RECOGNITION SYSTEMS USING BOOLEAN FUNCTIONS

6.2.1 IBM 1418

The IBM 1418 is a machine which reads numerals and special symbols printed in a single font[181, 271]. In the version of the IBM 1418 described in 1962 by Greanias[181], characters are binarised and fed bit by bit into a 17 column by 10 row shift register, arranged as in Section 2.3.2. Each of the 170 squares in Table 6.7 corresponds to a bistable element in the shift register. The elements are indexed 1, . . ., 170, and some of the index numbers are shown in Table 6.7. For $j = 1, \ldots, 170$, we define a Boolean variable x_j such that $x_j = \mathrm{T}$ or $x_j = \mathrm{F}$ according as the jth shift register element is '1' or '0'. Here '1' corresponds to *black* and '0' to *white*.

Instead of using one numerical discriminant function per class, the IBM 1418 uses one Boolean discriminant function, $f_r(X)$, per class. For example, for the recognition class of the numeral '4' the Boolean discriminant function is

$$\begin{aligned} f_4(X) = {} & \bar{x}_{62} \,.\, \bar{x}_{79} \,.\, (\bar{x}_5 \vee \bar{x}_{107}) \,.\, (x_{92} \vee x_{109} \vee x_{127}) .\, [(\overline{x_{107} \vee x_{125}}) \vee \\ & (x_{91} \,.\, x_{92})] \,.\, (x_{92} \vee x_{93}) \,.\, (x_{93} \vee x_{110}) \,.\, (x_{58} \vee x_{59}) \\ & .\, (x_{55} \vee x_{72}) \,.\, (x_{75} \vee x_{76}) \,.\, (x_{41} \vee x_{42}) \,.\, (x_{24} \vee x_{25}) \\ & .\, (x_{23} \vee x_{40}) \,.\, (\bar{x}_{37} \vee x_7) \,.\, [x_{92} \vee x_{93} \vee Z_{14} \,.\, Z_{15}] .\, \bar{Z}_3 \\ & .\, \bar{Z}_{16} \,.\, \bar{Z}_{34} \,.\, \bar{Z}_{51} \end{aligned}$$

For the recognition class of the numeral '7', the Boolean discriminant function happens to be more complicated:

$$\begin{aligned} f_7(X) = {} & Z_3 \,.\, Z_4 \,.\, Z_5 \,.\, Z_9 \,.\, Z_{15} \,.\, \bar{Z}_{16} \,.\, Z_{24} \,.\, (Z_{12} \vee Z_{13}) \,.\, \bar{Z}_{29} \\ & .\, (\bar{Z}_{21} \vee \bar{Z}_{22}) \,.\, (x_{39} \vee x_{56}) \,.\, \bar{x}_{106} \,.\, (x_{57} \vee \bar{x}_{90}) \,.\, (x_8 \vee x_{25}) \\ & .\, \{[(x_{54} \vee x_{61} \vee x_{125}) \,.\, x_{39}] \vee x_{74} \,.\, \bar{x}_{73}\} \,.\, \{(\overline{x_4 \vee x_{90}}) \\ & \vee (x_{38} \,.\, x_{39})\} .\, (\bar{x}_{125} \vee \bar{x}_{129}) \,.\, (\bar{Z}_{22} \vee x_{43} \,.\, x_{60} \,.\, x_{94} \,.\, x_{126}) \\ & .\, [\bar{Z}_{13} \vee x_{40} \,.\, x_{57} \,.\, x_{74} \vee (\overline{x_{59} \vee x_{76} \vee x_{93}}) \vee (\overline{x_{42} \vee x_{59} \vee x_{76}})] \\ & .\, [\bar{Z}_{11} \,.\, (x_{55} \vee x_{72}) \vee Z_1 \vee Z_2] \,.\, (\bar{x}_{90} \vee x_{55} \vee \bar{x}_{61}) \end{aligned}$$

Table 6.7. ELEMENTS OF SHIFT REGISTER OF IBM 1418

1	18	35	52	69	86	103	120	137	154
2	19								155
3		37							
4			55	72					
5		39				107			
6	23	40			91	108	125		
7	24	41	58	75	92	109			
8	25	42	59	76	93	110	127		
9					94	111			
10			61	79					
11			62						
12									
13									
14									
15									168
16									169
17								153	170

The Z's are Boolean functions, such as $Z_i = \overline{x}_9 \,.\, \overline{x}_{10} \,.\, \overline{x}_{26} \,.\, \overline{x}_{27}$ and $Z_j = x_{76} \,.\, x_{92} \,.\, x_{108}$, which are used in $f_r(X)$ for more than one class. The Z's detect small white areas, black line elements, and other fairly simple configurations. Greanias[181] does not disclose details of the Z's but mentions that the IBM 1418 uses roughly 50 Z's altogether.

The Section 2.3.2 shift register technique is used so that there is no need for exact pre-alignment of characters. Nevertheless there is a time interval during which a character is expected to pass into and out of alignment with the recognition system. During this time interval the truth values of $f_1(X), \ldots, f_r(X), f_s(X), \ldots, f_z(X)$ are determined after each step of the character through the shift register. X is assigned to the sth class if

(1) after at least one step, $f_s(X) = \mathrm{T}$, and
(2) after every step, $f_r(X) = \mathrm{F}$ for all r except $r = s$, and
(3) the total number of *black* bits in the input character exceeds a prescribed minimum.

If these conditions are not satisfied for any value of s, the input character is rejected.

The IBM 1275 is a more recent IBM machine which uses Boolean functions in character recognition[235, 450a]. It recognises the 10 numerals and four special symbols in one of two fonts.

6.2.2 Peephole masks for small areas

A function which is *true* when and only when at least two of x_i, x_j, x_k, x_l are *true* is a simple example of a *threshold function.* The IBM 1418 uses only a few threshold functions[271], but several other important commercial print recognition systems use threshold conditions more extensively. In several of these systems, binarised characters are fed into a shift register as in Section 2.3.2. Elements of the shift register are represented by small squares in Figure 6.6. To introduce the recognition technique,

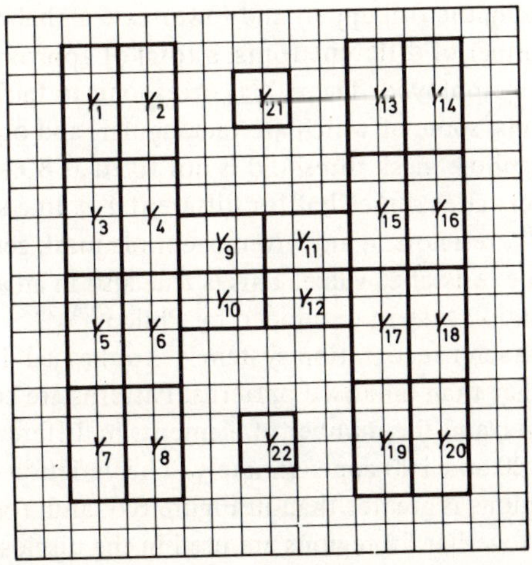

Figure 6.6. *Example of Y regions for recognition of* 'H'

let us consider an example in which the eight elements within the rectangular region marked Y_1 in Figure 6.6 are connected to the eight resistors of an eight-resistor peephole mask. The eight elements within the region Y_2 are connected to another eight-resistor peephole mask, and so on for the other Y's, except that for example the peephole mask for Y_9 includes only six resistors, and the peephole mask for Y_{21} includes only four. The peephole mask which is connected to the elements in Y_1 is connected so as to give its largest possible output when all of these elements are *black* (i.e. '1'). The peephole masks for regions $Y_2, \ldots, Y_{20}$ are also connected in this way. The peephole masks for regions Y_{21} and Y_{22} are connected so as to give their largest possible outputs when their constituent elements are all *white.*

Let us define Boolean variables $y_1, y_2, \ldots, y_{22}$ such that, for $j = 1, \ldots, 22$, y_j is *true* if the Y_j peephole mask yields at least 80% of its greatest possible output current, and *false* otherwise. The system recognises a character in the shift register as an 'H' if

$$(y_1 \vee y_2) \cdot (y_3 \vee y_4) \cdot (y_5 \vee y_6) \cdot (y_7 \vee y_8) \cdot (y_9 \vee y_{10}) \cdot (y_{11} \vee y_{12}) \cdot (y_{13} \vee y_{14}) \cdot (y_{15} \vee y_{16}) \cdot (y_{17} \vee y_{18}) \cdot (y_{19} \vee y_{20}) \cdot y_{21} \cdot y_{22}$$

is *true.* Typically there are five or six Boolean conditions of this sort for each recognition class. A character is assigned to the rth class if at least one of the rth class Boolean conditions is *true.* Note that the *or's* in the above Boolean condition for H's allow a good deal of raggedness in the limb width.

For recognising the full upper- and lower-case alphabet and numerals printed in a number of different fonts, a total of approximately 400 different Y's are employed. These Y's correspond to fairly small black and white regions, some of which are rectangular, and others roughly curved. The peephole mask threshold is not fixed at 80% for all Y's, and instead this level varies somewhat for different Y's. In a system disclosed by Scan-Data[391], resistors in any given peephole mask generally do not all have the same resistance value. This is true also in an automatic terrain classification system developed by Philco[206, 207].

An NCR character recognition system[333] applies a Y-regions technique to analogue rather than binarised patterns. Patterns are composed of 32 x 30 elements, and the number of elements in different Y regions varies between 20 and 100 approximately. The variation in size and shape of the regions is greater than in Figure 6.6, and, for recognising the 10 numerals, altogether 22 regions are used in the disclosed version of the system.

In this NCR system, the document is raster scanned by a flying-spot scanner. During the scan the flying spot passes through a given *Y* region during specific time intervals. During these intervals the photomultiplier output is summed and stored by an integrating amplifier which is assigned to that *Y* region. There is one integrating amplifier per *Y* region, and, because a pattern element may lie in more than one *Y* region, the photomultiplier output at any given instant may be switched through into more than one integrating amplifier. During the entire scan of a character the photomultiplier output is summed in a 23rd integrating amplifier.

When the entire 32 x 30 element input pattern has been scanned, the outputs of the integrating amplifiers corresponding to the 22 *Y*'s are thresholded. The output of the 23rd integrating amplifier is used to bias the thresholds applied to the outputs of the other 22 integrating amplifiers so as to compensate for overall increases or decreases in brightness of the input pattern. Boolean variables $y_1, \ldots, y_{22}$ are defined as above: y_j is *true* if the output of the summing amplifier for Y_j exceeds the threshold applied to it, and *false* otherwise. Further Boolean variables are defined which are *true* or *false* according as the pre-threshold outputs of various integrating amplifiers do or do not exceed the pre-threshold outputs of others by more than a threshold amount. For each recognition class the system uses an elaborate Boolean discriminant function of these variables and the *y*'s. A pattern is assigned to the *r*th class if the *r*th class discriminant function is *true*. Note that whilst this system avoids the difficulties of binarisation on the one hand and the inaccuracies of delay lines on the other, it requires accurate pre-alignment of characters, since the Section 2.3.2 technique cannot be applied except with a shift register or delay line.

When we say that a pattern element is *white*, we mean (roughly) that the average whiteness of the document over a small area exceeds a binarising threshold. In Section 2.4.1 we saw that Dineen's smoothing technique works by summing over a small area after binarisation. This is very roughly equivalent to increasing the size of the scanning spot and thus decreasing the resolution of the system. In the *Y*-regions technique which has been introduced in the present section, the *Y* regions can be made quite large so as to have a smoothing (denoising) effect, and can be positioned, and designed in shape and size, so as to avoid crossing black/white boundaries of character limbs, thus avoiding loss of resolution.

6.2.3 The IBM 1975

The IBM 1975 was designed to recognise printed numerals and upper- and lower-case letters in more than 200 different fonts and uncontrolled print quality, for use by the American Social Security Administration[210]. If Boolean discriminant functions were used in the IBM 1975 as in the IBM 1418, these functions would be very complicated, because of the number of classes and the great variation of shape and quality of the characters within any given class. To avoid the use of exceedingly complicated discriminant functions, the IBM 1975 recognises characters in terms of features.

Characters to be recognised are binarised and fed into a 30 row by 17 column shift register, in which upper-case characters, after size normalisation, are not more than approximately 22 bits high. The process of binarisation is highly developed, and we have discussed part of it in Section 2.2.2. After binarisation, the first stage of the recognition process is the detection of features, and this is best introduced in terms of an example.

A 10 x 28 portion of the shift register is represented in Figure 6.7, where the region marked 'B_1' contains 4 pattern elements, and the regions marked 'B_5', 'B_6' and 'B_7' contain respectively 6, 3, and 3 elements. The region marked 'A_1' contains 2 pattern elements, and the numbers of elements in other 'A' and 'B' regions can be seen in Figure 6.7. Boolean functions $a_1, a_2, \ldots, b_1, b_2, \ldots$ are defined as follows. Function a_1 is *true* only if *all* the pattern elements in the region marked 'A_1' are *black*. Function a_2 is *true* if and only if *all* the elements in the region marked A_2 are *black*, and so on for the other A's. Function b_1 is *true* if and only if at least one of the elements in the region marked B_1 is *black*, and so on for the other B's.

To illustrate feature detection in the IBM 1975, Andrews *et al.*[20] have given details of the detection of the 'overhang' feature. The upper horizontal limb of 'T' sticks out further to the right than the lower serif of 'T', whereas the upper serif of 'I' sticks out as far to the right as the lower serif of 'I'. The 'overhang' feature is present in T's since the upper right portion overhangs the lower right portion of a 'T'. The 'overhang' feature is not present in I's since in 'I' the top right does not overhang the bottom right. Thus presence or absence of the 'overhang' feature distinguishes T's from I's. The 'overhang' feature is deemed present if a Boolean function such as

$$b_1 . b_2 . b_3 . b_4 . b_5 . \bar{a}_1 . \bar{a}_2 . \bar{a}_3 . \bar{a}_4 . \bar{a}_5 . \bar{a}_6 . \bar{a}_7 . \bar{a}_8 . \bar{a}_9 . \bar{a}_{10} . \bar{a}_{11} . \bar{a}_{12} . \bar{b}_9 . (\bar{b}_{10} \vee b_6) . (\bar{b}_{11} \vee b_7) . (\bar{b}_{12} \vee b_8) . (\bar{b}_{13} \vee \bar{b}_{14}) \qquad (6.13)$$

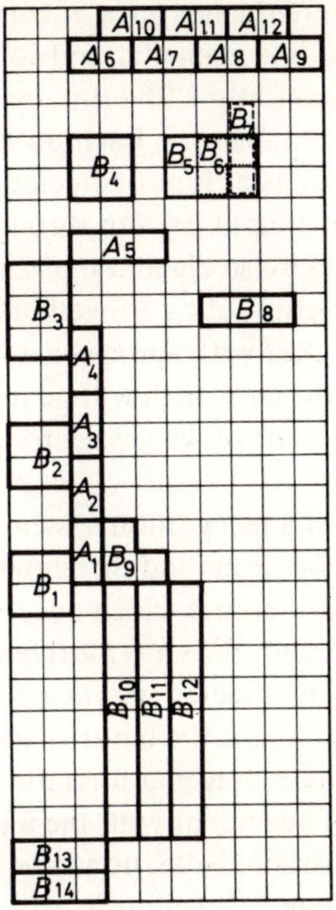

Figure 6.7. *Regions used in detecting the 'overhang' feature*

is *true* after at least one step of the character through the shift register, and absent otherwise. For this function to be *true*, there must be a black vertical limb passing up through regions B_1, B_2, B_3 flanked by a certain amount of white in regions A_1, A_2, A_3, A_4. There must also be black structure passing through B_4 and B_5, flanked above by a certain amount of white in $A_6, A_7, \ldots, A_{12}$. Function $(\bar{b}_{10} \vee b_6)$ requires that, if the bottom of the character extends down into B_{10}, then the top must extend into B_6, and $(\bar{b}_{11} \vee b_7)$ can be interpreted similarly. Function $(\bar{b}_{12} \vee b_8)$ requires that, if the horizontal serif at the base of the character extends into B_{12}, then there must also be a vertical serif extending down into B_8 from the top horizontal limb of the character. Function $(\bar{b}_{13} \vee \bar{b}_{14})$ ensures that the serif at the base of a tall 'I' will not pass below B_{10}, B_{11}, B_{12}.

The IBM 1975 employs altogether 96 features, such as line segments of various lengths and orientations, line endings and gaps in lines, blobs, features which detect different curvatures of corners, features which detect relative positions of line segments, and so on. The system transforms an input character into a 96-bit pattern, in which each bit corresponds to one of the 96 features. Each bit is '1' or '0' according as the corresponding feature is or is not detected in the input pattern after at least one step of the input pattern through the shift register. The 96-bit pattern is recognised by an elaborate piecewise linear system employing about 2000 weight vectors altogether[210], although a given 96-bit pattern is only matched with approximately 150 to 200 of them because of the use of a short cut which will be introduced below in Section 6.6.2. The components of weight vectors are restricted to the values +1, −1, and 0.

Scan-Data have patented a recognition system[391a] in which features are detected by elaborate Boolean (and threshold-logical) discriminants. The more or less right-angled corner which occurs at the top left of the characters 'D', 'E', 'F', 'P', and 'R' is a typical feature in this system. A feature is ignored unless it is detected within a prescribed zone within a rectangular region which contains the input character. In the IBM 1975, on the other hand, a feature is detected if its Boolean function is *true* for at least one position of alignment with the input character, and there is no restriction on this position. Note, however, that in the IBM 1975 'overhang' feature, the Figure 6.7 regions $B_1, B_2, B_3, B_{13}, B_{14}, A_1, A_2, A_3, A_4, A_6, A_7, \ldots, A_{12}$ are used for positioning the actual overhang with respect to the upright limb of the character 'T'.

6.3 INCOMPLETELY SPECIFIED BOOLEAN FUNCTIONS

In the truth table for an *incompletely specified* Boolean function, some of the entries in the $(N + 1)$th column are blank and undefined[303]. A completely specified function maps all possible X's on to values of $f(X)$, whereas an incompletely specified function maps only some of the possible X's onto values of $f(X)$. Incompletely specified functions arise in practice when the number of different X's which ever actually occur is less than 2^N. The truth table need not specify the truth value of $f(X)$ corresponding to any X which never occurs.

As a trivial example, let us say that recognition class R_1 consists of the three patterns TFF, TFT, TTF, and that recognition class R_2 consists of the three patterns FFF, FFT, FTF, and let us say that TTT and FTT never occur. A Boolean function which is *true* for all members of R_1 and *false* for all members of R_2 is incompletely specified, because it does not matter whether this function is *true* or *false* for TTT or FTT. We can complete an incomplete function in such a way as to allow the most economical implementation. For instance $f_1(X) = x_1$ is a completely specified function which is *true* for all members of R_1 and *false* for all members of R_2. If now we change our example by including TTT in R_2 and FTT in R_1, a Boolean function which is *true* for all members of R_1 and *false* for all members of R_2 is a completely specified Boolean function. In fact this is the Table 6.6 function, which is more expensive to implement than the function $f_1(X) = x_1$. This is a simple illustration of the idea that incompletely specified functions are cheaper to implement than completely specified functions, because, as remarked above, an incomplete function can be completed in such a way as to allow the most economical implementation.

As a practical example, let us consider the function $f_4(X)$ in Section 6.2.1. Here $f_4(X)$ is a Boolean function which (ideally) is *true* for all 4's, *false* for all other characters which the machine is to recognise, and either *true* or *false* for X's which never occur. Greanias estimates[181] that $f_4(X)$ is *true* for roughly 268 million different X's and this is less than 2^N by a factor greater than 250 million. Each of the 268 million patterns for which $f_4(X)$ is *true* is either a '4' or is a pattern which can be relied upon not to turn up in practice. To avoid $f_4(X)$ being *true* for any pattern which is not a '4', $f_4(X)$ would have to be made more complicated and expensive to implement and this would have no practical advantage.

6.4 IMPLEMENTATION OF BOOLEAN FUNCTIONS BY USING NUMERICAL FUNCTIONS

6.4.1 Introduction

We may regard a binary pattern X either as an array of non-numerical truth values, or as an array of numerical values such as 1 and 0. To implement a Boolean function $f(X)$ of X, we can use a numerical function $g(X)$ of the vector X, such that the numerical value of $g(X)$ satisfies a prescribed condition if and only if X is such that $f(X)$ is *true*[319].

For instance, consider $f(X) = \bar{x}_1 \vee x_2$, and let 1 and 0 be the numerical values corresponding to *true* and *false*. The function

$g(X) = 2x_1 - 2x_2 - 1$ satisfies the condition $g(X) < 0$ if and only if $f(X)$ is *true*. For any given X, '$g(X) < 0$' is *true* or *false* according as $f(X)$ is *true* or *false*. Instead of implementing $f(X)$ by means of logic elements, we can implement $f(X)$ by means of, for example, a resistor mask and threshold circuit which outputs a signal indicating that $f(X)$ is *true* if and only if $g(X) < 0$.

As a further example let us redefine $g(X)$:

$$g(X) = 4x_1x_2 - 5x_2x_3 + 3x_1 + 8x_3 + 1$$

It is easy to check that for any given X the proposition 'the numerical value of $g(X)$ is a multiple of four' is *true* or *false* according as the Table 6.6 function is *true* or *false*. To implement the Table 6.6 function, we can compute $g(X)$ and signal that the Table 6.6 function is *true* if and only if $g(X)$ is a multiple of four. From the point of view of implementation, conditions such as 'the value of $g(X)$ is a multiple of four', or 'the value of $g(X)$ is a prime number' or 'the value of $g(X)$ is an integral power of three' are less convenient than conditions such as '$g(X)$ is greater than zero'. In the following section Boolean functions are implemented by application of threshold conditions to linear functions.

6.4.2 Threshold functions

For the purposes of the present section it is convenient to augment any pattern $\boldsymbol{X}$ by including an $(N + 1)$th component which is always unity. As in Section 3.7.1, the augmented version of $\boldsymbol{X}$ is denoted by $\boldsymbol{Y}$. A Boolean function $f(X)$ is a *threshold function*[277] if there exists an $(N + 1)$-component weight vector, $\boldsymbol{W}$, such that

$Y . W > 0$ for all X such that $f(X)$ is *true*, and
$Y . W < 0$ for all X such that $f(X)$ is *false*.

In other words, a Boolean function $f(X)$ is a threshold function if the set of all X's for which $f(X)$ is *true* is linearly separable from the set of all X's for which $f(X)$ is *false*. Given the truth table of a threshold function, a separating hyperplane can be determined by the methods of Sections 3.7 or 3.8.

For the function $f(X)$ defined in Table 6.8, $\boldsymbol{Y} . \boldsymbol{W} > 0$ or $\boldsymbol{Y} . \boldsymbol{W} < 0$ according as $f(X) = \mathrm{T}$ or $f(X) = \mathrm{F}$, where $\boldsymbol{Y} = \{1, x_1, x_2, x_3\}$ and

Table 6.8. EXAMPLE OF A THRESHOLD FUNCTION

x_1	x_2	x_3	$f(X)$
F	F	F	T
F	F	T	F
F	T	F	F
F	T	T	F
T	F	F	T
T	F	T	T
T	T	F	T
T	T	T	F

$W = \{1, 3, -2, -3\}$, as Nilsson has shown on page 72 of Ref. 336 by application of the fixed increment rule. The value of $\boldsymbol{Y} \cdot \boldsymbol{W}$ can be computed by a resistor mask as in Section 1.6. A circuit can be designed to give one output voltage V_1 if the total current in the resistor mask exceeds zero, and a different voltage V_0 otherwise. The output voltages V_1 and V_0 signify respectively that $f(X)$ is *true* or *false*. This implementation of the Table 6.8 function is more economical in terms of numbers of components than an implementation by logic elements, such as that shown in Figure 6.8. Most threshold functions can be implemented more economically by means of a resistor mask and a threshold circuit than by means of a circuit of logic elements.

And and *or* functions are important threshold functions. Let us consider a circuit which gives an output signal indicating *true* if and only

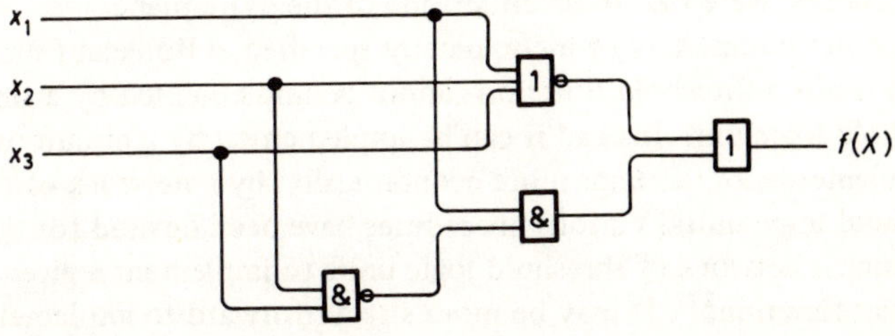

Figure 6.8. *A logic circuit which computes the Table* 6.8 *function*

if at least θ of its N inputs are *true*. If $\theta = 1$ the circuit implements the *or* function of its N inputs, and if $\theta = N$ the circuit implements the *and* function of its N inputs.

Not all Boolean functions are threshold functions; for example the Table 6.6 function is not a threshold function. For $N = 0, 1, \ldots, 7$, Table 6.9 gives approximately the numbers of Boolean functions which are threshold functions[463]. Table 6.9 also gives approximately the value of 2^{2^N}, which, as mentioned in Section 6.1, is the total number of different Boolean functions of N variables. From Table 6.9 we see that the proportion of Boolean functions which are threshold functions rapidly decreases as N increases.

Table 6.9. NUMBER OF THRESHOLD FUNCTIONS OF *N* VARIABLES

N	2^{2^N}	*Number of threshold functions*
0	2	2
1	4	4
2	16	14
3	256	104
4	65 536	1882
5	$4{\cdot}3 \times 10^{9}$	$9{\cdot}5 \times 10^{4}$
6	$1{\cdot}8 \times 10^{19}$	$1{\cdot}5 \times 10^{7}$
7	$3{\cdot}4 \times 10^{38}$	$8{\cdot}4 \times 10^{9}$

If the truth table of an incompletely specified Boolean function has not more than $2N$ entries in the $(N + 1)$th column, this function can probably be implemented by means of a threshold logic unit (which is, for example, a resistor mask plus threshold circuit, as in Section 3.9.4). This follows from Section 3.9.3. Note that in, for instance, Section 3.7.1, we only discussed the separation of R_1 from R_2, and there was no need to consider patterns which, belonging to neither of these classes, were free to lie either side of the hyperplane.

Whether completely or incompletely specified, a Boolean function which is not a threshold function cannot be implemented by a single threshold logic unit. Instead it can be implemented by a circuit of logic elements, or, perhaps more economically, by a network of threshold logic units. Various procedures have been devised for designing a network of threshold logic units to implement a given Boolean function[277]. It may be more straightforward to implement a function by means of logic gates (NOR's, NAND's etc.) because the design is easier to understand intuitively and to modify if necessary, and because logic gates can be purchased ready made in integrated circuits.

6.4.3 Polynomial discriminants

Not all Boolean functions are threshold functions, but all Boolean functions can necessarily be implemented numerically by means of polynomial discriminants. This is of remarkably little practical use, but it is of theoretical interest as a link with the polynomial techniques of Chapter 5.

Corresponding to any given Boolean function $f(X)$ we define a numerical function $g(X)$ such that $g(X) = 1$ or 0 according as $f(X)$ is *true* or *false*. We expand $g(X)$ in terms of a complete set of orthonormal functions $\phi_0(X), \ldots, \phi_{2^N-1}(X)$, as in Section 5.1.1. For any given X we compute the value

$$g(X) = \sum_{j=0}^{2^N-1} w_j \phi_j(X) \tag{6.14}$$

and decide that $f(X)$ is *true* or *false* according as $g(X) = 1$ or 0. For instance, if the ϕ's are the N-dimensional generalisation of functions (5.1), then, from Section 5.1.1, $w_j = g(X_j)$. By multiplying out the ϕ's as at the right-hand side of (5.1), we see that (6.14) is polynomial[319].

Although *any* Boolean function can be implemented in this way, this is usually not the most economical implementation. For example, for the function specified by Table 6.8 and the ϕ functions (5.1), (6.14) becomes

$$g(X) = \phi_0(X) + \phi_4(X) + \phi_5(X) + \phi_6(X)$$
$$= 1 - x_2 - x_3 + x_1x_2 + x_1x_3 + x_2x_3 - 2x_1x_2x_3$$

But the Table 6.8 function can be implemented more economically by means of a threshold logic unit.

In Section 3.7.1 a pattern whose representative point lay *on* the dichotomising hyperplane was rejected, and patterns not lying on the hyperplane were assigned to one or other class. In the present section $f(X)$ is *true* for all patterns lying on the polynomial surface $g(X) = 1$, and $f(X)$ is *false* for all patterns lying on the polynomial surface $g(X) = 0$. All N-element patterns lie on one or other of these two polynomial surfaces. In this respect (6.14) differs from the numerical discriminant functions which have been introduced in previous chapters. Note that the polynomial discriminants which were discussed in Chapter 5 were of order n, whereas (6.14) is generally of order N.

6.4.4 Numerical discriminants in the multiclass case

Suppose that we wish to design a machine to recognise z classes of N-element binary patterns. In principle, though usually not in practice, we can construct a table which has $N + 1$ columns. Any pattern which ever occurs in our recognition problem occupies the first N entries in a unique row in this table. The $(N + 1)$th entry in any given row is a symbol indicating to which class we wish the machine to assign the pattern in that row. For patterns which occur but which do not belong to any of the z classes, the $(N + 1)$th entry signifies *reject*. For patterns which never occur there is no row in the table. Let us call this table the *classification* table for our recognition problem.

From the classification table it is always possible to construct z truth tables, one per class, each truth table having the same number of rows and columns as the classification table. In the truth table for the rth class, for all patterns belonging to the rth class the $(N + 1)$th entry is *true* and for all patterns in the classification table which do not belong to the rth class the $(N + 1)$th entry is *false*. The incompletely specified function expressed by the rth class truth table can be implemented by means of a Boolean discriminant such as $f_4(X)$ or $f_7(X)$ in Section 6.2.1.

In practice it is not usually possible to construct the classification table for reasons indicated in the penultimate paragraph of Section 3.2. Instead, functions such as $f_4(X)$ and $f_7(X)$ in Section 6.2.1 are arrived at by a combination of direct intuition and trial and error, as explained by Greanias[181]. But for the present purposes it is convenient to think in terms of the classification table as a theoretical construction.

Instead of implementing the rth class truth table by means of a Boolean discriminant function, we can use polynomials discriminants as in Section 6.4.3. Therefore it is *always* possible to implement the classification table by means of a numerical discriminant system, though the Section 6.4.3 polynomials are usually uneconomical.

The most economical implementation of a classification table would generally be linear. Not all Boolean functions are threshold functions, and, analogously, not all possible classification tables can be implemented by a multiclass linear system such as, for instance, the Section 3.7.3

system. When applied to binary patterns, all of the multi-class numerical discriminant systems which have been mentioned in previous chapters can be regarded as implementations of classification tables.

If the classification table for a given problem were available explicitly, the practical choice between Boolean and numerical implementation might be determined mainly by economy, although reliability of the hardware is another important factor, and Boolean hardware tends to be more reliable than analogue hardware. To appreciate why Boolean discriminant functions are widely used in commercial reading machines, we must also take account of the fact that the classification table is usually not explicitly available in practice. It is easier to embody human intuition and imagination in Boolean than in numerical systems.

The classification table is perhaps useful for clarifying ideas about the *reject* category. There are *two* classes of patterns which do not belong to any of our z recognition classes. The first is the class of rejects which is the $(z + 1)$th class in the classification table. For instance, a mutilated character which could be a '3' or could be an '8' should, in many recognition systems, be rejected, and would therefore be entered in the *reject* category in the classification table. This is the class of patterns for which we wish to *ensure* rejection.

The second class of patterns not belonging to any of our z classes consists of patterns which can be relied upon not to turn up, and which are not entered in the classification table. If one of these patterns were to turn up, we would not care how our machine classified it. For instance, in a machine for recognising the 10 numerals, if the input pattern were 'S', we probably would not mind if the machine classified it as '5' rather than *reject*. The class of patterns which never occur usually has many members, each without an entry in the classification table. This makes implementation of the classification table cheaper; just as implementation of incompletely specified Boolean functions tends to be cheaper than implementation of completely specified Boolean functions.

6.5 NON-NUMERICAL SEQUENTIAL RECOGNITION

6.5.1 A simple decision tree

To determine which of the 16 possible 4-bit patterns is identical with an unknown 4-bit pattern X, we can simply use 16 resistor masks corresponding to the 16 patterns, and find which mask matches X perfectly.

It may be possible to match X with all 16 masks simultaneously, but in some circumstances this is not possible. An obvious alternative is to compare X with the 16 4-bit patterns in turn until one is found which is identical to X. On average X will be identified after eight comparisons, if X is chosen randomly in a number of trials.

It is more efficient to identify X by means of a sequential process such as that indicated in Figure 6.9. In Figure 6.9 the circled numbers represent states of a machine, and they can be thought of as labels in a computer programme. The state of the machine is initially state 1, and the state changes to 2 or 9 according as $x_1 = 1$ or 0. Suppose for instance that $x_1 = 0$, so that the machine is in state 9. The state changes to 10 or 13 according as $x_2 = 1$ or 0. Suppose that $x_2 = 1$ and $x_3 = 1$, so that the state changes from 9 to 10 to 11. If $x_4 = 0$, the state changes to '0110'. The machine cannot reach state '0110' unless $X = \{x_1 x_2 x_3 x_4\} =$ 0110. Similarly the machine cannot reach '1101' unless $X = 1101$, and so on for all other 4-bit patterns. Any 4-bit pattern directs the system to one of the 4-bit patterns at the right-hand side of Figure 6.9. An unknown 4-bit pattern X can be recognised as the 4-bit pattern in Figure 6.9 to which it directs the machine. This process identifies X after only *four* steps, one bit being examined at each step. This is more efficient than the process of comparison mentioned above which takes eight steps on average to identify X. The relative efficiency of the technique which is exemplified in Figure 6.9 is greater when N is larger.

Figure 6.9 indicates conditions for state-to-state transitions of a machine and is accordingly called a *transition diagram.* A transition diagram which has the branching shape of Figure 6.9 is called a *tree*[258]. The circles in Figure 6.9 are the *nodes* of the transition diagram or tree. The nodes represented by circles containing 4-bit patterns in Figure 6.9 are *terminal nodes.* The numbering of non-terminal nodes in Figure 6.9 is arbitrary: the system would work equally well if the numbering were changed.

6.5.2 Programme dominated sequence

In Sections 3.9.4, 5.6.1, and 6.2.3 we have encountered recognition systems in which an input pattern is transformed into a τ-bit pattern and the τ-bit pattern is recognised. Each of the τ bits is '1' or '0' according to the result of a binary test applied to the input pattern.

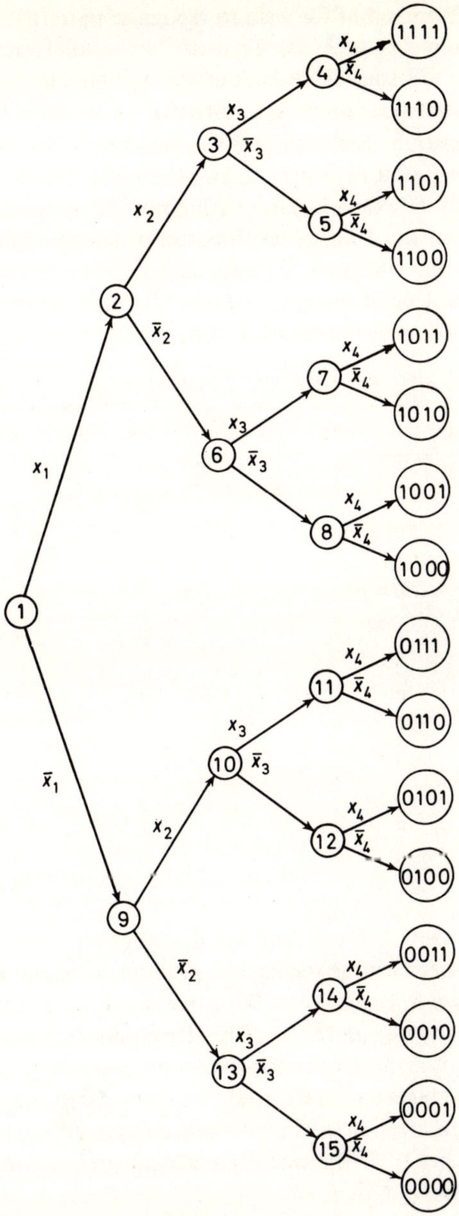

Figure 6.9. *A simple decision tree*

Suppose for example that we wish to recognise patterns belonging to 16 recognition classes by using τ tests. The smallest possible value of τ in this case is 4 since $2^4 = 16$, but we are unlikely in practice to be able to devise four tests such that no two patterns belonging to different recognition classes are transformed into the same 4-bit pattern. Instead we may find it necessary to employ more than four tests. Suppose, by way of example, that we employ 10 tests altogether, and that the results of the 10 tests on all patterns belonging to the rth class are as shown in the rth row of Table 6.10 for $r = 1, \ldots, 16$. In Table 6.10, '–' means '1 or 0' and for $j = 1, \ldots, 10$, z_j is defined such that $z_j = 1$ or 0 according as the result of the jth test is 1 or 0.

Table 6.10. TEST RESULTS FOR SIXTEEN CLASSES

z_1	z_2	z_3	z_4	z_5	z_6	z_7	z_8	z_9	z_{10}	*Class*
1	–	1	1	–	–	–	–	0	–	R_1
–	0	0	–	–	–	–	–	0	0	R_2
1	–	1	0	–	–	–	0	–	1	R_3
–	0	0	1	–	–	–	–	–	1	R_4
–	–	1	0	–	1	–	1	–	–	R_5
–	1	0	–	1	–	–	–	–	–	R_6
–	0	1	1	–	–	–	–	1	–	R_7
–	0	0	0	–	–	–	–	–	1	R_8
0	–	1	0	–	–	1	0	–	–	R_9
–	1	1	1	–	–	–	–	1	–	R_{10}
0	–	1	1	–	–	–	–	0	–	R_{11}
–	1	0	–	1	–	–	–	–	–	R_{12}
1	–	1	0	–	–	–	0	–	0	R_{13}
–	–	1	0	–	0	–	1	–	–	R_{14}
–	–	1	0	–	–	0	0	–	–	R_{15}
–	0	0	–	–	–	–	–	1	0	R_{16}

An input pattern can be recognised in terms of test results by means of the tree shown in Figure 6.10. This tree identifies a pattern in not less than three and not more than five steps, one test result being used at each step. This is more efficient than a process which compares the results of the 10 tests with each row of Table 6.10 in turn and recognises the input pattern after eight comparisons on average. Generally speaking the relative efficiency of the tree is greater the greater the number of recognition classes.

By way of example, Table 6.10 has been constructed so that each of the 10 tests is indispensable for discriminating between a pair of classes.

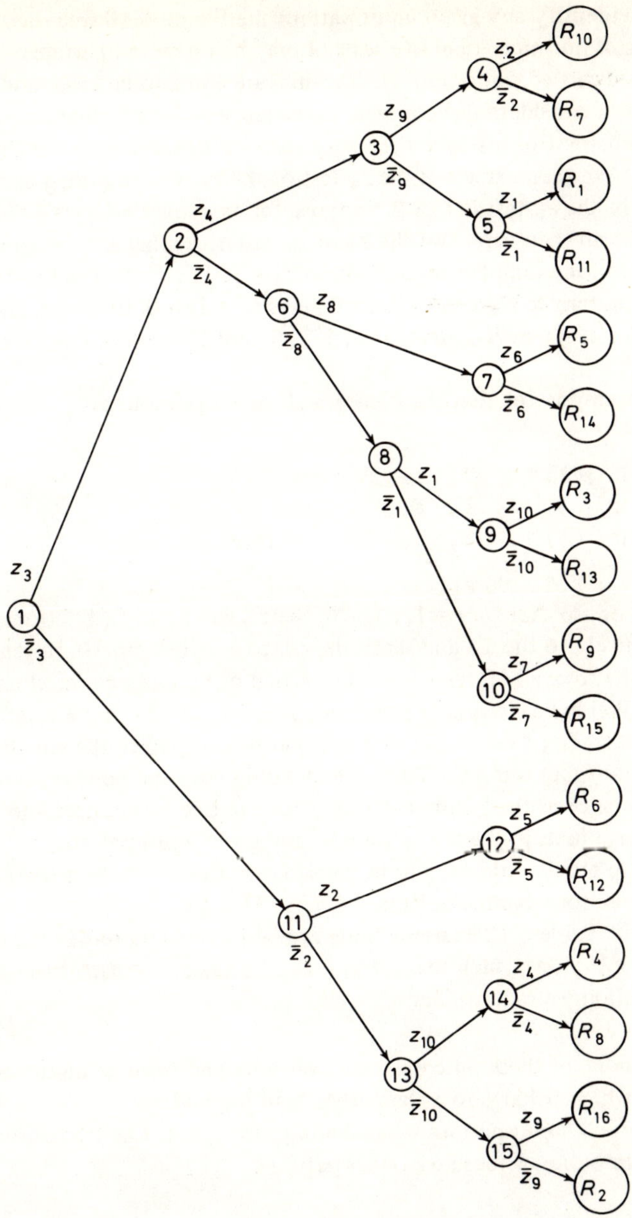

Figure 6.10. *A decision tree which uses the results of* 10 *binary tests*

But to identify any given input pattern the Figure 6.10 tree uses the results of not more than five tests. It may be possible to arrange that tests are carried out only if their results are going to be used, and this can be of considerable economic importance if the carrying out of tests is expensive. For instance the system can start by carrying out the z_3 test. It can then carry out the z_4 test or the z_2 test according as the result of the z_3 test is 1 or 0. Suppose for example that $z_3 = 1$. The system can then carry out the z_9 or z_8 test according as $z_4 = 1$ or 0. Suppose for example that $z_4 = 0$ and $z_8 = 1$. The system can assign the input pattern to R_5 or R_{14} according as $z_6 = 1$ or 0. In recognising a member of R_5 or R_{14}, tests 1, 2, 5, 7, 9, and 10 need not be carried out.

It is easy to see that the Figure 6.10 tree assigns X to

R_1 if $f_1(X) = z_1 \,.\, z_3 \,.\, z_4 \,.\, \bar{z}_9 = true$,
R_2 if $f_2(X) = \bar{z}_2 \,.\, \bar{z}_3 \,.\, \bar{z}_9 \,.\, \bar{z}_{10} = true$,
R_3 if $f_3(X) = z_1 \,.\, z_3 \,.\, \bar{z}_4 \,.\, \bar{z}_8 \,.\, z_{10} = true$,

and so on, so that for $r = 1, \ldots, 16$, the z's and $\bar{z}$'s in $f_r(X)$ correspond respectively to the 1's and 0's in the rth row of Table 6.10. Instead of using the tree, all 10 tests could be carried out on a given input pattern X, parallel logic circuits or peephole masks could determine which of $f_1(X), \ldots, f_{16}(X)$ was *true*, and X could be assigned to the rth class such that $f_r(X)$ was *true*. This system would have the same recognition performance as the Figure 6.10 tree, but the tree would have the advantage that, in the recognition of any given input pattern, not more than five tests would have to be carried out. For this reason trees have been used for example in Refs. 12, 173, 371, 445.

In the Table 6.10 example there are 64 possible patterns of test results $z_1, \ldots, z_{10}$ such that $f_5(X) = z_3 \,.\, \bar{z}_4 \,.\, z_6 \,.\, z_8 = true$. For correct recognition we require that

(1) none of these 64 patterns is ever obtained from an input pattern which belongs to a class other than R_5, and
(2) every input pattern which belongs to R_5 must be transformed into one of these 64 10-bit patterns.

If condition (1) is not satisfied we can increase the number of intermediate nodes between the initial node and the terminal node which is labelled R_5 in Figure 6.10, so that assignment to R_5 depends on the results of more tests. If condition (2) is not satisfied we can employ more than one terminal node for R_5, and a pattern X can be assigned to R_5 if it leads to any one of the terminal nodes which are associated with R_5. Here R_5 has been discussed only by way of example, and corresponding remarks apply for all $R_1, \ldots, R_{16}$.

In a sequential process of the Figure 6.10 type, the order in which tests are carried out is determined *by* the tree, and the sequence is therefore said to be *programme dominated.* The sequence of bits in Section 6.5.1 is also programme dominated, and note that all four bits are always used in the recognition of any given pattern. In Section 6.5.1 the bits were actually used in the order x_1, x_2, x_3, x_4; but we could have designed a tree which would do the job of the Figure 6.9 tree just as efficiently using the bits in any other order (if all patterns have equal *a priori* probability).

Table 6.10 is a decision table because it specifies the decision (in this case the class assignment) appropriate to the test results in each row. The classification table mentioned in Section 6.4.4 is a further example of a decision table. (It is usual to write a decision table so that results of a given test lie in the same row rather than in the same column, but for present purposes it might be confusing to follow this convention, because we have been discussing truth tables. In writing truth tables, the opposite convention is usually followed: successive columns correspond to $x_1, x_2, \ldots$ as in Section 6.1.)

Feigenbaum[140] (cf. Ref. 405) has used a procedure which automatically generates a decision tree of the Figure 6.10 sort. This procedure has the merit of simplicity, but it is not claimed to yield an optimal tree. Further procedures are available which, given a decision table, automatically construct a tree which is in some sense optimal[354a, 354b, 369a].

Before leaving the topic of programme dominated sequences it is perhaps worth noting, for the sake of unifying ideas, that a curve follower is a highly specialised programme dominated sequential system. By following the black/white edge of a character, as in Section 2.4.2, it is possible to find the lengths and positions on the document of all edge segments whose compass directions lie, for example, in the range N to NE, or NE to E, and so on. To obtain this data with a purely parallel system would be expensive. The curve follower only examines those parts of the document which contain black/white edges, whereas a parallel system would examine the entire region containing the character. Analogously the Figure 6.10 tree carries out not more than five tests to identify an unknown pattern, whereas a logically equivalent parallel system requires all 10 tests to be carried out.

6.5.3 Data dominated sequence

Although a curve follower is itself a programme dominated system, its output may be a natural sequence of symbols representing directions of the black/white edge of a character. There is also obvious natural sequence in speech. A sequential system which uses the variables in the order in which they occur is a *data dominated* sequential system. In a programme dominated system, information which directs the choice of tests is in some sense fed back from the decision making apparatus to the source of data, as in Figure 6.11(a). In a data dominated sequential system this feedback is characteristically absent, as in Figure 6.11(b).

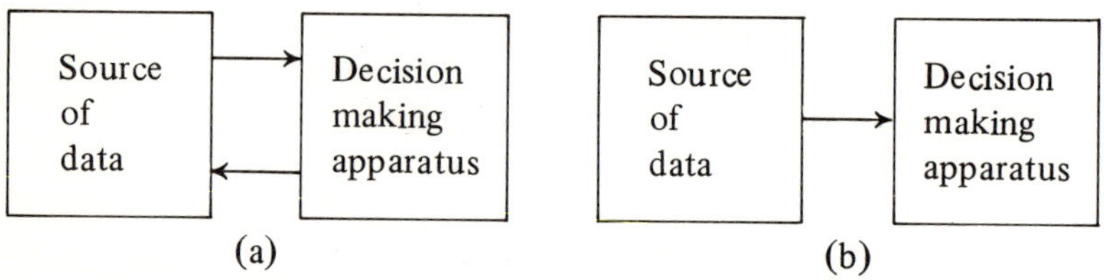

Figure 6.11. *Feedback in sequential decision making: (a) present and (b) absent*

To introduce an important type of data dominated sequential recognition system[54] let us consider an example. In this example the problem is to recognise the *word* 'success' even when it is misspelt 'suces', 'suxess', 'succes', 'sucess', 'sucsess', 'sucses', 'sucksess', and even when letters are irregularly spaced by any number of spaces:

su cc ess, s u c e s, etc[13].

In our example problem, letters and spaces have already been recognised by a character recognition machine. The output of this character recognition machine at any time is a 7-bit code word which represents a letter or space: e.g. '0000000' represents 'space', '0000001' represents 'A', '0000010' represents 'B', and so on. Thus the input to the *word* recognition system is a string of 7-bit code words. This string could be recognised by means of a sequential process for which Figure 6.12 is the transition diagram.

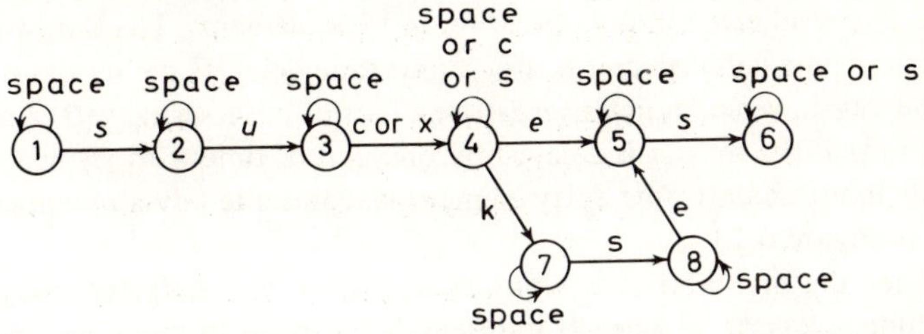

Figure 6.12. *A transition diagram for recognising versions of the word 'success'*

The Figure 6.12 process starts at node 1. If the first 7-bit code word in the string represents 'space', the process remains at node 1. Indeed the process remains at node 1 until the code word for 's' occurs, whereupon the process proceeds to node 2. If, while the process is at node 1, any code word not representing 'space' or 's' occurs in the string of code-words coming from the character recognition machine, the process terminates and the system signals that the string does not contain the word 'success'. If node 2 has in fact been reached the process remains there so long as successive code words represent 'space', and the transition to node 3 only occurs when 'u' occurs in the string. If, while the process is at node 2, any code word not representing 'space' or 'u' occurs in the string, the process terminates and the system signals that the string does not contain the word 'success'; and a similar rejection condition applies at all subsequent nodes. Transition from node 3 to node 4 occurs when either 'c' or 'x' occurs in the string. The process remains at node 4 if 'space' or 'c' or 's' occurs. The letter 'e' causes transition from node 4 to node 5. Alternatively, 'k' causes transition from node 4 to node 7. The system signals that the input string contains a variant of the word 'success' if and only if the process is at node 6 after the last code word in the string has been reached.

'succccccesssssss', 'suxcsc scscsccs e ss s', etc.,

would be recognised as versions of 'success', but probably no semantically different word would be recognised as 'success'. Nodes 7 and 8 allow combinations of letters such as in 'suckses', but 'k' must be followed by 's'. Figure 6.12 has been designed to require that 'k' be followed by 's' merely to illustrate the implementation of such a requirement.

To introduce a very simple hardware embodiment of Figure 6.12, let us assume that successive code words emerge from the character recognition machine at regular unit time intervals, and let us ignore any time delays inherent in the operation of logic elements. The hardware uses unit time delay elements. For a unit time delay element, a plot of output signal versus time differs from a plot of input signal versus time only in that the output is delayed by one unit of time with respect to the input. A unit time delay element is represented by a rectangular box in Figure 6.13.

When the first 7-bit code word emerges from the character recognition machine, a logical '1' pulse of unit length is applied to the *or* gate which is labelled 'starter pulse' in Figure 6.13. *Logical 1* means the voltage which represents *true,* and *logical 0* means the voltage which represents *false*. If the first code word to emerge from the character recognition machine represents 'space', the input to delay element 'A' is logical 1. The input to delay element 'A' continues to be logical 1 so long as successive code words emerging from the character recognition machine represent 'space'. If after some number (possibly zero) of spaces the next code word represents 's' the input to delay element 'B' is logical 1. The input to delay element 'B' continues to be logical '1' so long as successive words represent 'space'. If after some number (possibly zero) of spaces the next code word represents 'u', and then if after some number (possibly zero) of spaces the next code word represents either 'c' or 'x', the input to delay element 'D' is logical 1, and so on. It is easy to see that the output from the delay element labelled 'F' in Figure 6.13 is logical 1 if and only if the Figure 6.12 sequential process is at node 6. For a sequence of letters such as scusxes the output of delay element 'F' in Figure 6.13 is never logical 1. Figure 6.13 presupposes that each 7-bit code word is decoded, that is, transformed into a representation in which there is a separate channel for each different character which a code word can represent, and in which only one such channel is at logical 1 at any given time. Figure 6.13 also presupposes that signals in these channels remain at logical 1 for one unit of time.

In Section 8.3 we shall have more to say about recognition systems of this sort.

6.6 DECISION MAKING STRATEGIES

We now briefly consider some sequential decision making strategies which are applicable in numerical discriminant systems.

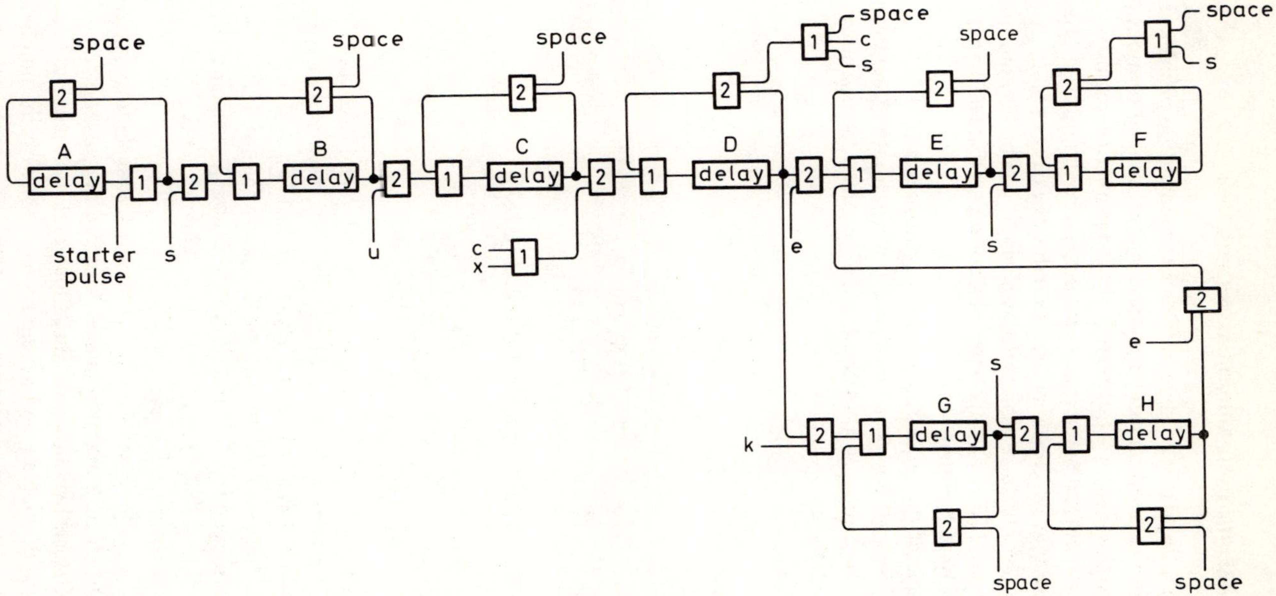

Figure 6.13. *A simple hardware implementation of the system whose transition diagram is shown in Figure* 6.12

6.6.1 Sequential probability ratio test

For simplicity, let us consider a two-class recognition problem in which recognition is based on results of various tests applied to input patterns. In the simplest case a set of tests is chosen prior to recognition. The tests are performed on an input pattern in a predetermined order, and we assume that we can compute estimates of $P(R_1/X)$ and $P(R_2/X)$ from the test results. For instance, we would be able to compute $P(R_1/X)$ and $P(R_2/X)$ if the test results were statistically independent or normally distributed.

The idea of the sequential probability ratio test[155, 156, 453] is that after a few of the tests have been performed, we compute $P(R_1/X)$ and $P(R_2/X)$ from the results of these tests. We assign the unknown pattern X to R_1 or R_2 according as

$$\frac{P(R_1/X)}{P(R_2/X)} > \rho_1 \tag{6.15}$$

or

$$\frac{P(R_1/X)}{P(R_2/X)} < \rho_2 \tag{6.16}$$

where ρ_1 and ρ_2 are prescribed thresholds. If

$$\rho_2 < \frac{P(R_1/X)}{P(R_2/X)} < \rho_1 \tag{6.17}$$

we perform a further test on the input pattern and take the results of this test, together with the results of previous tests, as data for a new computation of $P(R_1/X)$ and $P(R_2/X)$. If (6.17) is still found to be true, a further test is performed on the input pattern, $P(R_1/X)$ and $P(R_2/X)$ are recomputed, and so on. Otherwise X is assigned to R_1 or R_2 according as (6.15) or (6.16) is true. Wald's theory[453] leads to specific values of ρ_1 and ρ_2.

In this technique, tests are performed successively until a fairly confident recognition can be made. To avoid the possibility of the number of tests becoming infinite, Chien and Fu[77] and Fu[155] suggested that ρ_2 should increase and ρ_1 should decrease with the number of tests performed. The general advantage of a sequential probability ratio test is that on average it performs fewer tests than a parallel system using the same repertoire of tests, the same formula for estimating $P(R_1/X)$ and $P(R_2/X)$, and achieving the same reject and substitution error rates.

6.6.2 Cascaded decision making

In the sequential probability ratio test, different unknown patterns may be subjected to different numbers of tests during recognition. We now consider a technique which is applicable *after all* of the tests in a fixed repertoire of tests have been performed. In this technique, different unknown patterns are always subjected to *all* of a fixed set of tests.

Let us consider, for example, a piecewise linear system as in Section 4.1, employing 10 weight vectors for each recognition class. If $\boldsymbol{Y} \cdot \boldsymbol{W}_{rj}$ is computed for all $r = 1, \ldots, z$ and $j = 1, \ldots, 10$ in turn, this will be a fairly time-consuming process if z is large. To speed up the process of finding the largest $\boldsymbol{Y} \cdot \boldsymbol{W}_{rj}$, we compute the average weight vector

$\boldsymbol{W}'_r = \frac{1}{10}\sum_{j=1}^{10} \boldsymbol{W}_{rj}$ for $r = 1, \ldots, z$. We start the process of recognising an unknown pattern by computing $\boldsymbol{Y} \cdot \boldsymbol{W}'_r$ for $r = 1, \ldots, z$. We then compute $\boldsymbol{Y} \cdot \boldsymbol{W}_{rj}$ for each of the 10 weight vectors associated with each of the six classes which have the largest values of $\boldsymbol{Y} \cdot \boldsymbol{W}'_r$, and assign $\boldsymbol{X}$ to the class which has the largest $\boldsymbol{Y} \cdot \boldsymbol{W}_{rj}$. The $\boldsymbol{Y} \cdot \boldsymbol{W}_{rj}$'s are not computed for classes other than the six classes with the largest $\boldsymbol{Y} \cdot \boldsymbol{W}'_r$, and this may save time. *Six* is a number of classes which has been mentioned only by way of example. The smaller the number of classes with highest $\boldsymbol{Y} \cdot \boldsymbol{W}'_r$ for which we compute $\boldsymbol{W} \cdot \boldsymbol{Y}_{rj}$'s the greater the economy in time, but the higher the risk that the greatest $\boldsymbol{Y} \cdot \boldsymbol{W}_{rj}$ is associated with a class which has been ruled out because $\boldsymbol{Y} \cdot \boldsymbol{W}'_r$ is relatively small.

In Liu and Shelton's multifont print recognition system[283], which recognised 51 classes, $\boldsymbol{Y} \cdot \boldsymbol{W}_{rj}$'s were computed for the 10 classes with the highest $\boldsymbol{Y} \cdot \boldsymbol{W}_r$. The average number of weight vectors per class was nine, and the use of the two-stage process reduced by roughly 80% the time which would otherwise have been used in computing $\boldsymbol{Y} \cdot \boldsymbol{W}_{rj}$'s. A two-stage process of this type provides an example of *cascaded* decision making. The IBM 1975 uses a refined cascade process[37] and only computes $\boldsymbol{Y} \cdot \boldsymbol{W}_{rj}$ for approximately one in ten of the $\boldsymbol{W}_{rj}$'s in recognising an unknown pattern, as mentioned in Section 6.2.3. Casey and Nagy[72] have used cascaded decision making in the recognition of printed Chinese characters.

In a cascaded decision system, each stage (we hope) determines a set of recognition classes to which the input pattern does *not* belong; and recognition classes belonging to this set are not considered at subsequent stages of the cascade. Glucksman[174] has used a cascade process in which the second stage can be understood as follows. Glucksman has suggested that, if no member of the rth class training set is admitted by the first stage as a member of the sth class, then it is likely that no member of the rth class will be admitted by the first stage as a member of the sth class. In this case, if

(1) no member of the rth class training set has been admitted by the first stage as a member of the sth class, and
(2) for an unknown pattern X, the first stage admits both the rth and the sth classes

then X is unlikely to be a member of the rth class, and accordingly Glucksman's second stage rejects the rth class. In Glucksman's second stage, this rule is applied for all $r, s = 1, \ldots, z$.

6.6.3 Normalisation

Whilst studying sequential recognition, it is perhaps worthwhile to reconsider the normalisation techniques which were introduced in Section 2.3. These techniques are of two main types, characterised respectively by *exhaustive trial* and *measurement*. The Section 2.3.2 shift register technique is an example of an exhaustive trial technique, since alignments are tried in turn. A further example is provided by a commercial print recognition machine which, if it cannot confidently recognise a character, adjusts the binarising threshold and tries again. If it still cannot confidently recognise the character it adjusts the binarising threshold and tries again, and so on, until a binarising threshold is found which leads to confident recognition[11].

In *measurement* techniques, measurements are made on the input pattern and the pattern is normalised in accordance with these measurements, not by a process of trial and error. Centre of gravity and centre of black techniques illustrate this. A further measurement technique is that where we find the smallest rectangular box into which a character will just fit, and then adjust the size of the character so that the box becomes a standard size[353, 374]. This is essentially a two-stage recognition process.

For each size and position of the box, or, in other words, for each different box, there is a class of characters which will just fit snugly in the box. Let B_i be the class of all characters which will just fit in the ith box, and note that B_i includes patterns which belong to the z recognition classes $R_1, \ldots, R_r, \ldots, R_z$. In the first stage of the two-stage process of recognition, an unknown pattern X is classified as a member of one of the classes $B_1, \ldots, B_i, \ldots$. As a result of this classification X is (if necessary) altered in size and position so that it just fits into a standard box. The resulting pattern is then submitted to a set of resistor masks, or logic circuits, or to some other recognition system, which constitutes the second stage of the two-stage process of recognition.

If pattern X is a printed character, one of its limbs may be shortened due to imperfect printing, and as a result X may be assigned to the wrong one of the classes $B_1, \ldots, B_i, \ldots$. This can also happen if a spurious black mark lies very close to the character on the document. Assigning X to the *wrong* one of the classes $B_1, \ldots, B_i, \ldots$ *means* that X is altered to a size which is not the standard size for which the second-stage system has been designed. To avoid this we must redefine $B_1, \ldots, B_i, \ldots$ so that B_i is the class of characters which, after eliminating all spurious marks, and replacing all parts which are accidentally missing, will just fit in the ith box. The only safe way to recognise spurious black marks *as* spurious black marks is to recognise the character first, so that we know what its shape should be; and the same is true for the replacement of missing black parts of a character. This means that we cannot use the new definition of $B_1, \ldots, B_i, \ldots$ without first recognising X as belonging to one of $R_1, \ldots, R_z$. In other words, the first stage of the two-stage recognition process cannot safely be performed until after the second stage has reached a decision. In spite of this obvious logical and practical difficulty, normalisation by measurement is used commercially as outlined in Sections 2.3.1 and 2.3.3, and is tolerably successful in many applications.

Chapter 7

FEATURES

7.1 INTRODUCTION

In the automatic recognition of good-quality print such as that on the pages of this book, differences between members of any given recognition class arise mainly from the processes of transducing characters into discrete binary patterns[23a]. In the automatic recognition of poorer quality print, such as that which is produced by a high-speed printer or by an imperfect typewriter, important differences between members of any given recognition class may arise from differences in the accidents of printing, such as the spattering of ink, smudging, and distribution of voids. Hand-printed characters tend to have less spattering and fewer voids than low-quality machine-printed characters; and the differences between, for example, different hand-printed 2's are differences in distortion rather than in mutilation. The problem of recognising hand-printed characters is rather like a problem of recognising fairly good-quality machine-printed characters in an unlimited number of different fonts all mixed up together.

The recognition techniques which have been introduced in Chapters 3, 4, 5, and 6 are general techniques which have not been designed specifically to cope with major distortions of patterns..The present chapter introduces techniques which have been devised specifically for the recognition of characters printed by hand. Thus the present chapter is primarily concerned with the recognition of shapes which are subject to distortion.

7.2 ZONED FEATURES

7.2.1 Recognition in terms of edges

The Nippon Electric Company, a Japanese Company commonly referred to by the abbreviation NEC, have patented a system[337]* in which an

*To avoid giving an arbitrary name to this system we shall refer to it as *the* NEC system, although it is not the only hand-print recognition system patented by NEC (see for example Ref. 252a). Similarly, the Hitachi system which is introduced in Section 7.2.2.1 should not be assumed to be the only, or even the most successful, recognition system devised by Hitachi.

unknown pattern is brought into all possible alignments with a 3 x 3 window, using the Section 2.3.2 shift register technique. Let us denote the nine elements of the window by

$$\begin{matrix} x_1 & x_4 & x_7 \\ x_2 & x_5 & x_8 \\ x_3 & x_6 & x_9 \end{matrix}$$

and let us define four Boolean functions

$$V = x_4 . x_5 . x_6 . (\overline{x}_2 \vee \overline{x}_8) \qquad I = x_3 . x_5 . x_7 . (\overline{x}_1 \vee \overline{x}_9)$$

$$H = x_2 . x_5 . x_8 . (\overline{x}_4 \vee \overline{x}_6) \qquad D = x_1 . x_5 . x_9 . (\overline{x}_7 \vee \overline{x}_3)$$

The function V is *true* when the 3 x 3 window contains a roughly vertical piece of edge such as

$$\begin{matrix} 0 & 1 & 1 \\ 0 & 1 & 1 \\ 0 & 1 & 1 \end{matrix} \quad \text{or} \quad \begin{matrix} 1 & 1 & 1 \\ 1 & 1 & 0 \\ 1 & 1 & 0 \end{matrix} \quad \text{or} \quad \begin{matrix} 0 & 1 & 0 \\ 0 & 1 & 0 \\ 0 & 1 & 0 \end{matrix}$$

H, I, or D is *true* according as the window contains a roughly horizontal, or incrementally sloping, or decrementally sloping edge.

The 3 x 3 window scans through a total of 15 columns and 15 rows of pattern elements. This 15 x 15 array is partitioned into nine zones, each comprising 5 x 5 elements. We define four Boolean functions corresponding to each of the nine zones. For $i = 1, \ldots, 9$, the four functions corresponding to the ith zone are T_{iV}, T_{iH}, T_{iI}, and T_{iD}. Function T_{iV} is defined such that T_{iV} is *true* if and only if V is *true* for at least four positions of the centre element of the 3 x 3 window within the ith zone. Function T_{iH} is defined such that T_{iH} is *true* if and only if H is *true* for at least four positions of the centre element of the 3 x 3 window within the ith zone, and the others T's are defined similarly. Since there are nine zones and four T's per zone, an input pattern is transformed into a 36-element binary pattern, in which each element corresponds to one of the T's. The 36-element binary pattern is recognised by means of Boolean discriminants. For example, indexing the nine zones

$$\begin{matrix} 1 & 2 & 3 \\ 4 & 5 & 6 \\ 7 & 8 & 9 \end{matrix}$$

the Boolean discriminant function for 3's is

$$\begin{aligned} f_3(X) = {} & \overline{T}_{1D} \cdot \overline{T}_{1V} \cdot \overline{T}_{1I} \cdot T_{1H} \cdot T_{2H} \cdot T_{3H} \cdot \overline{T}_{4D} \cdot \overline{T}_{4V} \cdot \overline{T}_{4I} \cdot \overline{T}_{4H} \\ & \cdot \overline{T}_{5D} \cdot \overline{T}_{5V} \cdot \overline{T}_{5I} \cdot T_{5H} \cdot (T_{6D} \vee T_{6V} \vee T_{6I} \vee T_{6H}) \\ & \cdot \overline{T}_{7D} \cdot \overline{T}_{7V} \cdot \overline{T}_{7H} \cdot \overline{T}_{8D} \cdot \overline{T}_{8V} \cdot T_{8H} \cdot \overline{T}_{9D} \cdot \overline{T}_{9H} \end{aligned}$$

An input pattern X is recognised as a '3' if $f_3(X)$ is *true*. This is merely a simple example showing what sort of Boolean discriminants are used.

Munson[323] and Munson *et al.*[324] have described a system which detects edges by means of peephole masks such as the one indicated in Figure 2.14. As mentioned in Section 2.4.2, a threshold circuit associated with each of these peephole masks gives a binary output. The peephole masks are grouped into 84 sets. All peephole masks which belong to any given set have the same orientation and are positioned within the same small zone of the 24 x 24 element input pattern. The 84 sets correspond to 84 different choices of orientation of the peephole masks and position of the zone. The binary outputs from all of the threshold circuits associated with peephole masks which belong to any given one of the 84 sets are *or*'ed together. Thus a 24 x 24 element input pattern is transformed into an 84-bit pattern in which, for $j = 1, \ldots, 84$, the jth bit is '1' if the output of the threshold circuit for at least one of the peephole masks in the jth zone-and-orientation is '1', and '0' otherwise. The 84-bit pattern is recognised piecewise linearly.

The systems of Munson *et al.* and NEC transform an input pattern into a new pattern by means of edge detection, and we shall now discuss the advantages of this. Suppose for example that one million different hand-printed 2's are subjected to such a transformation. It is hoped that the number of different patterns resulting from this transformation will be very much less than one million, or, in other words, that there will be less variability among patterns resulting from this transformation than among input patterns. One reason for employing the transformation is to achieve a reduction of variability, and a less important reason is to reduce the number of elements in the patterns which are subjected to the final processes of recognition.

To see *how* an edge-detection transformation reduces variability, we must consider examples. For instance the 2's in Figures 7.1(a) and (b) might both produce, in the NEC system, $T_{1H}, T_{2H}, T_{3D}, T_{5H}, T_{6I}, T_{7I}, T_{7H}, T_{8H}, T_{9H}$ all *true* and all other T's *false*, so that Figures 7.1(a) and (b) would both be transformed into the same 36-bit pattern. When Figures 7.1(a) and (b) are binarised into 15 x 15 bit patterns, the Hamming distance between these two patterns is great. The way in which the transformation changes Figures 7.1(a) and (b) into the same 36-bit pattern is exemplified in the top left-hand zone. The line segment in this zone in Figure 7.1(a) slopes less and is higher than the segment in Figure 7.1(b), but the transformation ignores this difference. The Figure 7.1 example is unusual in that it produces the same output pattern from two input patterns. More commonly, in two different 2's, some, but not all, of the nine zones will contain line segments which will not be distinguished in this transformation.

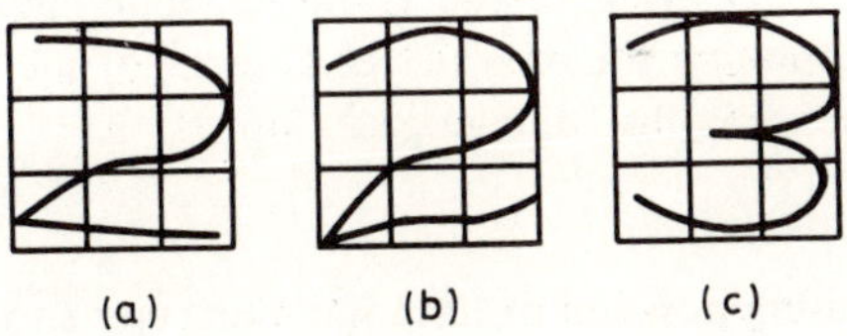

Figure 7.1.

An edge-detection transformation is unnecessarily elaborate for eliminating the differences between Figures 7.1(a) and (b). Instead we could simply binarise the characters on a 3 x 3 grid: if the total amount of black within one of the zones in Figure 7.1 exceeded a prescribed threshold, the corresponding bit in the 9-bit pattern would be '1' and otherwise '0'. The threshold could be chosen so that Figures 7.1(a) and (b) would yield the same 9-bit pattern. But Figure 7.1(c) would also produce this same 9-bit pattern, which would of course be disastrous. A transformation which is designed to ignore differences between members of the same recognition class must not ignore all differences between members of different recognition classes.

An edge detection system such as the NEC system might transform the '5' in Figure 7.2(a) and the '6' in Figure 7.2(b) into the same 36-bit pattern. One way of avoiding this type of disaster might be to work with a larger number of smaller zones; for instance 6 x 6 instead of 3 x 3. If each of the zones in Figure 7.1 were divided equally into four new zones, and if the new 6 x 6 zones were used in the same way as the 3 x 3 zones, Figures 7.1(a) and (b) would not both be transformed into the same 6 x 6 x 4 bit pattern, and thus the usefulness of the transformation would be reduced.

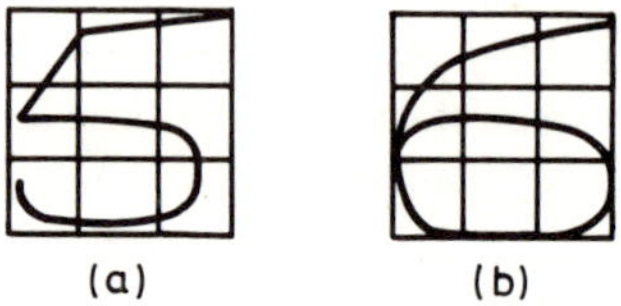

Figure 7.2.

The NEC system would ignore the fact that the middle left-hand zone contains a /– shape in Figure 7.2(b) but only a ∠ shape in Figure 7.2(a). Instead of attempting to resolve the confusion of Figures 7.2(a) and (b) by the use of smaller zones, we can attempt to resolve this confusion by detecting ├ and L shapes, limb ends, and so on, and base recognition on the presence or absence of such features from quite large zones, as in the following section.

7.2.2 Schemes using position of limb junctions and ends

7.2.2.1 Implementation

In 1959 Bomba[50] described a recognition system which worked with 60 x 90 element binary patterns. Peephole masks such as the five shown in Figure 7.3 were matched in all possible alignments with the input pattern. The small squares in Figure 7.3 correspond to pattern elements. For a peephole mask to *match* the unknown pattern in a given alignment,

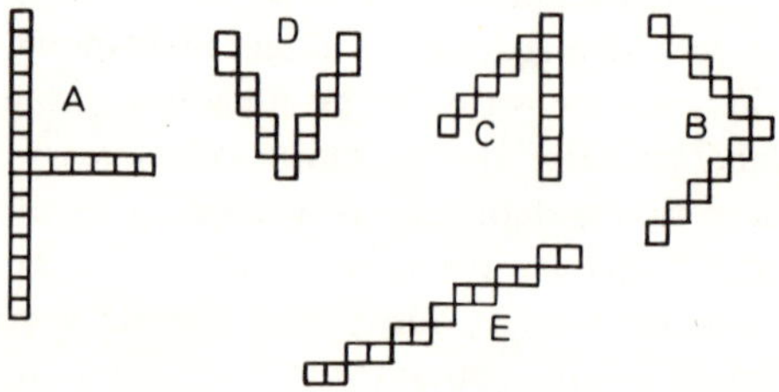

Figure 7.3. *Bomba's features*

all or almost all of the squares in that peephole mask had to coincide with *black* elements in the input pattern. In addition to the peephole masks shown in Figure 7.3, Bomba used peephole masks differing from that labelled 'A' in Figure 7.3 in that they were rotated through 180° and ±90° with respect to 'A'. Bomba also used 'B' and 'D' rotated through 180° and 'E' rotated through 90°, ±30°, ±45°, and ±60°. Mask 'E' detects a straight line, and a horizontal row of 15 elements would, for example, be one of the 'rotations' of 'E': the term 'rotation' is applied loosely because of the rectangular grid.

Bomba divided the 60 x 90 array into 3 x 3 zones, each of 20 x 30 elements. Characters were recognised by means of a decision tree as in Section 6.5.2. The questions at the nodes were such as 'does the input pattern match a vertical line peephole mask in every one of three vertically aligned zones?' and 'does the input pattern match a +90° or −90° rotation of peephole mask 'A' in any zone?', and so on. The tree had more than one terminal node for some of the recognition classes: to recognise 34 classes, Bomba's tree had 44 terminal nodes.

To reduce the numbers of noisy black and white bits in an input pattern, Bomba use a smoothing technique similar to Dineen's (Section 2.4.1). He then reduced all limb widths to approximately four pattern elements. This was necessary since the limb width of input characters varied from 4 to 10 pattern elements, and, for example, peephole masks such as those labelled 'A', 'B', 'C', or 'D' in Figure 7.3 would match any solitary vertical limb (as in the character '1') which was more than six elements wide. Bomba did *not* reduce limbs to single-element width as in Section 2.4.3 because, for example, slight curvature of the thinned limbs would prevent the peephole masks from matching the input pattern.

Whereas Bomba used non-overlapping rectangular zones, other workers have used radial zones as in Figure 7.4 [417] or overlapping rectangular zones[26].

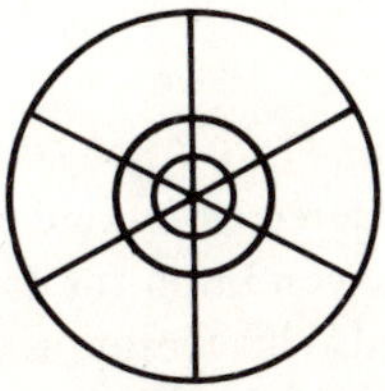

Figure 7.4. *Polar zones*

Parks[343] has described a system which uses features such as +, Y, Y, ├, L, V, L, and limb endings in all of the eight orientations 0°, 45°, 90°, . . ., 315°, except, for example, that only 0° and 45° orientations of the '+' feature are used, since its 0° and 90° orientations are indistinguishable. To avoid binarisation, Parks' system starts by making all possible alignments of the 0°, ±45°, and 90° orientations of the peephole mask

```
– – –
+ + +
– – –
```

with the *analogue* input pattern, cf. Figure 2.15 (p. 43). The output of the peephole mask in a particular orientation and alignment is the sum of the pattern elements coincident with the +'s minus half the sum of the elements coincident with the –'s. The system labels each pattern element *H, V, I*, or *D*, according as the horizontal, vertical, or incrementally or decrementally sloping peephole mask which is centred on that element produces the largest output; except that, if the greatest output is not greater than the least by at least a prescribed amount, then that element is left unlabelled, (cf. Refs 117, 229, and page 171 in Ref. 370).

A '+' feature is deemed present in the input pattern if

(1) at least four of the six elements in the zone marked 'α' in Figure 7.5(a) are labelled as indicated, and
(2) at least four of the six elements in the zone marked 'β' in Figure 7.5(a) are labelled as indicated, and
(3) at least four of the six elements in the zone marked 'γ' in Figure 7.5(a), are labelled as indicated, and
(4) at least four of the six elements in the zone marked 'δ' in Figure 7.5(a) are labelled as indicated, and
(5) *N*'s must occur at at least seven of the eight points labelled '*N*' in Figure 7.5(a).

'*N*' stands for 'neither *H* nor *V* nor *I* nor *D*'. As a further example to illustrate how features are detected by one of the versions of Parks' system, the following is the condition for detection of a leftward-pointing horizontal line end. This feature is deemed present if at least three of the four *H*'s and 21 of the 22 *N*'s in Figure 7.5(b) are detected in the input pattern.

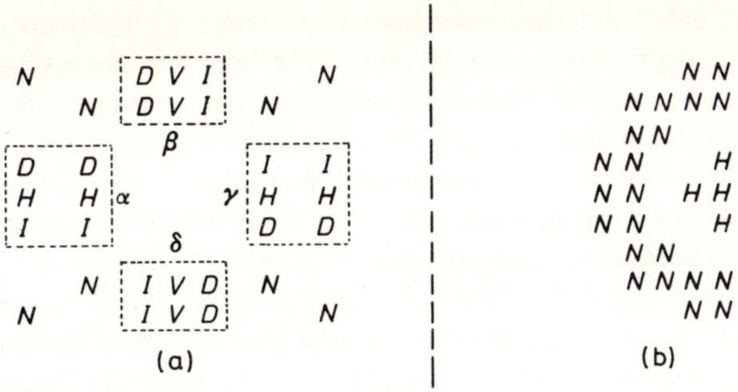

Figure 7.5. *Versions of Parks' features:* (*a*) '+' and (*b*) *leftward-pointing horizontal line end*

Parks has experimented with several recognition mechanisms. One of these is a decision tree in which the question at one node might be for example 'is there either an acute bend '∠' or a line ending pointing SW at the bottom left-hand corner of the character?'. Suppose that there is in fact an acute bend at the bottom left-hand corner. The system stores the position coordinates of this bend. The next node in the tree might ask, for example, 'is there a line-ending pointing E, NE, or SE anywhere within a rectangular zone five pattern elements high and eight wide, such that the bottom left-hand corner of this zone is situated three elements to the right and two elements below the position at which the feature at the previous node was located?'. This illustrates the idea of using the exact position of a feature to locate the zone in which the system searches for the features which are specified at the next node. The system generally uses a zone of different dimensions and location for each different node.

Hitachi[215], a Japanese Company, have patented a recognition system which detects features such as those indicated in Figure 7.6, where ! ,

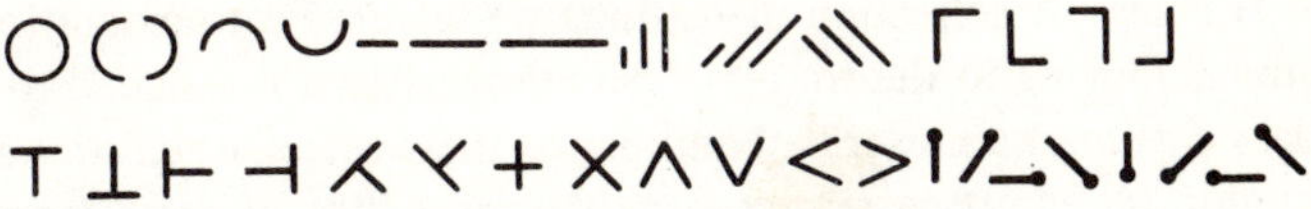

Figure 7.6. *Features used by Hitachi*

/ etc. represent variously orientated line endings. These features are detected optically in parallel, multiple images being formed for this purpose by means of mirror tunnels.

In discussing Bomba's and Parks' systems, we have not considered any procedures by which the system is *designed*. In the Hitachi system, part of the detailed design procedure is of interest. Both for the purposes of this procedure, and for the purposes of recognition, input characters are at least roughly positioned and (optically) size normalised so as just to fit into a standard rectangular box. The same design procedure is applied for all recognition classes and all features. By way of example, let us consider the recognition class '2', and the feature 'short horizontal line'. The procedure consists of examining, say, 50 different specimens of '2', and entering dots in the box shown in Figure 7.7(a) to record the positions of the centre of 'short horizontal line' in each of the specimen 2's. An envelope is then drawn round the dotted regions in Figure 7.7(a) to demarcate the regions labelled 'z' in Figure 7.7(b). The envelope can either be drawn manually by inspection of Figure 7.7(a), or alternatively the dots in Figure 7.7(a) can be optically defocused and photographed. The defocused spots can be superimposed photographically to yield a photograph which is transparent only in the regions marked 'z' in Figure 7.7(b).

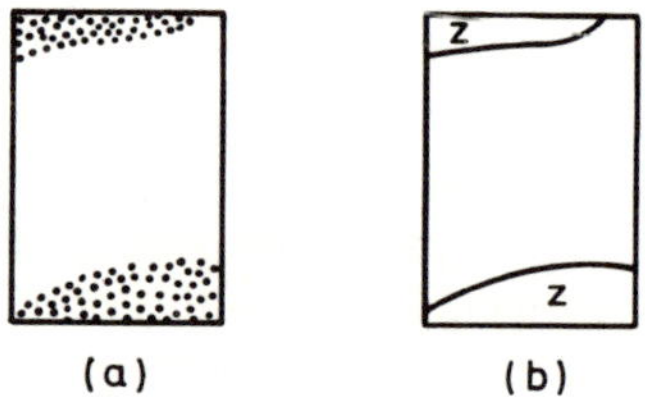

Figure 7.7. *Zone of occurrence*

The two regions marked 'z' in Figure 7.7(b) together constitute the *zone of occurrence* of '–' in '2', and we use this same term for the regions in which other features occur in other characters. The zones of occurrence, for example, of ' ⊃' in '2' and of '–' in '3' differ from the zone of occurrence of '–' in '2'.

A simplification of the recognition rules can be expressed in terms of the *r*th class. A collection of features are selected for recognition of patterns belonging to the *r*th class. An input pattern is assigned to the *r*th class if at least a prescribed number of these selected features are detected in the input pattern within their respective *r*th class zones of occurrence.

7.2.2.2 Discussion

Figure 7.8 shows copies of numerals written without constraint by different people[442]. We see that, for instance, when there is not a loop

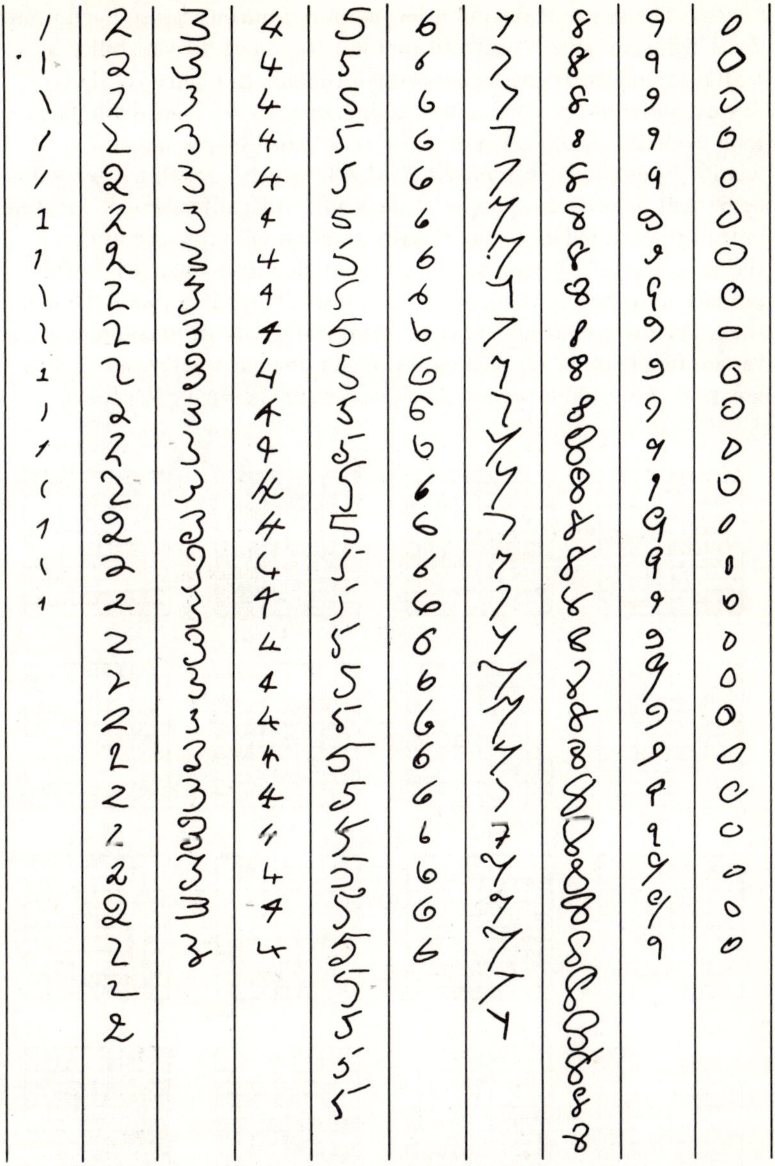

Figure 7.8. *Copies of numerals hand-printed by different people*

at the bottom left of a '2', there is not simply a standard '∠' shape instead. The shape of the lower left corner of unconstrained hand-printed 2's is highly variable[464]. As a further illustration of the variability of features in unconstrained hand-printed characters, Figure 7.9 shows a few examples of the portion where the upper stroke joins the bottom loop in closed-loop 6's. Figure 7.9 was obtained by placing a 12 x 12 window over sixteen 6's binarised 30 x 22 which were all written without constraint by different people[442]. It is quite difficult to design a feature detector which reliably signals that a junction of limbs such as that shown in Figure 7.9 is present in an input character when it is in fact present, and does not signal that it is present when it is absent. One of the problems is to decide what to count and what not to count as a variant of a feature. For instance, it is not obvious whether a near-miss junction |/ should be counted as a variant of the Figure 7.9 feature or

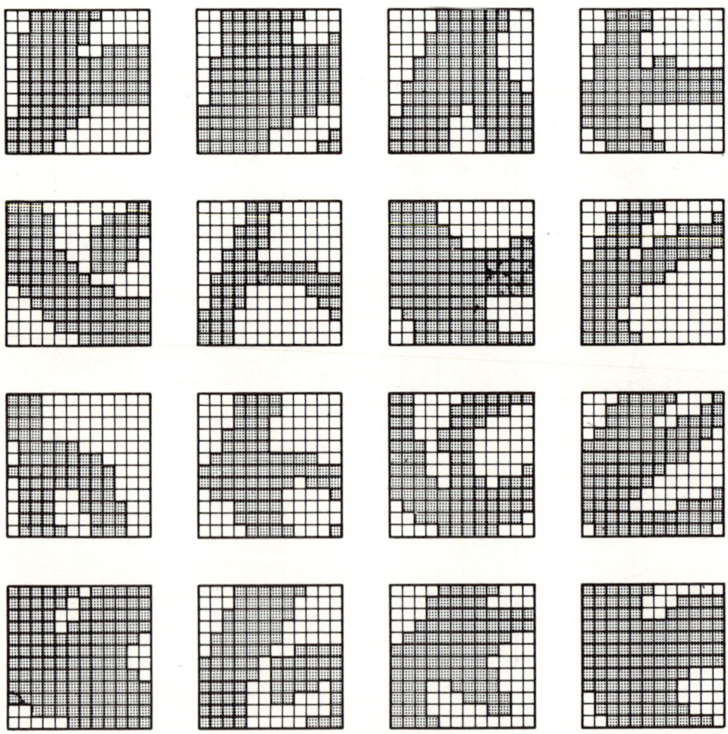

Figure 7.9. *Examples of limb junctions in the numeral* '6'

as a variant of a further feature, or perhaps not recognised as a variant of any feature. Such problems are resolved in practice by intuition and laborious experimental trial and error. Details of the more successful hand-printed character recognition machines which detect limb ends, bends, and junctions by methods like those of Section 7.2.2.1 do not appear to have been published, e.g. Refs 180a, 231a, and 400. But it is probably true to say first that these systems are restricted to the recognition of characters written in accordance with rules of constraint, and secondly that they use feature detectors which are considerably more elaborate than those mentioned in Section 7.2.2.1.

From Figure 7.8 we see, for example, that the line ending at the top left of an unconstrained hand-printed '3' may point in any direction, or be replaced by a small closed loop. In the Section 7.2.2.1 systems it may be necessary to detect roughly the orientation of this line ending, and then discard the information as to the orientation and merely record that some sort of line ending has been detected in the upper part of the character. The inefficiency of first acquiring and then discarding information, e.g. orientation information, is to some extent avoided in the recognition system which is the subject of Section 7.4.1.

7.3 GRAPH REPRESENTATION TECHNIQUES

7.3.1 Introduction

A *graph* consists of a finite non-empty set P of elements which are called *points,* and a set E of unordered pairs of distinct points which belong to P[201]. The two points which belong to any member of E are said to be mutually *adjacent*.

It is often helpful to represent a graph by a diagram in which each member of P is represented by a distinct dot or point, and each member of E is represented by a line between the two points to which it corresponds. A diagrammatic representation of a graph is itself called a *graph*, and a member of E is called a *line.* There is usually no difficulty in the ambiguous use of the terms *line, point,* and *graph* to mean either a pictorial representation of a line, point, or graph, or to mean that which is represented. In the pictorial representation of a graph, the positions of the points and the curvatures of the lines are chosen for intuitive convenience, and are not exactly determined by the mathematical definition of the graph. In this respect a graph differs from a pattern. The relative positions of the elements of a pattern are fixed: if we change the position of one element relative to all the others we generally change the pattern.

An *isomorphism* between the graph (P_1, E_1) and the graph (P_2, E_2) is a 1:1 correspondence between P_1 and P_2 such that any two points which are adjacent in (P_1, E_1) correspond to two points which are adjacent in (P_2, E_2), and any two points which are adjacent in (P_2, E_2) correspond to two points which are adjacent in (P_1, E_1). If there exists at least one isomorphism between (P_1, E_1) and (P_2, E_2), then (P_1, E_1) and (P_2, E_2) are *isomorphic.*

A simple, but generally impractical, method of determining whether two graphs (P_1, E_1) and (P_2, E_2) are isomorphic is as follows. First we arbitrarily assign index numbers 1, 2, . . ., p to the p points of P_1. We then construct the adjacency matrix of the graph (P_1, E_1). The adjacency matrix of the graph (P_1, E_1) is the matrix

$$\mathbf{A} = \begin{bmatrix} a_{11}, \ldots, a_{1j}, \ldots, a_{1p} \\ \vdots \quad\quad \vdots \quad\quad \vdots \\ a_{i1}, \ldots, a_{ij}, \ldots, a_{ip} \\ \vdots \quad\quad \vdots \quad\quad \vdots \\ a_{p1}, \ldots, a_{pj}, \ldots, a_{pp} \end{bmatrix}$$

in which, for $i, j = 1, \ldots, p$, $a_{ij} = 1$ if the ith and jth points of P_1 are adjacent and $a_{ij} = 0$ otherwise. Similarly, we index the points of P_2 and construct an adjacency matrix for the graph (P_2, E_2). If this adjacency matrix is not identical to the adjacency matrix $\mathbf{A}$, we index the points of P_2 differently and construct a new adjacency matrix for the graph (P_2, E_2). If this adjacency matrix is not identical to $\mathbf{A}$, we again index the points of P_2 differently and construct a new adjacency matrix for the graph (P_2, E_2), and so on, until the adjacency matrix of (P_2, E_2) is found to be identical to $\mathbf{A}$, or until the points of P_2 have been indexed in all of the $p!$ possible ways. If it is possible to index the points of P_2 such that the adjacency matrices of (P_1, E_1) and (P_2, E_2) are identical, then (P_1, E_1) and (P_2, E_2) are isomorphic. Except when p is small, the number, $p!$, of possible ways of indexing the points of P_2 is prohibitively large, and in practice we must use a more efficient procedure to determine whether two graphs are isomorphic[104].

The *degree* of a point in a graph (P, E) is the number of members of E to which that point belongs. Thus the sum of the entries in the ith row or the ith column of the adjacency matrix of (P, E) is the degree of the ith point of P.

7.3.2 Representation without using attributes

In a graph (P, E), E consists of pairs of distinct members of P, and therefore no line joins a point to itself. A *pseudograph* consists of a set P of points and a set of lines joining pairs of points which belong to P[201]. In a pseudograph, the two points which are joined by a line need not be distinct, so that loops are permitted; and furthermore two points may be joined by more than one line. For instance, Figure 7.10(a) is an example of a graph and Figure 7.10(b) is an example of a pseudograph. In the adjacency matrix of a pseudograph, the (i, j)th entry is the number of lines between the ith and jth points.

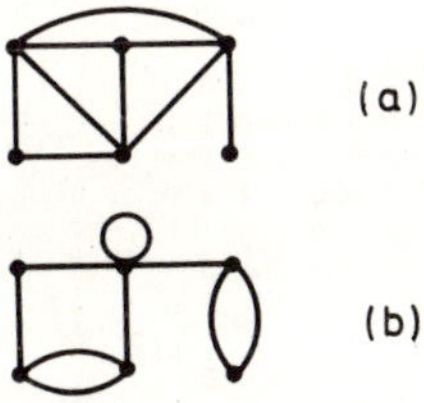

Figure 7.10. *Arbitrary examples of* (*a*) *a graph and* (*b*) *a pseudograph*

For purposes of character recognition, Sherman[404] thinned characters as in Section 2.4.3. Sherman regarded the thinned limbs of a character as the lines, and regarded the junctions and ends of the thinned limbs as the points, of a pseudograph. Bends and corners, that is, junctions of only two limbs, were ignored, so that a pseudograph contained no point of degree two. Limb ends and junctions of three or more limbs are arbitrarily labelled a, b, c, . . ., f in Figures 7.11(a), (b), and (c), and the pseudographs corresponding to Figures 7.11(a), (b), and (c) have seven, three, and three points respectively.

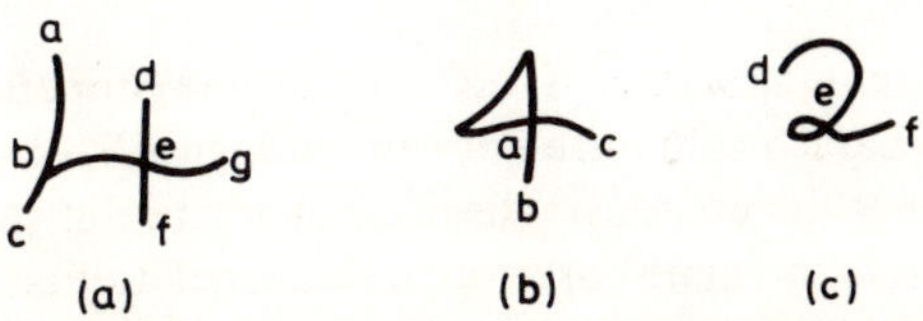

Figure 7.11. *Characters with Sherman's graph points arbitrarily labelled*

Sherman explored the idea that, if the pseudographs of two characters are isomorphic, this should be used as evidence for deciding that these two characters belong to the same recognition class. In Figure 7.12 each row includes a collection of characters whose pseudographs are mutually isomorphic. Figure 7.12 suggests that, except in special cases such as '8' and '0', pseudograph isomorphism is not an obviously useful property for distinguishing between character shapes, because there are too many different characters per row in Figure 7.12.

Characters	Adjacency matrix	Partition
3706521	01 10	2 x 1st
379521	0 0 0 1 0 0 0 1 0 0 0 1 1 1 1 0	3 x 1st, 1 x 3rd
475	0 0 0 0 1 0 0 0 0 1 0 0 0 0 1 0 0 0 0 1 1 1 1 1 0	4 x 1st, 1 x 4th
447	0 0 0 0 0 0 1 0 0 0 0 0 0 1 0 0 0 0 0 0 1 0 0 0 0 1 0 0 0 0 0 1 0 1 1 0 0 0 0 1 0 0 1 1 1 0 1 0 0	5 x 1st,1 x 3rd, 1 x 4th
4 1	0 1 0 0 0 0 1 0 1 0 1 0 0 1 0 1 0 1 0 0 1 0 0 0 0 1 0 0 0 0 0 0 1 0 0 0	4 x 1st, 2 x 3rd
42869	0 1 0 1 1 1 0 1 0	2 x.1st, 1 x 4th
0		no points
8	2	1 x 4th
86094	0 1 1 1	1 x 1st, 1 x 3rd

Figure 7.12. *Adjacency matrices and partitions for some hand-printed numerals*

Isomorphism is an unnecessarily complicated property for distinguishing between characters in different rows in Figure 7.12. Instead we can use the fact that the pseudographs of all characters in any given row in Figure 7.12 have the same partition, as indicated in that row, and that the partition for different rows is different[404]. The *partition* of a graph or pseudograph is a list of the degrees of the points of that graph or pseudograph[201]. For instance, the partition of Figure 7.10(a) is 4 + 4 + 4 + 3 + 2 + 1, and this can be written 3 x 4th, 1 x 3rd, 1 x 1st. (The fact that, in Figure 7.12, pseudographs which have the same partition are isomorphic, is only a fortuitous result of their simplicity. It is not generally true that graphs of pseudographs which have the same partition are isomorphic, e.g. 3 , 8 .)

7.3.3 Graph representation using attributes

Let us distinguish between the following three types of techniques.

(1) Rules are prescribed for constructing a graph or pseudograph from any given pattern. Let G_X be the graph or pseudograph which is constructed from an unknown pattern X, and let G_r be the graph or pseudograph which is constructed from a known reference pattern X_r. If G_X is isomorphic to G_r, this fact is used as evidence for assigning X to the same class as X_r.

(2) Rules are prescribed for constructing a graph or pseudograph from any given pattern, and further rules are prescribed for assigning attributes to each point and/or line of the graph or pseudograph. If there exists an isomorphism between G_X and G_r such that corresponding points and/or lines have the same attributes, then X is assigned to the same class as X_r.

(3) As in type (2), rules are prescribed for constructing a graph or pseudograph from any given pattern, and further rules are prescribed for assigning attributes to each point and/or line of the graph or pseudograph. If there exists an isomorphism between G_X and G_r such that the attributes of corresponding points and/or lines differ only within prescribed limits, then X is assigned to the same class as X_r.

Types (2) and (3) are just two of the possible generalisations of type (1). Type (1) is the special case of type (2) where there are no attributes, and type (2) is the special case of type (3) where is no tolerance for differences in attributes. Sherman's technique[404] is an example of type (1): perhaps a confusing example because a thinned character is used as a pictorial representation of its pseudograph. Barrow and Popplestone[30] have provided an example of a type (3) technique. The following paragraphs introduce, in a simplified form, the technique of Grimsdale *et al.*[190, 191], which provides a further example of a type (3) technique. The techniques of Sherman and Grimsdale *et al.* differ not only in their type, but also in their rules for constructing a graph from a pattern.

By means of a watchbird technique (*see* Section 7.4.2), Grimsdale *et al.*[190, 191] divided up a character into chunks of black such that no chunk contained a sharp bend or junction of limbs. For instance an 'R' might be divided up as in Figure 7.13(a), where the six chunks are arbitrarily indexed a, b, . . ., f. For a given character, Grimsdale *et al.* (in effect) constructed a graph in which there was one point per chunk,

Figure 7.13. *(a) A segmented character; (b) Graph constructed from Figure* 7.13*(a)*

and two points were joined by a line only if they corresponded to touching chunks. The graph constructed from Figure 7.13(a) is shown in Figure 7.13(b). As a further example, Figures 7.14(a) and (b) show respectively a stylised '2' and a stylised '5', and each of these is divided

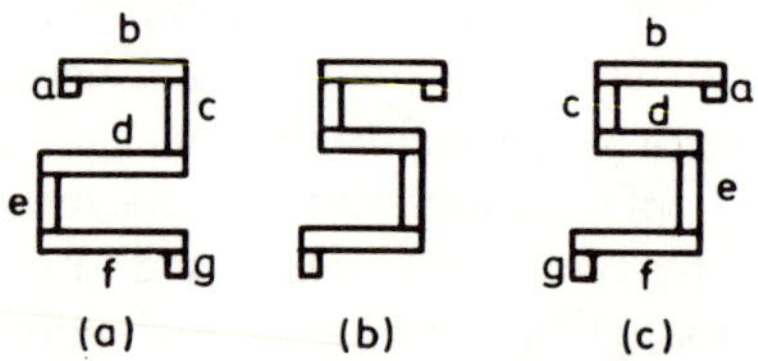

Figure 7.14. *Segmented stylised characters*

up into seven chunks. The chunks in Figure 7.14(a) are arbitrarily labelled a, b, . . ., g. The adjacency matrix for the graph constructed from Figure 7.14(a) is

	a	b	c	d	e	f	g
a	0	1	0	0	0	0	0
b	1	0	1	0	0	0	0
c	0	1	0	1	0	0	0
d	0	0	1	0	1	0	0
e	0	0	0	1	0	1	0
f	0	0	0	0	1	0	1
g	0	0	0	0	0	1	0

the rows and columns being labelled to show which row and column corresponds to which chunk. The information which is set out in the adjacency matrix can be expressed more concisely in the form of an adjacency table which has one row per chunk. For instance, the sixth row of Table 7.1 tells us that chunk f touches chunks e and g.

Table 7.1. ADJACENCY TABLE FOR FIGURE 7.14(a)

a	b
b	a, c
c	b, d
d	c, e
e	d, f
f	e, g
g	f

In the system of Grimsdale *et al.*, attributes were associated with each point and with each line in the graph which was constructed from a given character. The attributes associated with a point were measurements of the length, curvature, and orientation of the chunk corresponding to that point. We shall not give full details of the attributes of lines, but shall introduce the following simplification, for use in the Figure 7.14 example. In this simplification, each line in the graph has one of four possible attributes, TL, TR, BL, or BR. A line has the attribute TL if the points which it joins represent a roughly vertical and a roughly horizontal chunk, such that the *top* end of the vertical chunk touches the *left* end of the horizontal chunk. A line has the attribute BR if the points which it joins represent a roughly vertical and a roughly horizontal chunk, such that the *bottom* end of the vertical chunk touches the *right* end of the horizontal chunk. Similarly, TR and BL indicate *top right* and *bottom left* joins. Table 7.2 shows the attributes associated with the lines in the graph constructed from Figure 7.14(a). For instance, the entry in the column headed 'TR' and the row headed 'c' signifies that the *top* of chunk 'c' is connected to the *right* end of chunk 'b'.

The following is a simplification of one of the methods of recognition. For each recognition class, graphs and attributes are obtained from training set patterns and stored. Let G_{ri} be the graph obtained from the *i*th pattern in the *r*th class training set. A graph G_X and attributes are

Table 7.2. JOIN-CLASSIFIED ADJACENCY TABLE FOR FIGURE 7.14(a)

	TL	TR	BL	BR
a	b			
b	a	c		
c		b		d
d	e			c
e	d		f	
f		g	e	
g		f		

obtained from an unknown pattern X and X is assigned to the rth class if there exists an isomorphism between G_X and G_{ri} such that

(1) the attributes (length, curvature, and orientation) associated with corresponding points in G_X and G_{ri} differ only within prescribed limits, and
(2) the attributes (TL, TR, BL, BR) associated with corresponding lines in G_X and G_{ri} are identical.

To illustrate the usefulness of condition (2), suppose that Figure 7.14(a) is a training set pattern whose graph and attributes have been stored, and suppose that Figure 7.14(b) is an unknown pattern which is to be recognised. It is possible to index the chunks of Figure 7.14(b), as shown in Figure 7.14(c), such that the adjacency table of the graph constructed from Figure 7.14(c) is identical to Table 7.1, and let us assume that this isomorphism satisfies condition (1). Thus the lengths, curvatures, and orientations of the chunks labelled 'a' in Figures 7.14(a) and (c) differ only within prescribed limits; the lengths, curvatures and orientations of the chunks labelled 'b' in Figures 7.14(a) and (c) differ only within prescribed limits, and so on. However, condition (2) is not satisfied, because the join-classified adjacency table constructed from Figure 7.14(c) is not identical to Table 7.2. Thus Figure 7.14(c), which is a stylised '5', is not assigned to the same recognition class as Figure 7.14(a), which is a stylised '2'.

7.3.4 Graphs with points corresponding to single black bits

In the present section, a point in a graph corresponds not to a chunk of black but to a single black bit in a binary pattern, and a line in a graph corresponds to a pair of black bits. As in the technique of Grimsdale *et al.*, an attribute is associated with each line. Specifically, in the present section, the attribute associated with a line is the relative position of the two bits which correspond to that line. By working with single bits we obtain finer control over character shape than is possible in a technique such as that of Grimsdale *et al.*, and since there is no segmentation into chunks, there is no risk of *erroneous* segmentation into chunks.

As usual, let X_{ri} be the *i*th pattern in the *r*th class training set, and let X be an unknown pattern. We construct a graph, G_{ri}, whose points correspond 1:1 to the black bits in X_{ri}, and whose lines correspond to arbitrarily chosen pairs of black bits in X_{ri}. We assign X to the *r*th class if

> it is possible to construct a graph G_X whose points correspond 1:1 to the black bits in X, such that
> (1) there exists an isomorphism between G_X and G_{ri} such that
> (2) the relative position of the two bits in X_{ri} which correspond to any given line in G_{ri} differs only within prescribed limits from the relative position of the two bits in X which correspond to the corresponding line in G_X.
>
> (7.1)

We find it convenient to prescribe the allowed variations of relative position of pairs of corresponding points by explicitly listing the allowed variations of relative position. Let L be the list of allowed relative positions. In order to re-state (7.1) precisely in terms of L, and in order to prepare for Section 7.3.5, we now make some definitions.

A *bit location* is a location which may contain either a *black* or a *white* element of a pattern. Let S be the array of bit locations on which the binary pattern X_{ri} is written, and let T be the array of bit locations on which X is written. Let Q be the set of all pairs of bit locations, such that in any member of Q one bit location belongs to S and the other to T. Let $F_{ri} = \{F_{ri1}, \ldots, F_{rij}, \ldots, F_{ri\phi}\}$ be the set of all pairs of black bits in X_{ri} which correspond 1:1 to lines in G_{ri}. We shall denote elements of S by α's and elements of T by β's. For $j = 1, \ldots, \phi$, let α_{j1}, α_{j2} be the locations of the two black bits in F_{rij}. In a 1:1 correspondence between the black bits of X and X_{ri}, let β_{j1} and β_{j2} respectively be the bit locations in T which correspond to α_{j1} and α_{j2}. We assign X to the rth class if

$$\left.\begin{array}{l}\text{there exists a 1:1 correspondence between the black bits of}\\ X \text{ and } X_{ri} \text{ such that, for all } j = 1, \ldots, \phi,\\ \qquad\qquad \{\{\alpha_{j1}, \beta_{j1}\}, \{\alpha_{j2}, \beta_{j2}\}\} \in L\end{array}\right\} \quad (7.2)$$

where $\in$ means *belongs to.* If $\{\{\alpha_{j1}, \beta_{j1}\}, \{\alpha_{j2}, \beta_{j2}\}\} \in L$, then the relative position of α_{j1} and α_{j2} differs only within prescribed limits from the relative position of β_{j1} and β_{j2}: we prescribe the limits of variation of relative position by prescribing the set L. If X is assigned to the rth class by (7.2) then X is also assigned to the rth class by (7.1). The statement of (7.1) is looser and more general than the statement of (7.2).

To illustrate (7.2), suppose that X_{ri} is the '5' shown in Figure 7.15(a), and that the members of F_{ri} are the 14 pairs of bits which are indicated by lines in Figure 7.15(b). The black bits in Figure 7.15(b) are indexed 1, 2, . . ., 12. Two heavy squares joined by a dotted line in any of Figures 7.16(a), . . ., (k) indicate a pair $\{\alpha_i, \beta_k\}$ or a pair $\{\alpha_j, \beta_h\}$. In the present example we stipulate that, if the relative position of α_i and α_j is as shown on S and the relative position of β_k and β_h is as shown on T, in Figure 7.16(a), then $\{\{\alpha_i, \beta_k\}, \{\alpha_j, \beta_h\}\} \in L$. If the relative position of α_i and α_j is as shown on S, and the relative position of β_k and β_h is as shown on T, in Figure 7.16(b), then $\{\{\alpha_i, \beta_k\}, \{\alpha_j, \beta_h\}\} \in L$. In the same way,

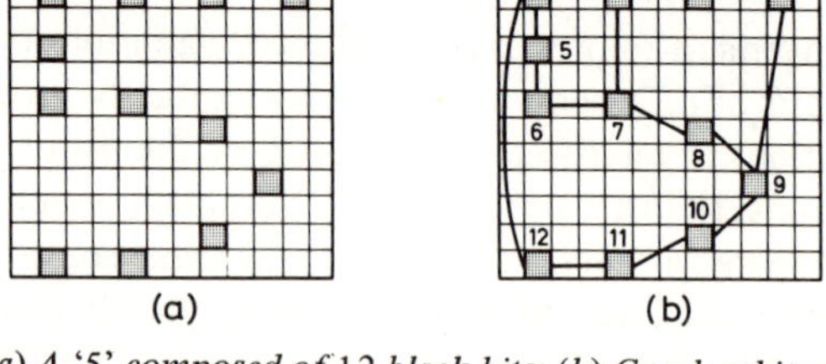

Figure 7.15. *(a) A '5' composed of* 12 *black bits; (b) Graph arbitrarily constructed from Figure* 7.15*(a)*

further members of L are defined in terms of Figures 7.16(c), (d), . . ., (k). We also stipulate that, if the relative position of β_k and β_h is the *same* as the relative position of α_i and α_j, then $\{\{\alpha_i, \beta_k\}, \{\alpha_j, \beta_h\}\} \in L$. In this example, the set L has no members other than those which we have stipulated. The only patterns which are recognised as '5' via

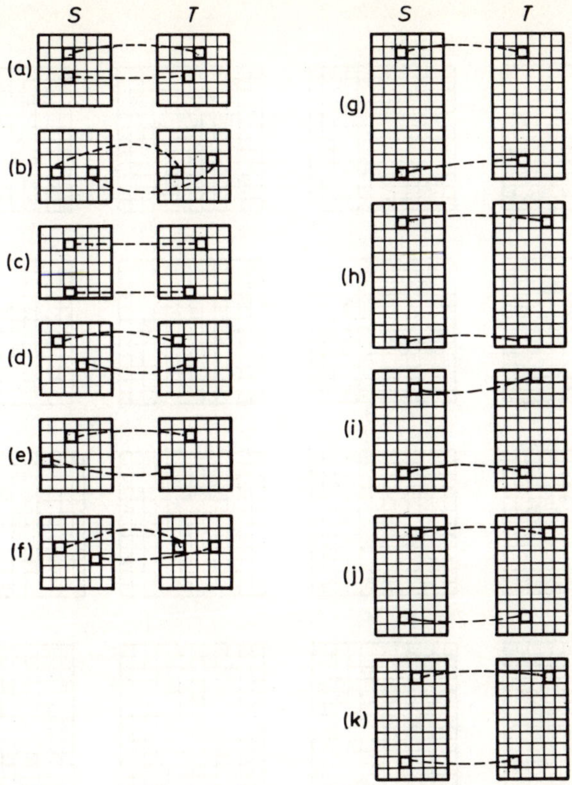

Figure 7.16. *Allowed variations of relative positions of points. Only parts of S and T are shown*

Figure 7.15(b) by (7.2) are the 47 patterns which are shown in Figure 7.17 and any pattern which differs from any one of the Figure 7.17 patterns only in shift.

[To *generate* the Figure 7.17 patterns, we can first generate all patterns which (7.2) would assign to the rth class *if* the pairs $\{4, 12\}$, $\{3, 7\}$, and $\{1, 9\}$ did not belong to F_{ri}. This is straightforward because in a generated pattern the relative position of the bits corresponding to $\{11, 12\}$ in Figure 7.15(b) does not depend on the relative position of the bits corresponding to $\{10, 11\}$, which does not depend on the relative position of the bits corresponding to $\{9, 10\}$, and so on. We can then reinstate $\{4, 12\}$, $\{3, 7\}$, and $\{1, 9\}$ in F_{ri} and reject any of the generated patterns which would not be recognised by (7.2).]

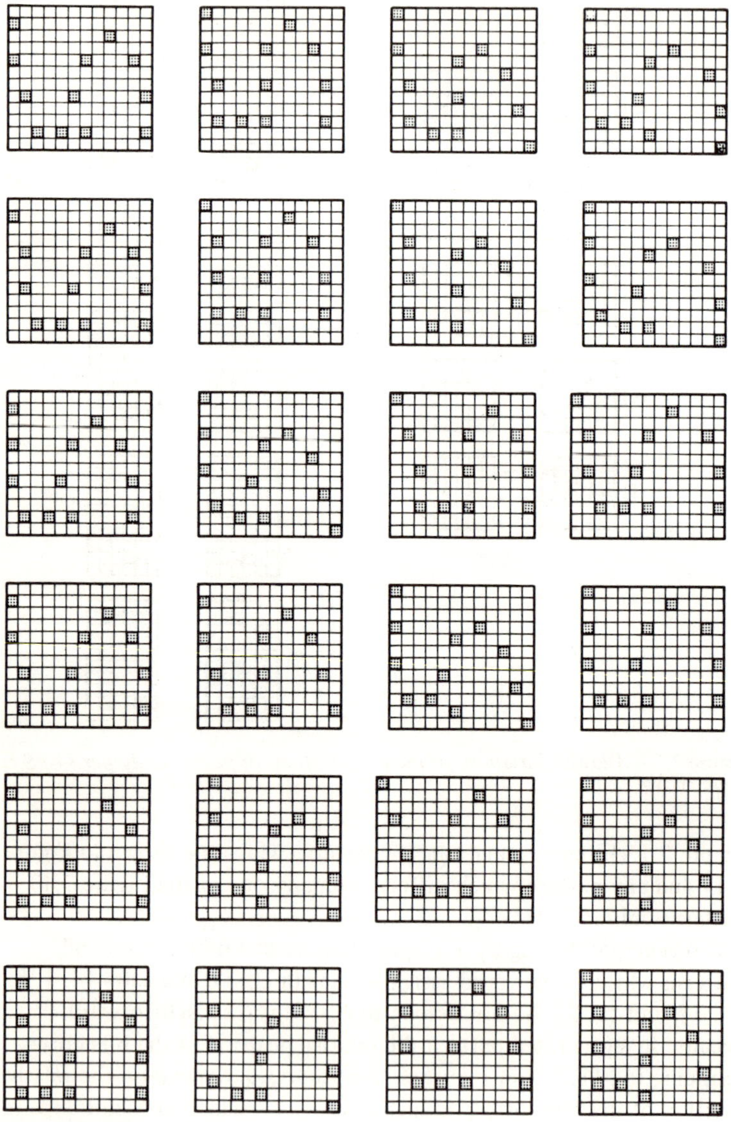

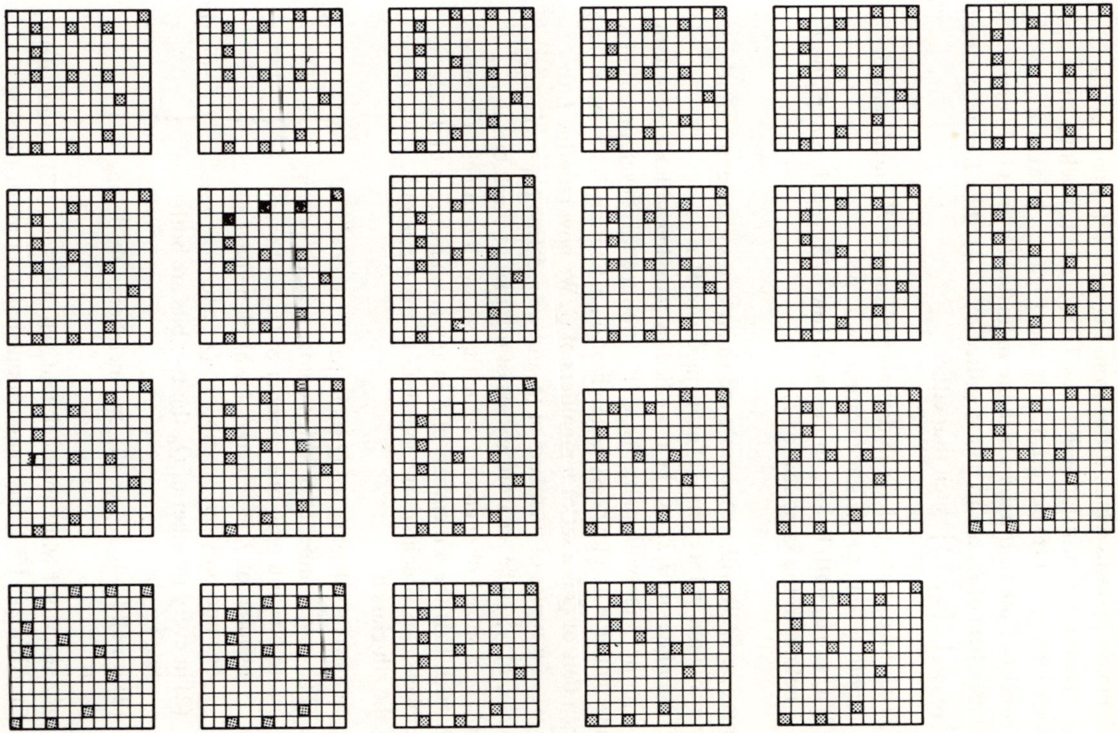

Figure 7.17. *Characters recognised as '5' by rule (7.2) via Figure 7.15(b)*

To illustrate one of the limitations on the set of all classes of patterns which can possibly be recognised by (7.2), let R_r be the class of all binary patterns which differ from Figure 7.18(a) only in size and/or position. For instance, Figures 7.18(c) and (d) belong to R_r and Figures 7.18(e) and (f) do not. Let us take Figure 7.18(a) as X_{ri}, and let F_{ri} consist of the four pairs which are indicated by lines in Figure 7.18(b). If all members of R_r are to be recognised by (7.2), then L must contain *all* $\{\{\alpha_i, \beta_h\}, \{\alpha_j, \beta_k\}\}$ such that either

(1) α_i and α_j both belong to the same column of S, and β_h and β_k both belong to the same column of T, or
(2) α_i and α_j both belong to the same row of S, and β_h and β_k both belong to the same row of T.

In this case (7.2) will erroneously recognise non-square configurations such as Figures 7.18(e) and (f) as members of R_r.

This failure of (7.2) can be remedied by working with n-tuples with $n > 2$, rather than with pairs. We shall introduce this development in a manner which will allow easy generalisation in Section 7.3.5. An *n-tuple* of members of Q is a set of n members of Q. We now redefine L to be a set of n-tuples of members of Q, and we redefine $F_{ri} = \{F_{ri1}, \ldots, F_{rij}, \ldots, F_{ri\phi}\}$ to be an arbitrary set of n-tuples of black bits in X_{ri}. Let Q_c be a subset of Q and let Φ_j be the set of all n-tuples of members of Q_c such that the n members of S in any given member of Φ_j are the n members of S which are the locations of the n bits in F_{rij}. We assign X to the rth class if

> there exists a subset Q_c of Q such that
> (1) every member of S which contains black belongs to one and only one member of Q_c, and every member of T which contains black belongs to one and only one member of Q_c, and
> (2) in every member of Q_c the two bits are both black; and
> (3) for all $j = 1, \ldots, \phi$, the one member of Φ_j belongs to L. (7.3)

It is easy and worthwhile to check that, when $n = 2$, (7.3) is equivalent to (7.2). Although (7.3) has been formulated in terms of the single training set pattern X_{ri}, an unknown pattern X can be assigned to the rth class if (7.3) is satisfied for *any* of the rth class training set patterns $X_{r1}, \ldots, X_{ri}, \ldots, X_{rt_r}$.

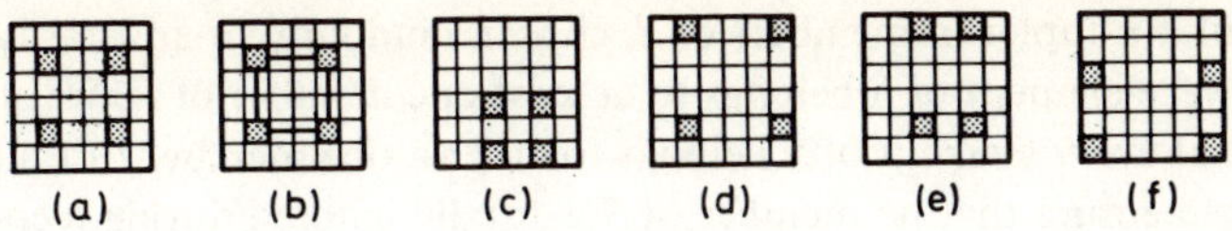

Figure 7.18.

A list of all of the members of a set *extensively* defines that set. Another way of defining a set is to specify a property possessed by all of the members, and by no non-members of that set. A set which is defined in this way is defined *intensively.* Figure 7.16 provides an extensive definition of the set L which is used in the Figure 7.17 example (except that Figure 7.16 explicitly lists only the relative, not the absolute, positions of pairs of elements of S and T). We now give an example in which the set L is defined intensively, and the economic problems of extensive definition are thereby avoided. In this example we intensively define L to be the set of all n-tuples

$$\{\{\alpha_1, \beta_1\}, \ldots, \{\alpha_h, \beta_h\}, \{\alpha_i, \beta_i\}, \{\alpha_j, \beta_j\}, \{\alpha_k, \beta_k\}, \ldots, \{\alpha_n, \beta_n\}\}$$

such that, for all $h, i, j, k = 1, \ldots, n$, if $d'_{hi} < d'_{jk}$ then $d_{hi} < d_{jk} + e$, where e is a constant, d_{hi} is the Euclidean distance between α_h and α_i, and d'_{hi} is the Euclidean distance between β_h and β_i. If $n = 4$ and the set $\{F_{ri1}, \ldots, F_{ri\phi}\}$ consists of all possible 4-tuples of black bits of X_{ri}, then (7.3), using this set L, makes the same classification decisions as a rule proposed by Simon *et al.*[407b], using the same training set patterns and value of e. By changing the value of e, we intensively define different sets L; but the total number of different sets L which we can define in this way is very much smaller than the total number of sets L which we can (in principle) define extensively. To avoid restriction on the choice of the set L, and for logical simplicity, L will be defined extensively in the following section.

7.3.5 Black bits and white bits

A pattern X can be assigned to the rth class by (7.1), (7.2), or (7.3) only if X and X_{ri} have the same number of black bits. We now generalise (7.3) so that 1:1 correspondence between the black bits of X and X_{ri} is no longer necessary. For this purpose we find it expedient to make active use of white bits as well as black bits.

As in Section 7.3.4, the pattern X is on the array S, and the pattern X_{ri} is on the array T. Again, L is a set of n-tuples of members of Q, and F is a set of ϕ n-tuples of members of S, chosen randomly or arbitrarily except that every element of S belongs to at least one member of F. We stipulate that every element of S belongs to at least one member of F in order to ensure that no member of S is totally ignored during recognition. Q_c is a subset of Q, and for $j = 1, \ldots, \phi$, Φ_j is the set of all n-tuples of members of Q_c such that the n members of S in any member of Φ_j are the members of S which constitute the jth member, F_j, of F.

A generalisation of (7.3) is: assign X to the rth class if there exists a subset Q_c of Q such that

$$\left.\begin{array}{l} \text{(1) every member of } S \text{ belongs to at least one member of} \\ \quad Q_c\text{, and every member of } T \text{ belongs to at least one} \\ \quad \text{member of } Q_c\text{, and} \\ \text{(2) in every member of } Q_c \text{ the two bits are both black} \\ \quad \text{or both white, and} \\ \text{(3) for all } j = 1, \ldots, \phi\text{, every member of } \Phi_j \text{ belongs to } L. \end{array}\right\} \quad (7.4)$$

We shall arrive at (7.4) from first principles in Section 10.3.

To illustrate (7.4) we use a one-dimensional example, since a two-dimensional example would contain too many bits to be worked by hand. In our example X_{ri} is the 9-bit pattern which is shown in Figure 7.19(a), where black and white bits are represented by '1' and '0' respectively. In our example, $n = 3$, and F consists of the four triples labelled F_1, F_2, F_3, and F_4 in Figure 7.19(b). The set L is the union of two sets L_1 and L_2. Figure 7.19(c) represents a member of L_1, three members of Q being indicated by dotted lines. L_1 consists of *all* triples of members of Q such that the three members of S have relative positions as shown on S in Figure 7.19(c), and the three members of T have the relative positions shown on T in Figure 7.19(c), where heavy squares represent bit locations. L_2 consists of all triples of members of Q such that the members of S have relative positions as shown on S in Figure 7.19(d), and the three members of T have relative positions as indicated in Figure 7.19(d).

By specifying X_{ri}, F, and L, we specify the class of patterns which will be recognised by (7.4). To obtain an intuitive impression of the efficacy of (7.4), we wish to look at the complete set of all patterns which (7.4) recognises; and in order to look at this set we must first generate its members. This can be done by means of the following two steps.

Suppose that the pattern X_{ri} on S and the pattern X on T are such that X is assigned to the rth class by (7.4) and let us consider a set Q_c

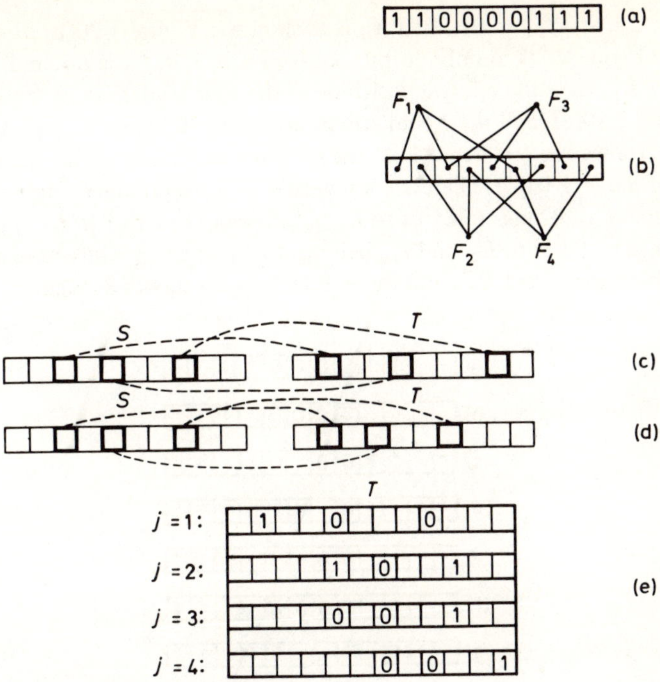

Figure 7.19. *One dimensional illustration of rule* (7.4)

which satisifes (7.4). Let $Q_{c1}, \ldots, Q_{ck}, \ldots, Q_{c\gamma}$ be all the subsets of Q_c such that every member of S belongs to one and only one member of Q_{ck}. Every member of Q_c necessarily belongs to at least one of the subsets $Q_{c1}, \ldots, Q_{ck}, \ldots, Q_{c\gamma}$, and therefore every member of T belongs to a member of at least one of the subsets $Q_{c1}, \ldots, Q_{ck}, \ldots, Q_{c\gamma}$. Let T_k be the set of all members of T such that any member of T_k belongs to at least one member of Q_{ck}. For $k = 1, \ldots, \gamma$, let X_k be the set of all bits of X such that any bit in X_k is in a member of T_k. It is important that every bit in X belongs to at least one of the subsets $X_1, \ldots, X_k, \ldots, X_\gamma$ of X.

Let f_{jk} be the member of Φ_j which is composed only of members of Q_{ck}. In the Figure 7.19 example, if, for all $j = 1, 2, 3, 4, f_{jk} \in L_2$, then X_k must be identical to X_{ri} or differ from X_{ri} only in shift. This, and the following remarks, follow from the fact that, in Figure 7.19(b), F_3 overlaps F_1 which overlaps F_4 which overlaps F_2. If, for $j = 1, 3, 4,$

$f_{jk} \in L_2$, and $f_{2k} \in L_1$, then X_k is as shown in Figure 7.20(b) or differs from Figure 7.20(b) only in shift. If, for $j = 2, 3, 4$, $f_{jk} \in L_2$, and $f_{1k} \in L_1$, then the relative positions of the four triples are as shown in Figure 7.19(e), and these four triples do not make up an X_k because for instance the left-hand '1' of the $j = 2$ triple coincides with the middle '0' of the $j= 1$ triple. There are altogether $2^4 = 16$ possible combinations wherein f_{1k} belongs to L_1 or to L_2, f_{2k} belongs to L_1 or to L_2, f_{3k} belongs to L_1 or to L_2, and f_{4k} belongs to L_1 or to L_2. Only nine of these combinations yield X_k's and these nine X_k's are shown as Figures 7.20(a), . . ., (i).

(a)			1	1	0	0	0	0	1	1	1	
(b)			1		0	0	0	0		1	1	
(c)			1	1	0	0		0	1		1	1
(d)		1		1	0		0		0	1	1	1
(e)			1		0	0		0		1	1	1
(f)			1		0	0	0	0		1		1
(g)		1	1		0			0	1			1
(h)	1		1	0		0	0	0		1	1	
(i)	1	1		0	0		0	0	1		1	1

Figure 7.20. *Subpatterns allowed by rule* (7.4)

We have seen that, in any pattern X which is assigned to the rth class by (7.4), every bit must belong to at least one of $X_1, \ldots, X_k, \ldots, X_\gamma$. We can *generate* all patterns which are recognised by (7.4) by superimposing all possible combinations of Figures 7.20(a), . . ., (i) in all possible relative positions, except that a '1' must not be superimposed on a '0', and a '0' must not be superimposed on a '1'. For instance, Figure 7.20(b) can be superimposed on a copy of itself which has been shifted one bit to the left, and the result is shown as Figure 7.21(a). Figure 7.20(a) cannot be superimposed on a copy of itself which has been shifted one place to the left, since this would involve superimposing 1's on 0's and 0's on 1's. Figure 7.21(f) can be obtained by superimposing Figure 7.20(h) on a copy of Figure 7.20(i) which has been shifted one bit to the right. The only patterns of less than 14 bits which are assigned to the rth class by (7.14) are the seven patterns which are shown in Figure 7.21. The presence of 0's as well as 1's in Figures 7.20(a), . . ., (i) restricts the ways in which Figures 7.20(a), . . ., (i) can be combined to make up patterns. If there were no 0's there would be no restriction, and the result would generally be disastrous.

(a)		1	1	0	0	0	0	1	1	1				
(b)		1	1	0	0	0	0	1	1	1	1			
(c)	1	1	1	0	0	0	0	1	1	1	1			
(d)	1	1	1	0	0	0	0	0	1	1	1			
(e)	1	1	1	0	0	0	0	0	1	1	1	1		
(f)	1	1	1	0	0	0	0	0	0	1	1	1	1	
(g)		1	1	0	0	0	0	0	1	1	1	1		

Figure 7.21. *Patterns recognised by rule* (7.4)

Unfortunately, (7.4) assigns to the rth class any pattern X which is made up of any combination of the patterns shown in Figure 7.21. For instance, (7.4) assigns to the rth class the pattern

11000011100001111000001111

which is made up of Figures 7.21(a), (c), and (e), with the right hand 1's of Figure 7.21(a) overlapping two of the left-hand 1's of Figure 7.21(c) and two of the right-hand 1's of Figure 7.21(c) overlapping two of the left-hand 1's of Figure 7.21(e). One way of dealing with this difficulty is to define Q_L to be the set of all members of Q such that in any member of Q_L the position of the element of S differs by not more than ± 5 elements from the position of the element of T. We then stipulate that L_1 and L_2 only contain triples of members of Q_L, the relative positions of these members being as indicated in Figures 7.19(c) and (d). The result of this restriction on L is that only the seven patterns shown in Figure 7.21, and a few patterns differing from these only in shift, are assigned to the rth class by (7.4).

7.3.6 A necessary condition for isomorphism

We have not yet discussed any detailed procedure by which (7.3) or (7.4) could be used in the recognition of a pattern. Because of the large amount of computation which is involved if the number of bits is large, it is desirable for the recognition procedure to be implementable by highly parallel special purpose hardware. To introduce one such procedure, let us return to the problem of determining whether two graphs are isomorphic. For solving this problem various procedures have been devised, and these make use of conditions which must necessarily be satisfied if an isomorphism exists[104, 445a]. We now consider one such condition.

Let $G_A = (P_A, E_A)$ and $G_B = (P_B, E_B)$ be two graphs, such that P_A and P_B are the sets of points, and E_A and E_B are the sets of pairs of points, of G_A and G_B respectively. Let Q_0 be the set of all pairs of points such that in any member of Q_0 one point belongs to P_A and the other point belongs to P_B, and both of the points have the same degree. Let m_i be the degree of the points belonging to the ith pair, q_i, in Q_0. Let K_0 be the set of all pairs of members of Q_0 such that in any member of K_0 the two points in P_A constitute a member of E_A and the two points in P_B constitute a member of E_B. We define Q_g and K_g inductively as follows. For $g = 1, 2, 3, \ldots,$ a member q_i of Q_{g-1} belongs to the subset Q_g of Q_{g-1} if and only if q_i belongs to at least m_i members of K_{g-1}. A member of K_{g-1} belongs to the subset K_g of K_{g-1} if and only if it contains two members of Q_g. Let Q_w be the first set in the sequence $Q_0, Q_1, \ldots, Q_w$ such that $Q_w = Q_{w-1}$. If G_A and G_B are isomorphic then

every point in P_A and every point in P_B belongs to at least one member of Q_w (7.5)

If this condition is satisfied it does *not* follow that G_A and G_B are isomorphic.

To see that (7.5) is a necessary condition for isomorphism, let us consider a point a_0 in P_A such that in the graph G_A the point a_0 is adjacent to the points $a_1, \ldots, a_i, \ldots, a_m$. Let us consider an isomorphism between G_A and G_B such that the points $b_0, b_1, \ldots, b_i, \ldots, b_m$ in G_B correspond to the points $a_0, a_1, \ldots, a_i, \ldots, a_m$ in G_A. For all $i = 0, \ldots, m$, $\{a_i, b_i\} \in Q_0$. For all $i = 1, \ldots, m$, $\{a_0, a_i\} \in E_A$ and $\{b_0, b_i\} \in E_B$, and therefore $\{\{a_0, b_0\}, \{a_i, b_i\}\} \in K_0$. Therefore $\{a_0, b_0\} \in Q_1$, and similarly we can see that, for $i = 1, \ldots, m$, $\{a_i, b_i\} \in Q_1$. Therefore, for $i = 1, \ldots, m$, $\{\{a_0, b_0\}, \{a_i b_i\}\} \in K_1$, and hence $\{a_0, b_0\} \in Q_2$. Similarly we can see that, for $g = 3, 4, \ldots,$ $\{a_0, b_0\} \in Q_g$. If $Q_g = Q_{g-1}$, then $K_g = K_{g-1}$, and $Q_g = Q_{g+1} = Q_{g+2} = \ldots,$ and there is no advantage in continuing the series $g = 1, 2, \ldots$

beyond $g = w$. Since for *any* point a_0, $\{a_0, b_0\} \in Q_w$, and for *any* point b_0, $\{a_0, b_0\} \in Q_w$, it follows that (7.5) is necessarily satisfied if G_A and G_B are isomorphic. (Because Q_{g+1} is a subset of Q_g, w must be finite.)

After slight modification, condition (7.5) becomes a condition which is necessarily satisfied if X is assigned to the rth class by rule (7.4). Let L and F be defined as in Section 7.3.5. Let Q_0 now be the set of all members of Q such that in any member of Q_0 the two bits are either both black or both white. Let L_0 be the set of all members of L such that

(1) any member of L_0 consists of n members of Q_0, and
(2) in any member of L_0 the n bit locations in S constitute a member of F.

Let α and β respectively be the bit locations in S and T which constitute the ith member, q_i, of Q_0, and let m_i be the number of members of F to which α belongs. Let us define Q_g and L_g inductively as follows. For $g = 1, 2, 3, \ldots$, a member q_i of Q_{g-1} belongs to the subset Q_g of Q_{g-1} if and only if q_i belongs to at least m_i members of L_{g-1}. A member of L_{g-1} belongs to the subset L_g of L_{g-1} if and only if it contains n members of Q_g. Let L_w be the first set in the sequence $L_0, L_1, \ldots, L_w$ such that $L_w = L_{w-1}$. If rule (7.4) assigns X to the rth class, then X is assigned to the rth class by the rule: assign X to the rth class if

$$\left.\begin{array}{l}\text{(1) every member of } F \text{ belongs to at least one member of } L_w;\\ \text{(2) every member of } T \text{ belongs to at least one member of } L_w\end{array}\right\} \quad (7.6)$$

To see this, let us suppose that the patterns X_{ri} and X on S and T are such that X is assigned to the rth class by (7.4). Let $Q_{c1}, \ldots, Q_{ck}, \ldots, Q_{c\gamma}$ be defined as in Section 7.3.5, and let $\{\alpha_0, \beta_0\}$ be any member of Q_{ck}. Let m_i be the number of members of F to which α_0 belongs, and let $\alpha_{j1}, \ldots, \alpha_{jh}, \ldots, \alpha_{jn}$ be the elements of the jth member of F to which α_0 belongs. For all $h = 1, \ldots, n$ and all $j = 1, \ldots, m_i$, let β_{jh} be the element of T such that $\{\alpha_{jh}, \beta_{jh}\} \in Q_{ck}$. Every member of Q_c, and therefore every member of Q_{ck}, belongs to Q_0. Therefore, for all $j = 1, \ldots, m_i$, $\{\{\alpha_{j1}, \beta_{j1}\}, \ldots, \{\alpha_{jn}, \beta_{jn}\}\} \in L_0$. Therefore $\{\alpha_0, \beta_0\} \in Q_1$. Since $\{\alpha_0, \beta_0\}$ is *any* member of Q_{ck}, it is true that, for all $h = 1, \ldots, n$ and $j = 1, \ldots, m_i$, $\{\alpha_{jh}, \beta_{jh}\} \in Q_1$. Therefore, for all $j = 1, \ldots, m_i$, $\{\{\alpha_{j1}, \beta_{j1}\}, \ldots, \{\alpha_{jn}, \beta_{jn}\}\} \in L_1$, and hence $\{\alpha_0, \beta_0\} \in Q_2$. Similarly we can see that, for $g = 3, 4, \ldots, w$, every member of Q_{ck} belongs to Q_g, and, as before, there is no advantage in continuing the series $g = 1, 2, 3, \ldots$ beyond $g = w$.

Let f_{jk} be as defined in Section 7.3.5. Every member of Q_{ck} belongs to Q_w, and therefore, for all $j = 1, \ldots, \phi$, f_{jk} consists of n members of Q_w, and $f_{jk} \in L_w$. For all $j = 1, \ldots, \phi$, the set $\{f_{j1}, \ldots, f_{jk}, \ldots, f_{j\gamma}\}$ must have at least one member, and therefore condition (1) in rule (7.6) is satisfied. As we saw in Section 7.3.5, every member of T belongs to at least one of the subsets $Q_{c1}, \ldots, Q_{ck}, \ldots, Q_{c\gamma}$. Every member of Q_{ck} belongs to at least one of $f_{1k}, \ldots, f_{jk}, \ldots, f_{\phi k}$, and therefore condition (2) in rule (7.6) is satisfied. Thus we have established that, if X is assigned to the rth class by (7.4), then X is also assigned to the rth class by (7.6). But it does *not* follow that, if X is assigned to the rth class by (7.6), then X is assigned to the rth class by (7.4).

Rule (7.6) has the advantage that it can be implemented remarkably simply, though generally at great cost, in highly parallel hardware. We postpone introducing this hardware implementation until Section 8.5.1 because it provides an example of a microcellular array. The usefulness of (7.6) depends on the cost of implementation, and also on whether in practice we can determine a set L so as to achieve low error rates in recognition. Section 10.3 introduces a technique for determining a set L automatically.

7.4 SEQUENTIALLY DETECTED FEATURES

7.4.1 An IBM curve follower system

A curve follower system for recognising hand-printed characters was described in 1963 by Greanias *et al.*[184], and this system subsequently evolved into the hand-printed character reader which forms part of the IBM 1287 and 1288 reading machines[374]. These are of commercial and historic importance because they are among the first commercially available machines to offer a tolerably successful hand-print reading facility. The hand-printed characters which these machines read are the numerals 0, . . ., 9 and the letters C, S, T, X, and Z, but letters must only be written on a document in locations where the machines expect letters rather than numerals.

7.4.1.1 Design principles

In all versions of the system the external black/white contour of an input character is traced round by a flying-spot contour follower as in Section 2.4.2. During this preliminary scan the maximum height and width of the character are measured and stored. We can think of these measurements as determining the height and width of a rectangular box into which the character will just fit horizontally and vertically. This box is divided into 4 x 5 zones, as in Figure 7.22.

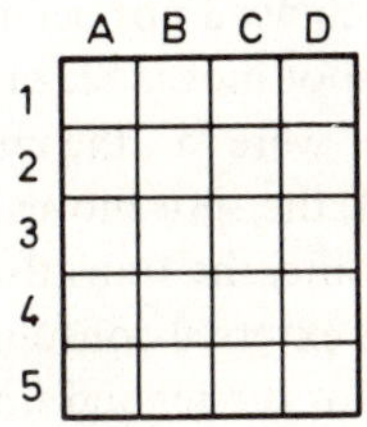

Figure 7.22. *Rectangular box divided into* 20 *zones*

The external contour of the character is then traced round a second time by the flying-spot contour follower, starting from approximately half way down the right-hand side of the character. The rate of progress of the spot is adjusted[134] so that, whatever the size of the original character, the spot will take approximately six time units to cross one of the zones in Figure 7.22 from side to side. This adjustment is important because, as we shall see, the system uses a measurement of the *time* spent moving in a given direction as a measurement of the *length* of a black/white edge in that direction.

During the (clockwise) second tracing of the contour the direction of movement of the spot is continuously determined[202]. The system[374] in the IBM 1287 does not make use of the precise direction[186], but only uses the fact the direction lies between $-15°$ and $+15°$, or between $15°$ and $45°$, and so on in multiples of $30°$. An early version of the system[134] used multiples of $45°$ instead of $30°$. We shall concentrate our discussion on this early version, because full details have been disclosed[134], and we shall use the compass bearings N, NE, E, etc., to represent the eight possible coarsely quantised directions of motion of the scanning spot.

The stream of data from the direction determining circuits is fed in parallel to 59 different data dominated sequential circuits, each of which is designed to determine the presence or absence of a different feature in the input character. For example, the (slightly simplified) transition diagram for detecting the feature which is called 'top of '2', '3', '7' ' is shown in Figure 7.23. At the start of the second tracing of the contour, this feature detector starts at node 1 of Figure 7.23. If, while the circuit is at node 1, the scanning spot moves N, or NE, or NW in column B, or C, or D and row 1 or 2 in Figure 7.22 for three time units continuously, the circuit undergoes transition to node 2. If, while the spot is at node 2, the spot moves W, or NW, or SW anywhere in rows 1 or 2 of Figure 7.22 for a total of six time units, not necessarily continuously, the transition to node 3 occurs. 'ITU' in Figure 7.23 means *integrated time units,* that is, time units which need not occur continuously. If, while the circuit is at node 2, the spot moves SE or E in row 1, as might happen if the input character were '5', the circuit returns to node 1. If, while the circuit is at node 3, the spot moves E anywhere in row 1 continuously for two time units, the transition to node 4 occurs. If the circuit is at node 4 when the external contour of the input character has been completely traced for the second time, the 'top of '2', '3', '7' ' feature is deemed present in the input character. In Figures 7.23, 7.26, and 7.27, it is to be understood that if, while the circuit is at a given node, none of the conditions for transition from that node are satisfied, then the system remains at that node.

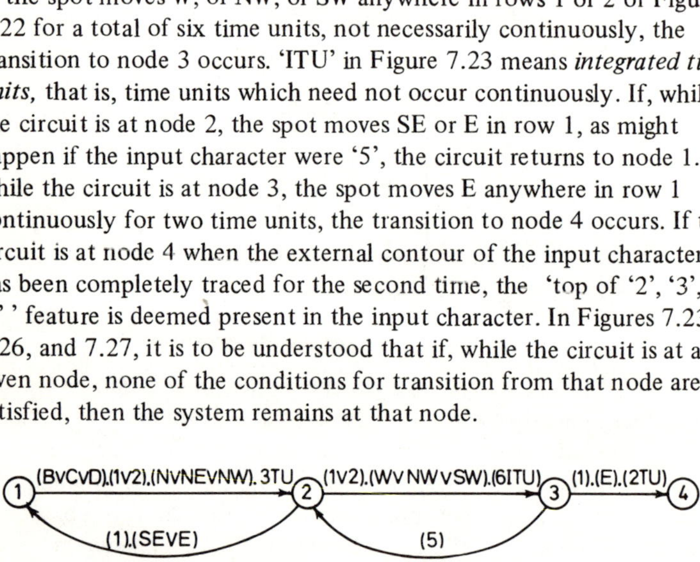

Figure 7.23. *Transition diagram for detection of 'top of* '2', '3', '7' ' (V *represents the logical 'or'*)

The feature detector for 'top of '2', '3', '7' ' is a fairly typical example of a feature detector in this system. A feature is deemed present or absent according as its detector circuit is or is not at a prescribed node when the external contour has been completely traced for the second time. Thus an input character is transformed into a binary pattern comprising one bit per feature, each bit being '1' or '0' according as the corresponding feature is or is not present in the input character. This binary pattern is recognised by parallel Boolean logic circuits. For instance, a character is recognised as '3' if the 'top of '2', '3', '7' ' feature and the 'cusp of 3' feature are present and either 'bottom curved tail of '3', '5', '9' ' is present or 'rounded bottom of '6' or '8' ' is absent.

The Boolean discriminant function for '3' happens to be unusually simple (in Ref. 134). For instance, in Ref. 134, the Boolean function for '9' is a function of 42 variables, the value of each variable being determined by the presence or absence of a feature. In the IBM 1287 [374] the Boolean function for 9's, $f_9(X)$ is something like

$$f_9(X) = f_{91}(X) \vee f_{92}(X) \vee f_{93}(X) \vee f_{94}(X)$$

where $f_{91}(X)$ is *true* if the input character is shaped like 9 , $f_{92}(X)$ is *true* if the input character is shaped like 9 , $f_{93}(X)$ is *true* if the input character is shaped like 9 , and $f_{94}(X)$ is *true* if the input character is shaped like 9 . The functions $f_{91}(X), f_{92}(X), f_{93}(X)$, and $f_{94}(X)$ are Boolean discriminants for subclasses of the class of nines. Subclass discriminants are also used in the recognition of other classes.

The contour follower only traces round the *external* black/white contour of a character, and this may not yield sufficient information to distinguish, for example, between

0 and 1 , or 9 and 8 , or 0 and θ , or 7 and 9 .

If for a given input character the Boolean discriminant functions for the classes '0' and '1' both turn out to be *true*, the system sweeps the flying spot horizontally right across the input character, and counts the number of times the spot meets black. For 0 the scan meets black twice, and for 1 once, and the input character is accordingly recognised as '0' or '1'. The characters 9 , 8 are also resolved in this way; and the other two examples mentioned above are resolved by a vertical scan[374].

7.4.1.2 *Hardware implementation of feature detectors*

After the contour of the input character has been traced for the first time, analogue voltages proportional to the maximum height and width of the input character are applied across resistance divider networks as indicated in Figure 7.24. In order to deflect the scanning spot to any given position on the document it is necessary to apply horizontal and vertical deflection voltages; and, conversely, these voltages are measures of the position coordinates of the spot. If, for example, the horizontal deflection voltage, when suitably scaled, lies between v_2 and v_3 in Figure 7.24, then the scanning spot lies in column B in Figure 7.22. If, for example, the vertical deflection voltage, when suitably scaled, lies between the voltages on terminals v_9 and v_{10} in Figure 7.24, then the flying spot lies in row 4 in Figure 7.22. Using this idea, special circuitry provides the truth values of nine Boolean variables, one for each of the five rows, and one for each of the four columns, of Figure 7.22. For instance, if the spot lies in column B and row 4 of Figure 7.22, the variables corresponding to row 4 and column B are *true* and the remaining seven variables are *false*. In this case we say, for brevity, that '4' and 'B' are *true*.

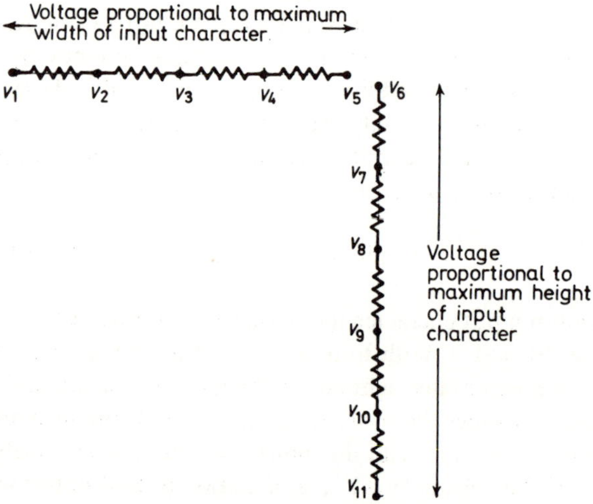

Figure 7.24. *Division of maximum height and maximum width voltages*

Similarly, in Ref. 134, the direction detector determines the values of eight Boolean variables, of which seven are *false* at any given time. For instance, while the spot is moving East, only 'E' is *true*.

To illustrate the implementation of a feature detector, an implementation of Figure 7.23 is shown in Figure 7.25[134]. Prior to the recognition of an input character, bistable elements i, n, and r in Figure 7.25 are set to state '0' by means of a signal on channel R. During the tracing of the contour, *and* gate d is activated (i.e. in state '1') only if the spot is moving N, NE, or NW in column B, C, or D and row 1 or 2. Timer circuit e only produces output '1' if *and* gate d remains activated continuously for three time units. When timer unit e produces output '1', this switches bistable element i to state '1'. If the spot then moves

E or SE in row 1, *or* gate h is activated, and bistable element i is thereby reset to state '0'. Timer circuit m produces output '1' only after *and* unit l has remained activated for a total of six time units, not necessarily continuously. It should now be easy to see that bistable element r is in state '1' only after the Figure 7.23 process has reached node 4. Note that, when *and* gate p in Figure 7.25 is activated, *and* gate g is also activated, so that bistable i is reset to state '0', but this does not cause bistable n to switch from state '1' to state '0'.

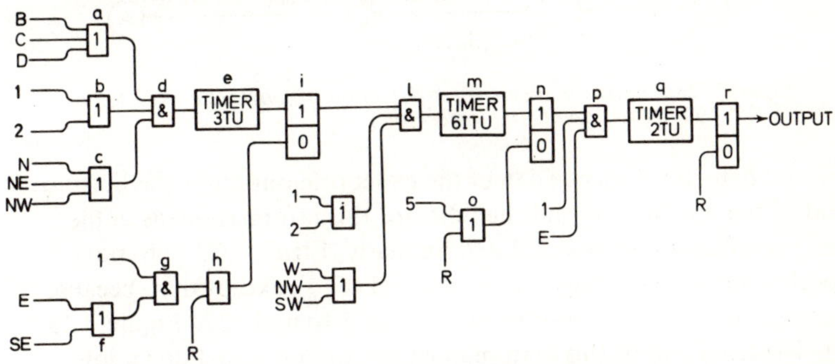

Figure 7.25. *Logic diagram for detection of 'top of '2', '3', '7' '*

Note also that Figure 7.25 is an asynchronous circuit which employs bistables, whereas Figure 6.13 employs unit time delays instead of bistables. This is because, in Figure 7.25, a transition to a new node occurs if the specified conditions are fulfilled, and if these are not fulfilled the system remains at its present node. In Figure 6.13, on the other hand, if none of the conditions for re-entry or exit from the present node are obeyed, the sequential process stops and the system signals that the input word is not a version of 'success'.

7.4.1.3 Discussion

Figure 7.26 is a transition diagram[134] for detecting the feature 'bottom curved tail of '3', '5', '9' '. The condition for transition from node 1 to node 2 would be satisfied while the spot traversed the underside of the bottom of 0 , 6 , or 2 , moving from right to left. The spot would subsequently work round the top of any of these three characters, and then satisfy the conditions for transition from node 2 to node 3 to node 4 while traversing the upper edge of the bottom stroke of the character from left to right. But nodes 3 and 4 would not in fact be reached, because whilst the spot was working round the top of e.g. ‘2’, the condition for transition from node 2 to node 1 would have been satisfied. Thus ‘bottom curved tail of ‘3’, ‘5’, ‘9’ ’ is not detected in a ‘2’. But this feature may be found present in a ‘3’, whatever the orientation of the bottom end of the bottom limb of the ‘3’, or even if the bottom terminates in a small loop as in 3 . The Figure 7.26

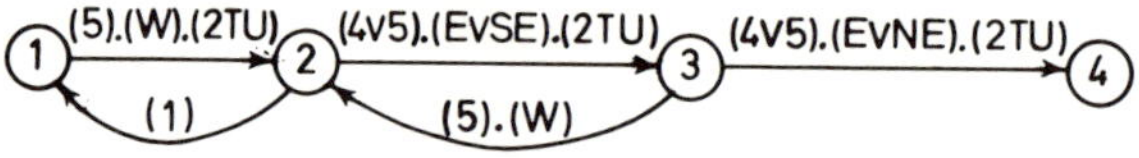

Figure 7.26. *Transition diagram for detection of ‘bottom curved tail of ‘3’, ‘5’, ‘9’ ’* (V *represents the logical ‘or’*)

feature detector does not detect the exact orientation of the bottom end of the bottom line and then discard this information, as in the last paragraph of Section 7.2.2.2. Similarly, Figure 7.23 does not specify the detailed shape of the top end of ‘3’, except that, because of the condition for transition from node 3 to node 2 in Figure 7.23, the left-hand end of this feature must not be connected down into row 5, as in 8 .

As a further example, Figure 7.27 is the transition diagram for the ‘cusp of 3’ feature detector[134]. It is an instructive exercise to draw many shapes which would be recognised by Figure 7.27 as ‘cusp of 3’, and consider how these shapes could all be recognised by a feature detector of the sort discussed in Section 7.2.2.1.

It is worth noting that the choice of features in this system is entirely *ad hoc.* The features are tailor-made for the repertoire of characters which the machine is to recognise. On the other hand, in some of the systems discussed in Section 7.2 the features are chosen without much regard for the characters to be recognised, and could just as well be used for recognising Greek or Cyrillic letters instead of Arabic numerals.

A disadvantage of contour or centre-line tracers is their sensitivity to accidental breaks in character limbs, due for instance to faulty ink-flow in a ball-point pen. Gaps of less than a certain size can be jumped over, but this introduces the risk of closing a gap which ought to be left open, as in 5 → 6 . To cope with the differently positioned breaks in the contours of 9 , 9 , 9 , separate logic has to be used for each of these shapes, as mentioned above. To cope with 5 , the part ɔ can be recognised as a shape in its own right, and then the ‾ can be located and recognised separately[302]. To reduce the cost of recognising characters containing gaps, the writer for the IBM 1287 is asked[235] to use an HB pencil, to close loops, and to connect lines, e.g. as in 5 as opposed to 5 .

Further, the writer is asked to write big so that each character nearly fills the preprinted box in which it must be written, and to block-print characters without ornate loops and curls; but in fact the IBM 1287 can recognise a wide range of character shapes in which these rules have not been obeyed. The writer is also asked[235] to separate horizontally adjacent characters by at least 0·020 in. If the gap is much smaller than this, the contour follower is liable to jump from one character to the next and trace the contour of two characters as though it were the contour of one. To deal with this, an IBM patent[185] discloses a technique for recognising the shape of the contour where two characters meet, and artificially segmenting the two characters where such a shape is detected.

We shall briefly discuss the linguistic aspect of this system in Section 8.3.2.1.

7.4.2 Watchbird techniques

A curve follower can be used to extract information from a pattern and, if required, this information can be used in the recognition of the pattern. The contour follower itself does not recognise the pattern. Watchbird techniques are further techniques for extracting information from patterns, and this information may or may not be used in recognition. The term *watchbird* is taken from Rabinow[359]. Watchbird techniques are sometimes known as *stream-following* techniques. It is convenient here to introduce simple watchbird techniques in terms of character recognition.

Consider a '9' scanned from left to right by a vertical raster, and binarised so that if the binarised pattern were stored it would be as shown in Figure 7.28. In a watchbird system, the whole pattern need not be stored. Instead, the stream of data from the scanner and binariser is compared with a copy of the same stream of data which has been delayed by the time period of one vertical scan. At any instant the recognition circuitry is fed with two pattern elements, these being the element scanned at that instant and the element which

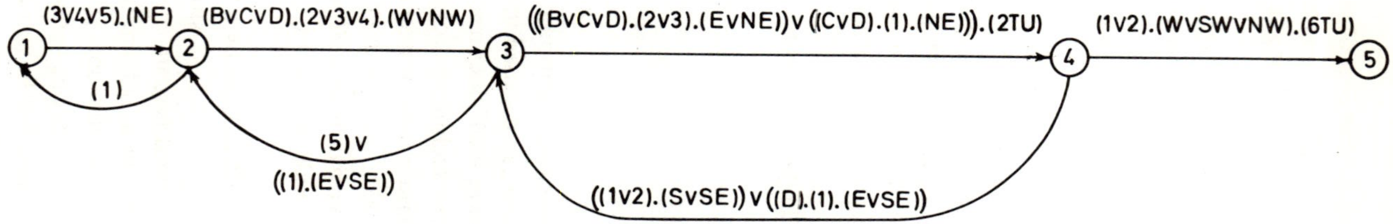

Figure 7.27. *Transition diagram for detection of 'cusp of 3'* (V *represents the logical 'or'*)

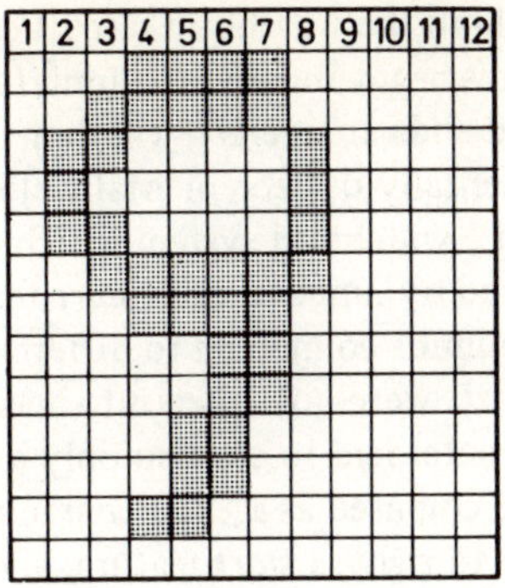

Figure 7.28. *A binarised* '9'

would appear immediately to the left of this in Figure 7.28. Let us denote these two elements by x_{at} and x_{bt} respectively, and stipulate that the scan proceeds from the top to the bottom of the character.

If, during the course of a scan, x_{at} changes from white to black and back from black to white during an interval while x_{bt} remains white, then the scan has encountered the *start* of a piece of character limb which was not encountered in the previous scan. This happens during the scanning of column 2 of Figure 7.28. If x_{at} changes from black to white and back to black during an interval while x_{bt} remains black, then a piece of limb which was present in the previous scan has *forked* out into two pieces in the present scan. This *fork* feature is encountered during the scanning of column 3 of Figure 7.28.

If x_{bt} changes from black to white to black while x_{at} remains black, a *join* feature is present: that is, two limbs have converged to a single piece of black This *join* feature is encountered during the scanning of column 8 of Figure 7.28. If x_{bt} changes from white to black to white while x_{at} remains white, the scan has encountered the *end* of a limb. This *end* feature is encountered during the scanning of column 9 of Figure 7.28.

It is possible to compare the times at which, for example, successive scans meet the top of the '9' in Figure 7.28, and from this we can deduce that the top of the '9' slopes upwards through columns 3 and 4. By comparing the times at which the scans of columns 4 and 5 meet black for the *third* time we can deduce that the tail of the '9' slopes upwards through columns 4 and 5. This introduces the general idea of tracing the progress of limbs through successive scans. A special circuit, which Rabinow[359] calls a *watchbird* circuit, can be assigned to each limb. For a given limb the watchbird circuit can be made to determine which features begin and end the limb (e.g. whether the limb starts at a *fork* and ends at an *end*), whether the limb starts horizontally, or incrementally or decrementally sloping, and so on.

Perotto[346] described a watchbird system which determined the *forks* and *joins* connected by limbs to each *start* feature, and took no notice of *joins* between limbs connected to different *start* features. For recognition purposes, *ends* were not taken into account. To be recognised as '0' or '4' a character had to contain only a *start* connected to a *fork* and a *join.* To be recognised as a '2', a character had to contain, when scanned from left to right, a *start* feature, and also, at a lower vertical level, a second *start* connected to a *fork.* A '3' had to contain three *starts.* A '5' had to contain a *start* connected to a *fork*, and a lower *start not* connected to a *fork* or *join.* Among the ten numerals, '0' and '4' were the only two which were not distinguished by rules of this sort, and, instead, '0' was distinguished from '4' by means of special circuitry for detecting a long vertical limb roughly in the middle of the input character.

To guard against noise, that is, the presence of spurious black or white elements, Perotto suggested ignoring

(1) white gaps of less than a prescribed length between black parts of a vertical scan, and
(2) black limbs consisting of less than a threshold number of black elements between *start* and *end*, and
(3) white 'lakes' consisting of less than a threshold number of white elements between *join* and *fork*, and
(4) horizontal gaps in limbs when such gaps were of less than a prescribed length.

To measure the size of a white lake, a circuit can count the total number of time instants in successive scans when the scan is in white between the two black limbs which enclose the lake.

Let c_i be the number of white bits in the ith column between the top black bit in the ith column of scan and the highest row which has contained a black bit in any previous column of scan. In an RCA patent[363] the sum of c_i over all columns of scan is called the *top cavity* of the input character. For instance, 'T' is distinguished from 'Y' by using the fact that 'T' has a small or zero top cavity, whilst 'Y' has a relatively large top cavity. This RCA system[363] measures the squareness of various corners, e.g. for distinguishing between 'O' and 'D'; and also measures the total width of the input character, e.g. for distinguishing between the numeral '0' and the letter 'O'. One of the features used for distinguishing between 'C' and 'O' is the presence of a *join* in 'O' but not in 'C'. For each recognition class, there is a prescribed list of features, some of which must be present and others of which must be absent for assignment of the input character to that class.

Other watchbird techniques have been disclosed by IBM[287, 372] Farrington[446], Siemens[407], Marconi[226], REI[88], Grimsdale and Bullingham[190], Rosenfeld and Pfaltz[381], and Shelman and Hodges[401].

7.4.3 Sequentially detected strip features

In a system developed by Toshiba* for recognising hand-printed Arabic numerals on envelopes in the Japanese mail, characters are scanned by a vidicon camera, binarised, stored, and thinned[169]. If the height of a thinned character exceeds a prescribed limit, the height and width of that character are halved. Thinning a character before, rather than after, this rough size normalisation, reduces the chance of flooding small loops, as in '8', when the size of the character is halved. After thinning, and, if necessary, halving the size of the input character, the pattern which is the input pattern to the recognition system always consists of 36 columns and 40 rows of bits.

The recognition process has three main stages. In the first stage a 3 x 3 window is successively aligned with the input pattern so that the central element of the window coincides successively with each element in the second row of the input pattern, then successively with each element in the fourth, sixth, etc., rows of the input pattern. In other words, the 3 x 3 window scans every other row of the input pattern, and therefore scans 20 rows altogether.

In any given alignment of the window, the 3 x 3 bit pattern in the window is assigned to one of seven classes, which are called *B, V, I, D, H, L, X,* respectively. '*V*' is the class of all 3 x 3 bit patterns which contain a roughly vertical piece of character limb. '*I*' and '*D*' are respectively classes of 3 x 3 bit patterns containing roughly incrementally and decrementally sloping limb segments. For instance,

$$\begin{array}{ccc}1&1&0\\1&1&0\\0&1&1\end{array} \quad \text{and} \quad \begin{array}{ccc}0&0&0\\1&1&0\\0&0&1\end{array} \quad \text{and} \quad \begin{array}{ccc}1&1&0\\1&1&1\\0&0&1\end{array}$$

*Toshiba is a trade name of the *To*kyo *Shiba*ura Electric Company.

would all be classified as '*D*'. '*H*' and '*L*' are classes of roughly horizontal segments: in '*H*' the horizontal black segment lies mainly in the upper half of the 3 x 3 window, and in 'L' the horizontal black segment lies mainly in the lower half. '*B*' stands for blank, and a 3 x 3 bit pattern is assigned to '*B*' if it contains no black bits or very few black bits. '*X*' is the class of non-blank 3 x 3 bit patterns in which segment direction is not tolerably clear. *Every* 3 x 3 bit pattern belongs to one of these seven classes. A given 3 x 3 bit pattern is assigned to one of these seven classes by means of intuitively designed parallel logic circuits.

The system not only assigns a 3 x 3 bit pattern to one of the seven classes *B, V,* etc., but also records whether the black elements in the 3 x 3 window are connected by black to black elements above but outside the window. For introductory simplicity, let us temporarily forget about vertical connectivity, and return to it later.

When the centre of the 3 x 3 window scans along a row of the input pattern, all successive 3 x 3 bit patterns within a strip 3 rows high and 36 columns wide are classified as 'B', 'V', or 'I', etc. If the strip does not contain any part of the input character, the strip contains only *B*'s. If the strip passes through the top of an '8', for example, then the strip may perhaps contain a string of *B*'s, then a '*V*', then some *H*'s, then another '*V*', and then more *B*'s. This tells us that the strip contains a roughly ⌒ shaped piece of character. Alternatively the strip may perhaps contain some *B*'s, two *I*'s, five *H*'s, a '*D*', and then some more *B*'s. This also tells us that the strip contains a roughly ⌒ shaped piece of character. Indeed there are many different sequences of *B*'s, *V*'s, etc., which, if found in a strip, would indicate that the strip passes through a roughly ⌒ shaped piece of character.

A strip passing through the upper loop of '8' below the ⌒ at the top might encounter two very roughly parallel pieces of character limb. The strip might for instance contain any one of the sequences shown in Table 7.3.

These are of course only a very few examples and there are many sequences which would tell us that the strip contained only a pair of very roughly parallel black segments. The presence of sequences such as . . . *B I I H B* . . . in the above examples reflects the fact that the thinning procedure is not applied repeatedly until a single-element limb width is obtained, but instead is stopped after one application, which may result in imperfect thinning.

The transition diagram shown in Figure 7.29 can be used for detecting any of the eight sequences in Table 7.3. The successive

Table 7.3. EXAMPLES OF POSSIBLE SEQUENCES IN A STRIP THAT CONTAINS TWO VERY ROUGHLY PARALLEL PIECES OF CHARACTER LIMB

B	*B*	*V*	*B*	*B*	*B*	*B*	*V*	*B*	*B*	*B*	*B*	*B*
B	*B*	*B*	*B*	*V*	*B*	*B*	*B*	*V*	*B*	*B*	*B*	*B*
B	*B*	*V*	*B*	*B*	*B*	*B*	*B*	*V*	*X*	*L*	*B*	*B*
B	*V*	*B*	*B*	*B*	*B*	*B*	*B*	*V*	*X*	*X*	*V*	*B*
B	*B*	*L*	*I*	*I*	*B*	*B*	*B*	*V*	*B*	*B*	*B*	*B*
B	*I*	*I*	*H*	*B*	*B*	*B*	*V*	*V*	*B*	*B*	*B*	*B*
B	*B*	*B*	*I*	*I*	*B*	*B*	*B*	*I*	*B*	*B*	*B*	*B*
B	*B*	*L*	*V*	*B*	*B*	*B*	*B*	*L*	*I*	*B*	*B*	*B*

inputs to the sequential system are the successive *B*'s, *V*'s, etc., derived from a strip. It is decided that the strip contains roughly parallel segments of black if the system is at node 7 when the end of a sequence is reached. Although Figure 7.29 is only a very simple example, it classifies many different sequences as containing roughly parallel black segments.

Katsuragi *et al.*[249] have intuitively classified shapes which may be encountered in strips into 19 classes. For instance, a strip which contains little or no black is classified as BLANK. A strip which contains roughly parallel black segments is classified as PAL. A strip which contains a roughly ⌒ shaped piece of black is classified as CAP. A strip which contains a roughly ◡ shaped piece of black is classified as CUP. A strip which contains a single roughly vertical piece of black is classified as VRT. A strip which contains a single roughly incrementally sloping piece of black is classified as INC. A strip which contains a single horizontal piece of black is classified as BAR. A strip which contains a roughly horizontal piece of black and then, to the right of this, as in _|, a roughly vertical piece of black, is classified as BAV. A strip which contains three roughly vertical pieces of black is classified as TRI, and so on. The shape in any given strip is assigned to one of these 19 classes by means of a data dominated sequential system of the Figure 7.29 sort, using at least one different transition diagram for each of the 19 classes.

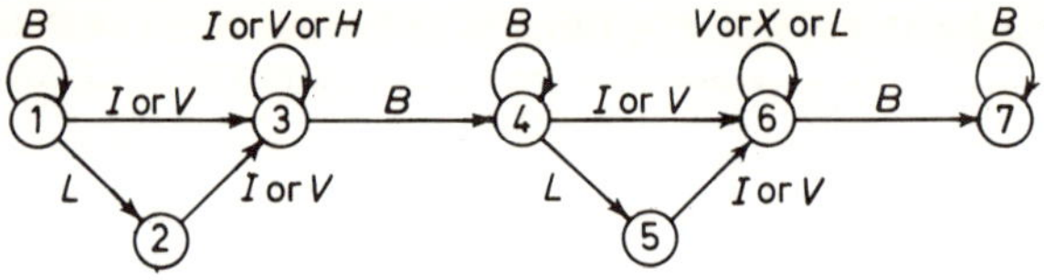

Figure 7.29. *Drastically simplified transition diagram for detection of* PAL

The first stage of the character recognition process consists of scanning 20 strips with a 3 x 3 window and classifying the 3 x 3 bit patterns. The second stage consists of assigning the sequence in each strip to one of the 19 shape classes. For instance, working from the top to the bottom of an '8' the sequence of strip classifications might perhaps be seven BLANK's and then BLANK, BAR, CAP, PAL, PAL, CUP, CAP, PAL, PAL, PAL, CUP, BLANK, BLANK. The third stage of the character recognition process consists of assigning the sequence of 20 strip classifications to one of 10 recognition classes corresponding respectively to the 10 numerals. For this purpose further data dominated sequential circuits are used, and an example of a transition diagram for recognising 8's is shown in Figure 7.30. Figure 7.30 is a drastic simplification of an example given by Genchi *et al*[169].

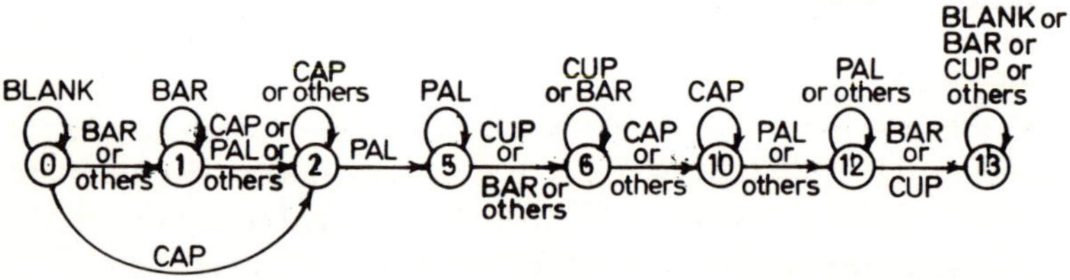

Figure 7.30. *Drastically simplified transition diagram for recognition of the character* '8'

In Figures 6.12 and 7.29 we have used the convention that, if the system is at a given node and the next input to the system does not satisfy any condition for transition either to a new node or back to the given node, then the sequential process stops, and the input sequence is not classified as belonging to the recognition class which is associated with the transition diagram. This is *not* the case in Figure 7.30 and in the transition diagrams which are used for recognising characters in the Toshiba system[169, 249]. One of the conditions for exit from each node in Figure 7.30 is *others. Others* means 'any strip classification other than those which are explicitly listed in the conditions for exit from or re-entry to the node'. For example, for node 0 in Figure 7.30, *others* means 'any strip classification other than BLANK, BAR, or CAP'. While working through a transition diagram, the system counts the number of times when the strip classification is one of the *others*, and at the end of the sequence this number is the *penalty count* for the transition diagram. The input character is assigned to the recognition class which corresponds to the transition diagram with the lowest penalty count; unless the lowest count is associated with more than one recognition class, or is greater than or equal to two, in which the case the input character is rejected. The transition diagrams used in practice are very much more complicated than Figure 7.30, and more than one transition diagram is used for each class. Each transition diagram recognises only a subclass.

Kiji and Hoshino[252a] have described a further system in which horizontal strips of a character are classified and the vertical sequence of strip classifications is recognised by sequential circuits. As in the Toshiba system, the transition diagrams are devised intuitively and are modified and improved by trial and error. In order to speed up this design process, computer aided design can be used[225], for instance to provide the designer quickly with detailed diagnostic information when the recognition process fails, and to provide rapid and convenient means of correcting transition diagrams. To facilitate correction, in the Toshiba system the transition diagrams are not implemented as in Figure 6.13, but instead are stored in a computer core store[321].

Let us now return to the question of vertical connectivity in the Toshiba system. The shapes 5 and 3 are identical except for the position of the bar at the top relative to the ʒ . The Toshiba system, in the simplified form in which we have introduced it, could not be relied on to distinguish between this 5 and 3 : working from top to bottom, both characters might yield a sequence such as BLANK, BAR, INC, INC, ... This is because the relative positions of the pieces of black in successive strips have been ignored.

To remedy this, the Toshiba system records whether the black contents of each 3 x 3 window are connected by black to black in the strip above[249]. By using this information in the strip-classifying transition diagrams, each of the 19 classes of strip shapes is subdivided into three subclasses, roughly according as black within the strip is connected to the left, right, or middle of the black shape in the strip above. Instead of working with 19 classes of strip shapes, the character recognition transition diagrams work with 3 x 19 = 57 subclasses of strip shapes.

For instance, INC-L might be used as a transition condition in a character recognition transition diagram, where INC-L means 'INC connected to the left part of the black in the previous strip'.

By taking account of vertical connectivity the system can to some extent track the progress of black limbs through successive strips, as in watchbird techniques. In Section 7.4.2, features such as *end, fork, join,* and *start* are detected sequentially, and let us briefly compare this with feature detection in the Toshiba system. Instead of scanning the input pattern with a 3 x 3 window, a simple watchbird technique effectively scans the input pattern with a 2 x 1 window, which at any time contains x_{at} and x_{bt}, in the notation of Section 7.4.2. Instead of assigning a pattern within a 3 x 3 window to one of seven classes, the watchbird system assigns a pattern within a 2 x 1 window to one of four classes, each class consisting of only one pattern. Let us denote these four classes, that is, patterns, by

$$B = (x_{bt} = 0) . (x_{at} = 0) \qquad C = (x_{bt} = 1) . (x_{at} = 1)$$

$$D = (x_{bt} = 0) . (x_{at} = 1) \qquad E = (x_{bt} = 1) . (x_{at} = 0)$$

For example, the *join* feature in Section 7.4.2 can be detected by a sequential process of which Figure 7.31 is the transition diagram[305]. A *join* is detected by reaching node 3 in Figure 7.31.

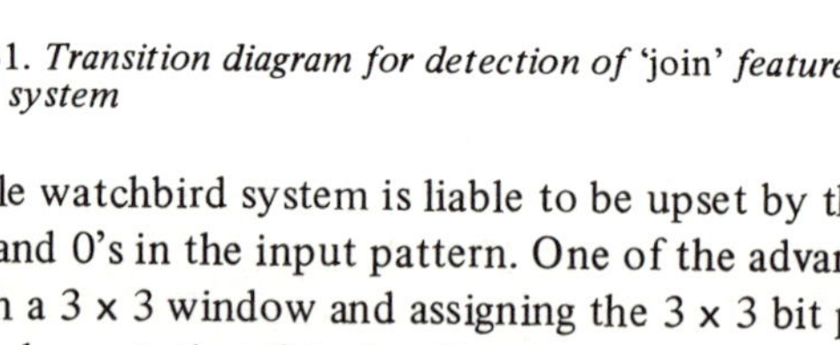

Figure 7.31. *Transition diagram for detection of* 'join' *feature in a simple watchbird system*

This simple watchbird system is liable to be upset by the presence of spurious 1's and 0's in the input pattern. One of the advantages of scanning with a 3 x 3 window and assigning the 3 x 3 bit pattern to one of seven classes is that this classification may not be upset by the presence of a few spurious 1's and 0's. In other words, the use of a 3 x 3 window instead of a 2 x 1 window has a denoising effect. By the use of seven classes instead of four, more information is extracted from the input character.

Since the Toshiba system measures neither length nor proportion of character limbs, it may perhaps not be easy for the system to resolve pairs of characters such as those shown in Figure 7.32.

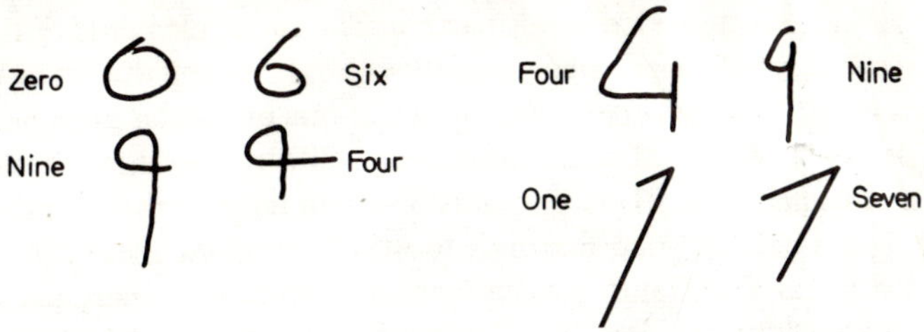

Figure 7.32. *Examples of pairs of characters differing only in proportion*

The Toshiba system must, in its transition diagrams, explicitly provide for different versions, such as

of the bottom of the character '3', whereas this may not be necessary in the Section 7.4.1 system. On the other hand, breaks in different places in the external contours of e.g. 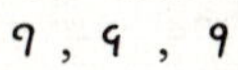 can be provided for in the Toshiba system by allowing alternative transition conditions in a single transition diagram, whereas in Section 7.4.1 these different breaks call for drastically different recognition logic.

7.5 DISCUSSION OF FEATURES

7.5.1 Classes of subpatterns

For the sake of unifying ideas, some but by no means all, of the recognition systems of Chapters 5, 6, and 7 can be discussed in terms of classes of subpatterns. A *subpattern* is a subset of the elements which constitute a pattern. More precisely, a *subpattern* is a subarray of the array of elements which constitute a pattern. For example the 1's and 0's in Figure 5.6 constitute a subpattern. In the terminology of Sections 5.2 and 5.3, an *n*-tuple state is a subpattern.

The following paragraphs are concerned with classes of subpatterns. Instead of repeatedly using the phrase *class of subpatterns*, it is convenient to use the term *f-class*. An *f-class* is a class of subpatterns. The term *class* is often used to mean *recognition class*, and the prefix *f-* in *f-class* avoids any ambiguity between recognition classes and classes of subpatterns. Systems which can be regarded as using *f*-classes in the recognition of patterns are of three main types, which are discussed in Sections 7.5.2, 7.5.3, and 7.5.4 respectively.

7.5.2 Negating systems

In the Section 5.6.1 system, let us consider one particular alignment of the jth peephole mask with an input pattern, such that the jth peephole mask perfectly matches the input pattern. The set of elements of the input pattern which can *not* be changed without causing the jth peephole mask *not* to match the input pattern in this particular alignment is a subpattern. The class of subpatterns which differ from this subpattern only in position (i.e. shift) is an f-class. We shall refer to this f-class as the jth f-class because it corresponds to the jth peephole mask. The Section 5.6.1 system transforms an input pattern into a binary pattern in which the jth bit is '1' or '0' according as at least one subpattern belonging to the jth f-class is or is not included in the input pattern.

Let C be the union of all regions marked A or B in Figure 6.7 (p. 145). Thus C is the set of all bit locations such that any member of C belongs to at least one of the A or B regions in Figure 6.7. In the Section 5.2 sense, C is an n-tuple. Let D be the set of all states of C such that when C is in a state belonging to D, then the function (6.13) is *true*. Let E be the set of all subpatterns such that a member of E is a member of D or differs from a member of D only in position. The *overhang* feature is present in an input pattern if and only if a subpattern which belongs to E is included in the input pattern. The IBM 1975 transforms an input pattern into a binary pattern in which the bit associated with the overhang feature is '1' or '0' according as a subpattern which belongs to the f-class E is or is not included in the input pattern.

Let us now define C_j to be the set of pattern elements for which the corresponding weights are non-zero in the jth threshold logic unit in the first layer of an α-perceptron. Let D_{j1} be the set of states of C_j which cause the jth threshold logic unit to give output '1', and let D_{j0} be the set of states of C_j which cause the jth threshold logic unit to give output '0'. The first layer of an α-perceptron transforms an input pattern into a τ-bit pattern in which, for $j = 1, \ldots, \tau$, the jth bit is '1' or '0' according as a subpattern belonging to the f-class D_{j1} or to the f-class D_{j0} is included in the input pattern.

In the Stanford Research Institute edge detector system which was mentioned in Section 7.2.1, an input pattern is transformed into an 84-bit binary pattern which the jth bit is '1' if the output of the threshold unit for at least one alignment of a peephole mask in the jth zone-and-orientation is '1', and '0' otherwise. Let D_{ji} be the set of 4 x 8 bit subpatterns such that, if and only if the input pattern includes a member of D_{ji}, then the output of the threshold unit for the peephole mask in the ith alignment in the jth zone-and-orientation is '1'. Let E_j be the union of the D_{ji}'s over all alignments in the jth zone-and-orientation. That is, $E_j = D_{j1} \cup D_{j2} \cup \ldots \cup D_{ji} \cup \ldots \cup D_{js}$. In this system an input pattern is transformed into an 84-bit pattern in which the jth bit is '1' or '0' according as the input pattern does or does not include at least one subpattern belonging to the f-class E_j.

Let us re-define D_{ji} to be a set of states of the n-tuple which is labelled 'A' in Figure 7.3. In particular, let D_{ji} be the set of all states of 'A' which *match* the peephole mask which is associated with 'A'. Different values of i correspond to different alignments of 'A' with the input pattern. One of the questions in Bomba's tree[50] can be asked in the form 'does the input pattern contain any subpattern which belongs to the f-class E_j?', where E_j is the union of all D_{ji}'s over a prescribed zone. Bomba's system gives the same recognition performance as a system which

(1) transforms an input pattern into a binary pattern in which the jth bit is '1' if and only if the input pattern contains at least one subpattern which belongs to the jth subclass, and
(2) recognises the pattern resulting from step (1) by means of a tree of the Section 6.5.2 sort.

In spite of differences in implementation, the recognition systems which have been mentioned in this section are all examples of *negating* systems. As we shall see in Section 10.2, the distinction between negating and non-negating systems is important from the point of view of the automatic determination of f-classes. Loosely speaking, a *negating* system is a system in which there are values of j, r, and s, such that, if an input pattern X includes a subpattern belonging to the jth f-class, this inclusion is used as evidence in favour of assigning X to the rth recognition class, and as evidence *against* assigning X to the sth recognition class. More precisely, a negating system is, or is equivalent to, a system which

(1) transforms an input pattern X into a τ-bit binary pattern Z in which the jth bit is 1 or 0 according as at least one subpattern belonging to the jth f-class is or is not included in the input pattern, and
(2) recognises Z by either
    (a) using a Boolean discriminant $f_r(Z)$ and assigning X to the rth class if $f_r(Z)$ is *true* and $f_s(Z)$ is *false* for all $s \neq r$, or

(b) using a numerical discriminant $g_r(Z)$ and assigning X to the rth class if $g_r(Z) > g_s(Z) + \rho$ for all $s \neq r$, where ρ is a reject threshold, and

(3) To formulate condition (3) let Z_1 be a τ-bit binary pattern in which the jth bit is '1', and let Z_1' be the τ-bit pattern which is generated from Z_1 by changing the jth bit in Z_1 from '1' to '0'. Let Z_0 be a τ-bit pattern in which the jth bit is '0', and let Z_0' be the τ-bit pattern which is generated from Z_0 by changing the jth bit in Z_0 from '0' to '1'. According to condition (3) there must exist values of j, r, and s, where $r \neq s$, and there must exist patterns Z_1 and Z_0 such that

(a) if condition (2)(a) holds, then

$$f_r(Z_1) = true \text{ and } f_r(Z_r') = false \text{ and } f_s(Z_0) = true \text{ and } f_s(Z_0') = false$$

or

(b) if condition (2)(b) holds, then

$$g_r(Z_1) > g_r(Z_1') \quad \text{and} \quad g_s(Z_0) > g_s(Z_0')$$

For instance, in the Section 5.6.1, system, the f-classes are automatically selected *so that* if X includes any member of the jth f-class, this inclusion can be used as evidence *for* assigning X to any member of one set of recognition classes and *against* assigning X to any member of another set of recognition classes. In the IBM 1975, if X contains the *overhang* feature, that is, if X contains a subpattern belonging to the *overhang* f-class, this is used as evidence *for* recognising X as 'T' and *against* recognising X as 'I'. In Bomba's tree[50], the presence of a horizontal line feature in any one of the three top 30 x 20 bit zones is used as evidence *for* the input pattern being 'T' or '3', and *against* the input pattern being 'L' or 'A'.

The term *feature* is used very broadly in the literature on pattern recognition[262a, 274]. We are concerned in Section 7.5 with systems in which it can reasonably be said that the jth *feature* is present or absent from the input pattern according as a member of the jth f-class is or is not included in the input pattern. A feature is associated with an f-class in the same way that a character is associated with a recognition class. In Section 7.5 we are concerned with systems in which a recognition class is a set of variants of a character; and a set of variants of a feature is an f-class.

7.5.3 Non-negating systems

A *non-negating* system is a system which transforms a pattern X into a pattern Z in which the jth bit is '1' or '0' according as at least one subpattern belonging to the jth f-class is or is not included in the input pattern, and recognises X by recognising Z.

For instance, Bledsoe and Browning's system (Section 5.3) is a non-negating system which is not a negating system. In Bledsoe and Browning's system, let A_{rj} be the set of all states of the jth n-tuple which occur in at least one member of the rth class training set. Let a_{rj} be a binary variable such that $a_{rj} = 1$ or 0 according as the input pattern does or does not include a member of the f-class A_{rj}, and let m be the total number of n-tuples. An input pattern is assigned to the rth class if, for all $s \neq r$,

$$\sum_{j=1}^{m} a_{rj} > \sum_{j=1}^{m} a_{sj}$$

The value of $\sum_{j=1}^{m} a_{sj}$ cannot be decreased by changing any a_{sj} from $a_{sj} = 0$ to $a_{sj} = 1$, and therefore condition (3)(b) in Section 7.5.2 cannot be satisfied. (If it happens by chance that A_{sj} contains all of the states of the jth n-tuple which do not belong to A_{rj} and no state of the jth n-tuple which does belong to A_{rj}, Bledsoe and Browning's system does not exploit this by using $a_{sj} = 1 - a_{rj}$.)

The Hitachi system which was mentioned in Section 7.2.2.1 is a further example of a non-negating system. The f-classes in this Hitachi system are similar to those of Bomba's system, except that zones of occurrence are used instead of Bomba's rectangular zones. For recognition of characters belonging to the rth recognition class, m_r f-classes are chosen. Let b_{rj} be a binary variable such that $b_{rj} = 1$ or 0 according as the input pattern does or does not include a subpattern belonging to the jth of the m_r f-classes which are used in the recognition of characters belonging to the rth class. The input pattern is assigned to the rth class if $\sum_{j=1}^{m_r} b_{rj} > \rho_r$, where ρ_r is a prescribed threshold. $\sum_{j=1}^{m_s} b_{sj}$ cannot be decreased by changing any b_{sj} from $b_{sj} = 0$ to $b_{sj} = 1$, and therefore condition (3)(b) in Section 7.5.2 cannot be satisfied. In this Hitachi system, the *absence* of a feature is not used as evidence for assigning the input pattern to the rth class. (Because of this, a 2 which contains all the features of 7 may not be correctly recognised. Bledsoe and Browning's system does not have this disadvantage.)

7.5.4 Relational systems

A *relational* system is a system in which an input pattern X is assigned to the rth recognition class only if X contains a combination of subpatterns which belongs to a (perhaps implicitly or intensively) prescribed set of combinations of subpatterns.

As a very simple abstract example, let us consider the three f-classes

$$F_\alpha = \{\alpha_1, \ldots, \alpha_\delta\}, F_\beta = \{\beta_1, \ldots, \beta_\delta\}, F_\gamma = \{\gamma_1, \ldots, \gamma_\delta\}$$

A non-negating condition is: assign X to the rth class if X contains any member of F_α and any member of F_β and any member of F_γ. According to this, X is assigned to the rth class if X contains *any* one of the δ^3 combinations $\alpha_1\beta_1\gamma_1, \alpha_1\beta_1\gamma_2, \alpha_1\beta_2\gamma_1, \ldots, \alpha_\delta\beta_\delta\gamma_\delta$. On the other hand, a relational condition is: assign X to the rth class if X contains any combination of subpatterns belonging to the set

$$\gamma = \{\alpha_1\beta_1\gamma_1, \alpha_3\beta_2\gamma_2, \alpha_6\beta_3\gamma_8, \ldots, \alpha_9\beta_7\gamma_9\}$$

where γ generally does not contain all of the δ^3 possible combinations comprising one member of each of F_1, F_2, and F_3. In the special case where γ does contain all of the δ^3 possible combinations, the relational condition is also a non-negating condition.

The Toshiba system of Section 7.4.3 is a relational system which cannot usefully be regarded as a non-negating system. In the Section 7.4.3 system, CAP, CUP, BAR, etc., are the names of f-classes of 3 x 36 bit subpatterns. The system does not recognise an input pattern X by recognising a pattern Z in which one of the bits is '1' or '0' according as X does or does not contain *any* subpattern belonging to the f-class CAP, another of the bits is '1' or '0' according as X does or does not contain *any* subpattern belonging to the f-class CUP, and so on. According to Figure 7.30, X is recognised as an '8' if X contains a member of BLANK *which is followed by* a member of BAR *which is followed by* a member of CAP, and so on.

The system of Grimsdale *et al.* (Section 7.3.3) is a further example of a relational system. Suppose, for introductory simplicity, that only one reference pattern per recognition class is used in the system, and let X_r be the reference pattern for the rth recognition class. X_r is segmented into a number, say n_r, of chunks of black, and let us denote these chunks of black by $\gamma_{10}, \gamma_{20}, \ldots, \gamma_{io}, \ldots, \gamma_{n_r o}$ respectively. For $i = 1, \ldots, n_r$, let $F_i = \{\gamma_{i1}, \gamma_{i2}, \ldots, \gamma_{i\delta_i}\}$ be the set of all chunks of black which differ from γ_{io} only within prescribed limits of length, curvature, and orientation. X is assigned to the rth class if X is segmented into n_r chunks which can be indexed $1, \ldots, n_r$ so that

(1) for all $i = 1, \ldots, n_r$, the ith chunk of X belongs to F_i, and
(2) if the ith and jth chunks of X_r form, for instance, a 'BL' join, then the ith and jth chunks of X form a 'BL' join, and vice versa.

This is not a non-negating system, because condition (1) is not sufficient: X is assigned to the rth class only if condition (2) is also satisfied. Condition (2) restricts positional *relationships* of the chunks of X.

The systems of Sections 7.3.4 and 7.3.5 are relational. For instance, in Section 7.3.4 let $F'_{rij} = \{F'_{rij1}, F'_{rij2}, \ldots, F'_{rijk}, \ldots, F'_{rij\delta_j}\}$ be the set of all n-tuples of black bits on T such that $F_{rij} \cup F'_{rijk}$ consists only of bits in members of the union of the n members of Q which constitute a member of L. Here X is assigned to the rth class if (7.2) is satisfied: it is not sufficient for X merely to include one member of each of $F'_{ri1}, \ldots, F'_{ri\phi}$.

Loosely speaking, a non-negating system is a restricted case of a relational system, in which all combinations of members of f-classes are allowed. A negating system is a restricted case of a non-negating system in which it is useful to use the absence of a given feature as evidence for assigning a pattern to a given recognition class.

The logical structure of a relational system is usually more elaborate than that of a non-negating system, and it is sensible to ask whether a relational system can be expected to have any practical advantage over a non-negating system. We shall not attempt to answer this question in general terms, but in Section 10.3.3 we shall see analytically that the relational rule (7.6) does have an advantage over a specific non-negating rule[443a]

It is perhaps worth noting that relational systems such as those of Toshiba and Grimsdale *et al.* do not use zones; whereas in the systems of Section 7.2, recognition depends on the detection of subpatterns within prescribed zones. In Section 7.2, recognition depends on the positions of subpatterns, and the spatial arrangement or ordering of subpatterns is roughly implied by the positioning of subpatterns. In the systems of Toshiba and Grimsdale *et al.*, recognition depends on the spatial ordering or arrangement of subpatterns, and the relative positions of subpatterns are roughly implied by their spatial ordering.

7.5.5 Recognition of distorted shapes

The main purpose of the present section is to suggest *why* f-classes have been found useful in the recognition of distorted shapes[443a]. To be specific, let us confine our attention to rubber-sheet distortions. When the jth of the possible rubber-sheet distortions operates on the pattern X, we denote the resulting pattern by $D_j(X)$. The inverse distortion D_j^{-1} changes $D_j(X)$ back to X:

$$D_j^{-1}(D_j(X)) = X$$

Let $V = \{D_1, \ldots, D_j, \ldots, D_\beta\}$ be the set of all possible rubber-sheet distortions such that no member of V alters the recognition class of any pattern in any of the classes $R_1, \ldots, R_r, \ldots, R_z$.

Even if the distortions $D_1, \ldots, D_j, \ldots, D_\beta$ were known in practice, the number β would be so large that it would not be practical to try out each j in turn and assign X to the rth class if, for any i, $D_j(X) = X_{ri}$, where as usual, X_{ri} is the ith member of the rth class training set.

A more practical technique is to choose a set $\{F_{ri1}, \ldots, F_{rik}, \ldots, F_{ri\phi}\}$ of subpatterns of X_{ri}, and for each $k = 1, \ldots, \phi$ define the f-class

$$E_{rik} = \{D_1^{-1}(F_{rik}), \ldots, D_j^{-1}(F_{rik}), \ldots, D_\beta^{-1}(F_{rik})\}$$

If $D_j(X) = X_{ri}$, or in other words, if $D_j^{-1}(X_{ri}) = X$, then X can be assigned to the rth class. If, for any j, $D_j^{-1}(X_{ri}) = X$, then X necessarily contains at least one subpattern in each of the f-classes $E_{ri1}, \ldots, E_{ri\phi}$. If $F_{ri1}, \ldots, F_{ri\phi}$ are chosen so that no pattern belonging to the sth class (where $s = 1, \ldots, z, s \neq r$) contains at least one subpattern in each of $E_{ri1}, \ldots, E_{ri\phi}$, then we can safely assign X to the rth class if X contains at least one subpattern in each of the f-classes $E_{ri1}, \ldots, E_{ri\phi}$. The practical usefulness of this simple archetypal non-negating recognition rule (cf. Ref. 361a) depends on the cost of equipment for determining whether X contains at least one subpattern in each of $E_{ri1}, \ldots, E_{ri\phi}$. Practical techniques for determining whether X contains any member of a given (usually intensively defined) f-class have been considered above in previous sections. It is usual to reduce system complexity by normalising X at least for position and possibly for size.

For recognition of the numeral '7' we might perhaps use a subpattern F_{rik} which consists of a leftward pointing line-ending at the top left of the character, and for later reference let us denote the corresponding f-class by E_1 instead of E_{rik}. For recognition of the numeral '1', to prevent misrecognition as '7', we might perhaps use a subpattern F_{rik} which consists of an upward-pointing line-ending at the top of the character, flanked on the left by a considerable white area, and let us denote the corresponding f-class by E_2. If an unknown pattern X were found to contain any subpattern belonging to E_2, this might, in the non-negating system introduced above, satisfy one of a set of ϕ conditions for recognising X as a '1'. However, it might be more economical, and just as effective in practice, to discard the f-class E_2, and instead of using the condition that X must contain at least one member of E_2, use the condition that X must *not* contain any member of E_1. After this modification had been made, the system would be a *negating* system. Analogous modifications might be made for other f-classes, and we could regard the resulting system as a system which transforms the input pattern X into a τ-bit binary pattern, in which the jth bit is '1' or '0' according as X does or does not include at least one member of the jth f-class. Instead of recognising a τ-bit pattern by looking it up in a decision table, it is generally more economical to use numerical or non-trivial Boolean discriminants.

In the non-negating and negating systems which have been introduced in the present section, an f-class consists of distorted versions of a reference subpattern. The 'overhang' f-class in the IBM 1975 (Section 7.5.2) accords at least roughly with this, in that it consists of a set of subpatterns which are quite similar to each other in shape. But the reasoning of the present section is not the only reasoning which leads to the use of f-classes, and for example the f-classes used in Bledsoe and Browning's system (Section 7.5.3) or those used in Stearn's system (Section 10.2.2.2) do not generally consist of distorted versions of reference subpatterns. Even in a system which can be understood in terms of the present section, to achieve minimum error rates at minimum cost it may not be necessary for an f-class to be precisely a set $\{D_1^{-1}(F_{rik}), \ldots, D_\beta^{-1}(F_{rik})\}$. For instance, in Bomba's system[50], rectangular zones can be regarded as providing, in some cases, a very rough approximation to zones of occurrence in a system such as the Hitachi system[215].

To understand the system of Grimsdale *et al.* (Section 7.3.3) in terms of distortions, let us say that the reference pattern X_{ri} is partitioned by the watchbird technique into ϕ chunks $F_{ri1}, \ldots, F_{rik}, \ldots, F_{ri\phi}$ of black. Let us assume that the watchbird technique partitions a pattern $X = D_j^{-1}(X_{ri})$ into the ϕ chunks $D_j^{-1}(F_{ri1}), \ldots, D_j^{-1}(F_{ri\phi})$. Further, let us assume that each of the distortions $D_1, \ldots, D_\beta$ is such that, if and only if a pair of chunks of X_{ri} touch, then the corresponding pair of chunks of $X = D_j^{-1}(X_{ri})$ touch; and that the join-classification (TL, TR, etc.) of corresponding pairs of touching chunks is the same. Still further, let us assume that, for any $j = 1, \ldots, \beta$, for any $r = 1, \ldots, z$, for any $i = 1, \ldots, t_r$, and for any $k = 1, \ldots, \phi$, the length, curvature, and orientation of the chunk $D_j^{-1}(F_{rik})$ differ from the length, curvature, and orientation of the chunk F_{rik} only within limits which are known to us and which serve as the prescribed limits in condition (1) in Section 7.3.3. If these assumptions are true, and if an unknown pattern X is such that, for some j, $X = D_j^{-1}(X_{ri})$, then it must obviously be possible to construct graphs from X and X_{ri} which satisfy conditions (1) and (2) in Section 7.3.3. [But if conditions (1) and (2) are satisfied it does not necessarily follow that, for some j, $X = D_j^{-1}(X_{ri})$.]

An assumption of distortion continuity is implicit in the assumption that if and only if a pair of chunks of X_{ri} touch then the corresponding chunks of $D_j^{-1}(X_{ri})$ touch. To introduce a further recognition technique which makes use of an assumption that characters are subject to continuous distortions, let us say that, if the distortion D_j is applied to a rubber sheet, then the point (x, y) on the undistorted rubber sheet is moved to position (x', y') on the distorted rubber sheet. If D_j is continuous, and if we move the point (x, y) continuously round (for instance) the external black/white contour of $D_j^{-1}(X_{ri})$, then (x', y') will move continuously round the external contour of X_{ri}.

Let us construct round the unknown pattern X and round the training set pattern X_{ri} the smallest rectangles whose boundaries do not intersect any black, as in Figure 7.1. Let us divide these rectangles into (for instance) 3 x 3 zones, and index these zones $1, \ldots, i, \ldots, 9$, as in Section 7.2.1. For simplicity, let us assume that for any j, if and only if (x, y) is in the ith zone, then (x', y') is in the ith zone. In this case, if, for some j, $D_j(X) = X_{ri}$ and D_j is continuous, then the sequence of zones through which the point (x, y) passes while continuously traversing the external contour of X must be the same as the sequence of zones through which (x', y') passes. This suggests a recognition technique in which the external contour of each training set pattern X_{ri} is traced, and the system records the sequence of zones through which the contour passes. The contour of an unknown pattern X is traced, and the sequence of zones through which the contour passes is compared with the sequences obtained from training set patterns. If X yields the same sequence as X_{ri}, then X is assigned to the rth class. To illustrate the power of this simple rule (cf. Section 7.4.1), note that, at whatever point the contour traversal starts, Figures 7.1(b) and 7.1(c), and also Figures 7.2(a) and 7.2(b) yield different sequences, so that these characters are distinguished without the detection of contour slope or more-elaborate features within zones.

Brown[65] described a system which recorded the sequence of indices of the zones through which the stylus passed while a character was being written. When the stylus was lifted at the end of a stroke, a special symbol was introduced into the sequence. The sequence which was obtained from an unknown character was compared with sequences which had been obtained from training set characters. If X and X_{ri} yielded the same sequence, then X was assigned to the rth class. Brown's system is said to be an *on-line* or a *real-time* recognition system, because it processes stylus position data during the writing of a character. Further real-time character recognition techniques are described in Refs 38, 112a, 121, 163, 193, 313, and 433, and generally speaking, real-time recognition of hand-printed characters has been found easier and cheaper than recognition which is not in real time. Refs 131, 154, 313a, and 466 describe techniques for real-time recognition of cursive script, and Mermelstein and Eden's technique of cursive script recognition will be introduced in Section 8.4.

7.6 CROSSING COUNTING TECHNIQUES

In the systems of Sections 3.10, 5.6.2, 9.1, 9.4.2, and 9.5, an input pattern is transformed into a non-binary pattern, and none of these systems can usefully be regarded as a member of any of the categories of Section 7.5. The crossing counting systems which are outlined in the present section are (mostly) further examples of systems which do not belong to any of the categories of Section 7.5. We first mention some of the older techniques which are only of historical interest.

In 1954 Rohland[373] described a system which scanned an input character with a 24 column x 16 row vertical raster. Five further raster scans were also used, their scanning lines being inclined at 90°, ± 35°, and ± 19° to the vertical respectively. Let us consider the vertical raster by way of example: the procedure which was used for the vertical raster was also used for the other five rasters.

The system counted the black elements in each column of the vertical raster. If the count for a given column exceeded seven it was called a *long* count, and if it exceeded four it was called a *short* count (so a long count was also a short count). If a short count was detected in a column, the system ignored the occurrence of a short count in any of the next three columns of the scan. Similarly, if a long count was detected in a column, long counts in the next three columns were ignored, because the first long count was sufficient to indicate the presence of a fairly long piece of character limb parallel to the columns of the raster scan. Rohland's system simply counted the number of not-ignored long and short counts for each raster. Recognition was accomplished by a tree of the Section 6.5.2 type, in which the nodal questions were such as 'does the horizontal raster have at least two long counts?', or 'does the +35° raster have at least three short counts?'.

A system described by Weeks[457] also used six differently orientated raster scans. Each raster consisted of 64 lines, but only six of these lines were actually used in recognition. These six lines were selected so that they lay equally spaced between the first and last of the 64 lines which were found to contain any black; as, for example, in Figure 7.33.

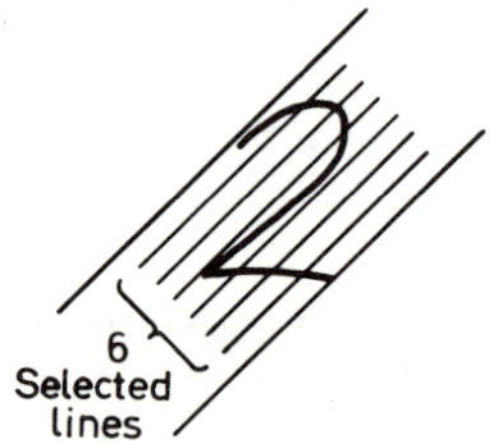

Figure 7.33. *Weeks' six selected lines*

The system counted the number of times each of the six selected lines of each of the six rasters crossed black. A count larger than three was treated *as* a count of three, and thus for each line of each raster there were four possible counts: 0, 1, 2, 3. The system transformed an input character into a 6 x 6 x 4 = 144-bit binary pattern, in which any given bit was '1' or '0' according as a given line in a given raster did or did not cross black a given number of times. The 144-bit pattern was recognised by the method of Section 3.3.

Johnson[239] and Dimond[121] described systems in which numerals were written or printed round two dots as shown in Figure 7.34(a). Figure 7.34(b) shows seven black lines a, b, . . ., g radiating from the two dots used in Figure 7.34(a). A character was recognised according to the lines a, b, . . ., g which it did or did not cross. For instance the character '1' crosses only b and d, '2' crosses, a, b, c, f, e, and so on. (In Dimond's system[121] line g sloped down to the left somewhat, and line f sloped up to the left.)

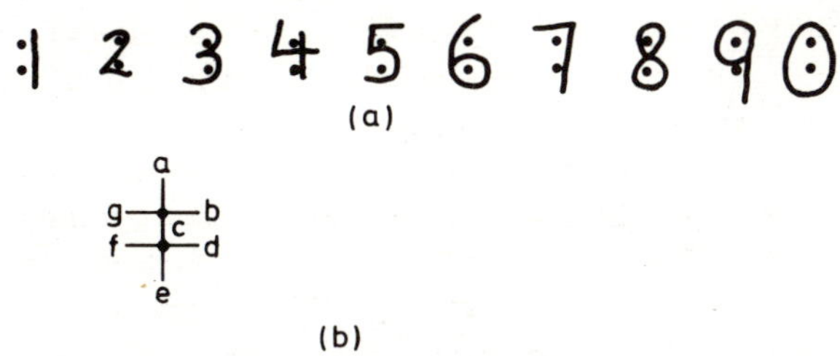

Figure 7.34. (*a*) *Characters written round dots;* (*b*) *Lines which are crossed*

More recently, Glucksman[174, 257] developed a technique in which the input pattern was the binary pattern filling a rectangular box which just fitted round the input character. For every white element in the input pattern, the system obtained four counts. These four counts were respectively the numbers of times when a line pointing N, E, S, or W from a given white point crossed a character limb. A count which was greater than two was treated *as* a count of two. For each of the $3^4 = 81$ possible combinations of counts, e.g. 1, 1, 2, 1; 0, 1, 2, 0; etc., the system counted up the total number of white elements in the input pattern which manifested this particular combination of counts. Thus the input pattern was transformed into a vector with 81 components, each component being the number of white elements having a particular combination of counts. The 81-component vector was recognised by, for example, a linear discriminant system.

Whereas Johnson and Dimond counted crossings with lines emanating from *two* fixed points, and Glucksman counted crossings with lines emanating from *all* white points, an early IBM system[371] counted crossings with lines emanating from a *few* automatically selected white points. An input character was scanned with a vertical raster, and recognition was accomplished by a tree of the Section 6.5.2 type. The question at the first node in the tree was 'does the input character contain a *triple intersection?*'. A *triple intersection* was deemed present in the input character if two successive vertical lines of scan had three intersections with character limbs. If the input character was found to contain a triple intersection, the tree asked next 'does the input character contain *lower left inlet*?'. To explain this, let us denote by S_2 the second of the two successive vertical lines of scan which intersect three black limbs. Let S_{2U} be the set of white bits in S_2 between the top and middle black sections, and let S_{2L} be the set of white elements in S_2 lying between the middle and bottom black sections. *Lower left inlet* was deemed present in the input character if, from at least one bit in S_{2L}, a horizontal line extending leftwards did not cross any black. *Upper right inlet* was deemed present if, from at least one bit in S_{2U}, a horizontal line extending rightwards did not cross any black. *Upper left inlet* was similarly defined. The characters '3', '5', '9' were expected to possess *lower left inlet,* and '2', '6', '8' were not. '2' was expected to have *upper left inlet,* and '6' and '8' were not. '6' was expected to have *upper right inlet,* and '8' was not.

A further crossing counting system was described by Doyle[125]. Doyle smoothed input patterns by a method similar to Unger's (Section 2.4.1), and recognition was based on the results of various tests applied to smoothed characters. The outcome of a test was a string of not more than 12 integers. For example, one test consisted of scanning the input character with a vertical raster, and, for each line of scan, counting the number of black limbs which were crossed. The sequence of numbers of intersections with black in successive vertical lines, after removing adjacent repetitions, was the *outcome* of this test. For instance, the numbers of intersections with the character '0' might be 11222211, and, after removing adjacent repetitions, the outcome of this test would be 121. Another one of Doyle's tests differed from this only in that a horizontal rather than a vertical raster was used.

In yet another of Doyle's tests, a vertical raster was used, and the first vertical line of the raster to intersect black was stored. After each subsequent vertical line, the stored line was updated as follows. For all *i,* that is, for all bits in a line of scan, if the *i*th bit in the line of scan was black, then the *i*th bit in the stored line was changed to black, regardless of whether it was previously black or white. If the *i*th bit in the line of scan was white, then the *i*th bit in the stored line was left unchanged. (In other words, updating consisted of *or*'ing the latest line of scan into the stored line.) After each line of scan, and after the updating operation, the number of separate black sections in the updated stored line was ascertained. If this number was less than the number in the previous updated stored line, or if the raster had by then scanned half of the input character, scanning ceased, and the outcome of the test was the number of separate black sections in the penultimate version of the updated stored line. Doyle used altogether four tests of this sort, employing respectively horizontal rasters scanning from top to bottom and bottom to top, and vertical rasters scanning from left to right and right to left. Note that when, for instance, a left-to-right vertical raster is used, an element is white in the updated stored line only if a horizontal line extending leftwards from the corresponding element in the latest line of scan does not meet any black. The IBM system mentioned above[371] used and developed this technique for determining whether various *inlets* etc., were present in the input character.

Doyle used further tests besides those which we have mentioned. The outcomes of the tests determined the components of a binary vector. Each component of this vector was '1' or '0' according as a particular test did or did not yield a particular outcome. For instance, one component of this vector would be '1' only if the outcome of a given one of Doyle's tests was '121', another component would be '1' only if the outcome of this test was '131', another component would be '1' only if the outcome of this test was '2321', and so on. The binary vector was recognised by the method of Section 3.3, and indeed one purpose of Doyle's work was to try out this method, the tests being chosen merely because they were easy to implement on a digital computer.

Gamba and his associates have experimented with various different techniques[165] for transforming an input pattern into a vector with many binary components. For instance, one technique[166] uses a different pair of randomly drawn lines for each test (cf. Novikoff[339]). These lines may be curly and/or broken. The result of each test is '1' or '0' according as the number of intersections of the input character with a given one of the random lines is or is not greater than the number of intersections with the other. The vector composed of the test results is recognised by the method of Section 3.3.

Most of the crossing counting techniques which we have mentioned do not measure the distances along a line between points where that line meets black. In a further family of techniques, distances to intersections are measured[408, 419]. In the simplest (but not the most useful) technique of this sort, a character is placed in a square or circular box,

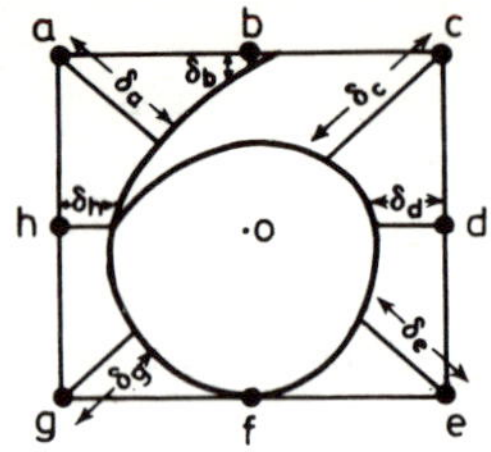

Figure 7.35. *Radial distances to the edge of a character*

as in Figure 7.35. In Figure 7.35, the point o is the centre of the box, and a, b, . . ., h are arbitrary points on the edge of the box. The length δ_a is the distance between a and the point where the line ao first meets black, δ_b is the distance between b and the point where the line bo first meets black, and $\delta_c, \ldots, \delta_h$ are defined similarly. Recognition techniques are applied[78, 294] to the vector $\{\delta_a, \ldots, \delta_h\}$.

Chapter 8

CONTEXTUAL, LINGUISTIC, AND ARRAY TECHNIQUES

8.1 CONTEXT

8.1.1 Context using complete words

The recognition systems which we have so far considered assign an input character to a recognition class without taking account of the context of the input character. Accuracy of recognition can generally be improved by taking account of context, and we now outline a few of the methods by which this has been done.

Bledsoe and Browning's method[45] of using context could be applied in many numerical discriminant systems, that is, in systems where an unknown pattern X is assigned to the rth class if $g_r(X) > g_s(X)$ for all s except $s = r$, where, for present purposes, $g_a(X), \ldots, g_r(X), g_s(X), \ldots, g_z(X)$ are the numerical discriminant functions for the letters a, b, . . ., z respectively. Bledsoe and Browning's context method requires the storage of a dictionary containing all the words which the machine is to recognise. In the recognition of an unknown word, the system only actually refers to stored words which contain the same number of letters as the unknown word. Suppose for instance that the unknown word has four letters, X_1, X_2, X_3, and X_4. For each four-letter word in the dictionary, the system sums the values of the discriminant functions appropriate to the letters in the dictionary word. For instance, for the dictionary word 'able' the system computes the sum $g_a(X_1) + g_b(X_2) + g_1(X_3) + g_e(X_4)$. For the dictionary word 'them', the system computes the sum $g_t(X_1) + g_h(X_2) + g_e(X_3) + g_m(X_4)$, and so on for all other four-letter words in the dictionary. The unknown word is recognised as the dictionary word for which the sum is highest.

Statistical considerations suggest that the logarithm of the *a priori* probability of a word should be added to the sum for that word. For instance, for the dictionary word 'able' the sum

$$g_a(X_1) + g_b(X_2) + g_l(X_3) + g_e(X_4) + \log(\textit{a priori}\text{ probability of 'able'})$$

should be computed; for the dictionary word 'them' the sum

$$g_t(X_1) + g_h(X_2) + g_e(X_3) + g_m(X_4) + \log(\textit{a priori}\text{ probability of 'them'})$$

should be computed, and so on for all other four-letter words in the dictionary. Again, the unknown word should be recognised as the four-letter word for which the sum is highest.

To see this mathematically, let ω be the number of letters in a given input word. According to the maximum likelihood decision rule[1a, 127], the letters which constitute the input word should be assigned respectively to the classes $R_{r_1}, \ldots, R_{r_i}, \ldots, R_{r_\omega}$ such that $P(r_1, \ldots, r_\omega \mid X_1, \ldots, X_\omega)$ is greater than for any other assignment of letters to recognition classes. In this, $P(r_1, \ldots, r_\omega \mid X_1, \ldots, X_\omega)$ is the conditional probability that the ω letters belong respectively to the classes $R_{r_1}, \ldots, R_{r_\omega}$, given that the letters of the input word are the patterns $X_1, \ldots, X_\omega$ respectively. According to Bayes' rule,

$$P(r_1, \ldots, r_\omega \mid X_1, \ldots, X_\omega) = \frac{P(r_1, \ldots, r_\omega) \,.\, P(X_1, \ldots, X_\omega \mid r_1, \ldots, r_\omega)}{P(X_1, \ldots, X_\omega)} \quad (8.1)$$

where $P(r_1, \ldots, r_\omega)$ is the *a priori* probability of the word whose letters belong respectively to the classes $R_{r_1}, \ldots, R_{r_\omega}$. In the recognition of print or hand print, but probably not in the recognition of cursive script, it may be useful to assume that the precise shape of any character in the input word does not depend on the class to which any other character in the input word belongs.

In this case we have

$$P(X_1, \ldots, X_\omega \mid r_1, \ldots, r_\omega) = \prod_{i=1}^{\omega} P(X_i \mid r_i)$$

For maximisation purposes we can ignore $P(X_1, \ldots, X_\omega)$ in (8.1), since this is the same for all possible class assignments of $X_1, \ldots, X_\omega$. Thus, taking logs as in Section 3.3, $X_1, \ldots, X_\omega$ should be assigned to $R_{r_1}, \ldots, R_{r_\omega}$ such that

$$\log P(r_1, \ldots, r_\omega) + \sum_{i=1}^{\omega} \log P(X_i \mid r_i) \text{ is maximised}$$

In the recognition systems of, for example, Sections 3.3, 3.4, 4.6.1, 5.1, and 5.2, the numerical discriminant is (we hope) a function which is at least roughly maximised if log $P(X_i|r_i)$ is maximised. In such systems, $X_1, \ldots, X_\omega$ should be assigned to $R_{r_1}, \ldots, R_{r_\omega}$ such that

$$\log P(r_1, \ldots, r_\omega) + \sum_{i=1}^{\omega} g_{ri}(X_i) \text{ is maximised}$$

where $g_{r_i}(X)$ is the discriminant for the class R_{r_i}.

Garry[167] and Duda and Hart[127] have employed rules of this sort, except that they have used arbitrary measures of confidence instead of numerical discriminants. If the dictionary is available before the document is read (which is not the case in Duda and Hart's work), it is unnecessary to try putting together all possible class assignments for $X_1, \ldots, X_\omega$ so as to make up words which are not in the dictionary. Instead, to recognise an unknown word, we can work through the dictionary computing the appropriate sum for each word in the dictionary, and storing only the word which has the highest sum found so far.

An alternative method of using context has been developed for the IBM 1975. The IBM 1975 used by the American Social Security Administration is required to recognise about one million different names, including the name 'JANES'. There is a chance the 'O' in 'JONES' will be misrecognised as 'A' by the character recognition machine, so that 'JONES' will be misrecognised as 'JANES'. Fosdick *et al.*[148] and Hennis[210] have described a scheme for reducing the *total* number of errors of this sort, and a simplified version of this scheme is as follows. Two lists of names are stored, and the first of these lists contains names which are unlikely to be confused with other names due to misrecognition of characters. If a name belonging to this list is the apparent output of the character recognition machine, this name is accepted as the final output of the system. The second list contains names which are most likely to occur as the result of misrecognition. If a name belonging to the second list is the output from the character recognition machine, this name is changed to what is likely to be a correct version, e.g. 'JANES' or 'JONSS' is changed to 'JONES' and the corrected version is the final output of the system. This process of correction is only applied to names for which there is statistical confidence that, on average, many more errors will be put right than correct names made wrong. Any name for which the ratio of the probability of being correct to the probability of being the result of misrecognition is within a prescribed range is placed in neither list, and the system always rejects such names (cf. Baskin and Bonner[33]).

8.1.2 Context using *n*-grams

The time taken to look up a word in a dictionary may be reduced by storing, for example, 'thick-er-est-en-ens' as a single composite entry rather than as five separate entries 'thick', 'thicker', etc. A well-known development of this idea is to store the dictionary in the form of a tree rather than a list. But even when such ideas are applied, the use of a large dictionary is still costly, either in time taken to look up words, or in hardware, or in both.

Instead of working with a dictionary of complete words, it is generally more economical to work with digrams, trigrams, etc., although this yields a smaller reduction in error rates than when complete words are used[451]. For present purposes a *symbol* is a letter or a space. A *digram* is a pair of consecutive symbols. A *trigram, tetragram,* . . ., *n-gram* are respectively a set of 3, 4, . . ., *n* consecutive symbols. For instance, # CA, CAT, AT # are trigrams included in the word # CAT #, where # stands for *space*.

A simple method is to store the *a priori* probability of each digram which ever occurs. Let us consider the recognition of the word $\#X_1X_2X_3X_4\#$, and suppose that the initial '#' (i.e. space) has already been recognised. To recognise X_1, the system evaluates the numerical discriminants $g_a(X_1), \ldots, g_r(X_1), \ldots, g_z(X_1)$, and assigns X_1 to the rth class such that $g_r(X_1) . P(\#r)$ is greatest, where $P(\#r)$ is the *a priori* probability of occurrence of the digram composed of # followed by a member of the rth class. Suppose for instance that X_1 is recognised as 'C'. Then X_2 is assigned to the rth class such that $g_r(X_2) . P(Cr)$ is greatest. Suppose for instance that X_2 is recognised as 'A'. Then X_3 is assigned to the rth class such that $g_r(X_3) . P(Ar)$ is greatest, and so on for the remaining characters in the word. A technique of this sort has been applied in speech recognition by Denes[114], but it has the disadvantage that errors tend to propagate along the string of symbols which constitute a word[1a, 143].

Carlson[69] has considered a problem in which one of the letters in a name is a character which has been rejected by a character recognition machine and the other characters in the name have all been correctly recognised by the character recognition machine. Values of numerical discriminants are not available from the recognition machine. To make a good guess at the recognition class of a rejected character, Carlson uses trigrams, and to obtain estimates of *a priori* probabilities of trigrams, he uses a large repertoire of names. For each trigram which occurs in any name in the repertoire, Carlson's system counts the total number of names in the repertoire which include this trigram. This number, divided by the total number of names in the repertoire, is used as an estimate of the *a priori* probability of the trigram.

To illustrate the use of trigram probabilities, let us consider the name MIC*AEL, where * stands for *reject*. Carlson's system replaces '*' by 'A' and takes the sum of the *a priori* probabilities of ICA, CAA, AAE as the score for 'A'. The system then replaces '*' by 'B' instead of 'A' and takes the sum of the *a priori* probabilities of ICB, CBA, BAE as the score for 'B'. The system then replaces '*' by 'C', and so on; and finally '*' is replaced by the letter whose score is largest. Performance is improved by using two separate *a priori* probabilities for each trigram, according as the trigram is or is not the final trigram in a name.

Thomas and Kassler[434] have considered a problem in which, in an English word, each character is either recognised correctly or classified as a reject, and no further information is available from the recognition machine. Suppose for example that the output of the character recognition machine is '#PIG*ON#'. Like Carlson, Thomas and Kassler substitute in turn all letters of the alphabet for the rejected character. This gives #PIGAON#,#PIGBON#, etc. The tetragrams #PIG, PIGA, IAGO, GAON, AON# are looked up in a list containing all tetragrams which ever occur in English words. If these five tetragrams are all present in this list, #PIGAON# is provisionally accepted as a possible word, and otherwise it is rejected. This process is repeated for the words #PIGBON#, . . .,#PIGZON#, and some of these are provisionally accepted and others rejected.

The provisionally accepted words are then subjected to a second test, which is designed to reject words which would not be found in a dictionary of complete words. Roughly speaking, this second test uses two main lists of n-grams, where n is variable. Corresponding to each n-gram in the first list, there is a set of n-grams in the second list. Each n-gram in the second list includes the n-gram to which it corresponds in the first list†. When any n-gram in the first list is found in a word

†Thomas and Kassler regard what we have called the *second list* as a list of permissible contexts for the n-grams in the first list. In their formulation, an n-gram in the second list does not actually include the corresponding n-gram in the first list, but, instead, the position of the first-list n-gram relative to the second-list n-gram is symbolically indicated.

which has been accepted by the tetragram test, this word is now rejected unless it also contains one of the n-grams in the second list which correspond to this n-gram in the first list.

This use of two lists is a solution to the problem of deciding *which* variable-n n-grams in a candidate word should be checked for presence in a list. This problem can be avoided by using a fixed value of n and stipulating that *all* n-grams must be checked, as Riseman and Ehrich[369b] have as done with digrams and Thomas and Kassler[434] have done with tetragrams. But any fixed value of n is sometimes not big enough to be useful, and is sometimes unnecessarily big. For instance, a tetragram or even a 5-gram test would accept the spurious word 'SPATENT', since 'SPATE' and 'PATENT' are legitimate English words; whereas a digram test would reject the spurious word 'PQN'.

A character recognition machine is not the only possible source of errors in words which it reads. Another important source is the writer, e.g. the typist, of the document which is read. A character recognition machine may perhaps misrecognise or reject a character, but it is generally less likely to pass over a character without making any response at all. A typist, on the other hand, is liable to miss out characters or to put in too many, so that a written word may contain the wrong number of characters. None of the techniques which we would have mentioned so far can cope with spurious omissions and insertions of characters, but this problem has been tackled by, for example, Alberga[8], Alter[13], and Szanser[429].

We have only considered the use of context in recognising characters in words or names. Character recognition machines are often used for recognising arbitrary strings of characters such as account numbers. Further characters, known as check characters, may be incorporated in a string, such that a prescribed arithmetical test is satisfied only if all the characters in the string have been recognised correctly[197, 219, 248]

8.2 SCENE ANALYSIS

In modern syntactic linguistics, a string of symbols is not only recognised but is also analytically described. It has been suggested[254, 331] that linguistic techniques may perhaps be useful for the formal description or analysis of patterns or scenes. A *scene* is a field of view which may contain many objects. *Scene analysis* is the technical term for the description of a two- or three-dimensional scene. A full review of techniques of scene analysis would be beyond the scope of this book, and the following paragraphs merely note some of the respects in which the problems of scene analysis differ from those pattern recognition problems which we have previously encountered.

8.2.1 Multiplicity of possible classifications of a given object

To recognise an object as a cube is to assign the name 'cube' to this object. It may not be necessary to assign such a detailed name to an object in a scene analysis problem. For instance, for purposes of avoiding collision with an object, a mobile automaton[147] might simply recognise an object *as an object,* rather than as a 'cube' or 'tall pillar', etc.

If an automaton has been instructed to locate all cubes within a given scene, it might be convenient to classify all objects in the scene either as cubes or as not-cubes. For instance,there might be no advantage in distinguishing between a tetrahedron and a dodecahedron, since these are both not-cubes. Similarly, if an automaton has been instructed to locate all objects with height less than a given value h, it might be convenient to classify all objects in the scene as 'taller than h' or 'shorter than h', and to ignore details of the shapes of objects.

In these examples, objects are classified, but the class to which a given object may be usefully be assigned differs from example to example.

8.2.2 Shape

8.2.2.1 No shape

In character recognition we are concerned with the shapes of characters, and very loosely we can say that '2' is a 'two' by virtue of its shape. In aerial photographs, lakes and woods are generally not distinguishable by differences in their shapes, but they may be distinguished by differences in texture[205] and perhaps colour[461, 464a]

8.2.2.2 Analytically describable variations in shape

The range of different shapes manifested by different unconstrained hand-printed 2's cannot be expressed in terms of a few concise mathematical formulae. But the shape of a two-dimensional image of a three-dimensional object varies in accordance with the laws of perspective, and, for instance, the range of shapes of images of a cube seen from different points of view *can* be specified mathematically[204]. Roberts[370] has described a system which, given a photograph of an object, can automatically produce a line drawing of this object as it would be seen from a different point of view. Given a television picture of a room containing simple objects, the SRI automaton[128] can produce a map showing where objects are situated on the floor, and this can be used in choosing a path of motion such that the automaton will not collide with any object.

8.2.3 Segmentation of a scene

To locate lines of print on a page, a machine can make use of the horizontal strip of white between successive lines. Once a line of print has been located it can be segmented into characters by the methods introduced in Section 2.3.3. For determining which faces belong to which bodies in Figure 8.1, methods such as those of Section 2.3.3 are not applicable: for instance it is no good simply looking for white gaps between different bodies. Guzman[194] has tackled this problem by a method which involves classifying the shapes of all vertices, that is, of all junctions of two or more lines, in a scene such as Figure 8.1. The following is a simplified introduction to Guzman's technique.

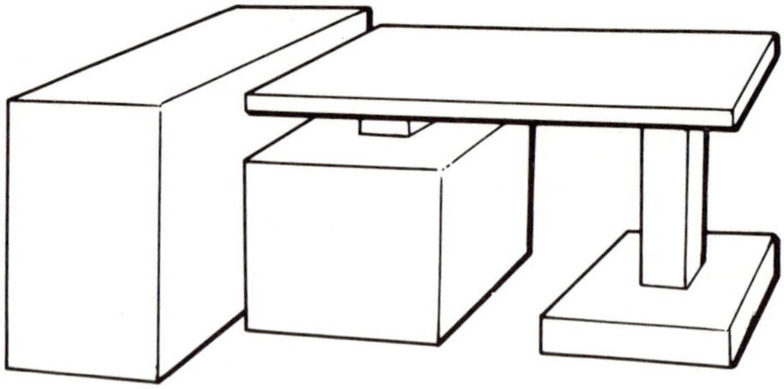

Figure 8.1. *Line drawing of a scene composed of parallelepipeds*

If a vertex is roughly of the 'Y' shape shown in Figure 8.2(a), Guzman's programme *links* the regions A and C, and also links the regions B and C, and also the regions A and B. The idea is that two regions are linked if they meet at a vertex whose shape suggests that these two regions are probably parts of faces belonging to the same body. If a vertex is roughly of the shape shown in Figure 8.2(b), regions D and E and also regions F and G are linked. Rules of this sort are also applied to further classes of vertex shapes.

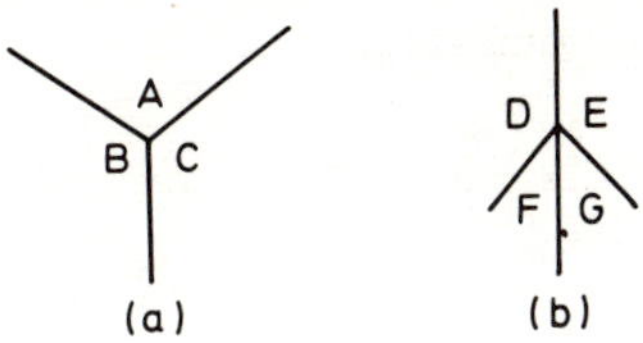

Figure 8.2. *Examples of vertex shapes*

When all links have been found, they are used for forming nuclei such that each nucleus is a set of regions which are probably faces, or parts of faces, of the same body. If two regions are connected by at least two links, these regions are classified as belonging to a single nucleus which consists of these two regions. If a region and a nucleus are connected by at least two links, they are classified as belonging to a single, larger, nucleus. If two nuclei are connected by at least two links, they are classified as belonging to a single, larger, nucleus. (Two nuclei are said to be connected by one link if there is one link between a region in one nucleus and a region in the other nucleus.) The process of developing nuclei stops when no further nuclei or regions are classified as belonging to larger nuclei. The system then outputs lists of the regions belonging to each final nucleus; and usually each such list turns out to be a list of faces, or partly obscured faces, of the same body. This constitutes a solution to the segmentation problem which confronts a machine attempting to recognise objects such as those shown in Figure 8.1. The technique of Guzman[194] has been extended by Huffman[230a] and by Falk[138a].

Whereas Guzman's programme starts from a list of the regions in a scene and determines which of these belong to the same body, the system of Brice and Fennema[59] starts from a television picture of a scene, and first divides this television picture into regions having roughly equal grey scale value. These regions are then merged so as to make up larger regions which are likely to be images of faces of objects. Finally, Brice and Fennema's system applies rules of Guzman's sort for determining which regions belong to the same object.

In Figure 8.1 there are cases where one object partly obscures or occludes the view of another. Occlusion is a common source of difficulty in practical scene analysis: for instance, one chromosome may lie on top of another on a microscope slide, or a cloud may hide terrain in an aerial photograph. The problem of occlusion also arises in character recognition when a typist has typed one character on top of another in an attempt to remedy a typing error.

8.3 PICTURE SYNTAX

8.3.1 Generative grammars

8.3.1.1 Finite-state grammars

A Boolean function, $f(X)$, of N variables, dichotomises the set of 2^N possible N-bit patterns into two classes: one of these is the class of X's for which $f(X)$ is *true* and the other is the class of X's for which $f(X)$ is *false*. The truth table for $f(X)$, or a Boolean algebraic expression for $f(X)$, *defines* these two classes. In previous chapters, classes of patterns have also been *defined* in terms of numerical discriminant functions, and a common example of this is the definition of the class of all X's such that $g_s(X) > g_r(X)$, for all r except $r = s$, where $g_1(X), \ldots, g_r(X), g_s(X), \ldots, g_z(X)$ are numerical discriminant functions. We now consider the problem of defining classes of patterns in which the number of elements per pattern is not constant. We treat this as part of the more general problem of defining classes of strings in which the number of symbols per string is not constant.

A *symbol* is a primitive entity which may be a lexical character or a concatenation of lexical characters. For instance, the letter 'h' may serve as a symbol, or the arbitrary concatenation of letters 'PAL' may serve as a symbol, or the word 'house' may serve as a symbol, or the numeral '1' may serve as a symbol. A *vocabulary* is a finite non-empty set of symbols. A *string* is a sequence of symbols which belong to a vocabulary[54]. For instance, the sequence of letters which make up a word is an example of a string. The sequence of words which make up a phrase, or a clause, or a sentence, is a further example of a string. The sequence 1100001110011110 is an example of a string. The sequence BLANK, BAR, CAP, PAL, PAL, . . . is an example of a string.

One way of defining a class of strings is to specify the rules of operation of a machine which recognises all the members, and no non-members, of this class. It is sometimes more convenient to define a class of strings by specifying the rules of operation of a machine which *generates* all of the members, and no non-members, of this class. For instance, any member of the class R, and no non-member of the class R, can be generated by a machine which carried out the following rules of operation. The machine first writes the symbol σ and then replaces this by 0A or by 0B. Suppose for instance that the machine replaces σ by 0A. The machine then replaces A by 0A or by 0B, to yield 00A or 00B respectively: suppose for instance that the result of this is 00A. The machine then replaces A by 0A or by 0B, to yield 000A or 000B respectively: suppose for instance the the result of this is 000B. The machine then replaces B by 1B or 1 to yield 0001B or 0001: suppose for instance that the result of this is 0001B. The generative process continues in this manner, that is, B is replaced by 1B or 1. When B is in fact replaced by 1, the generative process terminates. If, during the generative process, the machine replaces σ or A by 0A m times and replaces B by 1B n times, the result is a string of $m + 1$ 0's followed by $n + 1$ 1's, where m and n are non-negative integers. By making different choices of m and n, the machine can generate all members of R and no non-members of R; and the rules of operation of the machine therefore constitute a definition of the class R.

These rules can be expressed symbolically:

$$\left.\begin{array}{lcl} \sigma & \rightarrow & 0\mathrm{A} \mid 0\mathrm{B} \\ \mathrm{A} & \rightarrow & 0\mathrm{A} \mid 0\mathrm{B} \\ \mathrm{B} & \rightarrow & 1\mathrm{B} \mid 1 \end{array}\right\} \qquad (8.2)$$

The expression A → 0A means 'replace A by 0A', and the expression A → 0A | 0B means 'replace A either by 0A or by 0B'. The arrow means 'replace by' or 'rewrite as', and the vertical bar means 'or'. Rules (8.2) are examples of *rewrite rules* or *productions.* The symbol 'σ' is called the *initial symbol,* because the generative process begins by writing σ. Any symbol which occurs in any string after termination of the generative process is a *terminal symbol.* In the present example the only terminal symbols are 0 and 1. Any symbol which is used in the generative process and which does not occur in any string after termination of the generative process is a *non-terminal symbol.* In the present example the only non-terminal symbols are σ, A, and B.

Let R be the class of all strings which consist of any number (greater than zero) of 0's followed by any number (greater than zero) of 1's. For instance, 000000001, 00111, 0000111111, are strings which belong to R. Figure 8.3 is a transition diagram of the Section 6.5.3 sort, and the sequential process starts at node 1. If and only if, after the last symbol in the input string has been processed, the system is at node 3, then the input string belongs to the class R. We can *define* R as the class of all strings such that the Figure 8.3 system is at node 3 when the last symbol in the string has been processed. An advantage of this definition of R is that it tells us how to design a machine which distinguishes between members and non-members of R.

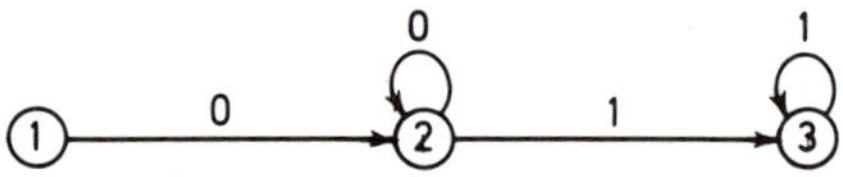

Figure 8.3. *Transition diagram for recognition of members of the class R*

It is very important that we can *not* define R by listing all members of R, as in a truth table, because the number of members of R is unlimited. Because there may be *any* number (greater than zero) of 1's and 0's in a member of R, we can *not* distinguish members of R from non-members of R by means of parallel logic circuits as in Section 6.1, nor by direct application of the numerical discriminant techniques which were introduced in Chapters 3, 4, and 5.

Let R' be the set of all strings belonging to R such that in any string belonging to R' the number of symbols (i.e. 0's and 1's) is exactly 100. The number of members of R' is limited, and R' could be defined by listing all its members. Members of R' could be distinguished from non-members of R' by means of parallel logic circuits or by means of numerical discriminants. But, for instance, parallel logic circuits would be very much more costly than the Figure 8.3 sequential system, and would in this sense be an inefficient and inappropriate means of distinguishing between members and non-members of R'. In the Section 7.4.3 recognition system, the number of positions of the 3 x 3 window in any given strip is always the same, and therefore members of the *f*-class PAL could be distinguished from non-members by means of parallel logic circuits, although this would be unnatural and expensive compared with the Figure 7.29 sequential technique.

A set of non-terminal and terminal symbols and rewrite rules is called a *finite-state grammar* if each of the rewrite rules is of the form $J \rightarrow xK$ or $J \rightarrow x$, where J and K are non-terminal symbols and x is a terminal symbol[54]. According to this, rules (8.2) are the rewrite rules of a finite-state grammar which defines the class R. The term *grammar* is used here in a technical sense which is not the same as in old-fashioned linguistics.

As a further example, the following is a finite-state grammar which generates all the strings and only the strings which the Figure 7.29 sequential system recognises as 'PAL'.

Initial Symbol: σ
Non-terminal Symbols: σ, 1, 2, 3, 4, 5, 6, 7
Terminal Symbols: B, L, H, V, I, X
Rewrite Rules:

$$\begin{aligned}
\sigma &\rightarrow B1 \mid I3 \mid V3 \mid L2 \\
1 &\rightarrow B1 \mid I3 \mid V3 \mid L2 \\
2 &\rightarrow I3 \mid V3 \\
3 &\rightarrow I3 \mid V3 \mid H3 \mid B4 \\
4 &\rightarrow B4 \mid L5 \mid I6 \mid V6 \\
5 &\rightarrow I6 \mid V6 \\
6 &\rightarrow V6 \mid X6 \mid L6 \mid B7 \\
7 &\rightarrow B7 \mid B
\end{aligned}$$

It can be proved that the class of strings which can be generated by *any* given finite-state grammar can be recognised by an appropriate sequential system of the Section 6.5.3 sort[54, 222b].

8.3.1.2 Context-free grammars

One of the aims of syntactic linguistics is to define the set of all strings which are syntactically permissible sentences in a given language. This aim would clearly be accomplished if the linguist were to formulate rules of operation of a machine which would automatically recognise all syntactically permissible sentences and not recognise any syntactically non-permissible sentences in the given language. Alternatively, this aim would also be clearly accomplished if the linguist were to formulate rules of operation of a machine which would generate all the syntactically permissible sentences and no syntactically non-permissible sentences in the given language[24, 289].

Because of the simplicity of finite-state grammars, it is sensible to enquire whether a finite-state grammar could possibly generate all of the sentences which would be syntactically permissible in a given natural language. It is in fact quite easy to give examples of classes of English sentences which cannot possibly be generated by a finite-state grammar. For instance, let us stipulate that in the sentence

(i) People who say that S_1 are liars.

S_1 is any English sentence. Indeed S_1 might be the sentence (i), and this would give

(ii) People who say that people who say that S_1 are liars are liars.

We could substitute (i) for S_1 in (ii), and then substitute (i) for S_1 in the result of this, and so on *ad infinitum.* By this means we could generate a class of sentences which would be semantically preposterous, but syntactically permissible. Successive sentences would be strings of the form *aSb, aaSbb, aaaSbbb,* . . .. This class of strings could not be generated by means of a finite-state grammar, because a finite-state grammar has no means of ensuring that the number of *a*'s before the S is equal to the number of *b*'s after the S[79]. But this class of strings could easily be generated by application of the rewrite rule $S \rightarrow aSb$.

By means of the rewrite rule

$$S \rightarrow 00 \mid 11 \mid 1S1 \mid 0S0$$

a class of strings can be generated such that the second half of each string is, so to speak, the mirror image of the first half, e.g. 1001, 110011, 1011111101, 11100011000111. This is another example of a class of strings which cannot be generated by a finite-state grammar, nor be recognised by a sequential machine of the Section 6.5.3 type[79].

Rewrite rules such as $S \rightarrow aSb$ and $S \rightarrow 1S1$ are not allowed in a finite-state grammar, but are allowed in a context-free grammar. A *context-free grammar*[54] is a set of non-terminal and terminal symbols and rewrite rules of the form $J \rightarrow \omega$, where J is a non-terminal symbol and ω is a (non-empty) string of terminal and/or non-terminal symbols subject to the restriction that $\omega \neq J$. The following is a very simple example of a context-free grammar:

Initial Symbol:	σ
Non-terminal Symbols:	σ, VP1, NP1, NP2, NC1, NC2, NC3, VC1, AC
Terminal Symbols:	player, captain, giraffe, contest, prize, John, Mary, won, lost, abandoned, the, a

8.3.1.3 Context-dependent grammars

We have seen that there are classes of strings which can be generated by context-free grammars but not by finite-state grammars. Thus context-free grammars are more general than finite-state grammars. Similarly, context-dependent grammars are more general than context-free grammars, because there are classes of strings which can be generated by context-dependent but not by context-free grammars[54].

A *context-dependent grammar* is a set of non-terminal and terminal symbols and rewrite rules of the form $\gamma_1 J \gamma_2 \rightarrow \gamma_1 \omega \gamma_2$, where J is a non-terminal symbol, ω is a (non-empty) string of terminal and/or non-terminal symbols, and γ_1 and γ_2 are strings of non-terminal and/or terminal symbols. The strings γ_1 and/or γ_2 may be *empty* that is, they may contain no symbols. A context-free grammar is a context-dependent grammar in which γ_1 and γ_2 are empty in all rewrite rules.

As a very simple example, the following is a context-dependent grammar which defines the same class of sentences as was defined by (8.3).

Initial Symbol:	σ
Non-terminal Symbols:	σ, NP3, VP1, NC1, NC2, NC3, VC1, AC
Terminal Symbols:	player, captain, giraffe, contest, prize, John, Mary, won, lost, abandoned, the, a
Rewrite Rules:	$\sigma \rightarrow$ NP3 VP1
	VP1 $\rightarrow$ VC1 NP3
	NP3 VC1 $\rightarrow$ AC NC1 VC1 | NC3 VC1
	VC1 NP3 $\rightarrow$ VC1 AC NC2
	NC1 $\rightarrow$ player | captain | giraffe
	NC2 $\rightarrow$ contest | prize
	NC3 $\rightarrow$ John | Mary
	VC1 $\rightarrow$ won | lost | abandoned
	AC $\rightarrow$ the | a

In this, the context-sensitive rules preclude such nonsense as 'the prize won the player'; whereas rules (8.3) preclude such nonsense by using NP1 and NP2 instead of NP3. From the point of view of parsing, the distinction between NP1 and NP2 is somewhat artificial and therefore undesirable, since NP1 and NP2 correspond to noun phrases of the same sort: article + noun.

Rewrite Rules:

$$\left.\begin{array}{l}\sigma \rightarrow \mathrm{NP1} \quad \mathrm{VP1} \\ \mathrm{VP1} \rightarrow \mathrm{VC1} \quad \mathrm{NP2} \\ \mathrm{NP1} \rightarrow \mathrm{AC} \quad \mathrm{NC1} \mid \mathrm{NC3} \\ \mathrm{NP2} \rightarrow \mathrm{AC} \quad \mathrm{NC2} \\ \mathrm{NC1} \rightarrow \text{player} \mid \text{captain} \mid \text{giraffe} \\ \mathrm{NC2} \rightarrow \text{contest} \mid \text{prize} \\ \mathrm{NC3} \rightarrow \text{John} \mid \text{Mary} \\ \mathrm{VC1} \rightarrow \text{won} \mid \text{lost} \mid \text{abandoned} \\ \mathrm{AC} \rightarrow \text{the} \mid \text{a} \end{array}\right\} \quad (8.3)$$

This simple grammar generates, and thereby defines, a class of 96 strings which are sentences such as ‘John lost the contest’ and ‘a giraffe won the prize’.

Figure 8.4 is a graphical record of the process of generation of the sentence ‘the captain won the contest’ by rules (8.3). For instance, the lines extending from σ to NP1 and VP1 indicate that the rule $\sigma \rightarrow$ NP1 VP1 was used in generating the sentence. The lines extending downward from VP1 indicate that the rule VP1 $\rightarrow$ VC1 NP2 was used; and the lines extending downward from NP1 indicate that the rule NP1 $\rightarrow$ AC NC1 was used, and so on. Any word joined by a line to NC1, NC2, or

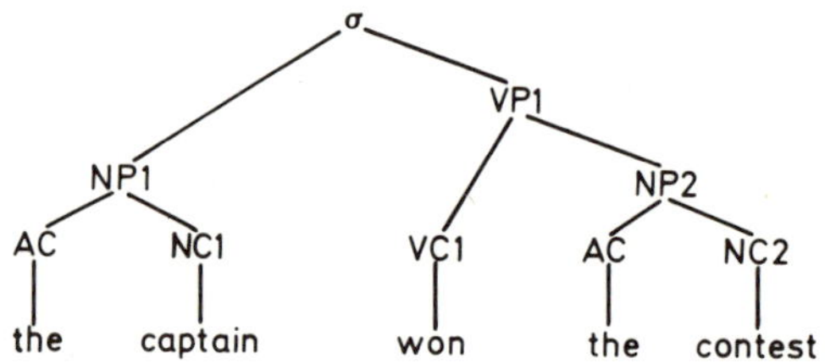

Figure 8.4. *Parse tree for a sentence generated by rules* (8.3)

NC3 is a noun, any word joined by a line to VC1 is a verb, and any word joined by a line to AC is an article. Any sequence of words which stems from NP1 or NP2 is a noun phrase, and any sequence of words which stems from VP1 is a verb phrase. Thus Figure 8.4 provides a parse of the sentence ‘the captain won the contest’, because it tells us which words are nouns, verbs, or articles, and which phrases are noun phrases or verb phrases. Figure 8.4 is the *parse tree* or *rule tree* for ‘the captain won the contest’[289]. A parse tree is a *structural description* of a sentence.

A *phrase structure grammar*[54] is a set of non-terminal and terminal symbols and rewrite rules of the form $\omega_1 \rightarrow \omega_2$, where ω_1 and ω_2 are strings of non-terminal and/or terminal symbols such that ω_1 contains at least one non-terminal symbol. Context-dependent, context-free, and finite-state grammars are phrase structure grammars which conform to the restrictions which have been introduced above.

The class of all strings which a given phrase structure grammar can generate is the class which that phrase structure grammar defines. The rewrite rules of a given phrase structure grammar can be used in recognising whether or not any given string is a member of the class of strings which that phrase structure grammar defines. The manner in which rewrite rules are used in recognition is, except in special cases, more complicated that the manner in which rewrite rules are used in generation, and will not be discussed here[149, 223].

8.3.1.4 *Transformations*

The passive versions of the 96 sentences generated by rules (8.3) constitute a class of 96 passive sentences. This class of 96 passive sentences can be defined by means of an appropriate phrase structure grammar. It is more elegant to define this class of 96 passive sentences by applying just one rule to each sentence generated by rules (8.3). This rule says that, if a sentence consists of $\omega_1 \omega_2 \omega_3$, where ω_1 and ω_3 are noun phrases and ω_2 is a verb, then the sentence can be rewritten 'ω_3 was ω_2 by ω_1'. This (simplified) *transformation* rule can be written symbolically

$$\begin{array}{ccc} \text{NP} & \text{V} & \text{NP} \\ | & | & | \\ \omega_1 & \omega_2 & \omega_3 \end{array} \Rightarrow \omega_3 \text{ was } \omega_2 \text{ by } \omega_1 \qquad (8.4)$$

This rule transforms one terminal string into another, on condition that the original string has a prescribed structural description. A transformation rule such as (8.4) differs from any rule in a phrase structure grammar in that it rewrites terminal strings, and also in that it takes account not only of the string which it transforms, but also, at some level, of the structural description of this string. In a phrase structure grammar, a rewrite rule only takes account of the string which it rewrites, regardless of any previous versions of this string during the generative process[79].

Under prescribed structural conditions, other transformation rules swap one terminal string for another, add or delete symbols, permute the order of symbols, and combine strings[24].

In the generation of sentences, phrase structure grammars generate terminal strings, and then transformation rules are applied to these terminal strings in order to generate further terminal strings. The process of recognising a string or sentence is the reverse of this generative process, in that transformation rules are applied first, and then phrase structure rules are applied[149].

In character recognition, operations such as normalising, smoothing, and thinning are tenuously analogous to transformations, in that they change one pattern into another, they are applied prior to the final processes of recognition, and (we hope) they simplify the final processes of recognition.

8.3.2 Pattern grammars

8.3.2.1 Strings

In the Toshiba system of Section 7.4.3, the *f*-classes PAL, CAP, etc., are defined by finite-state grammars, and a finite-state grammar for a simplified version of PAL was formulated in Section 8.3.1.1.

By tracing round the black/white edge of a character, we can obtain a string of directions such as E, SE, E, E, SE, S, SW, SW, . . ., as mentioned in Section 2.4.2, and such strings can be classified by means of phrase structure grammars[139, 269]. The Section 7.4.1 system provides important practical examples of this which are not restricted to finite-state grammars.

A string is a sequence of discrete symbols, but the input to the feature detectors in the Section 7.4.1 system is *not* a sequence of discrete symbols. The contour direction may change, for instance from E to SE, at *any* time, not at one of a sequence of discrete time instants. The scanning spot may move from one zone to another, for instance from B4 to B5, at *any* time, not at one of a sequence of discrete time instants. In the Section 7.4.1 system, the time scale is continuous, not discrete. To render the Section 7.4.1 system amenable to linguistic analysis, we can replace the feature detectors in Section 7.4.1 by string-recognition circuits, without making any change whatsoever to recognition performance.

By way of example, let us consider the 'cusp of '3' ' detector whose transition diagram is shown in Figure 7.27 (p. 207). Let us feed the input to the Figure 7.27 feature detector into a circuit which outputs the symbol '*a*' as soon as the condition (3 ∨ 4 ∨ 5). (NE) is satisfied, which outputs the symbol '*b*' as soon as the condition (1) is satisfied, and so on, as indicated in Table 8.1. Any one of the Table 8.1 conditions

Table 8.1. SYMBOLS PRODUCED WHEN TRANSITION CONDITIONS IN FIGURE 7.27 ARE SATISFIED

Condition	*Symbol*
(3 ∨ 4 ∨ 5) . (NE)	*a*
(1)	*b*
(B ∨ C ∨ D). (2 ∨ 3 ∨ 4) . (W ∨ NW)	*c*
(5) ∨ ((1) . (E ∨ SE))	*d*
(((B ∨ C ∨ D) . (2 ∨ 3) . (E ∨ NE)) ∨ ((C ∨ D) . (1) . (NE))) . (2TU)	*e*
(1 ∨ 2) . (S ∨ SE) ∨ (D) . (1) . (E ∨ SE)	*f*
(1 ∨ 2) . (W ∨ SW ∨ NW) . (6TU)	*g*

may be satisfied continuously during a time interval of several microseconds, but the corresponding symbol is produced only once. The string of symbols forms the input to a sequential circuit whose transition diagram is shown in Figure 8.5. In Figure 8.5, β stands for *a* or *d* or *e* or *f* or *g*, δ stands for *a* or *b* or *c* or *f* or *g*, ϕ stands for *a* or *b* or *c* or *d* or *e*, and τ stands for *a* or *b* or *c* or *d* or *e* or *f* or *g*. If and only if the Figure 8.5 process is at node 5 when the last symbol in the input string has been processed, then that string belongs to the class 'cusp of '3' '. In Figure 7.27 it is understood that the process remains at a given node until a condition for transition to a different node is satisfied,

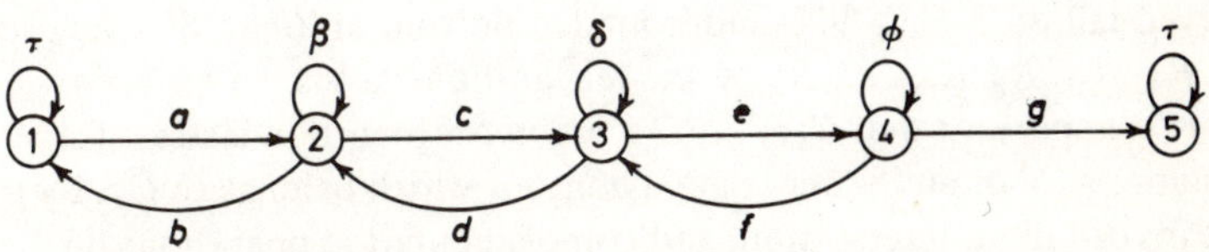

Figure 8.5. *A symbolic transition diagram correponding to Figure 7.27*

and no loop from a node to itself is explicitly shown. Such loops are shown in Figure 8.5, for purposes of analysis. It is easy to see that any black/white contour which would satisfy the Figure 7.27 condition for 'cusp of '3' ' would yield a string of symbols which would satisfy the Figure 8.5 condition for 'cusp of '3' '; and any black/white contour which would not satisfy the Figure 7.27 condition for 'cusp of '3' ' would not yield a string of symbols which would satisfy the Figure 8.5 condition for 'cusp of '3' '.

It is also quite easy to see that the class of strings which are classified by Figure 8.5 as 'cusp of '3' ' is precisely the class of strings which are generated by the following context-free grammar:

Initial Symbol: σ
Non-terminal Symbols: $\sigma, \psi, \alpha, \beta, \gamma, \delta, \epsilon, \phi$
Terminal Symbols: $\lambda, a, b, c, d, e, f, g$

Rewrite Rules:

$$\sigma \to \psi a \alpha c \gamma e \epsilon g \psi$$
$$\psi \to a\psi \mid b\psi \mid c\psi \mid d\psi \mid e\psi \mid f\psi \mid g\psi \mid \lambda$$
$$\alpha \to \beta\alpha \mid b\psi a\alpha \mid \lambda$$
$$\gamma \to \delta\gamma \mid d\alpha c\gamma \mid \lambda$$
$$\epsilon \to \phi\epsilon \mid f\gamma e\epsilon \mid \lambda$$
$$\beta \to a \mid d \mid e \mid f \mid g \mid \lambda$$
$$\delta \to a \mid b \mid c \mid f \mid g \mid \lambda$$
$$\phi \to a \mid b \mid c \mid d \mid e \mid \lambda$$

λ is the null symbol: for instance $\beta\lambda = \beta$ and $a\lambda c = ac$.

Similarly, there is a context-free grammar which defines the class of black/white contours which Figure 7.23 recognises as 'top of '2', '3', or '7' '; and there is a context-free grammar which defines the class of contours which Figure 7.26 recognises as 'bottom curved tail of '3', '5', '9' '. For $i = 1, 2, \ldots, 59$, let C_i be the class of contours which are recognised by the ith feature detector in the Section 7.4.1 system. In particular, let C_1, C_2, C_3, and C_4 respectively be the classes of contours which are recognised as 'cusp of '3' ', 'top of '2', '3', or '7' ', 'bottom curved tail of '3', '5', '9' ', and 'rounded bottom of '6' or '8' '. As usual, let $R_1, \ldots, R_r, R_s, \ldots, R_z$ be the recognition classes.

It is important that $C_1, \ldots, C_{59}$ are *not* recognition classes: for instance a '6' or an '8' may have a contour which belongs to C_4. By means of union, intersection, and complementation operations on $C_1, \ldots, C_{59}$, the Section 7.4.1 system defines a class R'_r which (ideally) includes every member of R_r and no member of any R_s (where $s = 1, \ldots, z, s \neq r$). A character is assigned to R_r if it belongs to R'_r; and (ideally) no character which belongs to R'_r but not to R_r ever occurs in practice (cf. Section 6.4.4). For instance, in Section 7.4.1.1 we mentioned that in Ref. 134 a character was recognised as a '3' if its contour belonged to C_1 and C_2 and either to C_3 or not to C_4. Figure 8.6 represents this recognition condition by means of a Venn diagram, in which any point in the rectangle labelled C_i represents a member of C_i, for $i = 1, 2, 3, 4$. Any point within the hatched area in Figure 8.6 (ideally) corresponds either to a '3' or to a pattern which is not a '3' and which can be relied upon not to turn up in practice.

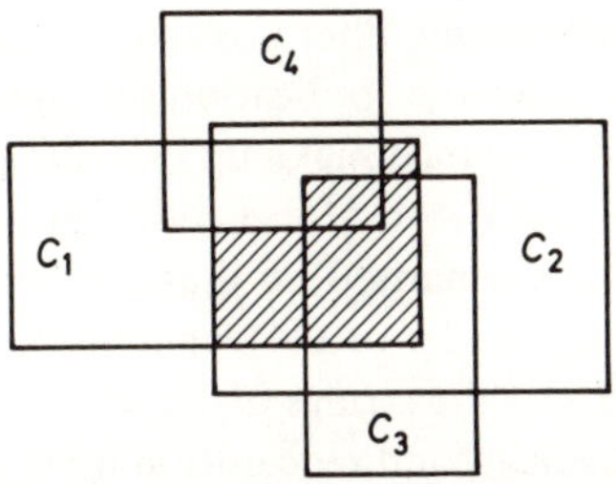

Figure 8.6. *Venn diagram to illustrate recognition condition for* 3's

The Section 7.4.1 system achieves economy by defining R'_r in terms of $C_1, \ldots, C_{59}$ instead of defining R'_r directly by means of a phrase structure grammar. The Section 7.4.1 system capitalises on the fact that, for instance, the top curved portion of a hand-printed '2' may be identical to the top curved portion of a hand-printed '3'. In various speech recognition systems, however, R'_r is defined directly by means of sequential circuits (e.g. in Section 9.6.3). The Section 7.4.1 system does not in fact recognise strings of discrete symbols, but achieves the same recognition performance as a system which recognises strings of discrete symbols, in a manner which we have indicated above. Similarly, the speech recognition systems in Refs 171, 296, and 432 do not in fact recognise strings of discrete symbols, but they can be shown to achieve the same recognition performance as systems which transform speech waveforms into strings of symbols and then recognise these strings sequentially. These systems classify strings directly into classes $R'_1, \ldots, R'_r, \ldots, R'_s, R'_z$ such that R'_r (ideally) includes every member of R_r and no member of any R_s. In these systems the classes $R'_1, \ldots, R'_z$

are in effect defined by phrase structure grammars. In practice $R'_1, \ldots, R'_z$ are defined more cheaply than $R_1, \ldots, R_z$, and there is no advantage in defining $R_1, \ldots, R_z$ rather than $R'_1, \ldots, R'_z$.

The fact (Section 6.4.4) that, in many pattern recognition problems, various patterns can be relied upon not to turn up in practice, is often of vital economic importance. But there are pattern recognition problems in which we cannot rely on any pattern not to turn up in practice: for instance in automatic signature verification and speaker identification[238a]. In automatic signature verification a machine is required to distinguish authentic signatures from all possible forgeries and indeed from all possible patterns which are not authentic signatures. Similarly, in linguistics, a machine is required to distinguish syntactically admissible strings from *all* other possible strings.

We now briefly consider the application of linguistic techniques directly to the 1's and 0's which make up one-dimensional binary patterns. For instance, hand-sent Morse code can be sampled at regular discrete time instants and binarised, so that dots and dashes become strings of 1's and the remainder of the signal becomes 0's. In hand-sent Morse code, the lengths of the strings of 1's and 0's depart substantially from their prescribed values, and recognition must be based on the *proportions* of the lengths of various strings[178]. These proportions generally vary non-trivially

By means of the rewrite rule $S \rightarrow 0S111 \mid 0111$, we can generate all strings which are composed of n_0 0's followed by n_1 1's, such that $n_1/n_0 = 3$. But a phrase structure grammar is surely an inept and prohibitively inefficient means of defining the class of all strings which are composed of n_0 0's followed by n_1 1's, such that, for example $3 \leqslant n_1/n_0 \leqslant \frac{22}{5}$. This class of strings is very much simpler than any recognition class in hand-sent Morse code, and because of the problem of non-trivial variation of proportion, the prospects for the useful application of linguistic techniques directly to binarised hand-sent Morse code do not appear to be good.

As a further simple illustration of the problem of proportion, the seven strings 110000111, 1100001111, 11100001111, 1110000111, 111000001111, 1110000001111, 11000001111 can be distinguished from *all* other strings by means of a grammar whose rewrite rules are

$$\sigma \rightarrow 11A \mid 111A \mid 11100000111 \mid 1110000001111 \mid 110000111$$

$$A \rightarrow 00001111 \mid 000001111$$

But this grammar is scarcely more than an explicit list of the seven strings. This same class of seven strings was defined less trivially, and perhaps more promisingly, in Section 7.3.5.

8.3.2.2 Two-dimensional grammars

Figure 8.7 shows the rewrite rules of a simple arbitrary example of a two-dimensional grammar which generates thirty-six 6 x 6 bit binary patterns. The set of A's make up a region, and according to one of the rewrite rules in Figure 8.7 the A's region may be subdivided into the I's region and the J's region. When this rewrite rule is used in generating a pattern, the structural description of the generated pattern indicates that the A's region is subdivided into the I's and J's regions.

The subdivision of regions at successive levels of structural description is a familiar idea. For instance, at one level, a map may show national boundaries; at another level, a map may show county boundaries; at yet another level a map may show parish boundaries, and so on. This hierarchic structural description of a geographic locality is useful although it is pictorial (iconic) rather than symbolic. Anatomical drawings provide further examples of this. For instance, at one level, a drawing might show the shape of the human head; at another level, a drawing might show the outline shape and positions of the eyes, ears, nose, and mouth; and at yet another level a drawing might show parts of the eyes, ears, etc.[281]

It is usually the case that a map is a map of a unique geographic locality. An anatomical drawing, on the other hand, may be a general representation of the anatomy of many individuals, and may not be intended to represent the anatomy only of one unique individual. A general drawing of this sort does not define explicitly and precisely the *variations* in anatomy which occur among different individuals. Because it may be useful to describe anatomy hierarchically in terms of the subdivision of regions, we might perhaps consider the possibility of defining precisely the variations in anatomy which occur among different individuals (e.g. for purposes of automatic recognition) by means of a grammar of the sort trivially exemplified in Figure 8.7. This is not a good idea, because among different individuals the proportions, for instance the ratios of the distances between eyes, ears, and mouth, generally vary non-trivially. This variation of proportion is a two-dimensional counterpart of the variation of proportion which

```
           AAAAAA       CCCCCC
           AAAABB   |   CCCCCD
           AABBBB   |   CCCDDD
σ  ──────→ AAABBB   |   CCDDDD
           AABBBB   |   CCDDDD
           AABBBB       CCCDDD

AAAAAA            KKKKKK          IIIII
AAAA              KHKK      |     IIII
AA      ──────→   HH        |     IJ
AAA               HHH       |     IJJ
AA                HH        |     JJ
AA                HH              JJ

KKKKKK  ──────→   100100    |     101111
K  KK             1  01     |     1  10

 H                 1               0          1
HH                11        |     10    |    00
HHH     ──────→   000       |     111   |    000
HH                10        |     00    |    11
HH                11              10         01

IIIII             110011    |     011001
IIII    ──────→   1100      |     0110
I                 1         |     0
I                 1         |     0

 J                 1        |      0
 JJ     ──────→    11       |      10
JJ                01        |     10
JJ                00        |     00

  BB                11              00           10
BBBB              1111      |     1101   |     0000
 BBB    ──────→    111      |      001   |      010
BBBB              0011      |     1100   |     1100
BBBB              1001            0100         1111

CCCCCC            101101          101000
CCCCC             01110     |     10100
CCC     ──────→   101       |     000
CC                00        |     01
CC                01              01
CCC               011             001

   D                 1               1            0
 DDD               111      |      100   |      010
DDDD    ──────→   0011      |     0110   |     1100
DDDD              0010      |     0111   |     1000
 DDD               000             011          110
```

Figure 8.7. *Example of a two-dimensional grammar*

was mentioned above at the end of Section 8.3.2.1. A grammar of the Figure 8.7 sort could only cope with non-trivial variation of proportion by using a prohibitively large number of rewrite rules and of alternatives, that is, of |'s, in each rewrite rule. In the two-dimensional case, just as in the one-dimensional case, phrase structure grammar appears to be an inept means of defining non-trivial ranges of proportion.

In the scene analysis system of Brice and Fennema[59] (Section 8.2.3) a television picture is described hierarchically. For instance, a picture of a cube is subdivided into faces, and faces are subdivided into regions of roughly equal grey scale value. This system, which has only a limited ability to distinguish between different shapes, produces a hierarchical structural description without using explicitly stored conventional rewrite rules. The Figure 8.7 grammar, on the other hand, precisely defines a class of patterns by means of explicitly listed conventional rewrite rules.

In a phrase structure grammar, a non-terminal symbol may be rewritten by a string which consists of more than one symbol. For instance, the rule $Y \rightarrow hijk$ would allow the string $XhijkZ$ to be generated from the string XYZ. In this, X and Z are, so to speak, pulled apart to make room for $hijk$. In the two-dimensional case, the rewrite rule

$A \rightarrow \begin{matrix} 1 & 0 \\ 0 & 1 \end{matrix}$ could not be applied to the A in

$$\begin{matrix} 1 & 1 & 0 & 1 & 1 \\ 1 & 0 & 1 & 1 & 0 \\ 0 & 1 & A & 1 & 0 \\ 1 & 0 & 1 & 0 & 1 \\ 0 & 0 & 0 & 1 & 1 \end{matrix}$$

because if the digits surrounding A were pulled apart to make room for

$\begin{matrix} 1 & 0 \\ 0 & 1 \end{matrix}$ in place of A, this would introduce gaps between digits and the

pattern would be spoilt[380]. For this reason there is no rewrite rule of the form $S \rightarrow aSb$ or $S \rightarrow aS$ in the (isotonic) Figure 8.7 grammar, and no rewrite rule in Figure 8.7 can be used more than once in the generation of a particular pattern.

Kirsch[254] and Dacey[109] have formulated two-dimensional grammars in which a rewrite rule can be applied more than once during the generative process. It is convenient to introduce this work in terms of an example in which the rewrite rules are not the rewrite rules of a phrase structure grammar. Specifically, starting from a single black square surrounded by an unlimited number of white squares, the rules (i), (ii), (iii) in Figure 8.8 generate all possible right triangles such as those shown in Figure 8.9, provided that rules (i), (ii), (iii) are applied as follows:

(1) apply rule (i), then
(2) apply rule (ii) as many times as possible, then
(3) apply rule (iii), then
(4) either stop or do (1), (2), (3), (4) again.

This simple procedure does not immediately provide a useful structural description of a right triangle. A more obviously sensible structural description can be obtained by using the following idea.

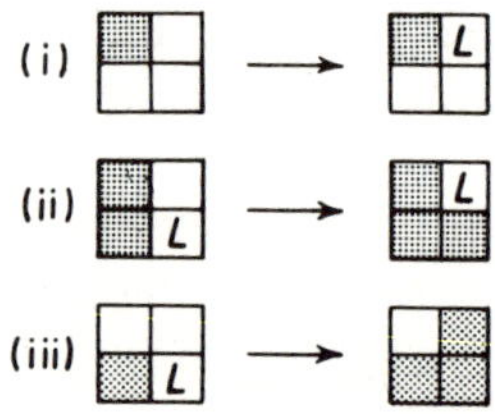

Figure 8.8. *Rewrite rules for generating right triangles*

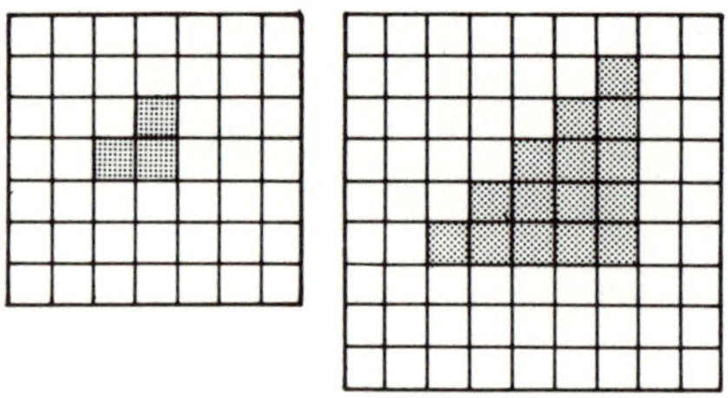

Figure 8.9. *Examples of right triangles*

Figures 8.10(a) and (b) show two 3 x 3 portions of a right triangle. The 3 x 3 pattern in Figure 8.10(a) is such that its centre element lies on the hypotenuse of the right triangle. The 3 x 3 pattern in Figure 8.10(b) is such that its centre element does not lie on an edge of the right triangle. By centring a 3 x 3 window on each black element in turn, a machine can label the elements of a right triangle as shown in

Figure 8.10(c). In Figure 8.10(c), elements lying on the hypotenuse are labelled '*H*', elements not lying on an edge are labelled '*I*', and so on. The triangle grammars of Kirsch and Dacey can be thought of as applying this labelling technique during the process of generating a right triangle, and the result is a right triangle labelled as in Figure 8.10(c). This labelling constitutes a sensible structural description of a right triangle.

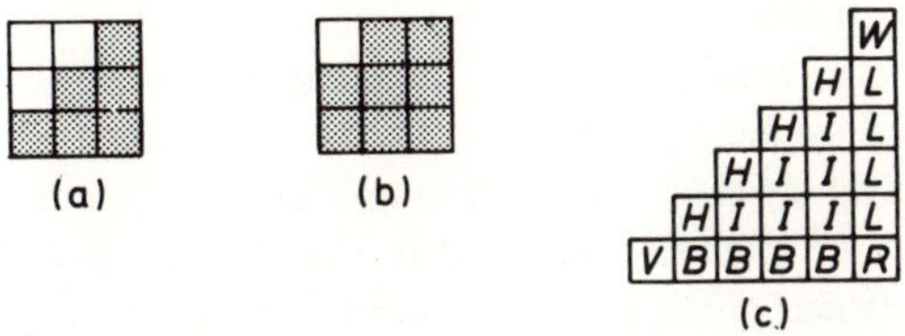

Figure 8.10. *Labelling of elements of a right triangle*

The triangle grammars of Kirsch and Dacey avoid trouble with gaps by conjoining black elements to the outside of a black figure[380]. To generate pictures composed mainly of lines, Narasimhan[330, 331] and Shaw[398] have formulated grammars in which at every step of the generative process a line is added to a collection of lines. Further picture grammars are mentioned in reviews by Miller and Shaw[315] and Fu and Swain[158].

8.3.2.3 Graph grammars

The systems of Section 7.3 provide rules for constructing a graph from a pattern. Typically, graphs $G_{r1}, G_{r2}, \ldots, G_{ri}, \ldots, G_{rt_r}$ are constructed from the rth class training set patterns $X_{r1}, X_{r2}, \ldots, X_{ri}, \ldots, X_{rt_r}$ respectively. If, subject to restrictions on corresponding lines and/or points, the graph G_X which is constructed from an unknown pattern X is isomorphic to one of $G_{r1}, \ldots, G_{rt_r}$, then X is assigned to the rth class. A single graph is used in the recognition of many patterns. For instance, only the single graph shown in Figure 7.15(b) (p. 188) is used in Section 7.3.4 for recognising all of the fives which are shown in Figure 7.17. In the Figure 7.15(b) example, the attributes which are associated with the lines of the graph are relative positions of points, and accordingly the relative positions of black bits in the fives in Figure 7.17 are constrained.

These are classes of patterns in which relative positions of bits, or lengths of lines, are not of definitory importance. For instance, all possible diagrams of series parallel networks constitute one such class. All possible diagrams which are, in the graph theoretic sense, trees, constitute another such class. In these examples, what matters for the purposes of distinguishing the given class from all other classes is the adjacency of lines, not the proportions of lengths of lines. These are examples where a recognition class consists of pictorial representations of graphs which belong to a particular class of graphs.

There are classes of graphs (e.g. the class of all possible trees) which can be defined by means of graph grammars. The most natural graphic generalisation of a phrase structure grammar is a web grammar, and to introduce this we must explain what is meant by a *labelled directed* graph. In a *labelled* graph a separate symbol is associated with each point, and the symbol associated with any given point is the *label* or *name* of that point[201]. In a *directed* graph, every line has an order or direction. The order or direction of the line which joins two points *a* and *b* is either (*b, a*) or (*a, b*) and this is represented diagrammatically by *a* ←— *b* or by *a* —→ *b* respectively. A *web* is a labelled directed graph[382]

From any one-dimensional string of symbols we can construct a web whose points correspond 1:1 to the symbols in the string, such that each symbol in the string is the label of the corresponding point in the web, and such that two points in the web are joined by a (left to right) directed line if and only if the corresponding symbols are immediate (left to right) neighbours in the string. For instance, for the string *abcd*, the web is as shown in Figure 8.11(a). Since a phrase structure grammar defines a class of strings, and since we can construct a one-dimensional web corresponding to any given string, we can use a phrase structure grammar to define a class of one-dimensional webs.

Pfaltz[351] and Rosenfeld and Pfaltz[382] have devised grammars which define classes of webs, where the webs are not merely one-dimensional concatenations of labelled points. By a way of example, Figure 8.11(b) shows a rewrite rule of a very trivial web grammar. This generates all webs of the form indicated in Figure 8.11(c).

Web grammars are a clear generalisation of phrase structure grammars, and they have the merit of mathematical tractability. But their usefulness is restricted to cases where proportions of lengths of lines are not of definitory importance and recognition classes consist of pictorial representations of webs which belong to a grammatically defined class

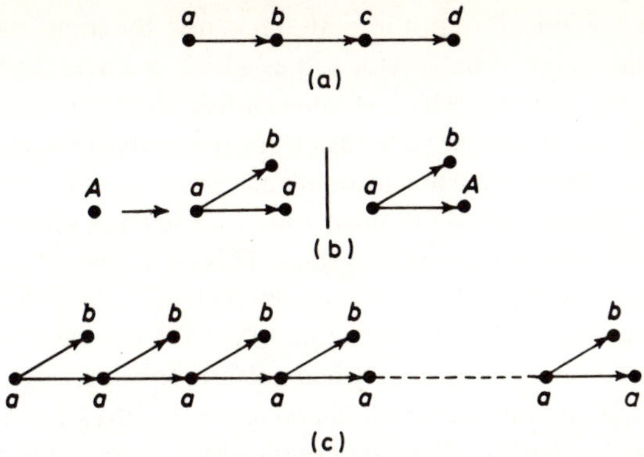

Figure 8.11. (*a*) *Web corresponding to the string abcd;* (*b*) *Rewrite rule in a trivial web grammar;* (*c*) *Web generated by Figure* 8.11(*b*) *rewrite rule*

of webs. In Section 7.3 the set $\{G_{r1}, \ldots, G_{rt_r}\}$ of graphs is defined by storing these graphs individually, rather than by means of a graph grammar. To recognise all possible pictorial representations of the webs generated by Figure 8.11(b), it would not be practical to store all of these webs individually, since their number is unlimited, and instead a grammatical definition of this class of webs is appropriate. On the other hand, when Section 7.3 techniques are used in cases where proportions of lengths of lines is of definitory importance (e.g. in Figure 7.17), the graphs $G_{r1}, \ldots, G_{rt_r}$ are not webs , and the class $\{G_{r1}, \ldots, G_{rt_r}\}$ cannot be defined by a web grammar.

8.3.2.4 Grammatical inference

A grammatical inference problem is a problem of designing a machine which, given a training set of strings belonging to a class R, automatically determines whether or not any further given string belongs to R. In 1972, solutions are available only for severely restricted grammatical inference problems[396], and we will not discuss this work in general terms. But we will encounter a basic example of a grammatical inference problem in Section 10.3.7.2.

8.4 ANALYSIS BY SYNTHESIS

According to the doctrine (*see* for example Refs 115, 132, 196, 279, and 423) of *analysis by synthesis*, a pattern is automatically synthesised so as to be more or less identical to a pattern to be recognised. The recognition machine does not directly recognise the input pattern, but instead obtains a set of parameter values which characterise the process of synthesising a pattern which is more or less identical to the input pattern. This set of parameter values is itself a pattern which is subsequently recognised by conventional pattern recognition techniques.

This transformation* is intended to reduce pattern variability and thus to simplify the recognition system. This idea is based on the hope that, when a word is written, the parameters which characterise the physical processes of writing are simpler than the parameters which characterise the word as a geometrical pattern on paper. Similarly, it is hoped that the parameters which characterise the physical processes of speaking are simpler than the parameters which characterise the spoken sound in the frequency domain[196, 279]. These hopes are in turn based on the fact that speech sounds or written characters are constrained by the anatomical apparatus which generates them, and on the idea that these constraints may simplify quantitative description of the generative process more than they would simplify quantitative description of the generated pattern[133, 447]

Bell *et al.*[36] have applied analysis-by-synthesis techniques to speech spectra. Since we have not yet discussed speech, we shall illustrate the analysis-by-synthesis approach by outlining the cursive script recognition system of Mermelstein and Eden[310]. *Cursive script* is the technical term for joined-up handwriting, in contradistinction to hand printing.

In Mermelstein and Eden's system[310] the horizontal and vertical co-ordinates of a pen are continuously recorded during the cursive writing of a word. Let us denote the x (i.e. horizontal) and y (i.e. vertical) components of the velocity of the pen point at time t by $\dot{x}_t$ and $\dot{y}_t$ respectively. While a word is written, plots of $\dot{x}_t$ and $\dot{y}_t$ versus time are produced by the recording apparatus. A word is recognised by recognising the plots obtained while it is being written. Mermelstein and Eden's system does this by artificially generating plots which are automatically adjusted to be very similar to the plots which are produced naturally while the word is being written. The input to the last stage of Mermelstein and Eden's recognition system is *not* a geometrical pattern of grey scale values, and it is *not* the plots of $\dot{x}_t$ and $\dot{y}_t$ versus t. Instead it is the set of parameter values which precisely determine the artificially generated plots.

*Here and henceforward the term *transformation* is used in the non-linguistic sense in which it has been used in previous chapters.

In the generative process, the artificially generated plots are adjusted stroke by stroke to match the naturally produced plots. A *stroke* is, for these purposes, a portion of the $\dot{x}_t$ and $\dot{y}_t$ versus t plots extending from one time instant when $\dot{y}_t = 0$ to the next time instant when $\dot{y}_t = 0$. Using this definition of *stroke,* the natural plots are segmented into strokes. Corresponding to each stroke in the natural plots, a stroke is artificially generated. The $\dot{y}_t$ component of an artificially generated stroke consists of two quarter-wave sinusoids, which may differ from each other in frequency and in phase but not in amplitude, and the same is true for the $\dot{x}_t$ component. The parameters such as amplitude and frequency of the sinusoids are automatically adjusted so that the artificially generated stroke matches the corresponding natural stroke in that a local minimum of a mean square error function is obtained. The values of altogether 12 parameters characterise each artificially generated stroke. Because the natural stroke matches the artificial stroke, the 12 parameter values which characterise the artificial stroke also characterise the natural stroke. For each class in a prescribed set of classes of strokes, the Section 3.4 normality assumption method yields an estimate of the probability that a given stroke belongs to that class.

Mermelstein and Eden performed experiments in which their system was required to recognise a limited repertoire of whole words. The word recognition process started with the first stroke of the first letter of the word to be recognised. This stroke was assigned to its most likely stroke class, the second stroke was assigned to its most likely stroke class, and so on. After each step in this process, the sequence of stroke class names so far generated was checked to make sure that it belonged to at least one of the words in the stored repertoire of words. If it was found that the sequence did not belong to any word in the repertoire, the last stroke class name which had been added to the sequence was replaced by the name of the next-most-likely stroke class, provided that the likelihood of this stroke class exceeded a prescribed threshold. If the resulting sequence still did not belong to any word in the repertoire, the last stroke class name was replaced by the one next most likely to it, provided that the likelihood of this stroke class exceeded the prescribed threshold. If this prescribed threshold was not exceeded, the system worked through alternative above-threshold choices of the previous stroke in the sequence, and so on. If this process did not lead to a sequence belonging to a word in the repertoire, the whole process was repeated with a lower threshold. When, finally, this process did lead to a complete sequence which fully corresponded to one of the words in the repertoire, the sequence was recognised *as* that word.

In earlier work using similar techniques, Eden[132, 133] showed that, if the artificially generated stroke sequence, that is, the artificially generated plots of $\dot{y}_t$ and $\dot{x}_t$ versus t, were used to control a pen, the word written on paper by the machine very closely resembled the same word written by the human hand. In Mermelstein and Eden's recognition system[310] the practical reason for generating strokes artificially was not to reproduce human handwriting, but to obtain parameters characterising natural strokes. It would have been difficult to obtain the values of descriptive parameters of a natural stroke by direct measurement of the natural $\dot{y}_t$ and $\dot{x}_t$ versus t plots. Similarly, Bell *et al.*[36] generated speech spectra because otherwise it would have been difficult to obtain accurate descriptive parameters of natural speech spectra by direct measurement.

A generative grammar most emphatically does *not*[80] purport to describe the physical processes by which strings of words are generated by humans. The formulation of rules for generating strings is merely a means of defining classes of strings. These classes can be defined just as precisely, though in practice generally not so conveniently, by the formulation of rules for recognising strings belonging to these classes. To recognise an input string as a member of a class of strings, it is not necessary to generate a string which is identical to the input string[149, 223].

The analysis-by-synthesis approach to pattern recognition, on the other hand, does purport to describe, or at least to take cognisance of, the physical processes by which patterns are generated by humans[423]. But matching a synthetic pattern to a natural one is not the only possible way to make use of knowledge of physical processes of generating patterns. Moreover, a disadvantage of matching an input pattern to an artificially generated pattern is that this is generally a time-consuming process.

8.5 ITERATIVE ARRAY TECHNIQUES

This chapter ends with a brief introduction to a family of hardware techniques.

8.5.1 Microcellular arrays

In Figure 8.12, the squares represent cells and the lines represent two-way interconnections between cells. By way of introduction, suppose first that each cell in Figure 8.12 contains the logic circuit which is shown in Figure 8.13(a). According to Figure 8.13(a), each cell in Figure 8.12 has a ninth input channel which is labelled 'A' and is not shown in Figure 8.12. Initially the bistable element in every cell is in state '0'. If a logic element is in state '1', that element is said to be *activated.* The nine inputs to a cell are all fed to an *or* gate, and activation of this *or* gate causes activation of the bistable element, and thus of the eight output channels of the cell. If the 'A' channel of only one of the cells in Figure 8.12 is activated, the neighbours of this cell become activated, and then the neighbours of the neighbours, and so on. In other words, activation propagates outwards from the cell whose 'A' channel has been activated. This example introduces the notion of propagation in a network, but in a form which is too simple to be useful.

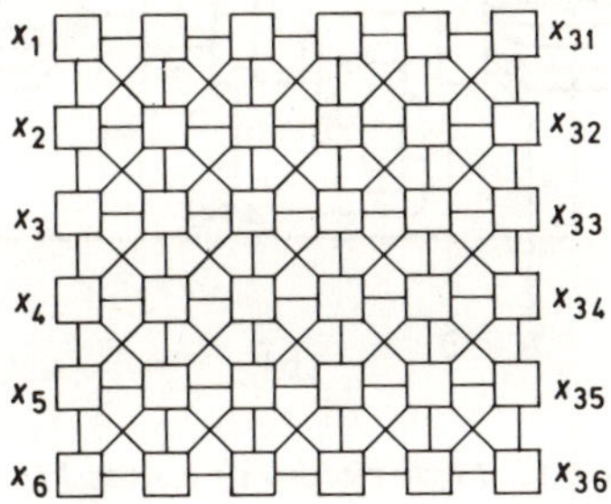

Figure 8.12. *A cellular network*

In Figure 8.13(b), the Figure 8.13(a) cell has been elaborated so as to include a second bistable element with input channel labelled 'B'. To introduce an idea, let us say that all bistables in a Figure 8.12 network using Figure 8.13(b) cells are initially set to state '0', and then a 6 x 6 bit binary pattern is fed into the network. This is done by setting the 'B' channel of each cell to '1' or '0' according as the corresponding pattern element is black or white, so that the 6 x 6 bit pattern is stored in the S_2 bistables of the 36 cells. Suppose that the pattern element in cell x_3 in Figure 8.12 is black, and that we wish to know, for instance, whether there is a continuous path of black cells from cell x_3 to cell x_4. This question can be answered by applying a '1' signal to the 'A' channel of cell x_3. If, by propagation, this causes activation of the S_1 bistable in cell x_{34}, then there is a black path between x_3 and x_{34}, and otherwise there is not. McCormick[304] has proposed using this idea for

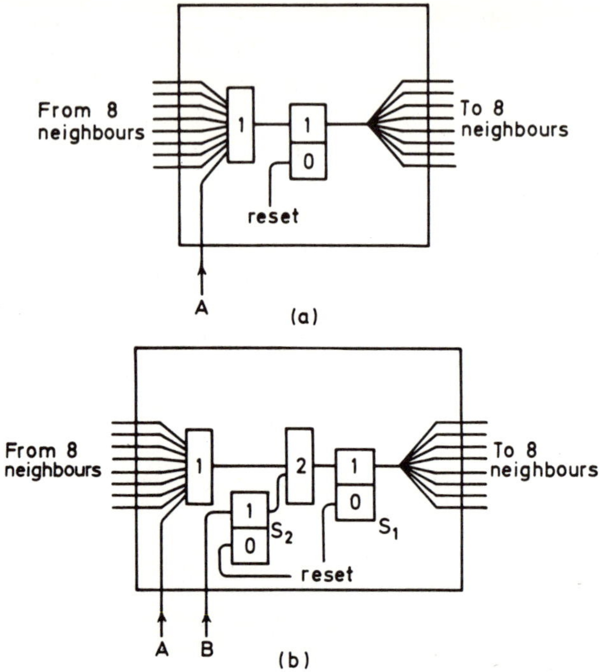

Figure 8.13. *Logic circuits of cells in Figure 8.12*

determining whether or not two given events in a bubble chamber are connected by a track.

Another application is in determining whether a black element in a binarised character is the result of ink spattering or whether it is a *bona fide* part of a character. An NCR patent[334] discloses a system in which activation propagates outwards from an original black element to all black elements within a prescribed area which are connected directly or via intermediate black elements to the original black element. If, within the prescribed area, the total number of black elements activated by propagation is less than a threshold, then the original element is deemed to be due to ink spattering, and it is eliminated. This is used before a process of alignment by left justification (Section 2.3.3). Spurious black elements at the left side of a character would cause misalignment if they were not eliminated by the propagation test.

The *medial axis transformation*[48, 322, 352] provides a further example of a propagation technique. In this, activation propagates in all directions through black at uniform velocity, starting simultaneously from all points lying on boundaries between black and white. The locus of all points at which wave fronts of propagation meet is the *medial axis* of the character or other figure which is being investigated. The medial axis is a skeleton, that is, a thinned version (cf. Section 2.4.3) of the original figure.

It is possible to record the times at which wavefronts of propagation meet at successive points on the medial axis. Using this time information, the original figure can be roughly reconstructed from its medial axis. This is done by propagating activation outwards in all directions from points on the medial axis. Propagation does not start simultaneously from all points on the medial axis, but, instead, starts from the last point and works back to the first point, the timing being precisely the reverse of the timing of the formation of the medial axis. When the first point is reached, propagation ceases, and the wave front of propagation is then roughly the shape and size of the original black/white contour.

Glucksman[173] has developed a character recognition technique which, like the medial axis transformation, requires a rather more complicated network than has been described above. In Glucksman's system, activation is propagated rectilinearly through white portions of a pattern, and there is no propagation through black. To introduce this system, let us consider the recognition of the three letters T, H and U. If activation is propagated eastwards from all white elements on the west edge of a pattern, and westwards from all points on the east edge, propagation will not reach the regions between the vertical limbs of H or U, and using an obvious optical analogy these regions can be said to lie in shadow, since black is opaque. There is no shadow in T under these conditions, and this fact can be used to distinguish T from H and U. If, in addition to the previous propagation, activation is propagated southwards from the north edge of a pattern, there is shadow in H but none in U, and hence these characters can be distinguished. Glucksman has elaborated this idea so that more classes of characters can be recognised, and recognition is not limited to ideal conditions.

Propagation was also essential in a recognition system devised by Unger in the late 1950's, and we shall return to this below.

In the examples which we have so far considered, there is propagation of activation through black or white. We now consider an example in which there is propagation of deactivation[443a]. Specifically, this example is an implementation of rule (7.6) in Section 7.3.6, and to introduce this we shall use the notation of Section 7.3.6. In this example, X and X_{ri} are 6-bit patterns. The terminals $\alpha_1, \ldots, \alpha_6$ in Figure 8.14 are the elements of S, and the terminals $\beta_1, \ldots, \beta_6$ are the elements of T. There is one cell, represented by a square in Figure 8.14, corresponding to each member of Q. The network also includes a set L' of n-input *and* gates, and the members of L' correspond 1:1 to the members of L. For clarity, the members of L' are not shown in Figure 8.14.

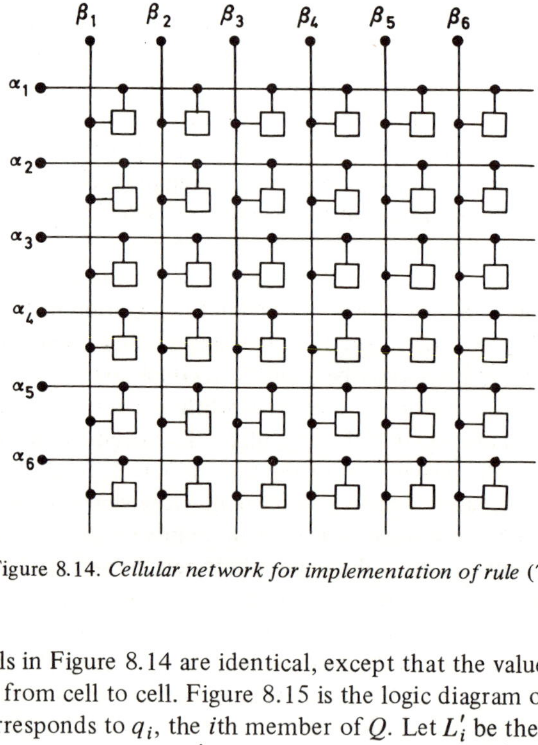

Figure 8.14. *Cellular network for implementation of rule* (7.6)

All cells in Figure 8.14 are identical, except that the value of m_i may vary from cell to cell. Figure 8.15 is the logic diagram of the cell which corresponds to q_i, the ith member of Q. Let L_i' be the set of all *and* gates which belong to L', such that any member of L_i' corresponds to a member of L which includes q_i. The output of the threshold gate ν in Figure 8.15 provides one input to each *and* gate which belongs to L_i'. The output of every *and* gate which belongs to L_i' is one of the inputs to the threshold gate μ.

The pattern X_{ri} is fed onto the terminals $\alpha_1, \ldots, \alpha_6$, and the pattern X is fed onto the terminals $\beta_1, \ldots, \beta_6$. For instance, β_6 is in state '1' or '0' according as the right-hand bit in X is black or white. Initially a '1' signal is applied to the channel which is marked 'start' in Figure 8.15, and this is done in all cells. Thus, for all i, the output of the threshold gate ν is '1' only if $q_i \in Q_0$. The only *and* gates in L' which then produce output '1' are those which correspond to the members of L_0.

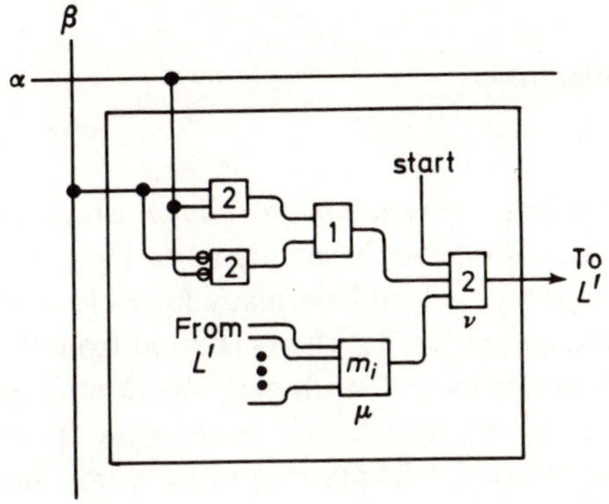

Figure 8.15. *Logic circuit of a cell in Figure* 8.14

Therefore the threshold gate μ produces output '1' or '0' according as q_i does or does not belong to Q_1. A '0' signal is then applied to the *start* channel in all cells, so that the threshold gate ν produces output '1' only if $q_i \in Q_1$. The result is that only members of L' which correspond to members of L_1 produce output '1'. The result of this is that ν produces output '1' only if $q_i \in Q_2$, and so on. This iterative process continues (asynchronously) until there is no change in the output of the threshold gate ν in any cell. To implement rule (7.6), X is then assigned to the rth class if

(1) for all $j = 1, \ldots, \phi$, at least one member of L' which corresponds to a member of Φ_j produces output '1', and
(2) every column in Figure 8.14 contains at least one cell in which the output of the threshold unit ν is '1'.

In this section we have considered only a few examples of cellular networks. Because of their possibly high speed of operation, and their amenity (if there are not too many logic elements per cell and interconnections between cells) to cheap implementation in integrated circuits, cellular networks have been the subject of much research[317].

Most of this research has been outside the field of pattern recognition: for instance, Kautz *et al.*[250] have designed cellular networks for tasks such as matrix inversion, linear programming, and data sorting.

8.5.2 Macrocellular arrays

Minnick[317] distinguishes between *microcellular* arrays, which, like those which we have just considered, have only a few logic elements per cell, and *macrocellular* arrays, which have many logic elements per cell. In an ordinary digital computer, data is transferred from the store to the central processor where logic or arithmetic operations are performed, and the result may be transferred back to the store. Transfers to and from the central processor take place word by word, and a word does not usually consist of more than 50 bits. For processing patterns consisting of hundreds or even thousands of elements, word by word processing may be unacceptably slow. In this case it may be preferable to perform computations pattern by pattern instead of word by word. To save the time taken in transferring words or patterns to and from the central processor, it is possible to do logic and arithmetic operations in the store rather than in the central processor. Many systems of this sort turn out to involve macrocellular arrays, for which Minnick[317] has provided a bibliography. Like microcellular research, most of the macrocellular work has been outside the field of pattern recognition, but a number of programmable macrocellular systems have been developed for pattern processing or recognition purposes, e.g. Refs 73, 177, 180a, 304, 357a, and 445.

By way of example, let us briefly consider Unger's spatial computer[445]. This consisted of an array of identical cells, as in Figure 8.12, there being one cell per pattern element, and all cells being connected to a single master control unit. Each cell contained a number (e.g. seven) of storage elements (bistables). These were called MR1, MR2, MR3, . . ., except for one of them which was not wired up in the same way as the others and which was called the PR (meaning Principal Register).

Logic operations were carried out pattern by pattern, not word by word. The master control unit issued instructions to all cells at once, and at any given time all cells received the same instruction. The instructions were obtained from a stored programme, as in a conventional computer. The programme was not stored in the cellular array, but in a separate random access store.

To illustrate the working of the system we outline a programme for detecting downward pointing line endings, as might be found at the bottom of P, T, or F. Specifically, the programme detects any piece of edge wherein a vertical white/black edge at least two elements long with white on the left meets the left end of a horizontal black/white edge at least two elements long with black on top whose right-hand end meets the bottom of a vertical black/white edge at least two elements long with black on the left, e.g. as shown in Figure 8.16(a) or (b).

```
0 1 1 1 0        0 1 1 0
0 1 1 1 0        0 1 1 0
0 1 1 1 0        0 0 0 0
0 0 0 0 0
   (a)             (b)
```

Figure 8.16. *Examples of downward pointing line endings*

Suppose for instance that the input pattern is as shown in Figure 8.17(a).

Downward pointing line endings can be detected by means of the following steps:

(1) For each '1' in the input pattern, enter a '1' in the PR of the corresponding cell in the cellular array. Similarly, for each '0' in the input pattern, enter a '0' in the PR of the corresponding cell, so that the overall effect is that the input pattern is stored in the PR's.
(2) In every cell, copy the contents of the PR into MR1, so that the overall effect is that a copy of the input pattern [Figure 8.17(a)] is stored in the MR1's and the pattern in the PR's remains unchanged.
(3) Replace the contents of each PR by the contents of the PR immediately to its left. In other words, shift the pattern in the PR's one element to the right.
(4) Invert the pattern in the PR's: in other words, if a PR contains '1', replace this by '0', and vice versa. The resulting pattern in the PR's is as shown in Figure 8.17(b).
(5) In each cell, replace the contents of the PR with the *and* of the contents of the PR and MR1. The result is as shown in Figure 8.17(c), where there is a '1' only in positions lying on vertical white/black edges in Figure 8.17(a).

0	0	0	0	0	0	0	0	0
0	0	0	0	0	0	1	1	0
0	1	1	1	0	0	0	1	0
0	1	1	1	0	1	1	1	0
1	1	1	1	0	0	0	0	0
0	0	0	0	0	1	1	1	0
0	1	1	0	0	1	1	1	0
0	1	1	0	0	1	1	1	0
0	1	1	1	0	0	0	0	0
0	0	0	0	0	0	0	0	0

(a)

1	1	1	1	1	1	1	1	1
1	1	1	1	1	1	1	0	0
1	1	0	0	0	1	1	1	0
1	1	0	0	0	1	0	0	0
1	0	0	0	0	1	1	1	1
1	1	1	1	1	1	0	0	0
1	1	0	0	1	1	0	0	0
1	1	0	0	1	1	0	0	0
1	1	0	0	0	1	1	1	1
1	1	1	1	1	1	1	1	1

(b)

0	0	0	0	0	0	0	0	0
0	0	0	0	0	0	1	0	0
0	1	0	0	0	0	0	1	0
0	1	0	0	0	1	0	0	0
1	0	0	0	0	0	0	0	0
0	0	0	0	0	1	0	0	0
0	1	0	0	0	1	0	0	0
0	1	0	0	0	1	0	0	0
0	1	0	0	0	0	0	0	0
0	0	0	0	0	0	0	0	0

(c)

0	0	0	0	0	0	0	0	0
0	0	0	0	0	0	0	0	0
0	1	0	0	0	0	0	0	0
0	1	0	0	0	0	0	0	0
0	0	0	0	0	0	0	0	0
0	0	0	0	0	1	0	0	0
0	1	0	0	0	1	0	0	0
0	1	0	0	0	1	0	0	0
0	1	0	0	0	0	0	0	0
0	0	0	0	0	0	0	0	0

(d)

0	0	0	0	0	0	0	0	0
0	0	0	0	0	0	0	0	0
0	0	0	0	0	0	0	0	0
0	0	0	0	0	1	1	1	0
1	1	1	1	0	0	0	0	0
0	0	0	0	0	0	0	0	0
0	0	0	0	0	0	0	0	0
0	0	0	0	0	1	1	1	0
0	1	1	1	0	0	0	0	0
0	0	0	0	0	0	0	0	0

(e)

Figure 8.17. *Illustration of operation of Unger's spatial computer*

(6) In each cell, replace the contents of the PR with the *and* of the contents of the PR and the contents of the PR of the cell immediately above.

(7) In each cell, replace the contents of the PR with the *or* of the contents of the PR and the contents of the PR of the cell immediately below. The resulting pattern in the PR's is shown in Figure 8.17(d). Figure 8.17(d) differs from Figure 8.17(c) only in that isolated 1's have been removed. Figure 8.17(d) contains all the vertical white/black edges of Figure 8.17(a) which are at least two elements long.

(8) Store the pattern in the PR's [i.e. Figure 8.17(d)] in the MR2's.

(9) Copy the pattern in the MR1's into the PR's and repeat steps (3) to (7) modified so as to detect horizontal black/white edges containing at least two black elements, with black on top. Store the result, which is shown in Figure 8.17(e), in the MR3's.

(10) Copy the pattern in the MR1's into the PR's and repeat steps (3) to (7) modified so as to detect vertical black/white edges containing at least two black elements, with black on the left. Store the result in the MR4's.

(11) Having found edges with the required length and orientation, the final problem is to determine which, if any, of these edges are connected together in the required manner. The first step towards this is to copy the pattern [Figure 8.17(e)] from the MR3's into the PR's, and then

(12) Between every pair of adjacent PR's which both contain 1's, open a communication channel for later use.

(13) *And* the pattern in the PR's with the pattern [Figure 8.17(d)] in the MR2's, leaving the result in the PR's.

(14) From any PR which contains '1', propagate 1's to all PR's connected to this by channels opened in step (12), subject to the restriction that only channels between horizontally adjacent cells may be used. The result of this differs from Figure 8.17(e) only in that the upper two rows of 1's have been eliminated.

(15) In each cell, replace the contents of the PR with the *and* of the contents of the PR and MR4. If, after this, the PR in any cell contains a '1', decide that the input pattern contains the required edge sequence, that is, a downward pointing line ending.

To achieve character recognition, Unger used routines of the above sort for detecting features such as 'horizontal cavity open above', 'hole', 'right vertical edge', etc. These routines were developed to cope with the raggedness of real characters. A Section 6.5.3 tree was used in recognition, and not more than nine features had to be detected in order to recognise any given alphanumeric character. Before starting the recognition process, Unger's spatial computer smoothed the input pattern by applying the rules which were formulated in Section 2.4.1. The price for the versatility of Unger's computer was approximately 170 gate inputs and 11 memory elements per cell, as well as the cost of the master control unit and associated store.

Chapter 9

COEFFICIENT ANALYSIS

9.1 HIGHER MOMENTS

In a visual pattern, let $f(x, y)$ be a measure of blackness at the point (x, y). The higher moments of the pattern are defined by

$$M_{pq} = \iint x^p y^q f(x, y)\, dx dy$$

where $p, q = 0, 1, 2, \ldots$, and integration is over the entire pattern. Blackness can be regarded as analogous to mass. M_{00} is the total blackness or mass of the pattern, M_{20} and M_{02} can be thought of as moments of inertia of the pattern about the y and x axes, and so on. It can be proved[228] that the infinite sequence $M_{00}, M_{10}, \ldots, M_{pq}, \ldots$, where $p, q = 0, 1, 2, \ldots, \infty$, is uniquely determined by $f(x, y)$, and conversely that $f(x, y)$ is uniquely determined by the infinite sequence $M_{00}, M_{10}, \ldots, M_{pq}, \ldots$.

For recognition purposes it is of course impractical to work with an infinite sequence of moments, but at the cost of loosing uniqueness, we can use the values of a chosen set of moments[12, 228]. Given an input pattern, we can evaluate, for instance, 22 of its moments. The values of these moments can be regarded as the components of a 22-component vector, and ordinary pattern recognition techniques can be applied to this vector. One possible advantage of applying pattern recognition techniques to this vector rather than directly to the input pattern is that the total number of components of the vector may be less than the total number of elements in the input pattern, and yet the vector may contain enough information for recognition purposes[266]. A further advantage is that the vector can quite easily be normalised so that, if the overall blackness, position, height, width, orientation, or even the perspective[172], of the input pattern is altered, the vector obtained from it remains unchanged[412].

For introductory purposes, let us confine out attention to N-element binary patterns in which $f(x, y) = 1$ or 0. In this case the moments are defined by

$$M_{p,\,q} = \Sigma\, x^p y^q \tag{9.1}$$

where the summation is over all pattern elements which are '1', that is, which are black. Thus M_{00} is the total number of black elements in the input pattern.

Let $\bar{x}$ and $\bar{y}$ be the coordinates of the centre of gravity of the input pattern. Thus $\bar{x}$ is the average of the x-coordinates of all black elements, and $\bar{y}$ is the average of the y-coordinates of all black elements. From (9.1),

$$M_{10} = \Sigma x \text{ and } M_{01} = \Sigma y$$

whence,

$$\bar{x} = M_{10}/M_{00} \quad \text{and} \quad \bar{y} = M_{01}/M_{00}$$

A vector whose components are moments given by (9.1) does not remain unchanged when the input pattern is shifted, but a vector whose components are moments given by

$$\Sigma(x - \bar{x})^p \,.\, (y - \bar{y})^q \tag{9.2}$$

does remain unchanged when the input pattern is shifted. It is easy to see this, since, if we change x, y to $x + b, y + d$, then $(x + b) - (\overline{x + b}) = x - \bar{x}$ and $(y + d) - (\overline{y + d}) = y - \bar{y}$. But, if we alter the height and breadth of the input character, the moments given by (9.2) do not remain unchanged.

To remedy this, or, in other words, to normalise for height and width as well as shift, we use moments defined by

$$m_{pq} = \sum \left(\frac{x - \bar{x}}{[\overline{(x - \bar{x})^2}]^{1/2}} \right)^p \cdot \left(\frac{y - \bar{y}}{[\overline{(y - \bar{y})^2}]^{1/2}} \right)^q \tag{9.3}$$

instead of (9.2). If x is changed to $ax + b$, then

$$\frac{(ax + b) - (\overline{ax + b})}{[\overline{(ax + b - \overline{ax + b})^2}]^{1/2}} = \frac{x - \bar{x}}{[\overline{(x - \bar{x})^2}]^{1/2}}$$

and $(y - \bar{y})/[\overline{(y - \bar{y})^2}]^{1/2}$ also remains unchanged when the height and breadth of the input pattern are changed. This normalisation is achieved by dividing by the root mean square of $x - \bar{x}$ rather than by the mean of $x - \bar{x}$, because the mean of $x - x$ is zero.

To normalise for the total number of black elements in the input pattern, we divide the (9.3) moments by m_{00}. Note that $m_{10} = m_{01} = 0$ and $m_{20}/m_{00} = m_{02}/m_{00} = m_{00}/m_{00} = 1$, and since these five normalised moments do not depend on the input pattern they are not useful for recognition: they have been used up in the process of normalisation. We will not give details of orientation or shear normalisation[12, 71], but the general idea is to rotate one or both of the axes so that in the new coordinate system the $p = 1, q = 1$ moment is zero, which means that this moment also is used up.

Alt[12] based character recognition on the values of 22 normalised moments such that $2 < p + q < 7$. A disadvantage of basing recognition on the values of moments is that this tends to give undue preponderance to the parts of a character lying furthest from the centre of gravity.

However, the method of moments suggests methods of normalisation for position, size, shear, orientation, and perspective, which can be used even when recognition is *not* directly based on the values of moments[71]. For instance, a pattern can be normalised for position by shifting it until its centre of gravity coincides with a prescribed point, as in Section 2.3.1, and linear or other recognition techniques may be applied directly to the shifted pattern, *not* to its moments. As a further example, a pattern can be normalised for height by adjusting its vertical scale so that $\overline{(y - \bar{y})^2}$ assumes a prescribed value, and, after this adjustment, linear or other recognition techniques may be applied directly to the pattern.

9.2 SLIT SCANNING TECHNIQUES

The importance of slit scanning techniques is commercial rather than theoretical. Section 9.2.1 serves as a link between Section 9.2.2 and the method of moments.

9.2.1 Weighted filter slit scanning

Philco-Ford have disclosed a character recognition technique[354] in which, in the simplest embodiment, a document is moved past a reading head in a light-tight box. A vertical slit of light, roughly the height of the characters, is focused onto the document, and the system is aligned so that, as the document moves, the slit sweeps along the line of characters to be read. Light reflected from the document is measured by three photomultipliers. The first of the three photomultipliers simply measures the total light reflected from the document. A photographic transparency whose transmission coefficient is $\theta_1(y)$ is interposed between the document and the second photomultiplier, the y axis being parallel to the length of the slit. A photographic transparency whose transmission coefficient is $\theta_2(y)$ is interposed between the document and the third photomultiplier. The outputs of the three photomultipliers are differentiated with respect to time. An input character is transformed into a six-component vector whose components are

(1) the number of maxima in the differentiated output of the first photomultiplier,
(2) the number of minima in the differentiated output of the second photomultiplier,
(3) and (4): the same as (1) and (2) but for the second photomultiplier,
(5) and (6): the same as (1) and (2) but for the third photomultiplier.

These numbers of maxima and minima are the total numbers that occur during the scanning of the input character by the slit. The input character is recognised by recognising the six-component vector obtained from it. This is particularly easy if all characters belonging to a given recognition class are transformed into the same six-component vector. It is then of course only necessary to compare the vector obtained from the input character with stored reference vectors, one per class, and find which reference vector is identical to that obtained from the input character.

The obvious link between this method and the method of moments is that if, for instance, $\theta_1(y) = y$ and $\theta_2(y) = y^2$, then the photomultipliers measure instantaneous moments of the slit. Indeed Giuliano *et al.*[172] have proposed implementing the method of moments by illuminating not just a thin slit but an entire character and measuring the reflected light via transparencies whose transmission coefficients are proportional to x, y, xy, x^2y, or to xy^2, etc.

9.2.2 Slit scan methods for stylised fonts

Figure 9.1 contains drawings of the numerals in a font called E13B which was designed to be recognised by slit scan methods. These characters were originally designed for use on bank cheques, for purposes

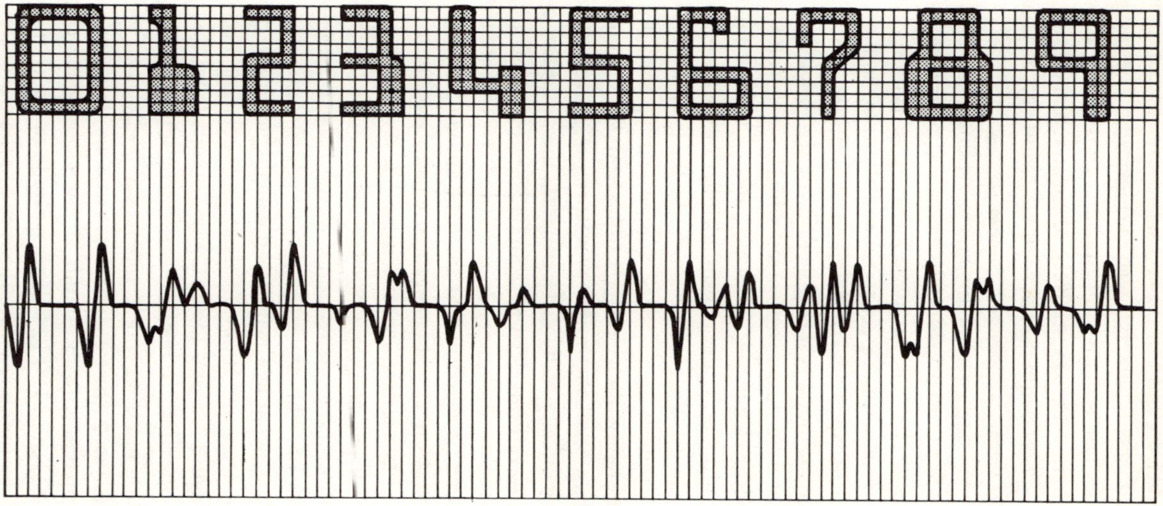

Figure 9.1. E13B *Numerals and their slit scan waveforms*

of automatic sorting. Characters printed on cheques are liable to be written over and dirtied, and this is one reason why characters are usually printed in magnetic ink and read magnetically. The magnetic reading system does not 'see' dirt and characters written by hand on top of the magnetic characters. Alternatively, the characters can be printed in ink which is opaque to infra-red light, and can be read optically using infra-red.

In a magnetic reading system, a document bearing a horizontal line of characters is transported horizontally past a stationary reading head like the reading head of a tape recorder. The output from the reading head is the differential with respect to time of the total amount of ink within a vertical slit-shaped area of the document. In the optical counterpart of the magnetic system, the document is brightly illuminated and is transported past a vertical slit which is arranged so that only light from within a narrrow slit-shaped area of the document reaches a photomultiplier. If the photomultiplier output is differentiated by a suitable RC circuit, the result is similar to the output of the magnetic system. In both the magnetic and optical systems, the slit extends above and below the characters to be read. We shall now discuss methods of recognition of the output waveform, regardless of whether it is obtained magnetically or by differentiating the output of a photomultiplier. Waveforms derived from E13B numerals would be roughly as shown below the numerals in Figure 9.1. Note that the characters have been designed so that the total amount of ink within a very thin vertical slit does not change appreciably except at the positions indicated by vertical lines in Figure 9.1.

One method[55] of recognition of waveforms is cross correlation with reference waveforms, using one reference waveform per recognition class, as in Section 3.5. This method has been implemented by feeding the waveform into a delay line, which is the analogue counterpart of a shift register. The delay line is tapped at intervals corresponding to the vertical lines in Figure 9.1, and the analogue voltages from the tapping points constitute the input to resistor mask recognition circuitry.

Cross correlation has been widely superseded by Boolean techniques. In one such technique[288] the signal derived from an input character is continuously compared with thresholds set for instance at ±15%, ±30%, ±45%, ±60%, ±80%, and ±100% of the magnitude of the first peak in the waveform. Let t_0 be the time of the first peak in the waveform, and let $t_1, t_2, \ldots$ be the times corresponding to subsequent successive vertical lines in Figure 9.1. At each of the times $t_1, t_2, \ldots$, the system stores the results of comparing the waveform with all the thresholds, positive and negative. This stored data provides the inputs to a Boolean discriminant system which is implemented by parallel logic circuits. For instance, one of the inputs to the logic circuits indicates whether it is *true* or *false* that the waveform exceeds the 45% threshold at t_3; and another input indicates whether it is *true* or *false* that the waveform is more negative than the −60% threshold at t_4, and so on. Characters are recognised according as appropriate Boolean functions are *true* or *false*, as in Section 6.2.1.

Instead of storing the quantised instantaneous amplitude at t_1, t_2, . . ., an IBM system[51] separately integrates the positive and negative portions of the waveform over time intervals corresponding roughly to intervals between midpoints between successive vertical lines in Figure 9.1, and stores the quantised results of integration for each time interval. The stored data is recognised by Boolean discriminants. The effect of integration is to make the adverse effect of noise less than in a system where the instantaneous quantised amplitudes at t_1, t_2, . . . are used as the basis of recognition.

A practical difficulty is that, owing to inaccuracy of printing or to the document not moving past the reading head at precisely the prescribed speed (e.g. because of slipping), the vertical lines in Figure 9.1 are not aligned with the reading head at precisely the prescribed times relative to the time when the leading edge of the character reaches the reading head. To overcome this timing difficulty it is possible to determine the exact times at which various peaks in the waveform occur, and to synchronise the timing circuitry accordingly[51, 338].

Alternatively, it is possible to use a recognition technique which depends less critically on timing, so that the timing circuitry need not be adjusted during the recognition of a character. In one such system[95], a single bistable element is of central importance. The waveform derived from a character is fed through a low-pass filter to reduce noise. At the time when any positive peak in the filtered waveform exceeds a threshold, a 'set' pulse is applied to the bistable. If the bistable is already in state '1', the 'set' pulse does not change the state of the bistable; but if the bistable is in state '0', the 'set' pulse switches the bistable into state '1'. At the time when any peak in the filtered waveform goes more negative than a negative threshold, a 'reset' pulse is applied to the bistable. If the bistable is already in state '0', the 'reset' pulse does not change the state of the bistable; but if the bistable is in state '1', the 'reset' pulse switches the bistable to state '0'. The first peak in the waveform is used to trigger timing circuitry which then produces a sequence of timing pulses, such that each pulse occurs at a time corresponding to the midpoint between successive vertical lines in Figure 9.1, it being assumed that the vertical lines in Figure 9.1 conform to their nominal timing. When each timing pulse occurs, the state of the bistable is fed into a 7-bit shift register. After the character, which moves from left to right, has been completely scanned by the reading head, seven timing pulses have occurred, and the seven bits in the shift register are a record of the states of the bistable at the times of the seven timing pulses. The 7-bit pattern in the shift register is the same for all members of any given recognition class, and is different for different recognition classes. For instance, if the input character is 4 , the leading edge of the character switches the bistable to state '1', and the negative peak which follows two vertical lines later switches the bistable to state '0'. The positive peak which follows two vertical lines later switches the bistable to state '1', and the final negative peak switches the bistable to state '0'. Thus the 7-bit pattern for 4 is 0110011. Similarly the 7-bit patterns for 3 , 2 , 1 , are 0000011, 0001001, 0000111 respectively, and so on for the other recognition classes. Recognition is achieved by comparing the 7-bit pattern with one reference 7-bit pattern per class.

E13B is not the only font which has been designed to be magnetically readable; CMC7 is another such font. Figure 9.2 shows drawings of '2' and '4' in CMC7. A *stroke* in a CMC7 character is a slit-shaped portion which

(1) is the height of the character, and
(2) is the width of one of the bars in Figure 9.2, and
(3) contains at least one black vertical bar.

Any CMC7 character consists of seven strokes. The horizontal intervals between strokes are restricted to two different lengths, specifically, twice the width of a stroke and 10/3 the width of a stroke. These are known respectively as *short* and *long* intervals. In the CMC7 numerals, every character has four short and two long intervals, and these are differently positioned in the different characters, as in Figure 9.2.

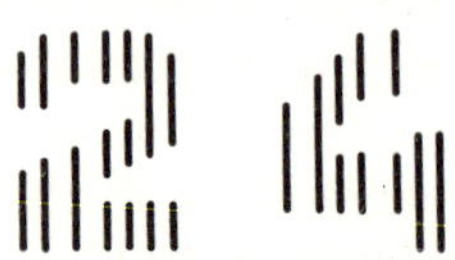

Figure 9.2. *Drawings of the* CMC7 *numerals* '2' *and* '4'

CMC7 characters, and other characters composed of vertical strokes[170], can be recognised by means of a technique which is similar to that which we have most recently introduced. To illustrate this, we shall outline a system in which a bistable element is switched on by a positive peak in the signal from the reading head, and off by a negative peak[94]. A positive peak also triggers timing circuitry which subsequently delivers two pulses. The first pulse occurs at a time which is ideally the time of the centre of the stroke which triggered the timing circuitry. When this pulse occurs, the state of the bistable is fed into a shift register. The second pulse occurs at a time corresponding ideally to 7/2 stroke widths after the triggering of the timing circuitry. If the bistable is in state '0' when the second pulse occurs, a '0' is fed into the shift register; but if the bistable is in state '1' the contents of the shift register remain unchanged. Owing to the timing of the second pulse, a '0' is fed into the shift register only if the stroke which triggered the timing circuitry is followed by a long interval. Every stroke triggers the timing circuitry, and therefore, when a character has passed completely beneath the reading head, the pattern of 0's and 1's in the shift register is the pattern of long and short intervals in the input character. For instance, for '2' and '4' the shift register contains 111010110 and 1110111010 respectively (in these bit patterns, bits from left to right correspond to intervals from right to left). For each recognition class the pattern in the shift register is unique, and can therefore be recognised trivially. Since the timing circuitry is triggered afresh by each stroke, it is less sensitive to inaccuracies of document speed and printing than is the corresponding E13B system.

An advantage of CMC7 is that it includes alphabetic characters (by using three long intervals per character), whilst E13B is restricted to numerals and four special symbols.

To introduce a further technique for recognising the output of a slit scan reading head, we must anticipate the ideas of the next section. The signal from the reading head is amplified and fed in parallel to, say, n filters, each of which transmits only the frequencies lying within a particular frequency band, different filters corresponding to different frequencies[113]. The output of each filter is separately squared and integrated over the period during which a character passes completely under the reading head. At the end of this period, the output of any given integrator is a measure of the total amount of energy present in the signal from the reading head within the frequency band of the corresponding filter. The outputs from the integrators are compared with thresholds $\theta_1, \theta_2, \ldots, \theta_k, \ldots, \theta_m$ which are prescribed functions of the total energy in the signal from the reading head. This total energy is measured by squaring and integrating the signal from the reading head without the interposition of any filter. Recognition is accomplished by Boolean discriminants implemented by parallel logic circuits. The inputs to these circuits are binary signals indicating whether it is *true* or *false* that the output from the jth frequency band integrator exceeds θ_k, for $j = 1, 2, \ldots, n$ and $k = 1, 2, \ldots, m$. This technique is claimed[113] to be insensitive to noise which is due, for example, to ink spattering and to accidental variations in the distance between the reading head and the document being read.

Generally speaking, character recognition may be made cheaper if characters are specially designed, that is, are *stylised,* to facilitate automatic recognition. For this reason stylised fonts are in widespread commercial use. Two classes of techniques are employed for reading stylised characters. One class comprises slit scanning techniques of the sort discussed in the present section. The other class comprises two-dimensional reading techniques. In these, stylised characters are read by methods such as those which we have discussed in Chapters 1, 6, and 7, the recognition process being simplified because of stylisation. We will not discuss details of two-dimensional reading of stylised characters.

9.3 FOURIER TRANSFORMATION

9.3.1 Discrete Fourier series

A visual pattern is a spatial distribution of grey (or colour) scale values, and this distribution has a characteristic shape. A probability distribution is a distribution of probability values, and this distribution has shape in N-dimensional space. Some of the techniques which have been used for describing probability distributions have also been used for describing spatial distributions of grey scale values. One such technique is the method of moments. For instance, variances and covariances are moments.

The method of potentials which we discussed in Section 4.6.1 is a method of approximating a probability distribution in N-dimensional space. Kazmierczac[251] has applied a related method of potentials directly to two-dimensional visual patterns. In Kasmierczac's technique an interpolation function spreads out from each black pattern element.

A third technique which has been applied both to probability distributions and to visual patterns is orthonormal expansion[21], and Fourier series expansion is an example of this. Before discussing Fourier expansion, let us consider a point P moving at constant speed in a circular path of radius a. Let the time taken to go once completely round the path be $2\pi/\omega$ s, so that the point goes completely round the path $\omega/2\pi$ times per s. Then $2\pi/\omega$ is the *period* of the motion, $\omega/2\pi$ its *frequency*, and ω its *angular frequency*.

If the moving point lies on the u axis at time $t = 0$, then at a subsequent time, t, the point P lies at ωt radians to the u axis, as shown in Figure 9.3. At time t the projection of the position vector on the u axis is $a \cos \omega t$. The top plot in Figure 9.4 is a plot of $a \cos\omega t$ *versus* t, and the bottom plot is a plot of $a \sin\omega t$, which is the projection of the position vector on the v axis. The middle plot is of $a \cos(\omega t + \phi)$ *versus* t, and it can be seen that the addition of the constant angle ϕ shifts the middle plot along the t axis relative to the top plot. Here ϕ is the *phase angle* between the top and middle plots. The three curves in Figure 9.4 are *sinusoids.*

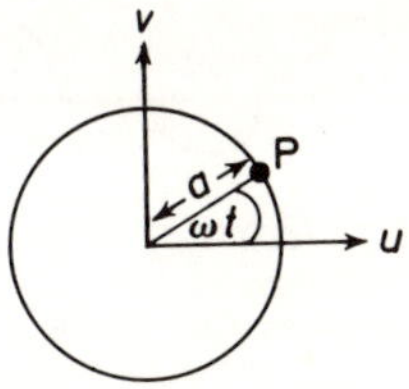

Figure 9.3. *A point moving in a circular path*

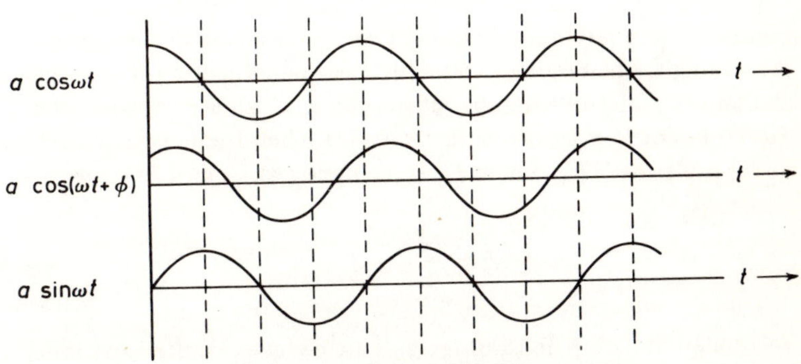

Figure 9.4. *Plots of sinusoids differing in phase*

At time t, the coordinates of the moving point are (a cosωt, a sinωt). Alternatively, the position of the point is expressed by the complex number a (cosωt + i sinωt). In fact the series expansion of $e^{i\omega t}$ is the same as the series expansion of (cosωt + i sinωt), i.e.

$$e^{i\omega t} = \cos \omega t + i \sin \omega t \tag{9.4}$$

and the position of the point at time t is $ae^{i\omega t}$. Note that the functions $ae^{in\omega t}$, where $n = 0, \pm 1, \pm 2, \pm 3, \ldots$, are orthonormal in that

$$\frac{\omega}{2\pi} \int_{-\pi/\omega}^{\pi/\omega} e^{in\omega t} \cdot e^{in'\omega t}\, dt = \begin{cases} 1 & \text{if } n = -n' \\ 0 & \text{if } n \neq -n' \end{cases} \tag{9.5}$$

A waveform is said to be *periodic* if it consists of an infinite sequence of repetitions of the same segment. Figure 9.5 shows part of a plot of an arbitrary periodic function of time, $f(t)$. Let us denote the period, that is, the time duration of the repeated segment, by T_B, and let $\omega_B = 2\pi/T_B$.

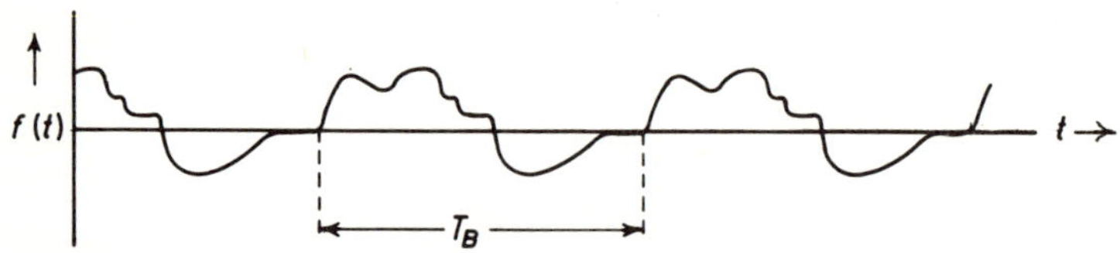

Figure 9.5. *A section of an arbitrary periodic function*

The justification and statement of the conditions of Fourier expansion will be found elsewhere[56, 341], and the following paragraphs contain only a very brief revision of elementary Fourier Theory. According to the Fourier expansion, a periodic function $f(t)$ is equal to the sum of an infinite number of sinusoids, which are known as the *harmonics* or *Fourier components* of $f(t)$. Their frequencies are restricted to multiples of $1/T_B$, where T_B is the period of $f(t)$. In symbols,

$$f(t) = \sum_{n=-\infty}^{\infty} g_n e^{in\omega_B t} \tag{9.6}$$

[cf. equation (5.5)]. In (9.6) the g_n's are complex coefficients which determine the amplitude and phase of the harmonics. The g_n's can be determined by integrating the product $f(t)e^{-i\omega_B t}$ over one period. Using (9.6) and then interchanging the order of summation we have

$$\int_{-\pi/\omega_B}^{\pi/\omega_B} f(t)\, e^{-in\omega_B t}\, dt = \int_{-\pi/\omega_B}^{\pi/\omega_B} \sum_{n'=-\infty}^{\infty} g_{n'} e^{in'\omega_B t} \,.\, e^{-n\omega_B t}\, dt$$

$$= \sum_{n'=-\infty}^{\infty} g_{n'} \int_{-\pi/\omega_B}^{\pi/\omega_B} e^{in'\omega_B t} \,.\, e^{-in\omega_B t}\, dt$$

$$= \frac{2\pi g_n}{\omega_B}$$

by using (9.5). Thus

$$g_n = \frac{\omega_B}{2\pi} \int_{-\pi/\omega_B}^{\pi/\omega_B} f(t) e^{-in\omega_B t}\, dt \tag{9.7}$$

and similarly it can be shown that

$$g_{-n} = \frac{\omega_B}{2\pi} \int_{-\pi/\omega_B}^{\pi/\omega_B} f(t) e^{in\omega_B t}\, dt \tag{9.8}$$

Expressions (9.7) and (9.8) do not immediately provide the most efficient computer programme for determining the g_n's, and a very much more efficient computational procedure, known as the *fast Fourier transform*, is explained in Refs 92 and 96.

Since sines and cosines may be more familiar than complex exponentials, let us manipulate (9.6) into an expression in terms of sines and cosines[241]. From (9.7) we have

$$g_n e^{in\omega_B t} = \frac{\omega_B}{2\pi} e^{in\omega_B t} \int_{-\pi/\omega_B}^{\pi/\omega_B} f(t)\, e^{-in\omega_B t}\, dt$$

and using (9.4) this becomes

$$g_n e^{in\omega_B t} = \frac{\omega_B}{2\pi} (\cos n\omega_B t + i \sin n\omega_B t) \int_{-\pi/\omega_B}^{\pi/\omega_B} f(t) [\cos(-n\omega_B t) + i \sin(-n\omega_B t)] dt$$

$$= \frac{\omega_B}{2\pi} (\cos n\omega_B t + i \sin n\omega_B t) \left[\int_{-\pi/\omega_B}^{\pi/\omega_B} f(t) \cos(n\omega_B t) dt - i \int_{-\pi/\omega_B}^{\pi/\omega_B} f(t) \sin(n\omega_B t) dt \right] \qquad (9.9)$$

and similarly we find that

$$g_{-n} e^{-in\omega_B t} = \frac{\omega_B}{2\pi} (\cos n\omega_B t - i \sin n\omega_B t) \left[\int_{-\pi/\omega_B}^{\pi/\omega_B} f(t) \cos(n\omega_B t) dt + i \int_{-\pi/\omega_B}^{\pi/\omega_B} f(t) \sin(n\omega_B t) dt \right] \qquad (9.10)$$

When equations (9.9) and (9.10) are added the imaginary terms cancel out to give

$$g_n e^{in\omega_B t} + g_n e^{-in\omega_B t} = \frac{\omega_B}{\pi} \cos(n\omega_B t) \int_{-\pi/\omega_B}^{\pi/\omega_B} f(t) \cos(n\omega_B t) dt + \frac{\omega_B}{\pi} \sin(n\omega_B t) \int_{-\pi/\omega_B}^{\pi/\omega_B} f(t) \sin(n\omega_B t) dt \qquad (9.11)$$

Equation (9.6) can be rewritten

$$f(t) = g_0 + \sum_{n=1}^{\infty} (g_n e^{in\omega_B t} + g_{-n} e^{-in\omega_B t})$$

By substituting (9.11) in this we obtain

$$f(t) = g_0 + \sum_{n=1}^{\infty} b_n \cos(n\omega_B t) + \sum_{n=1}^{\infty} c_n \sin(n\omega_B t) \tag{9.12}$$

where

$$b_n = \frac{\omega_B}{\pi} \int_{-\pi/\omega_B}^{\pi/\omega_B} f(t) \cos(n\omega_B t)\, dt$$

and

$$c_n = \frac{\omega_B}{\pi} \int_{-\pi/\omega_B}^{\pi/\omega_B} f(t) \sin(n\omega_B t)\, dt$$

and, from (9.7) or (9.8),

$$g_0 = \int_{-\pi/\omega_B}^{\pi/\omega_B} f(t)\, dt$$

which is the average of $f(t)$ over a period. Equation (9.12) expresses $f(t)$ as the sum of a series of sine and cosine sinusoids with frequencies $n\omega_B/2\pi$, where $n = 1, 2, 3, \ldots$. This is known as the *Fourier series* for $f(t)$. The difference in angular frequency between successive sinusoids in this series is

$$\Delta\omega = (n+1)\omega_B - n\omega_B = \omega_B = 2\pi/T_B \tag{9.13}$$

9.3.2 Fourier integral

We can tackle the case where $f(t)$ is not periodic by regarding the period as infinitely long[270]. It is convenient now to define $\omega = n\omega_B = n\Delta\omega$, so that (9.7) and (9.8) can be expressed by the single equation

$$g_\omega = \frac{\Delta\omega}{2\pi} \int_{-\pi/\Delta\omega}^{\pi/\Delta\omega} f(t)\, e^{-i\omega t}\, dt \tag{9.14}$$

Substitution of (9.14) into (9.6) gives

$$f(t) = \frac{1}{2\pi} \sum_{\omega=-\infty}^{\infty} \left[\int_{-\pi/\Delta\omega}^{\pi/\Delta\omega} f(t) \mathrm{e}^{-\mathrm{i}\omega t} \, \mathrm{d}t \right] \mathrm{e}^{\mathrm{i}\omega t} \Delta\omega$$

As the period of $f(t)$ tends to infinity,

$$\lim_{\Delta\omega \to 0} f(t) = \frac{1}{2\pi} \sum_{\omega=-\infty}^{\infty} \left[\int_{-\pi/\Delta\omega}^{\pi/\Delta\omega} f(t) \mathrm{e}^{-\mathrm{i}\omega t} \, \mathrm{d}t \right] \mathrm{e}^{\mathrm{i}\omega t} \, \mathrm{d}\omega$$

$$= \int_{-\infty}^{\infty} g(\omega) \, \mathrm{e}^{\mathrm{i}\omega t} \, \mathrm{d}\omega \tag{9.15}$$

where

$$g(\omega) = \frac{1}{2\pi} \int_{-\infty}^{\infty} f(t) \mathrm{e}^{-\mathrm{i}\omega t} \, \mathrm{d}t \tag{9.16}$$

$g(\omega)$ is the *Fourier transform* of $f(t)$, and $f(t)$ is the *Fourier transform* of $g(\omega)$ The function $g(\omega)$, which is generally complex, is sometimes known as the *spectrum* of $f(t)$. According to equation (9.15), $f(t)$ is composed of an infinite series of sinusoids, with successive sinusoids differing infinitesimally in frequency. The spectrum $g(\omega)$ gives the amplitude and phase at angular frequency ω.

We have been concerned with a function $f(t)$ of time. If we had worked with displacement x instead of time t and with $k = 2\pi/\lambda$ instead of $\omega = 2\pi/T$, where λ is the *wavelength*, the spatial counterpart of the *period*, we would have obtained

$$f(x) = \int_{-\infty}^{\infty} g(k) \mathrm{e}^{\mathrm{i}kx} \, \mathrm{d}k \tag{9.17}$$

and

$$g(k) = \frac{1}{2\pi} \int_{-\infty}^{\infty} f(x) \, \mathrm{e}^{-\mathrm{i}kx} \, \mathrm{d}x \tag{9.18}$$

which are the one-dimensional spatial counterparts of (9.15) and (9.16) respectively.

9.3.3 Fourier theorems

For later use, we now revise three of the well-known theorems of Fourier theory[56, 341].

(1) *Addition theorem.* If $g_1(k)$ and $g_2(k)$ are respectively the Fourier transforms of two functions $f_1(x)$ and $f_2(x)$, then the Fourier transform of $f_1(x) + f_2(x)$ is

$$\int_{-\infty}^{\infty} [f_1(x) + f_2(x)]\,\mathrm{e}^{-ikx}\,\mathrm{d}x = \int_{-\infty}^{\infty} f_1(x)\mathrm{e}^{-ikx}\,\mathrm{d}x + \int_{-\infty}^{\infty} f_2(x)\mathrm{e}^{-ikx}\,\mathrm{d}x$$

$$= g_1(k) + g_2(k)$$

(2) *Shift theorem.* If $g(k)$ is the Fourier transform of $f(x)$, then the Fourier transform of $f(x - \alpha)$ is

$$\frac{1}{2\pi}\int_{-\infty}^{\infty} f(x-\alpha)\,\mathrm{e}^{-ikx}\,\mathrm{d}x = \frac{1}{2\pi}\int_{-\infty}^{\infty} f(x-\alpha)\,\mathrm{e}^{-ik(x-\alpha)}\,.\,\mathrm{e}^{-ik\alpha}\,\mathrm{d}(x-\alpha)$$

$$= \mathrm{e}^{-i\alpha k} g(k)$$

(3) *Cross correlation theorem.* The cross correlation function, $C_{12}(\beta)$, of two functions $f_1(x)$ and $f_2(x)$ is defined[270] by

$$C_{12}(\beta) = \int_{-\infty}^{\infty} f_1(x) f_2(x+\beta)\,\mathrm{d}x \qquad (9.19)$$

In the case where $f_1(x)$ and $f_2(x)$ are discrete,

$$C_{12}(\beta) = \sum_{-\infty}^{\infty} f_1(x) f_2(x+\beta)$$

and we have encountered a normalised version of this in Section 3.5. In the present section we consider the case where $f_1(x)$ and $f_2(x)$ are continuous. Let $g_1(k)$ and $g_2(k)$ be the Fourier transforms of $f_1(x)$ and $f_2(x)$ respectively. According to the cross correlation theorem, the Fourier transform $D_{12}(k)$ of $C_{12}(\beta)$ is given by

$$D_{12}(k) = 2\pi g_1^*(k) \, . \, g_2(k)$$

where the asterisk denotes the complex conjugate. (The complex conjugate of any complex number $u + \mathrm{i}v$ is $u - \mathrm{i}v$.) To prove the cross correlation theorem (p. 36 in Ref. 270) we substitute

$$f_2(x+\beta) = \int_{-\infty}^{\infty} g_2(k)\, \mathrm{e}^{\mathrm{i}k(x+\beta)}\, \mathrm{d}k$$

into (9.19) and reverse the order of integration. This gives

$$C_{12}(\beta) = \int_{-\infty}^{\infty} f_1(x) \int_{-\infty}^{\infty} g_2(k) \mathrm{e}^{\mathrm{i}k(x+\beta)}\, \mathrm{d}k\, \mathrm{d}x$$

$$= \int_{-\infty}^{\infty} g_2(k) \int_{-\infty}^{\infty} f_1(x) \mathrm{e}^{\mathrm{i}kx}\, \mathrm{d}x \, . \, \mathrm{e}^{\mathrm{i}k\beta}\, \mathrm{d}k$$

$$= \int_{-\infty}^{\infty} g_2(k) \, . \, 2\pi g_1^*(k) \mathrm{e}^{\mathrm{i}k\beta}\, \mathrm{d}k \tag{9.20}$$

by using (9.18). Using β instead of x as the spatial variable in (9.17), the Fourier transform $D_{12}(k)$ of $C_{12}(\beta)$ is such that

$$C_{12}(\beta) = \int_{-\infty}^{\infty} D_{12}(k) \mathrm{e}^{\mathrm{i}k\beta}\, \mathrm{d}k \tag{9.21}$$

and by comparing this with (9.20) we establish that

$$D_{12}(k) = 2\pi g_1^*(k) g_2(k) \tag{9.22}$$

9.4 PATTERN RECOGNITION BY FOURIER OPTICS

9.4.1 Fourier transformation by Fraunhofer diffraction

Fourier transformation by Fraunhofer diffraction is the starting point of our elementary introduction to Fourier optics in pattern recognition. In Figure 9.6, the vertical line labelled X represents a side view of a plane in which the x direction is parallel to X and the y direction is normal to the paper on which Figure 9.6 is drawn. Suppose that this plane is illuminated with parallel coherent monochromatic light at an angle θ as indicated in Figure 9.6, and let us consider a ray incident on this plane at $x = 0$. At a distance δ backwards along this ray, the phase differs by $2\pi\delta/\lambda$ from the phase at $x = 0$, where λ is the wavelength of the light. Since the wavefront is plane, the phase at Q is the same as the phase at P; and let x be the distance of Q from $x = 0$. Now $\delta = x \sin\theta$, and it is convenient to define $\alpha = (2\pi \sin\theta)/\lambda$. Thus, if the amplitude at $x = 0$ is $ae^{i\omega t}$, then the amplitude at P and Q is $e^{i(\omega t - \alpha x)}$.

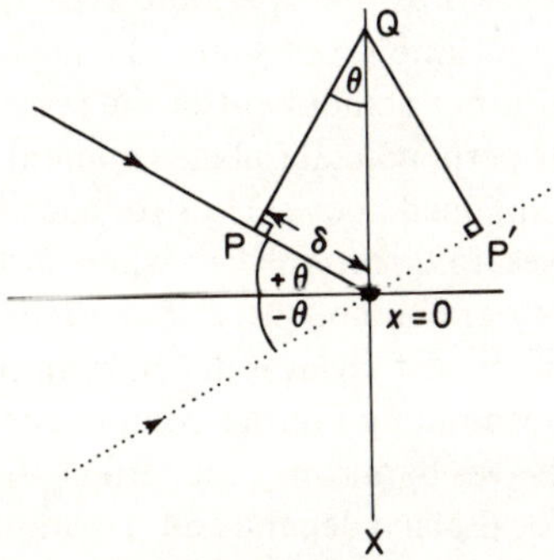

Figure 9.6.

Suppose that the plane is also illuminated with parallel coherent monochromatic light with the same wavelength as before, but at an angle $-\theta$, as indicated by the dotted line in Figure 9.6, and such that the phase of the $+\theta$ and $-\theta$ beams of light is the same at $x = 0$. At the point Q the phase of the light from the $-\theta$ beam is the same as the phase at P′, which is $2\pi\delta/\lambda = \alpha x$ ahead of the phase at $x = 0$. The total complex amplitude at Q due to both beams is

$$ae^{i(\omega t - \alpha x)} + ae^{i(\omega t + \alpha x)} = ae^{i\omega t}(e^{i\alpha x} + e^{-i\alpha x})$$

$$= 2ae^{i\omega t}\cos\alpha x \qquad (9.23)$$

This is the complex amplitude at *any* point (x, y).

Suppose now that the x, y plane contains a photographic transparency or mask whose transmission coefficient is $2 \cos\alpha x$. If the x, y plane is illuminated with parallel monochromatic coherent light, of amplitude $ae^{i\omega t}$, in a direction perpendicular to the x, y plane, the light emerging from the mask has amplitude $2ae^{i\omega t}\cos\alpha x$. But this is precisely what would be obtained if two waves were travelling at $\pm\theta$, as in Figure 9.6. Indeed the light emerging from the mask *is* in fact composed of plane waves travelling at $\pm\theta$. From (9.23) we see that the angle θ depends not only on the wavelength of the light but also on the wavelength of the transmission coefficient of the transparency.

If the x, y plane contains a mask which has an aperiodic transmission coefficient, for instance if the mask is a transparency of the character '2', then, according to (9.17), generalised to two dimensions, the mask can be regarded as the sum of an infinite number of sinusoidal masks, with transmission coefficients given by the two-dimensional generalisation of (9.18). In other words, the aperiodic mask is equivalent to the superimposition of an infinite set of sinusoidal masks, there being one sinusoidal mask per Fourier component of the aperiodic mask. Each sinusoidal mask treats perpendicular plane coherent monochromatic light in the manner explained above. Thus for each Fourier component we get two plane waves, in directions $\pm\theta$, where θ depends on the wavelength of the Fourier component, in accordance with (9.23). The complex amplitude of these $\pm\theta$ waves depends on the complex amplitude of the corresponding Fourier component.

If we focus these waves by means of a perfect lens, the amplitude at a given point in the focal plane depends on the amplitude of the wave emanating in a particular direction from the mask. Thus the complex amplitude at a given point in the focal plane of the lens depends on the complex amplitude of a single Fourier component of the mask. If, in Figure 9.7, the focal length of the lens L2 is f, then the complex amplitude at a point R in the focal plane which is at distance $u = f \tan\theta$ from the optic axis depends on the complex amplitude of the Fourier component which is associated with the angle θ. The spatial distribution, i.e. the pattern, of complex amplitude in the focal plane is the Fourier transform of the pattern which is embodied in the mask. The pattern in

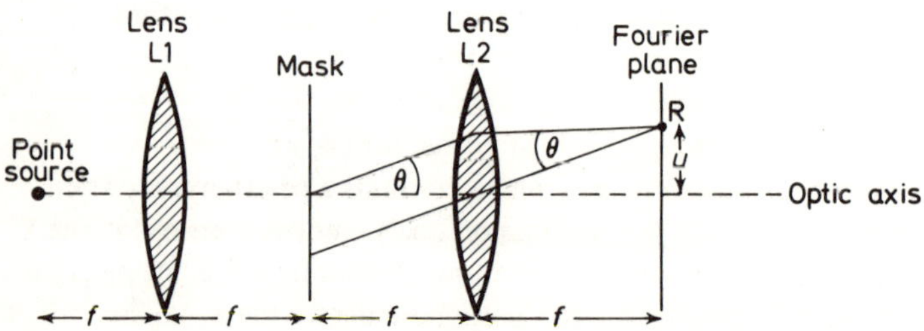

Figure 9.7. *A simple set-up for Fraunhofer diffraction*

the focal plane is the *Fraunhofer diffraction* pattern of the mask. The focal plane of the lens L2 is known as the *Fourier plane,* or, alternatively, as the *Fraunhofer plane,* of L2.

Let us return for a minute to Figure 9.6, and to the situation where the x, y plane is illuminated from $+\theta$ and $-\theta$. If we retard the phase of the light in the $+\theta$ beam by ϕ radians, and advance the phase in the $-\theta$ beam by ϕ radians, then the amplitude incident at any point (x, y) is

$$a\mathrm{e}^{\mathrm{i}[\omega t-(\phi+\alpha x)]}+a\mathrm{e}^{\mathrm{i}(\omega t+\phi+\alpha x)}=2a\mathrm{e}^{\mathrm{i}\omega t}\cos(\alpha x+\phi)$$

Thus we see that the phase change in the incident light causes a phase change (i.e. shift) in the distribution of amplitude in the x, y plane. Conversely, if the x, y plane contains a transparency or mask with transmission coefficient $2\cos\alpha x$, and, if this mask is illuminated perpendicularly with parallel coherent monochromatic light, then the effect of moving the mask in the $\pm x$ direction is to change the phase of the light diffracted into directions $\pm\theta$. If this light is focused as in Figure 9.7, the magnitude of the amplitude at point R remains unchanged when the mask is moved in the $\pm x$ direction, but the phase at R depends on how much the mask is shifted in the x direction. Of course the mask must remain within the field of view of the lens and within the collimated beam of light.

9.4.2 Recognition of Fourier transforms of characters

Figure 9.8 shows Fraunhofer diffraction patterns obtained[23] from the characters 0, . . ., 9, A, . . ., Z. To obtain the Figure 9.8 patterns, the original characters were photographed and a transparency of each character in turn was used as the mask in the Figure 9.7 set-up. The Figure 9.8 photographs record the pattern of light *intensity* in the Fourier plane, but do not record *phase*. As explained above, the Fraunhofer diffraction intensity pattern remains unchanged when the transparency of the character is moved in its own plane. Because of this position invariance, we might consider recognising an unknown character by recognising its Fraunhofer diffraction pattern[224]. Besides the advantage that it would be unnecessary to position the input character accurately prior to recognition, this would also have the advantage that we could ignore various spatial frequency bands in the input character[240]. A spatial frequency band can be blanked out by an opaque annulus or disc parallel to, and immediately in front of, the

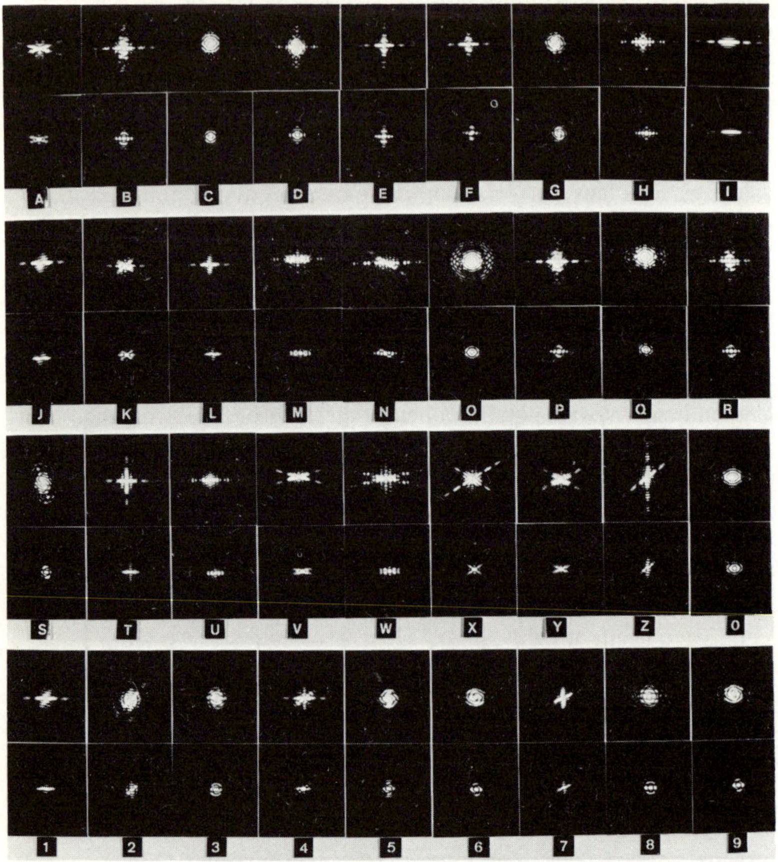

Figure 9.8. *Fraunhofer diffraction patterns obtained from characters. There are two photographs of the diffraction pattern of each character, and in the lower photograph the film was less exposed than in the upper photograph. From Reference 25, with permission*

Fourier plane, and centred on the optic axis. In particular, noise such as ink spatter round the input character gives rise to high spatial frequencies which can be ignored by ignoring all parts of the diffraction pattern which lie more than a suitable distance from the optic axis. On the other hand, because the letters 'O' and 'Q' differ only in detail, we might improve discrimination between them by blanking out parts of the diffraction pattern which lie nearest to the optic axis, since these correspond to low spatial frequencies and coarse spatial structure in the input character[221]. A further possible advantage of this technique of character recognition is that, by varying the frequency of the light, e.g, by obtaining light from a rotating prism or diffraction grating, it might be possible to recognise an input character regardless of its size, at least within 2:1 limits of size variation[224].

Unfortunately the overwhelming disadvantages of this technique are:

(1) In our discussion of Figure 9.6 we saw that each spatial frequency produces beams of light at $\pm \theta^\circ$. This means that the diffraction pattern remains unchanged if the input character is rotated through 180°. Thus the diffraction patterns for '6' and '9' may be identical.
(2) The diffraction (intensity) pattern is not only independent of the position of the input character, but is also to an important extent independent of the positioning of limbs *within* a character[221]. For instance, 'H' and 'T' consist of horizontal and vertical lines, and have similar diffraction patterns, as can be seen in Figure 9.8.
(3) The surface of paper has irregularities which are of the same order of magnitude as the wavelength of light, and these produce strong unwanted diffraction effects if we attempt to obtain a diffraction pattern from light reflected from paper. Therefore a character must be converted into the form of a transparency, either photographically or by soaking the document in oil[164], or a special photoelectric device must be used[356]. A photographic process allows reduction of the size of an input character to microfilm proportions, the Fraunhofer diffraction pattern thereby being increased to a manageable size[224].
(4) If the Fraunhofer diffraction pattern is to be recognised by optical matching with reference Fraunhofer diffraction patterns in the form of transparencies, these transparencies must have a tolerably accurate grey scale, which is difficult to achieve.

This last disadvantage has been overcome by focusing the diffraction pattern of an unknown character onto a ground glass screen which randomises the phase of the light, and takes the place of the point source in Figure 9.7. Light passing through the ground glass screen is rendered parallel by the lens L1 and then falls on a transparency of a reference character (*not* a reference diffraction pattern). This reference transparency (e.g. of '2') can be binary, so that there is no grey scale trouble[23]. Light diffracted by the reference transparency passes through a further lens, L2, and a photomultiplier measures the amount of light focused onto the optic axis. The photomultiplier output is large only if the input character is the same as the reference character, or is the same as the reference character rotated through 180°.

To understand loosely why this is so[285], let us consider a bright spot lying at a position given by the vector $\boldsymbol{r}$ on the ground glass screen, such that the origin lies on the optic axis. The bright spot acts as a coherent source, and if the reference character is the same as the input character, diffraction by the reference character produces, in the Fourier plane of L2, bright spots at positions $\pm\boldsymbol{r}$ *relative* to the given bright spot on the ground glass screen. The $-\boldsymbol{r}$ spot lies on the optic axis. Since this is true for all bright spots on the ground glass screen, there is high intensity on the optic axis in the Fourier plane of L2 if the input character is the same as the reference character, and recognition can be based on this. If the ground class screen were removed, phase information would be conserved, position invariance would be lost, and the input character would have to be accurately aligned with the reference character.

The use of the ground glass screen does not surmount disadvantages (1), (2), and (3), and character recognition by Fraunhofer diffraction patterns does not appear to be a practical proposition. But it may be useful to transform a character (or other pattern) into a further pattern and recognise the Fourier transform of this further pattern. For instance, in Section 7.4.1 the direction of motion of a contour-following spot was continuously determined and was quantised into 8 or 12 directions. Suppose now that the angular direction ψ is not quantised and that we plot $(\psi - 2\pi t/T)$ versus time, t, where T is the time taken to trace once completely round the external contour. This plot is periodic if the spot traces many times round the external contour, and we can apply recognition techniques to the discrete Fourier transform of this periodic plot[60, 466a]. If phase is ignored, and if the speed of the spot is adjusted so that T always has the same value[182], whatever the input pattern, then the Fourier transform of the periodic plot is invariant to the orientation, size, and location of the input character, chromosome, or blood cell, etc. Noisy variations in the contour can be ignored by ignoring high frequencies.

Instead of recognising a diffraction pattern obtained from an input pattern or from a pattern derived from the input pattern, it may be expedient to recognise a pattern which is obtained *from* a diffraction pattern which in turn is derived from an input pattern[273, 369]. For instance, Lendaris and Stanley[273] have obtained a Fraunhofer diffraction pattern from a small area of an aerial photograph. The total intensity in the diffraction pattern between the inner and outer circumferences of an annular region centred on the optic axis is a measure of the total amplitude of frequencies within a particular frequency band, irrespective of orientation, in the chosen area of the aerial photograph. Lendaris and Stanley have obtained from a set of concentric annuli a set of total intensities; and this set of intensities constitutes a pattern which is characteristically different according as the chosen area of the aerial photograph contains, for instance, orchard or natural woodland.

9.4.3 Fraunhofer holography in pattern recognition

Before discussing Fraunhofer holography, let us revise an elementary formula concerning complex numbers. Any complex number can be expressed in the form $be^{i\beta}$, and note that

$$be^{i\beta} \times be^{-i\beta} = b^2 \tag{9.24}$$

If $be^{i\beta}$ is in fact the sum of two complex numbers according to

$$B = be^{i\beta} = a_1 e^{i\nu_1} + a_2 e^{i\nu_2} = A_1 + A_2$$

then the complex conjugate of $be^{i\beta}$ is

$$B^* = be^{-i\beta} = a_1 e^{-i\nu_1} + a_2 e^{-i\nu_2}$$

and using (9.24) and multiplying out we see that

$$B^2 = B^*B = (a_1 e^{-i\nu_1} + a_2 e^{-i\nu_2})(a_1 e^{i\nu_1} + a_2 e^{i\nu_2})$$

$$= a_1{}^2 + a_2{}^2 + a_1 a_2 e^{i(\nu_1 - \nu_2)} + a_1 a_2 e^{-i(\nu_1 - \nu_2)} \tag{9.25}$$

$$= |A_1|^2 + |A_2|^2 + A_1 \, |A_2| \, e^{-i\nu_2} + A_1^* \, |A_2| \, e^{i\nu_2} \tag{9.26}$$

A photograph of a Fraunhofer diffraction pattern records only the spatial distribution of light intensity in the Fourier plane, and phase information is lost. Holography is based on a trick which allows photographic recording of phase information as well as intensity information. The trick is to photograph the interference pattern which is formed when a diffraction pattern is illuminated with light from a source which is phase locked to, or is the same source as, that which gives rise to the diffraction pattern[118, 425]. Because phase information is retained, we can make use of the cross correlation theorem of Section 9.3.3.

Figure 9.9 is a diagram of a simple set-up for producing an interference pattern in the Fourier plane of lens L2[176]. This set-up differs from Figure 9.7 in that it includes an additional lens L3 which focuses light to a point lying at a distance x_s from the optic axis, so that parallel light is incident at an angle $\tan^{-1}(x_s/f)$ onto the Fourier plane of L2. At the instant $t = 0$ the amplitude distribution in the Fourier plane due to this beam of light is $ae^{i\gamma u}$, where a and γ are constants, and the u axis in the Fourier plane is as indicated in Figure 9.9.

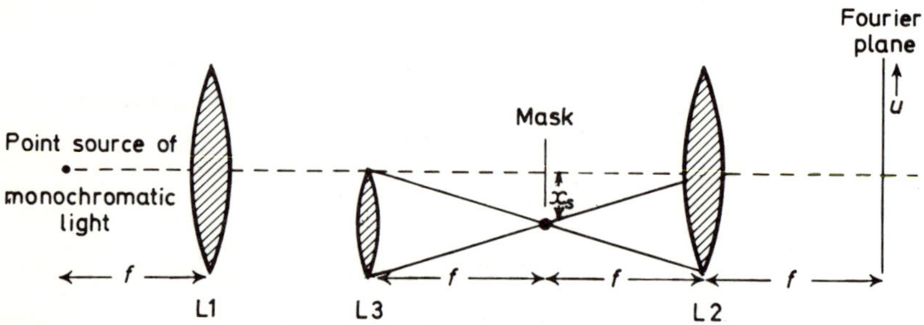

Figure 9.9. *A simple set-up for obtaining a hologram*

The pattern in the mask in Figure 9.9 is generally two-dimensional, but for introductory simplicity let us forget about the dimension which is perpendicular to the plane of the paper on which Figure 9.9 is drawn. Generalisation to include this dimension is in fact straightforward. Let us denote the transmission coefficient of the mask by $f_1(x)$. In Section 9.4.1 we saw that the lens L2 focuses the Fourier transform of $f_1(x)$ onto the Fourier plane of L2. It is convenient to express the Fourier transform of $f_1(x)$ as $g_1(u)$.

The total complex amplitude at any point in the Fourier plane is the sum of $g_1(u)$ and the amplitude $ae^{i\gamma u}$ due to the light which has passed through the lens L3. The pattern of amplitude in the Fourier plane is an *interference* pattern. If we photograph this interference pattern, we in fact record photographically (approximately) the intensity, that is, the square of the amplitude, at each point. Thus the photograph, which is called a *hologram*, records

$$|g_1(u) + ae^{i\gamma u}|^2 = |g_1(u)|^2 + a^2 + g_1(u)ae^{-i\gamma u} + g_1^*(u)ae^{i\gamma u} \quad (9.27)$$

[here we have used formula (9.26)].

To determine whether a second photographic transparency $f_2(x)$ is in fact the same as $f_1(x)$, Vander Lugt *et al.*[449] place the $f_2(x)$ transparency between lenses L1 and L2 in the set-up shown in Figure 9.10, and they place the hologram obtained from $f_1(x)$ between lenses L2 and L4. The Fourier transform $g_2(u)$ of $f_2(x)$ is focused by L2 onto the hologram so that the complex amplitude distribution of light emerging from the hologram is the product of $g_2(u)$ and the transmission coefficient of the hologram, which is given, approximately, by (9.27). The amplitude distribution over the output plane in Figure 9.10 is the Fourier transform of the complex amplitude distribution of light emerging from the hologram[272]. Thus, according to the addition theorem (Section 9.3.3), the amplitude distribution in the ouput plane of Figure 9.10 is $F_1 + F_2 + F_3$, where F_1 is the Fourier transform of $g_2(u)(|g_1(u)|^2 + a^2)$, F_2 is the Fourier transform of $g_1(u)g_2(u)ae^{-i\gamma u}$, and F_3 is the Fourier transform of $g_1^*(u)g_2(u)ae^{i\gamma u}$. Here F_1 is simply $f_2(x)$ attenuated by the factor $|g_1(u)|^2 + a^2$. According to the shift theorem, F_2 is a function centred at $x = -\alpha$. According to the shift

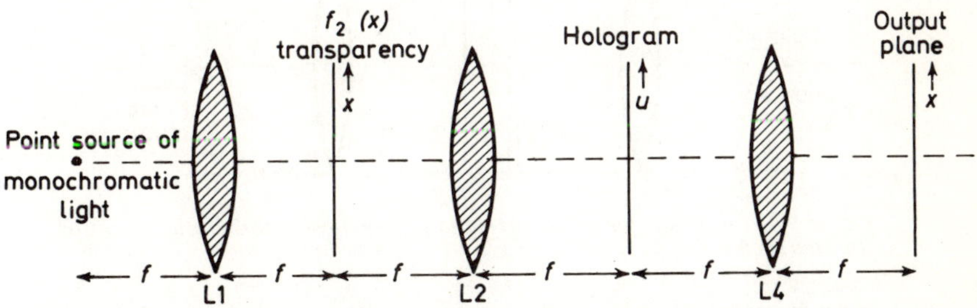

Figure 9.10. *A simple set-up for holographic cross correlation*

theorem and the cross correlation theorem, F_3 is the cross correlation function of $f_1(x)$ and $f_2(x)$, centred at $x = +\alpha$. The distance x_s, and thus γ, must be made big enough to prevent the cross correlation function F_3 from overlapping F_1 in the output plane.

Figure 9.11 shows a simple non-holographic and indeed *non-coherent* optical set-up for cross correlating two functions $f_1(x, y)$ and $f_2(x, y)$.

If the $f_2(x, y)$ transparency is displaced by x_d, y_d relative to the position of the $f_1(x, y)$ transparency, the Figure 9.11 photomultiplier measures

$$\iint f_1(x, y) f_2(x + x_d, y + y_d)\, dx\, dy \tag{9.28}$$

To determine the cross correlation function, that is, the dependence of the cross correlation coefficient (9.28) on x_d, y_d, the two transparencies must be aligned in all possible relative positions in turn, which is generally impractical. To avoid mechanical shifting and to obtain the cross correlation function instantaneously, it is possible to use an extended source instead of a point source, as explained in Section 5.3 of Rosenfeld's book[378]. Rosenfeld remarks that the amplitude of light emanating from an extended source generally depends upon direction, and the central region of the transparency is unduly weighted. Holography provides an alternative method of obtaining a complete cross correlation function instantaneously. If the point $x = \gamma$, $y = 0$ is taken as the origin, the amplitude at (x_d, y_d) in the output plane of Figure 9.10 depends on the value of (9.28) for the displacement x_d, y_d. In the output plane of Figure 9.10, the values of (9.28) for all displacements are displayed simultaneously, in the form of an amplitude distribution.

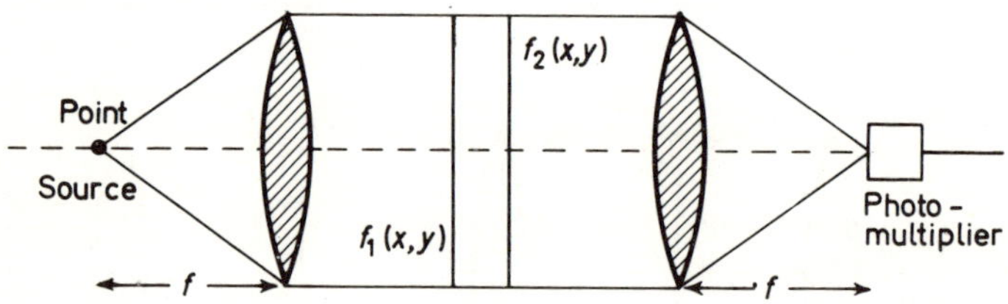

Figure 9.11. *A set-up for cross correlation using mechanical displacement of transparencies*

An advantage of holographic cross correlation is that we can ignore or attenuate arbitrarily chosen bands of spatial frequencies without incurring disadvantages (1) and (2) of Section 9.4.2. For character recognition, more sharply peaked cross correlation functions can be obtained by attenuating lower spatial frequencies, so that the higher frequencies, which are associated with details of patterns, become more important[40]. In the less exposed Fraunhofer patterns in Figure 9.8 it can be seen that the lower spatial frequencies (regions nearest the optic axis) tend to be associated with higher intensities. By suitably overexposing the film, Binns *et al.*[40] saturated the higher intensity regions without saturating the lower intensity regions. This increased the relative importance of the lower intensity, and thus the higher frequency, regions of the hologram.

In character recognition, if $f_2(x, y)$ is the character 'F' and $f_1(x, y)$ is 'E', the maximal value of (9.28) may be the same as when $f_2(x, y)$ is 'F' and $f_1(x, y)$ is also 'F', (cf. Section 1.1). We can mitigate this difficulty by normalising as in Section 3.5, so that the value of the normalised cross correlation coefficient

$$\frac{\iint f_1(x, y) f_2(x + x_d, y + y_d)\, dx\, dy}{\left(\iint f_1^2(x, y)\, dx\, dy\right)^{1/2} \left(\iint f_2^2(x, y)\, dx\, dy\right)^{1/2}} \qquad (9.29)$$

is equal to unity when $x_d = y_d = 0$ and $f_1(x, y) = f_2(x, y)$.

Several holographic character recognition schemes have been proposed, e.g. Refs 120, 130, 221, and 449. In one of these schemes, the reference patterns are arranged in a two-dimensional array such as

1 2 3
4 5 6
7 8 9

and a single hologram of this whole array is obtained. Using this hologram in the Figure 9.10 set-up, with a single unknown character as the $f_2(x)$ transparency, the cross correlation functions of the input character with the nine reference numerals are obtained in parallel in the output plane. The output plane contains nine fairly bright regions, one per numeral, and the input character is assigned to the class associated with the region which contains the brightest point after normalisation. If the $f_2(x, y)$ transparency of the input character is moved in its own plane, the entire cross correlation pattern in the output plane move proportionately. This method does *not* share the position invariance of the Section 9.4.2 method. The tolerance for movement of the reference hologram has been investigated by Vander Lugt[448].

Instead of holographically cross correlating a single input character with an array of reference characters, we can holographically cross correlate an array of input characters with a single reference character. It is possible to do this with whole words instead of reference characters. For instance, a reference hologram might be obtained from a transparency of the single word 'diffraction'. If the $f_2(x, y)$ transparency in Figure 9.10 was a transparency of a whole page of text, a bright spot would appear in the output plane in any position corresponding to a position of the word 'diffraction' in the text. A less bright spot would mark the occurrence of the word 'fraction' in the text. A still less bright spot would mark 'action', and so on. This technique is probably of greater interest for picking out targets in aerial photographs than for character recognition.

North American Rockwell[365] have disclosed a target identification system in which, in the simplest embodiment, a diffraction pattern $g_1(u)$ of a transparency of an aerial photograph $f_1(x)$ is obtained in the Fourier plane of a lens as in Figure 9.7. The v axis is perpendicular both to the u axis and the optic axis. A photograph of a target is used as the input transparency in a second Figure 9.7 set-up, arranged so that its Fourier plane differs from the $g_1(u)$ Fourier plane only by a slight rotation about the v axis, and the two optic axes meet in the Fourier plane. The resulting interference pattern in the Fourier plane is photographed. This photograph is a hologram which records

$$|g_1(u) + g_3(u)\,e^{i\phi u}|^2 = |g_1(u)|^2 + |g_3(u)|^2 + g_1^*(u)g_3(u)\,e^{i\phi u} + g_1(u)g_3^*(u)e^{-i\phi u} \quad (9.30)$$

where $g_3(u)$ is the Fourier transform of the target, and the factor $e^{i\phi u}$ arises from rotation about the v axis. When this hologram is used in place of the mask in the Figure 9.7 set-up, the Fourier plane of L2 contains the $f_1(x), f_3(x)$ cross correlation function, which has bright spots corresponding to positions of the target in the photograph $f_1(x)$. This technique has been developed so as to allow a target in the photograph to differ in size and orientation from the reference target. A more interesting development is to detect the position of the target in the aerial photograph by measuring the fringe spacings in the u and v directions in the plane where the $g_1(u)$ and $g_3(u)$ diffraction patterns interfere. The interference pattern is not actually photographed[365].

Gabor[164] proposed a character recognition system in which an interference pattern (9.30) was photographed. In this, $g_1(u)$ was the Fourier transform of a single reference character, $f_1(x)$, and $g_3(u)$ was the Fourier transform of an array, $f_3(x)$, of point sources. The hologram (9.30) was used in a set-up which was somewhat similar to the Figure 9.10 set-up, with a single unknown character $f_2(x)$ as the input transparency. The Figure 9.10 output plane contained the Fourier transform of $g_2(u)\,|g_1(u)+g_3(u)e^{i\phi u}|^2$, and, from (9.30), one of the terms in this was the Fourier transform of

$$g_2(u)g_1^*(u)g_3(u)e^{i\phi u} \tag{9.31}$$

If $f_2(x)=f_1(x)$ and if $g_1(u)g_1^*(u)$ were constant, that is, independent of u, then the Fourier transform of (9.31) would be $f_3(x)$ somewhat shifted. In this case the pattern $f_3(x)$ of bright spots would appear in the Figure 9.10 output plane, and detection of this pattern (e.g. by an array of photocells) would signify that $f_1(x)=f_2(x)$, in which case $f_2(x)$ could be assigned to the same recognition class as $f_1(x)$.

Unfortunately $|g_1(u)|^2$ is generally not independent of u, and this means that the output plane generally does not contain $f_3(x)$ when $f_1(x)=f_2(x)$. To mitigate this difficulty a filter with transmission coefficient $1/|g_1(u)|^2$ can be combined with the hologram so that the Fourier transform of $g_2(u)g_1^*(u)g_3(u)\,e^{i\phi u}\,|g_1(u)|^{-2}$ appears instead of the Fourier transform of (9.31) in the Figure 9.10 output plane[426]. In practice, however, two patterns $f_1(x)$ and $f_2(x)$ are seldom precisely identical, and the photographic and optical systems depart from their ideals. The result is that this does not appear to be a useful technique for character recognition[120].

Linear techniques such as those introduced in Chapter 3 generally give lower error rates than are obtained by simple non-weighted mask matching as in Chapter 1. The holographic techniques which we have so far discussed are essentially non-weighted mask matching techniques, but this is *not* a basic limitation of holography. For instance, holograms can be generated by a digital computer[21, 286], and thus it is possible to compute a weight vector $\boldsymbol{W}$ by Chapter 3 techniques and obtain a computer generated hologram of the function $f_1(x, y)=\boldsymbol{W}$. This hologram could be used to produce in the Figure 9.10 output plane the integral counterpart of the discrete dot product $\boldsymbol{W}\,.\,\boldsymbol{X}$, where $\boldsymbol{X}=f_2(x, y)$. Apart from the possibility of frequency filtering, holographic implementation would have the advantages of avoiding the noise which, in, for instance, flying-spot scanner or retina systems, arises from optical/electrical transduction and spatial sampling on a finite grid. In practice, computer generated holograms do not appear to have been used in character recognition; and perhaps one reason for this is the overriding disadvantage that light reflected from paper is unsatisfactory for holographic purposes.

9.5 AUTOCORRELATION

9.5.1 Two-term autocorrelation

The two-term autocorrelation function $A(x_d, y_d)$ of a function $f(x, y)$ is defined by[270]

$$A(x_d, y_d) = \int_{-\infty}^{\infty}\int_{-\infty}^{\infty} f(x, y)\, f(x + x_d, y + y_d)\, \mathrm{d}x\, \mathrm{d}y \tag{9.32}$$

Comparing this with (9.19) we see that the autocorrelation function of $f(x, y)$ is the cross correlation function of $f(x, y)$ with itself. To introduce some of the properties of the autocorrelation function, let us suppose that two identical transparencies of $f(x, y)$ are arranged for cross correlation with each other as in Figure 9.11. For any given displacement x_d, y_d, the photomultiplier provides a measure of $A(x_d, y_d)$. By fixing the position of one transparency and moving the other successively into all displacements, we could obtain a plot of $A(x_d, y_d)$ *versus* x_d, y_d, and this would be a plot of the autocorrelation function of $f(x, y)$. The photomultiplier output depends only on the *relative* displacement of the two transparencies and therefore the plot of $A(x_d, y_d)$ *versus* x_d, y_d would remain unchanged if the fixed transparency were originally placed in a different position. In other words, the autocorrelation function of $f(x, y)$ is invariant to displacements of $f(x, y)$ in the x, y plane.

If the second transparency is moved by an amount x_d, y_d relative to the first transparency, the relative position of the two transparencies is the same as it would be if the second transparency had not been moved and the first transparency had been moved $-x_d, -y_d$ relative to the second transparency. Therefore the photomultiplier output is the same in both cases and

$$\iint f(x, y)\, f(x + x_d, y + y_d)\, \mathrm{d}x\, \mathrm{d}y = \iint f(x - x_d, y - y_d)\, f(x, y)\, \mathrm{d}x\, \mathrm{d}y$$

or, in other words,

$$A(x_d, y_d) = A(-x_d, -y_d)$$

This means that the autocorrelation function of $f(x, y)$ is 180° symmetrical and thus remains unchanged when $f(x, y)$ is rotated about the optic axis through 180°.

For any given $x_d, y_d, A(x_d, y_d)$ is given by (9.32). In the course of integration, noisy black and white marks are to some extent cancelled out, and because of this we can expect the autocorrelation function of, for instance, a character, to be rather less noisy than $f(x, y)$. Horwitz and Shelton considered the possibility of recognising an unknown character by first obtaining its autocorrelation function and then cross correlating this autocorrelation function with one reference autocorrelation function per recognition class[224]. The merit of this would arise from the position invariance and the denoising effect of autocorrelation.

It is of course impractical to obtain an autocorrelation function by using two transparencies as in Figure 9.11, and other methods are available. From Section 9.3.3, the two-dimensional version of the cross correlation theorem tells us that the cross correlation function $C_{12}(x_d, y_d)$ is the Fourier transform of

$$D_{12}(u, v) = 2\pi g_1^*(u, v) g_2(u, v)$$

Hence, when $f_1(x, y) = f_2(x, y) = f(x, y)$, the autocorrelation function of $f(x, y)$ is the Fourier transform of

$$2\pi g^*(u, v) g(u, v) = 2\pi \, |g(u, v)|^2$$

Thus the autocorrelation function of $f(x, y)$ is the Fourier transform of the square of the Fourier transform of $f(x, y)$[270]. This means that the Fraunhofer diffraction pattern obtained from a photographic transparency of the Fraunhofer diffraction pattern of $f(x, y)$ is the autocorrelation function of $f(x, y)$. But this is an unnecessarily tortuous way of obtaining the autocorrelation function of a character, and simpler optical techniques are available which use incoherent polychromatic light. In these techniques, light from an extended source passes through a transparency of $f(x, y)$ and is reflected back through this transparency by one[263] or more[220] mirrors.

Horwitz and Shelton have described an electronic technique for obtaining autocorrelation functions without requiring transparencies[224], and this technique is most easily introduced in the case where characters are binary. A character is vertically raster scanned, binarised, and fed bit by bit into a two-dimensional shift register, as in Section 2.3.2. Let us say that the binary character is m elements high and m elements wide. In this case the raster and shift register are made at least $2m - 1$

elements high by m elements wide. Let us say that the input is at the bottom left-hand corner of the shift register. Before any character is fed in, the shift register is set to contain only 0's.

Each element in each of the bottom m rows of the shift register provides an input to a separate *and* gate. The other input to each of the $m \times m$ *and* gates is derived from the bottom left-hand corner element of the shift register (the input element). A separate counter circuit is assigned to each *and* gate, and a counter is incremented by unity every time the corresponding *and* unit gives output '1' after a step of the character through the shift register. After the last '1' bit in the character has been fed into the shift register, the input element, and therefore all *and* gates, are not again activated by this character. The values in the counters then constitute a discrete form of the autocorrelation function of the input character.

To understand how this works, let us consider the *and* gate which is connected to the shift register element which is situated in the dth column from left and the eth row from bottom of the shift register. The output of this *and* gate is

$$f(x_j, y_k) \cdot f(x_{j+\mathrm{d}}, y_{k+\mathrm{e}})$$

and after the last '1' bit in the character has passed into the shift register, the counter associated with this *and* gate contains

$$\sum_{j=1}^{m} \sum_{k=1}^{m} f(x_j, y_k) \cdot f(x_{j+d}, y_{k+e}) \qquad .$$

which is the value of the discrete autocorrelation function for the particular displacement d, e. The raster is made at least $2m - 1$ elements high in order to prevent the top of the $m \times m$ character appearing in the bottom of the bottom $m \times m$ window in the shift register before the bottom of the character has disappeared out of the top of this window (cf. Section 2.3.2).

To combat the ambiguity of '6' and '9', Horwitz and Shelton suggested making use of the numbers contained in the counters before the input character has passed completely into the shift register[224]. Another way of dealing with 180° ambiguity is by multiple auto-correlation.

9.5.2 Multiple autocorrelation

The nth order multiple autocorrelation function of $f(x, y)$ is defined by[307]

$$N(x_2, y_2, x_3, y_3, \ldots, x_n, y_n) = \int_{-\infty}^{\infty}\int_{-\infty}^{\infty} f(x, y)\, f(x + x_2, y + y_2)\, f(x + x_3, y + y_3) \ldots f(x + x_n, y + y_n)\, \mathrm{d}x\, \mathrm{d}y \qquad (9.33)$$

This can be visualised in terms of n transparencies of $f(x, y)$ in the Figure 9.11 set-up, these being arranged successively in all possible relative alignments. Alternatively, we can note that

$$f(x, y)\, f(x + x_2, y + y_2) \ldots f(x + x_n, y + y_n) \qquad (9.34)$$

is the product of the values of the function $f(x, y)$ at n points. In other words, (9.34) is the product of the elements of an n-tuple, and (9.33) is the sum of this product over all alignments of this n-tuple with $f(x, y)$. To implement the discrete binary nth order autocorrelation function, we can replace the 2-input *and* gates by an appropriate set of n-input *and* gates in Horwitz and Shelton's shift register technique.

If the n-tuple associated with displacements $(x_2, y_2, \ldots, x_n, y_n)$ is itself 180° symmetrical, as it necessarily is in the $n = 2$ case, then the value of (9.33) for these particular displacements is unchanged if $f(x, y)$ is rotated through 180°. But this is not the case if the n-tuple is not 180° symmetrical, and therefore the complete nth order autocorrelation function, which involves all possible n-tuples, is not invariant to 180° rotation of $f(x, y)$.

For pattern recognition purposes it may be unnecessary to evaluate (9.33) for all possible values of $(x_2, y_2, \ldots, x_n, y_n)$, (cf. Alt's use[12] of 22 higher moments rather than all possible higher moments). Clowes and Parks[91] and Clayden *et al.*[90] intuitively chose a set of M n-tuples and evaluated a discrete version of (9.33) for each of these. An input pattern was thus transformed into an M-component vector, which was recognised by the cross correlation method of Section 3.5. Instead of Horwitz and Shelton's shift register, Parks[342] used a delay line, to cope with non-binary patterns; and instead of *and* units he used multiplier units, one for each of the M chosen n-tuples. Experimentally it was found best to invert the value of $f(x, y)$ at some of the elements of some of the n-tuples. The resulting recognition system was the system outlined in Section 5.6.2.

9.6 SPEECH RECOGNITION

9.6.1 Introduction

The remainder of this chapter is devoted to a cursory introduction to the research literature on speech recognition[232, 280]. We shall be more concerned with logical structure than with acoustic detail.

The vocal chords produce sound in the throat in roughly the same way that the lips produce sound in a trumpet. Air pressure blows the lips apart, and tension in the lips closes them together again. This cycle is repeated so long as there is sufficient air pressure and sufficient tension in the lips. The result is an almost periodic variation in air pressure and volume, which produces an audible sound. The spectrum of sound produced by the vocal chords is rich in harmonics, and these excite resonances in cavities situated between the vocal chords and the lips and nostrils. The principal cavities are the mouth, the nasal cavity which is between the nostrils and the throat, and the pharyngeal cavity which is between the vocal chords and the back of the mouth[143]. When the vocal chords vibrate, the sound which we actually hear has a spectrum with energy maxima at the resonant frequencies of the vocal tract. These maxima are known as *formants*, and the three or four formants of lowest frequency are the most important in speech recognition. The frequencies of the formants depend on the positions of, for instance, the lips, tongue, and jaw. Thus the frequencies of the formants vary during speech, and to some extent the vowel sounds which we actually hear are determined by their formant frequencies. For a male speaker, the *pitch* frequency, that is, the fundamental frequency of vibration of the vocal chords, is usually in the range 90–140 Hz, and the first three formants are typically at 500 Hz, 1500 Hz, and 2500 Hz respectively.

The vocal chords are not the only source of speech sounds. For instance, the hissing sound at the beginning of the spoken word 'snap' is produced by forcing air through clenched teeth; and the final consonant of 'snap' is associated with an explosive release of air pressure by the lips.

A *spectrograph* is a device which provides in visible form the energy spectrum of successive short time-segments of speech[143]. The output of a spectrograph is known as a *spectrogram,* and consists of a succession of vertical strips. Each strip is a representation of the energy spectrum of a short time-segment of speech. Frequency increases from the bottom to the top of a strip, and the energy at any given frequency is represented by the blackness of the strip at that frequency. From left to right, successive strips relate to successive time-segments. Figure 9.12 shows a spectrogram of the utterance 'A bird in the hand is worth two in the bush'. The roughly horizontal black bands which are most conspicuous during vowel sounds indicate formants. Figures 9.13 and 9.14 show samples from the amplitude/time waveform of the utterance 'A bird in the hand is worth two in the bush'. The top plot in Figure 9.13 is the speech waveform of the complete word 'bird', and the lower plot is the speech waveform of the word 'bush', the time axis being horizontal. Each of the plots in Figure 9.13 covers 300 ms. The five amplitude/time plots in Figure 9.14 are 40 ms samples from the speech waveforms of /ir/ in 'bird', /n/ in 'in', /i/ in 'is', /bu/ in 'bush', and /sh/ in 'bush': the top sample is from /ir/ and the bottom sample is from /sh/.

Rough short-time spectra can be obtained from a set (known as a *bank*) of tuned filters, whose outputs are rectified, integrated, and sampled periodically, e.g. every 10 ms. The output of an integrator is a measure, over a short time, of the amplitude or energy in the frequency band of the corresponding filter. This apparatus for obtaining a succession of short-time spectra is known as a *spectrum analyser*. The instantaneous output of a spectrum analyser is essentially a one-dimensional pattern, comprising one element per integrator. We shall call this one-dimensional pattern a *spectral section,* and we shall assume that adjacent elements in this pattern correspond to adjacent frequency bands.

The amplitude of the harmonics of sound produced by the vocal chords decreases as the frequency increases. It is often expedient to compensate for this by interposing between the microphone and the spectrum analyser a *pre-emphasis* circuit which amplifies sound by a factor which increases, e.g. by 6 or 9 dB per octave, as the frequency increases.

9.6.2 Spoken word recognition by time–frequency pattern recognition

By storing successive spectral sections we obtain a two-dimensional pattern which is analogous to a spectrogram. A system described by Denes and Mathews[116] (cf. Ref. 133a) recognised this (analogue) pattern

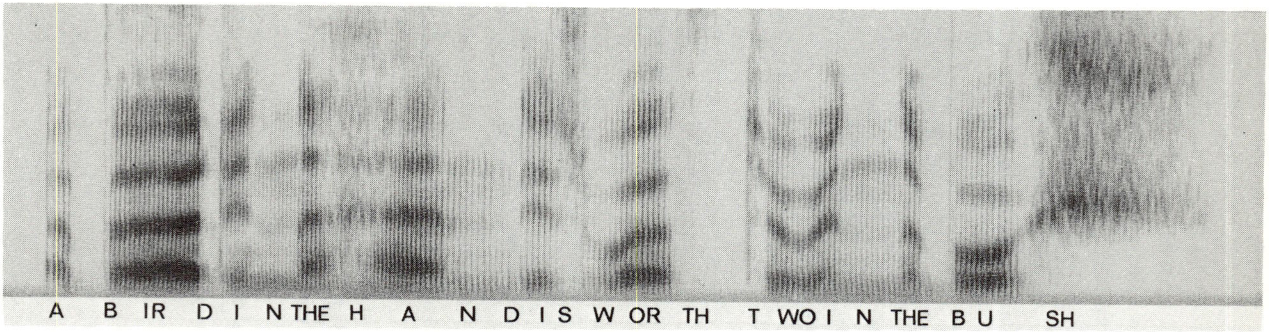

Figure 9.12. *Spectrogram of 'A bird in the hand is worth two in the bush'.* (*By courtesy of J.S.R.U. Crown Copyright*)

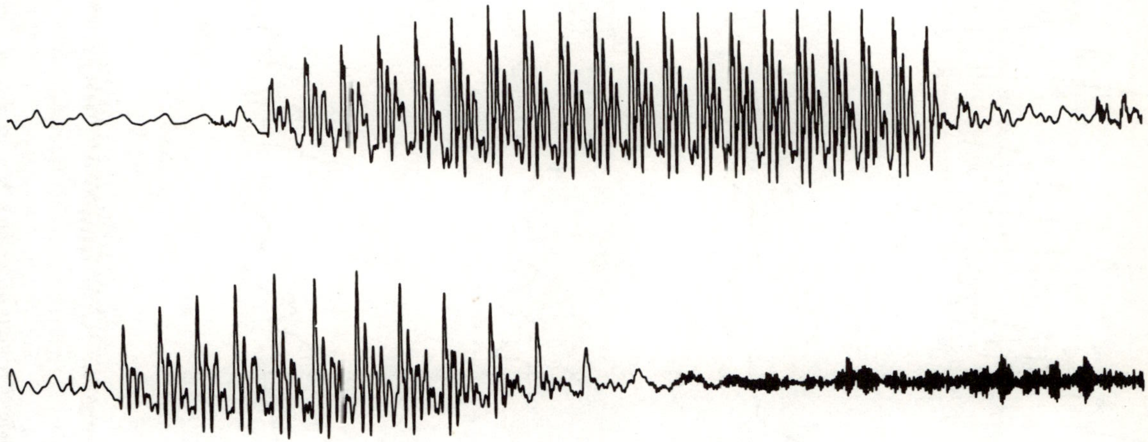

Figure 9.13. *Amplitude/time plots of 'bird'* (*upper plot*) and *'bush'* (*lower plot*). (*By courtesy of J.S.R.U. Crown Copyright*)

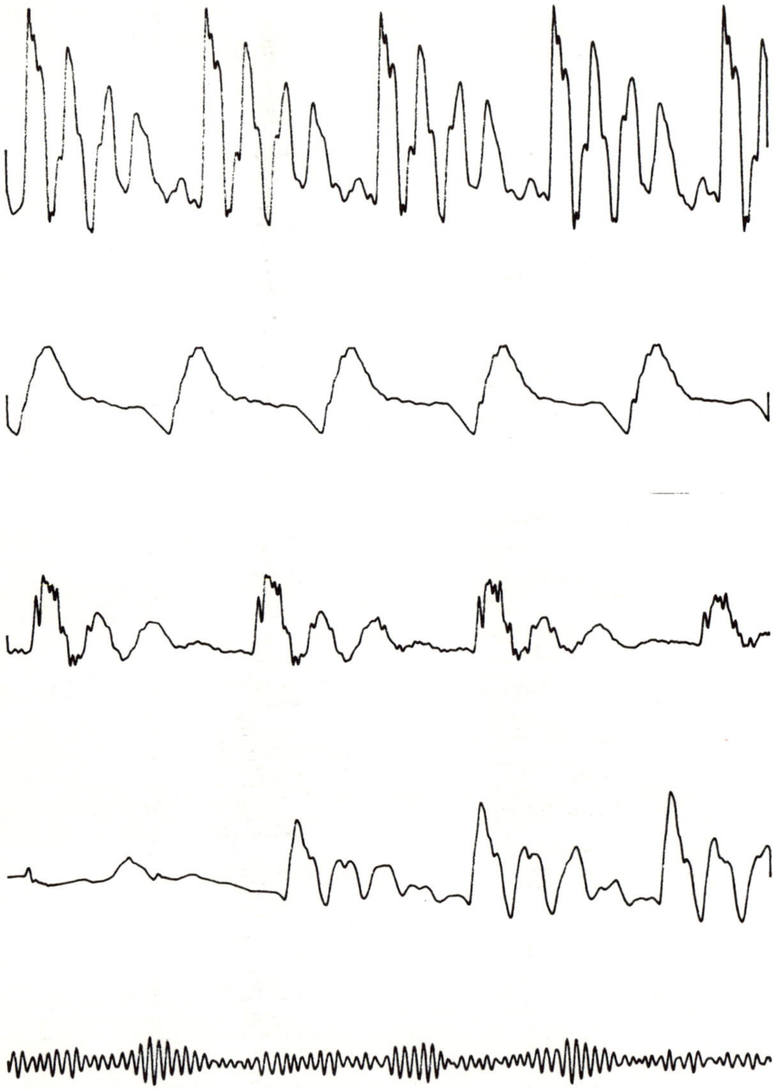

Figure 9.14. *Amplitude/time plots of samples from/ir/, /n/, /i/, /bu/, and /sh/.* (*By courtesy of J.S.R.U. Crown Copyright*)

obtained from a spoken digit by means of cross correlation as in Section 3.5. Denes and Mathews obtained better results by normalising so that the number (60) of spectral sections per spoken word was the same for all spoken words. Time normalisation by uniform alteration of the time scale does not take account of the fact that when a speaker increases his speed of speaking he tends to reduce the duration of vowels more than he reduces the duration of consonants[467].

Olson and Belar binarised the spectral sections obtained from an eight-filter spectrum analyser, and thereby obtained a sequence of 8-bit patterns[340]. Their system did not store all of these 8-bit patterns, but only stored a given 8-bit pattern if it differed from its immediate predecessor. A maximum of five 8-bit patterns was stored, and the resulting 40-bit pattern was recognised by simple Boolean discriminants. Olson and Belar tried binarising spectral sections in various different ways:

(1) By assigning '1' to any element greater than both its neighbours and assigning '0' to all other elements.
(2) By assigning '1' to any element greater than a prescribed one of its neighbours, and assigning '0' to all other elements. Here 1's corresponded to an amplitude/frequency slope which had a prescribed sign.
(3) By assigning '1' to any element exceeding a prescribed threshold and assigning '0' to all other elements.

Ross[381] used a four-filter spectrum analyser and converted the four output signals to a logarithmic scale. From each logarithmic spectral section a 5-bit pattern was obtained. In this the first four bits corresponded to the four filters: one of these bits was '1' only if the corresponding log output exceeded a weighted sum of the other three log outputs by at least a prescribed margin. The fifth bit was '1' or '0' according as the highest frequency log output exceeded a weighted sum of the lowest two by at least a prescribed margin. Thus a sequence of 5-bit patterns was obtained from a spoken word. A 5-bit pattern was stored only if it differed from its immediate predecessor, and only four 5-bit patterns were stored altogether. The 20-bit pattern obtained in this way from a spoken word was recognised by a nearest-neighbour method, as in Section 4.3. Like Olson and Belar, Ross used only a *sequence* of different spectral sections, and did not use the exact times of occurrence of these spectral sections, so that there was no need for time normalisation. Time information has been used in an elaboration of Ross' technique[314].

Following the binarisation method (1) of Olson and Belar, King and Tunis[253] and Ide *et al.*[233] binarised spectral sections obtained from a 16-filter spectrum analyser. Thus a spoken word was converted into a sequence of 16-bit patterns containing 1's at formant frequencies. This entire sequence was stored as a two-dimensional pattern and recognised by a linear discriminant system with weights determined by an error correcting procedure.

By means of resonating optic fibres, a speech sound can be converted into a two-dimensional visual pattern. Tscheschner[438] has proposed to recognise such patterns by optical mask matching, and Cutler *et al.*[108] have proposed to recognise such patterns by holographic cross correlation.

9.6.3 Independent classification of spectral sections

In the systems which we have so far mentioned, a spoken utterance was converted into a two-dimensional pattern which was recognised as a whole. We now outline some systems in which spectral sections are independently classified. In the terminology of Section 7.5.1, classes of spectral sections are *f*-classes.

Dudley and Balashek[129] asked speakers to sustain the vowel sounds in 'seat', 'sit', 'set', 'ah', 'coat', and 'cool', and the four consonants in 'sun' and 'ruff'. For various repetitions, i.e. specimens, of each of these 10 sounds, Dudley and Balashek stored spectral sections obtained from a 10-filter spectrum analyser. For each of the 10 different sounds all of the stored specimen spectral sections were averaged, and hence for each of the 10 sounds a separate 10-element average pattern was obtained. While a word to be recognised was being spoken, each successive spectral section was recognised as one of the 10 sounds by cross correlation with the 10 10-element average patterns as in Section 3.5. The system counted the number of sections recognised as each of the 10 sounds while the input word was being spoken. This gave 10 counts, which constituted a further 10-element pattern. This 10-element pattern, and thus the spoken word, was recognised by the method of Section 3.5. Note that information as to the *sequence* of spectral sections was not used in recognition.

By means of a minimum distance rule (cf. Section 3.4) Shearme and Leach[399] assigned each spectral section to one of 20 *f*-classes, so that a spoken word was transformed into a string of symbols, each symbol indicating membership of a segment in a particular one of the 20 *f*-classes. This string was recognised by a nearest-neighbour method.

In a system for recognising spoken Italian digits, Gilli and Meo binarised the outputs of a 17-filter spectrum analyser[171]. At any given time the 17-bit pattern from the spectrum analyser was assigned to one of 21 *f*-classes (or rejected) by means of Boolean discriminants. For example, the 17-bit patterns in one of the 21 *f*-classes were characteristic of the /e/ sound in 'zero'; the 17-bit patterns belonging to another one of the 21 *f*-classes were characteristic of the second vowel in 'zero', and so on. Not all 17-bit patterns were classified: for instance, the 17-bit patterns corresponding to the consonants in 'zero' were not assigned to any of the 21 *f*-classes.

A word was recognised as 'zero' if the spectrum analyser output was classified as '/e/ in zero' for at least 5 time units during the first 12 time units after the start of the word, and if the spectrum analyser output was classified as '/o/ in zero' for at least 3 time units some time after the 12th time unit after the start of the word. This recognition condition was implemented by a sequential circuit of the Figure 7.25 sort, and the recognition conditions for the other digits were also implemented in this manner.

As a further example, a digit was recognised as 'tre' if

(1) the spectrum analyser output was classified as '/t/in tre' for at least 2 time units, and then
(2) the spectrum analyser output was classified as '/r/ in tre' for at least 3 time units, and then
(3) some time before the 20th time unit after the start of the word the spectrum analyser output was classified as '/e/ in tre' for at least 3 time units.

Note that in recognising 'tre' the system required both the consonants and also the vowel, whereas in recognising 'zero' the system did not require the consonants, and instead merely required that the vowel sounds were *included in* the spoken word during prescribed time intervals. A further spoken digit recognition system using asynchronous sequential circuits of the Figure 7.25 sort has been described by Martin *et al*[296].

In the remainder of this section we shall outline a few further systems which used independent classification of spectral sections in the recognition of speech sounds (e.g. vowels) which were *not* whole words.

Forgie and Forgie[146] used a 35-filter spectrum analyser in a spoken vowel recognition system. The first formant was expected to lie in the range 215–890 Hz, and this range was split up into four bands, 215–315 Hz, 315–465 Hz, etc. The range of the second formant was also divided into four bands. It is roughly true to say that for each spectral section the system found which of the four first-formant bands and which of the four second-formant bands contained the largest total amplitude.

If, for instance, the largest total amplitude in the range of the first formant was in the band 315–465 Hz, and if the largest total amplitude in the range of the second formant was in the band 1230–1700 Hz, then the vowel sound was the vowel in 'bit' or the vowel in 'boot' or the vowel in 'Bert'. To decide between these alternatives, a decision tree was used: if the ratio of the total amplitude in the range 2150–3350 Hz to that in the range 1230–1700 Hz exceeded a prescribed threshold, then the spectral section was classified as belonging to the vowel in 'bit', and otherwise a further test was performed. Specifically, if the ratio of the total amplitude in the range 3350–5250 Hz to that in the range 1230–1700 Hz exceeded a prescribed threshold, then the spectral section was classified as belonging to the vowel in 'boot', and otherwise as belonging to the vowel in 'Bert'. This example illustrates the two main stages of operation of the system. The first stage was a rough measurement of the frequencies of the first and second formants, and this yielded a short-list of vowels which could have given rise to these measurements. The second stage used a decision tree to resolve the vowel sounds in the short-list. At each node in a tree, a ratio of total amplitudes within prescribed ranges was compared with a threshold. The frequency ranges and thresholds were determined intuitively in the light of a careful study of the observed spectra of vowel sounds (in the context 'b–t').

In a vowel recognition system of Hemdal and Hughes[209], spectral sections were obtained from a (computer simulated) 35-filter spectrum analyser. Each spectral section was classified as belonging to a vowel or consonant by applying various tests: for instance, low total spectral energy below 350 Hz and relatively high energy above 4 kHz, or relatively low total energy over all frequencies, would cause a spectral section to be classified as belonging to a consonant. If a spectral section was classified as a vowel the computer approximately determined the frequencies F_1, F_2, F_3 of the first three formants by finding the frequencies of energy maxima within the frequency ranges associated with these formants. A 4-bit pattern was then obtained from the spectral section by answering the following four yes/no questions:

$F_1 < 500$ Hz? $2{\cdot}38F_1 + F_2 < 2830$ Hz?

$F_2 > 1170$ Hz? $(F_2 - F_1)/(F_3 - F_2) < 1$?

It was found that not more than two different vowels would yield the same 4-bit pattern, and that two vowels which yielded the same 4-bit pattern could be distinguished by their duration (greater or less than 133 ms). In this, *duration* was the time during which spectral sections yielded the 4-bit pattern associated with the pair of vowels. A sound was not recognised as a vowel unless its duration was at least 100 ms. Recognition depended on several further conditions, such as the condition that if one vowel sound followed another (making a diphthong) then this pair of vowels had to be one of nine specified pairs.

Energy maxima at formant frequencies are not always sharply peaked, but are sometimes broad and flat and therefore difficult to locate. On the other hand, when an energy maximum is sharply peaked it may lie between the frequencies of two adjacent filters, so that the peak is not evident in the spectrum analyser output. A spectral section contains no more than three or four important peaks, and if any one of these is not detected, the result may be disastrous in a system which depends on detection of peaks. Because most frequencies in a spectral section are located where energy increases or decreases with frequency, Nelson *et al.*[335] and Martin *et al.*[296] made extensive use of energy/frequency *slope* in the recognition of speech sounds. The *slope* of a filter is positive or negative according as the output of this filter is greater or less than the output of the adjacent filter of lower frequency. For instance, the /s/ and /f/ sounds in 'sit' and 'fit' are both characterised by absence of negative slope from the entire spectral section, and are distinguished from each other by the absence of energy from the low frequencies of the /f/ spectrum. Further, the ratio of the sum of all slopes below 2500 Hz to the sum above 2500 Hz tends to be less for /f/ than for /s/.

Klein *et al.*[256] have described various experiments with 12 different Dutch vowels, each spoken by 50 different male speakers. For instance, for each of the 12 x 50 = 600 vowel specimens, a spectral section was obtained from an 18-filter spectrum analyser. Each spectral section defined a point in 18-dimensional space, and Klein *et al.* calculated the centre of gravity of the 600 points corresponding to the 600 vowel specimens. The 12 points corresponding to each speaker were shifted in the 18-dimensional space so as to make their centre of gravity coincide with the centre of gravity of the 600 points. The original set of 600 points was thus translated into a new set. The Karhunen–Loève expansion (Section 3.10) was applied to this new set of 600 points, this set being treated as a single set. By means of the eigenvectors corresponding to the four largest eigenvalues, each of the 600 spectral sections were translated into a four-element pattern; and the four-element patterns were recognised by the normality assumption method of Section 3.4. In further experiments[355a], the Karhunen–Loève expansion reduced each spectral section to a three-element pattern. Successive three-element patterns made up a single two-dimensional pattern which was recognised as a whole, as in Section 9.6.2.

9.6.4 Zero crossings

Ewing and Taylor[138] described a programme which counted the number, Z_1, of zero crossings, that is, the number of times the amplitude/time plot of the input speech waveform passed through zero, during each short time interval in a succession of short time intervals. The programme also counted the number, Z_2, of zero crossings per time interval in a plot of the differential of the speech waveform with respect to time. A plot of $Z_2 - Z_1$ *versus* time was recognised by a minimum Euclidean distance rule (Section 3.4). An advantage of basing recognition on zero crossings is that this is cheaper than using a spectrum analyser.

During a single spoken vowel or consonant, Lavington's system[267] determined the short time (e.g. 10 ms) interval for which Z_2 was greatest. Recognition was based on three measurements over this particular interval. These were measurements of the maximum amplitude of the speech signal and the values of Z_1 and Z_2.

In 1951 Peterson[350] showed spectrographically that Z_1 and Z_2 are not, as had previously been suggested[74], true measures of the frequencies of the first two formants. To obtain better approximations to these two frequencies, Davis *et al.*[112] fed the input speech signal into two filters. One filter transmitted all frequencies below 900 Hz and the other transmitted all frequencies above 1000 Hz. The number Z_f of zero crossings per time interval in the output of the first filter was quantised into six levels (200–300, 300–400, 400–500, 500–600, 600–700, 700–800 Hz), and the number Z_s of zero crossings per time interval in the output of the second filter was quantised into five levels (500–1000, 1000–1500, 1500–2000, 2000–2500, 2500–3000 Hz). At any instant the quantised values of Z_f and Z_s specified an element in a 6 x 5 = 30 element grid. During an input word, the system recorded the total time for which each of these elements was specified by the speech signal. The resulting array of 30 time values was recognised by cross correlation as in Section 3.5.

Instead of counting zero crossings per time interval, various authors have measured the time, τ, between successive zero crossings. For instance, given a vowel sound, Bezdel and Chandler's programme[39] determined the number of τ's in the range $t_1 - t_2$, the number of τ's in the range $t_2 - t_3$, and so on, and the resulting histogram was recognised by, for example, a minimum Euclidean distance rule.

Teacher *et al.*[432] described a word recognition system which had the advantage of economical hardware implementation. This system measured the time τ_E between the zero crossing associated with the opening of the vocal chords and the zero crossing immediately following this (in the pre-emphasised speech waveform). The system also measured the highest peak amplitude, A, between these two zero crossings. During sounds such as /s/ where the vocal chords were not vibrating, that is, when there was no *voicing*, the system measured the time τ_E between a zero crossing where the gradient of the speech waveform was steep and the next zero crossing. Again the highest peak amplitude, A, between these two zero crossings was measured. The value of $1/2\tau_E$ was quantised into 18 levels, A was quantised into eight levels, and a third parameter, V, which at any time was a measure of the extent to which the speech sound was voiced, was quantised into four levels.

Words were recognised by data dominated sequential circuits, with one circuit per word. For recognition of a word, the corresponding circuit required that

(1) $1/2\tau_E$, A, and V were within prescribed ranges of values for at least T_1 ms, and then
(2) $1/2\tau_E$, A, and V were within prescribed ranges of values for at least T_2 ms, and then
(3) up to four further stages like (2) but of course with different ranges and minimum time requirements.

9.6.5 Autocorrelation of speech

A speech waveform is usually highly repetitive, and it would be impractical to recognise a speech waveform simply by, for instance, cross correlation with standard waveforms. Spectral analysis and zero crossings analysis avoid some of the redundancy of speech by transforming a speech waveform into a less repetitive pattern. Autocorrelation is the basis of some further methods of avoiding some of the redundancy of speech waveforms.

Purton[358] fed an input speech waveform into a high-pass filter and also into a low-pass filter (adjusted so that both filters transmitted 1000 Hz with equal attenuation). The output of each filter was binarised and fed into a separate shift register. The stepping frequency of the shift register associated with the low-frequency filter was 2 kHz, and the stepping frequency of the shift register associated with the high-frequency shift register was 8 kHz. The total number of stages in the two shift registers was 18. At each step of each shift register, the output of each shift register stage was multiplied by the three-level-quantised amplitude of the corresponding filter output, and the result was integrated. The 18 integrators were sampled every 25 ms, yielding an 18-element pattern each time. Successive 18-element patterns made up a single two-dimensional pattern which was recognised linearly.

Cannon[68] fed speech sounds into an 'artificial ear'. This was a device in which speech sounds travelled a distance dependent on their frequency before being attenuated to zero amplitude. For instance, 10 kHz signals were damped out near the beginning of the device, and 100 Hz signals would reach the end. This device was tapped at four points along its length. During a vowel sound, the signals from the four tapping points were autocorrelated for the first 4 ms after the opening of the vocal chords. The vowel was recognised by cross correlation of the four autocorrelation functions with average reference autocorrelation functions.

9.6.6 Segmentation in speech recognition

Before discussing segmentation is speech recognition, let us briefly return to character recognition. In Section 6.6.3 we saw that normalisation techniques in character recognition are of two types: normalisation by *measurement* and normalisation by *exhaustive trial*. Segmentation techniques can be classified similarly. When a word is segmented into characters by the detection of white columns between successive characters, segmentation *precedes* recognition, just as normalisation by measurement precedes recognition. When, as in Section 2.3.2, a character in context is shifted through all positions and is recognised when it matches a mask in one position, segmentation is *contemporaneous* with recognition, as in normalisation by exhaustive trial. This cannot be used in all character recognition systems. For instance, the Toshiba hand-print system (Section 7.4.3) and the IBM 1975 system (Section 6.2.3) require segmentation *prior* to recognition: if parts of two characters were included in the same 3 x 36 strip in the Toshiba system, the result would be disastrous.

In the systems outlined in Section 9.6.3, spectral sections were assigned to *f*-classes, so that a speech signal was transformed into a string of *f*-class names. A set of successive sections with the same *f*-class name could be regarded as a single segment of the spoken utterance, but such segments were not treated as entities in the recognition process. In the spoken digit recognition systems of von Keller[450b] and Sholtz and Bakis[406], on the other hand, segmentation of this sort was used to split up an utterance into vowels and consonants, and these segments were treated as entities in the recognition process.

Sholtz and Bakis[406] worked with a (computer simulated) bank of 40 filters which produced a spectral section for every 10 ms of speech. A spectral section was classified as *silence* if its total power was below a threshold. A section which was not *silence* was classified as vowel or consonant according as the ratio of the total power in the band 0–800 kHz to the total power in the band 7–8 kHz did or did not exceed a threshold (actually 44·5). Consonants were classified into three classes, {/s/, /z/}, {/f/, /v/, /θ/}, {stop}, by means of decision trees which asked questions about the ratio of the total power within various bands, the ratio of the total power within successive spectral sections, and the position of the section in the spoken word (e.g. beginning of word?, preceded by vowel?, etc.).

For each section classified as belonging to a vowel, eight power ratios were measured, e.g. ratio of power in band 600–1400 Hz to power in band 1500–6000 Hz, ratio of power in band 0–200 Hz to total power, ratio of power in band 200–400 Hz to total power, etc. Each of these eight ratios was generally found to vary with time during the duration of a vowel segment, i.e. during a succession of vowel sections. The plot of the first ratio *versus* time, t, was approximated by a quadratic expression $at^2 + bt + c$, where a, b, c were chosen to give optimal least squares fit. A further six of the power ratios were also approximated in this way, and the last power ratio was approximated by $et + f$, so that 23 parameters $a, b, c, \ldots$ were used in approximating the power ratio *versus* time plots. The duration of the vowel segment was used as a 24th parameter. The 24-component vector obtained from a vowel segment was assigned by a linear discriminant system to one of 11 classes: one class for each of 10 vowels, and a reject class. Note that the values of the 24 parameters could not be computed until *after* the spoken digit had been segmented into vowels and consonants. The 24 values characterised a vowel segment as a single entity, rather than as a sequence of independent spectral sections.

In the Section 9.6.3 systems, a given spectral section was assigned to one and only one out of a plurality of f-classes. Bobrow and Klatt[49] have devised a recognition system in which 15 tests are applied to each spectral section and the result of each test may be +1, 0, or, for some tests, −1. The outcome of a given test applied to a given spectral section is a Boolean function of thresholded outputs, or of thresholded functions of outputs, of the filters in the given spectral section and the immediately preceding section. For instance, for the ith spectral section, the result of a test which is called 'voice' is '1' if the log of the output of the second-from-lowest filter exceeds 34 units (or* the log of the output of the second-from-lowest filter exceeds 29 units and the result of test 'voice' for the $(i-1)$th section is '1') and otherwise the result of test 'voice' is '0'. The test 'voice' is intended to give result '1' for spectral sections produced when the vocal chords are vibrating, that is, when the speech sound is *voiced*, and '0' for all other spectral sections. Another one of the tests is designed to give the result '1' for a spectral section which sounds /a/-like, '−1' for a section which is not voiced, and '0' for a section which is voiced but not /a/-like. Similarly, the system tests whether a spectral section is /i/-like, /u/-like, fricative-like, and so on, these tests being based mainly on the comparison of power ratios with thresholds.

For a given utterance, the test 'voice' might for instance produce a sequence of results

0 0 0 1 1 1 1 0 1 1 1 1 1 1 1 0 0 0 0 0 0

where each bit corresponds to one spectral section. Bobrow and Klatt's

*The use of two thresholds, 34 and 29, provides a 'hysteresis' margin which is designed to prevent the result of test 'voice' from fluctuating insignificantly between '1' and '0' over successive sections. This hysteresis idea is used in other tests besides the test 'voice'.

programme removes successive repetitions from this sequence, to yield 0 1 0 1 0. The test '/a/-like' might produce

$$-1\ -1\ -1\ 0\ 0\ 0\ 0\ -1\ 0\ 0\ 0\ 1\ 1\ 1\ 1\ -1\ -1\ -1\ -1\ -1\ -1$$

and successive repetitions would be removed to yield −1 0 −1 0 1 −1. Similarly, all other tests produce strings of 1's, 0's, and −1's, and successive repetitions are removed. The *set* of strings produced by the 15 tests is recognised by the independence assumption method of Section 3.3, applied as in Doyle's character recognition system (Section 7.6). For instance, for each recognition class the system stores separately the conditional probability of the outcome 01010 of the test 'voice', the outcome 0101010 of the test 'voice', and so on, for all outcomes of all tests.

The removal of successive repetitions gives invariance to changes in the rapidity of speech. Before repetitions are removed, the result of any test can be regarded as segmenting the spoken utterance. For example, the test '/a/-like' segments a spoken utterance into segments which are not voiced, segments which are /a/-like, and segments which are voiced but not /a/-like. To tell which of these three types of segment a given spectral section lies in, we only need to see whether the result of the test '/a/-like' for this section is '−1', '1', or '0'. But this segmentation is not *used* in the sense that segmentation was used in the system of Sholtz and Bakis, where measurements were made on segments *after* segmentation.

It is roughly true to say that a *phoneme* is a basic unit of spoken speech which is analogous to a *letter* in written language. For instance, the spoken word 'bird' consists of three phonemes, /b/, /ir/, and /d/. In English there are approximately 40 phonemes. Speech consists of a string of phonemes, and a given phoneme may occur in many spoken words, just as the letter 'b' may occur in many written words. In cursive script, the shape of, for example, the letter 'b' is not unique, and the alternative shapes of 'b' constitute a recognition class. The exact shape of a 'b' in cursive script may depend upon its context. Similarly, a phoneme is not a unique acoustic unit, but a class of somewhat similar acoustic units. The precise acoustics of a phoneme generally depend strongly on its context. The variations of phonemes are so great that phonemes have been subclassified into *allophones*. An allophone is a set of mutually similar variants of a phoneme. For example[49], the versions of the phoneme /p/ in the spoken words 'peak', 'supper', 'spin', and 'top' are different allophones of /p/.

Just as it is usually practical to recognise printed words via segmentation into letters, it may in some situations be practical to recognise spoken words via segmentation into phonemes[335, 387], although the phoneme has not finally been proved to be an optimal unit for automatic speech recognition[123]. Reddy[368] has described a computer based phoneme recognition system in which the actual amplitude/time speech waveform is fed into a computer. The waveform is divided into a succession of 10 ms *segments*. Successive 10 ms segments are merged to form larger segments (cf. Refs 59, 312) if they do not differ too much in intensity and zero crossing rates. This merging process results in the segmentation of the speech waveform into chunks which correspond roughly to phonemes[367]. Each chunk is then classified as a particular phoneme by means of a tree which asks questions concerning the duration of the chunk, the mean and standard deviation of its intensity, the means and standard deviations of its numbers of zero crossings per 10 ms, the frequency and amplitude of the first three formants, etc. When the decision tree requires values of formant frequencies and amplitudes, as it does in vowel classification, Reddy's programme finds the discrete Fourier series coefficients of a single pitch period, regarded as one period from an infinitely repetitive waveform, and this provides an approximation to the integral Fourier transform, which would be costly to compute. Fourier coefficients are computed for not more than two pitch periods per chunk. Reddy's system minimises the use of Fourier transformation in speech recognition, and in particular avoids the common practice of starting the speech recognition process with some sort of spectral analysis. In Reddy's system, segmentation into chunks necessarily precedes measurement of the means and standard deviations of intensity and zero-crossings rates of chunks. Segmentation *precedes* recognition, and Reddy's system provides an example of speech segmentation by *measurement.*

The remaining paragraphs of the present section contain a discussion of segmentation in relation to the use of context. In the contextual techniques of Section 8.1, there is no restriction on the detailed shapes of the character which make up a word: there is only restriction on combinations of names of recognition classes of characters. For instance, in the word

there is a tendency for the letters to become narrower towards the top, but none of the Section 8.1 techniques would take this into account in deciding between the legitimate English words 'WAITING' and

'WHITING'. In the Section 8.1 techniques, information as to the precise detailed shapes of characters is discarded before contextual rules are applied, so that dependence between detailed shapes of characters is not taken into account.

In the *perception* of speech, the importance of dependence between the precise acoustics of phonemes has been established beyond doubt. It has been shown that what we hear subjectively may depend on the precise acoustics of phonemes jointly, not independently. For instance, Cooper *et al.*[101] have shown that exactly the same burst of noise may be heard by a human subject as /p/ or /k/ according as the central frequency of the noise in this burst is below or not below the frequency of the second formant of the following vowel sound. Ladefoged and Broadbent[265] have performed experiments in which listeners hear exactly the same (synthetic) word in different (synthetic) contexts. Whether this word is heard as 'bit', 'bet', or 'bat' depends on the frequencies of the formants in the words that are used as context.

In the automatic recognition of spoken or written words, there are several ways of taking account of the dependence between the precise acoustics of phonemes or shapes of letters. One is to use a relational system in which, in a given word, the allowed combinations of variants of phonemes or letters are restricted. A simpler way of taking account of dependence is to recognise a word as a single unsegmented whole, as in Section 9.6.2. A further advantage of the Section 9.6.2 techniques is that they avoid errors which might arise from a process of segmentation. But the Section 9.6.2 techniques have the disadvantage of requiring a separate discriminant for each word, each discriminant requiring designing or training; and this disadvantage weighs more heavily the greater the number of different words which are to be recognised. The Section 9.6.2 techniques happen to be linear, but not all techniques which recognise words as unsegmented wholes are linear. For instance, Bobrow and Klatt's system[49] stores a separate conditional probability for each test result for each whole word or phrase which is to be recognised; and it can be argued that this system recognises an utterance without making use of segmentation, just as Doyle's system[125] (Section 7.6) recognises a written character without segmentation into features.

Although, due for instance to co-articulation, there is often significant dependence between the precise acoustics of speech segments, it may be possible, in limited practical applications, to obtain tolerably low error rates without taking account of dependence. When this is the case, different combinations of variants of segments may correspond to speech distortions which we wish to ignore. We gain some invariance to distortion by allowing all possible combinations of the variants of a prescribed set of segments. (Analogously, the simple non-negating system of Section 7.5.5 achieves invariance to distortion by assigning X to the rth class if X includes *any* member of E_{ri1} and *any* member of E_{ri2} and . . . and *any* member of $E_{ri\phi}$, but *see* Ref. 443a.) Independent classification of segments has economic advantages. One advantage arises from the fact that the variability of a segment is generally less than the variability of an unsegmented whole, so that discriminant systems for classifying segments tend to be cheaper than discriminant systems which classify unsegmented patterns. Another advantage arises from the fact that a given segment may occur in many different patterns. For instance, the same limb junction may occur in many different characters; and the same phoneme may occur in many different spoken words. It is of course more economical to use the same equipment for recognising a given phoneme in whatever word it occurs, rather than using different equipment for recognising the given phoneme in different words.

The shortest segments which are commonly used in automatic speech recognition are spectral sections. The Section 9.6.3 systems classify spectral sections independently, and this has the advantage that there is no risk of error in the process of segmentation, since every spectral section is a segment. If we use segments which are of longer duration than spectral sections, then we can take account of the precise acoustics of spectral sections within a segment, even when we find it expedient to ignore dependence between the precise acoustics of different segments. For instance, Sholtz and Bakis[406] obtain parameters which describe a voiced segment as a single whole, and the spectral sections which constitute a voiced segment are parametrised jointly, not independently. However, segmentation into chunks which are of longer duration than spectral sections generally incurs a risk of erroneous segmentation[429a].

Chapter 10

LEARNING

10.1 UNSUPERVISED LEARNING

10.1.1 Two-stage systems

To obtain training sets for use in the systems of Chapters 3, 4, and 5, a human operator may inspect many specimen patterns and either label each pattern according to its class, or sort the patterns into batches such that all patterns which belong to the same batch belong to the same recognition class. We shall refer to this labelling or sorting process as *preclassification.* When training sets contain many thousands of patterns, preclassification may be a laborious task, and errors may be made, so that patterns are mis-labelled or mis-sorted.

To reduce the amount of work required in preclassification, systems have been devised in which a small preclassified training set, of patterns from all recognition classes, is used for determining weight vectors. These weight vectors are used in the automatic classification of non-preclassified patterns which are subsequently used as training set patterns in the determination of improved weight vectors. Learning proceeds in two stages, and preclassified training set patterns are used only in the first stage[100].

Nagy and Shelton[216, 328] have described a two-stage print recognition system in which the second stage adapts the system to a single font. In the first stage one weight vector per recognition class is determined by the independence method of Section 3.3, applied to a preclassified training set which includes characters in, for instance, 12 different fonts. The second stage works with a training set, which we will denote by T, of characters in a single font. This single font is one of the fonts used in the first stage of the learning process. The patterns belonging to T are not preclassified.

Using weights determined by the first stage, and a fairly high reject threshold, the Section 3.3 recognition rule is applied to the patterns which belong to T. Let T_1 be the set of patterns belonging to T which are *not* classified as rejects by the Section 3.3 rule. New weights are now determined by the method of Section 3.3, using T_1 as the training set, the members of T_1 having been automatically labelled according to their recognition class. Using these weights and the Section 3.3 rule, recognition of all of the patterns belonging to T is again attempted, and let T_2 be the set of patterns which are *not* classified as rejects. New weights are now determined by the method of Section 3.3, using T_2 as the training set. This iterative procedure is repeated with training sets $T_3, T_4, \ldots, T_{i-1}, T, \ldots$. If, for any i, the number of rejects when T_i is the training set is greater than a prescribed fraction of the number of rejects when T_{i-1} is the training set, then the reject threshold is reduced by one unit in order to reduce the reject rate. The procedure stops either when the reject threshold or the reject rate reaches a prescribed minimum, or when the number of iterations reaches a prescribed maximum.

Nagy and Shelton applied this technique experimentally to binary patterns derived from characters as in Section 5.6.1, and found that the second stage yielded a considerable improvement in the recognition of characters in the single font which was used in this stage. A condition for the success of Nagy and Shelton's technique, and also of the following technique, is that the first stage of training must result in tolerably reliable recognition of patterns belonging to T: otherwise the second stage of training causes an explosive deterioration of recognition performance.

Ide and Tunis[234] have described a two-stage technique which is a development of the fixed increment procedure of Section 3.7.3. In the first stage, weights are determined by applying the method of Section 3.7.3 to a preclassified training set of patterns from all recognition classes. In the second stage, a modified fixed increment rule is applied to a non-preclassified training set. The procedure passes repeatedly through this non-preclassified training set, computing dot products between training set (augmented) patterns and weight vectors. For any given training set pattern, let the weight vectors giving the largest dot products be W_s and W_r, such that $Y \,.\, W_s \geqslant Y \,.\, W_r$. The procedure passes on to the next training set pattern and no weight vector is changed unless the condition

$$W_r \,.\, Y + \rho \leqslant W_s \,.\, Y \leqslant W_r \,.\, Y + \delta$$

is fulfilled, in which case W_s is changed to $W_s + Y$ and W_r is changed to $W_r - Y$. Here ρ is a reject threshold and δ is a dead zone threshold, and $\delta > \rho$. An interpretation of the condition for correction is that, if $W_s . Y > W_r . Y + \delta$, it is presumed that no correction is required. If $W_s . Y < W_r . Y + \rho$, we cannot be reasonably confident that Y belongs to the sth class, and it is better not to change any weight vector. The procedure continues to iterate until convergence , or until it becomes clear that convergence will not be attained.

Apart from reducing the labour of preclassification, a two-stage process may be useful when the hardware of a recognition system gradually develops faults or drifts out of adjustment. Second-stage learning can be used to make continuous adjustments to weights, thereby compensating gradual changes in the hardware[234]. This application of second-stage learning is sometimes called *tracking*.

10.1.2 Fully unsupervised learning

When a publisher produces a paperback edition of a hardback book, the laborious and costly job of typesetting may have to be done for the paperback. Optical character recognition has been used for reading a hardback into a computer system which automatically does the typesetting for the paperback. Different hardbacks may be printed in different fonts, and to avoid limitations on the choice of the fonts which the recognition machine could read, the recognition machine could learn each font. The advantage of unsupervised learning in this application, or in a similar application[23a], would be that there would be no need to repeat the onerous task of preclassification for each font. The approach of Nagy and Shelton[328] would have the disadvantage of requiring a realistically wide range of fonts to be read with tolerable reliability after the first stage of learning. Fully *unsupervised* systems, that is, systems which use no preclassified training set and have no first stage, do not suffer from this disadvantage. There is considerable literature on unsupervised learning, e.g. Refs 27, 53, 58, 99, 150, 326, 345, and 418; and as an introduction, the present section outlines two methods.

The first step in Ball and Hall's ISODATA procedure[28] is to choose arbitrarily a set of initial points in hyperspace. For the representative point of each training set pattern, the procedure finds the nearest initial point in hyperspace. Patterns which are nearest to the same initial point are assigned to the same (arbitrarily named) class. Classes containing fewer than a prescribed number of patterns are discarded. For each remaining class, ISODATA determines the mean and the standard deviation along every axis in hyperspace. If, for a given class,

(1) the standard deviation along any axis exceeds a prescribed limit, and
(2) the average distance between the mean and the members of the class exceeds a prescribed limit, and
(3) the class contains more than a prescribed number of members,

then the class is split into two new classes, for intance by means of a hyperplane which is perpendicular to the axis of greatest standard deviation, and which passes through the mean of the original class. On the other hand, if the means of two classes are separated by less than a threshold distance, then these two classes are lumped together to form a single new class, whose mean and standard deviations are computed. ISODATA only permits the lumping together of a controlled number of pairs of classes.

Splitting and lumping results in a new set of classes. The rules for splitting and lumping are applied to the new classes just as they were applied to the original classes. This results in a further set of classes, to which the same rules are applied, and so on, until, for instance, no condition for lumping or splitting is satisfied. The final set of classes are regarded as *clusters* in hyperspace. For application in pattern recognition it would be hoped that all patterns belonging to any given cluster would belong to the same recognition class. In this case, a human operator could determine the recognition class of a cluster by inspecting just one of its members. Inspecting one member of each cluster *after* the ISODATA process would be less onerous than preclassifying all training set patterns individually *before* applying a conventional learning process to preclassified training sets. It is instructive to compare ISODATA with Firschein and Fischler's technique of subclass determination (see Section 4.4).

The following is a version of one of Dorofeyuk's unsupervised learning algorithms[124], based on the method of potentials of Section 4.6.1. Let us denote the non-preclassified training set patterns by $X_1, \ldots, X_t$. The algorithm assigns X_1 to a class which we shall arbitrarily call R_a. The algorithm next selects the pattern X_i from $X_2, \ldots, X_t$ such that $f(d(X_i, X_1)) \geqslant f(d(X_j, X_1))$, for all $j = 2, \ldots, t$, except $j = i$, where $f(\ )$ is as in Section 4.6.1, and assigns X_i to R_a. Among the remaining training set patterns, the algorithm then finds X_j such that $\frac{1}{2}(f(d(X_j, X_1)) + f(d(X_j, X_i)))$ is largest, and assigns X_j to R_a. Among the remaining training set patterns, the algorithm then finds and assigns to R_a the pattern X_k such that

$$\frac{1}{n_a} \sum f(d(X_k, X_i)) \tag{10.1}$$

is maximal, where n_a is the present number of members of R_a, and summation is over all present members of R_a. Using a similar rule, the algorithm assigns further patterns to R_a, until there is no pattern left in $\{X_2, \ldots, X_t\}$ such that the value of (10.1) exceeds a prescribed threshold. The algorithm then assigns the first training set pattern which has not been assigned to R_a to a second class which we shall arbitrarily call R_b; and, using rules similar to those used for assigning patterns to R_a, assigns so-far-unassigned training set patterns to R_b, until the maximal value of the expression corresponding to (10.1) no longer exceeds a prescribed threshold. The algorithm then assigns the first training set pattern which has not been assigned to R_a or to R_b to a further class R_c, and so on until the training set is exhausted. One member of each class $R_a, R_b, \ldots$ can then be inspected by a human operator, and the name of each class can be changed from $R_a, R_b, R_c, \ldots$ to accord with the human's nomenclature. The recognition rule is as in Section 4.6.1.

10.2 AUTOMATIC DETERMINATION OF FEATURES

10.2.1 Introduction

In systems such as the IBM 1287 and 1975 and the Toshiba hand-print recognition system, the design of features takes up a great deal of human effort, and the complexity of the recognition system is finally limited by the limitations of the complexity which humans can grasp intuitively. It may be desirable to automate the determination of features, first to obviate the cost of human design effort, and secondly to obviate limitations on system complexity and thus on recognition performance. However, it may be impossible to automate the design of features such as are used in the IBM 1287 and 1975, and instead it may be necessary to choose the logical structure of the recognition system *so that* the features which the system uses are features which can be determined automatically.

In the systems mentioned in Section 7.5, a feature corresponds to an *f*-class,and a feature is said to be present in an input pattern if a member of the corresponding *f*-class is present in the input pattern. In such systems, the automatic determination of features is the automatic determination of *f*-classes. Sections 10.2.2 and 10.2.3 outline methods of automatically determining *f*-classes for use in negating and non-negating systems. Section 10.3 introduces a method of determining the set L which in turn determines the *f*-classes in the relational system of Section 7.3.5.

10.2.2 Negating systems

10.2.2.1 Selection techniques

A technique such as that of Section 5.5 can be used to select a set of *f*-classes from a repertoire of candidate *f*-classes. If the computational cost of the technique is to be kept within practical bounds, only a limited number of candidate *f*-classes can be processed (for instance, in Section 5.5, $I(v_j)$ can be computed only for a limited number of v_j's). The number of possible *f*-classes is generally astronomical, and the ratio of the number of useful *f*-classes to the total number of possible *f*-classes is usually exceedingly small. For this reason, candidate *f*-classes must not in practice be chosen randomly, and instead they must be chosen so that a tolerably large proportion of them will be selected as useful *f*-classes.

Kamentsky and Liu[243] showed experimentally that *f*-classes chosen from a set of candidates by the Section 5.5 selection technique yielded considerably lower error rates than were obtained with *f*-classes chosen at random from the same set of candidates. In these experiments, the candidates were *not* randomly chosen sets of subpatterns. Each candidate was a set of subpatterns differing from each other only in position.

The 'overhang' *f*-class in the IBM 1975 (*see* Section 7.5.2) contains many pairs of subpatterns which differ from each other not only in position. Automatic selection of *f*-classes such as those used in the IBM 1975 does not appear to be practical[20], because it does not appear possible to restrict the repertoire of candidates so that a tolerably large proportion of candidates are accepted, without at the same time precluding *f*-classes such as are used in the IBM 1975. Because of practical restrictions on numbers of candidates, the usefulness of automatic selection techniques is limited.

10.2.2.2 A method of building up f-classes

For introductory simplicity, let us consider a problem where there are only two recognition classes, R_1 and R_2, and we wish to determine an *f*-class $F = \{\gamma_1, \ldots, \gamma_\delta\}$ such that every pattern which belongs to R_1 contains a member of F, and no pattern which belongs to R_2 contains a member of F. Suppose for example that a subpattern γ_0 consists of four bits; specifically, $x_3 = 1, x_4 = 1, x_7 = 0$, and $x_9 = 0$. The subpattern γ_0 is included in the pattern X if and only if the *and* function $a_0 = x_3 . x_4 . \bar{x}_7 . \bar{x}_9$ is *true*. Similarly, for any subpattern there is a corresponding *and* function which is *true* if and only if that subpattern is included in X. Let $a_1, \ldots, a_\delta$ be the *and* functions which correspond in this way to the subpatterns $\gamma_1, \ldots, \gamma_\delta$ respectively. The problem of determining an *f*-class $F = \{\gamma_1, \ldots, \gamma_\delta\}$ is the same as the problem of automatically determining a function $f(X) = a_1 \vee a_2 \vee \ldots \vee a_\delta$ which is *true* if X belongs to R_1 and *false* if X belongs to R_2. If such a function can be determined, X can be assigned to R_1 or R_2 according as $f(X)$ is *true* or *false*.

In 1962 Bonner[52] published a heuristic method for the automatic determination of Boolean discriminants which were not restricted to *or*'ed *and* terms. Slagle *et al.*[409] give a bibliography of methods which, given the truth table of a Boolean function, automatically determine an expression of that function as an *or* function of *and* terms, this expression being in some sense economically optimal. These optimal methods are generally not practical in pattern recognition, because usually the number of bits per pattern is large, and the number of patterns which belong to no completely specified row of the classification table (Section 6.4.4) is very large. For use in pattern recognition, Stearns[420] devised a method which is not optimal, but which does not require an impractical amount of computation.

To introduce Stearns' method[420], let $R_1^* = \{X_{11}, X_{12}, \ldots, X_{1i}, \ldots, X_{1t_1}\}$ and R_2^* be training sets of R_1 and R_2 respectively. Stearn's method determines an f-class F such that every member of R_1^* includes a subpattern belonging to F and no member of R_2^* includes a subpattern belonging to F. It is convenient to say that the set of 1's and 0's which are the same in two patterns is a subpattern which is *common* to those two patterns. For instance, the subpattern which is common to 01011011 and 11001101 is –10–1––1. The subpattern which is common to –10–1––1 and 11011000 is –10–1–––. A subpattern is *contained* in a pattern if all the bits in the subpattern which are not '–' are the same as the corresponding bits in the pattern. For instance, –10–1––– is contained in 11001100 but not contained in 11000110.

Figure 10.1 is a flow diagram for Stearns' programme. During the operation of the programme, the symbols X_{1i}, γ, and γ' generally stand for different patterns or subpatterns at different times. For instance, the symbol X_{1i} initially stands for X_{12}, and might perhaps subsequently stand for X_{13}, X_{15}, X_{16}, and so on, as programme and data dictate. If, for instance, γ' is –10–1–––, then the result of the instruction 'replace γ by γ'' is that γ is –10–1–––. The programme sometimes enters γ in a list of members of F, and each time this happens, γ is a different subpattern. After a subpattern has been entered in the list of members of F, that subpattern remains unaltered when γ is subsequently redefined as a different subpattern.

It is quite easy to see that Stearns' programme is *guaranteed* to determine an f-class F such that every member of the original training set R_1^*, and no member of R_2^*, contains a subpattern belonging to F. Note that the programme *builds up* the f-class subpattern by subpattern, rather than selecting a whole f-class from a repertoire of candidate f-classes as in Section 5.5. A disadvantage of Stearns' method is that, if R_1^* and R_2^* contain many patterns, F may contain too many subpatterns, and some of these may have too many bits, to be practical.

10.2.3 Non-negating systems

The selection criterion in Section 5.5 requires ideally that $v_j = 0$ in all patterns belonging to half of the recognition classes. Stearns' technique requires that no member of F is included in any member of R_2^*. In a non-negating system, these requirements are unnecessary.

In Section 7.5.3, Bledsoe and Browning's system and the Hitachi system of Section 7.2.2 were mentioned as examples of non-negating systems, In Bledsoe and Browning's system the f-class A_{rj} is determined

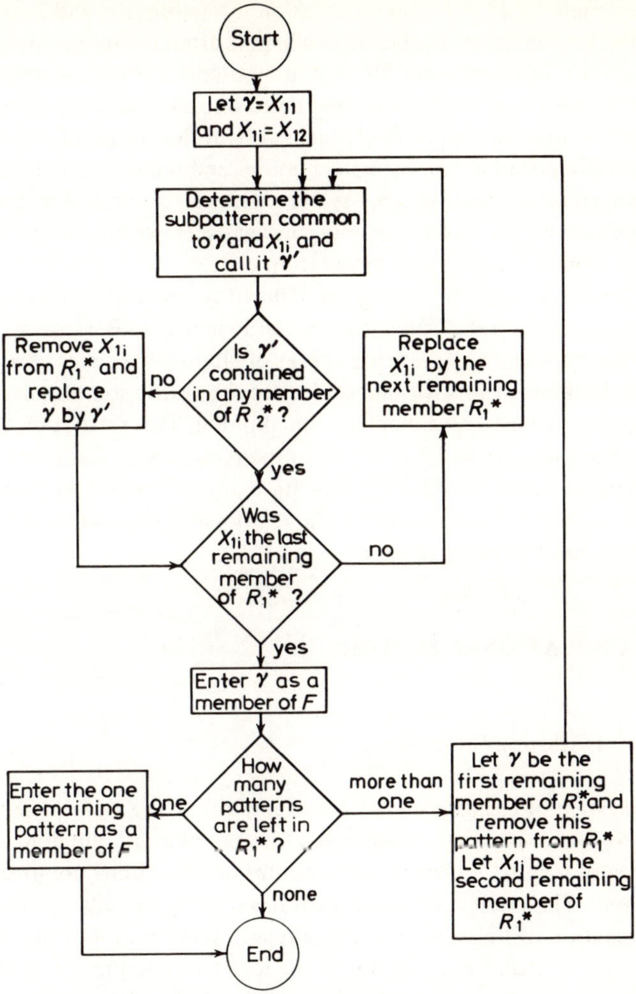

Figure 10.1. *Flow diagram for Stearns' programme*

simply by storing all states of the *j*th *n*-tuple which occur in at least one member of the *r*th training class set. It is important that *f*-classes are *built-up*, subpattern by subpattern, rather than *f*-classes being selected as wholes from a repertoire of candidates. In the Hitachi system, *f*-classes depend on zones of occurrence, and zones of occurrence are *built-up*, point-by-point, as explained by Section 7.2.2.1.

The simplicity of f-class determination in the Bledsoe and Browning and Hitachi systems is an advantage which is attended by the following disadvantage. In Bledsoe and Browning's system, an f-class is only used in the recognition of patterns belonging to one particular recognition class. It is a disadvantage of the Hitachi system that zones of occurrence are generally different for different features and recognition classes. A system such as the Section 5.6.1 system is more economical in that a given f-class may be used (positively or negatively) in the recognition of patterns from more than one recognition class.

In the Bledsoe and Browning and Hitachi systems, an f-class is a subset of a prescribed set of subpatterns. For instance, in Bledsoe and Browning's system, an f-class is a subset of all possible states of a given n-tuple. Systems of this sort are subject to the restriction that no two prescribed sets have any subpattern in common. This restriction ensures that no two f-classes which are used in the recognition of patterns belonging to a given recognition class have any subpattern in common. No such restriction is necessary in the relational system which is the subject of the following section.

10.3 A RELATIONAL SYSTEM

10.3.1 Distortions of patterns

In the system of Grimsdale *et al.* (*see* Section 7.3.3) a training set character is automatically fragmented into chunks, and the limits of variation of length, curvature, and orientation of a chunk are prescribed intuitively. The present section is concerned with the fully automatic determination of f-classes for use in a relational system. For introductory simplicity, we shall not make use of the idea (*see* Section 7.5.5) that distortions of characters are usually continuous. Furthermore, we shall be concerned with the mapping of individual bits of binary patterns, because this appears to be the simplest and most readily comprehensible type of mapping, although it does not immediately provide a successful practical technique of recognition. The general aim of Section 10.3 is to provide basic insight into the problem of recognising shapes which are subject to distortion. The specific aim is to provide a method of automatic determination of the set L for use in the system of Section 7.3.6.

As in Section 7.3.4, let X_{ri} be the ith pattern in the rth class training set, and let X be any unknown pattern which may occur in practice. Let S be the array of bit locations on which X_{ri} is written, and let T be the array of bit locations on which X is written. Let U be the union of S and T. A *partition* on U is a set of non-overlapping subsets of U whose union is U.

Let U_1 be the partition on U which has 25 subsets as indicated in Figure 10.2(a). In Figure 10.2(a), bit locations which are labelled with the same letter belong to the same subset of U_1, and bit locations which are not labelled with any letter belong to the same subset of U_1. Let B_1 be the set of 2^{25} pairs of patterns which can be generated by filling each subset of U_1 exclusively with black bits or exclusively with white bits. For instance, the pairs of patterns shown in Figures 10.2(b) and (c) are pairs which belong to B_1. The partition U_1 is such that, in any pair of patterns which belong to B_1, the pattern on T is a shifted version of the pattern on S.

Further partitions U_2, U_3, U_4, U_5, U_6, U_7, on U are indicated in Figures 10.2(d), (f), (h), (j), (l), (n) respectively, using the same convention as was used in Figure 10.2(a) for indicating the partition U_1. For instance, in Figure 10.2(d), bit locations which are labelled with the same letter belong to the same subset of U_2, and bit locations which are not labelled with any letter belong to the same subset of U_2. Correspondingly, B_2 is the set of 2^{25} pairs of patterns which can be generated by filling each subset of U_2 exclusively with black bits or exclusively with white bits. For instance, the pair of patterns shown in Figure 10.2(e) belongs to B_2. The partition U_2 is such that, in any pair of patterns which belongs to B_2, the pattern on T is a shifted version of the pattern on S.

For $k = 1, 2, 3, 4, 5, \ldots, B_k$ is the set of all possible pairs of patterns which can be generated by filling each subset of U_k exclusively with black bits or exclusively with white bits. U_3 is as indicated in Figure 10.2(f), and in any pair of patterns which belongs to B_3, the pattern on T is an enlarged version of the pattern on S. For instance, the pair of patterns shown in Figure 10.2(g) belongs to B_3. The partition U_4 is as indicated in Figure 10.2(h), and in any pair of patterns which belongs to B_4, the pattern on T is a sheared version of the pattern on S. For instance, the pair of patterns shown in Figure 10.2(i) belongs to B_4. The partition U_5 is as indicated in Figure 10.2(j), and in any pair of patterns which belongs to B_5, the pattern on T is a roughly enlarged version of the pattern on S. For instance the pair of patterns shown

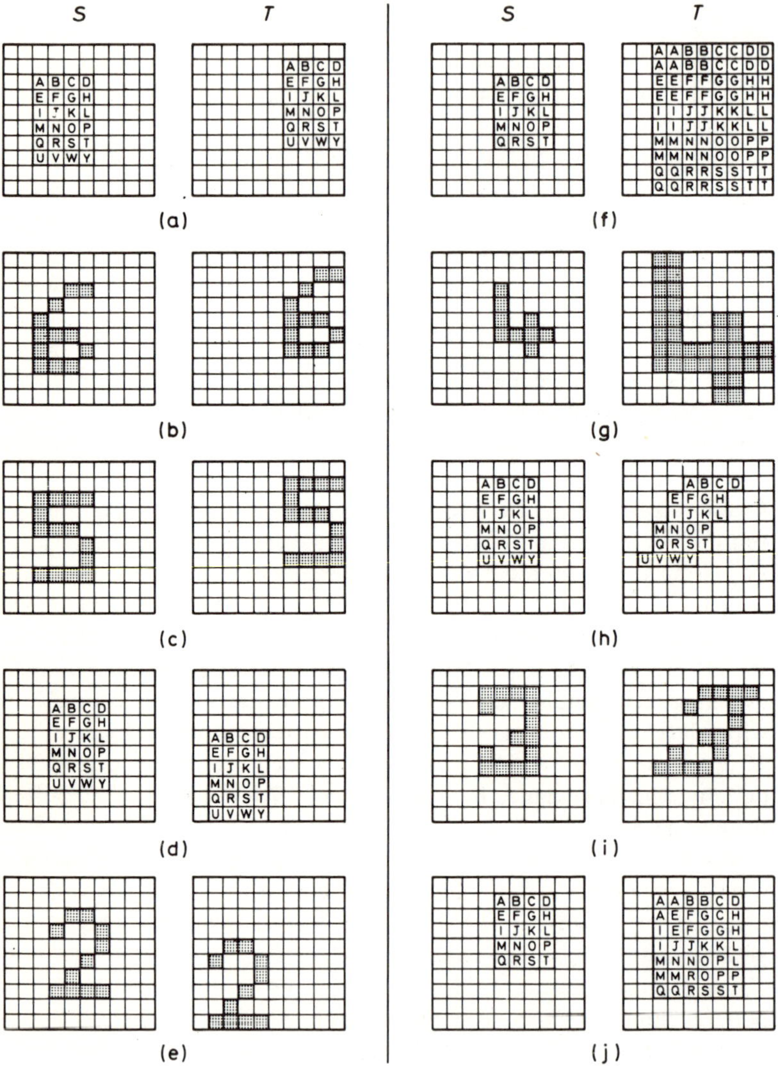

Figure 10.2. *Examples of distortions*

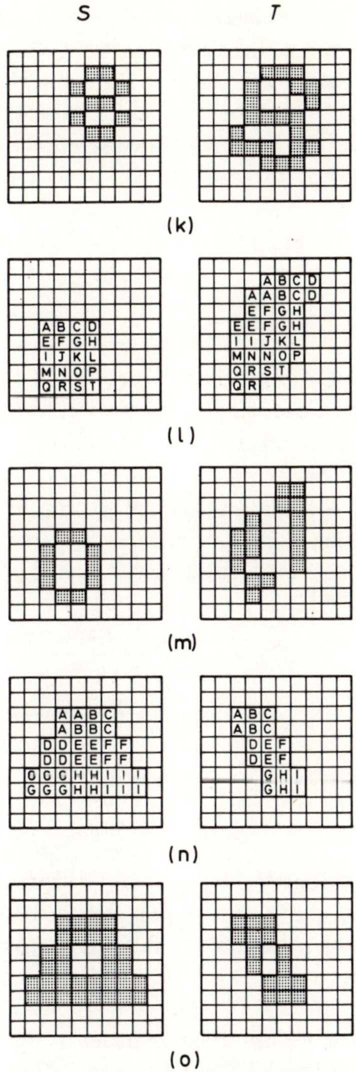

Figure 10.2. (*continued*)

in Figure 10.2(k) belongs to B_5. The partition U_6 is as indicated in Figure 10.2(l), and in any pair of patterns which belongs to B_6, the pattern on T is a roughly enlarged and somewhat sheared version of the pattern on S. For instance, the pair of patterns shown in Figure 10.2(m) belongs to B_6. The partition U_7 is as indicated in Figure 10.2(n), and in any pair of patterns which belongs to B_7, the bottom of the pattern on T is narrower than the bottom of the pattern on S, and somewhat sheared to the right. For instance, the pair of patterns shown in Figure 10.2(o) belongs to B_7.

We say that a partition U_h is a *subpartition* of a partition U_k if and only if

(1) $U_h \neq U_k$, and
(2) the intersection of any given subset U_{hj} of U_h with any given subset of U_k is either empty or identical to U_{hj}.

For instance, let $U_{(b)}$ be the partition which is indicated in Figure 10.3(b). Because U_1 is a subpartition of $U_{(b)}$, $B_{(b)}$ is a subset of B_1. For simplicity the following work concentrates on partitions such as U_1 and does not explicitly consider partitions such as $U_{(b)}$.

We define a set $V = \{U_1, \ldots, U_k, \ldots, U_\beta\}$ of partitions on U by saying that the partition U_k belongs to V if and only if

(a) U_k is such that, if $\{X_{ri}, X\} \in B_k$, then X belongs to the rth class, and
(b) no subpartition U_h of U_k exists such that, if $\{X_{ri}, X\} \in B_h$, then X belongs to the rth class.

The Figure 10.2 partitions $U_1, U_2, \ldots, U_7$ are intended to be examples of members of V. The partition shown in Figure 10.3(a) does not belong to V because condition (a) is (presumably) not satisfied; and $U_{(b)}$ does not belong to V because condition (b) is not satisfied, owing to the existence of U_1.

Just using intuition, we can draw on paper a large number of somewhat different hand-printed 2's, but we cannot draw all of the shapes which we would happily recognise as '2'. If, for example, patterns are binarised 40 x 40, we cannot say how many binarised patterns we would intuitively recognise as '2'. Similarly, just using intuition, we can specify a large number of partitions belonging to the set

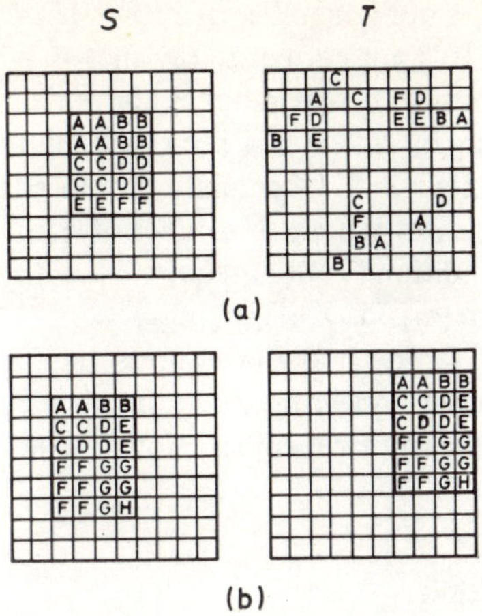

Figure 10.3. *Examples of partitions which do not belong to V*

$V = \{U_1, \ldots, U_\beta\}$: for instance, we can specify those partitions which are associated with shift, with elongation, and with shear. But we cannot intuitively specify *all* of the partitions $U_1, \ldots, U_\beta$, nor do we know the value of β.

Because any partition in V satisfies condition (a) for membership in V, an unknown pattern X could be assigned to the rth class if

$$\{X_{ri}, X\} \in B \tag{10.2}$$

where $B = B_1 \cup B_2 \cup \ldots \cup B_k \cup \ldots \cup B_\beta$ is the union of the sets $B_1, \ldots, B_\beta$ which correspond respectively to the members $U_1, \ldots, U_\beta$ of V. In practice, however, we do not know all of the partitions $U_1, \ldots, U_\beta$, just as we do not know all of the shapes which we would recognise as '2'. To use rule (10.2), or to use a rule which is roughly equivalent to rule (10.2) we must first solve the problem of designing a system which, given a training set of members of B, can automatically determine whether or not any further pair of patterns $\{X_{ri}, X\}$ belongs to B. In the following pages, this problem is tackled step by step, successive steps being progressively less simplified. In Section 10.3.5 we consider how a training set of members of B may be obtained in practice.

It is convenient, as a shorthand, to use conventional set theoretic symbols. In particular, $|Z|$ means the *number of members* of the set Z. If $Z = \{E, D\}$, where $D = \{d_1, d_2, d_3\}$ and $E = \{e_1, e_2, e_3\}$, then E is a member of Z, but e_1 is not a member of Z: $Z = \{E, D\}$ is not the same as the union $E \cup D$. It is not correct to say that $A = \{d_1, e_1\}$ belongs to Z, but, to avoid verbosity, it is sometimes convenient to say that A belongs to Z, meaning by this that A is included in the union $E \cup D$. We have already used this in the formulation of (7.6) (1): the member $\{\alpha_{j1}, \ldots, \alpha_{jn}\}$ of F is not strictly a member of $\{\{\alpha_{j1}, \beta_{j1}\}, \ldots, \{\alpha_{jn}, \beta_{jn}\}\}$, and condition (7.6)(1) requires that $\{\alpha_{j1}, \ldots, \alpha_{jn}\}$ be included in the union $\{\alpha_{j1}, \beta_{j1}\} \cup \{\alpha_{j2}, \beta_{j2}\} \cup \ldots \cup \{\alpha_{jn}, \beta_{jn}\}$ for at least one member of L. The symbolic expression $Y \supseteq W$ means that every member of the set W belongs to the set Y and possibly $Y = W$. $Y \not\supseteq W$ means that at least one member of W does not belong to Y.

10.3.2 Single partition

As a first simplification, suppose that we are provided with a training set B_k^* of members of B_k, and that we are not told the partition U_k. Let us consider the problem of automatically determining whether or not any given pair of patterns is a member of B_k.

As in Section 7.3.4, let Q be the set of all pairs of bit locations, such that in any member of Q one bit location belongs to S and the other bit location belongs to T. Let J_k be the set of all members of Q such that in any given member of J_k the two bits are both black or both white in *every* member of B_k^*. An unknown pair of patterns can safely be assigned to B_k if

the two bits in every member of J_k are both black or both white in the unknown pair of patterns. } (10.3)

If this condition is not satisfied, the unknown pair of patterns should be rejected, or, in other words, no decision should be made as to whether this pair does or does not belong to B_k.

To see that (10.3) never assigns to B_k a pair of patterns which does not in fact belong to B_k, let J_k' be the set of all members of Q such that in any member of J_k' the two bit locations belong to the same subset of U_k. In any member of J_k' the two bit locations both contain black or both contain white in any given member of B_k^*. Therefore $J_k' \subseteq J_k$, and, if (10.3) is satisfied, the two bits in any given member of J_k' are both black or both white in the unknown pair of patterns. Therefore, in the unknown pair of patterns, every subset of U_k is filled entirely with white bits or entirely with black bits. Thus we see that, if (10.3) is satisfied, the unknown pair of patterns belongs to B_k.

Rule (10.3) may reject a pair of patterns which in fact belongs to B_k, but it never assigns to B_k a pair of patterns which does not belong to B_k, even if this pair does not belong to B_k^*. Rule (10.3) is a simple example of a rule which is guaranteed never to recognise wrongly a non-member of the training set.

Rule (10.3) is perhaps the simplest solution to our simplified problem. For later reference, we now introduce a further solution which is more elaborate than (10.3). Let N_q be the set of all possible n-tuples of members of Q. Thus any set of n members of Q is a member of N_q. We shall say that a member of N_q is *isochromatic* in a given pair of patterns if in every one of the n members of Q which constitute this member of N_q the two bits are either both black or both white in the given pair of patterns. For instance, a member of N_q is isochromatic if the first member of Q contains two white bits, the second member of Q contains two black bits, . . ., the nth member of Q contains two black bits. A member of N_q is *not* isochromatic if, in any one of the n members of Q, one bit is white and the other is black.

Let H_k be the set of all members of N_q such that any given member of H_k is isochromatic in every member of B_k^*. Thus H_k is the set of all possible n-tuples of members of J_k. An unknown pair of patterns can safely be assigned to B_k if

every member of H_k is isochromatic in the unknown pair of patterns. (10.4)

If this condition is not satisfied, the unknown pair of patterns should be rejected.

Since every member of J_k belongs to at least one member of H_k, and since $J_k \supseteq J'_k$, every member of J'_k belongs to at least one member of H_k. Therefore, if (10.4) is satisfied, the two bits in every member of J'_k are both black or both white, and the unknown pair of patterns must belong to B_k. Rule (10.4) is the same as rule (10.3) when $n = 1$.

10.3.3 Many partitions: separate training sets

We now consider a problem in which separate training sets of members of each of $B_1, \ldots, B_k, \ldots, B_\beta$ are provided, but we are not told the partitions $U_1, \ldots, U_\beta$. The problem is to determine automatically whether or not any given pair of patterns belongs to B, where, as before, B is the union $B = B_1 \cup B_2 \cup \ldots \cup B_\beta$.

A simple solution to this problem would be to determine J_k for each $k = 1, \ldots, \beta$ in turn, and decide that an unknown pair of patterns belongs to B if

for any $k = 1, 2, \ldots, \beta$, (10.3) is satisfied. (10.5)

Unfortunately this is impractical, because it involves applying (10.3) separately for each $k = 1, \ldots, \beta$, and β is presumably a very large number. In the following paragraphs we seek a solution, or at least a rough solution, which does not require separate computation for each $k = 1, \ldots, \beta$ in order to determine whether or not a given unknown pair of patterns belongs to B.

Let ν be the smallest of the numbers $|J_1|, \ldots, |J_k|, \ldots, |J_\beta|$, and let J be the union $J = J_1 \cup J_2 \cup \ldots \cup J_k \cup \ldots \cup J_\beta$. A simple but very poor rule is: assign the unknown pair of patterns to B if

in at least ν members of J the two bits are either both black or both white in the unknown pair of patterns. (10.6)

In recognition, this rule does not require separate computation for each $k = 1, \ldots, \beta$, and it is easy to see that any pair of patterns which is assigned to B by (10.5) is also assigned to B by (10.6). But (10.6) may assign to B pairs of patterns which are not assigned to B by (10.5), and, in particular, (10.6) may assign to B pairs of patterns which do not belong to B.

Let μ be the smallest of the numbers $|H_1|, \ldots, |H_k|, \ldots, |H_\beta|$, and let H be the union $H = H_1 \cup H_2 \cup \ldots \cup H_k \cup \ldots \cup H_\beta$. A further rule is: assign the unknown pair of patterns to B if

at least μ members of H are isochromatic in the unknown pair of patterns. (10.7)

Like (10.6), (10.7) does not require separate computation for each $k = 1, \ldots, \beta$, in the recognition of an unknown pair of patterns. To determine the members of H we could determine the members of $H_1, \ldots, H_\beta$ separately as in Section 10.3.2. This is impractical because β is presumably a very large number, and we shall tackle this difficulty in Section 10.3.4. Meanwhile, we shall assume that the members of H are determined by determining the members of $H_1, \ldots, H_\beta$ separately.

H_k consists of all possible n-tuples of members of J_k. If, in a given unknown pair of patterns, the two bits in any given member of J_k are both black or both white, then $|H_k|$ members of H_k are isochromatic in the unknown pair of patterns. Since $|H_k| \geqslant \mu$, and $H_k \subseteq H$, a pair of patterns which is assigned to B by (10.5) is also assigned to B by (10.7), whatever the value of n. But (10.7) may assign to B pairs of patterns which do not belong to B.

To see the advantage of (10.7) over (10.6), let us restate (10.6): assign the unknown pair of patterns to B if

> there exists a subset of J' of J such that $|J'| = \nu$ and in every member of J' the two bits are both black or both white in the unknown pair of patterns. (10.8)

Let us restate (10.7): assign the unknown pair of patterns to B if

> there exists a subset H' of H such that $|H'| = \mu$ and every member of H' is isochromatic in the unknown pair of patterns. (10.9)

Let us consider any set H' which satisfies (10.9), and let J'' be the set of all members of Q such that any given member of J'' belongs to at least one member of H' If $|J''| < \nu$, then $|H'| < \mu$, and (10.9) is not satisfied. If (10.9) is satisfied, $|J''| \geqslant \nu$, and therefore J'' is, or includes, a set J' which satisfies (10.8). Thus a pair of patterns which is assigned to B by (10.9) is also assigned to B by (10.8).

Let us now consider any set J' which satisfies (10.8), and let H'' be the set of all possible n-tuples of members of J'. Because $|J'| = \nu$, $|H''| = \mu$. A member of H'' is not necessarily a member of H, and therefore a pair of patterns which is assigned to B by (10.8) or (10.6) is not necessarily assigned to B by (10.9) or (10.7). It seems reasonable to assume that, as n increases, there is a decrease in the probability that any given member of N_q belongs to H; and that there is therefore a decrease in the probability that any given member of H'' belongs to H. According to this, the advantage of (10.7) over (10.6) is that, by increasing the value of n, we can reduce the probability that (10.7) will assign to B a pair of patterns which does not belong to B. Yet, whatever the value of n, a pair of patterns which would be assigned to B by (10.5) is assigned to B by (10.7).

If, as we have stipulated, N_q contains all possible n-tuples of members of Q, then the number of members of N_q is generally impractically large if $n > 1$. If, for the sake of economy, we now stipulate that N_q does not contain all possible n-tuples of members of Q, but , instead , that N_q contains a randomly chosen set of n-tuples of members of Q, then there is a danger that μ will be a small number, possibly zero. The smaller the value of μ, the greater the chance that (10.7) will assign to B a pair of patterns which does not belong to B.

To mitigate this difficulty, we do not stipulate that N_q is a randomly chosen set of n-tuples of members of Q. Instead we stipulate that N_q is a set of n-tuples of members of Q chosen as follows. Let F be a set of ϕ n-tuples of members of S, chosen randomly except that every member of S belongs to at least one member of F. In a member of N_q there are n members of S and n members of T. We stipulate that, henceforwards, N_q is the set of all possible n-tuples of members of Q such that in any member of N_q the n members of S constitute a member of F. In the sense explained at the end of Section 10.3.1, any member of N_q contains a member of F: it is convenient to say informally that a member of F *belongs to* a member of N_q.

To see the advantage of introducing the set F, recall that H_k is the set of all members of N_q which are n-tuples of members of J_k. We assume that any subset in any of $U_1, \ldots, U_\beta$ contains at least one member of S and at least one member of T. If this is true, it follows that each member of S belongs to at least one member of J_k. Therefore each member of F belongs to at least one member of H_k, and this in turn means that H_k must have at least ϕ members. The members of N_q have been chosen so as to ensure that $\mu \geqslant \phi$.

Section 10.3.4 introduces a development of this work in which it is not possible to ascertain the value of μ. By way of preparation for this development, we can use instead of rule (10.7) the following rule: assign the unknown pair of patterns to B if

$$\left.\begin{array}{l}\text{at least } \phi \text{ members of } H \text{ are isochromatic in the unknown}\\ \text{pair of patterns.}\end{array}\right\} \quad (10.10)$$

Because $\mu \geqslant \phi$, a pair of patterns which is assigned to B by (10.7) is also assigned to B by (10.10); but (10.10) may assign to B a pair of patterns which (10.7) would not assign to B.

We now consider a succession of elaborations of (10.10), each elaboration being a rule which necessarily assigns to B any pair of patterns which (10.5) assigns to B. Successive elaborations reduce the chance of assigning to B a pair of patterns which does not belong to B. The first two elaborations are trivial.

If each subset of each of $U_1, \ldots, U_\beta$ contains at least one member of S and at least one member of T, then, for any given k, any given member of S belongs to at least one member of J_k, and any given member of T belongs to at least one member of J_k. Because any given member of J_k belongs to at least one member of H_k, it follows that any given member of S belongs to at least one member of H_k, and any given member of T belongs to at least one member of H_k. Therefore any unknown pair of patterns which is assigned to B by (10.5) is also assigned to B by the rule: assign the unknown pair of patterns to B if

(1) at least ϕ members of H are isochromatic in the unknown pair of patterns, and
(2) in the unknown pair of patterns, each member of S belongs to at least one isochromatic member of H, and each member of T belongs to at least one isochromatic member of H. (10.11)

Because of condition (2), a pair of patterns which is assigned to B by (10.10) may not be assigned to B by (10.11).

We have seen above that each member of F belongs to at least one member of H_k. In a pair of patterns which is assigned to B by (10.5), every member of H_k is isochromatic. Therefore any unknown pair of patterns which is assigned to B by (10.5) is also assigned to B by the rule: assign the unknown pair of patterns to B if

(1) each member of F belongs to at least one member of H which is isochromatic in the unknown pair of patterns, and
(2) in the unknown pair of patterns, each member of T belongs to at least one isochromatic member of H. (10.12)

Any pair of patterns which is assigned to B by (10.12) is also assigned to B by (10.11), but the converse is not true.

If an unknown pair of patterns is assigned to B by (10.5), then there exists k in the range $k = 1, \ldots, \beta$ such that J_k is a set Q_c which satisfies (7.4), provided that the set H is used in place of the set L. Fulfilment of (7.4)(1) follows from the assumption that each subset of each of the partitions $U_1, \ldots, U_\beta$ includes at least one member of S and at least one member of T. Fulfilment of (7.4)(2) is obvious. Fulfilment of (7.4) (3) follows from the fact that, if the unknown pair of patterns is assigned to B by (10.5), then every member of H_k is isochromatic in the unknown pair of patterns, and $\Phi_j \subseteq H_k$.

Since any pair of patterns which satisfies (10.5) also satisfies (7.4), it follows from the reasoning of Section 7.3.6 that any pair of patterns which satisfies (10.5) also satisfies (7.6), and in terms of the set B we restate (7.6): assign the unknown pair of patterns to B if

$$\left.\begin{array}{l}\text{(1) every member of } F \text{ belongs to at least one member of } L_w \text{, and} \\ \text{(2) every member of } T \text{ belongs to at least one member of } L_w\end{array}\right\} \quad (10.13)$$

where L_w is as defined in Section 7.3.6, and we are using $L = H$. Here L_0 is the set of all members of H which are isochromatic in the unknown pair of patterns, and $L_w \subseteq L_0$. Therefore any pair of patterns which is assigned to B by (10.13) is also assigned to B by (10.12). The advantage of (10.13) is that a pair of patterns which is assigned to B by (10.12) is not necessarily assigned to B by (10.13). [Rule (10 12) is a *non-negating* rule, whereas rule (10.13) is *relational.*]

10.3.4 Many partitions: mixed training sets

In Section 10.3.3 we assumed that the training sets of members of $B_1, \ldots, B_\beta$ were provided separately, so that it was possible to ascertain immediately to which of the sets $B_1, \ldots, B_\beta$ a given member of a training set belonged. In other words, any given member of a training set was preclassified as a member of a particular one of the sets $B_1, \ldots, B_\beta$. In the present section, for reasons which will become clear in Section 10.3.5, we no longer assume that members of training sets are preclassified. The training sets of members of $B_1, \ldots, B_\beta$ are now randomly shuffled up together, and it is not possible to ascertain immediately to which of the sets $B_1, \ldots, B_\beta$ a given member of a training set belongs. As in Section 10.3.3, we are not told the partitions $U_1, \ldots, U_\beta$, and the problem is to determine automatically whether or not any given pair of patterns belongs to B.

Let $B_1^*, \ldots, B_k^*, \ldots, B_\beta^*$ be the training sets of members of $B_1, \ldots, B_k, \ldots, B_\beta$ respectively, and let $B^* = B_1^* \cup B_2^* \cup \ldots \cup B_k^* \cup \ldots \cup B_\beta^*$ be the training set of members of B. Let t be the smallest of the numbers $|B_1^*|, \ldots, |B_k^*|, \ldots, |B_\beta^*|$, and let M_0 be the set of all members of N_q such that any member of M_0 is isochromatic in at least t members of B^*.

As n increases, it becomes less likely that an n-tuple which does not belong to H will belong to M_0. To see this, let $\{q_1, \ldots, q_i, \ldots, q_n\}$ be a member of N_q which does not belong to H. Let B_i' be the set of all members of B^* in which the two bits in q_i are both black or both white. The n-tuple $\{q_1, \ldots, q_i, \ldots, q_n\}$ is isochromatic in members of B^* which belong to the intersection $B'' = B_1' \cap B_2' \cap \ldots \cap B_i' \cap \ldots \cap B_n'$. As n increases, $|B''|$ generally decreases, so that it becomes increasingly likely that $|B''| < t$ and thus $\{q_1, \ldots, q_n\} \notin M_0$. On the other hand it is easy to see, from the definition of M_0, that $M_0 \supseteq H$, whatever the value of n.

We could simply use the set M_0 as the set L in Section 7.3.6, and use (10.13) for determining whether an unknown pair of patterns belongs to B. But we can do better than this, as follows. Suppose that H_k is used as the set L in Section 7.3.6, and that the unknown pair of patterns is in fact a member of B_k^*. As before, H_k is the set of all members of N_q which are n-tuples of members of J_k. From the definitions of Q_0 and L_0 in Section 7.3.6, $Q_0 \supseteq J_k$, and, since $L = H_k$, $L_0 = H_k$. Let $\{\alpha, \beta\}$ be any member of J_k, and let m_i be the number of members of F to which α belongs. Any member of F belongs to at least one member of H_k, and therefore $\{\alpha, \beta\}$ belongs to at least m_i members of H_k. Therefore, since $H_k = L_0$, $Q_1 \supseteq J_k$ and $L_1 = H_k$. Similarly we can show that $H_k = L_w$.

In general, the set L_w depends on the choice of the unknown pair of patterns, and it is convenient now to use subscripts to distinguish between the L_w's which are obtained with different unknown pairs of patterns. In particular, let L_{kiw} be the L_w which is obtained when the ith member of B_k^* is used as the unknown pair of patterns. Let L_{jw} be the L_w which is obtained when the jth member of B^* is used as the unknown pair of patterns.

We have seen that, if $L = H_k$, and a member of B_k^* is used as the unknown pair of patterns, then $H_k = L_w$. In other words, if $L = H_k$, then $H_k = L_{k1w} = L_{k2w} = \ldots = L_{kiw} = \ldots = L_{k|B_k^*|w}$. If $L = H$ then, since $H_k \subseteq H$, it follows that $H_k \subseteq L_{k1w}, H_k \subseteq L_{k2w}, \ldots, H_k \subseteq L_{kiw}, \ldots, H_k \subseteq L_{k|B_k^*|w}$. Similarly, if $L = M_0$, then, since $H_k \subseteq H \subseteq M_0$, it follows that $H_k \subseteq L_{k1w}, H_k \subseteq L_{k2w}, \ldots, H_k \subseteq L_{kiw}, \ldots, H_k \subseteq L_{k|B_k^*|w}$. Therefore, if $L = M_0$, any member of H_k belongs to every one of the $|B_k^*|$ members of the set $\{L_{k1w}, \ldots, L_{k|B_k^*|w}\}$.

Because $t \leqslant |B_k^*|$, it follows that any member of H_k belongs to at least t members of the set $\{L_{1w}, L_{2w}, \ldots, L_{jw}, \ldots, L_{|B^*|\,w}\}$. Therefore, if $L = M_0$, any member of H belongs to at least t members of the set $\{L_{1w}, \ldots, L_{|B^*|\,w}\}$. Therefore $M_1 \supseteq H$, where M_1 is the set of all members of M_0 such that any given member of M_1 belongs to at least t members of the set $\{L_{1w}, \ldots, L_{|B^*|\,w}\}$ when $L = M_0$. Similarly we can show that $M_2 \supseteq H$, where M_2 is the set of all members of M_1 such that any given member of M_2 belongs to at least t members of the set $\{L_{1w}, \ldots, L_{|B^*|\,w}\}$ when $L = M_1$. Similarly we can show that $M_3 \supseteq H$, where M_3 is the set of all members of M_2 such that any given member of M_3 belongs to at least t members of the set $\{L_{1w}, \ldots, L_{|B^*|\,w}\}$ when $L = M_2$. Let M_ω be the first set in the series $M_0, M_1, M_2, M_3, M_4, \ldots$ such that $M_\omega = M_{\omega-1}$. Each set in this series includes H, and therefore $M_\omega \supseteq H$. Because $|M_0|$ is finite and $M_g \supseteq M_{g-1}$ for all $g = 1, 2, 3, \ldots$, the value of ω must be finite. Because $M_0 \supseteq M_\omega \supseteq H$, the number of members of M_ω which do not belong to H is generally less than the number of members of M_0 which do not belong to H. When (10.13) is used for determining whether an unknown pair of patterns belongs to B, it is desirable that the number of members of L which do not belong to H should be as small as possible. Therefore it is preferable to use $M_\omega = L$ instead of $M_0 = L$ in the computation of L_w for use in (10.13).

The members of M_ω can be determined by the following iterative procedure:

(1) Assign to M_0 all members of N_q which are isochromatic in at least t members of B^*.
(2) Using $L = M_0$, compute $\{L_{1w}, \ldots, L_{|B^*|\,w}\}$.
(3) Assign to M_1 all members of M_0 which belong to at least t members of $\{L_{1w}, \ldots, L_{|B^*|\,w}\}$.
(4) Using $L = M_1$, compute $\{L_{1w}, \ldots, L_{|B^*|\,w}\}$.
(5) Assign to M_2 all members of M_1 which belong to at least t members of $\{L_{1w}, \ldots, L_{|B^*|\,w}\}$.
(6) Continue the series $M_1, M_2, \ldots$ until $M_\omega = M_{\omega-1}$.

10.3.5 Training sets

We now consider the problem of obtaining the training set B^*. Let $R_1^*, \ldots, R_r^*, \ldots, R_z^*$ be preclassified training sets of patterns belonging to the recognition classes $R_1, \ldots, R_r, \ldots, R_z$ respectively; and let C^* be the set of all pairs of patterns belonging to $R_1^*, \ldots, R_z^*$ such that in any given member of C^* the two patterns belong to the same recognition class. A member of C^* is not necessarily a member of B. For instance, the pair of characters 7 , 7 , may not be related by any of the distortions $U_1, \ldots, U_\beta$, and therefore may not belong to B. Let C_{B^*} be the intersection $C_{B^*} = C^* \cap B$, and let $C_{\bar{B}^*}$ be the set of all members of C^* which do not belong to B.

It is not practical to use C_{B^*} as the training set B^*, because we do not know whether any given member of C^* belongs to C_{B^*} or to $C_{\bar{B}^*}$. If we simply use C^* as the set B^*, and if $|C_{\bar{B}^*}| \ll |C_{B^*}|$, it is possible that, if the jth member of $B^* = C^*$ is in fact a member of $C_{\bar{B}^*}$, then, because this member of $C_{\bar{B}^*}$ does not belong to B, the set L_{jw} may be empty when, for instance, $L = M_1$. In this case, this member of $C_{\bar{B}^*}$ will make no further contribution to the determination of M_ω. Thus it is possible that, when C^* is used as the training set B^*, $|M_\omega|$ is not very much larger than it would be if C_{B^*} were used as the training set B^*.

Henceforward we shall use C^* as the training set B^*. The value of t is not available, and instead of t we use a number which is to be optimised by experimental trial and error.

10.3.6 Degeneration

10.3.6.1 Degeneration in recognition

To recognise an unknown pattern X, we could pair X with each training set pattern in turn. Each of the pairs $\{X_{11}, X\}$, $\{X_{12}, X\}$, $\ldots, \{X_{ri}, X\}, \ldots, \{X_{z\,|R_z^*|}, X\}$ could be tested for membership of B by using (10.13) with $L = M_\omega$, and X could be recognised in accordance with (10.2). This would require computation of L_w for each of the pairs $\{X_{11}, X\}, \ldots, \{X_{ri}, X\}, \ldots, \{X_{z\,|R_z^*|}, X\}$ in turn. This requirement for a generally impractical amount of computation can, at the cost of worsening error rates, be avoided by using the idea of *degeneration*, as in Section 5.3.

Let L_{ri0} be the set of all members of L which are isochromatic in $\{X_{ri}, X\}$, and let L_{r0} be the union

$$L_{r0} = L_{r10} \cup L_{r20} \cup \ldots \cup L_{ri0} \cup \ldots \cup L_{r\,|R_r^*|\,0}$$

For $g = 1, 2, 3, \ldots$, let Q_{rg} be the subset of Q such that q_i belongs to

Q_{rg} if and only if q_i belongs to at least m_i members of L_{g-1}, where m_i is the same as in Section 7.3.6. Let L_{rg} be the set of all members of L_{rg-1} such that any member of L_{rg} contains n members of Q_{rg}; and let L_{rw} be the first member of the sequence $L_{ro}, L_{r1}, L_{r2}, \ldots$ such that $L_{rw} = L_{rw-1}$.

Instead of using (10.2), we could assign X to the rth class if

$$\left.\begin{array}{l}\text{(1) every member of } F \text{ belongs to at least one member} \\ \quad \text{of } L_{wr}, \text{ and} \\ \text{(2) every member of } T \text{ belongs to at least one member} \\ \quad \text{of } L_{wr}.\end{array}\right\} \tag{10.14}$$

Since $L_{ro} \supseteq L_{rio}$, it follows that $L_{rw} \supseteq L_{riw}$, and if X is assigned to the rth class by (10.2) using (10.13), then X is also assigned to the rth class by (10.14), but unfortunately the converse is not true. Rule (10.14) has the advantage that L_{rw} is computed only once for the rth class, whereas rule (10.2) requires separate computation of L_{riw} for each member of R_r^*.

Furthermore, if (10.14) is used, it is not necessary to store the rth class training set, and instead we only need store the sets $A_{r1}, \ldots, A_{rj}, \ldots, A_{r\phi}$, where A_{rj} is the set of all states of F_j which occur in at least one member of R_r^*, and F_j is the jth member of F, (cf. Section 7.5.3). To see this, note that the member $\{\{\alpha_1, \beta_1\}, \ldots, \{\alpha_n, \beta_n\}\}$ of L belongs to L_{ro} if and only if there exists a value of j in the range $j = 1, \ldots, \phi$ such that

(1) $\{\alpha_1, \ldots, \alpha_n\} = F_j$, and
(2) the state of $\{\beta_1, \ldots, \beta_n\}$ in X is the same as a state of $\{\alpha_1, \ldots, \alpha_n\}$ which belongs to A_{rj}.

Using this, the members of L_{ro} can be determined from X and $A_{r1}, \ldots, A_{rj}, \ldots, A_{r\phi}$.

10.3.6.2 Degeneration in determination of M_0

The members of M_0 could be determined as follows:

(1) Obtain all members of C^* by pairing all members of R_r^*, for $r = 1, \ldots, z$.
(2) Work through all members of N_q in turn and assign to M_0 any member of N_q which is isochromatic in at least t members of C^*.

This is in fact an unnecessarily laborious method of determining M_0, and we now introduce a degenerate method which gives exactly the same result, that is, exactly the same set M_0, without pairing all members of R_r^* for all $r = 1, \ldots, z$.

Let $\{\{\alpha_1, \beta_1\}, \ldots, \{\alpha_n, \beta_n\}\}$ be any member of N_q, and let the 2^n possible states of $\{\alpha_1, \ldots, \alpha_n\}$ and $\{\beta_1, \ldots, \beta_n\}$ be indexed so that $\{\alpha_1, \ldots, \alpha_n\}$ and $\{\beta_1, \ldots, \beta_n\}$ are in the *same* state if and only if $\{\{\alpha_1, \beta_1\}, \ldots, \{\alpha_n, \beta_n\}\}$ is isochromatic. Let ν_{hri} be the number of members of R_r^* in which $\{\alpha_1, \ldots, \alpha_n\}$ is in the ith state, and let ν_{jri} be the number of members of R_r^* in which $\{\beta_1, \ldots, \beta_n\}$ is in the ith state. It is easy to see that $\nu_{hri} \times \nu_{jri}$ is the number of pairs of members of R_r^* in which $\{\alpha_1, \ldots, \alpha_n\}$ and $\{\beta_1, \ldots, \beta_n\}$ are both in the ith state, so that $\{\{\alpha_1, \beta_1\}, \ldots, \{\alpha_n, \beta_n\}\}$ is isochromatic. Thus the total number of pairs of members of R_r^* in which $\{\{\alpha_1, \beta_1\}, \ldots, \{\alpha_n, \beta_n\}\}$ is isochromatic is

$$\sum_{i=1}^{2^n} \nu_{hri} \times \nu_{jri}$$

and the total number of members of C^* in which $\{\{\alpha_1, \beta_1\}, \ldots, \{\alpha_n, \beta_n\}\}$ is isochromatic is

$$\sum_{r=1}^{z} \sum_{i=1}^{2^n} \nu_{hri} \times \nu_{jri} \qquad (10.15)$$

The members of M_0 can be determined by the following procedure:

(1) For all possible n-tuples, that is, for all h, including $h = j$, determine the values of $\nu_{h11}, \nu_{h12}, \ldots, \nu_{h12^n}, \nu_{h21}, \ldots, \nu_{h22^n}, \ldots, \nu_{hz2^n}$.

(2) For each member of N_q in turn, compute the value of expression (10.15), and assign to M_0 any member of N_q for which the value of expression (10.15) is not less than t.

In this, the set N_q consists of all members of F paired with all possible n-tuples of elements of T: but this has been stipulated only for the sake of theoretical tractability, and adequate results may perhaps be obtained by using a large number, rather than all possible, n-tuples of elements of T.

10.3.6.3 Degeneration in determination of M_ω

Determination of M_ω by the procedure given at the end of Section 10.3.4 would involve much computation, and we now give a procedure for determining a set M'_ω which, at the cost of worsening error rates, can be used instead of M_ω as L in Section 7.3.5 or Section 10.3.6.1. The advantage of using M'_ω is that the determination of M'_ω requires less computation than the determination of M_ω. Note that M_ω or M'_ω only has to be determined once for given R^*, and does not have to be determined again for each unknown pattern which is recognised. Therefore the problem of reducing the computation in the determination of M_ω is not so important as the problem of avoiding the computation required by (10.2) and (10.13).

Let P be the set of all pairs of bits such that in any given member of P

(1) the two bits are either both black or both white, and
(2) the two bits are in the same member of Q.

A member of Q is a pair of bit *locations*, whereas a member of P is a pair of bits. As usual, let q_i be the ith member of Q. Let p_{i1} be the member of P which consists of two black bits in q_i, and let p_{i0} be the member of P which consists of two white bits in q_i. Let p_{iy} be any member of P whose two bits are in q_i: thus $y = 1$ or 0.

Let K_{r0} be the set of all n-tuples of members of P such that, in any member of K_{r0},

(1) the n members of P are respectively in the n pairs $\{\alpha_1, \beta_1\}$, . . ., $\{\alpha_n, \beta_n\}$ which constitute a member of M_0, and
(2) the n members of P are such that the state of $\{\alpha_1, . . ., \alpha_n\}$ occurs in at least one member of R_r^* and the state of $\{\beta_1, . . ., \beta_n\}$ occurs in at least one member of R_r^*.

Let P_{r1} be the subset of P_{r0} such that p_{iy} belongs to P_{r1} if and only if p_{iy} belongs to at least m_i members of K_{r0}, where m_i is the same as in Section 7.3.6 (*see* p. 197). For $g = 1, 2, . . .$, let K_{rg} be the set of all members of K_{rg-1} such that any given member of K_{rg} contains n members of P_{rg}. Let P_{rg} be the subset of P_{rg-1} such that p_{iy} belongs to P_{rg} if and only if p_{iy} belongs to at least m_i members of K_{rg-1}. Let K_{rw} be the first member of the series $K_{r0}, K_{r1}, K_{r2}, . . .$ such that

$K_{rw} = K_{rw-1}$. Let δ_{hjri} be a variable which has the value 1 if, when $\{\alpha_1, \ldots, \alpha_n\}$ and $\{\beta_1, \ldots, \beta_n\}$ are both in the ith state, the pairs of bits in $\{\alpha_1, \beta_1\}, \ldots, \{\alpha_n, \beta_n\}$ constitute a member of K_{rw}, and $\delta_{hjri} = 0$ otherwise.

A procedure for determining the set M' is

(1) Compute M_0 by the method of Section 10.3.6.2, and compute K_{rw} for all $r = 1, \ldots, z$.
(2) Assign to M'_1 all members of M_0 such that

$$t \leqslant \sum_{r=1}^{z} \sum_{i=1}^{2^n} \delta_{hjri} \times \nu_{hri} \times \nu_{jri} \tag{10.16}$$

(3) Using M'_1 instead of M_0, compute K_{rw} for all $r = 1, \ldots, z$.
(4) Assign to M'_2 all members of M'_1 such that (10.16) holds.
(5) Continue the series $M'_2, M'_3, \ldots$ until $M'_\omega = M'_{\omega-1}$.

From the construction of M'_ω it is obvious that $M_0 \supseteq M'_\omega$. To see that $M'_\omega \supseteq M_\omega$, let L_{fw} be the set L_w when the fth member of B^* is used as the unknown pair of patterns in Section 7.3.6. Here we are using the subscript f in place of the subscript j which was used in Section 10.3.4, to avoid confusion. Let K'_{fw} be the set of all n-tuples of members of P such that, in any member of K'_{fw},

(1) the n members of P are respectively in the n pairs $\{\alpha_1, \beta_1\}$ $\ldots, \{\alpha_n, \beta_n\}$ which constitute a member of L_{fw}, and
(2) the n members of P are such that the state of $\{\alpha_1, \ldots, \alpha_n\}$ is the state of $\{\alpha_1, \ldots, \alpha_n\}$ in the fth member of B^*.

The procedure given at the end of Section 10.3.4 assigns to M_g all members of M_{g-1} which belong to at least t members of the set $\{L_{1w}, \ldots, L_{|B^*|w}\}$. Thus a member of M_{g-1} is assigned to M_g if it contains a member of each of at least t of the sets $K'_{1w}, \ldots, K'_{fw}, \ldots, K'_{|B^*|w}$. If the two patterns which constitute the fth member of B^* belong to R^*_r, then $K'_{fw} \subseteq K_{rw}$. Therefore, from the definition of δ_{hjri}, it follows that δ_{hjri} has the value 1 if the pairs of bits in $\{\alpha_1, \beta_1\}$, $\ldots, \{\alpha_n, \beta_n\}$ constitute a member of K'_{fw}. Therefore any member of M_{g-1} which contains a member of each of at least t of the sets K'_{1w}, $\ldots, K'_{|B^*|w}$ is such that (10.16) holds. Hence it follows that $M'_g \supseteq M_g$ and $M'_\omega \supseteq M_\omega$.

10.3.7 Discussion

10.3.7.1 The value of n

In the recognition system of Section 10.3.6.1, if the value of n is very small, error rates may be high, and if n is not very small, e.g. if $n > 3$, the system may be economically impractical. To avoid this difficulty we can redevelop the system so that it maps black/white boundaries rather than individual bits, and so that it exploits continuity of distortions.The theory has been outlined above in its simplest form, not in its most practical form.

10.3.7.2 A grammatical inference problem

Figure 10.4 shows a few of the rewrite rules of a grammar (cf. Figure 8.7) which generates all the pairs of patterns which belong to B. In Section 10.3.4 we have considered the grammatical inference problem: given some members of B, but not give the rules of the grammar which generates B, determine whether or not any given pair of patterns belongs to B. In Section 10.3.4 we did not attempt to determine the rewrite rules of a grammar which generates B. Indeed it does not appear to be possible to determine the rewrite rules automatically, and, even if it were possible, it would not be practical to use the rewrite rules in a conventional manner in recognition, because the number β is very large. (cf. the problem of proportion at the end of Section 8.3.2.1.)

10.3.7.3 Normalisation by exhaustive trial

Let T_k be the partition on T such that each subset of T_k is the intersection of T with a subset of U_k. If, in an unknown pattern X, each subset of T_k contains only 1's or only 0's, then it is easy to construct a pattern X_k on S such that in $\{X_k, X\}$ each subset of U_k contains only 1's or only 0's, and therefore $\{X_k, X\}$ belongs to B.

Recognition rule (10.2) gives the same results as the procedure: for each $k = 1, \ldots, \beta$ (where possible) construct X_k from X, and assign X to the rth class if, for any $i = 1, \ldots, |R_r^*|$,

$$X_k = X_{ri} \qquad (10.17)$$

Construction of X_k from X can be regarded as *normalisation* of X with respect to the *distortion* U_k. Recognition using (10.17) exemplifies the familiar process of normalisation by *exhaustive trial* (Section 6.6.3).

There may be more than one value of k such that a given pattern X is correctly recognised by (10.17). But the values of k when different unknown patterns – different X's – are recognised by (10.17) are generally different. In other words, different patterns are normally recognised after normalisation for different distortions. In this sense, different patterns are generally recognised by (10.17) after different transformations.

Section 5.6.1 provides a simple example of a system in which any unknown input pattern is transformed into a further pattern whose elements are the results of tests which have been applied to the input pattern. This transformation is the same whatever the unknown input pattern: the same peephole masks are used in the same way whatever the input pattern. In a system such as this, the transformation is required to be such that transformed patterns can be recognised reliably by means of an economical discriminant system.

For reliable recognition of, for instance, unconstrained hand-printed numerals, 0, . . ., 9 and letters A, . . ., Z, it may never be possible to find *one* transformation which can be applied to *all* input patterns so that patterns resulting from the transformation can be recognised directly and reliably by means of an economical discriminant system. Instead it may be necessary to employ the more powerful technique of using a generally *different* transformation for every different input pattern, as in normalisation by exhaustive trial (cf. Ref. 175). It would be economically prohibitive to normalise by exhaustive trial for all of the distortions U_1, . . ., U_β where β is large. In Section 10.3.3 we have attempted to obtain more or less the same results as would be obtained by normalisation by exhaustive trial, but without separate computation for each of $U_1, \ldots, U_\beta$. Note in particular that, in trial, (10.17), the distortions on X_{ri} and X. In a system such as the Section 5.6.1 system, the transformed pattern depends only on X.

For introductory simplicity, rule (10.2) has been used as the starting point of the theory of Section 10.3. A rule which maximises or minimises a score may give better practical results than (10.2) or (10.17). A very simple example of this is the rule: for each $k = 1, \ldots, \beta$, for each $r = 1, \ldots, z$, and for each $i = 1, \ldots, |R_r^*|$, compute the Hamming distance between X_{ri} and X_k, and assign X to the class

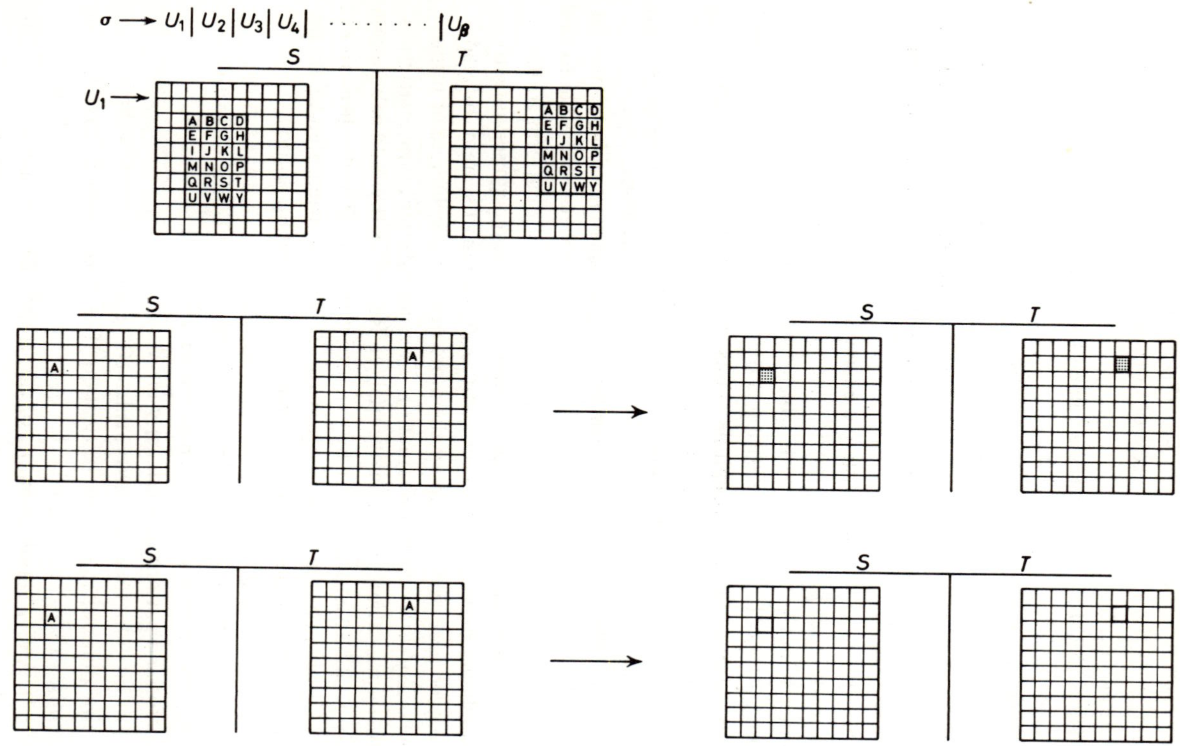

σ → U1 | U2 | U3 | U4 | .... | Uβ
S
T
U1 →
A B C D
E F G H
I J K L
M N O P
Q R S T
U V W Y
A B C D
E F G H
I J K L
M N O P
Q R S T
U V W Y
S
T
A
A
S
T
S
T
A
A
S
T

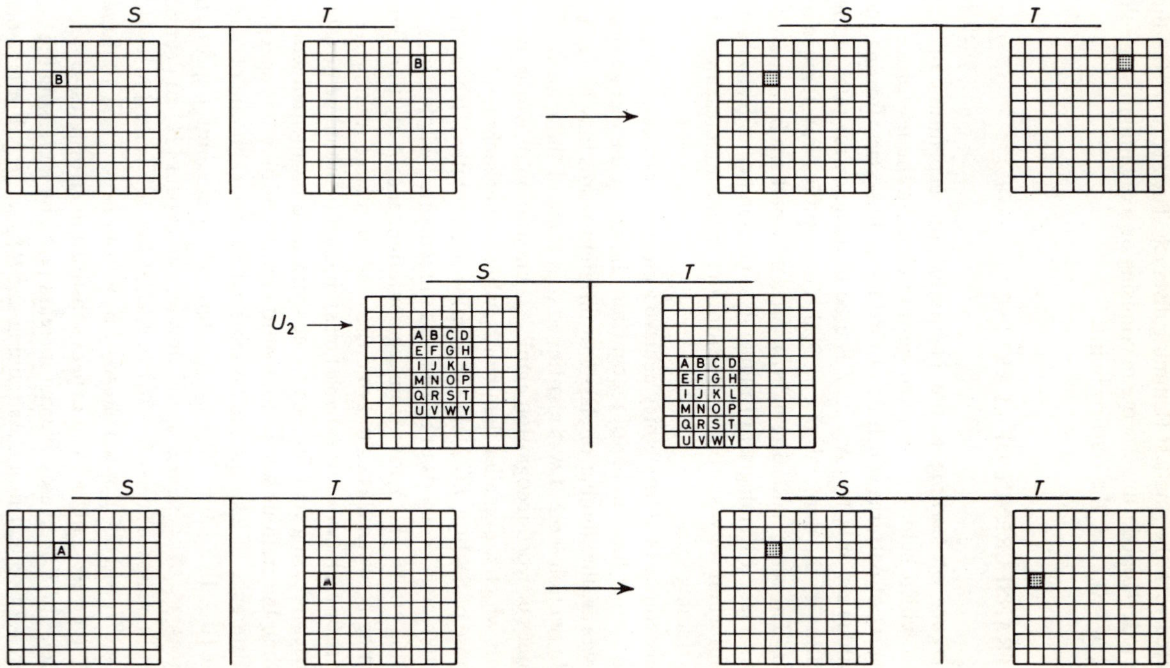

Figure 10.4. *A few of the rewrite rules of a grammar which generates all members of B*

associated with the smallest Hamming distance. The Section 10.3 theory can be redeveloped using a score maximising or score minimising rule, instead of (10.2), as the starting point.

10.4 TRANSFERENCE OF LEARNING

Transference of learning is the facilitation of recognition of patterns which belong to one recognition class by the use of a training set of patterns which do not belong to that class. For instance, if a training set of letters A, . . ., Z is used to reduce error rates in the recognition of the numerals 0, . . ., 9, this exemplifies transference of learning. The same reduction of error rates may perhaps be achieved by using a larger training set of numerals. Transference of learning may be useful when we wish to reduce error rates without increasing the size of training sets.

Transference of learning may achieve a greater reduction of error rates the larger the number of recognition classes. In the recognition of whole words, the number of classes of different words may be very large. In Section 9.6.6 it was mentioned that some of the known techniques of word recognition employ segmentation of words into segments which are smaller than words, whilst other techniques (e.g. those of Section 9.6.2) do not employ segmentation. It may be useful to recognise words or syllables as unsegmented wholes, thus mitigating errors which arise from segmentation, and to use transference of learning between classes to avoid the need for a large training set of members of each (word or syllable) class. Indeed it should be possible for a machine using transference to recognise an unsegmented word even when the training set for that word consists of only one specimen.

Transference of learning can be achieved by the technique of Section 10.3. In Section 10.3 we can, up to a certain limit, expect $|H_k|$ to decrease as $|B_k^*|$ increases, and thus we can expect $|H|$ to decrease as $|B^*|$ increases. The set $L = M_\omega$ or the set $L = M'_\omega$ is used instead of the set H, and C^* is used instead of B. We can expect $|L|$ to decrease as $|C^*|$ increases, and we can expect substitution error rates to decrease as $|L|$ decreases. We can increase $|C^*|$ by increasing the number, z, of recognition class training sets $R_1^*, \ldots, R_z^*$. For instance, when $z = 10$, $|C^*|$ will be smaller, and therefore substitution error rates will be larger, than when $z = 36$. When $z = 36$, the error rates in the recognition of patterns belonging to $R_1, \ldots, R_{10}$ can be expected to be lower than when $z = 10$, in which case recognition of patterns belonging to $R_1, \ldots, R_{10}$ is improved by transference. A simplified version of the Section 10.3 system has provided a poor, but apparently positive, experimental demonstration of transference[443].

In loose general terms, the underlying idea is as follows. Roughly *as if* in normalisation by exhaustive trial, (10.17), the distortions $U_1, \ldots, U_\beta$ are used in the recognition of patterns. The Section 10.3 system behaves very roughly *as if* it automatically determines $U_1, \ldots, U_\beta$ from a training set of characters. Since all recognition classes are subject to the same distortions $U_1, \ldots, U_\beta$, it does not matter which recognition classes provide the training set C^* from which $U_1, \ldots, U_\beta$ are determined. For instance $U_1, \ldots, U_\beta$ may be determined from training sets only of the letters A, . . ., Z and then be used in the recognition of the numerals 0, . . ., 9.

Section 10.3 does not provide the only possible means of achieving transference, and as a very trivial example we now introduce a further system which exhibits transference. In this example, the problem is to recognise whole words, and the system stores all of the different words which are to be recognised. Let us say that each of the stored words is randomly assigned to one of the two sets, D_1 or D_2. The words belonging to D_1 are segmented into characters, and these characters are used as a training set from which one weight vector per character recognition class is determined. If these weight vectors are used in Section 8.1.1 for recognition of words belonging to D_2, this exemplifies transference, because the words which belong to D_2 have not been used in determining weight vectors.

In general, transference can be achieved by learning something which is useful in recognition and independent of recognition class.

10.5 ASSOCIATIVE MEMORY

To provide a background for a general discussion of learning in pattern recognition, we now very briefly discuss computer memory. There are two sorts of computer memory: conventional and associative. In a conventional memory, an item is stored at an address which is not determined *by* the item. For instance, the number of a patent may serve as the address of the patent specification in a patent library, but the number of the patent is not determined by the technical content of the specification.

A *content addressed* or *associative* memory differs from a conventional memory in that a stored item, or a portion of a stored item, is used as the address of that item[199]. A telephone directory is essentially a collection of name/number pairs. We use a name alphabetically to find a required name/number pair. This exemplifies associative addressing, since part (the name) of a stored item (the name/number pair) is used to locate (or address) that item.

To illustrate more clearly what is meant by conventional and associative memory let us consider the storage of binary patterns. In this context, a binary pattern is usually called a *word*. By way of example, Figure 10.5 shows five columns of four cells, the cells being as shown in Figure 10.6, except that connections to channels C and D for cells in the left-hand column are interchanged as indicated in Figure 10.5.

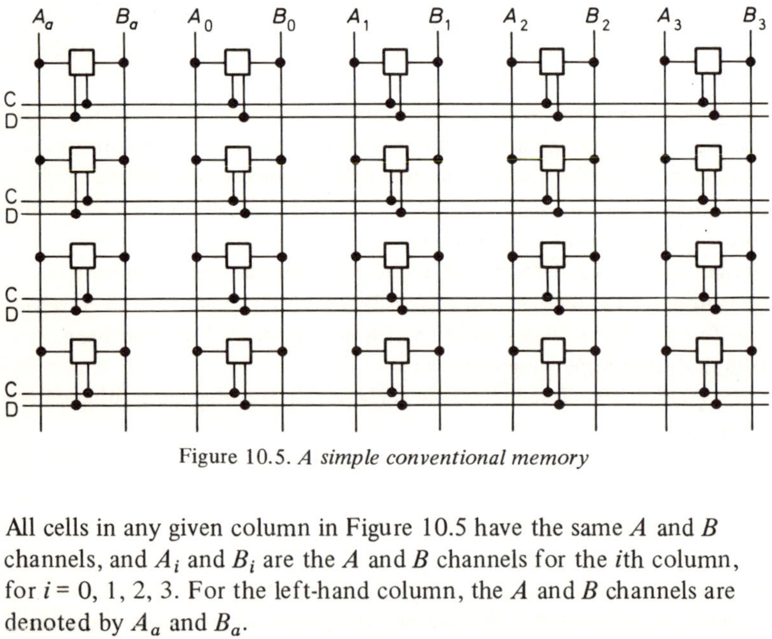

Figure 10.5. *A simple conventional memory*

All cells in any given column in Figure 10.5 have the same A and B channels, and A_i and B_i are the A and B channels for the ith column, for $i = 0, 1, 2, 3$. For the left-hand column, the A and B channels are denoted by A_a and B_a.

If all A and B channels except B_a and A_i are in state '0', then the 4-bit pattern in the bistables in the left-hand column of Figure 10.5 is copied into the bistables in the ith column. Conversely, if all A and B channels except A_a and B_i are in state '0', then the 4-bit pattern in the ith column is copied into the left-hand column. Transfers of this sort are useful when logical and arithmetical operations are done on the

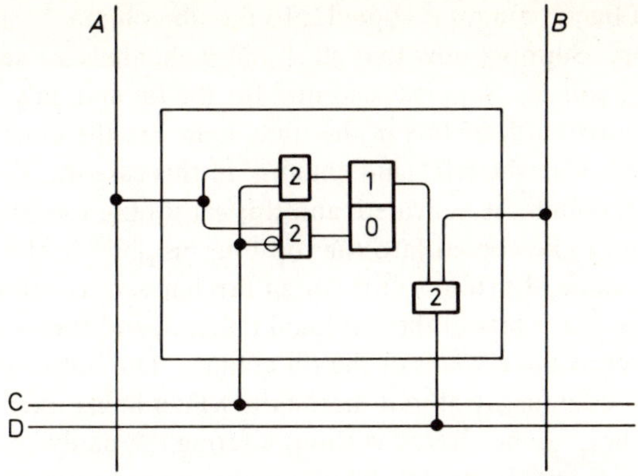

Figure 10.6. *Logic circuit of any cell in Figure* 10.5

pattern in the left-hand column. The raw data for these operations can be obtained from the right-hand columns, and the results can be returned to these columns. Instead of having four storage columns of 4-bit words, a big digital computer might have 256 000 columns of 36-bit words.

In order to store or retrieve a pattern in or from the *i*th column, it is necessary to specify the value of i, so that A_i or B_i can be activated. In a conventional memory system, one value of i is permanently associated with each storage column, and successive columns have successive i-values. The i-value of a column is its *address*. In a conventional memory, if there are M storage columns, the range of addresses is $i = 0, 1, 2, \ldots, (M - 1)$.

An essential difference between a conventional and an associative memory is that, in an associative memory, if there are M storage columns, the addresses of these columns are not confined to the range $0, \ldots, (M - 1)$. The address of a column, at least for the purpose of copying a pattern out of that column, is not permanently associated with that column, but is assigned arbitrarily, and can be altered at will without altering the hardware.

Figure 10.7 is a diagram of a simple associative memory. The cells marked 'X' are as shown in Figure 10.8, and all other cells in Figure 10.7 are as shown in Figure 10.6. Thus the top four rows of cells in Figure 10.7 constitute precisely the Figure 10.5 network. If all A and B channels are set to '0' except for B_a, B_b, and A_i, then the 7-bit pattern from the left-hand column is copied into the *i*th column, as in a conventional memory. Suppose now that all *A* and *B* channels are set to '0' except for A_a and B_b. Suppose also that for the *i*th and only the *i*th column, the bottom three bits in the *i*th column are the same as the bottom three bits in the left-hand column. In this case the 3-input *and* gate in the *i*th column is activated, and this causes the top four bits in the *i*th column to be copied into the top four bistables in the left-hand column. The value of *i* (if any) for which this happens is determined by the bottom three bits in the left-hand column, and therefore these three bits serve as the *address* of the *i*th column. The bottom three bits in the *i*th column are stored there rather than being fixed permanently, and they can be altered without altering the hardware. Note that the top four bits in the left-hand column are meaningless unless one of the 3-input *and* gates is activated.

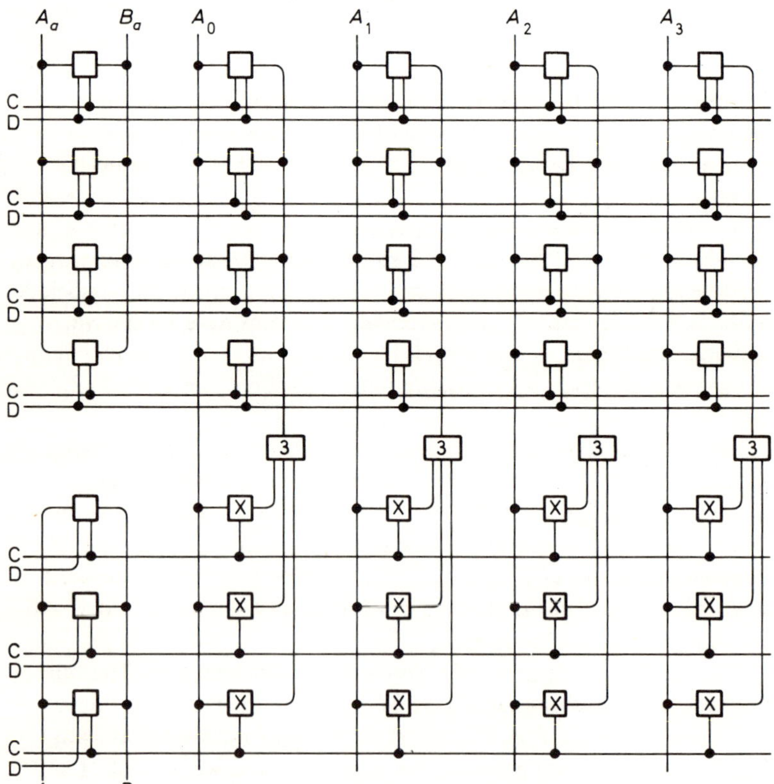

Figure 10.7. *A simple associative memory*

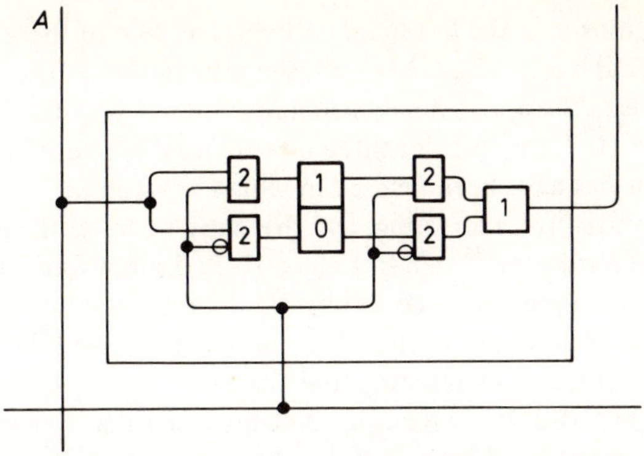

Figure 10.8. *Logic circuit of any cell marked 'X' in Figure* 10.7

Suppose, for instance, that we wish to store the pairs of binary numbers {010, 0110}, {011, 1010}, {110, 1111}, {111, 0100}, and that given the left-hand three bits of a pair we wish the associative memory to provide the right-hand four bits. The four (3 + 4)-bit patterns could be stored in the four right-hand columns of Figure 10.7, the leftmost bit of each pattern being at the bottom. If, for instance, the bottom three bits in the left-hand column were set to be 011, and all A and B channels were set to '0' except for A_a and B_b, then 1010 would be copied from the memory into the top four bistables of the left-hand column, as required. An alternative technique would be to use a conventional memory with eight 4-bit words, and store 0110 in the word with address 010, store 1010 in the word with address 011, and so on. The left-hand three bits would be the address of the right-hand three bits. This would have the disadvantage that four out of the eight words of store would be unused. In general, if we wish to store M words, each with an address which is a random N-bit pattern, an advantage of using an associative memory is that it only needs hardware for storing M words, rather than 2^N words, and this is important if $M \ll 2^N$. On the other hand, the hardware of associative memory is usually more elaborate and expensive than that of conventional memory. Furthermore, conventional memory, at the cost of a limited amount of serial searching, can be made to behave like associative memory by means of a technique called *hash coding*[223].

We have just considered an example in which the 3-bit patterns in the four pairs were all different. If two had been the same, two 4-bit patterns would sometimes have been candidates for being copied from storage columns into the left-hand column, and one of these 4-bit patterns would have to have been chosen arbitrarily. Arbitrary selection of this sort is necessary in many associative memory systems[199, 306].

In Figure 10.7, the bottom three bits are used for addressing. Associative memories have been devised in which *any* subset of the bits in a word can be used for addressing, and this subset can be changed without changing the hardware[135, 306]. In Figure 10.7, the top four bits of the *i*th column are copied into the left-hand column if the bottom three bits in the *i*th column are *identical* to the bottom three bits in the left-hand column. Instead of insisting that these two 3-bit patterns be *identical*, other associative memory systems insist that one of these patterns, regarded as a binary number, be greater than, less than or equal to, numerically the next higher to, or bear some other computable relationship to, the other[199].

10.6 SCIENTIFIC BASIS OF AUTOMATIC PATTERN RECOGNITION

10.6.1 Design of a recognition system without automatic learning

If we are to assign a handwritten character to the recognition class which the writer intended, we may perhaps need to know the context of that character in a word, the nationality (culture) and era (time in history) of the writer[464]; and perhaps, in some cases, it may also be necessary to be familiar with the writing habits of that particular writer and the circumstances under which the character was written. This illustrates the idea that membership of a given pattern in a given recognition class may be conditional on many factors, e.g. context, culture, era[262, 468]. To design a machine which could recognise *any* character which a human could recognise, it would presumably be necessary to take account of such factors. We do not yet know how to design a machine which could recognise *any* character which a human could recognise. Instead, at the present state of the art, we only attempt to design machines which recognise *limited* ranges of character shapes. Roughly speaking, the more we limit the ranges of character shapes, the less we need to use context in order to achieve reliable recognition.

In order to simplify the following introductory discussion, we shall rule out the use of context altogether. We shall consider a problem of designing a machine to recognise unconstrained hand-printed numerals on envelopes in the mail, there being only one numeral on each envelope. To be specific let us say that the numeral on any given envelope is written in a pre-printed box, and that the contents of this box are binarised 40 x 40. Let $\{X_1, X_2, \ldots, X_p\}$ be the set of all 40 x 40-bit patterns which ever occur in practice in this recognition problem.

We can regard the output of a recognition machine as a symbol which indicates the recognition or reject class to which the machine has assigned the input pattern. Let $\nabla_M(X)$ be the output of a given machine when the input pattern is X, and let Φ_M be the function

$$\Phi_M = \{\{X_1, \nabla_M(X_1)\}, \{X_2, \nabla_M(X_2)\}, \ldots, \{X_p, \nabla_M(X_p)\}\}$$

Let $\nabla_C(X)$ be the recognition or reject class to which the machine designer would intuitively assign X, and let Φ_C be the function

$$\Phi_C = \{X_1, \nabla_C(X_1)\}, \{X_2, \nabla_C(X_2)\}, \ldots, \{X_p, \nabla_C(X_p)\}$$

The classification table of Section 6.4.4 is an expression of Φ_C: in the row of the classification table which contains X, the $(N + 1)$th entry is $\nabla_C(X)$. We would regard a machine such that $\Phi_M = \Phi_C$ as a solution to our recognition problem. (Note that, since the use of context has been ruled out, we do not require the recognition machine to produce an estimate of the likelihood that X is a '0', an estimate of the likelihood that X is a '1', an estimate of the likelihood that X is a '2', and so on.)

In practice, the function Φ_C is unknown, and therefore we cannot deduce from Φ_C the design of a machine such that $\Phi_C = \Phi_M$. Instead, we can design the machine intuitively[181], and test experimentally whether $\nabla_M(X) = \nabla_C(X)$ for a large number of X's, preferably chosen at random from $\{X_1, \ldots, X_p\}$. If we find that $\nabla_M(X) \neq \nabla_C(X)$ for an intolerably large number of X's, we can modify the machine, and again test experimentally whether $\nabla_M(X) = \nabla_C(X)$ for a large number of X's. If we still find that $\nabla_M(X) \neq \nabla_C(X)$ for an intolerably large number of X's, we can again modify the machine, and so on. Modification of the machine can be based on an intuitive study of the actual cases where $\nabla_M(X) \neq \nabla_C(X)$. Because the number, p, of X's in the set $\{X_1, \ldots, X_p\}$ is astronomical, we cannot in practice test whether $\nabla_M(X) = \nabla_C(X)$ for *all* $X = X_1, \ldots, X_p$. In other words, it is not practical to test experimentally whether $\Phi_M = \Phi_C$; and this is why we have to make do with testing whether $\nabla_M(X) = \nabla_C(X)$ for a large number of X's.

This experimental design process is in fact a scientific process of hypothesis formation and testing. When we intuitively design the recognition machine, we implicitly hypothesise that the design of the machine is such that $\Phi_M = \Phi_C$. We test this hypothesis by testing experimentally whether $\nabla_M(X) = \nabla_C(X)$ for many X's. When we subsequently modify the machine, we modify the hypothesis.

For recognising numerals on envelopes, the detailed design of a machine such that $\Phi_M = \Phi_C$ may inevitably turn out to be very complicated. To mitigate the costly and burdensome work of designing a (presumably) very complicated machine by intuition and experimental trial and error, we can attempt to automate at least part of the process of designing the recognition machine. For instance, weights may be automatically determined from training sets by the methods of Chapter 3, and *f*-classes may be automatically determined by the methods of Section 10.2. In some cases, automation of the design process may have the advantage of avoiding limitations on recognition performance which would arise from limitations of a human designer's intuitive grasp of immensely complicated design.

10.6.2 Storing the classification table in associative memory

If Φ_c were available in practice, a very simple way of achieving $\Phi_M = \Phi_C$ automatically without intuitive design effort would be by storing the classification table in an associative memory. For instance, $\nabla_C(X)$ might be expressed by a 4-bit codeword. The Figure 10.7 associative memory could be modified so that a 40 x 40-bit pattern, instead of a 3-bit pattern, would serve as the address of a 4-bit codeword. The storing of pairs $\{X, \nabla_C(X)\}$ in the associative memory would be a crude sort of *learning*[422]. After learning, if the 40 x 40-bit input pattern was the pattern X, the 4-bit output codeword would be an expression of $\nabla_C(X)$. This technique is not practical, because the set $\{X_1, \ldots, X_p\}$ has an astronomical number of members, and, even if all of the pairs $\{X_1, \nabla_C(X_1)\}, \ldots, \{X_p, \nabla_C(X_p)\}$ were available, we could not afford to store them all in an associative memory.

It is not practical to use training sets containing many millions of patterns. If a practical machine is to learn to recognise 40 x 40-bit binarised numerals from envelopes, it must use a training set such that the ratio

$$\frac{\text{number of patterns in the training set}}{\text{number of patterns in } \{X_1, \ldots, X_p\}}$$

is very small, and yet we require that $\nabla_M(X) = \nabla_C(X)$ for (ideally) *all* $X = X_1, \ldots, X_p$. Therefore, a practical learning machine must *generalise,* that is, have the ability to recognise many patterns which do not belong to its training set. A simple associative memory, used as indicated above, is impractical because it does not generalise.

10.6.3 Learning in pattern recognition

In a learning system, let R^* be the training set of patterns from all recognition classes. After termination of learning, any of the systems of Chapters 3, 4, or 5 assigns an input pattern to a recognition class or rejects it. The output $\nabla_M(X)$ which the machine produces in response to an input pattern X depends on R^*, and this is true for all $X = X_1, \ldots, X_p$. In this sense, Φ_M is a function of R^*, which can be written $\Phi_M = \psi(R^*)$. The systems of Chapters 3, 4, and 5 provide examples of different ψ's, in that these systems determine Φ_M from R^* according to different rules.

To avoid substitution errors we require that $\psi(R^*) = \Phi_M = \Phi_C$. If R^* does not contain all X's which ever occur in practice, then a system such that $\psi(R^*) = \Phi_C$ is necessarily a system which *generalises,* because Φ_C is not merely the set of all pairs $\{X, \nabla_C(X)\}$ for X's belonging to R^*: Φ_C includes pairs $\{X, \nabla_C(X)\}$ for all X's which ever occur in practice.

If recognition classes were composed of patterns chosen at random, generalisation would be impossible, and, in this case, ψ would not exist such that $\psi(R^*) = \Phi_C$. The following discussion is restricted to problems where ψ exists such that $\psi(R^*) = \Phi_C$.

In practice, for instance in the numerals-on-envelopes problem, we do not know *a priori* the function Φ_C or a function ψ such that $\psi(R^*) = \Phi_C$. If we wish to use automatic learning, we can only proceed by intuitively suggesting a ψ, using this to determine Φ_M, and testing experimentally whether $\nabla_M(X) = \nabla_C(X)$ for a large number of X's preferably chosen at random from $\{X_1, \ldots, X_p\}$. If we find that $\nabla_M(X) \neq \nabla_C(X)$ for an intolerably large number of X's we can modify or change ψ and again test experimentally whether $\nabla_M(X) = \nabla_C(X)$ for a large number of X's. If we still find that $\nabla_M(X) \neq \nabla_C(X)$ for an intolerably large number of X's, we can again modify or change ψ, and so on. Like the design process in Section 10.6.1, this experimental process is in fact a scientific process of hypothesis formation and testing.

When we choose a ψ, we implicitly hypothesise that this ψ is at least roughly such that $\psi(R^*) = \Phi_C$. We test this hypothesis by testing experimentally whether $\nabla_M(X) = \nabla_C(X)$ for many X's. When we subsequently alter ψ, we alter the hypothesis.

We must use an experimental scientific, rather than a deductive mathematical, method in order to find ψ such that $\psi(R^*) = \Phi_C$, because we have no *a priori* knowledge from which to deduce ψ such that $\psi(R^*) = \Phi_C$. In Chapters 3, 4, and 5, learning algorithms, and thus ψ's, were deduced from mathematical considerations, but, in any of these systems, only experiment could establish whether or not $\nabla_M(X) = \nabla_C(X)$ for a tolerably large number of X's *not* belonging to R^* in a given practical problem, such as the numerals-on-envelopes problem.

In a learning system, Φ_M depends on R^*, but Φ_M does not *only* depend on R^*. Parts of the detailed design of a recognition system (e.g. weights) may be determined automatically from R^*, and other parts (e.g. normalisation, features, or other arbitary tests) may be determined by the non-automatic intuitive trial and error process of Section 10.6.1. Intuition is always used in the selection of learning algorithms, and in some systems intuitive selection of learning algorithms is computer assisted. Instead of using just one learning algorithm, better results may be obtained in practice by using many algorithms in one recognition system, the learning process being directed by a human operator, who, by means of graphical displays, watches the progress of learning, and chooses algorithms which seem appropriate to the data[389].

We have so far used the term *learning* without defining it. In the literature on automatic pattern recognition, the term *learning* usually means the determination of at least part of the detailed design of a recognition system by means of an automatic process which uses R^* as data. In this sense, *learning* is the automatic determination of Φ_M from R^*. In learning, training set patterns may or may not be stored in the recognition machine. For instance, in a nearest-neighbour system, training set patterns may be stored, whereas in the system of Section 3.7.3, training set patterns need not be stored. Mere storage of training set patterns, for instance as in Section 10.6.2, does not by itself immediately provide the generalisation which is indispensable in a practical problem such as the numerals-on-envelopes problem.

It remains to be seen whether or not any known automatic learning algorithm is a learning algorithm which is used in the brain. It is possible that the brain may use learning algorithms which have not yet been described in the literature on automatic pattern recognition. The term *recognise*, like the term *learn,* has been borrowed from psychology. Again, it is possible that the brain may use recognition algorithms which have not yet been described in the literature on automatic pattern recognition. Use of the term *classification* in place of *recognition* throughout this book would be an improvement, in that it would steer us clear of any linguistically implied claim that the pattern recognition processes used in the brain are the same as those used in any known artificial system[245, 390].

An automatic character recognition machine may have the advantage of reading many more documents per minute than a human operator. But, to achieve low error rates, machines which are at present available require characters to conform to constraints on quality and shape which are unnecessary for purposes of human reading. A human can recognise a very much greater diversity of shapes than any known artificial system can recognise. Looking ahead, there is no obvious and cogent reason why future artificial systems should not eventually take full account of context and recognise shapes and sounds which are as diverse as those which a human can recognise, although this may require big technical developments. Automatic pattern recognition has been the subject of major efforts only since the 1950's, and the eventual future accomplishments of automatic pattern recognition can be expected to be very much greater than the present accomplishments.

REFERENCES

Note: Copies of U.K. Patents may be obtained from the Patent Office, 25 Southampton Buildings, London WC2A 1AY.

1. ABDALI, S. K., 'Feature Extraction Algorithms', *Pattern Recognition,* **3** No. 1, Apr. 1971, 3–21.

1a. ABEND, K., 'Compound Decision Procedures for Unknown Distributions and for Dependent States of Nature', *Pattern Recognition,* Ed. L. N. Kanal, Thompson Book Co., Washington, D.C., 1968, 207–249.

2. ABEND, K., HARLEY, T. J., and KANAL, L. N., 'Classification of Random Binary Patterns', *IEEE Transactions on Information Theory,* **IT-11** No. 4, Oct. 1965, 538–544.

3. ABRAMSON, N., and BRAVERMAN, D., 'Learning to Recognise Patterns in a Random Environment', *IRE Transactions on Information Theory,* **IT-8** No. 5, Sept. 1962, S58–S63.

4. AIZERMAN, M. A., BRAVERMAN, E. M., and ROZONOER, L. I., 'Theoretical Foundation of the Potential Function Method in Pattern Recognition Learning', *Automation and Remote Control,* **25** No. 6, June 1964, 821–839.

5. AIZERMAN, M. A., BRAVERMAN, E. M., and ROZONOER, L. I., 'The Probability Problem of Pattern Recognition Learning and the Method of Potential Functions', *Automation and Remote Control,* **25** No. 9, Sept. 1964, 1175–1190.

6. AIZERMAN, M. A., BRAVERMAN, E. M., and ROZONOER, L. I., 'The Method of Potential Functions for the Problem of Restoring the Characteristic of a Function Converter from Randomly Observed Points', *Automation and Remote Control,* **25** No. 12, Dec. 1964, 1705–1714.

7. AIZERMAN, M. A., BRAVERMAN, E. M., and ROZONOER, L. I., 'The Robbins Monro Process and the Method of Potential Functions', *Automation and Remote Control,* **26** No. 11, Nov. 1965, 1882–1885.

8. ALBERGA, C. N., 'String Similarity and Misspellings', *Communications of the Association for Computing Machinery,* **10** No. 5, May 1967, 302–313.

9. ALBERT, A., 'A Mathematical Theory of Pattern Recognition', *Annals of Mathematical Statistics,* **34** No. 1, Mar. 1963, 284–299.

10. ALEXITS, G., *Convergence Problems of Orthonormal Series,* Pergamon, New York and London, 1961.

11. ALMEX, 'Character Readers', U.K. Pat. 1 166 759, Oct. 1969; *see also* U.K. Pat. 1 189 059, Apr. 1970.

12. ALT, F. L., 'Digital Pattern Recognition by Moments', *Optical Character Recognition,* Ed. G. L. Fischer, D. K. Pollock, B. Raddack, and M. E. Stevens, Spartan Books, New York, 1962, 153–179.

13. ALTER, R., 'Utilisation of Contextual Constraints in Automatic Speech Recognition', *IEEE Transactions on Speech and Audio,* **Au-16** No. 1, Mar. 1968, 6–11.

14. AMARI, S., 'A Theory of Adaptive Pattern Classifiers', *IEEE Transactions on Electronic Computers,* **EC-16** No. 3, June 1967, 299–307.

15. AMERICAN STANDARD *Graphic Symbols for Logic Diagrams,* AIEE 91-ASA Y 32.14, 1962. Available from: Order Department IEEE, 345 East 47th Street, New York, NY 10017.

16. AMOS, S. W., and BIRKINSHAW, D. G., *Television Engineering,* 2nd edn, **1**, Ch. 14, Iliffe, London, 1963.

17. ANDERSON, R. L., 'Optical Character Recognition – A Survey', *Datamation,* July 1969, 43.

18. ANDERSON, T. W., *Introduction to Multivariate Statistical Analysis,* Wiley, New York and London, 1958.

19. ANDERSON, T. W., and BAHADUR, R. R., 'Classification into Two Multivariate Normal Distribution Functions with Different Covariance Matrices', *Annals of Mathematical Statistics,* **33** No. 2, June 1962, 420–431.

20. ANDREWS, D. R., ATRUBIN, A. J., and HU, K. C., 'The IBM 1975 Optical Page Reader, Part III: Recognition Logic Development', *IBM Journal of Research and Development,* **12** No. 5, Sept. 1968, 364–371.

21. ANDREWS, H. C., *Computer Techniques in Image Processing,* Academic Press, New York and London, 1970; *see also IEEE Transactions on Computers,* **C-20** No. 9, Sept. 1971, 1045–1051.

22. ARKADEV, A. G., and BRAVERMAN, E. M., *Teaching Computers to Recognise Patterns,* Academic Press, New York and London, 1967.

23. ARMITAGE, J. D., and LOHMANN, A. W., 'Character Recognition by Incoherent Spatial Filtering', *Applied Optics,* **4** No. 4, Apr. 1965, 461–467.

23a ASCHER, R. N., KOPPELMAN, G. M., MILLER, M. J., NAGY, G., and SHELTON, G. L., 'An Interactive System for Reading Unformatted Printed Text', *IEEE Transactions on Computers,* **C-20** No. 12, Dec. 1971, 1527–1543.

24. BACH, E., *An Introduction to Transformational Grammars,* Holt, Rinehardt and Winston, New York, 1964.

25. BAKIS, R., U.K.Pat. 1 030 835, May 1966; U.S. Pat. 3 350 505, Oct. 1967.

26. BAKIS, R., HERBST, N. M., and NAGY, G., 'An Experimental Study of Machine Recognition of Hand-Printed Numerals', *IEEE Transactions on Systems Science and Cybernetics,* **SSC-4** No. 2, July 1968, 119–132.

27. BALL, G. H., 'Data Analysis in the Social Sciences', *1965 Fall Joint Computer Conference,* AFIPS Conference Proceedings, **27** Pt 1, 533–559.

28. BALL, G. H., and HALL, D. J., 'ISODATA, An Iterative Method of Multivariate Data Analysis and Pattern Classification', *1966 IEEE Communications Conference, Digest of Technical Papers* **II** (IEEE Catalogue No. 19C30), 116–117.

29. BALM, G. J., 'An Introduction to Optical Character Reader Considerations', *Pattern Recognition,* **2** No. 3, Sept. 1970, 151–166.

30. BARROW, H. G., and POPPLESTONE, J. R., 'Relational Descriptions in Picture Processing', *Machine Intelligence,* **6**, Ed. B. Meltzer and D. Michie, Edinburgh University Press, 1971, 377–396.

31. BARTZ, M. R., 'The IBM 1975 Optical Page Reader Part II: Video Thresholding System', *IBM Journal of Research and Development,* **12** No. 5, Sept. 1968, 354–363; *see also* U.K. Pat. 1 219 334, Jan. 1971.

32. BASHKIROV, O. A., BRAVERMAN, E. M., and MUCHNIK, I. B., 'Potential Function Algorithms for Pattern Recognition Learning Machines', *Automation and Remote Control,* **25** Dec. 1964, 629.

33. BASKIN, H. B., and BONNER, R. E. (IBM), 'Specimen Identification Techniques', U.K. Pat. 1 028 288, May 1966; U.S. Pat. 3 273 130, Sept. 1966.

34. BAULDREAY, J., and MILBRANDT, E., 'Solving Registration Problems in Optical Character Recognition', *Electronics,* **5** Jan. 1962, 77–81.

35. BAUMGARTNER, R. J., and BOND, M. F. (IBM), 'Character Recognition Systems', U.K. Pat. 1 144 319, Mar. 1969; U.S. Pat. 3 526 876, Sept. 1970; *see also* U.S. Pat. 3 517 387, June 1970.

36. BELL, C. G., FUJISAKI, H., HEINZ, J. M., STEVENS, K. N., and HOUSE, A. S., 'Reduction of Speech Spectra by Analysis-by-Synthesis Techniques', *Journal of the Acoustical Society of America,* **33** No. 12, Dec. 1961, 1725–1736; *see also Journal of the Acoustical Society of America*, **36** No. 2, Feb. 1964, 303–308.

37. BENE, J. F., and NELSON, P. F., 'Improvements in or Relating to Cross Correlation Apparatus', U.K. Pat. 1 102 359, Feb. 1968.

38. BERNSTEIN, M. I., 'A Method of Recognising Handprinted Characters in Real Time', *Pattern Recognition,* Ed. L. N. Kanal, Thompson Book Co., Washington, D.C., 1968, 109–114.

39. BEZDEL, W., and CHANDLER, H. J., 'Results of an Analysis and Recognition of Vowels by a Computer Using Zero Crossings', *Proceedings of the IEE,* **112** No. 11, Nov. 1965, 2060–2066.

39a. BIBERMAN, L. M., and NUDELMAN, S. (Eds), *Photoelectric Imaging Devices,* **I, II,** Plenum Press, New York and London, 1971.

39b. BIERMAN, A. W., and FELDMAN, J. A., 'A Survey of Results in Grammatical Inference', *Frontiers of Pattern Recognition,* Ed. S. Watanabe, Academic Press, New York and London, 1972, 31–54.

40. BINNS, R. A., DICKINSON, A., and WATRASEIWITZ, B. M., 'Methods of Increasing Discrimination in Optical Filtering', *Applied Optics,* **7** June 1968, 1047–1051.

41. BLACKWELL, D., and GIRSHICK, M. A., *Theory of Games and Statistical Decisions,* Wiley, New York and London, 1954.

42. BLAYDON, C. C., 'On a Pattern Classification Result of Aizerman, Braverman and Rozonoer', *IEEE Transactions on Information Theory,* **IT-12** No. 1, Jan. 1966, 82–83.

43. BLEDSOE, W. W., 'Further Results on N-tuple Pattern Recognition Method', *IRE Transactions on Electronic Computers,* **EC-10** Mar. 1961, 96–97.

44. BLEDSOE, W. W., and BISSON, C. L., 'Improved Memory Matrices for the *n*-tuple Pattern Recognition Method', *IRE Transactions on Electronic Computers,* **EC-11** June 1962, 414–415.
45. BLEDSOE, W. W., and BROWNING, I., 'Pattern Recognition and Reading by Machine', *Proceedings of the Eastern Joint Computer Conference,* 1959, 225–232.
46. BLOCK, H. D., 'The Perceptron: a Model of Brain Functioning', *Reviews of Modern Physics,* **34** No. 1, Jan. 1962, 123–134.
47. BLOCK, H. D., NILSSON, N. J., and DUDA, R. O., 'Determination and Detection of Features in Patterns', *Computer and Information Science,* Ed. J. T. Tou and R. H. Wilcox, Spartan Books, New York, 1964, 75–110.
48. BLUM, H., 'A Transformation for Extracting New Descriptors of Shape', *Models for the Perception of Speech and Visual Form,* Ed. W. Wathen-Dunn, MIT Press, Cambridge, Mass., and London, 1967, 362–380.
49. BOBROW, D. G., and KLATT, D. H., 'A Limited Speech Recognition System', *1968 Fall Joint Computer Conference,* AFIPS Conference Proceedings, **33**, 305–318.
50. BOMBA, J. S., 'Alphanumeric Character Recognition Using Local Operators', *Proceedings of the Eastern Joint Computer Conference,* 1959, 218.
51. BOND, M. F. (IBM), 'Character Recognition Apparatus', U.K. Pat. 1 118 790, July 1968; U.S. Pat. 3 528 058, Sept. 1970.
52. BONNER, R. E., 'A "Logical Pattern" Recognition Programme', *IBM Journal of Research and Development,* **6** No. 3, July 1962, 353.
53. BONNER, R. E., 'On Some Clustering Techniques', *IBM Journal of Research and Development,* **8** Jan. 1964, 22–32.
54. BOOTH, T. L., *Sequential Machines and Automata Theory,* Wiley, 1967.
55. BOOTH, W. T., MILLER, G. M., and SCHLEICH, O. A., 'Design Considerations for Stylised Font Readers', *Optical Character Recognition,* Ed. G. L. Fischer, D. K. Pollock, B. Raddack, and M. E. Stevens, Spartan Books, New York, 1962, 115–128; *see also* U.S. Pat. 3 111 645, Nov. 1963.
56. BRACEWELL, R., *The Fourier Transform and Its Applications,* McGraw-Hill, New York and London, 1965.
57. BRAVERMAN, E. M., 'Experiments on Machine Learning to Recognise', *Automation and Remote Control,* **23** Mar. 1962, 315–327; *see also* U.K. Pat. 1 230 834, May 1971.
58. BRAVERMAN, E. M., 'The Method of Potential Functions in the Problem of Training Machines to Recognise Patterns without a Teacher', *Automation and Remote Control,* **27** No. 10, Oct. 1966, 1748–1770.
59. BRICE, C. R., and FENNEMA, C. L., 'Scene Analysis Using Regions', *Artificial Intelligence,* **1** No. 3, Fall 1970, 205–226.
60. BRILL, E. L., HEYDORN, R. P., and HILL, J. D., 'Some Approaches to Character Recognition for Postal Address Reader Applications', *Proceedings of Automatic Pattern Recognition,* National Security Industrial Association, 1030 Fifteenth Street, Northwest, Washington, D.C., May 1969, 19–40.
61. BRINDLEY, G. S., *The Physiology of the Retina and Visual Pathway,* Arnold, London, 1960.
62. BRITISH COMPUTER SOCIETY, *Character Recognition 1967; see also Character Recognition 1971.*

63. BRITISH STANDARDS INSTITUTE, *Graphical Symbols for Electrical Power Telecommunications and Electronics Diagrams, Section 21: Pure Logic and Functional Symbols,* BS 3939, Mar. 1969; *BSI News,* July 1971, 25.
64. BRITT, R. H., 'A Practical Technique for Feature Extraction', *IEE/NPL Conference on Pattern Recognition,* IEE Conference Publication 42, July 1968, 347–354; *see also* U.K. Pat. 1 270 012, Apr. 1972.
65. BROWN, R. M., 'On-line Computer Recognition of Handprinted Characters', *IEEE Transactions on Electronic Computers,* **EC-13** No. 6, Dec. 1964, 750-752.
66. BRYCE, J. W. (IBM), 'Reading Machine', U.S. Pat. 2 240 546, May 1941.
67. BUSINESS PRESS, *Optical Character Recognition and the Years Ahead,* Business Press, Elmhurst, Ill., U.S.A., 1969.
68. CANNON, M. W., 'A Method of Analysis and Recognition of Voiced Vowels', *IEEE Transactions on Audio and Electroacoustics,* **AU-16** No. 2, June 1968, 154–158.
69. CARLSON, C., 'Techniques for Replacing Characters that are Garbled on Input', *1966 Spring Joint Computer Conference,* AFIPS Conference Proceedings **28,** 189–192.
70. CASEY, R. G. (Ed.), 'An Experimental Comparison of Several Design Algorithms Used in Pattern Recognition', *IBM Research Report,* RC1500, Nov. 1965.
71. CASEY, R. G., 'Moment Normalisation of Handprinted Characters', *IBM Journal of Research and Development,* **14** No. 5, Sept. 1970, 548–557.
72. CASEY, R. G., and NAGY, G., 'Recognition of Printed Chinese Characters', *IEEE Transactions on Electronic Computers,* **EC-15** No. 1, Feb. 1966, 91–101.
73. CHALMERS, J., and STEIN, A., 'Iterative Array for the Preprocessing of Handprinted Characters', *Electronics Letters,* **5** No. 18, 4th Sept. 1969, 431–433.
74. CHANG, S. H., 'Portrayal of Some Elementary Statistics of Speech Sounds', *Journal of the Acoustical Society of America,* **22** No. 6, Nov. 1950, 768–769.
75. CHATTEN, J. B., and TEACHER, C. F., 'Character Recognition Techniques for Address Reading', *Optical Character Recognition,* Ed. G. L. Fisher, D. K. Pollock, B. Raddack, and M. E. Stevens, Spartan Books, New York, 1962, 51–59.
76. CHERNOFF, H., and MOSES, L. E., *Elementary Decision Theory,* Wiley, New York and London, 1959.
77. CHIEN, Y. T., and FU, K. S., 'A Modified Sequential Recognition Machine Using Time-Varying Stopping Boundaries', *IEEE Transactions on Information Theory,* **IT-12** No. 2, Apr. 1966, 206–214.
78. CHIEN, Y. T., and FU, K. S., 'Selection and Ordering of Feature Observations in a Pattern Recognition System', *Information and Control,* **12** No. 10, Oct. 1968, 395–414.
79. CHOMSKY, N., *Syntactic Structures,* Mouton, 's Gravenhage, 1957.
80. CHOMSKY, N., *Aspects of the Theory of Syntax,* MIT Press, Cambridge, Mass., and London, 1965.
81. CHOW, C. K., "An Optimum Character Recognition System Using Decision Functions', *IRE Transactions on Electronic Computers,* **EC-6,** No. 4, Dec. 1957, 247.

82. CHOW, C. K., 'A Recognition Method Using Neighbour Dependence', *IEEE Transactions on Electronic Computers,* **EC-11** Oct. 1962, 683–690.
83. CHOW, C. K., 'Statistical Independence and Threshold Functions', *IEEE Transactions on Electronic Computers,* **EC-14** No. 1, Feb. 1965, 66–68.
84. CHOW, C. K., 'A Class of Non-Linear Recognition Procedures', *IEEE Transactions on Systems Science and Cybernetics,* **SSC-2** Dec. 1966, 101–108.
85. CHOW, C. K., 'An Optimum Recognition Error and Reject Tradeoff', *IEEE Transactions on Information Theory,* **IT-16** No. 1, Jan. 1970, 41–46.
86. CHOW, C. K., and LIU, C. N., 'An Approach to Structure Adaptation in Pattern Recognition', *IEEE Transactions on Systems Science and Cybernetics,* **SSC-2** No. 2, Dec. 1966, 73–80; *see also* U.K. Pat. 1 260 756, Jan. 1972 and U.S. Pat. 3 588 823, June 1971.
87. CHU, J. T., 'Optimal Decision Function for Computer Character Recognition', *Journal of the Association for Computing Machinery,* **12** No. 2, Apr. 1965, 213–226.
88. CHUANG, P. C., 'Recognition of Hand-printed Numerals by Two-stage Feature Extraction', *IEEE Transactions on Systems Science and Cybernetics,* **SSC-6** No. 2, Apr. 1970, 153–154.
89. CLAPPER, G. L. (IBM), 'Pattern Recognition System', U.K. Pat. 1 219 858, Jan. 1971.
90. CLAYDEN, D. O., CLOWES, M. B., and PARKS, J. R., 'Letter Recognition and Segmentation of Running Text', *Information and Control,* **9** No. 3, June 1966, 246–264.
91. CLOWES, M. B., and PARKS, J. R., 'A New Technique in Automatic Character Recognition', *Computer Journal,* **4** No. 2, Feb. 1961, 121–127.
92. COCHRAN, W. T., COOLEY, J. W., FAVIN, D. L., HELMS, H. D., KAENEL, R. A., LANG, W. W., NELSON, D. E., RADER, C. M., and WELCH, P. D., 'What is the Fast Fourier Transform?', *IEEE Transactions on Audio and Electroacoustics,* **AU-15** No. 2, June 1967, 45–55.
93. COGNITRONICS CORPORATION, 'Improvements in or Relating to Character Reading Apparatus', U.K. Pat. 1 175 391, Dec. 1969.
94. COLUMBIA CONTROLS RESEARCH CORPORATION, 'Character Recognition System', U.K. Pat. 1 194 585, June 1970; U.S. Pat. 3 548 374, Dec. 1970; *see also* U.S. Pat. 3 548 377, Dec. 1970.
95. COLUMBIA RIBBON AND CARBON MANUFACTURING COMPANY INCORPORATED, 'Improvements In or Relating to Character Reading System', U.K. Pat. 1 128 594, Sept. 1968.
96. COOLEY, J. W., LEWIS, P. A. W., and WELCH, P. D., 'The Finite Fourier Transform', *IEEE Transactions on Audio and Electroacoustics,* **AU-17** No. 2, June 1969, 77–83.
97. COOMBS, A. W. M., 'On the Construction of an Efficient Feature Space for Optical Character Recognition', *Machine Intelligence,* **4** Ed. B. Meltzer and D. Michie, Edinburgh University Press, 1969, 385–401.
98. COOPER, D. B., 'Adaptive Pattern Recognition and Signal Detection Using Stochastic Approximation', *IEEE Transactions on Computers,* **EC-13** No. 3, June 1964, 306–307.

99. COOPER, D. B., and COOPER, P. W., 'Nonsupervised Adaptive Signal Detection and Pattern Recognition', *Information and Control,* 7 No. 3, Sept. 1964, 416–444.

100. COOPER, D. B., and FREEMAN, J. H., 'On the Asymptotic Improvement in the Outcome of Supervised Learning Provided by Additional Non-supervised Learning', *IEEE Transactions on Computers,* **c-19** No. 11, Nov. 1970, 1055–1063.

101. COOPER, F. S., DELATTRE, P. C., LIBERMAN, A. M., BORST, J. M., and GERSTMAN, L. J., 'Some Experiments on the Perception of Synthetic Speech Sounds', *Journal of the Acoustical Society of America,* **24** No. 6, Nov. 1952, 597–606.

102. COOPER, P. W., 'Hyperplanes, Hyperspheres, and Hyperquadratics as Decision Boundaries', *Computer and Information Sciences,* Ed. J. T. Tou and R. H. Wilcox, Spartan Books, New York, 1964, 111–137.

103. COOPER, P. W., 'Fundamentals of Statistical Decision and Learning', in *Automatic Interpretation and Classification of Images,* Ed. A. Grasselli, Academic Press, New York and London, 1969, 97–129.

104. CORNEIL, D. G., and GOTLIEB, C. C., 'An Efficient Algorithm for Graph Isomorphism', *Journal of the Association for Computing Machinery,* **17** No. 1, Jan. 1970, 51–64.

105. COVER, T. M., 'Geometrical and Statistical Properties of Systems of Linear Inequalities with Applications in Pattern Recognition', *IEEE Transactions on Electronic Computers,* **EC-14** No. 3, June 1965, 326.

106 COVER, T. M., 'Estimation by the Nearest Neighbour Rule', *IEEE Transactions on Information Theory,* **IT-14** No. 1, Jan. 1968, 50–55.

107. COVER, T. M., and HART, P. E., 'Nearest Neighbour Pattern Classification', *IEEE Transactions on Information Theory,* **IT-13** No. 1, Jan. 1967, 21–27.

107a. CUTAIA, A. (IBM), 'Selective Character Centering Line Follow Logics', U.S. Pat. 3 587 047, June 1971.

108. CUTLER, C. C., JULESZ, B., and PENNINGTON, K. S. (WESTERN ELECTRIC COMPANY), 'Improvements in or Relating to Methods and Apparatus for Pattern Recognition', U.K. Pat. 1 191 004, May 1970.

109. DACEY, M. F., 'The Syntax of a Triangle and Some Other Figures', *Pattern Recognition,* **2** No. 1, Jan. 1970, 11–31.

110. DAMANN, J. E., 'Application of Adaptive Threshold Elements to Recognition of Acoustic-Phonetic States', *Journal of the Acoustical Society of America,* **38** No. 2, 1965, 213–223.

111. DAS, S. K., 'A Method of Decison Making in Pattern Recognition', *IEEE Transactions on Computers,* **c-18** No. 4, Apr. 1969, 329.

112. DAVIS, K. H., BIDDULPH, R., and BALASHEK, S., 'Automatic Recognition of Spoken Digits', *Journal of the Acoustical Society of America,* **24** No. 6, Nov. 1952, 637–642.

112a. DAY, A. M., PARKS, J. R., and POGBEE, P. J., 'On-line Written Input to Computers', *Proceedings of the Conference on Machine Perception of Pictures and Patterns,* National Physical Laboratory, Apr. 1972, The Institute of Physics and The Physical Society, London, 233–240.

113. DECLARIS, N., and GREESON, J. C. (IBM), 'Waveform Analysing Apparatus', U.K. Pat. 1 121 954, July 1968; U.S. Pat. 3 482 211, Dec. 1969.

114. DENES, P. B., ' The Design and Operation of a Mechanical Speech Recogniser at University College London', *Journal of the British Institute of Radio Engineers,* **19** No. 4, Apr. 1959, 219–229.

115. DENES, P. B., 'On the Motor Theory of Speech Perception', *Models for the Perception of Speech and Visual Form,* Ed. W. Wathen-Dunn, MIT Press, Cambridge, Mass., and London, 1967, 309–314.

116. DENES, P. B., and MATHEWS, M. V., 'Spoken Digit Recognition Using Time-Frequency Pattern Matching', *Journal of the Acoustical Society of America,* **32** No. 2, Nov. 1960, 1450–1455.

117. DEUTSCH, S., *Models of the Nervous System,* Wiley, New York and London, 1967.

118. De VELIS, J. B., and REYNOLDS, G. O., *Theory and Applications of Holography,* Addison-Wesley, Reading, Mass., and London, 1967.

119. DEVYATERIKOV, I. P., PROPOI, A. I., and TSYPKIN, Ya. Z., 'Iterative Learning Algorithms for Pattern Recognition', *Automation and Remote Control,* **28** No. 1, Jan. 1967, 108–117.

120. DICKINSON, A., and WATRASIEWICZ, B. M., 'Optical Filtering Applied to Postal Code Reading', *IEE/NPL Conference on Pattern Recognition,* IEE Conference Publication No. 42, July 1968, 207–213.

121. DIMOND, T. L., 'Devices for Reading Handwritten Characters', *Proceedings of the Eastern Joint Computer Conference,* 1957, 232–237.

122. DINEEN, G. P., 'Programming Pattern Recognition', *Proceedings of the Western Joint Computer Conference,* 1955, 94.

123. DIXON, N. R., and TAPPERT, C. C., 'Toward Objective Phonetic Transcription', *IEEE Transactions on Man–Machine Systems,* **MMS-11** No. 4, Dec. 1970, 202–210.

124. DOROFEYUK, A. A.,'Teaching Algorithms for a Pattern Recognition Machine Without a Teacher, Based on the Method of Potentials', *Automation and Remote Control,* **27** No. 10, Oct. 1966, 1728–1736.

125. DOYLE, W., 'Recognition of Sloppy, Hand-printed Characters', *Proceedings of the Western Joint Computer Conference,* 1960, 131.

126. DUDA, R. O., and FOSSUM, H., 'Pattern Classification by Iteratively Determined Linear and Piecewise Linear Discriminant Functions', *IEEE Transactions on Electronic Computers,* **EC-15** No. 2, Apr. 1966, 220–232.

127. DUDA, R. O., and HART, P. E., 'Experiments in the Recognition of Hand-printed Text: Part II-Context Analysis', *1968 Fall Joint Computer Conference,* AFIPS Conference Proceedings, **33**, 1139–1149.

128. DUDA, R. O., and HART, P. E., 'Experiments in Scene Analysis', *Proceedings of the First National Symposium on Industrial Robots,* IIT Research Institute, 10 West 35th Street, Chicago, Illinois 60616, U.S.A., Apr. 1970, 119–130.

129. DUDLEY, H., and BALASHEK, S., 'Automatic Recognition of Phonetic Patterns in Speech', *Journal of the Acoustical Society of America,* **30** No. 8, Aug. 1958, 721–732.

130. DYE, M. S., 'Character Recognition by Means of Optical Filtering', *The Marconi Review,* **32** No. 173, 1969, 111–128.

131. EARNEST, L. D., 'Machine Recognition of Cursive Script', *Proc. 1962 IFIP Congress,* 462–466.

132. EDEN, M., 'Handwriting and Pattern Recognition', *IRE Transactions on Information Theory,* **IT-8** Feb. 1962, 160.

133. EDEN, M., 'Handwriting Generation and Recognition', *Recognising Patterns,* Ed. P. A. Kolers and M. Eden, MIT Press, Cambridge, Mass., and London, 1968, 138–154.

133a. ELDER, H. A., 'On the Feasibility of Voice Input to an On-line Computer Processing System', *Communications of the Association for Computing Machinery,* **13** No. 6, June 1970, 339–346.

134. ESSINGER, P., and GREANIAS, E. C. (IBM), 'Character Recognition Apparatus Employing a Curve Follower', U.S. Pat. 3 303 465, Feb. 1967.

135. ESTRIN, G., and FULLER, R., 'Algorithm for Content Addressable Memories', *IEEE Pacific Computer Conference,* 1963, 118–130.

136. EVANS, T. G., 'Descriptive Pattern Analysis Techniques', *Automatic Interpretation and Classification of Images,* Ed. A. Grasselli, Academic Press, New York and London, 1969, 79–95.

137. EVEY, R. J., 'Use of a Computer to Design Character Recognition Logic', *Proceedings of the Eastern Joint Computer Conference,* 1959, 205–211.

138. EWING, G. D., and TAYLOR, J. F., 'Computer Recognition of Speech Using Zero Crossing Information', *IEEE Transactions on Audio and Electro-Acoustics,* **AU-17** No. 1, Mar. 1969, 37.

138a. FALK, G., 'Scene Analysis Based on Imperfect Edge Data', *Second International Joint Conference on Artificial Intelligence,* British Computer Society, London, Sept. 1971, 8–16.

139. FEDER, J., 'Languages of Encoded Line Patterns', *Information and Control,* **13** No. 3, Sept. 1968, 230–244.

140. FEIGENBAUM, E. A., 'The Simulation of Verbal Learning Behaviour', *Proceedings of the Western Joint Computer Conference,* 1961, 121–132; *see also Proc. 1962 IFIP Congress,* 401–404.

141. FIEDELMAN, 'A Survey of the Character Recognition Field', *Datamation,* **12** No. 2, Feb. 1966, 45.

142. FIRSCHEIN, O., and FISCHLER, M., 'Automatic Subclass Determination for Pattern Recognition Applications', *IEEE Transactions on Electronic Computers,* **EC-12,** Apr. 1963, 137–141.

143. FLANAGAN, J. L., *Speech Analysis, Synthesis, and Perception,* Springer-Verlag, Berlin and New York, 1965.

144. FLEGG, H. G., *Boolean Algebra and its Applications,* Blackie, London, 1964.

145. FONTIJNE, P., 'Principles of IBM Optical Character Readers', *Computer Weekly,* 14 Aug. 1969, 6.

146. FORGIE, J. W., and FORGIE, C. D., 'Results Obtained from a Vowel Recognition Computer Programme', *Journal of the Acoustical Society of America,* **31** No. 11, Nov. 1959, 1480–1489.

147. FORSEN, G. E., 'Processing Visual Data with an Automaton Eye', *Pictorial Pattern Recognition,* Ed. G. C. Cheng, R. S. Ledley, D. K. Pollock, and A. Rosenfeld, Thompson Book Co., Washington, D.C., 1968, 471–502.

148. FOSDICK, T., HAMBURGEN, A., and HENNIS, R. B. (IBM), 'Statistical Error Reduction in Character Recognition Systems', U.S. Pat. 3 492 653, Jan. 1970.

149. FOSTER, J. M., *Automatic Syntactic Analysis*, Macdonald/Elsevier, London, 1970.

150. FRALICK, S. C., 'Learning to Recognise Patterns without a Teacher', *IEEE Transactions on Information Theory*, **IT-13** No. 1, Jan. 1967, 57–64.

150a. FRASER, J. G., 'Further Comments on a Line Thinning Scheme', *Computer Journal*, **13** No. 2, May 1970, 221–222 (and Private Communication).

151. FREEMAN, H., 'On the Encoding of Arbitrary Geometrical Configurations', *IRE Transactions on Electronic Computers*, **EC-10** No. 2, June 1961, 260–268.

152. FREEMAN, H., 'Boundary Encoding and Processing', *Picture Processing and Psychopictorics*, Ed. B. S. Lipkin and A. Rosenfeld, Academic Press, New York and London, 1970, 241–266.

153. FRENCH, W. K. (IBM), 'Apparatus for Recognising a Speech Signal', U.K. Pat. 1 179 029, Jan. 1970.

154. FRISHKOPF, L. S., and HARMON, L. D., 'Machine Reading of Cursive Script', *Fourth London Symposium on Information Theory*, Ed. C. Cherry, Butterworths, London, 1961, 300–317.

155. FU, K. S., *Sequential Methods in Pattern Recognition and Machine Learning*, Mathematics in Science and Engineering, **52**, Academic Press, New York and London, 1968.

156. FU, K. S., 'Statistical Pattern Recognition', *Adaptive, Learning, and Pattern Recognition Systems, Theory and Applications*, Ed. J. M. Mendel and K. S. Fu, Academic Press, New York and London, 1970, 35–79.

157. FU, K. S., MIN, P. J., and LI, T. J., 'Feature Selection in Pattern Recognition', *IEEE Transactions on Systems Science and Cybernetics*, **SSC-6** No. 1, Jan. 1970, 33–39.

158. FU, K. S., and SWAIN, P. H., 'On Syntactic Pattern Recognition', *Software Engineering*, COINS III, **2**, Ed. J. T. Tou, Academic Press, New York and London, 1971, 155–182.

159. FUJITSU, 'Character Recognition System', U.K. Pat. 1 138 453, Jan. 1969.

160. FUJITSU, 'Pattern Feature Extracting System', U.K. Pat. 1 195 290, June 1970; *see also* U. K. Pat. 1 215 740, Dec. 1970.

161. FUKUNAGA, K., and KOONTZ, W. L. G., 'Application of the Karthunen–Loeve Expansion to Feature Selection and Ordering', *IEEE Transactions on Computers*, **C-19** No. 4, Apr. 1970, 311–318.

162. FULLER, R. H., and BIRD, R. M., 'An Associative Parallel Processor with Application to Picture Processing', *1965 Fall Joint Computer Conference*, AFIPS Conference Proceedings, **27** Pt I, 105–116.

163. FUNK, H. L., and KAMBIC, S. F. (IBM), 'Handwritten Character Representation Apparatus', U.K. Pat. 1 152 989, May 1969.

164. GABOR, D., 'Character Recognition by Holography', *Nature*, **208** No. 5009, Oct. 1965, 422–423; *see also* U.K. Pat. 1 143 086, Feb. 1969; U.S. Pat. 3 600 054, Aug. 1971.

165. GAMBA, A. (Philco), 'Pattern Recognition System Utilising Random Masks', U.S. Pat. 3 255 436, June 1966.

166. GAMBA, A., 'New Developments in Artificial Intelligence and Pattern Recognition', *Computer and Information Science*, Ed. J. T. Tou and R. H. Wilcox, Spartan Books, New York, 1964, 219–229.

167. GARRY, G. A. (IBM), 'Word Identifying Apparatus', U.K. Pat. 1 201 178, Aug. 1970; U.S. Pat. 3 533 069, Oct. 1970.

168. GASS, S. I., *Linear Programming Methods and Applications,* McGraw-Hill, New York and London, 1958.

169. GENCHI, H., MORI, K.-I., WATANABE, S., and KATSURAGI, S., 'Recognition of Handwritten Numerical Characters for Automatic Letter Sorting', *Proceedings of the IEEE,* **56** No. 8, Aug. 1968, 1292–1301; *see also* U.K. Pat. 1 180 290, Feb. 1970.

170. GENERAL ELECTRIC COMPANY, 'Improvements in Symbol Reading System', U.K. Pat. 1 182 712, Mar. 1970.

171. GILLI, L., and MEO, A. R., 'Sequential System for Recognising Spoken Digits in Real Time', *Acustica,* **19** No. 1, 1967/68, 38.

172. GIULIANO, V. E., JONES, P. E., KIMBALL, G. E., MEYER, R. F., and STEIN, B. A., 'Automatic Pattern Recognition by a Gestalt Method', *Information and Control,* **4**, Dec. 1961, 332–345.

173. GLUCKSMAN, H. A., 'A Parapropagation Pattern Classifier', *IEEE Transactions on Electronic Computers,* **EC-14** No. 3, June 1965, 434–443.

174. GLUCKSMAN, H. A., 'Multicategory Classification of Patterns Represented by High Order Vectors of Multilevel Measurements', *IEEE Transactions on Computers,* **C-20** No. 12, Dec. 1971, 1593–1598.

175. GOOD, I. J., 'Creativity and Duality in Perception and Recall', *IEE/NPL Conference on Pattern Recognition,* IEE Conference Publication No. 42, July 1968, 228–237.

176. GOODMAN, J. W., *Introduction to Fourier Optics,* McGraw-Hill, New York and London, 1968.

177. GOLAY, M. J. E., 'Hexagonal Parallel Pattern Transformations', *IEEE Transactions on Computers,* **C-18** No. 8, Apr. 1969, 733–740.

178. GOLD, B., 'Machine Recognition of Hand-Sent Morse Code', *IRE Transactions on Information Theory,* **IT-5** No. 1, Mar. 1959, 17–24.

179. GORBATENKO, G. G. (IBM), 'Digital to Analogue Converter', U.K. Pat. 1 179 839, Feb. 1970.

180. GORBATENKO, G. G., and MILLER, G. D. (IBM), 'Determining the Boundary Line Between Touching Characters', U.K. Pat. 1 125 866, Sept. 1968.

180a. GRAY, S. B., 'Local Properties of Binary Images in Two Dimensions', *IEEE Transactions on Computers,* **C-20** No. 5, May 1971, 551–561.

181. GREANIAS, E. C., 'Some Important Factors in the Practical Utilisation of Optical Character Readers', *Optical Character Recognition,* Ed. G. L. Fischer, D. K. Pollock, B. Raddack, and M. E. Stevens, Spartan Books, New York, 1962, 129–146.

182. GREANIAS, E. C. (IBM), 'Rotation and Size Invariant Shape Recognition Apparatus', U.S. Pat. 3 273 124, Sept. 1966.

183. GREANIAS, E. C., and MEAGHER, P. F. (IBM), 'Electronic Servo Apparatus', U.K. Pat. 1 018 634, Jan. 1966; *see also* U.S. Pat. 3 267 285, Aug. 1966, and U.S. Pat. 3 429 989, Feb. 1969.

184. GREANIAS, E. C., MEAGHER, P. F., NORMAN, R. J., and ESSINGER, P., 'The Recognition of Handwritten Numerals by Contour Analysis', *IBM Journal of Research and Development,* **7** No. 1, Jan. 1963, 14.

185. GREANIAS, E. C., LEM, D. J., and MEAGHER, P. F. (IBM), 'Apparatus for Determining the Boundary Between Two Touching Line Patterns', U.K. Pat. 1 153 012, May 1969.
186. GREANIAS, E. C., and NORMAN, R. (IBM), 'Apparatus for Resolving Space Curve Slopes into Angular Sectors', U.S. Pat. 3 297 988, Jan. 1967.
187. GRENANDER, U., 'Foundations of Pattern Analysis', *Quarterly of Applied Mathematics,* **XXVII** No. 1, Apr. 1969, 1–55.
188. GRIFFIN, E., 'An Optical Character Recognition System Using a Vidicon Scanner', *Optical Character Recognition,* Ed. G. L. Fischer, D. K. Pollock, B. Raddack, and M. E. Stevens, Spartan Books, New York, 1962, 73–84.
189. GRIFFIN, J. S., KING, J. H., and TUNIS, C. J., 'A Pattern-Identification Device Using Linear Decision Functions', *Computer and Information Science,* Ed. J. T. Tou and R. H. Wilcox, Spartan Books, New York, 1964, 169.
190. GRIMSDALE, R. L., and BULLINGHAM, J. M., 'Character Recognition by Digital Computer Using a Special Flying Spot Scanner', *Computer Journal,* **4** No. 2, July 1961, 129.
191. GRIMSDALE, R. L., SUMNER, F. H., TUNIS, C. J., and KILBURN, T., 'A System for the Automatic Recognition of Patterns', *Proceedings of the IEE,* **106** Pt. B, Mar. 1959, 210.
192. GRINOLD, R. C., 'Comment on "Pattern Classification Design by Linear Programming" ', *IEEE Transactions on Computers,* **C-18** No. 4, Apr. 1969, 378–379.
193. GRONER, G. F., 'Real-Time Recognition of Hand Printed Text', *1966 Fall Joint Computer Conference,* AFIPS Conference Proceedings, **29**, 591–601.
194. GUZMAN, A., 'Decomposition of a Visual Scene into Three Dimensional Bodies', *1968 Fall Joint Computer Conference,* AFIPS Conference Proceedings, **33** Pt. I, 291–304.
195. HALL, P. M., 'A Practical Optical Character Recognition System', *Electronics and Power,* Apr. 1968, 149; *see also Data Processing,* Jan.–Feb. 1968, 8–13.
196. HALLE, M., and STEVENS, K., 'Speech Recognition: A Model and a Program for Research', *IRE Transactions on Information Theory,* **IT-8**, Feb. 1962, 155.
197. HAMBURGEN, A. (IBM), 'Detection and Correction of Transposition Errors', U.S. Pat. 3 333 143, July 1967; *see also* U.S. Pat. 3 303 463, Feb. 1967.
198. HANDEL, P. W., 'Statistical Machine', U.S. Pat. 1 915 993, June 1933.
199. HANLON, A. G., 'Content-addressable and Associative Memory Systems–A Survey', *IEEE Transactions on Electronic Computers,* **EC-15** No. 4, Aug. 1966, 509–521.
200. HANNAN, W. J., 'The R.C.A. Multifont Reading Machine', *Optical Character Recognition,* Ed. G. L. Fischer, D. K. Pollock, B. Raddack, and M. E. Stevens, Spartan Books, New York, 1962, 3–14.
201. HARARY, F., *Graph Theory,* Addison-Wesley, Reading, Mass., and London, 1969.
202. HARDIN, W. W., and LEIMER, J. J. (IBM), 'Movement Direction Determining Apparatus', U.K. Pat. 1 165 720, Oct. 1969.

203. Hart, P. E., 'The Condensed Nearest Neighbour Rule', *IEEE Transactions on Information Theory,* **IT-14,** May 1968, 515.

204. HART, P. E., and DUDA, R. O., 'Perspective Transformations', *Artificial Intelligence Group Technical Note,* No. 3, Stanford Research Institute, Menlo Park, California 94025, U.S.A., Feb. 1969.

205. HAWKINS, J. H., 'Textural Properties for Pattern Recognition', *Picture Processing and Psychopictorics,* Ed. B. S. Lipkin and A. Rosenfeld, Academic Press, New York and London, 1970, 347–370.

206. HAWKINS, J. H., 'Image Processing Principles and Techniques', *Advances in Information Systems Science,* **3** Ed. J. T. Tou, Plenum Press, New York and London, 1970, 113–214.

207. HAWKINS, J. K., ELERDING, G. T., BIXBY, K. W., and HAWORTH, P. A., 'Automatic Shape Detection for Programmed Terrain Classification', *Proceedings of the Society of Photographic Instrumentation Engineers,* June 1966, XVI–1 to XVI–9.

208. HEASLEY, C. C., and FISCHER, G. L., 'Some Elements of Optical Scanning', *Optical Character Recognition,* Ed. G. L. Fischer, D. K. Pollock, B. Raddack, and M. E. Stevens, Spartan Books, New York, 1962, 15–26.

209. HEMDAL, J. F., and HUGHES, G. W., 'A Feature-Based Computer Recognition Programme for the Modelling of Vowel Perception', *Models for the Perception of Speech and Visual Form,* Ed. W. Wathen-Dunn, MIT Press, Cambridge, Mass., and London, 1967, 440–453.

210. HENNIS, R. B., 'The IBM 1975 Optical Page Reader, Part I: System Design', *IBM Journal of Research and Development,* **12** No. 5, Sept. 1968, 346–353.

211. HERSKOVITS, A., and BINFORD, T. O., 'On Boundary Detection', *Artificial Intelligence Memo,* No. 183, Project MAC, Massachusetts Institute of Technology, July 1970.

212. HIGHLEYMAN, W. H., 'An Analogue Method of Character Recognition', *IRE Transactions on Electronic Computers,* **EC-10,** Sept. 1961, 501–512; *see also* U.S. Pat. 2 978 675, Apr. 1961.

213. HIGHLEYMAN, W. H., 'Linear Decision Functions with Applications to Pattern Recognition', *Proceedings of the IRE,* **50,** June 1962, 1501–1514.

214. HILDITCH, C. J., 'Linear Skeletons from Square Cupboards', *Machine Intelligence,* **4** Ed. B. Meltzer and D. Michie, Edinburgh University Press, 1969, 403–420.

215. HITACHI Ltd., 'Pattern Recognition System', U.K. Pat. 1 123 564, Aug. 1968.

216. HO, Y. C., and AGRAWALA, A. K., 'On the Self Learning Scheme of Nagy and Shelton', *Proceedings of the IEEE,* **55** No. 10, Oct. 1967, 1764–1765.

217. HO, Y. C., and AGRAWALA, A. K., 'On Pattern Classification Algorithms Introduction and Survey', *Proceedings of the IEEE,* **56** No. 12, Dec. 1968, 2101–2114.

218. HO, Y. C., and KASHYAP, R. L., 'An Algorithm for Linear Inequalities and its Applications', *IEEE Transactions on Electronic Computers,* **EC-14** No. 5, 1965, 683–688.

219. HOEFS, G. H. (IBM), 'Character Checking', U.K. Pat. 1 162 607, Aug. 1969.

219a. HOFFMAN, R. L., and McCULLOUGH, J. W., 'Segmentation Methods for Recognition of Machine Printed Characters', *IBM Journal of Research and Development,* **15** No. 2, Mar. 1971, 153–165.

220. HOLDEN, S., 'Improvements in or Relating to Pattern Recognition', U.K. Pat. 1 207 679, Oct. 1970.

221. HOLEMAN, J. M., 'Holographic Character Reader', *Pattern Recognition,* L. N. Kanal, Thompson Book Co., Washington, D.C., 1968, 63–78; *see also* U.K. Pat. 1 151 190, May 1969.

222. HOLT, A. W., 'What was Promised – What we Have – and What is being Promised in Character Recognition', *1968 Fall Joint Computer Conference,* AFIPS Conference Proceedings, **33** Pt. 2, 1451–1458.

222a. HOLT, A. W., and HILL, J. D. (CDC), 'Recognition System for Reading Machine', U.S. Pat. 3 519 990, July 1970.

222b. HOPCROFT, J. E., and ULLMAN, J. D., *Formal Languages and their Relation to Automata,* Addison-Wesley, Reading, Mass., and London, 1969, 33.

223. HOPGOOD, F. R. A., *Compiling Techniques,* MacDonald Computer Monographs No. 8, MacDonald, London, 1969.

224. HORWITZ, L. P., and SHELTON, G. L., 'Pattern Recognition Using Autocorrelation', *Proceedings of the IRE,* **49** No. 1, 1961, 175–185.

225. HOSHINO, Y., and KIJI, K., 'Computer Aided Design of a Reader of Hand-printed Characters', *Proceedings of the International Joint Conference on Artificial Intelligence,* Ed. D. E. Walker and L. M. Norton, The Mitre Corp., Bedford, Mass., 01730, May 1969, 153–160.

226. HOSKING, K. H., 'A Feature Detection Method of Optical Character Recognition', *The Marconi Review,* **32** No. 172, 1969, 3–20; *see also* U.K. Pat. 1 195 695, June 1970.

227. HOWARD, P. H. (IBM), 'Character Recognition Employing Offset Registration Control Masks', U.S. Pat. 3 267 430, Aug. 1966.

228. HU, M. K., 'Visual Pattern Recognition Using Moment Invariants', *IRE Transactions on Information Theory,* **IT-8**, Feb. 1962, 179–187.

229. HUBEL, D. H., and WIESEL, T. N., 'Receptive Fields and Functional Architecture of Monkey Striate Cortex', *Journal of Physiology,* **195** No. 1, Mar. 1968, 215–243.

230. HUECKEL, M. H., 'An Operator which Locates Edges in Digitised Pictures', *Journal of the Association for Computing Machinery,* **18** No. 1, Jan. 1971, 113–125.

230a. HUFFMAN, D. A., 'Impossible Objects as Nonsense Sentences', *Machine Intelligence,* **6**, Ed. B. Meltzer and D. Michie, Edinburgh University Press, 1971, 295–323.

231. HUGHES, G. F., 'On the Mean Accuracy of Statistical Pattern Recognisers', *IEEE Transactions on Information Theory,* **IT-14** No. 1, Jan. 1968, 55–63.

231a. HUNT, D. J., 'A Feature Extraction Method for the Recognition of Hand-Printed Characters', *Proceedings of the Conference on Machine Perception of Pictures and Patterns,* National Physical Laboratory, Apr. 1972, The Institute of Physics and The Physical Society, London, 28–33.

232. HYDE, S. R., 'Automatic Speech Recognition: Literature Survey and Discussion', *Human Communication: a Unified View,* Ed. P. B. Denes and E. E. David, to be publ. McGraw-Hill, New York and London.

233. IDE, E. R., KIESSLING, C. E., and TUNIS, C. J., 'Some Conclusions on the Use of Adaptive Linear Decision Functions', *1968 Fall Joint Computer Conference,* AFIPS Conference Proceedings, **33** Pt. 2, 1117–1124.

234. IDE, E. R., and TUNIS, C. J., 'An Experimental Investigation of a Non-Supervised Adaptive Algorithm', *IEEE Transactions on Computers,* **EC-16** No. 6, Dec. 1967, 860–863.

235. INTERNATIONAL BUSINESS MACHINES, 'IBM System/360 Component Description and Operating Procedures, IBM 1287 Optical Reader', File No. S 360-03, Form A21-9064-4. 1968.

236. INTERNATIONAL BUSINESS MACHINES, 'IBM System/360 Component Description. IBM 1275 Optical Reader Sorter', File No. S 360-03, Form A19-0034-0, Jan. 1969.

237. INTERNATIONAL STANDARD ELECTRIC CORPORATION, 'Automatic Character Recognition Arrangement', U.K. Pat. 1 156 266, June 1969.

238. ITO, T., 'Note on a Class of Statistical Recognition Functions', *IEEE Transactions on Computers,* **C-18** No. 1, Jan. 1969, 76–79.

238a. JAYANT, N. S., 'A study of Statistical Pattern Verification', *IEEE Transactions on Systems, Man, and Cybernetics,* **SMC-2** No. 2, Apr. 1972, 238–246.

239. JOHNSON, R. B., 'Indicia Controlled Record Perforating Machine', U.S. Pat. 2 741 312, Apr. 1956.

240. JONES, C. M., KELLAHER, J. F., DILLARD, J. M., and BERNSTEIN, S. L., 'Fourier Transform Methods in Pattern Recognition', *CR Research Note AD 285794,* July 1962, Armed Services Technical Information Agency, Arlington Hall, Virginia, U.S.A.

241. JOOS, G., *Theoretical Physics,* 3rd edn, Blackie, London, 1958, 54.

242. KALAITH, T., 'The Divergence and Bhattacharyya Distance Measures in Signal Selection', *IEEE Transactions on Communication Technology,* **COM-TECH-15** No. 1, Feb. 1967, 52–60.

243. KAMENTSKY, L. A., and LIU, C. N., 'Computer-Automated Design of Multifont Print Recognition Logic', *IBM Journal of Research and Development,* 7 No. 1, Jan. 1963, 2–13.

244. KAMENTSKY, L. A., and LIU, C. N., 'A Theoretical and Experimental Study of a Model for Pattern Recognition', *Computer and Information Science,* Ed. J. T. Tou and R. H. Wilcox, Spartan Books, New York, 1964, 194.

245. KANAL, L. N., and CHANDRASEKARAN, B., 'Recognition, Machine "Recognition" and Statistical Approaches', *Methodologies of Pattern Recognition,* Ed. S. Watanabe, Academic Press, New York and London, 1969, 317–322.

245a. KANAL, L. N., and CHANDRASEKARAN, B., 'On the Dimensionality and Sample Size in Statistical Pattern Classification', *Pattern Recognition,* **3** No. 3, Oct. 1971, 225–234.

246. KANAL, L. N., and RANDALL, N. C., 'Recognition System Design by Statistical Analysis', *Proceedings of the 19th National Conference of the Association for Computing Machinery,* 1964, D2.5–D2.5–10.

247. KASHYAP, R. L., and BLAYDON, C. C., 'Recovery of Functions from Noisy Measurements Taken at Randomly Selected Points and its Application to Pattern Recognition', *Proceedings of the IEEE,* **54** No. 8, Aug. 1966, 1127–1129.

248. KATSURAGI, S. (Toshiba), 'Code Checking Systems', U.K. Pat. 1 170 160, Nov. 1969.

249. KATSURAGI, S., GENCHI, H., MORI, K., and WATANABE, S., 'Recognition of Handwritten Numerals Using Decision Graph', *Proceedings of the International Joint Conference on Artificial Intelligence,* Ed. D. E. Walker and L. M. Norton, The Mitre Corp., Bedford, Mass. 01730, U.S.A., May 1969, 161–170.

250. KAUTZ, W. H., PEASE, M. C., and GREEN, M. W., *Cellular Logic-in-Memory Arrays,* Final Report-Pt. I, Stanford Research Institute, Calif., May 1970.

251. KAZMIERCZAK, H., 'The Potential Field as an Aid to Character Recognition', *Information Processing,* Proceedings of a UNESCO Conference in Paris in 1959, Butterworths, London, 1960, 244–247.

252. KELLY, M. D., 'Edge Detection in Pictures by Computer Using Planning', *Machine Intelligence,* **6**, Ed. B. Meltzer and D. Michie, Edinburgh University Press, 1971, 397–409.

252a. KIJI, K., and HOSHINO, Y. (NEC), Electrical Character Recognition Systems, U.K. Pat. 1 253 302, Nov. 1971.

253. KING, J. H., and TUNIS, C. J., 'Some Experiments in Spoken Word Recognition', *IBM Journal of Research and Development,* **10** No. 1, Jan. 1966, 65–80.

254. KIRSCH, R. A., 'Computer Interpretation of Text and Patterns', *IEEE Transactions on Computers,* **EC-13** No. 4, Aug. 1964, 363.

255. KIRSCH, R. A., CAHN, L., RAY, C., and URBAN, G. H., 'Experiments in Processing Pictorial Information with a Digital Computer', *Proceedings of the Eastern Joint Computer Conference,* 1957, 221–229.

256. KLEIN, W., PLOMP, R., and POLS, L. C. W., 'Vowel Spectra, Vowel Spaces, and Vowel Identification', *Journal of the Acoustical Society of America,* **48** No. 4, Pt. 2, Oct. 1970, 999–1009.

257. KNOLL, A. L., 'Experiments with Characteristic Loci for Recognition of Handprinted Characters', *IEEE Transactions on Computers,* **C-18** No. 4, Apr. 1969, 366–372.

258. KNUTH, D. E., *The Art of Computer Programming,* **I**, Addison-Wesley, Reading, Mass., and London, 1968, 305.

259. KOCHEN, M., 'Automatic Question Answering of English-like Questions about Simple Diagrams', *Journal of the Association for Computing Machinery,* **16** No. 1, Jan. 1969, 26–48.

260. KOFORD, J. S., 'Adaptive Pattern Dichotomisation', *Technical Report,* No. 6201-1, Systems Theory Labs, Stanford Electronics Labs, Stanford University, Calif., Apr. 1964.

261. KOFORD, J. S., and GRONER, G. F., 'The Use of an Adaptive Threshold Element to Design a Linear Optimal Classifier', *IEEE Transactions on Information Theory,* **IT-12** No. 1, Jan. 1966, 42–50.

262. KOLERS, P. A., 'The Role of Shape and Geometry in Picture Recognition', *Picture Processing and Psychopictorics,* Ed. B. S. Lipkin and A. Rosenfeld, Academic Press, New York and London, 1970, 181–202.

262a. KOONTZ, W. L., and FUNUKAGA, K., 'A Non-Linear Feature Extraction Algorithm Using Distance Transformation', *IEEE Transactions on Computers,* **C-21** No. 1, Jan. 1972, 56–63.

263. KOVASZNAY, L. S., and ARMAN, A., 'Optical Autocorrelation Measurement of Two Dimensional Random Patterns', *Review of Scientific Instruments,* **28,** Oct. 1957, 793–797.

264. KUHL, F., 'Classification and Recognition of Handprinted Characters', *IEEE International Convention Record,* Pt. 4, Mar. 1963, 75–93.

265. LADEFOGED, P., and BROADBENT, D. E., 'Information Conveyed by Vowels', *Journal of the Acoustical Society of America,* **29,** 1957, 98–104.

266. LAMBERT, P. F., 'Designing Pattern Categorisers with Extremal Paradigm Information', *Methodologies of Pattern Recognition,* Ed. S. Watanabe, Academic Press, New York and London, 1969, 359–379.

267. LAVINGTON, S. H., 'Speech Recognition', U.K. Pat. 1 155 422, June 1969.

268. LECOURS, M., *Adaptive Spectral Analysis for Speech Sound Recognition,* Ph.D. Thesis, Faculty of Engineering, University of London, 1967.

269. LEDLEY, R. S., ROTOLO, L. S., GOLAB, T. J., JACOBSEN, J. D., GINSBERG, M. D., and WILSON, J. B., 'Fidac: Film Input to Digital Automatic Computer and Associated Syntax-Directed Pattern Recognition Programming System', *Optical and Electro-optical Information Processing,* Ed. J. T. Tippet, D. A. Berkowitz, L. C. Clapp, C. J. Koester, and A. Vanderburgh, MIT Press, Cambridge, Mass., and London, 1965, 591–615.

270. LEE, Y. W., *Statistical Theory of Communication,* Wiley, New York and London, 1960.

271. LEIMER, J. J., 'Design Factors in the Development of an Optical Character Recognition Machine', *IRE Transactions on Information Theory,* **IT-8,** Feb. 1962, 167–171.

272. LEITH, E. N., KOZMA, A., and UPATNEIKS, J., 'Coherent Optical Systems for Data Processing, Spatial Filtering, and Wavefront Reconstruction', *Optical and Electro-Optical Information Processing,* Ed. J. T. Tippet, D. A. Berkowitz, L. C. Clapp, C. J. Koester, and A. Vanderburgh, MIT Press, Cambridge, Mass., and London, 1965, 145–158.

273. LENDARIS, G. G., and STANLEY, G. L., 'Diffraction-Pattern Sampling for Automatic Pattern Recognition', *Proceedings of the IEEE,* **58** No. 2, Feb. 1970, 198–216.

274. LEVINE, M. D., 'Feature Extraction: a Survey', *Proceedings of the IEEE,* **57** No. 8, Aug. 1969, 1391–1407.

275. LEWIS, P. M., 'Approximating Probability Distributions to Reduce Storage Requirements', *Information and Control,* **2,** 1959, 214–225.

276. LEWIS, P. M., 'The Characteristic Selection Problem in Recognition Systems', *IRE Transactions on Information Theory,* **IT-8**, Feb. 1962, 171–178.

277. LEWIS, P. M., and COATES, C. L., *Threshold Logic,* Wiley, New York and London, 1967.

278. LI, K. P., DAMANN, J. E., and CHAPMAN, W. D., 'Experimental Studies in Speaker Verification Using an Adaptive System', *Journal of the Acoustical Society of America,* **40** No. 5, 1966, 966–978.

279. LIBERMAN, A. M., COOPER, F. S., HARRIS, K. S., MACNEILAGE, P. F., and STUDDERT-KENNEDY, M., 'Some Observations on a Model for Speech Perception', *Models for the Perception of Speech and Visual Form,* Ed. W. Wathen-Dunn, MIT Press, Cambridge, Mass., and London, 1967, 68–87.

280. LINDGREN, N., 'Machine Recognition of Human Language. Part I. Automatic Speech Recognition', *IEEE Spectrum,* **2** No. 3, Mar. 1965, 114–136.

281. LIPKIN, L. E., WATT, W. C., and KIRSCH, R. A., 'The Analysis, Synthesis, and Description of Biological Images', *Annals of the New York Academy of Science,* **128**, 31 Jan. 1966, 984–1012.

282. LIU, C. N., 'A Programmed Algorithm for Designing Multifont Character Recognition Logics', *IEEE Transactions on Electronic Computers,* **EC-13** No. 5, Oct. 1964, 586–593.

283. LIU, C. N., and SHELTON, G. L., 'An Experimental Investigation of a Mixed Font Recognition System', *IEEE Transactions on Electronic Computers,* **EC-15** No. 6, Dec. 1966, 916–925.

284. LOGINOV, N. V., 'Methods of Stochastic Approximation', *Automation and Remote Control,* **27** No. 4, Apr. 1966, 706–728.

285. LOHMANN, A. W. (IBM), 'Optical Character Recognition System', U.K. Pat. 1 057 450, Feb. 1967; U.S. Pat. 3 437 824, Apr. 1969.

286. LOHMAN, A. W., and PARIS, D. P., 'Computer Generated Spatial Filters for Coherence Optical Data Processing', *Applied Optics,* **7** No. 4, Apr. 1968, 651–655; *see also IBM Journal of Research and Development,* **13** No. 2, 1969, 160–169.

287. LOZIER, W. B., and LUCIANI, J. D. (IBM), 'Character Recognition System Using a Plurality of Delayed Scans for Determining Character Features', U.S. Pat. 3 482 210, Dec. 1969.

288. LUNDY ELECTRONICS AND SYSTEMS INCORPORATED, 'Waveform Recognition System', U.K. Pat. 1 172 367, Nov. 1969.

289. LYONS, J., *Introduction to Theoretical Linguistics,* Cambridge University Press, 1968.

290. MALABY, D. L. (IBM), 'Character Scanning Apparatus', U.K. Pat. 1 060 920, Mar. 1967.

291. MALABY, D. L. (IBM), 'Character Scanning Apparatus', U.K. Pat. 1 156 229, July 1969.

292. MANGASARIAN, O. L., 'Linear and Non Linear Separation of Patterns by Linear Programming', *Operations Research,* **13** No. 3, May-June 1965, 444–452.

293. MANN, A., HAMBURGEN, A., HOLT, A. W., UHLAND, J. C., and NUNLEY, L. J., 'Industrial Panel Discussion', *Proceedings of Automatic Pattern Recognition,* National Security Industrial Association, 1030 Fifteenth Street, Northwest, Washington, D.C., May 1969, 175.

294. MARILL, T., and GREEN, D. M., 'Statistical Recognition Functions and the Design of Pattern Recognisers', *IRE Transactions on Electronic Computers,* **EC-9** No. 4, Dec. 1960, 472–477.

295. MARILL, T., and GREEN, D. M., 'On the Effectiveness of Receptors in Recognition Systems', *IRE Transactions on Information Theory,* **IT-9,** Jan. 1963, 11–17.

296. MARTIN, T. B., ZADELL, H. J., GRUNZA, E. F., and HERSHER, H. B., 'Numeric Speech Translating System', *Proceedings of Automatic Pattern Recognition,* National Security Industrial Association, 1030 Fifteenth Street, Northwest, Washington, D.C., May 1969, 113–141.

297. MATSUSHITA ELECTRIC INDUSTRIAL COMPANY, 'Apparatus for the Automatic Following of Line Structured Patterns', U.K. Pat. 1 120 194, July 1968.

298. MATTSON, R. L., and DAMANN, J. E., 'A Technique for Determining and Coding Subclasses in Pattern Recognition Problems', *IBM Journal of Research and Development,* **9** No. 4, July 1965, 294.

299. MAYS, C. H., 'Adaptive Threshold Logic', *Technical Report,* No. 1557-1, Stanford Electronics Labs, Stanford University, Calif., Apr. 1963.

300. MAYS, C. H., 'Effect of Adaptation Parameters on Convergence Time and Tolerance for Adaptive Threshold Elements', *IEEE Transactions on Electronic Computers,* **EC-13** No. 4, Aug. 1964, 465–468.

301. MAYS, C. H., 'The Boundary Matrix for Threshold Functions', *IEEE Transactions on Electronic Computers,* **EC-14** No. 1, Feb. 1965, 65–66.

302. McCARTHY, T., MEAGHER, P. F., and NORMAN, R. J. (IBM), 'Character Recognition Apparatus', U.K. Pat. 1 121 023, July 1968; U.S. Pat. 3 460 091, Aug. 1969.

303. McCLUSKEY, E. J., *Introduction to the Theory of Switching Circuits,* McGraw-Hill, New York and London, 1965.

304. McCORMICK, B. H., 'The Illinois Pattern Recognition Computer – Illiac III'. *IEEE Transactions on Electronic Computers,* **EC-12** No. 6, Dec. 1963, 791–813.

305. McFERRAN, J. B., 'Feature Extraction for General Visual Patterns', *IEEE Conference Record of the Symposium on Feature Extraction and Selection in Pattern Recognition,* Oct. 1970, 125–134. Available from: Order Department IEEE, 345 East 47th Street, New York, NY 10017.

306. McKEEVER, B. T., 'The Associative Memory Structure', *1965 Fall Joint Computer Conference,* AFIPS Conference Proceedings, **27** Pt. 1, 371–388.

307. McLAUGHLIN, J. A., and RAVIV, J., '*N*th Order Autocorrelations in Pattern Recognition', *Information and Control,* **12** No. 2, Feb. 1968, 121–142.

308. MEISEL, W. S., 'Least-Square Methods in Abstract Pattern Recognition', *Information Sciences,* **1** No. 1, Dec. 1968, 43–54.

309. MEISEL, W. S., 'Potential Functions in Mathematical Pattern Recognition', *IEEE Transactions on Computers,* **C-18** No. 10, Oct. 1969, 911–918.

310. MERMELSTEIN, P., and EDEN, M., 'A System for Automatic Recognition of Handwritten Words', *1964 Fall Joint Computer Conference,* AFIPS Conference Proceedings, **26,** 333–343; *see also Information and Control,* 7, June 1964, 255–270.

311. MERRY, I. W., and NORRIE, G. O., 'Character Quality and Scanner Organisation', *The Computer Journal,* **4** No. 2, July 1961, 137–143.

312. MEURLE, J. L., 'Some Thoughts on Texture Discrimination by Computer', *Picture Processing and Psychopictorics,* Ed. B. S. Lipkin and A. Rosenfeld, Academic Press, New York and London, 1970, 371–379.

313. MILLER, G. M., 'On-Line Recognition of Hand-Generated Symbols', *1969 Fall Joint Computer Conference,* AFIPS Conference Proceedings, **35**, 399–412.

313a. MILLER, G. M., 'Real Time Classification of Handwritten Script Words', IFIP Congress 1971, Ljubljana, Booklet TA-2, Aug. 1971, 126–131.

314. MILLER, J. C., ROSS, P. W., and WINE, C. M., 'An Adaptive Speech Recognition System Operating in a Remote Time-Shared Computer Environment', *IEEE Transactions on Audio and Electro Acoustics,* **Au-18** No. 1, Mar. 1970, 26–31.

315. MILLER, W. F., and SHAW, A. C., 'Linguistic Methods in Picture Processing', *1968 Fall Joint Computer Conference,* AFIPS Conference Proceedings, **33**, 279–290.

316. MINNEMAN, M. J., 'Handwritten Character Recognition Employing Topology, Cross Correlation, and Decision Theory', *IEEE Transactions on Systems Science and Cybernetics,* **SSC-2** No. 2, Dec. 1966, 87–96.

317. MINNICK, R. C., 'Survey of Microcellular Research', *Journal of the Association for Computing Machinery,* **14** No. 2. Apr. 1967, 203–241.

318. MINSKY, M., 'Steps towards Artificial Intelligence', *Proceedings of the IRE,* **49** No. 1, Jan. 1961, 8–30.

319. MINSKY, M., and PAPERT, S., *Perceptrons,* MIT Press, Cambridge, Mass., and London, 1969.

320. MOHN, W. S., 'Two Statistical Feature Evaluation Techniques Applied to Speaker Verification', *IEEE Transactions on Computers,* **C-20** No. 9, Sept. 1971, 979–987.

321. MORI, K.-I., GENCHI, H., WATANABE, S., and KATSURAGI, S., 'Microprogramme Controlled Pattern Processor in a Handwritten Mail Reader-Sorter', *Pattern Recognition,* **2** No. 3, Sept. 1970, 175–183.

322. MOTT-SMITH, J. C., 'Medial Axis Transformations', *Picture Processing and Psychopictorics,* Ed. B. S. Lipkin and A. Rosenfeld, Academic Press, New York and London, 1970, 267–283.

322a. MUCCIARDI, A. N., and GOSE, E. E., 'A Comparison of Seven Techniques for Choosing Subsets of Pattern Recognition Properties', *IEEE Transactions on Computers,* **C-20** No. 9, Sept. 1971, 1023–1031.

323. MUNSON, J. H., 'Experiments in the Recognition of Handprinted Text: Part I, Character Recognition', *1968 Fall Joint Computer Conference,* AFIPS Conference Proceedings, **33** 1125–1138; *see also Pattern Recognition,* Ed. L. N. Kanal, Thompson Book Co., Washington, D.C., 1968, 115–139.

324. MUNSON, J. H., DUDA, R. O., and HART, P. E., 'Experiments with Highleyman's Data', *IEEE Transactions on Computers,* **C-17** No. 4, Apr. 1968, 399–401.

325. NADLER, M., 'An Analog-Digital Character Recognition System', *IRE Transactions on Electronic Computers,* **EC-12** No. 6, Dec. 1963, 814–821.

326. NAGY, G., 'State of the Art in Pattern Recognition', *Proceedings of the IEEE,* **56** No. 5, May 1968, 836–862.

327. NAGY, G., 'Feature Extraction on Binary Patterns', *IEEE Transactions on Systems Science and Cybernetics,* **SSC-5** No. 4, Oct. 1969, 273–278.

328. NAGY, G., and SHELTON, G. L., 'Self Corrective Character Recognition System', *IEEE Transactions on Information Theory,* **IT-12** No. 2, Apr. 1966, 215–222.

329. NAGY, G., and TUONG, N., 'Normalisation Techniques for Hand-Printed Numerals', *Communications of the Association for Computing Machinery,* **13** No. 8, Aug. 1970, 475–481.

330. NARASIMHAN, R., 'Syntax Directed Interpretation of Classes of Pictures', *Communications of the Association for Computing Machinery,* **9** No. 3, Mar. 1966, 166–173.

331. NARASIMHAN, R., 'On the Description, Generation, and Recognition of Classes of Pictures', *Automatic Interpretation and Classification of Images,* Ed. A. Grasselli, Academic Press, New York and London, 1969, 1–42.

332. NATHAN, R., 'Spatial Frequency Filtering', *Picture Processing and Psychopictorics,* Ed. B. S. Lipkin and A. Rosenfeld, Academic Press, New York and London, 1970, 151–163.

333. NATIONAL CASH REGISTER COMPANY, 'Character Recognition Device', U.K. Pat. 1 132 548, Dec. 1968.

334. NATIONAL CASH REGISTER COMPANY, 'Character Recognition Apparatus', U.K. Pat. 1 172 463, Dec. 1969.

335. NELSON, A. L., HERSHER, M. B., MARTIN, T. B., ZADELL, H. J., and FALTER, J. W., 'Acoustic Recognition by Analogue Feature-Abstraction Techniques', *Models for the Perception of Speech and Visual Form,* Ed. W. Wathen-Dunn, MIT Press, Cambridge, Mass., and London, 1967, 428–440.

336. NILSSON, N. J., *Learning Machines,* McGraw-Hill, New York and London, 1965.

337. NIPPON ELECTRIC COMPANY, 'Improvements in or Relating to Character Recognition Apparatus', U.K. Pat. 1 124 130, Aug. 1968.

338. NOBLE, D. L., and ANDREWS, D. R. (IBM), 'Improvements Relating to Character Recognition Apparatus', U.K. Pat. 1 023 810, Mar. 1966; *see also* U.K. Pat. 1 121 183, July 1968.

339. NOVIKOFF, A. B. J., 'Integral Geometry as a Tool in Pattern Recognition', *Bionics Symposium,* Wright Air Development Divison Report WADD60-600, 1960, 247–262.

340. OLSON, H. F., and BELAR, H., 'Phonetic Typewriter III', *Journal of the Acoustical Society of America,* **33** No. 11, Nov. 1961, 1610–1615.

340a. PALMIERI, G., 'Image Devices for Pattern Recognition', *Pattern Recognition,* **3** No. 2, July 1971, 157–168.

341. PAPOULIS, A., *The Fourier Integral and its Applications,* McGraw-Hill, New York and London, 1962.

342. PARKS, J. R., 'Automatic Recognition of Low Quality Printed Characters Using Analogue Techniques', *Radio and Electronic Engineer,* **34** No. 2, Aug. 1967, 67; *see also* U.K. Pat. 1 170 234, Nov. 1969.

343. PARKS, J. R., 'A Multilevel System of Analysis for Mixed Font and Hand-Blocked Printed Characters Recognition', *Automatic Interpretation and Classification of Images,* Ed. A. Grasselli, Academic Press, New York and London, 1969, 295–322.

344. PARZEN, E., 'On Estimation of Probability Density Function and Mode', *Annals of Mathematical Statistics,* **33** No. 3, Sept. 1962, 1065–1076.

345. PATRICK, E. A., and COSTELLO, J. P., 'On Unsupervised Estimation Algorithms', *IEEE Transactions on Information Theory,* **IT-16** No. 5, Sept. 1970, 556–569.

346. PEROTTO, P. G., 'A New Method for Automatic Character Recognition', *IEEE Transactions on Electronic Computers,* **EC-12**, Oct. 1963, 521–526.

347. PERVOZVANSKIY, A. A., 'Abstract Pattern Recognition as a Problem in Linear Programming', *Engineering Cybernetics,* **4**, July–Aug. 1965, 38–41.

348. PETERSON, D. W., 'Some Convergence Properties of a Nearest Neighbour Decision Rule', *IEEE Transactions on Information Theory,* **IT-16** No. 1, Jan. 1970, 26–31.

349. PETERSON, D. W., and MATTSON, R. L., 'A Method of Finding Linear Discriminant Functions for a Class of Performance Criteria', *IEEE Transactions on Information Theory,* **IT-12** No. 3, July 1966, 380–387.

350. PETERSON, E., 'Frequency Detection and Speech Formants', *Journal of the Acoustical Society of America,* **23** No. 6, Nov. 1951, 668–674.

351. PFALTZ, J. L., 'Web Grammars and Picture Description', *Technical Report 70-138*, Sept. 1970, Computer Science Center, University of Maryland, U.S.A.

352. PHILBRICK, O., 'Shape Description with the Medial Axis Transformation', *Pictorial Pattern Recognition,* Ed. G. C. Cheng, R. S. Ledley, D. K. Pollock, and A. Rosenfeld, Thompson Book Co., Washington, D.C., 1968, 395–407.

353. PHILCO CORPORATION, 'Improvements in and Relating to Apparatus for Recognition of Character and Like Electrical Signals', U.K. Pats 1 033 531 and 1 033 532, June 1966.

354. PHILCO-FORD CORPORATION, 'Character Recognition Apparatus', U.K. Pat. 1 124 454, Aug. 1968; *see also* U.S. Pat. 3 509 534, Apr. 1970.

354a. POLLACK, S. L., 'Conversion of Limited-Entry Decision Tables to Computer Programs', *Communications of the Association for Computing Machinery,* **8** No. 11, Nov. 1965, 677–682.

354b. POLLACK, S. L., HICKS, H. T., and HARRISON, W. J., *Decision Tables: Theory and Practice,* Wiley, New York and London, 1971.

355. POLONNIKOV, R. I., and ALEKSANDROV, V. V., 'A Procedure for Pattern Recognition', *Engineering Cybernetics,* No. 1, Jan./Feb. 1967, 92–106.

355a. POLS, L. C. W., 'Real-Time Recognition of Spoken Words', *IEEE Transactions on Computers,* **C-20** No. 9, Sept. 1971, 972–978.

356. POPPLEBAUM, W. J., 'Adaptive On-Line Fourier Transform', *Pictorial Pattern Recognition,* Ed. G. C. Cheng, R. S. Ledley, D. K. Pollock, and A Rosenfeld, Thompson Book Co., Washington, D.C., 1968, 387–394.

357. POTTER, R. J., 'An Optical Character Scanner', *Journal of the Society of Photographic Instrumentation Engineers,* **2** No. 3, Feb.-Mar. 1964, 75–78.

357a. PRESTON, K., 'Feature Extraction by Golay Hexagonal Pattern Transforms', *IEEE Transactions on Computers,* **C-20** No. 9, Sept. 1971, 1007–1014.

358. PURTON, R. F., 'Speech Recognition Using Autocorrelation Analysis', *IEEE Transactions on Audio and Electroacoustics,* **AU-16** No. 2, June 1968, 235–239.

359. RABINOW, J., 'Developments in Character Recognition Machines at Rabinow Engineering Company', *Optical Character Recognition,* Ed. G. L. Fischer, D. K. Pollock, B. Raddack; and M. E. Stevens, Spartan Books, New York, 1962, 27–51.

360. RABINOW, J., 'The Present State of the Art of Reading Machines', *Pattern Recognition,* Ed. L. N. Kanal, Thompson Book Co., Washington, D.C., 1968, 3–29.

361. RABINOW, J., 'Whither OCR?', *Datamation,* July 1969, 38.

361a. RABINOW, J., and GREENWALD, S., 'Multifont Reading Machines', U.S. Pat. 3 560 927, Feb. 1971.

362. RABINOW, J., HOLT, A. W., FISCHER, W., and MADER, L. W., 'High Speed Optical Identification of Printed Matters', U.S. Pat. 3 104 369, 1963.

363. RADIO CORPORATION OF AMERICA, 'Character Reader', U.K. Pat. 1 028 139, May 1966.

364. RAPHAEL SCAN DATA CORPORATION, 'Print Reading System', U.K. Pat. 1 179 144, Jan. 1970.

365. RAU, J. E. (North American Rockwell), 'Photo-Interpretation System', U.K. Pats 1 203 466 and 1 203 467, Aug. 1970.

366. RECOGNITION EQUIPMENT INCORPORATED, 'Digital Analog Retina Output Conditioning', U.K. Pats 1 115 909 and 1 115 910, June 1968; *see also* U.S. Pat. 3 509 533, Apr. 1970.

367. REDDY, D. R., 'Segmentation of Speech Sounds', *Journal of the Acoustical Society of America,* **40** No. 2, Aug. 1966, 307–312.

368. REDDY, D. R., 'Computer Recognition of Connected Speech', *Journal of the Acoustical Society of America,* **42** No. 2, Aug. 1967, 329–347.

369. REID, C. D., and REDMAN, J. D., 'Improvements in or Relating to Methods and Apparatus for Classifying Patterns', U.K. Pat. 1 172 539, Dec. 1969.

369a. REINWALD, L. T., and SOLAND, R. M., 'Conversion of Limited Entry Decision Tables to Optimum Computer Programs I: Minimum Average Processing Time', *Journal of the Association for Computing Machinery,* **13** No. 3, July 1966, 339–358.

369b. RISEMAN, E. D., and EHRICH, R. W., 'Contextual Word Recognition Using Binary Digrams', *IEEE Transactions on Computers,* **C-20** No. 4, Apr. 1971, 397–403.

370. ROBERTS, L. G., 'Machine Perception of Three-Dimensional Solids', *Optical and Electro-Optical Information Processing,* Ed. J. T. Tippet, D. A. Berkowitz, L. C. Clapp, C. J. Koester, and A. Vanderburgh, MIT Press, Cambridge, Mass., and London, 1965, 159–197.

371. ROCHESTER, N., JOHNSON, J. R., AMDAHL, G. M., and MUTTER, W. E. (IBM), 'Recognition of Recorded Intelligence', U.S. Pat. 2 889 535, June 1959; *see also* U.S. Pat. 3 271 761 Sept. 1966.

372. ROHLAND, W. S. (IBM), 'Character Sensing System', U.S. Pat. 2 877 951, Mar. 1959; *see also* U.S. Pat. 3 274 551, Sept. 1966.

373. ROHLAND, W. S. (IBM), 'Character Reader', U.S. Pat. 2 919 426, 1959.

374. ROHLAND, W. S., TRAGLIA, P. J., and HURLEY, P. J., 'The Design of an OCR System For Reading Handwritten Numerals', *1968 Fall Joint Computer Conference,* AFIPS Conference Proceedings, **33** Pt. 2, 1151–1162.

375. ROSEN, C. A., and HALL, D. J., 'A Pattern Recognition Experiment with Near-Optimum Results', *IEEE Transactions on Electronic Computers,* **EC-15**, Aug. 1966, 666.

376. ROSEN, J. B., 'Pattern Separation by Convex Programming', *Journal of Mathematical Analysis and Applications,* **10**, 1965, 123–134.

377. ROSENBLATT, F., *Principles of Neurodynamics,* Spartan Books, New York, 1962.

378. ROSENFELD, A., *Picture Processing by Computer,* Academic Press, New York and London, 1969.

379. ROSENFELD, A., 'Connectivity in Digital Pictures', *Journal of the Association for Computing Machinery,* **17** No. 1, Jan. 1970, 146–160.

380. ROSENFELD, A., 'Isotonic Grammars, Parallel Grammars, and Picture Grammars', *Machine Intelligence,* **6**, Ed. B. Meltzer and D. Michie, Edinburgh University Press, 1971, 281–294.

381. ROSENFELD, A., and PFALTZ, J. L., 'Sequential Operations in Digital Picture Processing', *Journal of the Association for Computing Machinery,* **13** No. 4, Oct. 1966, 471–494.

382. ROSENFELD, A., and PFALTZ, J. L., 'Web Grammars', *Proceedings of the International Joint Conference on Artificial Intelligence,* Ed. D. E. Walker and L. M. Norton, The Mitre Corp., Bedford, Mass. 01730, U.S.A., May 1969, 609–619.

383. ROSENFELD, A., and THURSTON, M., 'Edge and Curve Detection for Visual Scene Analysis', *IEEE Transactions on Computers,* **C-20** No. 5, May 1971, 562–569.

384. ROSS, P. W., 'A Limited-Vocabulary Speech Recognition System', *Journal of the Audio Engineering Society,* **15** No. 4, Oct. 1967, 414–418.

385. ROY, B. J., and SHERMAN, J., 'Two Viewpoints of the *k*-tuple Pattern Recognition Method', *IEEE Transactions on Systems Science and Cybernetics,* **SSC-3** No. 2, Nov. 1967, 117–120.

386. SAKAI, K., KATSURAGI, S., and WATANABE, S. (Toshiba), 'A Character Reader', U.K. Pat. 1 271 039, Apr. 1972.

387. SAKAI, T., and DOSHITA, S., 'The Automatic Speech Recognition System for Conversational Sound', *IEEE Transactions on Electronic Computers,* **EC-12** No. 6, Dec. 1963, 835–846.

388. SAKAI, T., NAGAO, M., and FUJIBAYASHI, S., 'Line Extraction and Pattern Detection in a Photograph', *Pattern Recognition,* **1** No. 3, Mar. 1969, 233–248.

389. SAMMON, J. W., 'Interactive Pattern Analysis and Classification', *IEEE Transactions on Computers,* **C-19** No. 7, July 1970, 594–616.

390. SAYRE, K. M., *Recognition: A Study in the Philosophy of Artificial Intelligence,* University of Notre Dame Press, Ind., 1965.

391. SCAN-DATA CORPORATION, 'Improvements in or Relating to Character Recognition Systems or Apparatus', U.K. Pat. 1 129 572, Oct. 1968.

391a. SCAN-DATA CORPORATION, 'Improvements in or Relating to Character Recognition Systems', U.K. Pat. 1 271 705, Apr. 1972.

392. SCARROTT, G. G., 'Devices for the Recognition of Printed Characters', U.S. Pat. 2 985 366, May 1961.

393. SCARROTT, G. G., and COOK, A. D., 'Improvements in Or Relating to Systems for Sensing and Recognising or Analysing Data', U.K. Pat. 1 127 741, Sept. 1968.

394. SEBESTYEN, G. S., *Decision Making Processes in Pattern Recognition,* Macmillan, London and New York, 1962; *see also IRE Transactions on Information Theory,* **IT-8** No. 5, Sept. 1962, S82–S91.

395. SEBESTYEN, G. S., and EDIE, J., 'An Algorithm for Non-Parametric Pattern Recognition', *IEEE Transactions on Electronic Computers,* **EC-15** No. 6, Dec. 1966, 908–915.

396. SEZAKI, N., and KATAGIRI, H., 'Character Recognition by Follow Method', *Proceedings of the IEEE,* **53** No. 5, May 1965, 510; *see also Proceedings of the IEEE,* **53** No. 10, Oct. 1965, 1656–1657.

397. SHADE, H. (IBM), 'Character Recognition Apparatus', U.K. Pat. 1 174 340, Dec. 1969.

398. SHAW, A. C., 'Parsing of Graph-Representable Pictures', *Journal of the Association for Computing Machinery,* **17** No. 3, July 1970, 453–481.

399. SHEARME, J. W., and LEACH, P. F., 'Some Experiments with a Simple Word Recognition System', *IEEE Transactions on Audio and Electroacoustics,* **AU-16** No. 2, June 1968, 256–261.

400. SHEINBERG, I., 'The Input 2 Document Reader', *Pattern Recognition,* **2** No. 3, Sept. 1970, 167–173.

401. SHELMAN, C. B., and HODGES, D., 'A General Purpose Programme for the Extraction of Physical Features from a Black and White Picture', *IEEE Conference Record of the Symposium on Feature Extraction and Selection in Pattern Recognition,* Oct. 1970, 135–144. Available from: Order Department IEEE, 345 East 47th Street, New York, NY 10017.

402. SHELTON, G. L. (IBM), 'Improvements Relating to a Scanner Threshold Adjusting Circuit', U.K. Pat. 1 093 079, Nov. 1967; Jan. 1972, 73–81. Sept. 1969.

403. SHEPARD, D. H., 'Scanning Apparatus', U.S. Pat. 2 978 590, Apr. 1961.

404. SHERMAN, H., 'A Quasi-Topological Method for the Recognition of Line Patterns', *Information Processing,* Proceedings of a UNESCO Conference in Paris in 1959, Butterworths, London, 1960, 232.

405. SHERMAN, R., and ERNST, G. W., 'Learning Patterns in Terms of Other Patterns', *Pattern Recognition,* **1** No. 4, July 1969, 301–314.

406. SHOLTZ, P. N., and BAKIS, R., 'Spoken Digit Recognition Using Vowel–Consonant Segmentation', *Journal of the Acoustical Society of America,* **34** No. 1, Jan. 1962, 1–5.

407. SIEMENS AKTIENGESELLSCHAFT, 'Improvements in or Relating to Apparatus for Use in the Automatic Recognition of Printed Characters', U.K. Pat. 1 132 486, Nov. 1968.

407a. SIEMENS AKTIENGESELLSCHAFT, 'Improvements in or Relating to Character Scanning Systems', U.K. Pat. 1 224 926, Mar. 1971.

407b. SIMON, J. C., CHECROUN, A., and ROCHE, C., 'A Method of Comparing Two Patterns Independent of Possible Transformations and Small Distortions', *Pattern Recognition,* **4** No. 1, Jan. 1972, 73–81.

408. SINGER, J. R., 'A Self Organising Recognition System', *Proceedings of the Western Joint Computer Conference,* 1961, 545–554.

409. SLAGLE, J. R., CHANG, C.-L., and LEE, R. C., 'A New Algorithm for Generating Prime Implicants', *IEEE Transactions on Computers,* **C-19** No. 4, Apr. 1970, 304–310.

410. SMITH, F. W., 'Pattern Classifier Design by Linear Programming', *IEEE Transactions on Computers,* **C-17** No. 4, Apr. 1968, 367–372.

411. SMITH, F. W., 'Design of Multicategory Pattern Classifiers with Two-Category Classifier Design Procedures', *IEEE Transactions on Computers,* **C-18** No. 6, June 1969, 548–551.

412. SMITH, F. W., and WRIGHT, M. H., 'Automatic Ship Photointerpretation by the Method of Moments', *IEEE Transactions on Computers,* **C-20** No. 9, Sept. 1971, 1089–1094.

413. SOCIETE D'ELECTRONIQUE ET D'AUMATISME, 'Pattern Recognition Apparatus', U.K. Pat. 1 143 585, Feb. 1969.

414. SOLARTRON, 'Typed Figures Translated into Computer Code', *Engineering* 15 Mar. 1957, 348–349.

415. SPECHT, D. F., 'Vectorcardiographic Diagnosis Using the Polynomial Discriminant Method of Pattern Recognition', *IEEE Transactions on Bio-Medical Engineering,* **BME-4** No. 2, Apr. 1967, 90–95.

416. SPECHT, D. F., 'Generation of Polynomial Discriminant Functions for Pattern Recognition', *IEEE Transactions on Electronic Computers,* **EC-16** No. 3, June 1967, 308–319.

417. SPINRAD, R. J., 'Machine Recognition of Hand-Printing', *Information and Control,* **8**, Apr. 1965, 124–142.

418. SPRAGGINS, J., 'Learning Without a Teacher', *IEEE Transactions on Information Theory,* **IT-12** , Apr. 1966, 223–229.

419. SPRICK, W., and GANZHORN, K., 'An Analogous Method for Pattern Recognition', *Information Processing,* Proceedings of a UNESCO Conference in Paris in 1959, Butterworths, London, 1960, 238.

420. STEARNS, S. D., 'A Method for the Design of Pattern Recognition Logic', *IRE Transactions on Electronic Computers,* **EC-9** No. 1, Mar. 1960, 48.

421. STECK, G. P., 'Stochastic Model for the Bledsoe–Browning Pattern Recognition Scheme', *IRE Transactions on Electronic Computers,* **EC-11,** Apr. 1962, 274–282.

421a. STEFANELLI, R., and ROSENFELD, A., 'Some Parallel Thinning Algorithms for Digital Pictures', *Journal of the Association for Computing Machinery,* **18** No. 2, Apr. 1971, 255–264.

422. STEINBUCH, K., and PISKE, U. A. W., 'Learning Matrices and Their Applications', *IEEE Transactions on Electronic Computers,* **EC-12** No. 5, Dec. 1963, 486.

423. STEVENS, K. N., and HALLE, M., 'Remarks on Analysis by Synthesis and Distinctive Features', *Models for the Perception of Speech and Visual Form,* Ed. W. Wathen-Dunn, MIT Press, Cambridge, Mass., and London, 1967, 88–102.

424. STEVENS, M. E., 'Automatic Character Recognition, A State of the Art Report', *Technical Note,* No. 112, National Bureau of Standards, Washington, D.C., May 1961.

425. STROKE, G. W., *An Introduction to Coherent Optics and Holography,* Academic Press, New York and London, 1966.

426. STROKE, G. W. and ZECH, R. G., 'A Posteriori Image-Correcting Deconvolution by Holographic Fourier Transform Division', *Physics Letters,* **25A** No. 2, 31 July 1967, 89–90.

427. SWONGER, C. W., 'Property Learning in Pattern Recognition Systems Using Information Content Measurements', *Pattern Recognition,* Ed. L. N. Kanal, Thompson Book Co., Washington, D.C., 1968, 329–347; *see also IEEE Transactions on Computers,* **C-20** No. 9, Sept. 1971, 1067–1075.

428. SWONGER, C. W., 'An Evaluation of Character Normalisation, Feature Extraction, and Classification Techniques for Postal Mail Reading', *Proceedings of Automatic Pattern Recognition,* National Security Industrial Association, 1030 Fifteenth Street, Northwest, Washington, D.C., May 1969, 67–85.

429. SZANZER, A. J., 'Automatic Error Correction in Natural Languages', *Information Storage and Retrieval,* **5**, 1970, 169–174; *see also ITL Review for Applied Linguistics*, No. 7, 1970, 49–56.

429a. TAPPERT, C. C., 'A Preliminary Investigation of Adaptive Control of the Interaction between Segmentation and Segment Classification in Automatic Recognition of Continuous Speech', *IEEE Transactions on Systems, Man, and Cybernetics,* **SMC-2** No. 1, Jan. 1972, 66–72.

430. TAUSCHEK, G., 'Reading Machine', U.S. Pat. 2 026 329, Dec. 1935; (appl. May 1929).

431. TAYLOR, W. K., 'Pattern Recognition by Means of Automatic Analogue Apparatus', *Proceedings of the IEE,* **106**, Pt. B, Mar. 1959, 198; *see also Control,* July 1960, 95–99.

432. TEACHER, C. F., KELLET, H., and FOCHT, L., 'Experimental, Limited Vocabulary Speech Recogniser', *IEEE Convention Record,* **15** Pt. 11-Speech, 1967, 169–173.

433. TEITELMAN, W., 'Real Time Recognition of Hand Drawn Characters', *1964 Fall Joint Computer Conference,* AFIPS Conference Proceedings, 26, 559–575.

433a. TELEFUNKEN, 'Circuit Arrangement for Ascertaining Among Several Conductors Upon Which Simultaneously Appear Different Voltages that which is the Highest Voltage', U.K. Pat. 1 231 618, May 1971.

434. THOMAS, R. B., and KASSLER, M., 'Character Recognition in Context', *Information and Control,* **10**, Jan. 1967, 43–64.

435. TOU, J. T., and HEYDORN, R. P., 'Some Approaches to Optimum Feature Extraction', *Computer and Information Science,* **2**, Ed. J. T. Tou, Academic Press, New York and London, 1967, 57–89.

436. TRICKETT, T., 'Designing Standard OCR Fonts', *Optical Character Recognition and the Years Ahead,* The Business Press, Elmhurst, Ill., 1969, 370–385.

437. TRIENDL, E. E., 'Skeletonisation of Noisy Hand Drawn Symbols Using Parallel Operations', *Pattern Recognition,* **2** No. 3, Sept. 1970, 215–226.

438. TSCHESCHNER, W., 'Device for Extracting Recognisable Features of a Speech Signal', U.K. Pat. 1 216 756, Dec. 1970.

439. TSYPKIN, Ya. Z., 'Adaptation, Training and Self Organisation in Automatic Systems', *Automation and Remote Control,* **27** No. 1, Jan. 1966, 23–61.

440. TSYPKIN, Ya. Z., Use of the Stochastic Approximation Method in Estimating Unknown Distribution Densities from Observations', *Automation and Remote Control,* **27** No. 3, Mar. 1966, 432–434.

441. UHR, L., and VOSSLER, C., 'A Pattern Recognition Programme that Generates, Evaluates, and Adjusts its Own Parameters', *Proceedings of the Western Joint Computer Conference,* 1961, 555–569.

442. ULLMANN, J. R., 'Experiments with the *n*-tuple Method of Pattern Recognition', *IEEE Transactions on Computers,* **C-18** No. 12, Dec. 1969, 1135–1137.

443. ULLMANN, J. R., 'Transference of Learning Between Recognition Classes', *IEEE Transactions on Computers,* **C-21** No. 2, Feb. 1972, 219–220.

443a. ULLMANN, J. R., 'Correspondence in Character Recognition', *Proceedings of the Conference on Machine Perception of Pictures and Patterns,* National Physical Laboratory, Apr. 1972. The Institute of Physics and the Physical Society, 34–44.

444. ULLMANN, J. R., and KIDD, P. A., 'Recognition Experiments with Typed Numerals from Envelopes in the Mail', *Pattern Recognition,* **1** July 1969, 273–289.

445. UNGER, S. H., 'Pattern Recognition and Detection', *Proceedings of the IRE,* **47**, Oct. 1959, 1737–1752; *see also Proceedings of the IRE*, **46**, Oct. 1958, 1744-1750.

445a. UNGER, S. H., 'GIT–A Heuristic Program for Testing Pairs of Directed Line Graphs for Isomorphism', *Communications of the Association for Computing Machinery,* **7** No. 1, Jan. 1964, 26–34.

446. UYEHARA, G. U., 'A Stream-Following Technique for Use in Character Recognition', *1963 IEEE International Convention Record,* Pt. 4, 64–74.

447. VAN DER GON, J. J. D., THURING, J. P., and STRAKEE, J., 'A Handwriting Simulator', *Physics in Medicine and Biology,* **6** No. 3, Jan. 1962, 407–414.

448. VANDER LUGT, A., 'The Effects of Small Displacements of Spatial Filters', *Applied Optics,* **6** No. 7, July 1967, 1221–1225.

449. VANDER LUGT, A., ROTZ, F. B., and KLOOSTER, A., 'Character Reading by Optical Spatial Filtering', in *Optical and Electro-Optical Information Processing,* Ed. J. T. Tippet, D. A. Berkowitz, L. C. Clapp, C. J. Koester, and A. Vanderburgh, MIT Press, Cambridge, Mass., and London, 1965, 125–141.

450. VAN EMDEN, M. H., 'Optimal Data Compression', *Machine Intelligence,* **6** Ed. B. Meltzer and D. Michie, Edinburgh University Press, 1971, 141–150.

450a. VAN STEENIS, H., 'The IBM 1275 Recognition System and Its Development', *Pattern Recognition in Biological and Technical Systems,* Ed. O-J. Grüsser and R. Klinke, Springer-Verlag, Berlin, Heidelberg, and New York, 1971, 253–261.

450b. VON KELLER, T. G., 'An On-Line Recognition System for Spoken Digits', *Journal of the Acoustical Society of America,* **49** No. 4, Pt. 2, Apr. 1971, 1288–1296.

451. VOSSLER, C. M., and BRANSTON, N. M., 'The Use of Context For Correcting Garbled English Text', *Proceedings of the 19th National Conference of the Association for Computing Machinery,* 1964, D2.4–1 to D2.4–13.

452. WADA, H., TAKAHASHI, S., LIJIMA, T., OKUMURA, Y., and IMOTO, K., 'An Electronic Reading Machine', *Information Processing,* Proceedings of a UNESCO Conference in Paris in 1959, Butterworths, London, 1960, 227–232.

453. WALD, A., *Sequential Analysis,* John Wiley, New York, 1947.

454. WATANABE, A., 'Karhunen–Loeve Expansion and Factor Analysis Theoretical Remarks and Applications', *Transactions of the Fourth Prague Conference on Information Theory, Statistical Decision Functions and Random Processes,* 1965, Czechoslovak Academy of Sciences, Prague, 1967, 635–660.

455. WATANABE, S., LAMBERT, P. F., KULIKOWSKI, C. A., BUXTON, J. L., and WALKER, R., 'Evaluation and Selection of Variables in Pattern Recognition', *Computer and Information Science,* **2**, Ed. J. T. Tou, Academic Press, New York and London, 1967, 91–121.

455a. WEAVER, J. A., *Reading Machines,* Mills and Boon, London, 1972.

456. WEE, W. G., Generalised Inverse Approach to Adaptive Multiclass Pattern Classification', *IEEE Transactions on Computers,* **C-17** No. 12, Dec. 1968, 1157–1164.

457. WEEKS, R. W., 'Rotating Raster Character Recognition System', *AIEE Transactions,* **80,** Pt. I, Communications and Electronics, Sept. 1961, 353–359.

458. WICKES, W. E., *Logic Design with Integrated Circuits,* Wiley, New York and London, 1968.

459. WIDROW, B., 'Generalisation and Information Storage in Networks of Adaline Neurons', *Self Organising Systems, 1962,* Ed. G. T. Jacobi, Spartan Books, New York, 1962, 435–463.

460. WILDE, D. J., *Optimum Seeking Methods,* Prentice Hall, Englewood Cliffs, N.J., 1964.

461. WILL, P. M., BAKIS, R., and WESLEY, M. A., 'Digital Image Processing for the Earth Resources Technology Satellite Data', *IFIP 1971,* Ljubljana, Booklet TA–6, Aug. 1971, 96–100.

462. WILSON, M. G. (IBM), 'Electrical Signal Handling Apparatus', U.K. Pat. 1 255 759, Dec. 1971.

463. WINDER, R. O., 'Enumeration of Seven-Argument Threshold Functions', *IEEE Transactions on Electronic Computers,* **EC-14** No. 3, 1965, 315–325.

464. WRIGHT, G. G. N., *The Writing of Arabic Numerals,* University of London Press, 1952.

464a. YACHIDA, M., and TSUJI, S., 'Application of Colour Information to Visual Perception', *Pattern Recognition,* **3** No. 3, Oct. 1971, 307–323.

465. YAU, S. S., and SCHUMPERT, J. M., 'Design of Pattern Classifiers with the Updating Property Using Stochastic Approximation Techniques', *IEEE Transactions on Computers,* C-17 No. 9, Sept. 1968, 861–872.

466. YOSHIDA, M., and OGATA, Y., 'Handwriting Analysis and Synthesis', *Journal of the Radio Research Laboratories, Japan,* **13** No. 65, Jan. 1966, 25–39.

466a. ZAHN, C. T., and ROSKIES, R. Z., 'Fourier Descriptors of Plane Closed Curves', *IEEE Transactions on Computers,* **C-21** No. 3, Mar. 1972, 269–281.

467. ZAYTSEV, V. G., and TYMOFEYEV, B. B., 'Speech Recognition', *Automatica,* No. 2, Kiev, 1965, 39–44; Translation JPRS: 31,350, Joint Publications Research Service, Building Tempo E, Adams Drive, 4th and 6th Streets S. W., Washington, D.C., 20443, U.S.A., Aug. 1965, 21–27.

468. ZUSNE, L., *Visual Perception of Form,* Academic Press, New York and London, 1970.

INDEX